The Great
American
Newspaper

The Rise
and Fall
of the

VILLAGE VOICE

The Great American Newspaper

KEVIN MICHAEL McAULIFFE

CHARLES SCRIBNER'S SONS · NEW YORK

Cartoons reprinted with the permission of Jules Feiffer. Copyright © 1956, 1957, 1958, 1959, 1960, 1961, 1962, 1963, 1964, 1965, 1066, 1967, 1968, 1969, 1970, 1971 by Jules Feiffer.

The excerpt from "Let Us Now Praise Mary Nichols" is reprinted with permission of *The Villager*. Copyright © 1975 by The Villager.

Excerpts from the articles by Paul Cowan, originally published in the *Village Voice,* are reprinted by permission of Paul Cowan. Copyright ©1972, 1974 The Village Voice, Inc.

Excerpts from articles by William Manville, originally published in the *Village Voice,* are reprinted by permission of William Manville. Copyright ©1961 The Village Voice, Inc.

Excerpts quoted in this book from material written by the following authors published in *The Village Voice* have been reprinted by permission of The Village Voice, Inc. which retains all copyrights therein:
Ken Auletta, Arthur Bell, Howard Blum, Jimmy Breslin, Nick Browne, Joe Coleman, Karen Durbin, Edwin Fancher, Frances Fitzgerald, Joe Flaherty, Stephanie Gervis Harrington, Richard Goldstein, David Gurin, Pete Hamill, Margot Hentoff, Nat Hentoff, Abbie Hoffman, Lenny Kaye, James Kempton, Jane Kramer, Seymour Krim, Steve Lerner, Barbara Long, Norman Mailer, Don McNeil, Jonas Mekas, Frederic Morton, Marlene Nadle, Jack Newfield, Mary Perot Nichols, Joel Oppenheimer, Robert Pasolli, Jerry Rubin, Ron Rosenbaum, Blair Sabol, Andrew Sarris, Marc Schleifer, Ken Sobol, Howard Smith, Jerry Tallmer, Phil Tracy, Lucian Truscott, Niccolo Tucci, Clark Whelton, Dan Wolf.

Copyright © The Village Voice, Inc. 1955, 1956, 1957, 1958, 1959, 1960, 1961, 1962, 1963, 1964, 1965, 1966, 1967, 1968, 1969, 1970, 1971, 1972, 1973, 1974, 1975, 1976.

Copyright © 1978 Kevin McAuliffe

Library of Congress Cataloging in Publication Data
McAuliffe, Kevin.
  The great American newspaper.
  1. The Village voice. I. Title.
PN4899.N42V535 071'.3 78-17217
ISBN 0-684-15602-4

O71.3
M114g

This book published simultaneously in the United States of America and in Canada - Copyright under the Berne Convention

All rights reserved. No part of this book may be reproduced in any form without the permission of Charles Scribner's Sons

1 3 5 7 9 11 13 15 17 19 20 18 16 14 12 10 8 6 4 2

PRINTED IN THE UNITED STATES OF AMERICA

195385

Foreword

THIS BOOK BEGAN AS AN IDEA FOR A masters project at the Columbia University School of Journalism in the summer and fall of 1974 and was finished in that form in the spring of 1975. An adapted excerpt from that paper was published in the *Columbia Journalism Review* that May, and the following summer Charles Scribner's Sons contracted for an expansion of the article into a book. Work on the book began the following spring, and the last page was typed, by candlelight, at approximately 2 A.M. Thursday, July 14, 1977, the New York blackout having begun some four hours before, exactly one year and thirteen days after the *first* page had been typed. So, for better or worse, four years of my life have been invested in writing the history of the *Village Voice,* a paper I much admired growing up but never wrote for. Perhaps this will make up for that.

Besides published sources of information and the *Voice* archives themselves, which I went through, start to finish, three times, there were various unpublished works that were of aid to me, at least for consulting purposes, and I would like to cite a Columbia masters project by Timothy Holt and a piece by Harper Barnes written for *New Times* in 1973 in particular.

There are people I should thank for their varied contributions along the way: David Otte, my agent; Elisabeth Crawford Perrier, who persuaded Scribners to buy the book originally; Doe Coover, her successor, its editor; Louise Webb, Marya Dull, and Mary Ann Compono, who retyped the manuscript; and not least John Keene, without whose legal acumen it might never have been published.

Thanks must go to the many people connected with the *Village Voice*'s history who gave me collectively many hours of their time for interviews and fact-checking, plus, in certain instances, vital, discreet documentation.

Thanks, most of all, to Dan Wolf, who broke two decades of circumspection and finally chose to let someone inside his head, and who made that someone me. However good this book is, it would not have been nearly so without the complete cooperation of the man who made the *Village Voice* what it was when it was something. I am in his debt, permanently, and glad to be.

Kevin McAuliffe
New York City
St. Patrick's Day, 1978

Introduction: *June 5, 1974*

JACK NEWFIELD HEARD ABOUT IT THE night before from author Peter Maas. The next morning, once word was out, it spread fast. Ely Kushel, the paper's accountant, got a call in his office at New York University, where he was on the faculty. It was from a broker who had been asking him for detailed financial statements about the newspaper, supposedly at the request of a bank that was being asked for some financing. "Ely," his caller said, "I want you to hear this from me first, because I was the one who asked you for the information." It turned out that the statements had not been requested by, and not turned over to, any bank at all.

Back at the offices of the paper, staff writers Lucian Truscott and Clark Whelton stepped off the elevator and were met by their editor, Dan Wolf, who took them aside, into the office of city editor Mary Nichols. "Sit down. Brace yourself. I've got news for you," he began. Farther down the hall, photo editor Fred McDarrah popped his head into the office of Brian van der Horst, co-writer of the "Scenes" column, and told him. Van der Horst thought it was a dumb joke by McDarrah. At home, Howard Smith, who wrote the column with Van der Horst and had been with the paper going back seventeen years, got a call from Wolf. "I have some very strange news," Wolf told him. "I think you'd better come over."

Word spread throughout the building, then outside, as members of the Family set about telling one another. Howard Blum phoned the office from Jones Beach and was told to get back to the office right away. In Britain, Letitia Kent, who had not written for the paper in six years, received two transatlantic telephone calls about it. That night, Marlene Nadle, who had been published by the paper off and on since 1963, was told by a friend over dinner in a Chinatown restaurant. She couldn't finish her meal. Nat Hentoff, one of its columnists, read the story in the *New York Post,* and his first thought was apprehension. Joe Flaherty, on the other hand, read it in the *Times* and had very quickly met up with his old friend Clay Felker, who asked him, "How do you feel? We're going to need you."

What had happened was that first thing that morning of June 5, 1974, the principal owners of the *Village Voice,* who were Carter Burden, councilman of the City of New York, and Bartle Bull, president, Taurus Communications, Inc., called the paper's editor, Wolf, and its publisher, Edwin Fancher, to a breakfast meeting at the

Brook Club on East 54th Street in Midtown Manhattan. And over that breakfast, while his partner Bull, who had been let in on what was up only at the last stages and only as a *fait accompli,* looked down and away, Burden apprised the paper's two founders of the contents of a press release that was still being written as he spoke.

"The companies that publish *New York* Magazine and the *Village Voice* today announced that they have merged," it began, stipulating that Bull, Wolf, and Fancher would all remain at their posts. For Wolf and Fancher, Clay S. Felker, editor and publisher, *New York* Magazine, was full of words of praise. "In its 20-year history," he announced, "the *Village Voice* under the direction of Dan Wolf and Ed Fancher has created a proud tradition of editorial innovation, independence and integrity in reporting and discussing the major issues of the city and country. They have assembled a unique and talented staff, which are the heart and soul of any publication. The merged company happens to be able to provide the backing to enhance the potential of the *Voice* and in doing so, broaden its scope and its audience. . . .

"We fully expect *New York* Magazine and the *Village Voice* to continue to compete with each other as they have in the past."

★ ★ ★

Dan Wolf and Ed Fancher were too stunned to say much of anything at that moment. It had happened too suddenly for either one of them to be thinking of their legal rights just yet, but they would start to do that in time. *Don't panic,* Fancher, the business side of their partnership, told himself. *It's not uncommon in business mergers for there to be no loss of control. For the parent corporation to be interested in just maximizing profits.*

He might as well have panicked.

★ ★ ★

"A marriage of sandals and Gucci loafers, of body odors and Bal à Versailles, of radical cheek and radical chic," *Time* called *New York*'s absorption of the "unremittingly quarrelsome, wordy, underedited" *Voice,* and could not have missed the point more. Clay Felker had not just bought himself any "alternative weekly" of run-on, first-person, advocacy journalism, of kinky classifieds, of sociopoliticocultural coverage of foreign films and feminism and rock and radical politics. He had bought "the" alternative weekly, the one that had made all the others possible, the one that had shown the way to a new kind of journalism in America.

He had also bought a publication that was three times as old and over twice as profitable as his own; in the fiscal year just ending, the *Village Voice* would clear $452,000 on sales of $4.6 million, a profit ratio of over 10 percent, well above normal in publishing. The *New York Times* might persist in calling it "a Greenwich Village weekly," but the fact remained that it was the first successful paper to be started in that city since the *Daily News* in 1918. Its own logo might identify it only as "The Weekly Newspaper of New York," but by now it was the most successful weekly newspaper in the country.

Those ramifications were not seen at the time, in 1974, just as they had not been foreseen in 1955, at the beginning.

I.
AT THAT POINT IN TIME

1. DWIGHT EISENHOWER WAS IN THE

White House, and if he died Richard Nixon would succeed him. Alger Hiss was in prison. If he died, someone would be found to succeed him.

There was good and there was evil. There was us and there was them. There was a way to do things, and there were things one did not do. There was no long hair. There were no drugs. There were no birth control pills. There were no black people. There was no such thing as dissent. It was the 1950s, and in America all was well.

Almost all was well. There was original sin. There was Communism.

★ ★ ★

There was also prosperity. There was a Cold War. As the burst of energy they had in the 1930s and 1940s went the way of the wartime alliance with Soviet Russia, the Left and the avant garde in America went into reverse. No one was waiting for Lefty anymore, and a lot of people were denying they ever knew him. The parade had begun before the House Un-American Activities Committee or Joe McCarthy himself, witnesses breaking down or being blacklisted, clinging to the Fifth or confessing, denouncing others or being denounced. The witchhunt was on everywhere, even television, where every week, on *I Led Three Lives,* government double agent Herbert Philbrick endured the scorn of loyal Americans and risked exposure to crack a cell of Reds sent over from Central Casting. "They" were the enemy. "They" were brainwashing our prisoners in Korea. "They" were stealing the secrets of our atomic bomb from us. "They" were everywhere. "We" had to be watching for them. The motif even worked its way into the classic science fiction film of the period, *The Invasion of the Body Snatchers,* as pods of alien beings landed on Earth to sprout full-blown likenesses of those whose personalities they would capture while the designated victims slept. "They" might look like us, "they" might talk like us, but "they" were not us, and "we" had to stop them before "they" took over.

And so America entered its modern phase by becoming a garrison state of the mind, making maximum anti-Communism, if not gospel, at least a national ideal all by itself. And the need to manifest one's own anti-Communism was obsessive: the descendants of emigrants and exiles and revolutionaries began taking loyalty oaths, and requiring them of one another, to so much as deliver a piece of mail. They practiced taking shelter from air raids underground and turned against those who asked why, or said no. The nation that had changed the course of human history by opening up a place for liberty and individualism and iconoclasm now changed the course of its own history in a long night of static sterility that stopped the evolution of an American culture dead in its tracks. It was a national epic of fatuity, a throwback of the first order, a spectacle of ludicrous conduct on such a mass scale it left the society in some ways permanently retarded. American life turned blank, banal, boring, and barren.

★ ★ ★

   . . . *The vulgarities of McCarthyism had withered the possibilities of a true dialogue between people. The best minds in America—radical and conservative—were repeating themselves. Up and down the countryside the elite of the Ivy League had taken flight into the reality of the conventional church, the community organization, the lawn mower. Practically no one was testing reality, and . . . those of us who started The Voice had long since been left cold by the dull pieties of official liberalism with its dreary, if unspoken, drive to put every family in a housing development and give each child his own social worker.*

There was no cross-fertilization of ideas because there were no new ideas; the people who might have been expected to think them up were on the defensive. Indeed, one of the stock clichés of the time was that "the end of ideology" was here, that the great seminal thinking had been done and the great problems solved, that from here on out all the American system would require were the sort of minor adjustments one might make with any machine that was functioning smoothly. There was no dialogue because dialogue meant differences of opinion, and above all else people wanted to go along, to play it safe, to be like everybody else. To be different was to be in danger. To be eccentric was to be alone. An entire generation went through life believing that the important things were to be accepted, to be processed by some institution that you identified yourself with, to go into business, make it up the corporate stepladder, and get a nice house in the suburbs. Their kids grew up on plastic rites of passage—Edsels and convertibles, Elvis Presley and the primitive stirrings of rock 'n' roll, D.A. haircuts and Davy Crockett caps, bobbie sox and hula hoops—but those were not, as has since been advertised, Happy Days. It was a surface happiness, cloaking fear and mistrust. You were afraid for yourself, suspicious of others. In pursuing that kind of happiness, people were running away from themselves, mindless, seeking sleep, trying to lose themselves in sameness. The books about that generation were aptly titled: *The Status Seekers. The Man in the Gray Flannel Suit. Organization Man. The Lonely Crowd.* This was the Silent Generation. It conformed. It policed itself.

★ ★ ★

There was a Silent Generation. There was also a Beat Generation. There was Organization Man, and there was the Angry Young Man.

If you were different in the 1950s, you were self-conscious about it. You were outnumbered, and you knew it. There was no such thing as an "alternate lifestyle." There was sex, but sex, fine and fun though it might be, had not come out of the closet yet, and no matter how much you believed in free love, something still so chancy, if it didn't make you feel dirty, could still make you feel guilty. There was politics, but causes were dead. It was a time to be cool, and to be cool you could not be committed. Your politics was yourself. If you couldn't take "society," if you stood out from the "square" world, it was because you couldn't cut it or make it there, and you admitted it. You were the one who was out of touch. So you dropped out. You just divorced yourself from the whole thing. You did like Hemingway, and took off for Europe and other foreign parts. Or you went off to Greenwich Village.

★ ★ ★

In the summer of 1970, William Welborne died.

Bill Welborne "lived a bohemian writer's life," wrote his friend Edwin Fancher in the *Village Voice,* the newspaper Fancher published, and where Welborne had worked in its early years. In the course of describing that life, Fancher described more, a time and a place that had passed.

> Bill was a writer. He was a child of the post-war '40s. He was one of the bright young men just out of the service (Air Corps), who made the scene at the New School writer's workshops. They studied on the GI Bill of Rights, but not for credit or a degree. They did their homework at the San Remo bar, talking endlessly about Faulkner and Sartre and the books they were going to write. And many of them, like Bill's friend Jimmy Baldwin, did write books. The Remo was where it was all happening then—for Styron, Kerouac, Broyard, and a hundred other young writers. Maxwell Bodenheim had been left over from the golden era of the bohemian '20s and would periodically invade the Remo to make drunken abusive declamations to the crowded bar. Joe Gould was usually a few doors up the street at the 'overflow' Minetta Tavern, holding forth with his 'oral history of the world.' The Remo closed just a few months ago and is empty now, but then it was the

international communications center for the young and hungry literati. Everyone there was trying to accumulate a few
hundred dollars to get to Europe—as in Hemingway's earlier
days—and the Remo was the last stop before boarding the
Holland-American Line in Hoboken, and the first stop on the
return. It was a gossip factory dispensing news of friends who
had left, or returned, or published, or divorced, or sold out, or
were making it with someone new.

The dropouts and the beatniks and the aesthetes and the outsiders
all went there, down below Union Square where all the forlorn
Communist Party rallies were held, below 14th Street where the streets
and the people got a little crazy, to Greenwich Village. With its low,
crowded brick buildings and its slow pace of life, it was a slice of Europe
in Manhattan, a haven for all that was lowlife and highbrow and
offbeat, the staging area for revolts against the bourgeois lifestyle, first
by the Bohemians, now by the Beats. It was a place contained, apart
from the mainstream of the society, and therefore special, where the
inhabitants could come and live and play and create, party and drink
and make love and smoke dope, write and paint and think and work odd
jobs and watch tourists watching them until they became famous or
went home or just settled down. The Beat poets and the abstract
expressionists were there. So were the novelists and the actors. So were
the dancers and the socialists. There were bongos and espresso in the
coffee houses, jazz in the clubs, and folk singing on the streets and
sidewalks. There was casual sex, sometimes with the other color, or
with the same sex. There was concern over disarmament and Little
Rock. And, as usual, the debate was being renewed, as it seemed to be
every ten years or so: Was the Village dying?
   But despite all that, the Village was thriving with a transfusion of
new blood in the 1950s. There was a new liberal ministry at the Judson
Memorial Church. The New School for Social Research on 12th Street
swelled with returning veterans taking courses on the GI Bill. The Off-
Broadway Theater movement had begun to challenge uptown producers and critics.
   They lived in walk-ups or tenements or cold-water flats with a
bathtub in the kitchen and paid anywhere from $16 to $26 a month for
rent; if they could clear $25 to $35 a week doing anything at all, they
could survive. They drank in the Continental atmosphere of Louis'
Tavern on West 4th Street or at Minetta's or at the Lion's Head in
Sheridan Square or at the White Horse Tavern with Dylan Thomas. At
the Cedar Tavern on University Place Joel Oppenheimer and other

Black Mountain poets were holding forth. So were the abstract expressionist painters—Willem deKooning, Larry Rivers, Jackson Pollock, Franz Klein. Then there was the San Remo, "where it was all happening," a restaurant on Macdougal Street near the border with Little Italy, compared by Mary McCarthy to the Café de Flore of Sartre and Beauvoir, where Maxwell Bodenheim would expound until he and his wife were murdered in 1954, where Allen Ginsberg and the creators of the Living Theatre, Julian Beck and Judith Malina, hung out before they were well-known.

They made the coffee house scene. At the Four Winds, or at the Limelight, run first by Helen Gee and then sold to Kelsey Marichal, or the Café LaMama, or the Caffe Cino on Cornelia Street. And, of course, at the Figaro, corner Bleecker and Macdougal. "The Figaro," wrote Howard Smith in the *Voice* when the café closed in January 1969, "was a good place for staying up all night while avoiding writing the great American novel. A nervous incubator where little teenyboppers were weaned from Brooklyn to their first affair."

It was the place where, after dropping out of some Midwestern university, you picked up a new style of education. Without realizing it you got street smart. It was a place where everyone was always saving up to go to Europe. Forever. But they either never went or always came back.

It was a place where balmy afternoons long-haired mothers sat around in the back garden nursing their kids. Where lots of writer-waiters and carpenter-painters took up with each others' wives after their first divorce.

The Figaro used to represent status. It was a warm place where everyone who ever hung around was handsome, groovy, great, and a waitress was instantly prettier if she worked there. A young poet was more inspired if he washed dishes until seven in the morning. If you got barred from the Figaro it could be fatal to your social equilibrium. It was the perfect womb for all the transient beautiful losers. And it was the kind of place you no longer had time for once you got busy and started to make it.

. . . But if you were young and ready to change the direction of your life, the place could become home.

They were all there. Norman Mailer and Dylan Thomas and James Baldwin and Jack Kerouac and Lorraine Hansberry and Calder Willingham and Vance Bourjaily. Dwight MacDonald and A. J.

Liebling and Paul Goodman and Anatole Broyard. The Clancy Brothers and Tommy Makem, singing their Irish folk songs and IRA
anthems. José Quintero, directing off-Broadway. Claes Oldenburg, who
would in a few years hold the first Happening. Dorothy Day, the
pacifist who put out the *Catholic Worker*. The roster of the talented
and the famous went on and on.

Michael Harrington would certify his credentials as a social critic
with the publication of *The Other America* in 1962, but in 1950 he was
a young, radical skeptic Catholic, "two years out of St. Louis and
goggle-eyed," as he put it when he reminisced about the event, the
night he was invited to a party at Norman Mailer's First Avenue loft.
There he met Marlon Brando; and Susan Sontag, who was then a
philosophy teacher; and the poet Denise Levertov; and the playwright
Maria Irene Fornes; and Alberto Moravia; and William Styron.

And Dan Wolf. And Ed Fancher.

2.

WHEN HE AND HIS FRIEND ED FANCHER

made the decision to go beyond talking about starting a paper in the Village and actually publish one, Dan Wolf was going on forty years old—though in its first issue he would lie and say he was only thirty-three. He was that self-conscious about it.

He was into middle age now, and had neither that much to show for his life nor quite figured out what to do with it. There was a massive barrier of shyness in front of him, this man with the facial features that reminded you of Eddie Cantor, and yet he had many friends in the Village, who once they got to know him saw that, then as now, what he was most of all was a fascinating conversationalist. He could talk with them, about anything, for hours, toking on his corncob pipe as he frequently did, and be brilliant. But conversation was not a job, and by this time it seemed he might never find a place for himself anywhere. There seemed no conventional route to success someone like him might take.

He knew it seemed that way, knew he lived very unrealistically. But he thought of himself as a romantic. He was never aware of time. And he was determined not to do the right things, not to live like the middle class.

Dan Wolf was born into middle-class life, in 1915 on the Upper West Side of Manhattan, but he had lived poor, especially in the Depression when one day his father, aged fifty-three and in the antiques business, dropped dead of a heart attack. After high school, he went to Europe, not college, and roamed around. He read his Hemingway, and from him gleaned, as he described it, the possibility of impossibility. When Pearl Harbor came, he was living at home. He went into the service as a Pfc. and got out as one, serving in New Guinea, Luzon, Okinawa, and Korea, securing captured enemy airfields with the intelligence section of the 75th Air Force. Combat, when he encountered it, exhilarated him as few experiences ever had. The day he came under air attack, instead of taking cover he came out to watch. He had, as Norman Mailer would say, death guts.

Dan Wolf met Mailer through Jean Malaquais when he enrolled to take a course the French novelist was teaching at the New School after the war, and they became so close that Mailer dedicated *The Deer Park* to Wolf among others. Mustered out of the service in 1946, Wolf had headed for the Village and lived on First Avenue near the Allen Street public baths (for a while, he could recall, next to a ballerina) before 51 Christopher Street, where he was now. To him it was both Montmartre and Montparnasse, the perfect place to be Bohemian and offbeat and antibourgeois. But he sensed a subtle difference now between the Bohemians who had been there and the Beats who were coming in, the Bohemians believing in the ideal of Art and that one should suffer to attain it, while to the Beats life was superior to art. To pick up changes in the mindset of a place, and be able to analyze them that way, so flexible and detached, was characteristic of his mind, with its many hinges, as was his belief that the hardest thing in this world is to be an individual, and his desire to stand apart from things. He had always been that way. In the thirties, when his generation was taking up collections for the Loyalists in Spain, he had never been a joiner or a signer. The night he went to a film being shown at the home of some Communists, one of the women there began showing off her fur coat, saying, "It was made in Russia," and he was so turned off by all their fawning he would tell the story even many years later as a vignette of an epiphany. Then again, when there was a controversy at the New School after the war over who would be permitted to join the American Veterans Committee, with one side seeking to exclude Fascists and the other seeking to exclude Communists, Wolf, though Jewish and not a Communist, was one of the few in favor of letting them both in.

He met Ed Fancher at the New School, too (in one of those cosmic courses, he cracked once, something like "Diet in the Light of World Conditions"), and when he left in 1950 Dan Wolf had not finished. He never did. The day in late 1954 he said to Fancher, "Let's start a paper in the Village," and Fancher said yes, he had written the sections of the *Columbia Encyclopedia* on Greek, Roman, and Arabic philosophy, he had written press releases for the Turkish Information Service in New York, he had freelanced writing and editing anything that came up, and he was planning to get married to Rhoda Lazare, a social worker and friend of Norman Mailer's sister Barbara since their days growing up in the Crown Heights section of Brooklyn. (The ceremony would take place on Thanksgiving Eve of 1955, with the reception held next door to the Fulton Fish Market.) He was, as sized up by his friend Mailer, a profoundly ambitious and dissatisfied man, one who could not accept another failure.

Of the two men, Wolf was the other-world type, Fancher the this-world one. Mailer's metaphor for Fancher was built around the fact that he had been a fullback at prep school: that was appropriate, Mailer said, because if you needed two yards straight ahead you'd want to give the ball to Ed Fancher. Prep school for Fancher had been at Lake Placid, after a childhood in Middletown, upstate New York, and before going off to the University of Alaska in Fairbanks, where he wrote a column for a local paper, *Jensen's Weekly*, about the campus. Then came a semester at Middlebury in Vermont, and the campaign with the ski troops of the 10th Mountain Division in Italy. While his friend Wolf continued to be a thinker and a drifter, dropping out of the New School, Fancher continued to be a doer and an achiever, going on to get his bachelor's and master's in psychology there. By the time he had agreed to be the publisher of this new paper, he had supervised a research project at Cornell Medical School, interned with the New Jersey Department of Mental Hospitals, taught psychology at New Rochelle High School, affiliated himself with something called the Institute of World Affairs, surveying the attitudes of foreigners residing in America, and set up his own, straight-Freudian practice there in the Village.

He was just past thirty, single again after an annulled marriage, living in a front-to-back railroad apartment upstairs from his friend Wolf, and into the Village scene—to make money on the side, he would pack people's things into his van and move them into the Village for $5. He was a booster of where he lived, eager to proselytize it and participate in the debate about its demise. "A lot of people think the Village died fifty years ago," he said at the start. "We don't. Those are the great days, this is the Golden Age." He also had an inheritance, $30,000 worth of stock in the Orange County Telephone Company left him by his grandfather, to use as seed money.

The decision to publish an avant-garde, iconoclastic, Bohemian weekly from out of the Village was, on the face of it, not a propitious one, and Fancher did not make it lightly. Three previous Village weeklies had folded—*Quill's Weekly* and *Bruno's Bohemia* in the 1920s, *Caricature* early in the fifties. So had two radical Left journals that, if not pegged for the Village per se, had certainly been aiming at that disaffected downtown sensibility for which it was known, first *New Masses* and, only recently, the metropolitan area afternoon daily *PM*.

Fancher's neighborhood might be, in words he chose for a speech twelve years later to the New York Press Association, not just "a central and vital district of New York City" but "a community unique in all America." It might be the nation's "center of innovation in the arts" and "a symbol in the American consciousness, just as Hollywood is," with "its tradition of rebellion and freedom" creating a magnet for "creative young people from all over the nation, and even the world," but putting over such a paper would be a lonely challenge.

The reason was that the Village was even more diversified than it seemed on the surface. It was not now, and never had been, the exclusive domain of an artistic colony. There was an Irish ethnic base, and a long strip where Little Italy became the South Village. There were longshoremen's bars, and bars where you could be beaten up, particularly if you were black and were there with a white girl. There were street gangs. There was organized crime—the Café Bohemia, a lesbian joint on Barrow Street, was a front, and author John Williams remembered later how at Conte's Restaurant downstairs in his building the "customers came generally in long, sleek, dark cars"—and there was the Tammany machine. And there was an increasing number of people who could see no difference between the two, as "The Bishop," Carmine G. DeSapio, ran the Democratic Party, and often the government, at the district, city, and state level from out of his Tamawa Club.

Most important to remember was that a blueblood business and banking community controlled the neighborhood's commercial life, and had succeeded in stifling the earlier newspaper ventures in the Village by denying them support and advertising. The paper that *was* thriving in the Village, the paper they *did* support, since 1933, was the *Villager*. "Reflecting the Treasured Traditions of this Cherished Community," said its masthead. "We feel the same responsibility to our neighbors that any small town community paper must feel," said its editor, Mrs. Emeline Paige, in a CBS television interview once. "It isn't our fault that some of our neighbors are fairly famous people." Every week it ran twelve to twenty-four pages of cake sales, weddings, births, deaths, home recipes, business news, press releases, a column by a cat, and headlines like MRS. SMITH'S TREE CARE REWARDED. And every week it reached, for free, its controlled circulation of 27,000. Dan Wolf and his friends might not know anyone who read the paper except for its apartment ads, but it was catering beautifully to the editorial tastes of those who *were* its advertising base.

So it would be a challenge. But, as Ed Fancher told the lawyers in depositions when he was suing its new owners twenty years later, "I'm a gambler. I didn't start the *Voice* except as a gamble." And there was a percentage, he thought, in accepting this particular challenge. Since the war there had been a building boom in the area, and he was anticipating the result: an alteration of the microcosm, an infusion of still newer blood, a new emerging force of young, degreed, white-collar professionals who would have an intellectual connection to the editorial product he would be offering, and no allegiance to the old established forces in the neighborhood that would be shunning it.

They began to collaborate, Wolf taking the free-form flights of imagination that provided the conceptual overview (at first he envisioned an international Bohemia's newspaper with a global network of stringers), Fancher taking care of the nuts-and-bolts (since he was after all the one who had taken a course in newspaper publishing), neither one of them having any idea really of what the hell they were doing or what they were getting themselves into. No puff pieces for advertisers, they agreed. That meant no birthdays even, no weddings, club meeting notices, "new business notes," none of that. No joining local organizations to gain acceptance. And, since they knew so many writers, and Dan Wolf didn't know what it was an editor was supposed to do anyway, they decided it would be a writer's paper. They would let the writers write, and if they liked it they would run it. That was all there was to it, they thought. They didn't even realize at that point that nobody else did it that way, and when they found out, it didn't matter. It might not be professional, but that was the way they wanted to do it.

★ ★ ★

The Village Voice was originally conceived as a living, breathing attempt to demolish the notion that one needs to be a professional to accomplish something in a field as purportedly technical as journalism. It was a philosophical position. We wanted to jam the gears of creeping automatism.

When they were finally over the hump, Edwin Fancher would look back and say, "We had the advantage of being extremely naive. If we had known anything at all about publishing we never would have started the paper." Not that nobody had tried to warn them. Hearing that someone in the Village was "plotting a gazette for intellectuals," Hearst columnist Louis Sobol, writing in the *New York Journal-American,* delivered one of his little seriatim chops, ". . . Looks like a dismal future."

★ ★ ★

The first thing they did was to get a name and some money. Both came from Norman Mailer. Even two full decades after their battles with him were over, their version of how it happened still did not agree with his. Theirs was that when they could not decide what to call their new venture, they made a list of possible titles, and Mailer picked the one thought up by a woman named Patricia Woods, an English teacher who had commuted to New Rochelle High School with Ed Fancher. His was that as he struggled rewriting his novel *The Deer Park* so that its pivotal character, Sergius O'Shaugnessy, might find his voice, the thought struck him that the Village, too, needed a voice. That was it, Mailer thought: *The Village Voice.* At any rate, it stuck. Mailer also agreed to match Ed Fancher's initial investment of

$5,000 and to become, with Wolf and Fancher, a 30 percent, founding stockholder. His lawyer, Charles Rembar, drew up corporate papers for the remaining 10 percent of stock, in lieu of a fee.

That was about all they heard out of Mailer for a while. Going through an intense personal crisis, feeling his personal life and his literary career both going south on him, Mailer had followed the astounding success of his first novel, *The Naked and the Dead,* with *Barbary Shore,* which got, as he himself said, "the worst reviews of a serious novel in years" when it came out in 1951, and *The Deer Park,* another bomb in the making that had been dropped by one publisher and rejected by seven others before Putnam took it. He was in the middle of his second bad marriage. And he was either stoned from smoking marijuana or speeding most of the time. He holed up for the summer touching up *Deer Park* one last time and read Vol. 1, No. 1, with, as he put it later in *Advertisements for Myself,* "the detachment of someone who had paid a nickel at a newsstand." That detachment was not going to last long.

They did their first hiring. A twenty-four-year-old Greek and Latin scholar at Columbia University, Joel Slocum, became their first business manager; he found for them their first office, a two-room walk-up on Greenwich Avenue above Sutter's Bakery. Florence Ettenberg, a pert, tiny, black-haired alumna of Queens College, where she had been editor of the paper, answered their ad in the *Times* and quit a $50 job with a radio-TV trade magazine for a $40 job with them as editorial assistant, which comprised, as she said looking back on it, "doing all the yucky things the guys didn't want to do." Her boss told her, "You're crazy. This is a great opportunity. You're never going to make any money," and her parents were a little amazed as she pedaled each morning on her bike from Park Avenue all the way down to the Village. But she became their first secretary, worked on developing circulation and advertising, and learned layout from a Virginia-born Village artist named Nell Blaine, who designed their first logo, plain white-and-black script on a gray block. She also rather quickly had a romance going with John Wilcock, the first of many that would develop under the various *Voice* roofs through the years.

John Wilcock was twenty-eight years old then, and, for $25 a week, was the paper's news editor. Born in England, he had lived through the Blitz and, beginning at sixteen, gotten into the newspaper business, first with the *Daily Mail* and the *Daily Mirror* in London, then across the ocean with the United Press's Toronto bureau, then as assistant editor of *Liberty* Magazine. For the last year he had been an assistant editor at *Pageant,* hanging around his favorite haunts in the Village—

Julius' Bar on 10th Street, Sam Kramer's drugstore—and getting into discussions with people about a new paper until he hooked up with Ed Fancher and Dan Wolf that spring.

The other editor, the associate editor, also at $25 a week, was Jerry Tallmer, and no other employee was as important in those early years. Ed Fancher had met Tallmer, a man built like a reed with a soft voice and a head of disobediently wavy hair, two years earlier at a cocktail party. When he called him again now in 1955, Tallmer was living at 62 Perry Street in the Village, a tenant of two ladies—one of them an anthropologist, the other an editor at Viking Press—who were friends of Fancher's and had introduced the two men. He was also thirty-four years old, had broken up with his first wife, and for the last year had been staring out his window looking at the pigeons, absolutely unable to write.

"Hello, this is Ed Fancher," said the voice on the phone. "Do you remember me?" Tallmer remembered a guy with a red beard who had wanted to save Greenwich Village by declaring all of it a national landmark. "Dan Wolf, Norman Mailer, and I are starting a paper. Are you interested?" Jerry Tallmer wanted to know if there was any money in it. No money, Edwin Fancher told him. Good-bye, Jerry Tallmer told Edwin Fancher.

A week went by. Jerry Tallmer, still staring at the pigeons, found himself strolling over to 22 Greenwich Avenue to see what the offices of the new paper looked like. When he got there, it was the rattiest sight he had ever seen. There it was, this loft, a big room with a few desks and typewriters, a tiny alcove in back with a sofa and a grubby bathroom, and John Wilcock ripping up pieces of paper and throwing them in the air. Jerry Tallmer was delighted.

Almost alone among all the people Ed Fancher and Dan Wolf knew, Jerry Tallmer knew something about newspapers—how to lay one out, how to write headlines, how to get ads and writers—from his days running the college paper at Dartmouth and working as an assistant editor for the *Nation*. As they went out to lunch at a Chinese restaurant, he asked them how much money they had. Five thousand, they told him. Well, if you had twice as much you'd have enough to make it, he said. But you don't, so maybe I'll be able to do a review now and then, but no more, and there they left it. Jerry Tallmer went home. And he began thinking: they'll need movie schedules in there. Next thing he knew, he was going around to the theaters himself, not telling Wolf and Fancher what he was doing, arranging with the managers to run the movie times, and going back to the office with that bit of news. When he did that Ed Fancher knew he was hooked, and soon Tallmer was putting in marathon hours for no pay, until the day, having picked up the extra financing he had recommended, they surprised him by putting him on salary—such as it was.

Throughout the summer they worked upstairs at 22 Greenwich, sometimes sixteen hours a day, sometimes more. Tallmer located a printer and recruited some writers. Other writers—or would-be writers—just streamed in, volunteering to work for nothing, which was fortunate since there was no money to pay them. Fancher, Wolf, Tallmer, and Wilcock, meanwhile, drew up lists of novelists, poets, and critics they would ask to contribute.

It was John Wilcock who came up with the suggestion of Gilbert Seldes. Seldes, the distinguished critic for the *New York Times Book Review,* had been, as far back as the 1920s with the publication of *The Seven Lively Arts,* a seminal culture critic, his range embracing popular culture—movies, comics, jazz—as well as academic-aesthetic standards. He was living on Manhattan's Upper East Side, and Jerry Tallmer was chosen to go see him. As Tallmer recalled it after Seldes's death in 1970:

> . . . I found him alone, padding around cheerfully, the furniture draped in dust covers.
>
> I seem to remember a dog. The man on whom I was calling put me at ease and I went into my pitch: ''Mr. Seldes, some of us down in the Village are at work on this new newspaper, and we haven't any money to pay you with, but the idea is . . .'' And then, after much perambulation: ''So if maybe once in a while you would care to write something for us, because maybe you could say it in *The Voice* and nowhere else. . . .''
>
> Gilbert Seldes stopped me, smiled, and said: ''I'll do it. On one condition. That I have a column once a week, every issue.''

And, just like that, America's newest weekly newspaper had writing for it one of America's best-known critics, every week, for no money.

Bill Fischer was running the Blue Mill Restaurant in the Village that summer of 1955 when one day his friend Ed Fancher came in for lunch. "What are you doing?" Fischer asked, and for the next hour Fancher told him. How he thought he was going to start a new newspaper. How the *Villager* was a dull sheet. How there was room for something else, a paper that could not only compete, but be a cultural magazine, go citywide, national, international.

This is ridiculous, Fischer said to himself, but charitably kept his thoughts where they were. *He has no experience.* When Fancher left, Fischer turned to his wife, and the two of them agreed: this was the most wild-eyed scheme they had ever heard.

Nevertheless, plans proceeded. They retained a distributor, Liberty News. And they set a target date for the first issue—Wednesday, October 26. Eleven days before that, the *New York Times* devoted a short article to the new venture, quoting Wolf that his new paper would be "neighborly without being small-town" and "very heavy on Off-Broadway theater." Four days later, on October 19, 1955, one week before publication, one of their ad salesmen walked in "and announced," as they reported the fact in their journal later, "the astounding fact that he had just sold our first ad."

One week later, they were ready. It appeared, subtitled "A Weekly Newspaper Designed to be Read," twelve pages for five cents, purportedly "on the newsstands of New York" but, as a practical matter, distributed or available in the West Village, Chelsea, Gramercy, Cooper-Stuyvesant, and the Lower East Side, all of them Lower Manhattan neighborhoods. The lead story: VILLAGE TRUCKER SUES COLUMBIA—a war buddy of Fancher's, thirty-six-year-old Fred Fleck, who had run the moving van service with him, had been expelled by the university's School of Social Work after writing an editorial critical of the school in its student paper, *The Process,* and was demanding $50,000. Also in the news, under the byline of Village writer Howard Fertig, was the arrest of a young robber from New Jersey. "Eight times in the past eight years some kid after easy money has made a target of John Tintor's liquor store on West 12th Street," Fertig reported. "The eighth—but first robber this year—walked into the store Saturday night and achieved the dubious distinction of being the first one to get caught . . . [He] was nabbed by police and taken to the Charles Street station." Also there was news of a New School speech, of a new priest sent to the Village from Assisi, of twenty to thirty families threatened with eviction by New York University getting a stay of a year, of a prize from the Village Arts Center to a subway doodler for his oil painting on a station wall "complete with hearts and arrows, swear-words, and signs saying 'Joe was here.' " There was a photo spread of folk singers in Washington Square, a notice that the Greenwich Village Association sought new members, an item headed "PEOPLE" that "thirty-five-year-old Jerry Zahn, owner of a service which provides animal actors for TV and film studios, is currently sharing his bathtub with a 15-lb. turtle which somebody casually left on his West 10th Street doorstep last week," and some very tacky, pseudo-*New Yorker* cartoons (one, by Muriel Jacobs, captioned "Why, you little rebel!"). In the back of the

book, there was Jerry Tallmer on Off-Broadway's *Threepenny Opera,*
Alan Bodian reviewing *Mr. Roberts,* Vance Bourjaily on the play *The
Diary of Anne Frank,* William Murray of the *New Yorker* panning *The
Man in the Gray Flannel Suit* (It is "comforting to feel that *Life*
Magazine's search for a happy heterosexual American author will not
be entirely fruitless," said Murray), and Michael Harrington, still of
the staff of the *Catholic Worker* at this point, with a review of Budd
Schulberg's book *Waterfront,* which had been the basis of Elia Kazan's
film, *On the Waterfront,* starring Marlon Brando, the year before.
There was Gilbert Seldes's column "The Lively Arts," a notice of the
Art Theatre's Charlie Chaplin Film Festival, and a column by Jerry
Tallmer's new wife Peggy, "The Village Shopper."

"Within the limitations of the given space, *The Village Voice* has
made an attempt, here in Vol. 1, No. 1," it said on the last page, "to be
comprehensive in covering or listing all such movies, plays, galleries,
and the like, that it feels fall properly within its 'beat.' It is, however,
quite possible that in the process of putting together a newspaper for
the first time, certain such events or places have been overlooked," and
the paper said it "would be grateful to be informed of any such
instances of neglect." It had taken great precautions that there would
be none. In its first issue, the *Voice* devoted forty-eight inches of space
to theater, twenty-eight to movies, twenty-five each to photography
and books, eighteen to art, ten to music, six to dance. The movie
schedules Jerry Tallmer had thought they would need, they had, for all
the movies playing in the Village—*Gigi, Summertime, Mr. Roberts,
Beauty and the Devil, Symphonie Pastorale, The Cabinet of Dr.
Caligari, Love Is a Many-Splendored Thing, When Tomorrow Comes,
Man on a Tightrope, The Adventures of Sadie, Man from Laramie,
Special Delivery, Bengazi.* Their advertising ratio: 20 percent. Half a
page of classifieds. Subscriptions, $2 a year. Projected, "a net paid
circulation . . . of at least 10,000"; actual circulation, 2,500.

Operating losses: $1,000 a week.

3. IF WE HAD KNOWN MORE WE CERTAINLY

would have suffered less. On the other hand, if we had been business-men or professionals we would probably have failed because it is not the way of the expert to pursue absurdities in a cool and resistant world.

★ ★ ★

Jerry Tallmer took one look at the first mail, and knew they were on to something: the letters were so much better written than any other paper's.

Not that it was all flattering. "Usually I am not one to discourage creative effort," Frances Bemis of West 13th Street began, but she was "startled and enraged" by this new publication. "Who can find time to read two Village publications?" she asked.

Robert DeNuncio of Macdougal Street was positively enraged. "Aside from your paper being dull, dessicant [*sic*], high-schooly, and utterly embarrassing, it proved wholly distasteful." He was particularly upset about the robbery story. "Haven't we enough *Daily Mirrors, Daily News', Posts,* and other offensive periodicals. Why all this hogwash about a poor youth caught stealing? Only 18 years old, and you moral righteous unartistic abortions have to follow the way of all papers. You claim your publisher to be a psychologist? What psychologist in his right mind would allow such damnation of youth! At least that 18-year-old was rebelling, and that's more than your paper has even dared venture."

"I like the format of the paper," said one favorable letter. "But for heaven's sake," and now the tone changed, "have the reviews up to date and have a little common sense in the writing. Other Village papers became too stodgy and would not break away from a small-town routine; and now you, with what appears to be too many inexperienced critics and writers, are attempting to go just the opposite. A happy medium would be fine." It was signed "A Reader," no address.

James Church wrote from upstate Poughkeepsie that the "tone is perfect." However, he noticed two mistakes—the use of *its* for *it's* and *renumeration* for *remuneration.*

The next week, the paper announced that it "welcomes letters, and will print as many as it can find space for," with the editors "exercising their privilege of condensation or omission" for "space and taste . . . these two grounds and one other. From this week on, no unsigned letters," or pseudonyms, such as the "New Reader" letter they were

19

printing. The week after that, in Vol. 1, No. 3, Robert Cowan of East 5th Street had praise that "in spite of your reviewers' glib pseudo attitudes, your paper is a welcome addition to the Village. Thank God it is not a paper full of aimless chitchat about Mrs. Whatsit's lovely teas." But Robert Gurdison of East 3rd Street wrote, "It must be fun to have a sounding board to do anything you want with. Aren't we clever though? The word, gentlemen—and ladies—is dilettantish." A whole new tradition had been born—the *Village Voice* letter column as community sounding board, as exchange of dialogue and dialectic with its writers, as a repository for random outrageous opinion. Letters like that would not stop coming for many, many years.

Dan Wolf would remember that "we were called pinkos when we came out, but we were very middle-of-the-road, really. We were radical journalistically, perhaps, but never politically." In fact, at the time, not even journalistically. Jerry Tallmer's back of the book worked right from the start. In December he celebrated the end of his writer's block. "Reviewers are certainly difficult people, and probably ought to be taken out and shot," he began, and launched into an expressive, ambivalent piece on why an Off-Broadway production of Chekhov's *Cherry Orchard* had been "mechanistic." A few weeks later he reviewed *Marty,* the film written by Paddy Chayevsky and starring Ernest Borgnine which would go on to win an Academy Award but which Tallmer, ahead of time, nominated as "The Least Humble and Most Aggravating of 1955."

"So it has turned into an essay, not a review," he admitted at the end. "So that's what the *Voice* is here for, isn't it? You know all about *Marty* already, anyway, and if you don't, you soon will. Go and see it and let me know what *you* think. I'd like to know; I really would." Tallmer had every Off-Broadway production reviewed at least once, needled the uptown critics for ignoring them, and continued to recruit new contributors who provided the paper with a cross-fertilization of ideas. One typical early piece, by Vance Bourjaily, began this way: "Paddy Chayevsky's *Middle of the Night* can't be dismissed lightly; it can, however, be dismissed heavily, and here we go."

But the news was another matter. In the front of the book, the *Village Voice* was, in its earliest days, a thoroughly ordinary newspaper. In the second issue, its lead story told readers there was "no such thing as 'an average Villager.' " With one scriptwriter paying as much as $90 for rent, "the traditional cold-water flat is evidently getting harder and harder to find," the survey found, and concluded with this quote from a twenty-three-year-old actor: "Usually I just look for jobs, but mostly I brood."

It continued that way. Advance word of a book by Dylan Thomas, and of publication of the memoirs by a Village-based priest of his time in Moscow. Eleanor Roosevelt stating her opposition to Communist China's admission to the United Nations "so long as China maintains troops in Korea and Viet Nam," and the naturalization of Marcel Duchamp as a citizen. An article on "the waterfront priest," Father John Corridan, dropping his fight against union corruption, and one on conditions at the Women's House of Detention. Headlines ran GREEN-WICH VILLAGE 'A WAY OF LIFE,' THE SEARCH FOR A VILLAGE APART-MENT, THE PRETTY GIRLS AT NUMBER 123, VILLAGERS REVEAL THE MEAL THEY'D MOST LIKE TO EAT, and VOICE ASKS VILLAGERS: IS THIS AREA NOISIER THAN REMAINDER OF CITY? There were man-in-the-street polls, personal items (two local clergymen appearing on the TV quiz show *The Big Surprise,* for instance), and interview pieces, in Q-and-A format, such as the ones by Millicent Brower, an aspiring actress and old friend of Norman Mailer's, on what men thought of "The Greenwich Village Girl" and what they in turn thought of "Those Village Men."

If it was John Wilcock who would later put down the *Voice* as "never far out" and only seeming to be so at the start from the hangover of McCarthyism, it was also John Wilcock who was largely responsible for the tone of that early *Voice*. Wilcock, with his jet black hair, his dour features, his tinny, almost squeal-pitched voice, his fascination with everything American from women to television, was a Bohemian, but he was not yet a freak. His background was in Fleet Street tabloids, hence lots of page-one police blotter stories (a thirteen-state alarm for a seventy-two-year-old Villager who may have lost his memory, the booking of a jail guard for abetting a prisoner's suicide, a fire near the Mercer Street station, the suicide of a Village actor, a fifteen-year-old boy killing himself with a rifle given him as a gift) and what Jerry Tallmer called his fondness for "man who" leads ("A man who once . . . today . . ."). He was still new to the scene, hence the ingenue, journalism-school tone of such pieces as VILLAGE TRUCKERS: THE LAST NICHE OF FREE ENTERPRISE. He was also not getting along with anybody else in the place. If Dan Wolf asked him to do something, he would snap back, "Don't tell me to do that, you do it." Dan Wolf took it as a kind of blackmail, because Wilcock knew what to do, and Wolf didn't, and Wolf knew Wilcock knew it.

They coexisted like that for eleven issues, the seed money going at a sickening clip until it was by now very nearly depleted. Wolf greeted the new year 1956 with an editorial that was ostensibly optimistic: "There have been a few shunners and a few who were outraged by our presence—some even before the first issue of the paper—but the smallness of their number has convinced us that the spirit of fair play is as characteristic of Greenwich Village as are all its other attributes." Yet in that same editorial Wolf had to take note of a letter to the editor from "one of our most valued contributors and friends," William Murray, criticizing them for rejecting a political piece he had written.

Meanwhile, they were making their first personnel changes. John Wilcock was eased out as news editor to be gradually replaced by Dan Balaban, a former economics teacher at Goddard and Briarcliff Junior College. But Wilcock stayed with the paper, getting a page 2 column, "The Village Square," that he could do what he wanted with—that was what he had really wanted all along—and that kept him in the office, it turned out, at least as much as ever. With all the tension surrounding Wilcock, Flo Ettenberg waited a while, then left, their romance continuing for another four years until she met her future husband on a vacation in Haiti at the same time Wilcock was wooing her long-distance with jewelry, roses, and telegrams. Gene Dauber was hired to take photographs and Ruth Blazy to handle classifieds; within months his place would be taken by two women, Molly Cook and Rubi Juster, and hers by the cantankerous Rose Ryan, who would last twenty years in the job. Ed Fancher's friend Bill Welborne took charge of circulation. Howard Fertig went out to Queens one night and knocked on the door of a promoter and marketing salesman whom he knew. His name was Joe Coleman, or Jack Coleman, or Joe Cohn, or Joseph K. Coleman, or just plain Joseph K., depending on what kind of a mood you caught him in, and Coleman had many moods. He came into the paper to run its sales staff, which at the time consisted of all poets, a situation that Fancher later remarked, only half-facetiously, "has led to four nervous breakdowns and eleven reorganizations." (One of them was named Harvey Shapiro. People in the office remembered him as the nervous, reluctant salesman sent to restaurants they believed were owned by the Mafia. Twenty years later he became the editor of the Book Review section of the Sunday *New York Times*.) Printers were switched to Washington, New Jersey, necessitating two consecutive all-nighters each week sandwiched around a ride across the state. Howard Bennett bought into the paper and his name appeared on the masthead as business manager.

And in that same first issue of 1956, Ed Fancher informed readers that "beginning with our next issue *The Village Voice* will have a weekly column contributed to our pages by Norman Mailer."

★ ★ ★

Even before this, an unspoken tension had entered into their relationship with Mailer. He was living on the Lower East Side with his second wife, Adele Morales. He had met and taken up with her right after she and Ed Fancher had broken up their affair. This was a point never articulated by any of them, but it was there, and they were all less close than they had been. And Mailer was, he himself would say later, as close to a nervous breakdown as he had ever been. Convinced beforehand that *Deer Park*, which had been physical agony for him to write, was going to restore the luster he had lost since *The Naked and the Dead*, he took out and designed himself a full-page ad in one of the early *Voices* displaying the worst pans it got. ("All over America *'The Deer Park'* is getting nothing but RAVES! 'Sordid and crummy'— Herman Kogan, Chicago *Sun-Times*. 'Disgusting'—Houston *Post*. 'The Year's Worst Snake-Pit in Fiction'—Frank O'Neill, Cleveland *News*. 'Moronic Mindlessness . . . Golden Garbage Heap.'—John Hutchens, N.Y. *Herald-Tribune*. 'A Bunch of Bums'—Scott O'Dell, L.A. *Mirror-News . . .*") As he would explain his actions later in *Advertisements for Myself,* "It was my way I now suppose of saying good-by to the pleasure of a quick triumph, of making my apologies for the bad flaws in the bravest effort I had yet pulled out of myself, and certainly for declaring to the world (in a small way, mean pity) that I no longer gave a sick dog's drop for the wisdom, the reliability, and the authority of the public's literary mind, those creeps and old ladies of vested reviewing. Besides," he added puckishly, "I had the tender notion—believe it if you will—that the ad might after all do its work and excite some people to buy the book." In the event, it did not.

Mailer was in a flaming funk, and in his search for something to do now he began coming more and more into the *Voice* office, peppering his partners with suggestions. Eventually, they reached the point where they had grown tired of listening to him. They also reached the point where they had run out of money. So two things were done.

The first was to bring in Howard Bennett. Mailer did not know Bennett well. Dan Wolf did, and he did not like him. But Edwin Fancher, who had met Bennett as well as Wolf at the New School after the war, had maintained separate friendships with each of them, and Bennett now convinced them all that he had money, good business savvy, and a lot of interest in their project. Actually, the amount of money he had was not large, in Dan Wolf's scornful appraisal the only job he had ever had was as a part-time librarian at the New School in exchange for taking courses, and he harbored secret dreams of supplanting his friend Fancher at the head of the business side of the operation. But Bennett, at the start of 1956, was in, and at the new stockholder's request Charles Rembar, Mailer's lawyer, was out. The stock, its value such as it was, was reorganized. Fancher dropped in another $10,000 to keep them going. Mailer matched his $10,000.

And Mailer began to write his column.

★ ★ ★

The column began as a dare, really, a chance, they thought, to give Norman a chance to act out his ideas, sublimate his anxieties, maybe even keep him busy. They did not know the half of it. Mailer, stoned out of his gourd from smoking dope perhaps a majority of his waking hours by now, had evolved a whole new persona for himself. He was "General Marijuana" now, his stock of "Mary Jane" was "a secret weapon," and this column of his was going to, unbeknownst to his business partners, become "the declaration of my private war on American journalism, mass communications, and the totalitarianism of totally pleasant personality." He was going to get back at television, literary critics, Cold War rhetoric, all at once, all by himself. He was going to shatter every convention, violate every sensibility there was. He was even going to attack his own audience. He would be outrageous. He would make a spectacle. He would raise obnoxiousness to an art form. He would commit preposterously antisocial acts on paper. He would insult everyone. He would test the outer limits of everything. He would be Mailer. Or so he thought.

"Do not understand me too quickly," the French novelist André Gide had said, and Mailer had admired the phrase, used it often. Now, he used it again, for a title—"QUICKLY: A Column for Slow Readers." The German émigré writer Thomas Mann had influenced him too, and it was Mann who had said that only the exhaustive was truly interesting, so Mailer turned in his copy, after deadline, twice as long as it was supposed to be. And he wasted no time getting started with the process of alienation.

> Many years ago I remember reading a piece in the newspapers by Ernest Hemingway and thinking: "What windy writing." That is the penalty for having a reputation as a writer. Any signed paragraph which appears in print is examined by the usual sadistic literary standards, rather than with the easy tolerance of a newspaper reader pleased to get an added fillip for his nickel.
>
> But this is a fact of life which any professional writer soon learns to put up with, and I know that I will have to put up with it since I doubt very much if this column is going to be

particularly well-written. That would take too much time, and it would be time spent in what is certainly a lost cause. Greenwich Village is one of the bitter provinces—it abounds in snobs and critics. That many of you are frustrated in your ambitions, and undernourished in your pleasures, only makes you more venomous. Quite rightly. If I found myself in your position, I would not be charitable either. Nevertheless, given your general animus to those more talented than yourselves, the only way I see myself becoming one of the cherished traditions of the Village is to be actively disliked each week.

At this point it can fairly be asked: "Is this your only reason for writing a column?" And the next best answer I suppose is: "Egotism. My search to discover in public how much of me is sheer egotism." I find a desire to inflict my casual opinions on a half-captive audience. If I did not, there would always be the danger of putting these casual opinions into a new novel, and we all know what a terrible thing that is to do.

"At any rate, dear reader," he concluded, "we begin a collaboration which may go on for three weeks, three months, or, the Lord forbid, for three-and-thirty years. I have only one prayer—that I weary of you before you tire of me. And therefore, so soon as I learn to write columnese in a quarter of an hour instead of the unprofitable fifty-two minutes this has taken, we will all know better if our trifling business is going to continue."

It was an auspiciously inauspicious beginning for what he wanted his column to say, but it was not all he said. In the middle there was this digression, this tangent, where the prose seemed to be barbed, not for the benefit of Mailer's readers, but for his confederates instead. *The Village Voice,*" he was saying, "which is remarkably conservative for so young a paper, and deeply patriotic about all community affairs, etc., etc., would not want me either if they were not so financially eager for free writing, and a successful name to go along with it, that they are ready to put up with almost anything. And I, as a minority stockholder in the *Voice* corporation, must agree that this paper does need something added to its general languor and whimsy."

Remarkably conservative for so young a paper. I, a minority stockholder. They were beginning to fight, and it was over this.

Mailer was beginning to see what a temperamental conservative his friend Wolf was, and it was true. To protect this experiment of theirs, Wolf—and Fancher too—felt they had to play it safe. Didn't Mailer see what a risk this was they were taking? The paper had to survive.

Mailer didn't see why it had to. He was beginning to think they saw him as an egocentric, and that was also true. What was certainly *not* true was that Mailer was any kind of temperamental conservative. Though he was capable of advocating any political point of view at any time, or, even better, many at once, he was temperamentally a revolutionary, always had been, always would be. Make the point, make a splash, he told them. Make this paper so radical, so far-out, so graphically shocking that when it folds it makes this giant éclat. So it folds. So what?

Dan Wolf was telling him no. *If we do that, this thing is going to go up in a puff of smoke. It'll blow up. It'll explode. The paper must survive.*

And Mailer was answering him, *You can't see, my friend, that there are more important things than* a fucking newspaper. *There's this whole media straitjacket, in New York, in America.* But even Mailer could see, or thought he could see, what was happening. Mailer wanted to be the editor of the paper so it could fail. Dan Wolf could not accept another failure in his life. He and his partner were worried about McCarthyism in the country and the Mafia in the Village. They had to contend with that, and with the *Villager* too. That was the competition. They were different enough from the *Villager* as it was. If they couldn't beat the *Villager* at covering local news, if they couldn't convince advertisers they were respectable, they couldn't last. If they couldn't last, they couldn't do anything. It was as simple as that. They wanted to put out a paper because they wanted to put out a paper. What did Mailer want?

Mailer wanted to put out a paper so he could go out like gangbusters with it, so he could lead one last rocks off–kamikaze–Pickett's Charge at the House of Eisenhower, maybe set off an earthquake underneath, maybe even start the process of insinuating those alien agents, anarchism and sex, inside. What Mailer could not know, what no one could possibly pick up on yet, was that, in just a very few years, all that was going to be happening anyway, in between commercials.

The next week, Mailer turned in an unbelievably prolix and periphrastic essay. About how "an old social idea is a lie." How "the act of writing something (which one expects or hopes will be published) . . . becomes—even at its best—all but a lie." How "four-fifths of gossip-columnists' spew" was "sheer premeditated falsity." About how "to communicate by way of the mass-media . . . is equivalent to communicating very little." And on. And on. And on.

Ed Fancher took one look at it, just as he and Wolf and Jerry Tallmer were ready for takeoff in Tallmer's car for the weekly expedition to the printer in New Jersey, and suggested that, maybe, it was going to be just a little bit much for some readers to get through. Mailer, "the

General," agreed—but did not withdraw the column. Instead, he merely prefaced it with an *achtung*.

> A WARNING: The column this week is difficult. True to my commitment to the *Voice,* I wrote it quickly. Because I do not want to lose all my readers at once, I suggest that all but the slowest readers pass me by this time. If you are not in a mood to think, or if you have no interest in thinking, then let us ignore each other until the next column. And if you do go on from here, please have the courtesy to concentrate. The art of careful writing is beginning to disappear before the mental impotence of such lazy audiences as the present one. . . .

That did it. The next issue, the *Voice* was bombarded with letters. Not responding to the column—hardly anyone had read that. Responding to that "warning" before it. Responding to Mailer in general.

He had one defender, Leo Stutzin of Brooklyn Heights—"Laurels to Mailer! At last someone has had the guts to look at things as they are, to see the Village as the stench-permeated seat of bitterness and frustration which it is, and publicly state it." Norman Rosten, also from the Heights, was a little more ambivalent. "Read *'Quickly'* slowly—and to my astonishment it had some very good things," he wrote. "Even some logic. What have you done to Mailer? I think the column is a good idea," he said, then added, referring to the young Mailer's picture that ran with the column—lumber shirt, baby face, big black curls in the hair—"but for Chrissakes get him a haircut."

The others, however, were not ambivalent, and they were not defenders. "This guy Mailer. He's a hostile, narcissistic pest. Lose him," advised one Phyllis Lind of West 87th Street. Elizabeth and Fritz Rikko of West 11th Street said that "as subscribers to *The Village Voice,* which we quite enjoy, we suggest that for the sake of the newspaper and its readership you eliminate the column by your arrogant, rude, and probably unintelligible stockholder, Norman Mailer." Lu Burke of Bleecker Street put it this way: "Society, Mr. Mailer, is people, and in this country most of us speak English." Finally, an irate Joe Jensen of Bank Street accused him of "getting yourself a 'reputation' by gutlessly imitating (prim term for thievery) Dos Passos in your ONE & ONLY book, and now *again* imitating by stencilling yourself upon the very overworked, tired, boring, creaky, mimeographed Henry Miller in your column. . . . It's a cinch your romance with yourself will be recorded as one of the most magnificent love stories in history.

"Curiously, will you have the *Voice* run this letter, too?" Jensen asked. "I doubt it," he answered himself. "Kiddo, you're not *that* contemptuous of public criticism." But it did run, all of them did, and in answer Mailer wrote this:

REPLY

I'm tempted to call my column "TONIC—A Charge for the Sluggish." Since the criticisms about my most indefensible personality have almost nothing to do with what I wrote last week, I suggest my correspondents read last week's column over again. Mailer, poor chap, does suffer from megalomania, but it is more or less true of all his work that it improves on second reading.

N.M.

In time, Mailer would concede that, as for this column, "rarely have ideas which were worth a clean show been given such a muscle-bound presentation." But for now, that was all he had to say. That, and complaints to his colleagues at the *Voice* that *inspired* in his copy had come out *inspiring* in the paper, and that there had been other typographical errors.

★ ★ ★

The week after that, having gotten it into his head—somehow—that this artillery barrage in the letter column meant that his campaign was *winning,* "the General" switched directions, and produced an undergraduate-level *roman à clef* parody of the American columnists' establishment. "COMMUNIQUÉS FROM THE MARSH MEDIA," he called it. Ed Sullivan became "Ed Sullen-Vain on C's of B.S.," Hedda Hopper of the *Daily News* became "Cheddar Chopper in the N.Y. Daily Nose," Max Lerner and Leonard Lyons of the *New York Post* became "Wax Burner" and "Learned Lions" of "the N.Y. Homely," Dorothy Kilgallen of the *Journal-American* was "Dorothy Kill-Talent in the N.Y. Churlish-American," and Niccolo Tucci, a *New Yorker* staff writer who was beginning to do some columns for the *Voice,* "Niche Touchee" of "the Village Void." The *Mirror*'s Walter Winchell himself was spoofed as "Voltaire Vein-Chill in the N.Y. Daily Rimmer":

Jail to you, Mr. and Mrs. Erotica and all the flips on Tea. . . . Several solovisions down in Greenwich Village where they put two holes in the doughnuts for the perverts are putting out a monthly rag called "Village Vices." Playwright Norman Mil-

ler—he scripted "Naked to the Death"—now Svengaling
those hammy hermits into Poverty Row where there are NO
holes in the doughnuts!!!

More letters followed—not one of them responding to his spoof.
Instead, readers were still obsessed with that second column. From
Glastonbury, Connecticut, reader Ruth McGray commented on the
"restrictions" Mailer had mentioned toward the end of it: "Without
being free to express the *raw* facts of life in his exuberant way, certainly
ulcers will result! Take care of him, please." In a long, rambling letter,
Robert A. Perlongo of West 12th Street tried "to understand" and
"sympathize" with him. Eli Siegel of Jane Street wrote a poem about
him "in the Metre of Tamburlaine."

Nor was that all. Reader Kenneth J. Schmidt of the Village, a regular
letter-writer who had already done a sendup of an interview the *Voice*
had done with a lady bullfighter, sent in a parody of his own, "Burp: A
Column for People Who Can Read, by Normal Failure," lampooning
both the ideas and the style of that second column. Mailer devoted the
first half of his fourth column to reprinting it, and had to admit that it
was superior to the satire he himself had done.

He rasped on. By Column Eight, in the issue of February 29, having
promised the week before, "Next week: The best column written so far
in this space," he was putting into print his admission that "this
column is beginning to bore me." Meanwhile, back at the office, his
relations with his colleagues had deteriorated almost to zero.

As his moods got blacker, he became more and more impossible.
Cover this. Cover that. Cover Sex. Murder. Dope. Revolution. Revolu-
tion. Dope. Murder. Sex. He spent two days drawing up a logo he
wanted the paper to use instead of the ones Nell Blaine had designed.
Besides her plain, original logo, she had done one showing slices of
Village life—bistros, Beats, bustling street corners—which the paper
ran sometimes. Mailer's version showed Village vignettes, too—Bowery
bums, dead bodies, abandoned babies, addicts shooting up. Jerry
Tallmer was convinced that he wanted to put out the *New York
Enquirer,* and Mailer could not stand Tallmer's long reviews. *YOU
WROTE THREE PAGES OF FUCKING SHIT ABOUT A PLAY
THAT CLOSED TWO WEEKS AGO,* Mailer hollered at him at one
point. Eventually, if they spoke in the course of a day, it was for one to
leave a harpoon in the side of the other. Even in the midst of one of his
column's *longueurs,* Mailer found a way to get a shot in: "Some time
I'm going to write a column when I'm drunk," he announced, "and
confess it as such to my readers." Then, in parentheses: "Since most

columnists write that way all the time, my action should prove offensive only to those with the highest sense of decorum. As, for example, Jerry Tallmer of this paper."

Undeterred and undaunted, he wrote a stylebook for the paper. Let's interview a criminal, a murderer or somebody, he said. Let's get some dialogue in this paper. He came by for the makeup of the front page one week. John Wilcock was laying out the dummy. Mailer thought he'd direct. Wilcock thought otherwise. "You can fire me," he blew up at Mailer, "but if you have the front page, you do it. I quit." Wilcock, Mailer knew, had made a shrewd guess; he, Mailer, wasn't about to lay out page one for the rest of his life. He respected Wilcock for that, and backed off.

Next, they thought maybe Norman could help with circulation problems. Fancher's buddy Fred Fleck, subject of the *Village Voice*'s first lead story on its first page one, had in the meantime been hanging around the office doing odd jobs and becoming convinced that they could do a better job delivering the papers themselves than their distributor could. He took Mailer to meet the people at Liberty News, convinced him the two of them could do it together, and then, their first Wednesday morning out together, picked a fight with Mailer and quit on the spot.

So now they had no distributor, and no Fred Fleck to do the distributing. All they had was Norman Mailer holding the bag. Nevertheless, for the next month the author of *The Naked and the Dead, Barbary Shore,* and *The Deer Park* got up on Wednesday mornings while it was still dark out and drove to locations all over Lower Manhattan delivering newspapers. He mapped out his own delivery routes by hand. He wasn't allowed to park in front of most newsstands, so he would have to double-park on the other side of the street and run across. "What's this stupid rag?" the owners would ask him, and he would have to wheedle with them to get the paper on the stands: "Look, just take it. But take five copies, not three." By the end of a month, the little old Jewish ladies who waited out in front of their stand for him in their babushkas were telling him in their Yiddish-inflected English, "The paper's doing a little better this week." Norman Mailer, in his brief career as a deliverer of newspapers, had been a success.

When Wanamaker's, the Village department store, had closed, it had been converted into an exhibition hall. There was an international floor show there that month, and the *Voice* had a stand inside. As their distributor of the moment, it was up to Mailer to see that they had copies of back issues there to give away as samples, so on the morning it opened he found himself lugging packets of back issues across town to the exhibit. Flo Ettenberg was with him. She was still getting used to Mailer, which required that she rehearse beforehand how cool she was going to be each time he would say "fuck" three times in one sentence. Suddenly, there on the streets, she put down her bundles and began laughing, uncontrollably, hysterically, without letup. Mailer stopped, too, wanting to know what was so funny. "Someday," she told him, in between new outbursts of laughing out loud, "I'm going to tell my grandchildren that I delivered papers with *Norman Mailer.*" Now Mailer, too, got the joke. "That's right," he said. "And they're going to ask you, 'Was that before or after *The Naked and the Dead?*' And you're going to say—'AFTER!' " And then he put down his bundles and broke up, too.

★ ★ ★

They found another distributor, and Norman was left with only his column again. He was still grinding his ax. "It is a relief to find myself sufficiently punch-drunk so that only the people who are closest to my life can hurt me any longer," he told his readers the week of April 4. "The obverse, of course, is that I enjoy hurting other people much more than I used to." When a friend, the psychoanalyst and author Robert Lindner (who had reviewed *Deer Park* favorably in the *Voice*), died at the age of forty-one, Mailer, with "no heart to write about him now," turned over his space that week to reprinting selections from Lindner's works. He issued an open challenge to debate any Village psychiatrist, got one hostile, condescending letter, and staged the debate anyway by breaking up the statements of his "Dr. Y" into dialogue form, where they were cleverly answered by "N.M."

He nominated Ernest Hemingway as the Democratic candidate for president, though allowing as how "I have not voted since 1948, and I doubt if I will vote in 1956." When six Marine Corps recruits drowned during training on Parris Island, Mailer, the ex-Marine, wrote his best column, exploring the double-edged ambivalences he felt about the Corps—how "I know I never felt so insignificant and so without dignity" as in boot camp, and yet how "I feel I give way to the anti-human plague of our time if I fail to recognize such obvious virtues as courage where courage indeed exists." He renamed the column "The Hip and The Square." He became more furious than ever with typos in his column. He became more furious than ever with his colleagues.

★ ★ ★

In this, he had an ally in Howard Bennett. Not that he and Bennett got along, or agreed on a vision of what the paper ought to be. It was simply that Bennett was fundamentally a critic, thought he should be advertising manager, and thought all advertising managers came into the office at four o'clock in the afternoon, which is what he did. *You spent sixteen hours trying to get an account that was already exclusively for the* Villager, he needled Fancher and Wolf during one of their battles. In what were now four-way office fights, Mailer and Bennett made up a coalition of the left and right against the center, Fancher and Wolf. While at all other times, Mailer and Bennett, with the latter's proclivity to criticize everybody and everything, couldn't stand one another.

Look, there was a murder in the Village the other day, Mailer snapped at one of these sessions. *You had nothing on it.*

Did the Villager? they answered back.

FUCK THE VILLAGER! he screamed at them.

The break was almost total. In the midst of one such fight right near the end, Mailer became so incensed with his friend Dan Wolf he let fly with a torrent of abuse that, in Mailer's subsequent, diplomatic description of the episode, cast aspersions on him both as an editor and as a man.

One reader wrote in from Queens, tabulating forty-three separate uses of the first person in a single column, but by the issue of April 25, the week after his piece on the Marines, Mailer was able to proclaim that "for the first time since I have been writing this column, the favorable letters outnumbered the unfavorable." That week he devoted his column to answering one from Bernard Zemble of Hillside, New Jersey, who asked him to "tell me, what is your definition of a hip person? A third-rate rape artist or a boy who digs Shakespeare, Milton and Freud?"

"Could be either," Mailer answered, and told him that "those who are Hip have a state of mind—a way of looking at life—which is altogether different from those who are Square." That "Hip is an American existentialism, profoundly different from French existentialism," that "its origins can be traced back into all the undercurrents and underworlds of American life, back in the instinctive apprehension and apperception of existence which one finds in the Negro and the soldier, in the criminal psychopath and the dope addict and jazz musician, in the prostitute, in the actor, in the—if one can visualize such a possibility—in the marriage of the call-girl and the psychoanalyst." That "the language of Hip, the argot of Hip, is virtually a new Basic

English, and the simple words which are the building blocks of its view of life, particularly such words as Man and Go and Make and Swing and Cool and Dig, have a primitive wealth of conceptual meaning which may possibly endure long after the television comedians and the gossip columnists and the hucksters have abused it almost to death." And, finally, that Hip "is still a vast human and historical distance from the philosophy which may follow it, a philosophy which may be imbedded some day in a four-letter word so famous and infamous that this newspaper would be destroyed if I were to put it into print."

All the ideas were there, mentioned in skeletal form, that he would develop into his seminal essay on that subculture and period, "The White Negro," and the subject so excited him that at the end he wrote, "I intend to continue writing about it for at least the next few weeks."

Just before that he had said, "Hip is not totally negative, and has a view of life which is predicated on growth and the nuisances of growth." Except that Mailer had originally written *nuances of growth,* not *nuisances* as it came out. Another typo.

★ ★ ★

Jerry Tallmer had proofread that line. At that time, their schedule on printing day began, after staying up late getting the stories in, the headlines written, and the dummies all laid out, at 4 A.M., with their drive, on perhaps three hours' sleep that would be all they would get before Wednesday, in Tallmer's car—at least until the bottom fell out of it—to the printing plant on the far side of New Jersey. On one such trip, along icy roads in the middle of that winter, the arguments between Mailer and his colleagues were very nearly settled, abruptly and forever. Four of them—Tallmer, Wolf, Fancher, and an editorial assistant named Susan Ryan—were in the car as it came over the steep hill that rose on the approach to the plant. They reached the crown, Tallmer applied his brakes, and they began to sail, down the hill, careening out of control on a sheet of ice, right toward another car that was on its way up. Tallmer had regained control of the wheel and they had slid safely into a snowbank. So the history of the *Village Voice,* and of its founders, did not come to an untimely end after only a few forlorn issues. But even when the trip was uneventful—and one hot day that summer, about to enter the Lincoln Tunnel, they turned around to find the back seat on fire—they would be there all day or most of the night, lucky to get back through the tunnels into the city without getting stuck in a traffic jam. And, dead tired from all this, Jerry Tallmer read over that line, noticed nothing wrong—after all, they reasoned later, *nuisance was* a word, maybe a better word than *nuance* to use here, and it certainly made sense that way—and passed it by.

Early that morning, they finally got back to New York, and Jerry Tallmer finally got to sleep. Sometime around noon, he woke up and went into the office. Right away the phone began to ring, and he picked it up. On the other end of the line, there was this voice.

"WHY DON'T YOU GET YOUR FINGER OUT OF YOUR ASS? WHY DON'T YOU GET YOUR FINGER OUT OF YOUR ASS?" It was Norman.

He had seen the typo, and for him this was the last straw. Jerry Tallmer had just put in another ninety-hour week, and for *him* this phone call was the last straw. He blew back at Mailer. This time, things were finished. Almost.

★ ★ ★

There was a debate going on in the pages of the *Voice* right at this time about *Waiting for Godot* in general, and the uptown Broadway production of it in particular. Jerry Tallmer had started it, concluding in his review that "the play as produced by Michael Myerberg on Broadway is not the play as written in Paris by Beckett, or as read by me, at any rate, here in New York." Herbert Berghof, the Villager and drama coach who had directed the play, was furious: "You probably do not know the original French version," he wrote, "nor do you base your statements upon correspondence with Mr. Beckett on the play—as I do," which was an interesting comment, because Barney Rosset of Grove Press, which had published the text of the play, also wrote Tallmer, "to tell you that both Beckett and I very much liked your review of *Godot.*"

Into this debate Mailer jumped at the beginning of his seventeenth column, in the issue of May 2—admitting right at the start that "I have not seen *Waiting for Godot* nor read the text."

Having stated his qualifications, he proceeded now to declare his interest. "What amuses me," he began, "is the deference with which everyone is approaching Beckett, and the fault of course, the part which is sad, is that none of the celebrators of Beckett have learned anything from Joyce (for whom Beckett worked as a secretary)." Not that Mailer knew his Joyce either—"like many of you who will read this, I have read perhaps half of *Ulysses* and fragments from *Finnegan's Wake.*" Then he extended the sport:

> But at the very least, the critics could have done a little rudimentary investigation into the meaning of the title of *Waiting for Godot,* and the best they have been able to come up with so far is that Godot has something to do with God. My congratulations. But Godot also means 'ot Dog, or the dog

> who is hot, and it means God-O, God as the female principle, just as Daddy-O in Hip means the father who has failed, the man who has become an O, a vagina. Two obvious dialectical transpositions on "Waiting for Godot" are To Dog The Coming, and God Hot for Waiting, but anyone who has the Joycean habit of thought could add a hundred subsidiary themes. As for example on Go, Dough! (Go, Life!)
>
> Nonetheless, I like To Dog The Coming as the best, because what I smell in all of this is that "Waiting for Godot" is a poem to impotence, and I suspect (again out of the ignorance of not having seen it) that Beckett sees man as hopelessly impotent, and the human condition as equally impotent. Given the caliber of the people who have applauded *Waiting for Godot,* I further suspect that the complex structures of the play and its view of life are most attractive to those who are most impotent.

And given the fact that Jerry Tallmer, associate editor of the *Village Voice,* was a critic, had liked *Godot,* had seen a Christ metaphor in it, had even called it "without any doubt the most serious piece of writing to come our way since the death of Joyce," a reader might further suspect that there was more to this Mailer passage than its specious reasoning and its tortured anagrams and its hip jive, that maybe "the caliber" of "those who are most impotent" was a classification meant to include him.

"Now, to make a most brutal transition," Mailer suddenly interjected. "Nearly all of the rest of this column is deeply depressing for me to write." And, under a separate heading, he brought up the matter of "The Nuisances of Growth."

"Errors in type-setting and proof-reading fall into two categories," he told his readers, "those which are obvious misspellings, and those (more serious and more interesting psychologically) where a word is left out or changed into another, and the meaning of the sentence thereby becomes altered. Yet the reader never knows that an error was made.

"Last week," he informed them, "a classic of this sort occurred," and he gave them both versions, his as written and as it appeared in the paper, to compare. Then he wrote this:

> In the four months I have been writing this column, similar (for me) grievous errors have cropped up in all but two of the pieces I have written, and these errors have made for steadily increasing friction between the Editor, an Associate Editor, and myself. Since no cliche is more true than that there are

two sides to every story, the Editor and Associate Editor, who are hard-working gentlemen, claimed that the fault was due to the fact that I am in the habit of turning in my column at the last minute, which undeniably increases their difficulties.

At any rate, we all had some words, some fairly sharp words, certain things were said which can hardly be unsaid, and the result is that this is to be my last column for *The Voice*—at least under its present policy.

Now, the quarrel was actually trivial, and I can take most of the blame for the way it went, but as happens so often, we were all of us at bottom arguing about something else—a much more serious difference of opinion which I have had with the Editor and Publisher.

They wish this newspaper to be more conservative, more Square—I wish it to be more Hip. We have compromised our differences for many weeks as best we could, and *The Voice* has perhaps suffered from the compromise. But, at present, since I am a minority stockholder and have no real voice in the control of anything except my column, I have decided that this contradictory association can go on no longer. If the paper is to become anything at all, it is necessary that I step out, for too many energies are being wasted in internal disputes. (Let me add that these disputes were not about my column. Although the Editor and Publisher agreed with very little in it, they allowed or submitted to a most rare freedom of the press.)

For those of you who are Hip and wish *The Voice* to be a Hip newspaper (which would make it the first in New York) I think I ought to add that the Editor and Publisher are very responsive to their readers' opinions, and if you make yourself heard, this newspaper will reflect your influence. If you do not, then the Editor and Publisher will prove to have been right—to have made a better objective estimate of the situation and of what interests readers—and so the fortunes of this newspaper will prosper more without me than with me. Perhaps there is room in Greenwich Village for two community newspapers—which has been their contention all along.

At any rate, this is a farewell column, and I for one am sorry it had to come to an end so abruptly. We may not have had the most pleasant of relationships, but it has been stimulating for me, and perhaps stimulating for some of you. I regret only that it became impossible to go on writing about the nature of The Hip and The Square, for that was fascinating to me, and I had finally found the subject (yes, after all these columns) which I wished to explore. So, regretfully, good-bye for awhile. I wonder in which form some of us will swing into communication again.

There was an "Encore" attached, in which, "as a last fillip," Mailer purported to reprint what he described as "the only poem I have ever written, a poem about potency and impotence (as well as other things), which is called *The Drunk's Bebop and Chowder,* and appeared in my novel, *The Deer Park.* Let us see how many typos are in this," he challenged. "If there aren't too many, try reading it aloud," he suggested to his readers. What followed were ten lines of sexual doggerel in a gibberish that could best be described as Typo English, which Mailer had devised, and which he insisted be followed word, such as they were, for word.

In that same issue there was also a Dan Wolf editorial alluding to the public resignation Mailer had made, and the stated reasons for it: "The one condition we agreed to, as Mr. Mailer declared in his first column, was that he would have complete editorial freedom. . . . We have always in the past lived up to our agreement not to edit or censor Mr. Mailer's copy, despite occasional serious reservations on our part about the matter. At his insistence now, we are also leaving intact the copy of this, his final column, despite reservations more serious than any to date."

That same day, May 2, the agreement between them was drawn up by Charles Rembar, Mailer's lawyer. There was really not all that much to agree to. Fancher and Wolf had 60 percent of the stock between them. Mailer and Bennett had 40 percent of the stock between them. There was no way Fancher and Wolf were surrendering control of the paper to Mailer and Bennett. And even if they had, there was no way Norman Mailer would have wanted Howard Bennett running the business side of *his* paper, and no way Howard Bennett would have wanted Norman Mailer in the paper *he* was running. But that problem could be handled later. For now, they agreed to these terms: Fancher and Wolf would retain 60 percent and control. Mailer and Bennett would retain 40 percent, and for that they would stay away from the office, not attempt to make editorial policy, and not contribute any more money. If Fancher and Wolf at any time could not maintain at least $4,000 in liquid assets, their 60 percent, and with it control of the paper, would revert to the other two. That was it. The partnership of Dan Wolf and Ed Fancher with Norman Mailer would continue, with him *in absentia.* Their friendship with him was over.

★ ★ ★

Mailer's defenders were out in force the next week. "Without Norman Mailer there is no *Village Voice*," Penny Funt of East 10th Street declared. Following Mailer's advice to write in, Ben Newman of Washington Place cast his vote "for a more Hip newspaper." A letter signed B. and F. Rubinstein of Boston, wishing the paper luck but cancelling two new subscriptions, said, "Without Mailer we just do not find *The Voice* interesting enough to bother with reading," and Julian Ludiner of East 5th Street lamented, "At last I found—and unhappily will not find again—excitement, frivolity, and seriousness in a small-town newspaper." From Joan Lorraine Smith of Bedford Street the message was, "Man you goofed—but really goofed."

To Maxwell Kenton of West 23rd Street, "It *is* one of the nuisances of growth that would lead you to question the value of his column. . . . You would be well advised to ask yourself: Why is the paper becoming successful?"

The man whose inquiry about "The Hip and The Square" had led to the whole final flap, Bernard Zemble of Hillside, New Jersey, told those at the paper to "go hang your head in shame. You now have a square, sterile newspaper." Even Joe Jensen of Bank Street, who had been so furious at the first two columns he had called Mailer a plagiarizer in love with himself, was "extremely sorry" to see him go now.

But the chorus of those glad to see him go was heard from, too. Bringing "the Square around to a Hip point of view," suggested Roy Lindberg of Third Avenue in Brooklyn, "is not necessarily best accomplished by shock treatments. . . . When a man comes up with a truly important idea, he no longer needs to march naked through Times Square in order to attract attention to himself."

A student at the Columbia School of Journalism, and a future New York journalist, A. Kent MacDougall, wrote from his place on West 112th Street, *"The Voice* is richer for the loss of the castrated bellow of N. Mailer. That the author of *Naked and the Dead* deteriorated to a point where he wrote such undisciplined gibberish is pitiful. Once I was a Mailer admirer. Now I feel like putting a quarter in his tin cup and saying a prayer over his departed literary genius." And Miss Leslie Stuart of Horatio Street "thought Norman Mailer's column quite bad, but he does have beautiful curls. How about compromising and continuing to print his picture only?"

To go with all this sampling of opinion pro and con in the letters column about the last appearance in the paper of Norman Mailer, there was—another appearance in the paper by Norman Mailer, in the form of a full-page advertisement (so the editors would not have to be responsible for what he said), saying, "It is never particularly pleasant for me to apologize, and in the present circumstances I loathe doing so. To announce a farewell appearance and then be on the scene again" was bad enough, but "for one artist to attack another" (though Beckett was, he made the point, "a minor artist") was "a crime, and for the first time in months I have been walking around with a very clear sense of guilt."

What had happened was that in the meantime Mailer had read the play, seen the play, read the play again, and come across an interview with the author in the *New York Times* where Beckett had indeed referred to "impotence" as his subject. Anyway, Mailer delivered himself of a huge essay about the play, its sense of (as he saw in it) Christ and sex and pessimism, and his interpretation of the characters Vladimir and Estragon as "a male and female homosexual" who "are so desperate they even speak wanly of hanging themselves, because this at least will give them one last erection."

But for his decision to quit, there was no apology. And there was no change of mind.

★ ★ ★

Norman Mailer went off to Europe, to get the Seconal and the Benzedrine out of his system, to clear his head up. From home he heard that the *Voice* was in trouble, and he felt glee, he laughed at their troubles. But when a year later he heard that Howard Bennett had sold out his stock and mounted a competitor, he found himself rooting for his old partners. Bennett's paper was *East,* a graphically ambitious, photo-offset weekly that had a lot in it of what would be called counterculture material ten years later, and it folded. Mailer returned to the United States, and his partners began to pay off their debt to him. In *Advertisements for Myself* he wrote an *apologia pro parte suae vitae,* ready by then to concede his errors, that, looking at it objectively, they not he had been right, and the friendship warmed up again, though it would never reach the intensity of the pre-paper days. Mailer even resumed contributing occasional pieces to the paper, still complaining about typos when he did. And, incrementally, he began to see it moving in the direction he had wanted it to go from the beginning. He knew that he had wanted to go too far too soon, that if he had been editor the paper would have failed, but on the other hand, he told himself, the fights had accomplished something too, gotten the paper talked about when it needed to be, kept Fancher and Wolf from failing by going to the other extreme, by being too conservative. And ulti-mately, it all seemed comic to him. It had never seemed comic to him then, when, he recalled, there was Tallmer with his vision for the paper and Wilcock with his and Fancher and Wolf with theirs and Bennett with his and Mailer with his, each of their visions absolute, none of them conceiving of a paper with more than a single, institutional point of view. The final irony, Mailer believed, was that they had all been right, that the paper reflected five or six different traditions, that every one of their ideas had found itself in the *Voice* eventually. It became, ultimately, a forum, which is all he had wanted all along, Mailer said, and he was glad to have had a hand.

★ ★ ★

That, of course, was Mailer's estimate of it, and perhaps he could not be expected to remember, as his partners would, how difficult that period had been with him, how unbearable it had been to be around him, getting into fistfights with people around town, hollering in rages at them, writing badly and behaving worse, his personality disintegrating, his talent bleeding out of him. It was as Mailer had said in his very first column when he made two statements, one that "I doubt very much if this column is going to be particularly well-written," and the other, about his partners, that "they are ready to put up with almost anything." He was right on both counts. The column had indeed been badly written, and his partners were ready to put up with anything. Almost anything.

"Self-expression usually ends as therapy," he wrote in *Advertisements for Myself.* Though he knew better, that he needed "a fallow year" after the strenuous undertaking of *The Deer Park,* "my readers suffered through more than one week, while the column served as therapy for me: I was eliminating some of the sludge of the past." And since "I sensed little of this at the time," breaking friendships was the next step.

But this period in his life would not be a total loss. Mailer would stage a comeback from this black funk writing better than ever, acclaimed within the decade, deservedly so, as the greatest living American writer, when any lesser talent could have been expected to self-destruct or go into permanent oblivion. Nor had he been without his prescience. He sensed early, in the dropout lifestyle of the Beatniks, in the prose of Jack Kerouac, in the new sensibility that went against the prevailing culture and that he called Hip, "an underground revolution on its way," and in his last column, several years ahead of time, he described it.

I feel the hints, the clues, the whisper of a new time coming. There is a universal rebellion in the air, and the power of the two colossal superstates may be, yes, may just be ebbing, may be failing in energy even more rapidly than we are failing in energy, and if that is so, then the destructive, the liberating, the creative nihilism of the Hip, the frantic search for potent Change may break into the open with all its violence, its confusion, its ugliness and horror. . . .

"The violence is better without than within," he thought, "better as individual actions than as the collective murders of society," just as he thought that more than anything else the revolution, when it came, would be, should be, a sexual revolution.

In all of this Norman Mailer had anticipated the sensibility of the 1960s, and when that sensibility dawned, when that revolution was ready, it would leave its tracks there in the pages of his very own newspaper. But this was still 1956, and Norman Mailer was leaving, and Dan Wolf was writing,

> Our idea for a paper was a ruggedly individualistic journal unhampered by surveys and statistics, a paper where people could speak to people in a community that is one of the most vital and knowledgeable in the world. What we really sought to find out six months ago was if there was any room for the free-est of free enterprise, or if caution was the only watch-word of the day. With 26 issues behind us we have our answer . . . unparallelled loyalty and doggedness can make a reality of any idea . . . not just a success but probably the best human experience any of us have known.

At the moment Dan Wolf was writing those words, the friendship and the partnership was breaking up, the paper would not stop hemorrhaging financially, and any week now they might go under.

4. THE VOICE, FROM THE VERY BEGIN-

ning, attracted talented people who found no place in the regular media. Even though the paper was based in Greenwich Village and fought many local and political battles, it quickly took on the character—in a very modest way—of a national newspaper. People began writing in from all parts of the country. We concluded that there is a "secret" group in America that is somehow vaguely uneasy about life in Peoria.

★ ★ ★

He was "not really sorry that Mailer's column has ended," wrote reader Walter Maundel, "but I absolutely agree with him that the *Village Voice* editors are taking a wrong direction. I think we are all sick of Charm," he told them, "particularly Village Charm."

> Sick of teeny weeny Village houses, philosophical bartenders, Saroyan policemen, serious discussions of serious movies, quaintness, friendliness, and *tedium vitae.*
>
> Sick of front-page stories (inevitably) about churches and ministers. Of pictures of the publisher drinking tea with the 8th Street Merchants' Benevolent Association. Of John Wilcock or Wilcox. Of most of your reviewers.
>
> I do not believe there is room for two "*Villager*"-type newspapers. And even if there is, why bother?

Now that the great Mailer contretemps had been settled, their way, now that they were on their own, the paper began to move, away from what it had been, in the direction Mailer and others had wanted it to move, but their way.

★ ★ ★

1956 . . . A special takeout section featuring photographs of 8th Street . . . For the summer, the paper goes monthly. . . . The ghost of a man named Alex Hamilton reported to be visiting the house at 27 Jane Street—to flush the toilet . . . Irreverent film reviews by Brigid Murnaghan, a tough-talking, hard-drinking beautiful blonde Bohemian girl . . . *Look Back in Anger* is panned by Millicent Brower. . . . In the September 26 issue, the paper publishes a poem by Steve Allen, host of the NBC weekly variety show originating live from New York. . . . Hungarian refugees stream into the Village, and Dan Wolf, in an editorial, pleads that more be let in:

> When we told the people of Hungary, day after day, that to live under Communism was worse than death, they believed us and acted accordingly. Moreover, they acted in a way that most Americans feel they would have to act if they were oppressed by Communism. . . . There is hope for the Hungarian people; oppressed or free, they know the things they are fighting for. The question is: is there any hope for us?

★ ★ ★

The money was not coming in, but the writers were, and their running commentary, like nothing seen before in an American newspaper, kept it going, for the next seven years. Four-letter words made it in, even *fuck,* Mailer's magic word, though no one was ever sure quite when and Wolf downplayed the development. Wit still came in the mail, such as in this dispatch from Queens: "This continuous inference that nothing happens out here. Things happen all the time in Queens. The garbagemen come every Tuesday, Thursday and Saturday." Muriel Jacobs drew for them (her best was of a Beatnik walking down the street holding his young son by the hand; the son, dressed like his father, had a toy beard strung across his chin). So did Hasse Nordenstrom, the Swedish cartoonist whom Dan Wolf never met, and Jim Frankfort, the Belgian-born American, under the acronym "Jaf," and Shel Silverstein, who also wrote pieces for them plus, in years to come, his own Rabelaisian repertoire of songs.

And the paper, meant to be a tribute to individuality, began to attract some highly individualistic writers.

Jean Shepherd was, then as now, a New York radio personality. Ed Fancher, prone to bouts of insomnia, would frequently stay up listening to his all-night show. Shepherd was a Villager himself, offbeat, eccentric—as a gimmick he decided to create a demand for a product that did not exist, and began mentioning a novel called *I, Libertine* on the air, starting the rumors in literary circles and the inquiries at bookstores. Fancher called him up, and Shepherd started to contribute to the *Voice.* He became a frequent figure around the office; his sketches of it appeared in the paper. And for nine years, from 1957 through 1965, he co-hosted, with the new distributor, Dan List, the Village Auto Rallye, a procession of antique cars through the streets one day each summer. Casper Citron, prior to becoming a night-time talk show host on another New York station, wrote, for a year between 1956 and 1957, the paper's first political column.

A young man from the Lower East Side—restless, aggressive, full of hostile energy, talent to burn, deeply into the theater, and starving— came in to see Jerry Tallmer, looking for something to write. His name was Charles Marowitz, and Tallmer sent him way over on the Lower East Side to the Emmanuel Brotherhood Church where a CBS producer named Joseph Papp was directing a makeshift Shakespeare company featuring such still-undiscovered talents as Colleen Dewhurst and Roscoe Lee Browne. Marowitz returned, raving that they had proved all you need for a theater is a plank and a passion. Since Marowitz spoke Yiddish, Tallmer told him to do a piece on the Yiddish theater in New York. He did, but this time he did not come back with a rave review; instead he rather bluntly pronounced Yiddish theater dead, and touched off a controversy with its partisans. Then he wrote a piece dismissing the Stanislavsky Method and the Actors Studio, which brought a rebuttal from actress Marta Curro, who had studied under Lee Strasberg there. In 1957, Marowitz moved to England, and, from Hampstead, caused another stir by putting down the English Bohemians and their "angryoungmanism," writing about how "it has become fashionable to grouse in the abstract, hurl invectives upon society, or slump into the corner of a coffee-bar and sit with a dazed, myopic, this-life-is-for-the-birds expression on your face. . . . American visitors to England seek me out and ask me to define angryoungmanism and to point out types—very much as the Greenwich Village tourists used to ask me to point out the queers!"

Katherine Anne Porter could be found in their pages. In the summer of 1956, she responded to a request to contribute with a letter from her place in Southbury, Connecticut, reminiscing about her days in the Village. Later, in fact, she did contribute, with a recollection of two characters from her Village days, Romany Marie, the self-styled "Gypsy Lady" and coffee house–restaurant proprietor who entertained and fed the Bohemians for over twenty years, and Joe Gould, one of those Bohemians. Ezra Pound was a contributor, too. So were e e cummings and Allen Ginsberg, and, "because poets are the only people who never get anything," Ed Fancher decided they, unlike the other writers, would get paid. "They get $2," he was quoted as saying. "When they ask for it." Henry Miller wrote a piece for the paper. So did critics Eric Bentley and Paul Goodman, too—but their stuff was rejected.

Niccolo Tucci was a staff writer at the *New Yorker,* looking to say something new in a new way, when he came across Ed Fancher at a cocktail party and began to tell Fancher what he would like to write. Fancher told him to write it instead, for the paper. Tucci did so, and in the third issue, that of November 9, 1955, began, not just his own column, but a permanent *Voice* tradition. "The Press of Freedom," he called it, and the title stuck, even into 1976, as a permanent heading in the paper, "open to articles from our readers" to be selected by the editors "on the basis of literacy and interest."

"The defense of the individual," that first column began, "must be the care of the individual, not of the State." The individual seemed to be what Tucci was always writing about. That, and totalitarianism, and communication, and a lot else that was often hard to tell in the intense, impressionistic prose.

Two weeks later, he followed that statement up with one on cultural freedom: "The Iron State is the Iron Lung State. No one needs an iron lung unless he is paralyzed." Other topics included "The Strapless Cocktail Party," "Negative Gravitation of the Will," the dilemma of the artist "selling out," and "The Blue-Haired Angels," those old ladies who pick up young boys. In three installments of writing about them Tucci covered a lot more ground, to wit:

> The male-devouring woman has always existed and always been disliked by men, except for those men who were slightly effeminate and for whom only such overpowering females had any appeal. Today's strong women are not the male-devouring type at all; they are innocent, adolescent, unintuitive, stupid girls who never grow up and who want their share in the world of love and want it right away, regardless of whether the man they choose likes them or not.
>
> Now if those men could only put those women in their place by telling them the unpleasant truth, all would be well on both sex fronts. . . . Why do these women act so stupidly? Because they never spend a minute trying to listen to the voice of their ancient, much-honored, now completely discredited feminine intuition. . . . If such women went straight to the rapist, as they go to the chiropodist and the psychoanalyst, they would be either killed or cured, and in both cases the world could only be improved by the practice. The shock would teach them something, they would get the real beating they so richly deserve and unknowingly crave. . . .

★ ★ ★

1957 . . . Gilbert Seldes defends Jackie Robinson's decision to quit baseball rather than accept a trade from the Dodgers to the Giants and attacks the press for attacking him. "You see, the newspapermen had been doing Mr. Robinson a favor all these years. Printing his name and everything. Not putting 'a Negro' after it every time he hit a home run or something. Treated him good, and look what he goes and done!'" . . . "The hero in modern America," he writes in the January 23 issue, "is not the philosopher who retires to his Walden to ponder the ways of man, nor the frontiersman who declares: 'I will go farther into the unknown.' In this day and age it is the man who says to the M.C. on a TV quiz show: 'I'll take the next question.' " . . . The *Voice* runs a story about just such a man, Charles van Doren. . . . In April, Wolf, Fancher, Tallmer, and Dan Balaban give their memories of how they heard FDR had died, on the twelfth anniversary of his death. . . . That October, there are paratroopers stationed in Little Rock, Soviet Sputniks circling the earth, and blacks complaining about discrimination right in the Village. Wolf asks, "Why are we so concerned with depriving Negroes of our housing when, in perhaps a year or so, we shall have to defend ourselves against invasions of green men from Mars with antennae in their heads?" . . . Seldes wants to know, "What is the Russian word for 'know-how?' I am not quite among those who are ready to junk the whole American system of free enterprise because the Soviet Union launched the first satellite. But I am ready to junk 95 percent of what we've been told about the natural-born, innate superiority of the American executive (in business or production) who responds to the only incentive that will ever get things done—which is profit." . . . That summer, old Bohemian Joe Gould, the ancient, hard-drinking, street-walking compiler of "The Oral History of Our Time," friend of cummings and Hemingway and William Carlos Williams and Saroyan and Malcolm Cowley and many others, dies after his committal to a mental institution. Dan Balaban goes to the funeral. "Finally, they bearded and buried Joe Gould," he opens his piece. "On Friday, August 23, he lay clean-shaven, hands folded, made up like a little wax doll." Balaban goes on to do a massive profile on the event, staying up all night to write about "A Bohemian Who Stayed On Too Long." . . . "Three itinerant poets came here to roost last week, but not for long," Balaban writes another time in a straight account of a visit to the Village paid by the avatars of Beat. "The 'San Francisco Poets'—Jack Kerouac, Allen Ginsberg, and Gregory Corso—told *The Voice* they were off to Tangiers to pursue their exciting destiny. 'We are witless madcaps,' they announced, 'who sing little insensible ditties.' " . . . At the end of the year, Balaban is off to write on his own. Eventually he winds up in New Jersey. . . . And Joe Coleman is there, with Corinne Grad, as the birthday party Mike Todd throws for Liz Taylor at Madison Square Garden degenerates into a food riot by the celebrities.

> . . . Men in tuxedos and women in gowns stumbled among the empty bottles, draining dregs for the free cham-

pagne. . . . Men who pride themselves on diner's cards and knowledge of the better restaurants fell and groveled over each other for pieces of ham, women who demand the right sauce with their Lobster Diavalo [*sic*] shrieked over tasteless, half-raw watery shrimp.

Men who make decisions that affect the lives of thousands in their industries ripped at each other and growled over 59-cent toys from Japan. They mounted the trucks that the whole mess had been brought in on, and threw apples at each other.

★ ★ ★

Nancy Hallinan, one of their writers, suggested Sy Krim to them. Seymour Krim, his full name was, and at that point in his life, recently released from the hospital after suffering a nervous breakdown, he was seeking a way out of the "joyless" literary criticism he had done for *Commentary* and other publications. With the *Voice* he got his chance. "The Nearsighted Cannoneer," he became. He wrote about sports. He wrote about jazz, and when he did he did not write what the paper's resident critic, Robert Reisner, wrote about it. He, in fact, did not tell the paper's audience what it wanted to hear at all. To Krim, they were in Mailer's phrase, "White Negroes"—literally.

Jazz is the music of the colored people. It came out of squalor, ignorance, the most ignoble and pathetic kind of conditions. . . . So we had white men and women imitating the Negro philosophy of life because they loved the music from which it inevitably and naturally came . . . the awful ignorance, poverty, violence, lack of constancy, me-firstism, and all the other symptoms that fair-minded people who know Negro life well—the inner lower-middle class communities of Harlem, or Newark, or Durham, North Carolina—see all too often. And that, too, is part of jazz.

When one reads *The Voice*'s graceful and worldly jazz columnist Mr. Reisner write about ''the titans'' of jazz, and all sorts of romantic business about the greatness and sophistication of jazz instrumentalists and the ''hipness'' of its philosophy, one can't help remembering nights in Harlem apartments of acquaintances where the music—the beautiful jazz music—came from unpaid $400 Philco combination radio-phonographs with the husband and wife at each other's throats over the money (before she got hit) and the four children screaming at the sight. Or the jealous husband, another time, who thought his drunken wife ''made'' a friend of his in the bathroom (where the john was stopped up and had been for two months because the landlord of this stinking trap wouldn't fix it) when he went out for a pint of whiskey. And again the slugging of the wife, the grappling on the kitchen floor, the screaming of the kids, and the final hop out of the first-floor window by a 5-year-old little toughie to get a cop on 125th Street and bring him back. And the cringing of the white man during all this.

. . . What would you white jazz-lovers say if you saw your own people, thousands of them, enslaved to the hocus-pocus of various Father Divines—still operating by the carload in Harlem and Philadelphia—buying furniture and especially the needed music-boxes, phonograph, or radio on time, time, time, the girls buying earrings and the men booze or sharp ties when the kids need medical help or the ex-wife is forced to 'go into the life,' become a prostitute, ''because my old man don't give a —— what happens to me''? . . . The white jazz-lovers . . . hear only the extract of the kind of life that produced this music—its sensuality, rhythm, humor, passion, even closeness and intimacy . . . [but] no matter how many Negro friends they number in Greenwich Village or in the entertainment or literary world . . . the background of jazz . . . would actually revolt some of its greatest propagandists.

"So what?" asked Herbert B. Lutz, a new stockholder in the newspaper, in a "Press of Freedom" piece he wrote in response. Lutz had no defense to make of the Beat jazz buff—a "hunk of atomic matter in the image of man without soul"—but he thought Krim was overdoing it, "idealizing our middle-class way of life," and he "gets on my nerves." Lutz continued on in his own vein with other pieces, reviving the "Press of Freedom" title Tucci had originally thought up, drawing his own share of irate mail. Krim continued too, writing about, years before it was ready to be staged, "The Revolt of the Homosexual," transcribing, Q-and-A-style, a mock interview of "Homosexual" by "Straight Guy." That one brought a response from David McReynolds—that "homosexuals *as a group* aren't going to lead any revolt because the last thing they want is to get involved in any real struggle" and they are "a tragic sub-culture which is every bit as sick as the larger society." McReynolds, a socialist and pacifist, also continued to contribute to the paper, in one piece deploring and analyzing the apoliticality of the Beats, envisioning the day they might march on City Hall and call "The Hipster General Strike."

★ ★ ★

Nat Hentoff was a jazz critic—he had written for *Downbeat*—and had been nothing else since before his move to New York from Boston, his hometown, in 1953. He was past thirty now, looking for someplace else to go to write about something else besides jazz before he got locked into a permanent stereotype, and he wasn't finding it. With the *Voice* he did. "Second Chorus," he called the column they gave him, but the title was all that was to be musical about it—his stipulation was that he be able to write about anything he wanted, *except jazz,* and he did exactly that. As it turned out, Hentoff had the presumption to be quite a political and cultural critic. His list of causes was long, his range of interests was wide, and there was almost no subject on which he did not feel qualified to comment—the civil rights movement, labor leader David Dubinsky and his International Ladies' Garment Workers Union, and, with ongoing rounds of press criticism evaluating their performance and their writers, the New York dailies. He did not even spare his own paper when it came to criticizing something; early in 1962 he publicly admonished it to "hire a competent jazz reviewer. And will the *Voice* never run regular editorials," he asked, "as this of all newspapers should?" Not everyone knew "by what possible measure a middle-brow jazz critic's assorted pronouncements on the New York press can be thought of as important," as a Harvard professor named Martin Peretz made clear he did not in a letter to the editor in September 1961. "Mr. Hentoff's articles," wrote the future contributor to the presidential campaign of Eugene McCarthy and publisher of the *New Republic,* "designed to make a point about the decline of the press, have made another with greater force. If one recalls A. J. Liebling's appraisals of newspaper performance in the *New Yorker,* it is the decline of criticism of the press that seems the most striking." But, though he tended to be testy, bumptious, and self-righteous, Hentoff was also dogged, passionate, always in earnest, and usually lively.

Of New York's various TV critics, he rated Jack O'Brian of the Hearst *Journal-American,* despite "troglodytic politics," second best. One who thought otherwise was Steve Allen. A frequent target of O'Brian's, Allen had already written an article attacking the man and his methods, and was looking to place it somewhere when Hentoff's piece appeared. Allen, who had contributed to the paper once already, came across it, and another *Voice* debate was under way. Under "The Press of Freedom," the paper printed his extended essay calling the critic "the neighborhood bully" of the industry. Allen cited the cases of not only himself but Arthur Godfrey, Jackie Gleason, Ed Sullivan, and

Dody Goodman, resident comedienne on Jack Paar's *Tonight* Show, as victims of that venom.

The article made news. It was mentioned, approvingly, in Hy Gardner's column (though not answered by Jack O'Brian in his) and even made a news item in that week's *Time*. And it drew a rebuttal from Hentoff attacking Allen's attack. Which drew a rebuttal from Allen counterattacking against Hentoff's attack on his attack, and ending, at last, "From here on, Nat, let's kick this around over a beer."

★ ★ ★

Howard Smith had spent the first eighteen years of his life in Newark, New Jersey, looking for a way out, looking to find a place where he would fit in and be himself, not quite sure what that place would be like when he found it. He was commuting from home to Pace College in Lower Manhattan, and on weekends driving into the Village, to look for apartments and girls, parking his car out of sight in order to hide its New Jersey plates. He lasted one semester at Pace, dropped out, and started making the Village scene—poetry readings, jazz sessions. And, in the fall of 1956, the Outdoor Art Show.

He figured it would be a good way to meet people, so he entered. The night before, he tossed off a series of watercolors, got them approved by a censorship board checking for nudes and antireligious themes, set up, and began selling them. While all this was going on, a man came up to the fence and called him over to ask a few questions. It was John Wilcock, and Howard Smith knew he worked for the *Village Voice;* Smith read the paper. He, not Wilcock, wound up asking the questions, until Wilcock wanted to know if he would like to come back to the office. Howard Smith put his stuff away, went back with Wilcock, and was introduced to Dan Wolf and Ed Fancher. Immediately, they liked him and he liked them. Immediately, Howard Smith knew there was something about them, he didn't know what, that made the chemistry right. They had a style, they were different, and he knew from that moment on he wasn't going to be floundering anymore. This was what he was looking for. This was the scene he had always wanted to make. He asked them for a job. We don't pay writers, they told him, but we're looking for somebody to be an office boy, for $35, maybe sixty hours a week. Howard Smith, who had never written anything anyway, not even for his school paper back at Weequahic High School, took the job, took an apartment in the Village with the money he earned, ran messages, bundled papers, did everything around the office—including, eventually, write.

Jack Kerouac was in town, giving a reading from his works, and the paper had no one to cover it. Except Howard Smith, who went to the reading, and then went back home, and sat down in front of his typewriter, with no idea how to write an article. Still, he tried.

> . . . His receding hair touseled, sweating enough to fill a wine cask, Kerouac looks like a member in good standing of the generation he called "beat." Anxious drags on cigarette after cigarette, walking around in tight little circles, fast quick talk to anyone nearby, swigs from an always handy drink, gulps of an always handy coffee, tighten Paisley tie, loosen tie, tighten.
>
> "What am I going to read?" . . . and he leafs through a suitcaseful and suddenly realizes no one remembered to bring a copy of his *On the Road.* . . .
>
> . . . The drink, the sweat, the smoke, the nerves are taking effect. It's time for him to go on. He . . . begins making his way through the maze of tiny night-club tables. They all came to see him, and a few tieless buddies from the old days, a little proud and a little jealous, the fourth estate, the agents, the handshakers, the Steve Allens, the Madison Avenue bunch trying to keep ultra-current; all treating him like a Carmine DeSapio or Floyd Patterson.
>
> He's shorter than they expected, this writer who has been likened to Sandburg but looks like a frightened MC on his first job. They applaud wildly for this 35-year-old who was drunk for the first three weeks that his book made the best-seller list. . . .

"Did you write this?" Jerry Tallmer asked when he brought the article in. "I didn't know you knew how to write. This is excellent." So Howard Smith became a writer—he sang carols on Christmas Eve with Dorothy Day and her Catholic Workers outside the Women's House of Detention on Sixth Avenue and wrote about the experience, and, as "Dear Aggy," he wrote an advice column. ("Dear Aggy: I have been working very hard every day for 40 years. Recently I was told that in Greenwich Village there are bohemians who never work. How do they do it? Sincerely, Tired-of-waiting. Dear Tired: How do we do what? Aggy") He became a photojournalist—his first photo story, done moving around with the Beat poets for *Escapade* Magazine, won an award from the New York Art Directors Club, and his second appeared in *Life.* And he became something of a personality—"Indigent young writer needs any kind of work that pays money. I can act, paint, sketch, write, cook, drive, clean, wait on tables, teach tennis, juggle, plus loads of other non-sensical attributes. . . . Please call before I starve," read the ad in the *Voice.* It was Smith's. So was "Send me $1 and I'll send you a poem from a hardworking Greenwich Village poet." So was "Writer doing a story about interesting parties. Invite me to yours." Dorothy Kilgallen saw that one and, without Smith's knowing it, mentioned it in her column. Next thing he knew, Howard Smith was being bombarded with invitations to parties all over town. And when he got married, and decided to travel, he placed an ad before his trip. He made it to ten foreign countries and twenty of the fifty states, and nearly all along the way he was able to stay with people who had answered it. There was a network of people out there, he discovered, whose only common tie was their long-distance link to Greenwich Village, this newspaper the *Voice.* Parties would be thrown for him, he would be treated as a celebrity by his hosts, as if some magic would rub off him onto them. Often, the only charge for staying someplace was telling them all about the Village.

★ ★ ★

1958 . . . The paper wins five awards from the New York Press Association, including second place for overall excellence among weeklies in New York State, and has a new subtitle on page one: "A Greenwich Village weekly." . . . Crime News: Howard Smith on the mugging of some actors in the Village, and gang fights . . . the son of S. J. Perelman confesses to rape and assault . . . a twenty-five-year-old man who passed himself off as a *Voice* photographer is arrested. . . . In June, Martin Luther King, Jr., gives the *Voice* an interview lamenting Southerners' delays in complying with desegregation. In September, Whitney North Seymour, Jr., Republican candidate for State Assembly and a future United States attorney, writes a Village realtor named Edmond Martin a public letter over Martin's notice "I am refusing to show apartments to Negroes at present on constitutional grounds." The "cherished dogma that renting to Negroes will panic whites and send property values plunging down received a sharp blow from Villagers," reports Michael Harrington in the *Voice* the next week, when thirty of Martin's tenants sign a statement against him. Then the paper runs a letter from the agent defending himself. Also in September, Steve Allen reappears in the *Voice,* writing an open letter to Governor Jim Folsom of Alabama, applauding him for his antisegregationist politics. . . . In the issue of June 25, the paper covers CBS's firing of Joseph Papp from his job on *I've Got a Secret* after he refuses to testify before the House Un-American Activities Committee. . . . "A show of cowardice," Niccolo Tucci calls CBS's handling of the episode. Soon, producer Papp surfaces again in the pages of the *Voice,* with his new endeavor, outdoor Shakespeare in Central Park, and "seeks Village Shelter for spouse and expected child" in an ad he takes for one of his actors. . . . Julian Beck and Judith Malina bring the Living Theatre back to the Village. . . . An exhibition is held to honor Edgard Varèse on his seventy-second birthday. . . . Another experimental composer, John Cage, writes a piece for the paper that begins, "What if I ask 45 questions?" asks forty-five questions, and ends. . . . Hentoff puts down the recent TV work of Edward R. Murrow. . . . The paper covers closely the successful campaign for Congress—first through a primary, then in the November election—of a young, handsome Manhattan Republican named John Lindsay. . . . "Flavia"—really Corinne Robbins, a writer for *Mademoiselle,* who did a feature on the *Voice* for her magazine and stayed around to write for the paper—begins the column "Voice Feminine," advising Village ladies about such matters as cooking and men. . . . During a snowstorm at year's end, the paper reports, at the Sheridan Square monument "one lass, green-stockinged and toreador-painted, climbed a full six feet up the local flagpole,·then took off after General Sheridan to kiss him full upon his snowy lips."

★ ★ ★

Bill Manville was working at an ad agency, living just north of the Village, reading the *Voice,* wondering what to do with this article he had written about barroom characters in the Village. He finally sent it in to Dan Wolf, and Wolf got back to him. As a one-time thing, Wolf told Manville, the article didn't interest him—but if Manville thought he could sustain his subject and characters for, say, six months, the paper would publish it. So Manville started a column, called it "Saloon Society," mailed it in every week—and, for the first few months, thought it was terrible. Boring. Tedious. Then things started to happen. He developed a central character, a composite based on, among others, George Hahn, a Village type who, for a while in 1957, held the title of promotions director at the *Village Voice.* And he came up with a name for him, thanks to a quiet type who worked at his agency, with a wife in Queens and the name Arthur Kugelman. "Make me famous," Kugelman told Manville. "Use my name. Make me the hero of this column you're writing." First Manville got Kugelman to sign a statement approving the use of his name. Then, as "A. E. Kugelman," the center of "Saloon Society," he made him famous—so famous that people began visiting Kugelman at his place out on Fire Island, inviting him to parties. When he finally went to one of them, he told his wife he was away on a business trip to Canada, said almost nothing, went off in the corner, and left early. I needed you there, he told Manville later; "I didn't have any of your jokes."

Manville was definitely a part of what he wrote about—"Bill Manville and 'Saloon Society' will be back next week, hangover or no hangover," the paper promised one week when he was missing. His column was his "Diary of a Year Beyond Aspirin," his characters "painters and psychologists, party girls, guitar players, Big Mary and Lou the Ladies Man, Fire Islanders, sexual engineers, bustups, runaways . . . and the man so high only dogs can dig him." His milieu was

> a world three martinis closer to the moon, a world of 8-day parties and four a.m. exuberance, a world in which to tear a lifetime to confetti. A world of people *engaged,* as the French say, in the attempt to take heaven by storm, a world of people who live on the contemporary sexual frontier, in their own lives and bodies, a solution to the problem of man's naked confrontation of woman.

He followed Kugelman and company through their travails. Through "A Flip's Marriage." Through "A Flip's Love Story," describing Kugelman himself:

> You know how he chased her year after year. She'd take up with a new guy, OK, man, he could stay cool, he'd say. He'd just smile and wait. Sure enough, you know, she'd get tired, she'd come back to him. He was the only one who understood her, she used to say. . . . And then the other night, we were in the Cherry Lane, a guy comes in, he says, hey, Al, Jeanne just got married. Al don't say anything. The guy says it again, Al, Jeanne just got married, I was at City Hall with them. Al says, tell her, she has any children, we're through.

And, to capture the way they spoke he came up with "A Flip's Dictionary." For *flip* itself, there were two meanings—as a common noun, "one who knows the price of everything and the value of Nothingness"; as a proper noun, "Prince of the Wasteland." These were some of his other definitions:

> APARTMENT, n. The raw material, which, by a creative act, can be made into a genuine Pad. The approved method for beginners is: bust the return buzzer so you have to walk down all six flights to let your guests in; stack chipped unwashed dishes in the kitchen sink; let cola bottles collect under the

bed; lose the can-opener so that the beer cans must be punched open with your graduation ball-point pen; have the utilities disconnected for lack of payment; stop the clocks, nail the window shades down, turn the hi-fi up so loud neighbors call the cops, and be confident that there will be no tomorrow.

DIVORCE, n. The bell that announces the start of the second round.

ENGAGEMENT, n. (arch.) A primitive rite, wherein a man and woman, for the amusement of society, demonstrate for a period of time their disinterest in what they are getting married for in the first place. The performance is marked at the beginnings by a notice in the newspapers; at the end, by the bankruptcy of the girl's father.

GAUGIN [*sic*], pr. n. The Jack Kerouac of the middle classes.

HANGOVER, n. The only evidence we have of the old-fashioned notion of a wrathful, punitive deity. . . .

TYPEWRITER, n. The first piece of interior decoration in a writer's pad. Its great expense is justified by the fact that it is useful for supporting paper-plate sandwiches and ashtrays at parties, and for flattening out curled-up photos held in reserve for the first dust jacket. The letters s, w, x and p are usually bent—a memento of the time the machine was thrown by the writer at his wife when she made a particularly unfair reply to the question of how come she still called herself a painter when she hadn't finished a canvas in three years. . . .

WEEK, a period of 15 meals, three nights of sleep and one love affair . . .

IMMATURE, adj. Being in a state of opposition to the clinically objective person making the judgment upon you. The widespread substitution of this word in our scientific civilization for the childish and emotional "I don't like you" is a great advance and one of the blessings of the universal expert knowledge of drugstore psychology in our time. The popularity of the term may in addition stem from the fact that it is unassailable; if you heatedly reply "But I am mature!" you stand immediately ashamed and convicted.

PARTY, n. . . . An entertainment which has been recently perfected. You go to it uninvited, bring your own whiskey, meet your ex-wife and her handsome new husband, and are

introduced to a girl with whom you will have an unhappy love
affair, get your feelings hurt when you discover your psychoanalyst is there but will not talk to you, and decide, while
swilling jars of aspirin the next morning, to give one yourself
as soon as possible.

In one column, Manville included what purported to be a letter from
a distraught Queens housewife: "Sometimes I wonder—is my husband
a flip? (signed) Worried." "No need to worry, madam," was Manville's
reply. "By definition, there are no flips in Queens."

But there could be flips anywhere, or people who thought they were,
and out of the blue one day Bill Manville got a call from a man who
introduced himself. He was from St. Louis, and had decided to fly to
New York, just like that. "I've been reading your column for two or
three months," he told Manville. "Turn me on." It so happened
Manville *was* going to a party that night, so he picked his visitor up and
took him to a building in the West 40s where, in the course of events,
the man found himself locked in the bathroom with a black girl who, in
those early days of dope, was getting herself off by chewing on Scotch
tape. Manville got him out of the bathroom, could tell just by looking
at him that he was scared to death, took him back to the airport, and
put him on the next plane. For five years after that, Manville heard
from the man—and his wife—every Christmas, how he was glad he had
done it, how he had gotten it out of his system, how Manville had saved
his marriage.

In 1961, Manville himself got married, and stopped writing his
column. He was off to Europe. Eventually he became a magazine
writer and novelist.

★ ★ ★

Jonas Mekas was thirty-four years old in 1958. He had
been born in Lithuania and lived through first its Russian occupation,
then its German invasion. He hid from the Wehrmacht's recruiting
patrols, broke out of two labor camps, and spent four years in a camp
for stateless persons with his brother Adolfas, publishing books of
poetry, before they both arrived in New York in 1949. His second night
in this new city, Jonas Mekas went up to Times Square, was swept up
into its overwhelming light show, saw a showing of the film classic *The
Cabinet of Dr. Caligari,* and made up his mind to stay rather than push
on to Chicago, where he and his brother were scheduled to take a job
arranged for them by one of their friends from the camp. He worked in
factories, on the docks, for a plumbing supplier, with a tailor, and

finally as a messenger for a photography studio. And within his first three weeks in New York he had borrowed $300 to buy a 16-mm. camera. He began shooting hand-held footage on the docks, and making a documentary on the Williamsburg section of Brooklyn where he was living. He took in the film showings at the Museum of Modern Art and the New York Film Society in the Village. Within a year, he had joined the Cinema 16 film society. And in 1955, the year the *Village Voice* was starting, Jonas Mekas moved to Orchard Street on the Lower East Side of Manhattan and began publishing, on the shoestring of money he was earning at the photography studio, the magazine *Film Culture*. For the next three years, he put it out erratically, attacking and then embracing several of the cultist underground movie-makers in New York, until Mekas became one of them.

Three years later he went into the offices of the *Voice* one day, and got to see Jerry Tallmer. Tallmer had read *Film Culture* and knew who he was. "Why doesn't the paper have a film column?" Mekas asked.

Because nobody wanted to write one, Tallmer told him. "Why don't you?" And he did. Jonas Mekas's "Movie Journal" covered commercial movies for the first few years, but more and more of it was devoted to his first love, the underground film. Another level of letter-writing dialogue was opened up—with readers complaining about his "flabbergastingly irresponsible reviews," his "truly monumental vulgarity," his stooping to "new depths of pretentiousness," his unwillingness to find anything good to say about "ANY movie that cost over $6.37 to produce." And in the issue of December 3, 1958, the paper ran a notice that, thanks to Mekas's reviewing, 20th Century–Fox had removed them from its press mailing list. It didn't matter to them; "with great pride we recommend you turn to page 6 for more of Mr. Mekas." It didn't matter to Mekas, either. He kept on, undaunted, making movies, writing his column, still putting out his own magazine whenever he could get it out. Before long, he had found two underground films by amateur filmmakers that he thought could demand, and get, wider attention. The first was *Shadows,* a film done by a struggling actor in the Village named John Cassavetes. *Film Culture* gave *Shadows* its first annual Independent Film Award and later in 1959 Cassavetes was starring in a private-eye TV series, *Staccato,* his career as an actor— and, it turned out, a director, too—under way. The next year, the winning film was *Pull My Daisy,* starring on camera, cavorting as themselves, Jack Kerouac, Allen Ginsberg, Gregory Corso, Peter Orlovsky, and Larry Rivers. And in 1961, the film of the year was Mekas's own *Guns of the Trees,* shot with a hand-held camera on the outskirts of the city, comparing the lives of two couples, one white (played by

Mekas's brother and girlfriend), the other black, with Allen Ginsberg reading his own poetry on the soundtrack. It took first prize that summer at the Free Cinema Festival in Porvetta Terme, Italy, beating out a new film called *Jules and Jim,* directed by a young Frenchman named François Truffaut. Mekas began to be called "the patron saint of underground cinema." He himself stopped calling it underground, and started calling it "The New American Cinema."

★ ★ ★

Since college, Marc Schleifer had been a poet, and as a friend of several of the major Beats, he wrote about them for the *Voice.* When Allen Ginsberg made one of his many visits to town, Schleifer did a rambling interview with him. When Gregory Corso ran out of money in Paris, Schleifer put that fact in the paper and organized a Corso Fund to rescue him. When Jack Kerouac debated the question "Is There a Beat Generation?" at Hunter College with author Kingsley Amis, anthropologist Ashley Montagu, and *New York Post* editor James Wechsler, Schleifer went and covered it.

Also since college, when he had thrown a party to honor the Queen on St. Patrick's Day, Schleifer had been the kind of nonconformist who specialized in bewildering and outraging other nonconformists. For instance, this Beat by night was by day employed at an advertising agency on Madison Avenue. And, though no "square" profession was held in more contempt downtown than advertising and no two words could summon up more contempt and scorn to those with the Village sensibility in the late 1950s than *Madison Avenue,* Marc Schleifer was proud of it. He even wrote a "Press of Freedom" defense of it, in which, besides making the case for the economic necessity of commercials, he took the offensive against liberals, such as Nat Hentoff, who criticized the industry, concluding with the metaphor that when the meal "is of superior quality, it is the master, not the butler, who is considered the gourmet. But if the master has vulgar taste and demands that he be served inferior fare, where is the justice in damning the butler?" Lawrence Alson, at the time Norman Mailer's brother-in-law, replied: "You ain't a butler at all, Mr. Schleifer. Folks have decided that's too high-falutin' for our vulgar and mediocre culture. They've voted you in as short-order cook. And some of them don't like what you're cooking. They claim they never ordered it. I know *I* didn't."

That didn't stop Schleifer. After spending six months in the field with his Army Reserve unit, he wrote an equally provocative article, about another cause dear to the hearts of all good liberals of the period—nuclear disarmament. Not only was Schleifer the infantryman against it; he came right out and said he preferred the bomb to any other kind of warfare. And he said why:

> If you've got any Sane Nuclear petitions to be signed, don't say it to the Infantry. I know the men I trained with for six months. They don't dig Rilke or Rupert Brooke, they don't dig "restoring international order," and they don't dig dying for democracy: they just dig foxholes.
>
> It is terror to think of being bayoneted in the stomach; it is terror to think of jellied-gasoline bombs that spill into trenches burning and suffocating all in their path; it is terror to think of a white-phosphorous shell that eats through flesh unless you dig each particle out; it is terror to think of the broken backs, castrations, and cripples left in the wake of anti-personnel mines, grenades, and mortar shells. It is terror to conceive of brainwashing for those who are captured, and the suffering and deprivation of those who survive. Compared to these deaths, these agonies, there is an almost sweet swiftness to atomic destruction.
>
> . . . If civilization sends its young men out to be killed once more, then civilization deserves to be destroyed.

Marc Schleifer would be on the scene for several more years, still writing and doing things that incensed liberals. Only this time he would have continued his line of thought so far he would be coming at them from the other direction, far, far to their left.

★ ★ ★

1959 . . . Jerry Tallmer is married again, and his new wife Louise takes over the "Voice Feminine" column. . . . "To offer a not altogether civil compliment," writes stockholder Norman Mailer in a letter in the issue of March 11, *"The Voice* is the most civilized paper in New York today." He is responding to Marta Curro, the actress, who has panned the first novel of Millicent Brower, *Voice* writer and aspiring actress and friend of Mailer, in the paper. . . . The next week, the paper apologizes for a typo in Mailer's letter and reprints an entire paragraph. Unfortunately, in its correction, *hashish* comes out *bashish,* and *Marta* becomes *Maria,* so the week after that, the paper corrects the correction. . . . An air-raid drill is scheduled for April 17, and in the issue just beforehand David McReynolds announces that "On Friday At 1:30 P.M. I Am Going To Break The Law"—he, Dorothy Day, and a few other protesters will sit on the benches at City Hall Park while the shelter sirens start to wail. When they are arrested and booked, *Voice* reporter Mary Perot Nichols covers their sentencing, as one of the protesters trades biblical quotations with the judge. Later, she catches up with conservative spokesman William F. Buckley, Jr., at one of his public appearances. Buckley, she writes, "acknowledged being a *Village Voice* reader—a newspaper which he found—Buckley smiled with a charming cocktail smile and groped for a word—'creepy.'" She also reports on conditions at the decrepit, notorious Women's House of Detention on Sixth Avenue. . . . That summer, during another air-raid drill, there are more protesters arrested—Julian Beck and Judith Malina, creators of the Living Theatre, among them this time. Their statement about spending time in jail, "All the World's a Prison," is published in the *Voice*. . . . And Nell Blaine, Village artist, designer of the first *Voice* logo, is stricken with polio.

★ ★ ★

Drugs were a concern Ed Fancher had, and he was not alone. He and Dan Wolf had become friendly with Howard Moody, the burly, butch-cut Marine veteran of World War II who had assumed the ministry of the Judson Memorial Church off Washington Square in 1956, when they served on a committee to put out a magazine about the church. By that time Moody was already into his so-called Ministry to the Arts—there was art, dance, and poetry either on the church premises or under its auspices, followed in 1960 by the opening of the Judson Memorial Theater, featuring the musicals of the Reverend Al Carmines. Moody was also coping—since its founding in 1892 his church had been situated between the neighborhoods of the old, established burghers and the new, emerging Italian-Americans— with a teenage population heavily into street gangs and heroin. In 1957, Moody wrote a guest editorial in the *Voice* about the situation, and he and Fancher founded something they called the Village Aid and Service Center on West 4th Street and Sullivan Street. Later, they were both involved with a coalition of voluntary antidrug agencies that Fancher served as acting chairman. Fancher, meantime, kept the pages of his paper open to the problem—it reported the crimes drugs caused, the activities of the narcotics committee, and the ideas for new approaches offered by various speakers brought in by local organizations. When New York Judge John M. Murtagh co-authored a book on addiction, they gave the review to Alexander King, a Villager, a writer— and, for ten years, an addict himself, which he freely admitted in the course of his review and its slashing attack on the Federal Bureau of Narcotics' hard-line commissioner, Harry J. Anslinger.

The recruitment of writers went on. Adam Margoshes began writing book reviews, wrote a "Press of Freedom" eulogizing Dr. Wilhelm Reich, the "discoverer" of "orgone energy," after Reich's death in a federal penitentiary, and then wrote under his own heading, "Fifth Column"—about the suicide of his Reich-thinking therapist, free love, homosexuality, his attempts to camouflage his Jewishness throughout his life, and the time, at DeWitt Clinton High School in 1933, when "I Was a Teen-Age Fascist."

★ ★ ★

His father had owned a steel company, but Michael Zwerin wanted to be a jazz musician, so he was in the Village, playing a few dates, making a living, even doing some writing for the *Villager.* He came into the offices one day, announced himself, said he'd like to write for the paper—and did, about music and jazz, as did Carman Moore, the music critic who was the first black writer to appear regularly in their pages. A beautiful Sarah Lawrence graduate named Suzanne Kiplinger was recommended to them by Bill Manville. She did an art column, and became one of their reporters. So did a writer, married to an architect, named Alan Bodian; when a "milling" and kite-flying rally planned by Jean Shepherd was disbanded by the police, Bodian was there and wrote the story. Margaret Marshall, literary editor of the *Nation,* did some writing for them. So did Dustin Rice, a professor of art at Columbia University and a friend of Jerry Tallmer's. And Kelsey Marichal, proprietor of the Limelight Café, was, under the *nom de plume* "Trencherman," their "Food Editor."

★ ★ ★

1960 . . . A riot breaks out at the Newport Jazz Festival, and a young Columbia graduate named Ken Sobol sends in this account of it to the *Voice:*

> The first sign we had that something unusual was up was on Sunday afternoon, while we were waiting in line to take the ferry across to Newport. A group of Delta Epsilon something or others came alongside in an open convertible, took one look at us, and screamed: 'Beatnik.' . . . It was not until later that we realized that Joe College has found himself a new scapegoat, and that to the frat mind, 'beatnik' now includes kike, nigger, pervert, junkie, and all other well-known forms of subversion. When we finally made it to the island, it became apparent that we had underestimated the odds. Instead of 4 to 1, it was more like 4000 to 1. Four of us (including the chicks) against

countless thousands of them. For the first time in my life,
Norman Mailer was beginning to make sense. . . .

. . . The Gaslight Café is closed down by the fire department, and an
ad in the *Voice* by its owner, John Mitchell, calls for witnesses; he is
being charged with assault and disorderly conduct. . . . That old
debate—Is the Village dying?—surfaces in the pages of the paper again,
as old Max Eastman himself is called on to review Allen Churchill's
nostalgic history of *The Improper Bohemians,* and Kenneth Rexroth
drops by the office to give his view—"The *Voice* is a more civilized organ
than Bruno's Weekly. The Village hasn't changed much. The place is
full of operators; it always was. It is expensive; it was in 1920. As far as
the Beat Group," says Rexroth, switching subjects, "let's all stop.
Right now. That has turned into a Madison Avenue gambit. When the
fall book lists come out, it will be as dead as Davy Crockett caps. This
stuff is strictly for the customers." . . . "It's a waste," Nat Hentoff calls
the Nixon-Kennedy race. Margaret Halsey writes an opinion piece
urging people to vote "no" and stay home. Joseph K. Coleman thinks
"there is evil" in Kennedy's "celebrity-oriented pitch," though he is
reconciled to him. But Dan Wolf, in a "without reservation" endorsement, predicts, "The somnolent 1950's will come to an end next week."

> We slept through them almost to the point of the Big Sleep,
> and when we were not dormant we frittered away our energies
> and let others steal our liberties in the most mirthless decade
> of them all.
> We assume that the election of John F. Kennedy, whom we
> support without reservation, will bring the decade to an end.
> Difficult as it has been for many of us to accept an ally from
> outside the ranks—one who is not a fellow fighter burdened
> with our shibboleths or bearing our stigmata—Kennedy,
> nonetheless, stands out today as the single most vital figure in
> American politics, barring none. He is, we believe, a commit-
> ted man. Committed more deeply than Stevenson, whose
> commitment must always be qualified by the nuances of a
> subtle mind.

And, Wolf concluded, "It is probably the happy measure of the
psychic health of this country that people are turning away from
Nixon. It never seemed credible to us, even from the beginning, that
Nixon, the Abominable No Man of our generation, could attain the
Presidency." Four years earlier, on Election Eve 1956, Wolf, in endors-

ing Stevenson, had written, "We think putting Richard Nixon within reach of the White House is heaping an undeserved indignity on this country. Nixon's precipitous rise in politics seems to us part of a growing immorality which places no limits on the aspirations of any man who has learned the art of 'selling' himself."

★ ★ ★

That unique dialogue with letter-writers continued. "If next week's front-page banner is 'Mailer on Baldwin on Krim,' I'm coming over to New York with a butcher knife," reader Richard Grossman of Philadelphia warned them. "I plan shortly to go to rot and ruin in the section of New York which your paper covers," wrote Jerry L. Watkins from Omaha, Nebraska. "So I figure a newspaper will come in handy." That was his way of asking to become a subscriber. And, in the issue of March 2, 1960, there was this missive, by Bill Manville:

> IDENTIFY LAMONT CRANSTON CLASSIFIED MATERIAL. SORRY NOT AT LIBERTY TO RESOLVE CONTROVERSY.
>
> > LOIS LANE
> > METROPOLIS

And this reply:

> DEAR SIR:
> BEN BUXTON IS NOT LAMONT CRANSTON STOP. I AM.
>
> > A. E. KUGELMAN

For its part, the paper responded in kind. Every issue for three years running it used this one-column filler item: "Special to the *Village Voice:* In 1938 the State of Wyoming produced one-third of a pound of dry edible beans for every man, woman and child in the nation."

As time went on a new mode of communication opened itself up—the ads. The personal notices, on page 2, and the classifieds, at $1.50 a line, became such a cheap outlet for creative writing that the flaky blurbs began to make news, not only in the *Voice* but elsewhere—as Howard Smith's "Writer doing a story about interesting parties" had done. There were ads for something called the Red Head Research Institute and for (in 1959) the Zen Teahouse, Second Avenue and 5th Street, first macrobiotic restaurant in the United States. Some of the others were classics:

"Controversial writer renounces Madison Avenue mercantile life for lonely full-time typewriter vigil. Thus poet faces poverty. Gain a key to creative knowledge, send donations to 'Impoverished Poet,' Box 285 . . ."

"Huge, slothful, unkempt but withal-charming young male genius, now unemployed and starving seeks job with desolate, inattentive boss . . ."

"At last! After years of study for the concert stage I am now prepared to offer my services as an accomplished male baby-sitter . . ."

"We need a regular part-time typist immediately. There's not much money but you'll have a miserable time . . ."

"Celia, love-apple—come back and I swear I shall change my uptown ways. I'll give up golf, bridge, and Lawrence Welk, and take you to the Royal Roost every night. Meet me there at 28 Cornelia Street tonight, and we'll discuss terms . . ."

"HELP WANTED FEMALE FULL-TIME PERMANENT POSITION. Divorced student, 27, with steady job seeks suitable spouse. Interesting diversified work: Washing, ironing, cooking, etc. Fringe benefits. Experience helpful but not necessary. Write: Box 87, Village Voice, NY 1, NY . . ."

"Staff member Life, but no time or fortune, needs unfurnished apartment . . ."

"Reformed pyromaniac needs one slightly charred paper drummer to love . . ."

"Space girl wanted—for vacancy in famous outer space corps. No experience necessary; but dancer, mime or actress preferred. Must be very extroverted. . . . If you qualify hail a flying saucer and come to see Sam Kramer . . ."

" . . . I was wrong. I love you. Please call . . ."

"Do you like parties? We'll invite you to ours if you'll invite us to yours. No creeps please . . ."

"Stubborn, penniless, aristocratic, unstable nitwit expects to hear from idiotic, irresponsible, temperamental broad who can't keep her mind on anything. If it's you, you might as well write back. I'll get hold of you sooner or later anyway."

That last ad was answered with another ad—"I've tried so hard to change"—and the two correspondents had coffee and got married. As for the paper, tacky and tame as these items might be by subsequent standards, they were for their time a sign that the paper was making contact with a new sensibility emerging out of the compulsory staleness of the fifties. No paper had ever had a readership that wrote letters and took out ads like these before, and no paper had ever printed anything like them. So, for its time, it earned the designation "way out," which is what some people called it, and why some people read it.

★ ★ ★

1961 . . . Norman Mailer is back in the paper again, writing about psychoanalysis and the theater again. It all starts with an Ed Fancher review of Genêt's *The Balcony*. In the issue of January 19, 1961, there is Mailer, saying, "Now that my old acquaintance and still business partner, Edwin Fancher, has come on stage as a critic, I think it is necessary that those of us who know him well rise to his defense and incarcerate his pen before he does himself damage." Fancher, says Mailer, is "an admirable fellow, hard-working, honest, and devoted to the orders of his heady profession." He also "has a mind like a 19th-century printing press. It is not his fault. He has been trained as a psychologist, and the language of psychology is totalitarian—its future function is to police society. Its unadmitted hope is to liquidate all psyches which do not obey its language. . . . Therefore grind your gears, dear Ed, and back off."

It was signed "Business love, Norman."

. . . Things are getting rougher in the Village: Just before the death in November 1960 of Lord Buckley, the comedian, the *Voice* reports that his cabaret card has been lifted (preventing him from performing in New York) and, just afterwards, that he had been shaken down to offer bribe money to get it back from the police. The next spring, John Mitchell, owner of the Gaslight, tells the paper that he has been forced to make payoffs to organized crime for two years. An overdose kills a Village junkie for the fifth time in three years. And, because of the "unsavory appearance" of the singers, Parks Commissioner Newbold Morris bans folk singing in Washington Square Park. At one demonstration to protest the ban, ten are arrested and twenty hurt; the next week, Howard Moody returns with a crowd 500 strong. There is no violence this time, and the ban is lifted. . . . The paper wins a George Polk Memorial Award for "significant achievement" in journalism from Long Island University, then wins the New York Press Association awards for general excellence, best front page, best feature, and excellence in advertising. . . . At the start of the year, the paper carries ads for the celebrated appearance, on February 4, 1961, of Lenny Bruce at Carnegie Hall; at the end of the year, for the first New York concert, to be held in the same place, by a new sensation, Bob Dylan. . . . At year's end, e e cummings is fighting eviction from his place on Patchen Street. . . .

In the issue of April 13, 1961, Nat Hentoff scorns "the equanimity of most American 'liberals' and nearly all the 'responsible' press about the now thoroughly open American financing and support of a Cuban invasion." In the aftermath of the disaster, Norman Mailer comes forth with an "Open Letter" to Fidel Castro and President Kennedy, a tome, printed in the *Voice,* in which Mailer alludes to the famous, favorable piece he had done for *Esquire* about Kennedy after the 1960 Democratic Convention: "In that piece, I may have made the error of sailing against the stereotype that you were a calculating untried over-ambitious and probably undeserving young stud who came from a very wealthy and much unloved family. . . . I mean: Wasn't there anyone around to give you the lecture on Cuba? Don't you sense the enormity of your mistake—you invade a country without understanding its music?"

At the beginning, Mailer makes two remarkable digressions. First, he says he has been thinking of running for mayor of New York—which in fact he will, eight years later. Also, he rebukes his model Ernest Hemingway, who, his career in twilight, has holed up in Ketchum, Idaho, and, though Mailer has no way of knowing it, cracked up mentally. "He no longer writes to us," Mailer confides somberly. "Maybe a letter once in a while. We do not talk about him. We feel he has deserted us and produced no work good enough to justify his silence. There are many of us who will curse him if he dies in silence."

Ten weeks after Mailer writes this, Ernest Hemingway goes downstairs at his home in Ketchum early one morning and blows his brains out.

★ ★ ★

After all this time, though he still liked Wolf and Fancher as little as they liked him, John Wilcock had never thought to stop writing his column for them, just as they had never thought to stop running it.

He was still around the office. In fact, they couldn't keep him out of there even when they wanted to. Wilcock was, if nothing else, irrepressible, and one of the ways he expressed that irrepressibility was to read other people's mail. After hearing him say, "I see you got a letter" once too often, they decided to stifle his curiosity. They locked the door on him.

That didn't stop him. He crawled through the transom over the door and got in anyway. When, to detect him, they arranged the letters on their desks in code and went over them later to determine that they had been rearranged in the night, they tried another tack. Jerry Tallmer left a stack of papers prominently on his desk one night, each one of them unfolding into another, until at the bottom there was this message: "Fuck you, John." They had no indication, after that night, that John Wilcock had ever seen the note—and, likewise, no indication that he had stopped either. And, when he was around the office during the day, he was apt to jump up and suddenly announce he was going home to watch a TV program. The others were astounded. None of them even owned a set.

Wilcock put that same irrepressibility, that same curiosity, into the paper, the paper that he always seemed to be carrying with him, leaving copies wherever he went, even the dentist. Sometimes that got the paper into trouble—as in February of 1956. Ted Joans, a Village regular, was a poet, artist, trumpet player, one of the old Bohemians who had joined the Beat movement and read his poetry to jazz. A black man, he would, many years later, reappear in the Village after a long absence, claiming to have been living in the real village of Timbuktu in Africa. He had also, according to Wilcock, been a researcher for Dr. Alfred Kinsey in the famous sex research study—except that Kinsey himself wrote in to say that "the story is completely fictitious and essentially libelous," forcing Wilcock to say that Joans still claimed to have worked for Kinsey, but "never on a personal basis. . . . It is possible the director [Kinsey] was never aware of his existence," and to apologize.

Before Norman Mailer ever wrote a book with that title, Wilcock made an advertisement for himself, ran it in the *Village Voice,* listed his experience, and offered $100 to anyone who would bring it "to some bigshot's attention, thereby getting me a job." He did not get a job, but he did get attention, and followed it with various other stunts, brainstorms, and "Reader Participation" schemes, all of them show-cased in his column, "The Village Square," which he numbered every week in order. He held an annual poetry contest, with poets as judges. He put in plugs for various enterprises, and gave his own return address. He posed questions and riddles, with $10 "for the first correct solution received at this office." He stayed in the office and called up the pay phone across the street just to see if someone would answer it. He dropped a stamped letter out the office window just to see if somebody would mail it. He put a message into a bottle and floated it into the water off the Staten Island Ferry just to see if it would wash ashore, and if someone would discover it and answer back. (Someone in New Jersey did.) He wrote to Ezra Pound, and Ezra Pound answered back. He urged everyone to concentrate at noon one Thursday, and he would attempt to transmit a message to them. He told his readers they could establish a clearinghouse for gift ties they had received, "Rent a Beatnik" for one of their parties, throw eggs over a house and have them land on grass without breaking, save up Green Stamps to buy a yacht, overpay their phone bills by a penny and trigger a computer malfunction, and pocket the premiums savings banks offered by starting a new account and then abruptly withdrawing it.

In October 1956, Wilcock, for a news story, tried to smuggle some women into the all-male bastion of McSorley's Saloon. It didn't work; NO ALE, JUST FAREWELL FOR TRIO, ran the headline. But John Wilcock's interest in women, and in womanizing, went unfazed. He was always writing about girls—new arrivals in the Village were a favorite subject—and how to get them. (One man's way, which Wilcock publicized, was to master the technique of correctly sizing up which pretty young females were waiting for a blind date and correctly impersonating him.) One of his columns was about going to the laundromat, finding a load marked "Sex," learning it belonged to a "Miss Sexton," and trying to find out who she was. One of his contests offered some lucky young lady a week-long "Greenwich Village Scholarship" with John Wilcock. One time he took a poll of young lovers to find out who still wore pajamas. Another time he asked for unaddressed love letters to be sent in to him, and matched them up.

His column could be about anything at all—what books Villagers were buying, what histories certain streets in the Village had, what Marilyn Monroe had been like the time he had interviewed her (charming). But usually it had something to do with the Beat scene. The first major *Voice* interview with the legendary nightclub comic Lenny Bruce was done, Wilcock explained, as "I fired questions at him one night between shows, put some paper into my typewriter, and recorded his answers verbatim as he shouted them to me while changing his shirt and taking a shave." The piece ran in the issue of June 15, 1961.

"How to Get By on $40 a Week" was the headline on the profile he did of a struggling Village artist getting by on an allowance from home, and soon he expanded on that idea. He began leaving New York to travel, making it around the world in thirty days the first time, eventually going all across Europe, North Africa, the Middle and Far East, North America—and all, he told the readers of his columns and of the many travel books he did later, on $5 a day. In January 1959 he was on Radio Athens helping to raise money for Skounda, an impoverished village in Greece. Three years later, he helped raise money for the adoption of a Korean girl named Lai Wah. And wherever he was he sent back reports to his *Voice* readers on what the scene was like there.

These were not, though, the only trips John Wilcock was taking. In the issue of August 3, 1961, he told readers of his column about taking the hallucinogenic drug psilocybin and of its fantastic effects.

But John Wilcock was the exception in the early years. The rule was that the writers were transient, producing for a while, passing through, and moving on. Only in 1962 was there the first break in that pattern. Dan Wolf found one writer who not only stayed but who, if she did not exactly develop a house style for the paper, certainly left the traces of its fundamental contribution to what came to be called the New Journalism. And he found another writer who became the first to leave, not because she had written herself out and no longer had something to say, but because her work had been read in the *Voice* and considered so good that the most esteemed magazine in America wanted her. This was the new pattern—writers coming to Dan Wolf, some staying and earning their reputation as New Journalists with him, others being discovered and recruited by the uptown, mainstream press, which increasingly tried to copy the tone of Dan Wolf's paper anyway. Either way, it meant Dan Wolf's paper had become a journal to be reckoned with.

J. R. Goddard, wacky Jack Goddard, was typical of the period. They met him through Gin Briggs, their staff photographer at the time; at the end of the fifties and the beginning of the sixties he wrote news for them. Goddard was a fan of Lord Buckley's—he did the story on the comedian's troubles after Buckley had died—and the first of a series of articles he did on Macdougal Street, "A Fruitcake's Version of Inferno," won the paper the 1960 award for best feature from the New York Press Association. Then he, too, went on his way, doing a novel, eventually winding up in California.

But before he left he introduced them to a tall, bony redhead, Stephanie Gervis. She began doing news features, covering John Henry Faulk's successful libel suit against the blacklisters who had driven him out of broadcasting, and the Anti-Communist Crusade of the ultraconservative evangelist Fred Schwarz. Her style was an unmistakable departure from the tacky tone the paper had gradually been growing out of since 1955. It was an authentic sixties voice, bridging the fifties sensibility the paper and its readers were leaving behind with the sensibilities that were to come. And, most important, it lasted. The tone she took became a trademark of the *Village Voice*. Her irreverence became institutionalized.

In the issue of October 25, 1962, the paper's seventh anniversary, her lead described a debate between the Village's congressman, liberal Republican John Lindsay, and his Democratic opponent. Instead of giving a straight account, she opened the piece, "If they ever put politicians on TV's 'To Tell the Truth,' and asked the real John Q. Liberal to stand up, Professor Milton B. Dworkin would be on his feet before you could say David Dubinsky. John Lindsay would probably just sit there." The next week, she broke the tension of the Cuban missile crisis as she began, "The chroniclers of the future may record that on the day the world almost came to an end, a cocktail party was in progress at the United Nations."

"In Greenwich Village, Sex Is Where You Find It," read the headline to her unserious treatment of a serious subject that summer of 1962.

> Poets, writers, sculptors, and painters (unless they have galleries on Bleecker Street) are strictly for aesthetic nourishment, and, of course, sex. . . . That leaves merchant seamen. I'm not quite sure what they're good for, unless of course, you decide some day that you want to be tattooed.

To get your singer, she advised, "Be sure you arrive early, get a seat near the stage, and prostrate yourself at your idol's feet."

> . . . When in the White Horse, be an intelligent, controversial conversationalist. To do this you must be omniscient; there's nothing you don't know or haven't read. Always argue on the side of the man you're after. He will soon realize that two can pontificate better than one.

She closed by recommending this "health food" cocktail:

> . . . Two tablespoons of powdered pot, one-half pound of hallucination mushrooms, two quarts of Irish whiskey, six black olives (finely chopped), a dash of mescalin, two teaspoons of poppy seeds, one herb bouquet (preferably from the Black Forest), four Preludin tablets (good for the diet), and two sticks of incense. Add ingredients to a cauldron of boiling water fetched from the Carmine Street swimming pool. Jump in.
> Swing, baby.

In May of the following year, the paper announced the wedding, in Paris, of Stephanie Gervis and Michael Harrington, a friend of Wolf's and Fancher's from old days in the Village. He had written for the very first issue of the *Voice,* and his book, *The Other America,* had just taken off to critical acclaim. And she, as Stephanie Harrington now, returned to the paper to become something of a permanent fixture. Unlike so many others who had wandered off, she stayed where she was. Like so many after her, she would eschew writing the Great American Novel for the Great American Newspaper.

★ ★ ★

She had grown up and spent her whole life in Providence, Rhode Island, and now, out of school, away from home and family, hanging out in the Village, drinking in the Limelight, Jane Kramer felt these surges of liberation, of dangerousness, of camaraderie. But she had to choose, either to return to Providence and marry her boyfriend, or to stay in New York. And, if she stayed in New York, what to do—to work for a publishing company, which she could do, or go to Columbia University for a master's, where she had been accepted. She went home to Providence, stayed there two weeks, knew she couldn't marry the boy, and left for good. For the next six weeks, she took the publishing job. Then, one day at lunch, she said to herself, "Fuck it," and never went back. Instead she went straight up to the Columbia campus, was told, "We've been expecting you," got her masters in seventeenth-century English literature and contemporary poetry, and, in the fall of 1961, landed a job writing for *The Morningsider,* the neighborhood newspaper taking in Columbia and its environs on the Upper West Side. There her stuff was read by, among others, Norman Mailer and Nat Hentoff. They liked it, Mailer showed some of her work to Dan Wolf, and, in the spring of 1962, for $30 a week—he could afford to pay a little now—he hired her. She was a staff writer, along with Stephanie Gervis; between them they formed an immediate friendship while writing, along with Mary Nichols, most of the news stories in the paper. And she amused Dan Wolf, this little Vassar girl with her charge accounts, like a visitor from another world in Greenwich Village— which is what she thought he thought of her.

She did profiles of personalities—of a robot maker, of Seymour Krim, of community organizer Jane Jacobs, of the Episcopal Village priest who had carried on and published a correspondence with the late author James Agee, of, in a eulogy after he died, e e cummings. She covered events—architects picketing over the planned demolition of Penn Station, patrons crowding into a Bowery jazz spot the night before its closing, the New York opening of Synanon for drug addicts, the theatrical chaos when CBS tried to film Salvador Dali at his own author's party, the literary chaos at a panel featuring William Saroyan, Bill Manville, Seymour Krim, Susan Sontag, and countless others who just jumped in.

She could give things a light treatment, too, as when she attended the training of the new Playboy Club's bunnies.

> The interview ended with a loud crash. Practical application was under way at the other end of the loft, and at one table the

serving bunny had just dropped her tray on the Chicago bunny mother. Alice cheerfully sponged the water off her Chinese dress—"All in a day's work," she said—but a mean-looking bunny from Chicago glared at the offender . . .

A bunny in costume stood over the table and gave the bunny pep talk to the girls. "Now, I can see that we have a very bright bunch of bunnies with us today," the bunny, whose name was Marion, said. "And I can see that they are going to take their orders beautifully and not drop any more trays. And I know that if they do drop their trays, they're going to drop them out there"—she pointed away from the table—"and not all over their bunny mother."

And, when seven leftist Brazilian students came over to her place, this was the piece she wrote:

"We are very nationalistic. We want to be ourselves. We want to be left alone to build our country," they said. "But we would also like to meet some American girls. You can arrange it, perhaps?"

"You are my first human contact here," a law student from Bahia breathed into my ear as he pinched my arm.

"You are my first human contact here," the president of the student body of Sao Paulo University breathed into my roommate's ear as he pinched her leg.

Then we all sat down to denounce America and have a beer . . .

They wanted to talk politics. I was thinking more in terms of a conga line. They won: "In our country, the man is always boss," they said.

"You are my first American leftist," whispered the law student from Bahia. "I would like to talk with you about socialism—alone—later." . . .

"Wall Street is gone," the Brazilians cheered. Everybody had another beer.

"Would you like my Brazilian cigarettes?" Bahia leaned over. "They are not the last souvenir I plan to leave with you before I go." . . .

He looked at the magazines on the coffee table. He had hoped to catch me reading Time. "Why, you have only leftist publications!" Beaming, he held up a copy of the Saturday Review.

One afternoon in early 1963, the phone at the paper's offices rang. It was for Jane Kramer. The man at the other end introduced himself. He was William Shawn, the editor of the *New Yorker*. He had been reading her articles in the *Voice,* he told her, and would she be interested in coming to work for the magazine?

Yes, she would, she said, and told Dan Wolf, and was on her way. For the first time, Dan Wolf had lost a writer, not because she had drifted away, but because she had been lured away. It was not to be the last time.

★ ★ ★

1962 . . . While Jane Kramer is coming to the attention of William Shawn in the pages of the *Voice,* Seymour Krim is saying in his column that "unless there is a revolution on 43rd Street, and it isn't likely, the *New Yorker* as we have known it has had it as a cultural force." While she is gently mocking the New York Playboy Club, John Wilcock is in a public, continuing argument with *Playboy* magnate Hugh Hefner, Wilcock accusing Hefner's New Orleans Playboy Club of racist practices. And while she and Mary Nichols have praise for urban planner–neighborhood organizer Jane Jacobs in their reporting, Jacobs's book, *The Death and Life of Great American Cities* (though it will go on to be regarded as a classic of its kind), gets a pan in the book review section. . . . Jacobs's book is not the only one that does badly with a *Voice* reviewer; Arthur Sainer receives Joseph Heller's new novel, *Catch-22,* very lukewarmly. . . . "VOICE BOOKS" is being headed up by a *New York Times* book reviewer, Eliot Fremont-Smith, in his spare time. It is a banner year for writing essays that go against the grain of Villagers' presumed political views, and Fremont-Smith writes one questioning the validity and wisdom of Israel's executing Adolf Eichmann. In another piece, ostensibly about Bob Dylan, he works in this comment: "Mr. Dylan is proof that not all of the young among us have yet accepted Bobby Kennedy as a model of making it." It is, in fact, a banner year for expressing doubts about the Kennedy administration in the pages of the *Voice.* A forty-fifth birthday party is thrown for the president at Madison Square Garden, featuring Frank Sinatra and Marilyn Monroe. The *Voice*'s Andrew Sarris is there. His piece, "No Biz Like Show Biz, And No Prexy Like JFK," asks: "Idea: Why not have Marilyn burst out of the cake next time? Superidea: Why not have a real orgy next time?" In December, after the missile crisis, Norman Mailer comes forth with another Open Letter, this one addressed to Kennedy alone. "Mr. President," wonders Mailer, "one does not know whether it pleases you that America is to a degree totalitarian." . . . In August, when Marilyn Monroe is a suicide, Charles Marowitz, back from England, denounces the sensationalist press coverage. . . . In the issue of November 8, a new heading, "WHAT'S ON," appears. A master list of cultural entertainment in the city, it becomes a permanent staple of the paper. . . . Four weeks later, two other new headings appear. They say, "LATE NEWS" and "NEWS BACKGROUND." They are bordered in black. They are only temporary. And they mean that Dan Wolf and Ed Fancher, after seven years of struggling, are on their way to becoming very rich men.

5. IT WAS NOT THE WRITING ALONE, HOW-

ever, that got them through this period. To be successful, they had to make the right friends, make the right enemies, spot—and spotlight— the right trends of the future. They did all that. There were four breaks in particular, four such reasons for their survival.

The first was Off-Broadway theater. Since about the turn of the decade, there had been a withdrawal of energy, a rebellion of sensibility, among the downtown theater types against the tastes—and the power to make tastes—that Broadway had. More and more, there were downtown shows staged by downtown actors and directors for down-town audiences—in cafés, in churches, in lofts in SoHo, as that neighborhood "south of Houston" Street came to be called. Anywhere, so long as it was off Broadway.

Off-Broadway became the umbrella title of this movement, and Jerry Tallmer, associate editor of the *Village Voice,* became one of its buffs. Off-Broadway was the place for new and different and excess talent in New York to go, to experiment, to be discovered—but, before 1955, there had not been much discovery, because no one had show-cased, had publicized, had championed the movement.

Jerry Tallmer had intended to, even before the *Village Voice* got off the ground. And, in the third week of its existence, as they looked for ways to keep themselves afloat and talked about the possibility of some kind of special salute to Off-Broadway, Jerry Tallmer came up with the idea of an awards ceremony.

"The Village Voice Theatre Awards," they were to be called, "annual in nature and" to "be given out by this newspaper in ceremonies to be held shortly after the end of this year."

Before they gave out the first awards, they changed the title. "The Village Voice Theatre Awards" needed a shorter, snappier name. Like Oscar. Like Emmy. Like Tony. Like . . . Obie. Jerry Tallmer thought it up. Off-Broadway. Acronym, OB. Obie. And they waited till the end of the theater season—till June 18, 1956—to hold their awards festivities at Helen Gee's Limelight Coffee House. Jerry Tallmer, Shakespearean actor Earle Hyman, and *Commonweal* critic Richard Hayes were the judges. Shelley Winters presented the awards—a slip of paper and no money. And the winners included several names who were about to become famous. Jason Robards, for his portrayal of Hickey in *The Iceman Cometh,* shared the best actor award with George Voskovec of *Uncle Vanya.* José Quintero, who directed Robards in *Iceman,* was best director. *Vanya* was cited as the best play, and *Threepenny Opera* as the best musical.

The term *Off-Broadway* was unfortunate, said Ed Fancher in his speech on awards night. In the next week's issue, Dan Wolf elaborated: "The theatre that is centered in Greenwich Village and the East Side is 'off nothing,' " Wolf wrote. "It is not secondary to Broadway. In conception, and at its best, it is new, different, and daring—a separate and very special force in the American theatre."

When the *Voice* decided to embrace Off-Broadway, the paper put the new theater movement on display for the first time. No longer was Off-Broadway a word-of-mouth phenomenon that could not break into print in the uptown, theater-district-oriented dailies. The *Voice* gave the new movement a forum, an outlet, made it aware of its own potential, provided its creators with a direct link to their natural, intended audience. In the process, people began to identify with the paper, because the paper was identified with something.

The man most responsible for all of that was Jerry Tallmer. Even more than that; for the first seven years, it could be said that Jerry Tallmer was as much the editor of the paper as Dan Wolf was. Certainly no one recruited or encouraged more writers in the early years—Hentoff and Krim especially—than he did, while Dan Wolf was still learning the ropes, feeling his way at the head of the paper, and striking some writers, Krim for one, as a bit too stiff and standoffish for them to communicate with. Likewise, no one put together, or had more control over, as much of the paper as Tallmer, with his back of the book, did.

And into his back of the book Jerry Tallmer threw all his energy. To drum up support for Off-Broadway, Tallmer gave it saturation coverage, at least one review of each downtown opening. He got a critical cross-fertilization of ideas, with different writers' sensibilities spreading over pages, debating shows, debating writers, debating directors, debating views on the theater. The flaps caused by Charles Marowitz's pans of Yiddish theater, the Method, and the Angry Young Men, or the long, lingering dialogue over whose interpretation and staging of *Waiting for Godot* was the correct one, were not isolated occurrences. If it was not Tallmer, belatedly going to see *The Bridge on the River Kwai* and finding in it a fifties-era antiheroic rebuttal to Hemingway, "this decade's glaringly obvious put-up-or-shut-up ultimatum to the decade of 'For Whom the Bell Tolls,' " then it was Lorraine Hansberry, critically looking at the shortcomings of her own play, *A Raisin in the Sun* ("a central character as such is certainly lacking"), and explaining her intent to link her protagonist to the one in Arthur Miller's *Death of a Salesman*. Or it was Marta Curro, the actress, the one who had defended the Method against Marowitz and done a book review that

Mailer didn't like, writing from the road how "Kerouac turned San Francisco into a garbage can for Midwestern losers," how during two months in Hollywood "I managed to lose my identity, the command of the English language, and a certain belief in God," how a visit to Disneyland "was the only brush with reality I'd had all summer."

That was the way Jerry Tallmer wanted it to be. He had his likes and dislikes, and he expected others to hold to theirs as strongly as he held to his. When uptown critics ignored Off-Broadway, he needled them for their snobbery, and retaliated in kind—"THEATRE UPTOWN," said the heading over the secondary, Broadway reviews. And when they did come, and panned what they saw, as they did in the summer of 1959 with a play by Jack Gelber about drug addiction called *The Connection,* Tallmer was ready with a perfervid review: "I pray that Mr. [Julian] Beck and Miss [Judith] Malina can keep the show alive until word-of-mouth overcomes the worst efforts of the (second-string, summertime) daily reviewers. If *The Connection* can't make it in Greenwich Village, or wherever people care deeply about imaginative theatre, then nothing can. But I think it can—if its producers, for their part, can hang on." Beck and Malina did hang on, and *The Connection* won Obies for playwright Gelber and star Warren Finnerty the next spring.

Tallmer may have saved that show singlehanded with his defense of it, but he was not the only one on the *Voice* who was close to the Off-Broadway theater; Howard Bennett, the departed, disgruntled stockholder, had been friends of Julian Beck and Judith Malina, the husband-and-wife team who owned the Cherry Lane Theatre and had founded the Living Theatre Company. Nor was he the only one there who could take credit for giving life to an Off-Broadway show; Herbert "Whitey" Lutz, who replaced Bennett as a stockholder, gave Edward Albee's *Zoo Story* its first American production.

A year later, looking to cast his *The American Dream,* Albee came across a photo in the *Voice* of an actor named Tom Hunter, and, on the strength of that alone, cast him in the lead. As things turned out, nothing much came of Tom Hunter, but the story of his discovery in the pages of the *Voice* was only the most unusual. It was not the first. It was not the last. For instance, among the stars of the future who made the pages of the *Voice* during their still-struggling year of 1956 were actor Robert Culp, comic Larry Storch, actor-singer-dancer Joel Grey, and, on his way to winning an Obie, veteran character actor Gerald S. O'Loughlin. It was always that way. Five years later, in 1961, the *Voice* was running pictures—showing them toiling away their apprenticeships in various Off-Broadway or downtown enterprises, all still relatively unknown yet, but all of them right on the verge of career breaks that would lead to Oscar nominations, Emmy nominations, Broadway leads, starring roles, audience and critical recognition—of singer Jerry Orbach, of actors Peter *(Joe)* Boyle, J. D. *(McCloud)* Cannon, William *(A Thousand Clowns, The Graduate)* Daniels, Knigh *(The Manchurian Candidate)* Deigh, Vic *(Combat)* Morrow, and Robert *(To Kill a Mockingbird)* Duvall. In 1962, the same thing—for actors George *(Advise and Consent)* Grizzard, Cicely *(East Side/West Side)* Tyson, James Earl *(Great White Hope)* Jones, for a strikingly unbeautiful Jewish girl with an inimitable singing style named Barbra Streisand, for two rapidly improving young comics working the Village clubs named Woody Allen and Bill Cosby. Even the byline on a review that year was of a well-known name to come—Tom Stoppard, his first great playwriting success with *Rosencrantz and Guildenstern Are Dead* five years in the future.

The Obies themselves were a powerful career-booster, a litmus test of discovering new talent. Lee Grant and Zero Mostel won Obies while still nourishing their comebacks after being blacklisted during the Red scare of the early fifties. Roy Scheider won an Obie before he landed his first important screen roles in *Klute* and *The French Connection,* Estelle Parsons before winning the Oscar for *Bonnie and Clyde,* Frank Langella before his unforgettable portrait of a supercilious paramour in *Diary of a Mad Housewife,* Brian Bedford before scoring in the Broadway success *Butley,* Diana Sands before *The Owl and the Pussycat.* George C. Scott and James Earl Jones and Hal Holbrook and Eli Wallach and Hume Cronyn and Godfrey Cambridge and Alan Arkin and Stacy Keach and Rip Torn won Obies. Tammy Grimes and Anne Jackson and Colleen Dewhurst and Jessica Tandy and Barbara Barrie and Rosemary Harris and Joan Hackett and Ruby Dee won them. In 1962, for her performance in the absurdist comedy *Oh Dad, Poor Dad, Mama's Hung You in the Closet and I'm Feeling So Sad,* an unknown named Barbara Harris won one, and her career took off. Obies went to name playwrights—Beckett, Genêt, Albee, Robert Lowell—but to newcomers and unknowns, too—Sam Shepard, Israel Horowitz, Terrence McNally, David Rabe. One went to Tom O'Horgan, the avant-garde director, before the fame of *Hair* made his name known to the general public.

Jerry Tallmer had been acquiring an apprentice of his own all this time. Their first summer "intern" at the paper was a Sarah Lawrence undergraduate named Betty Rollin—who, when she got a walk-on part in a school play, got her photo in the paper, and ultimately went on to become an NBC newswoman. Her boyfriend at the time was a twenty-one-year-old Yale dropout named Michael Smith, who, they recalled, looked the part—short sandy-colored hair, button-down shirt, seer-sucker suit, the nice young Yalie.

Betty Rollin introduced him to Dan Wolf and Ed Fancher. "I want to write. About anything," he told them. "What do you need? I'll do it." What they needed was just about anything, and that was what they let him write. Since they were starting up a sportscar column, they thought it would be a nice touch to let him review Kerouac's *On the Road*—in the sportscar column. Jerry Tallmer sent him to review a Joe Papp play. He did some general reporting and an interview with harpsichord maker Wolfgang Zuckermann. In the meantime, he had been studying acting with Stella Adler, and went off to act summer stock in Bucks County, Pennsylvania, do some work in London for the *Evening Standard,* make his way to Algeria to report for the *Voice* on the war for independence against the French there, and then return home to go back to the paper, as Jerry Tallmer's assistant, filling in as drama critic, doing layout with him at the printer.

Until one day Jerry Tallmer quit the paper.

His decision came without warning to them, but he had been thinking about it for some time. The *New York Post* was making him an offer, and he could not refuse. From the $25 he had been making at first, Jerry Tallmer had been raised to $40. In 1959, when he was about to get married again, he gathered up all his courage and asked them for $75, which they gave him, he thought, rather sullenly. Now he was up to $100 a week, and it was still not enough. His wife had had twins. He had been at this for seven years, eking out an income, and there was still no security. He was forty-one years old now, and there was no sign when, if ever, the paper would make money. No health plan, no benefits, no pension for his family, and, with the long hours he was still working every week, no time for them either. With the *Post,* he knew, he would have all that, security, and be in line to succeed Richard Watts as chief critic when Watts retired, too. His mind was made up, and one morning in 1962 he came into the office and told Dan Wolf of his decision.

It was a blow to Wolf, and it was unexpected. Almost from the beginning, since the tiffs with Wilcock and Mailer, it had been the three of them against it all, getting the paper out. They considered him as much a founder of the paper as they were. And they had never considered a future at the paper that did not include him. But, if he was going to go, he was going to go. Jerry Tallmer did not want to be talked out of leaving, and Dan Wolf did not try. The resignation was tendered, and accepted, quickly.

The first Michael Smith heard of it was at noontime, when Wolf took him for a walk, and, as they walked, told him quietly, the shock registering on Wolf's face, what had happened, and offered him Jerry Tallmer's job.

Michael Smith accepted on the spot, and for the next eleven years, four as a full-time associate editor, seven more alternating his stays in New York with trips on the road, he was around, and while he was, the scene changed still more, and got bigger. In the 1960s, theater downtown began to spread out, farther downtown, farther out, until there was a whole new movement going on, with a whole new name for it. Off-Broadway begat Off-Off-Broadway. There was experimental theater above and beyond the already-established experimental theater, by the Becks' Living Theatre, by Joe Chaikin's Open Theatre company, by the Performance Group, all across Lower Manhattan, but especially in the Village and SoHo cafés—the Cino, the Reggia, the Borgia, and most of all, Ellen Stewart's Café LaMama.

When the new phenomenon came, the paper was ready, and did what it had done for the first one—nurtured it, paraded it, absorbed it. In the fifties, the *Village Voice* had been the paper of Off-Broadway. In the sixties, it expanded to become the paper of Off-Off-Broadway, too, of *all* experimental or alternative theater. In 1964, Off-Off-Broadway plays were included in the Obies for the first time.

That year, the same week they won Obies for *The Brig,* a play about brutality in the Marine Corps, Julian Beck and Judith Malina were convicted of the crime of interfering with federal officers, while the "Best New American Play" award was going to *Dutchman,* whose black militant playwright Le Roi Jones had ridiculed the paper as "the downtown *Herald-Tribune."* Those were years of controversy surrounding the downtown theater movement, with the *Voice* often in the middle of it. They were also years of continued discovery, with the *Voice* once again often the vehicle. He had been struggling along, making the best of bit parts, for eight years before he won an Obie for a play called *The Journey of the Fifth Horse* in 1966, but inside of a year Dustin Hoffman had been cast by film director Mike Nichols in the title role of *The Graduate.* Two years later, the pattern repeated itself for another unknown, winner of an Obie for his part in *The Indian Wants the Bronx.* He went on from there to star in Joseph Papp productions, a movie, *The Panic in Needle Park,* and, four years later, in *The Godfather.* He was Al Pacino.

A whole new generation of character actors got started by winning Obies—Vincent Gardenia, John Heffernan, Roscoe Lee Browne, John Cazale, Cliff Gorman, Ron Leibman, Austin Pendleton, Moses Gunn, Hector Elizondo.

Likewise, in November 1964, a young black actor with the name Clarence Williams III was in the pages of the *Voice*, doing some Off-Broadway work; four years later he was starring in the TV series *Mod Squad*. In 1966, *Voice* readers could see two journeyman actors—Gene Hackman and Obie-winner James Coco—as they appeared in a new Murray Schisgal play, *Fragments;* in a year Hackman would be playing Warren Beatty's brother in *Bonnie and Clyde* and in four years Coco would be the star of Neil Simon's Broadway comedy *The Prisoner of Second Avenue*. That same year, six years before his initial Obie-winning success in Joseph Papp's staging of *Much Ado About Nothing* and eight years before he appeared on screen in *The Great Gatsby*, Sam Waterston made the *Voice*'s pages. The next year it was the turn of Charles Durning, half a decade before his performance in the play *That Championship Season* led to roles in *The Sting* and *Dog Day Afternoon* and secured his career as a character actor, and Ralph Waite, playing in a modern *Hamlet* years before he became the father on television's *The Waltons*.

As the *Voice* became involved in the Off- and Off-Off-Broadway scene, so did its critics, as individuals. Michael Smith and Arthur Sainer, in particular, were not just critics. They were participants, too, and they wrote advocacy criticism. Smith wrote and directed plays in the late sixties and early seventies; his first one was produced at the Café LaMama. Arthur Sainer, a rail-thin, soft-spoken man, was in his late thirties when he left his job at *TV Guide*, his marriage broke up, and, after holing up in a hotel on the Upper West Side for a time, he got an apartment on West 10th Street in the Village—out of which he had locked himself at two o'clock one morning in 1961. He was sitting there on the front steps, waiting for a locksmith to come, when Edwin Fancher came out of the building, on his way home after a date. Fancher stopped to talk. Sainer said he wanted to do some reviewing for the paper. He began covering theater, started going out to the printer, then did some reporting, and, for $30 a week, was their book editor— until they fired him. Too much like the *Times*, they said. But the connection had never been severed totally. In the years after 1964, he taught, lived in Vermont, came back to the city, began writing and directing Off-Off-Broadway plays, and reviewing in the *Voice* again.

Julius Novick, on the other hand, had never wanted to be anything other than a drama critic since before the day in 1958 when, still an undergraduate at Harvard, he had come into the office looking for a summer job. No, he was told, but if you want to write, go ahead, and Jerry Tallmer began giving him assignments. After seven years of spot reviewing, he became a regular reviewer in 1965. Besides writing for the paper Novick taught, had his own degree in directing from Yale Drama School, and wrote theater criticism for a wide range of publications. In the *Voice* he frequently took the tack that uptown, orthodox, conventional theater was not all that bad all the time, which made for interesting, dialectical counterpoints to what Sainer and others might be apt to say. For instance, when Kurt Vonnegut's play *Happy Birthday, Wanda June* opened in 1970, Novick found it "even funnier than *Cat's Cradle.*" Sainer said, "I went to it expecting the worst and I found it. . . . The play is manufactured, unfeeling, thoroughly conventional, and smugly tuned up to make itself an audience-pleaser." By the seventies, other critics had come along—Ross Wetzsteon, Audrey Berman, Michael Feingold, Erica Munk—all of them bringing with them their own, very different sensibilities, two or more of them often reviewing the same show and reaching verdicts totally at odds with one another. That kind of ongoing, in-house dialogue became a *Voice* trademark.

The Obies, meanwhile, became an event. Often, they were a show in themselves. In 1963, an Anti-Obie was awarded, to Lincoln Center, for "outstanding disservice to the American theatre." Internecine fighting among the critics selected to sit on Obie juries was something of a tradition, with feuds started and settled over who was to win what. In 1964, two years after he abstained on an Obie jury from giving an award to Samuel Beckett for his play *Happy Days,* Walter Kerr won the Anti-Obie for "his determined resistance to the works of Ibsen, Strindberg, Chekhov, Pirandello, O'Casey, Brecht, Sartre, Ionesco, Genêt, and Beckett, and for turning his skills instead to the promotion of a commodity theatre without relevance to dramatic art, the imagination, or our age." In 1969 an actor named Ching Yeh, for his acceptance speech, recited Hamlet's "to be or not to be" soliloquy—in his native language. Another year actress Lucy Silvray came on stage and thanked everyone for her Obie for playing, she said, the leg of her mother's friend Gladys that had been blown off in an explosion at a munitions factory in 1943. Only a few in the audience got it, that she was delivering an acceptance speech parody that Michael Smith had written for her beforehand. In 1970, the air-conditioning failed, the beer got warm, the crowd got unruly, and one recipient told one heckler, "Earn your right to be on stage, you loudmouth." The heckler, actually, had already been on stage that evening, to accept an Obie of his own. In 1972, the Obies' co-emcee was Groucho Marx himself. "A Night at the Obies" it was called, and a crowd of 500 packed into Art D'Lugoff's Village Gate to see him. Their reaction to him was mixed; Groucho engaged in leering at the female winners, cringed when the announcement was made that Jane Fonda's "Fuck the Army" Show had won an award, and kept whispering to Ross Wetzsteon, his co-host, "When is this goddamned thing going to be over?"

But in none of this, as it turned out, did Jerry Tallmer share, even though he was the one who had had the idea for it. After making the seminal contribution, after being present at the creation, after persevering all through the fifties, he missed out somehow. When the sixties and seventies came, when what he saw coming bore full fruit, they passed him by. The man who planted the seeds missed the harvest.

It was a matter of the most unfortunate timing, because when Jerry Tallmer left the *Village Voice* for the *New York Post* he very likely made the mistake of his life. He could not tell that at the time, of course, and no one would quarrel with his reasons for going. And, at the *Post,* he had everything he had never had at the *Voice*—everything except that position of freedom and influence, of being able to spot a trend coming and make it happen, of being in contact with an audience that read him assiduously, as the *Voice* audience did, and engaged him in dialogue. At the *Post,* Jerry Tallmer continued to be what he was, a very fine critic, but he never became the critic he could have been, never had the chance to do again what he had done for Off-Broadway at the *Voice,* never did succeed Richard Watts.

At the *Voice,* he had been Jerry Tallmer, associate editor of the *Village Voice.* At the *Post,* he was just Jerry Tallmer, one of the critics, another one of the writers. Not that he could necessarily have seen, in 1962, what his position at the *Voice* might mean someday. But in 1962, the paper hadn't made any money yet and didn't seem to have made any difference. So he left, and that was what made it unfortunate, because by leaving right then he missed out on making money, on what might have been, by a matter of months.

★ ★ ★

The second reason they made it was Jules Feiffer.

It was October 26, 1956, and they had been in business exactly a year to the day, when he walked in, very birdlike and defensive, John Wilcock remembered, showing some cartoons he'd done to Jerry Tallmer, while the rest of them looked over Tallmer's shoulder and flipped. This guy, Wilcock was thinking like all the others, was *good.*

He was good, but nobody had heard of him yet. Jules Feiffer was his name, he was twenty-seven then, and until five years before he had been living in an East Bronx walk-up with his Polish immigrant parents. Then he was drafted, and assigned to the Signal Corps in New Jersey, where he started his first comic strip—he'd wanted to be a cartoonist since he was a kid—about a four-year-old draftee named Munro. In 1953, mustered out of service, he began three years of wandering, living in Brooklyn Heights (the Village made him tense), going through psychoanalysis, picking up work here and there.

Except that the work Jules Feiffer was getting to do was not the work he wanted to do, and the work he wanted to do he was not getting a chance to do. He envisioned himself, alone in this nightmare of orthodoxy with this view of how it could all be satirized, how the whole thing was just so *absurd*—but he couldn't get anyone interested. He drew three complete books of cartoons—about Munro, about the Bomb, and about the conformity of the Silent Generation. "Come back when you have a name," he was told. The only work he got was doing shlock for art product houses and scripts for the Terry Town cartoon series on TV. By October of 1956 he was doing more and more of that all the time, and hating it more and more all the time, too. He was becoming, he knew it, a hack. And he knew about this paper the *Voice;* maybe they might want his sketches. To find out, he went in.

Tallmer was the first to see his drawings, and to this aspiring, uncomplimented cartoonist he couldn't have been nicer. "What you put in the *Voice* is up to you," Tallmer told him. "You decide. You want a panel, six panels, it's up to you." They struck an agreement that was typical of those early *Voice* years—Feiffer would appear every week, and, in exchange for doing without the pro forma $5 they offered him, he could do cartoons on anything he wanted. In other words, Jules Feiffer, who had had money without freedom, now, by choice, had freedom without money. It was a choice many others were going to make after him.

He wasn't particularly interested in politics, he told them. What he really wanted to do was a kind of cartoon equivalent to the writing Robert Benchley had done for the *New Yorker* in the thirties, but since this was the fifties it would have to be the kind of humor people were now beginning to call "sick." That was what he had called one of his unpublished books, and what he wanted his cartoon strip to be called: "Sick, Sick, Sick." He also didn't see himself in newspaper work for very long. The cartoon strip was to be a way of getting himself started in publishing; he would draw a few introductory cartoons and then begin the task of breaking down his books into serials.

He found out it wasn't that easy. He knew what he wanted to say, but he didn't know how to draw it, not right away, and so his humor came off a little tame at first; his first strip consisted merely of some businessmen waiting for a bus, with one crouched figure complaining— about being late to work, about a stomach ache, about everything— until someone else told him, "SHUT UP!"

But he got better, rapidly, and he changed his style, radically. Instead of narrow panels with tiny figures uttering small clouds of words in tightly lined darkness, Feiffer began drawing his characters boldly, freestyle, in white open space, and much bigger. Instead of showing situational humor or giving a cute conclusion, he began giving broader punchlines. Only a little while into it he discovered that the "introductory cartoons" had become an end in themselves, that he would never get around to breaking down those books after all. The point of the strip came to be more biting, outrageous, sardonic. Characters with slightly exaggerated features were making slightly exaggerated statements, sometimes in dialogue that led up to some rhetorical reductio, sometimes in monologue while they went through metamorphosis, strip by strip. It was a favorite technique of Feiffer's to show one character talking, alone, aging panel by panel, or repeating one key statement over and over, gradually making the statement, and the character, a little more ridiculous with each new panel and each new repetition and each new touch-up of his pencil. He took up neurosis and psychoanalysis, sex and the suburbs, having kids and making it with girls, always with this absurdist air, a "this-can't-possibly-be-happening-and-yet-it-is" mentality. Before there was such a thing known as "black humor," Jules Feiffer was into black humor.

His recurring hero was Bernard Mergendieler, inept, wimpy, hopeless, helpless Bernard Mergendieler, who could never win any of the girls he tried for nor any of the battles he got into with Miss Sacrosanct of the telephone company, who considered it a victory if he got out of bed all right in the morning. In one strip Bernard stood by himself, dreaming, gesturing, flashing his teeth, seeing himself as "a dictator . . . a titan . . . with a ruthless grasp on power and an iron grip on the helm of government," flashing his teeth. *"Then* could I meet girls." Once, Bernard got his girl, but it didn't work out. "I want to dance and *feel free,"* she told him. "To go *back* to Majorca and *gamble* and make *love.* And you want to go to *Queens* and live with your mother." Bernard responds: "You have any nice friends?" Another time, Bernard was thinking, fretting over how many different girls he had confessed his life story to and then lost: "All over the city girls who no longer like me are casually walking around with my life's confessions."

Feiffer was always putting his finger on people's phobias as he did then. He could identify every one of their unspoken urban neuroses, seemed to be able to describe every stereotype they'd ever met. The mama's boy's mama: "What's a mother for?" she asks, sending her son money when he asks her to, sending him to a shrink when he asks her to, not getting in touch and not sending any more money when his shrink says he should overcome his "mother influence. . . . So now it's over a month," she says. "He's depressed. He can't find a job. His psychiatrist is suing him. . . . But listen. So long as he's happy." The couple playing tennis: "Larry! What do you think you're *doing?"* she asks as he doubles over. "Hemorrhaging," he answers. The seductive Village blonde, monologuing: "After awhile, I found it hard to remember *one* from the *next.* I began to get worried about finding someone *right* and settling down. I *am* nearly twenty-*six* you know. . . . Well then my *father* of course would fly down and tell me how I was *destroying* my mother and if I don't *reform* he'd stop paying the rent. *You* know the scene—'Don't use that kind of language on me, I'm your *father!'* You know . . . So I said the hell with it and married Walter. I can use the vacation." The jazz fanatic, lecturing: "Most lay listeners hold the impression that our modern jazz idiom stems from the fusion of African and native American rhythms. Nothing could be further from the truth. Jazz was *really* invented by Steve Allen in 1955."

Feiffer could see the humor, pathetic as it might be, in everything. There was nothing he could not rank out somehow, no attitude that could not be satirized, no situation that he could not find an angle in worth spoofing. Even the existential *angst* of a man who could not bring himself to get out of bed in the morning. "It's not *healthy* to lie here," he exhorts himself. "Perhaps, I don't *really* want to get up, perhaps I feel that I have, at last, found my role. . . . So the *real* issue is not getting up or lying down—the *real* issue is how do I *honestly* feel about either move. Because without fully understanding my motivations, how can *either* act have any meaning for me? . . . I MUST DIG! I MUST PROBE! Pretty soon I'll have to start planning. I'll count to three." Even the existential *angst* in Christmas. With a chorus caroling "Sing Derry Derry down," Feiffer's narrator updated the tale of Virginia, the girl who wrote to Santa Claus. "And Santa Claus replied: 'Do *any* of us *truly* exist?' And he sent her a book on metaphysics instead of the doll house she really wanted. Moral: a truly bright child doesn't ask questions."

A Feiffer neurotic, afraid of a mean-looking dog, negotiated: "For instance, if I pet you would *that* make us friends?" he pleads. *"May* I pet you? Would you *snarl* at me if I pet you?" The dog lets him pet, and the neurotic is still unhappy: "Even when I'm able to *give* I feel I'm only being tolerated."

Sometimes Feiffer made his points with kids. For a while one summer, his spot was purportedly taken over by "Alvin Camus (age 5)," drawing scenes from his own life. During the height of the hula-hoop craze, Feiffer drew a little girl, spinning herself around, telling her story: "I spun my hoop like this. And soon all the boys were noticing me. So I spun my hoop like this. And then a crowd of men noticed me. And they all had a funny kind of grin. Then my mother came out and beat me up." And when in the spring of 1958 Marlon Brando's sympathetic portrait of a good Nazi in *The Young Lions* brought on a wave of World War II revisionist history, Feiffer drew two bright-eyed tots playing war. "I must be the good guy—the American," says one. "I must be the other good guy—the Nazi!" says the other. "I have the best uniform."

"I must be wishy washy but sensitive," says the first. "I must be mean and brutal—but there are reasons," smiles the other. "I must have to chase you. But I really want to be home raking up the old lawn," says the first child. "I must have to chase *you* too. But it's only because I'm made to," says the second. "I must kill you and win the war. It seemed right at the time," says the American. "I must die—misunderstood," says the Nazi, falling, shedding a tear, and then lying there, grinning. The child playing the American stares off dejectedly for a panel, then shouts: "NEXT TIME *I* MUST BE THE NAZI!"

"What I wouldn't give to be a nonconformist like all the others," one of his characters confessed, and Feiffer was as much against the orthodoxy of nonconformism as he was against the preexisting orthodoxy. Knowing the nonconformists as well as he did, he could put down their selling out as nobody else could. A Feiffer writer sat at his typewriter, expounding on the success of his book, *"The Naked Slasher Penthouse Caper.* The jacket was in *blood red* with the drawing of a chained, half naked girl holding a knife at the throat of a private cop in a trench coat. . . . The sub-head on the cover went—'When the seductress from the sanitarium hired detective Mike Yesterday all the rules had to be rewritten.' " The market changes, and he decides to call his next book *"Functional Aspects of the Moral Dichotomy In Judeo-Christian Man*—there's a painting of Mozart by Ben Shahn on the cover! And only when you turn to the inside do you see the sub-head—'When the seductress from Antioch hired anthropologist Mike Yesterday all of Darwin's theories demanded reappraisal' and just under that it reads—'A critical allegory of our time.' I've sold fourteen million copies. I've gotten dozens of offers to speak at universities, and 'Omnibus' is doing my life story. The hallmark of a professional is a profound knowledge of his market."

"Man, that's what a rebel is," went the Feiffer rebel. "I mean he don't talk up to no judge. He don't say it's a bad rap. Cause he *knows* he's guilty. Like to him just *living* is a crime. So he cuts out—you know, man—he *withdraws.* And he goes on his *own* and he says, 'Squares, I do not *know* you.' That's *rebellion,* man. And he learns a *new* tongue—like a different *language*—and when the squares come around he says '*What* are they saying?' That's *rebellion,* man. And soon he's *so* withdrawn he only hears *himself.* So he writes it in a book. And the squares say, 'hey—here's the latest!' So they *buy* his withdrawal and everyone makes a *mint. That's* rebellion, man." And as for rock 'n' roll, Feiffer drew a Presleyesque character on stage, mumbling, "Alwees S'pleash'r t'be here lad'z an' gen'lm'n—liket'sing a li'l song I wrote 'specially f'you," his fingers going "snap snap snap. 'Selllf Pity! BOOM! Smashed City! Referend me before you decide to end me!"

It was obvious early on that Dan Wolf and the *Voice* had captured a brilliant and original talent, one "alone and unafraid in a world made of the macrocephalic bromides of psychoanalysis, avant-gardism, progressive schooling, the hideous nuances of cocktail-party conversation, politics, television, togetherness, and the careful conformism of the equally careful outrageous," as Gilbert Millstein of the *New York Times* called Feiffer in a review of the first of those three unpublished books of his, when McGraw-Hill put it out in 1958. By then, stories were coming back to the office that up on Madison Avenue ad people were clipping Feiffer cartoons out of the paper and carrying them in their wallets, and the book sold out three printings in two months.

Before too long, Feiffer could not resist getting political. Those were, after all, the years of Eisenhower, and the General's ineffectuality finally became so offensive to Feiffer over the issue of civil rights and the 1957 Battle of Little Rock that he drew him, at a press conference, dispensing mindless evenhandedness: "I deplore the actions of extremists on both sides—those who blow up schools and those who want to keep them open." Another Feiffer cartoon showed two owlish, bespectacled cocktail party types discussing the dream one of them had had about a nuclear confrontation. At the height of the crisis, the dreamer recalls, "The President adopts a wait and see attitude."

After Eisenhower, Feiffer turned his pen on Richard Nixon. During the televised 1960 debates, Feiffer drew Nixon saying, "I believe Senator Kennedy believes what he believes sincerely as I believe that I believe what I believe sincerely," drew him with all his shadowy features and mock macho gestures and convoluted explanations, ridiculed him as a pompous ass with a fourth-rate mind. Not that Kennedy fared any better once he was in office. Feiffer seemed to take special delight in the clay feet and unfulfilled promises of liberal heroes.

That next summer, during the Berlin Wall crisis, Feiffer began to zero in on Kennedy's foreign policy. In one strip, "Marvin" expounds to his date how "by exchanging areas of exploitation we may *yet* be able to build the cold war to a stand still," and she answers him, "If President Kennedy could hear you now—I *swear* Marvin, there'd be no Arthur Schlesinger." But of course, there *was* an Arthur Schlesinger, a certified liberal intellectual in the service of this Cold Warrior, and Feiffer had already drawn him in one strip, rationalizing that "three or four years after the end of the Cold War, the American people may be ready to hear about it." In another strip, a prototype Kennedy-adviser figure explained himself: "Don't think I don't understand you idealists. *I* was an idealist myself before I joined the Administration. But then I learned politics is the art of the possible. We make our stand, introduce a bill milder than the stand we have taken, make a deal to water it down with amendments in order to get another watered-down bill we want out of committee. And then we get both bills on to the floor for a vote where they're defeated. This gives us an issue to campaign on while freeing us from having to implement a meaningless bill which would have cost us congressional votes on future measures that we might feel *equally* strongly about! It's easy to be principled," he concluded, "but it's another thing to get your program through." In yet another strip, more Schlesinger-like advisers did a "Cha Cha Cha" to the virtues of "pre-emptive liberalism" and "Defense Posture 2."

In what he saw as the spirit of the New Frontier, Feiffer offered "A Guide to Conversational Counterforce" to Americans planning to travel abroad. "ENGLAND: When they bring up Herman Kahn, Edward Teller, and nuclear deterrence (85 points), counter with Roy Welensky, Southern Rhodesia, and the continued sale of arms to South Africa. (90 points). FRANCE: When they bring up the CIA, civil rights and the radical right (80 points), counter with the OAS, suspension of the press and plastic bombs. (85 points). RUSSIA: When they bring up the stock market, the decline of capitalism and the Cuban fiasco (75 points), counter with Hungary, failing crops, and Mao Tse-tung. (85 points). GERMANY: When they bring up allied indecision on West Berlin (35 points), you may counter with latent Nazism and the fear of a new Hitler—but it will score you no points—they have never heard of either. A final word of advice: the best way to escape is to avoid speaking to anyone who understands English. Aloha!"

Feiffer's antiliberalism was brought to a head, and best brought out, by his attitudes toward their attitudes toward Castro. "I'm not basically anti-Castro," prattled the stodgy liberal, standing against a stool and dragging on his cigarette. "I just think if he wants our support the *least* he can do is meet us *half way.* Quite frankly we may as well recognize the fact that Americans don't dig revolutions anymore. After all, we've *had* ours. Why vulgarize it? I mean look what's happened to Cadillacs. Good Lord, if he *must* have his revolution, why couldn't he pick some *Communist* country? We'd have been with him 100%—Voice of America—Radio Free Europe—the *works!* But *no*—he has to pick one of *our* dictators. And without so much as a pre-revolt public relations campaign to soften up the opinion market. And then he has to popularize the *beard* thing. *Everybody* knows beards are a threat to the home. And that dirty *uniform* and those *Method* acting *mannerisms*— Good Lord, that might go well in the coffee houses but it *dies* in Cornwall, Connecticut!" Another ad-agency type, in another strip on the same subject, advocated "an extensive pre-revolt campaign in all emerging countries," complete with "free diner club memberships," and an *Andy Hardy* for Cuban TV, starring "a typical Cuban television family! house in the suburbs—two cars in the garage—and a wacky kid brother who looks like Raul Castro!"

He was not always so pointed. When Sputnik went into orbit, his cartoon character merely went "BLAST IT OUT OF THE SKY I SAY!" then, "We have committed the worst of all possible sins. . . . We were second." In another strip, he drew a Cold War metaphor—two guys, one big and one little, the big one saying, "I can punch you to jelly," the little one answering, "I can propagandize you to pieces," and the two of them agreeing, "How in the world could we ever get on without each other?" He could, in the fall of 1961, spoof the craven pro-Soviet neutralism of Indonesia's Sukarno as well as combative U.S. foreign policy, and before the heyday of black militancy and liberal guilt, he drew a cartoon showing two whites in a bar, facing each other, while two blacks move into the booth behind them and make loud threats until the frightened whites flee the place. At other times he could simply be inventively funny, such as he was in 1962, drawing in his strip the announcement of a new organization he called the Radical Middle, a sort of Eisenhowerism without Eisenhower. "Good morning, good afternoon, good evening," said their spokesman in one strip, a man totally without facial features. "Bold times call for bold answers. Within reason. In a manner of speaking. More or less. On the other hand."

Of all Feiffer's political cartoons in the early years, none was more famous than "BOOM," a four-page satire on the bomb and the arms race, a kind of nuclear fairy tale that ran in the *Voice* of October 29, 1958, to mark Feiffer's second anniversary with the paper.

"As soon as one country had discovered a bigger Bomb than its neighbor," went Feiffer's narration, "the first thing it did was call a disarmament conference." Soon, the earth is pockmarked by bomb tests. Public relations campaigns are telling people that BIG BLACK FLOATING SPECKS ARE VERY PRETTY GOOD FOR YOU. A patient tells his shrink, "All I dream about is big black floating specks," and the doctor tells him, "Adjust to it."

"So while half the people in the world worked on new, improved Bombs," the story goes on, "the other half worked on salves, medicants, and storm windows. And people saw the situation and said: THAT'S THE WAY THE SPEARMINT CHEWS and went about their business."

Ultimately, the biggest bomb of all is developed, but it needs to be tested. "So they had the test, and," the tale ends, showing the entire planet underneath a Hiroshima cloud, "it worked."

There was a demand for extra copies of "BOOM." Two months later, in London, *The Observer* ran it. Then *The Observer* began syndicating Feiffer in Britain. Syndication of the strip grew and grew; eventually Feiffer was appearing weekly in 100 different papers. And, as that happened, he branched out into other careers. Rembrandt Films made a movie out of the adventures of Munro, and won an Academy Award for it in 1961. Feiffer, thinking for so long a time that he was alone with his sensibility, began watching kindred comics like Mort Sahl and Nichols and May perform, and after a while he fell in with them. Mike Nichols produced a musical revue based on several of his cartoons in 1961. That same year his first play, *Crawling Arnold,* was produced. A novel, *Harry, the Rat with Women,* followed, then three plays—*God Bless, The White House Murder Case,* and, the most successful in its Off-Broadway run starring Alan Arkin in a 1969 Obie-winning role, *Little Murders*. That play was made into a movie, and then in 1971 Nichols made an original Feiffer screenplay into a film that followed two American men and their intertwined loves from college to middle age during changing sexual mores, called *Carnal Knowledge.*

Jules Feiffer had arrived, and he always remained unconvinced that he'd have ever been published anywhere by anybody if the *Voice* had not picked him up when it did.

★ ★ ★

The third reason was Washington Square Park.

Feiffer had a cartoon for it. A four-eyed alien being from a future century stood reviewing slides of New York City architecture in its various stages. On came slides of glass-slab highrises and housing projects; specimens of the nineteenth century, the speaker said. Then came a slide of an old brownstone; "one can only be left breathless by the brilliance of a society that was able to make such giant strides in a mere 150 years," he exulted.

Actually, it was the other way around—the brownstones had come first, then the housing projects and the glass slabs, and the distance traveled in 150 years had been strictly backward. Urban renewal was the order of the day in American cities, and in New York City urban renewal meant Robert Moses, the city's iron fist, its master builder, its power broker, who had been building what he wanted where he wanted and tearing down whatever he wanted for nearly thirty years.

But by the early fifties, there were chinks being perceived in the armor. After decades of a good, practically fawning press, Moses was getting heat from disclosures of corruption and incompetence in the Title I housing project he was administering. And when he had decided, early in the decade, that—supposedly to ease the flow of traffic downtown, which was his reason for destroying everything, it seemed—it would be necessary to put a highway over, under, or, best of all, *through* Washington Square Park, to coat the crossroads of the Village with blacktop and concrete, Robert Moses had set out on his North Africa campaign.

There had always been opposition to it from the people in the Village, but they were either too transient or too disorganized to do much. Besides, this was the era before demonstrations, and Moses was still only talking about it, only planning it. Mrs. Shirley Hayes, wife of an ad executive, and a Villager, had started the first committee against his road in 1952, and three years later the stalemate was still going on, with the *Village Voice* reporting in an early issue, the week of December 14, 1955, that she had led a crowd of fifty Villagers in voting to block all traffic through the park at a local mass meeting called to discuss the subject.

But she was not so alone any more, and she was not going to stay unpublicized as she had been. In Dan Wolf, she had an ally, and, in those early years, when he was so shy and reticent about declaring himself editorially about anything, he could always be counted on to break his silence on whether it was to be Moses and his cars or the Village and its people.

In just the third issue, Wolf wedded his paper to Mrs. Hayes's cause. If the highway goes through as planned, it will mean "the beginning of the end of Greenwich Village as a *community*," the fledgling editor protested.

> Of course, Greenwich Village will remain; maps and guide books will note it and nostalgia will breathe into it a spurious vitality. But all the same it will cease to be a reality . . .
>
> Washington Square Park is a symbol of unity in diversity. Within a block of the arch are luxury apartments, cold-water flats, nineteenth-century mansions, a university, and a nest of small businesses. It brings together Villagers of enormously varied interests and backgrounds. . . .

If it is reduced in size or made less accessible . . . Greenwich
Village will become no more than another characterless place
bearing a name. . . . New York is full of such places. . . . New
York's only breathing space south of 59th Street will have lost
its attraction.

Even in the days of the tacky news stories and the polls on
everything Villagers wanted to know about themselves, the paper
showed it had a cause. In the second issue, it began a postcard poll of
the Village, offering the various alternatives—the road Moses wanted, a
depressed roadway, an elevated one covering the park, leaving the park
as it was (at that time, Fifth Avenue buses were using it to turn
around), or closing it off to traffic completely. In mid-December, in the
same issue that carried a report on Mrs. Hayes's fifty-strong protest, it
announced VILLAGERS REJECT 'DITCH', TUNNEL, and disclosed that
seven out of every ten respondents wanted the park closed to traffic.
The paper was not only telling the people in its neighborhood that they
were diametrically opposed to Moses; it was telling them, too, that
they were numerous, something they might not have known before.

It continued to run news items about the endangered Village and on
the growing antihighway, save-the-Village movement. At the end of
May 1956 the paper reprinted some comments Moses lieutenant
Stuart Constable had just made in an interview granted to the *World-
Telegram & Sun*. "I don't care how those people feel," said Constable
about the Village's would-be road blockers. "They can't agree on what
should be done. They're a nuisance. They're an awful bunch of artists
down there."

"Anyone who joins in community action to preserve local traditions
and resources is always a terrible nuisance to the authorities," Dan
Wolf answered. "We hope there are thousands of nuisances like that
within a stone's throw of this office."

One year later, in the issue of May 1, 1957, the headline on the front
page ran, ROAD THROUGH 'SQUARE' LIKELY—BUT NO BLUEPRINT AS YET.
And Dan Wolf was writing, "The battle over Washington Square Park
has been going on for so many years that the whole subject has become
something of a bore. We suspect this is exactly what the Moses forces
have been waiting for all along. . . . The scheme to cut the park (and
the Village) in two is one more example of giving priority to automobiles over human beings. . . . [But] human beings can be stronger
even than Robert Moses, if they ever decide to get really angry about
it."

Nineteen fifty-seven was the year of compromise offerings, especially the proposal for a thirty-six-foot, two-lane roadway, with a twelve-foot mall to separate the two twelve-foot lanes of traffic, an idea that bore the distinction of being attacked in print by both Dan Wolf and Robert Moses. "Is a 12-foot mall necessary to divide two 12-foot roadways?" asked Wolf. "The [city planning] commission and everyone familiar with smart politics knows that the mall will become a third roadway when the pressure is off and the aroused Villagers have disbanded their organizations." And in even considering this form of diluted destruction, Wolf declared, the planning commission "thereby lost its claim to call itself a 'planning commission,' and became nothing more than another mediation board. The psychology of the mediator is very simple. If there are two widely divergent points of view, each backed by powerful forces, *you split the difference.*" That was not good enough for the Village.

It was not good enough for Moses, either, as he made clear in a "Dear Hulan" letter to the borough president of Manhattan, Hulan Jack, on October 9 of that year. Such a road, he wrote Jack, would be "ridiculously narrow and . . . in fact, no better than the present roadway. We must oppose a 36-foot roadway," he went on, "wherever it comes up and must as a matter of principle present in the City Planning Commission the arguments against any such inadequate roadway through Washington Square Park" that "ignores the new developments south of Washington Square"—most of them his doing, and themselves bitterly resented by the neighborhood's residents to start with. For Moses, it was all or nothing: he would settle for nothing less than a four-lane highway, twelve feet each lane, with a "center mall at least 5 feet wide." That would assure, he claimed, "safer crossing for passengers and greater safety for motorists." And on one point he was adamant: that "since the road must be divided at Washington Arch" anyway, "it should be divided all the way across the park."

Of course, that meant gutting the Village, but that was not Moses's primary concern. It *was* the primary concern, though, of Dan Wolf, and of Shirley Hayes, and of the many proliferating ad-hoc groups now being formed to stop the highway somehow. "A loud-mouthed minority," Hulan Jack called Mrs. Hayes and her various cohorts, people with "strange motives and sources we have not yet been able to determine." Dan Wolf had a comment. " 'Reason,' " he said, "is the acceptance by Villagers of the proposition that Washington Square is a traffic bottleneck and that something must be done about it NO MATTER HOW PAINFUL IT IS TO US."

On Christmas Eve, 1957, Robert Moses issued a statement on the still-stalled highway project. "The cold facts," it supposedly contained, and "those concerned and those responsible won't for long get away from them," he promised. For one thing, he said, "as traffic increases it is impossible to continue this pattern" around Washington Square "without crippling all uses of the Square as a possible park." And "closing the Square to all through traffic is completely unworkable." It was "an absurdity, can not be done legally anyway, and is contrary to established agreements and common sense." As for other suggestions made, such as widening the existing roads around the square and making them one-way, they "wouldn't work either." They "would cut off access to the Square, endanger lives, and destroy the value of the abutting property."

"Maybe letting this mess develop is the best way to educate the public under the democratic process," said Moses at the end of his statement, with a touch of the *hauteur* that he had displayed before toward public opinion. But just before that he had said something else, and introduced another, new reason for why the road had to go through and the park had to be split: "The developers of the Washington Square South apartments," when the entire urban renewal program got under way in the area around the park, "were formally, officially, and reliably promised," he said, "a Fifth Avenue address."

It may have been Moses's delayed admission of gladhanding favoritism behind the project, or it may simply have been that community organization was an idea whose time had come, but 1958 was the year of the turnabout. It was not compromise anymore. Now those nuisances, that awful bunch of artists who couldn't agree among themselves, that loud-mouthed minority, had gotten angry, as Dan Wolf had hoped they would, had become thousands of nuisances, and set out to prove that human beings *could* be stronger than Robert Moses.

There were new organizations—at least twenty-two of them now, ultimately collecting the signatures of 60 percent of the Village, 30,000 names in all, with their activities fully reported in the news sections and community bulletin board of Dan Wolf's paper. Marc Schleifer, the ad man and controversial *Voice* contributor, was doing some of the organizing. So was Jane Jacobs, the new voice for community control and alternative city planning for whom this was going to be the first of many such fights against Moses and the city, and a prelude to her writing *The Death and Life of Great American Cities*. On April 23 of that year, the antihighway organizers had a thirty-minute audience with Mayor Wagner at City Hall, and she was in the delegation. Endorsements and sponsorship for the committees began coming in from lustrous names and respected organizations. On May 14, Mrs.

Eleanor Roosevelt herself led a "no traffic" delegation to City Hall, and Margaret Mead was a sponsor of the march. After some waffling, Carmine DeSapio, seeing the potency the protesters had by now, brought his Tammany organization down on their side and momentarily allied himself with the Village Independent Democrats, the rump reformer group that had been formed to overthrow him. A Democratic district leader came out for the trial closing of the park to traffic, one of the suggestions offered by the antihighway people to prove their point, and the Americans for Democratic Action came out for it, too. Now Wagner, seeking a third term in 1961 and already edgy about whether he could count on DeSapio as an ally in such a race, had to worry about the political damage he might do himself by continuing to let Moses push the project.

Other figures got involved—Howard Moody of Judson Memorial Church, the editor of *Architectural Forum* Magazine, the manager of the Fifth Avenue Hotel, former New York police chief Francis W. H. Adams, social critic Lewis Mumford, housing expert and city planner Charles Abrams.

"A piece of unqualified vandalism," Mumford wrote in the *Voice* about Moses's road. And, in a front-page essay in the issue of July 2, 1958, Charles Abrams came up with the catchphrase, "the revolt of the urbs," to describe what was happening. The tag came to apply, not only to the struggle against the highway, but the one by the paper itself to find an audience. The "urbs" in revolt were precisely the people Ed Fancher had been aiming at from the beginning, the white-collar new breed he had thought would buy his paper, not the *Villager,* back when he had made his decision to put one out. Now, just as surely as it had become the paper of Off-Broadway, the *Voice* was the paper of the movement against Moses.

But neither Moses nor his partisans were preparing to yield. Quite the contrary. They were preparing to counterattack, and three weeks later, after mulling the proposal over for so long, the city Planning Commission suddenly gave its backing to a thirty-six-foot roadway.

There was outrage. From her summer vacation residence, Shirley Hayes telegrammed a protest to Wolf that he published in the paper. The Citizens Union endorsed her position. So did John Lindsay, the young Republican seeking election in the "Silk Stocking" 17th Congressional District. So, even, did Carmine DeSapio. The commissioners were "full of doubletalk," Wolf wrote bitterly in an editorial. "They have piously declared their dedication to preserving Greenwich Village, a 'stable and attractive neighborhood,' at the same time recommending a course of action best designed to destroy it."

And, he wanted to know, *"why wait* until midsummer, when so many people are out of town, to announce their decision? Was it so that it could be quickly acted on with a minimum of protest?"

It was a sneak attack, but the funds still had to be approved by the Board of Estimate, and before that could happen, Wolf wrote later, "the Village began to marshal its own force, which Mr. Moses has come to learn is considerable."

A massive, last-chance rally was scheduled by the highway's opponents for Thursday, September 18, outside City Hall. "After Six Long Years, THIS IS IT," read the headline in the *Voice* the day before. Fancher himself took part in the march, as a representative of the Joint Emergency Committee to Close Washington Square Park, and his paper pronounced the rally "a substantial victory" in its next issue. The momentum kept up through the public hearings of the Board of Estimate in late October. There, Hulan Jack, a voting member as borough president, suddenly reversed himself, making a motion to close the park to all but emergency traffic for at least thirty days. The motion passed, and Jack picked a committee of three—*two* of them members of the Joint Emergency Committee—to work out a permanent agreement.

The trial closing of the park was scheduled to start Saturday, November 1, 1958. Wolf sensed victory. "As late as last winter," he noted, "the cause was not an entirely respectable one." Four weeks later, he was sure. "This community never believed Mr. Moses' predictions, and welcomed a testing of his thesis," he wrote. Now, "even the handful of individuals in this community who originally opposed closing the Square have accepted it."

Nineteen fifty-nine was the year that Moses picked a fight with Joseph Papp, threatening to shut down free Shakespeare in Central Park. The situation inspired Feiffer to a cartoon that spring featuring an unseen "Moses" under questioning from a reporter standing outside his shut window: "Mr. Moses, Is It True That Unless the Shakespeare Festival Charges $2 Admission This Year, You Plan to Sell Central Park to O. Roy Chalk For a Housing Project?"

"Don't bother me! I'm typing!" came the answer.

It was also the year Moses lost that fight, the year that, in August, the Board of Estimate finally decided not to build a highway after all in Washington Square Park but rather to close it permanently to all traffic, and the year that Mayor Wagner finally called Moses off. It was the year of final victory.

Washington Square Park was only the first of many battles that were to be fought against Moses or the city, and the *Voice* kept reporting on all the fronts—Howard Moody's march to keep the square open to folk singers after the ban on them in 1961; Jane Jacobs's successful campaign to block the proposed bulldozing of sixteen square blocks in the West Village; the continuing eviction fights under Title I; the deplorable conditions at the Women's House of Detention on Sixth Avenue, and the attempts to have it torn down; the fate of the threatened landmark Jefferson Market Courthouse right next to the prison; the continuing attempts to resurrect and defeat the Moses dream, shared by many mayors over a forty-year period, for a Lower Manhattan Expressway.

And always the instrument seemed to be Mary Nichols.

She had come from Philadelphia, from a Main Line family, straight from Swarthmore to New York, to a place on the Italian strip of East Harlem, in 1948. She lived there, taking the Third Avenue Elevated down the East Side of Manhattan to the Village, to the San Remo or Louie's Tavern, on Saturday nights, until she married a landscape architect named Robert Nichols and moved there.

Mary Perot was now Mary Perot Nichols, and she was a housewife, just past thirty, with two little children, and no desire to be a writer of any kind, when she first got active in the fight against Robert Moses and the road he wanted to put through the park where she took her kids. She got more and more active, and as she did, she kept pestering Dan Wolf, "Why don't you do something about Washington Square Park?"

Until one day he came back with, "I can't stand listening to you anymore. Why don't you?" So she did.

With that, the *Voice* had a dogged, fearless reporter on its hands, a woman filled with all the old-fashioned ideas of the muckrakers—civic reform, a basic good-government idealism, belief in the power of the press—who loved every minute of what she was doing and took to being a journalist more than she had ever thought possible. Except for one thing; she could not write.

It fell to Dan Wolf to make her a writer. The man who didn't want to edit, didn't know how to, and didn't want to know, *had* to edit her. He went from rewriting her copy heavily to reassembling it to just coaching her on the fundamentals, and she proved a good learner. Even years later, she could remember Wolf, at five o'clock on a Monday afternoon, facing deadline, rewriting her, saying, "You said something dreadful," and always, the way she remembered it, taking the knife and giving it a little extra twist.

Twisting the knife came to be known as Mary Nichols's forte eventually, as she moved from covering the park to reporting on other

Moses matters to general community reporting and then on to the politics beat. By that time, she was one of the toughest reporters in town, on any paper. When, in 1964, after fudging the question for months, Robert Moses asked the Board of Estimate quickly and quietly for an $8.6 million appropriation, she was the one who correctly speculated that it was because the World's Fair, of which he had been placed in charge, was losing money. She "had seen at a glance truths about Moses' whole method of operation that no one, seemingly, had understood before," wrote Robert Caro in his 1974 biography of Moses, *The Power Broker*. And "her observations" in the *Voice* "were in many ways the most penetrating printed up to that time."

She was given a copy of a doctoral dissertation once on the history of the movement that finally defeated the Lower Manhattan Expressway, and when the narrative came to the mention of Assemblyman Louis DeSalvio, who had switched sides on the project and gone over to Moses, she scribbled in the margin, "Why not? He was always a crumb." That was her trademark, the tough talk and the good guys–bad guys mentality, and she got it covering politics and politicians. Late in 1958, when they decided down at the paper that they wanted, as they billed it, "an occasional column on the nature of the political scene," the problem was not whom to give the column to, but what to call it. At first it was going to be "Between the Ribs by Mary Fia," then by "Tony Stiletto," and then, for reasons nobody remembered, they came up with "Runnin' Scared," and no pseudonym. Just the byline, "Mary Perot Nichols."

Tough as she already was about politicians in those years, there was one for whom she had a soft spot, whom she admired, whom she believed in, and that was John Lindsay, the Manhattan Republican who gave up his seat in Congress to run for mayor on a Fusion-reform ticket in 1965. And when he won, he wanted her to come to work for him, which she did, leaving the *Voice*. Three years later, she was back again, and one thing was changed. Before Lindsay, Mary Nichols had believed politics was a matter of good guys and bad guys. After Lindsay, she believed it was a matter of bad guys and worse.

★ ★ ★

In the battle over Washington Square Park, the *Voice* had made the right friends, the "urbs." It had also made, though it did not know it at the time, the right enemies.

That was the fourth reason it survived—the fall of Carmine DeSapio.

★ ★ ★

"The Bishop," they called him, but behind the wavy gray hair and the dark sunglasses he always wore in public he looked more like a Godfather. Politically, that is exactly what he was. And Greenwich Village was his home base. His only official elective title was Democratic District Leader, First Assembly District South, and at that he was only one of two, since each district elected one man and one woman leader. But in his district Carmine DeSapio was *the* leader, and had been since 1939. He was also the chairman of something called the Tamawa Club, one of thirteen such clubs in the loose confederation known as "Tammany Hall," after the meeting place of the organization of Revolutionary War veterans to which it could trace its pedigree. Under Carmine DeSapio, Tamawa had become *the* club in Tammany, and under Carmine DeSapio, Tammany, after being nearly decimated in the 1930s by the investigations of the Seabury Commission and the reform, Fusion mayoralty of Fiorello LaGuardia, was making quite the comeback. With the help of Carmine DeSapio, Robert Wagner unseated an incumbent from his own party and was elected mayor of the City of New York in 1953. With the help of Carmine DeSapio, Averell Harriman had squeaked through to election as governor of New York State in 1954. And, having proved himself a kingmaker at the city and state level, Carmine DeSapio sat as New York's man on the Democratic National Committee.

To many reform-minded New Yorkers, the name DeSapio was synonymous with corruption and bossism, but the man was nothing if not entrenched right where he was, and the new newspaper inside his territory, the *Village Voice,* trod lightly regarding him at first. Like the *Villager,* the paper, notwithstanding its erstwhile policy to the contrary, ran puff pieces on him (when he received an award from a temple for using "the power entrusted to him in a truly democratic and brotherly spirit") and on a crony of his (Edgar T. Hussey, on the occasion of Hussey's taking over as president of the West Side Savings Bank).* Unlike the *Villager,* though, it also ran straight coverage on the formation and activities of the Village Independent Democrats, who split from DeSapio's organization in 1957 and dedicated themselves to the overthrow, once and for all, of Tammany. The VID, together with the Lexington Democratic Club, formed on the Upper East Side a few years earlier, was to be the nucleus of a whole new

---

*In 1973 the *Voice* identified Hussey as the banker who mortgaged gay bars connected to organized crime's traffic in narcotics.

reform movement in the Democratic Party of New York, but to the *Villager* it was a discreet nonevent.

During the Washington Square movement, the ambivalence continued. In late December of 1957, soon after fighting off the first primary challenge to his leadership by the reformers, DeSapio appeared to be waffling. Many suspected that his promises to protect the Village were as lukewarm as he could politically afford to make them, and that he secretly didn't mind if Robert Moses bulldozed anything Robert Moses wanted. At that point, Dan Wolf went public for the first time. "Carmine G. DeSapio visited last week's open meeting of the Greenwich Village Study, made a speech that indicated he was in favor of Greenwich Village, and departed," Wolf wrote. "There was nothing untoward, and certainly nothing unprecedented, about that. The only thing wrong with the picture was that Mr. DeSapio missed the point of the meeting."

> At the moment there is a feeling of despair, shared by a growing number of people, that Mr. DeSapio listens only to those groups that have the multiple purpose of telling him what he wants to hear, honoring him on regular occasions, and praising him, disproportionately, on all occasions. That the praise he hears is often insincere and that the facts he is told are often untrue must disturb even a man who has been in politics as long as he has.
>
> The nature of the Village is changing. Nothing said by sycophants can alter that. Nor can they alter the fact that more than a third of the Village Democrats voted against Mr. DeSapio—and for a virtually unknown candidate—in the September primary.

And when DeSapio did explicitly place himself in opposition to Moses's designs for the square, the powers that be in City Hall—powers, from Wagner on down, that he had made—appeared, for the first time, not to be listening to him. To Dan Wolf, it looked like a setup—DeSapio mollifying Mrs. Hayes and her cohorts by going along with them publicly, while privately going along with Moses—and he said so. "No politician is disgraced on his own doorstep," he reminded everyone.

But, even then, the *Voice*—and for that matter, the Village Independent Democrats—made up with him when he came through over the park. At one point, the VID, otherwise committed to toppling him, was his only visible source of political support. And Dan Wolf, who called him "the star of the proceedings" at the Great March on City Hall in

September of '58, praised him two months later "for having shown the judgment to play a crucial role in this fight."

Nineteen fifty-eight was also the year that DeSapio's heavyhanded tactics on the floor of the Democratic state convention against the reformers' candidate for the Senate nomination, Thomas Finletter, led to the Republicans' using "bossism" as their campaign issue and sweeping everywhere—Nelson Rockefeller over Harriman for governor, Kenneth Keating over DeSapio's hand-picked nominee, Manhattan district attorney Frank Hogan, for senator, and, right in DeSapio's own backyard, John V. Lindsay for Congress. Once again, the paper tried to have it both ways—to push DeSapio, but not too far. Mary Nichols left little doubt where she stood when she hosted a party for Lindsay in her own home on Carmine Street. The paper, for its part, endorsed Lindsay, and analyzed the results to mean that the Village "has seen in recent years a heavy influx of liberal, individualistic and egghead Democrats into what was previously a low-income, Tammany-domi-nated" domain. And yet that December Nichols reported, evenly enough, that at a meeting of the Village Independent Democrats "the heaviest share of the blame for the election debacle was not placed by the panelists on Tammany chief DeSapio, as might have been expected at a VID meeting, but on Governor Harriman, and, to some degree, on Mayor Wagner. . . . Mr. DeSapio was seen as less culpable than the organization he represents." But in the end, the paper could not have it both ways, and both they and DeSapio came to know it. If they were going to give aid and comfort to his enemies, even if only in the form of news coverage, if they were going to criticize him, even if they kept it muted and equivocal, if they were going to needle him, or even let others needle him, then, if Carmine DeSapio approved of the premises of his regime and wanted it to survive, they would have to be destroyed. And that is what Carmine DeSapio decided to have done.

They had never been getting either real estate or savings bank ads, even though it had been three years now they had been in business, and they had always assumed it was due to their general policy against being joiners and running puff pieces, or the advertisers' general conservatism, or the hold the *Villager* had, or John Wilcock's wiseass suggestion for ripping off the banks by pocketing the premium after opening and immediately closing an account with them, or whatever. But that was all they thought.

Now they found out otherwise. In the waning days of 1958, Mary Nichols had an interview scheduled with Leo Calarco, member of the Democratic State Committee and minion of Carmine DeSapio. She was there, not for the *Voice,* but for the Women's City Club, in connection with a report it was planning to publish on local school boards, and with her was another woman active in the club, Mrs. Willard Van Dyke. That proved to be important; it gave them a witness to what followed. They were talking to him, about schools, when suddenly Calarco changed subjects and launched a tirade at Mary Nichols about the newspaper she worked for.

"I'm here for other purposes," she reminded him, trying to get back to the interview. But there was no going back with Calarco, and he began running off at the mouth now. "I hate that paper," he told her. "You're inaccurate. We're going to put you out of business. We've been running around, turning off ads on you." For whom? she asked. For Carmine DeSapio, he told her.

She went back to the office and told Wolf and Fancher what he had said. And they waited for the right opportunity to do something about it.

DeSapio gave them the opportunity, one night in early January. Mrs. Gwen Worth, who had run on the VID slate against him in the 1957 primary, was up for secretary of the Greenwich Village Association. DeSapio, in a particularly gruesome display of blind machine power, had his supporters pack the meeting, vote in the wife of a Tamawa captain over her, and then leave. "The long arm of Carmine DeSapio has reached into the Greenwich Village Association," the *Voice* reported. Dan Wolf wrote an outraged editorial.

> If it can't win the Governorship or a seat in the Senate, Tammany Hall has at least proved that it can elect a Secretary in the Greenwich Village Association. . . . We don't suppose you can really count out a party that is able to infiltrate a local civic organization.
>
> This attempt to place in office a member of an organization that had enough public support to take an amazing 37 percent of the vote away from Carmine DeSapio and the massed power of the Tammany machine in the 1957 primary aroused the Democratic "regulars" to an effort they rarely make to win major elections.

Two weeks later, in the issue of January 28, he pressed the matter further, and wrote an editorial openly calling—before any primary challenge had begun—for DeSapio's defeat.

> Much of Tammany's political force grows out of the part of it that most subverts decent democratic government—its lack of

principles. . . . Thus it fought Roosevelt one year and em-
braced the New Deal the next; it hewed to the McCarthy line
when such was the way to win votes and declaimed fervently
for civil rights when the salability of the former line had
outworn itself.

The Tammany system actually has no relationship to the
Democratic voters of New York. It is made up of nothing more
than a handful of key people who dominate this city, hem in its
elected officials, inspect its buildings, buy and sell its land,
and appoint its judges. It is in every sense the "secret
government" of New York.

"The defeat of any Tammany symbol, DeSapio or another, by an
independent Democrat will open the door to a renovation of the party,"
Wolf wrote, and he warned:

The Democratic Party cannot go on forever intoning the
phrases of the New Deal. At one time or another it is going to
have to meet the extraordinary challenges which have developed during the past 25 years in our increasingly complex
urban society.

Let us start here in Greenwich Village—in the fight against
Tammany and DeSapio—to write a new Democratic Man-
ifesto. Who knows? It might strike fire—and spread.

Two weeks after that, in upstate Syracuse, Edwin Fancher rose to
speak in acceptance of an award for general excellence from the New
York Press Association to his newspaper. They figured the time was
right—DeSapio had made his move, they had burned their bridges
behind them. They would use this forum to accuse him, publicly.

Fancher stepped up to the podium, thanked his audience for their
award, and began by taking note of the fact that DeSapio had only the
week before given a speech of his own at a meeting of three press
organizations, in which he accused the press of failing "to fulfill its
political responsibility," of trying "to color, to camouflage, to empha-
size, to omit, and yes, to distort news," and threatened to "turn to TV"
to make his case if necessary. Then Fancher dropped his bombshell: at
home, DeSapio's attitude was just the same. "If they don't comply,
show them who's boss.

"We had few partisan political prejudices" at the beginning, the
publisher explained. "Indeed we knew that we had a lot to learn about
politics and we were prepared to take our time in learning it. On the

other hand, there were certain definite things that we knew we did *not* want to do with our newspaper, one of which was not to load it down with the self-serving publicity of local politicians of whatever party, or with weekly blurbs and photos celebrating the honors and awards forever being passed back and forth between them.

> But from the beginning we were aware of an undertow of resentment from certain political elements in the community who showed consternation over the emergence of a new individual voice. Virtually from the outset they were beating at our doors and clamoring over our phones in an attempt to twist us to partisanship in their favor, while at the same time we discovered an active, if underground campaign to discredit our pages and undermine our local advertising.
>
> Over the years since 1955 our refusal to play the role of house organ to the vested political interests of Greenwich Village has grown more and more intolerable to them. And if we were innocent when we started, it was these gentlemen who sent us to school—educated us, but not quite free of charge. We began to learn the facts of life, and we began to become politically oriented. . . . And if, over the years, we knew but could not prove that the vested political interests were trying to kill off our advertising, we now know it and can prove it.

The speech made page one of the *Times* the next morning, complete with the statement of Leo Calarco denying everything "categorically." Almost categorically, that is. Because while he "defied" the paper to prove what it said was true, he himself admitted telling Mary Nichols "that he not only would not recommend the newspaper to anyone, but also refused to buy it or read it." "If I don't like a product," Leo Calarco told the *New York Times,* I don't buy it. That's my privilege."

The primary campaign got under way that summer—and, with a week to go, there was an incident.

Gin Briggs was a young woman who had come all the way from Ponca City, Oklahoma, to Christopher Street in the Village, where she worked as the *Voice*'s staff photographer. One afternoon in late August 1959, she put a VID poster in the window of her apartment. Within hours, a crowd began to form in the street below. They cursed at her, shouted at her, taunted her that they were going to come up there after her and the sign. And that was only the beginning. The next day, after two visits to the house by a Tamawa captain were observed, her

landlord told her the sign was "against DeSapio and I can't have that":
it had to be down, or she had to be out, by midnight. His wife, the
landlady, then told her, "They'll break your window." She would not
say, no matter how many times Gin Briggs kept asking, who "they"
were. But she did say that the water was going to be shut off.

Even with this, Gin Briggs would not be moved. She refused to take
the sign down and threatened to sue anyone who tried to evict her. And
"all this happened," Dan Wolf reminded Village voters, "because one
poster appeared in one window on Christopher Street."

The incident made big news, gave Lorraine Hansberry the idea for a
roman à clef one-act play, *The Sign in Sidney Brustein's Window,* and
led a number of other Villagers to get in touch with the paper. In the
next issue, on Primary Eve, Wolf reported that they had been getting
"a surprising number of friendly calls from native-born Villagers, most
of whom were part of the Italian-American community. . . . They all
made—without exception—a single stipulation," according to Wolf.
"Never, never use our names."

> . . . "They can't find out how you vote?" He put it in the
> form of a question. We said no, and then asked him why he
> felt he had to be so secretive. He answered simply: "They'll
> put me out of business."

On Primary Day, DeSapio was reelected, but with only 53 percent of
the vote this time—a 10 percent slip in two years. The reformers were
gaining on him. The results "dealt a deathblow to the short-lived
legend of the 'new face on The Tammany Tiger,'" gloated Dan Wolf in
the aftermath. And looking toward 1961, when a new challenge could
be mounted against DeSapio and a new mayor was to be elected, Wolf
was talking about another Fusion ticket "to rescue the city from the
Big Swindle and return it to the spirit of the Little Flower," LaGuardia.

That was two years away, and in the meantime, with primaries for
the state committee coming up in June 1960—Calarco was giving up his
seat—DeSapio tried to split the movement by picking a reformer, Mrs.
Eleanor Clark French, to run with his choice to succeed Calarco. It
didn't work; a VID ticket headed by James Lanigan won the district
with 51 percent of the vote. Wolf called it "a political miracle" that
"marks the last stage in the domination of this district by DeSapio and
his lieutenants. Their wigwam is about to flip."

And "the Angel of Political Destruction is slated to be none other
than President-elect John F. Kennedy," wrote Mary Nichols six
months later. What Kennedy had done to get his party's nomination

was to use Connecticut boss John Bailey to establish a liaison with the boss of Buffalo, Peter Crotty, in order to sidestep DeSapio, Tammany, and the hostile New York State Democratic organization. Kennedy used Crotty to get to Bronx boss Charles Buckley, to Mayor Wagner after him, to the reformers after Wagner, and locked up the New York delegation solid while DeSapio stood still, publicly professing neutrality and privately holding out for Lyndon Johnson to make the race. Now that Kennedy was safely elected, with Johnson safely his vice-president, Nichols reported, his brother Robert had already held a meeting with Herbert Lehman, Eleanor Roosevelt, and other figures prominent in the reform movement to let them know that he had no preference as to who ran the party, them or DeSapio. The inference, though, was clear—anybody who could beat DeSapio was welcome to— and "DeSapio," she wrote, "who seems to have at least as many lives as a cat, may have reached the fatal ninth demise."

Perhaps, but then it seemed she may have spoken too soon. The reformers, after all, had no candidate for mayor, and over the winter things became complicated. Wagner and DeSapio broke off their alliance, Wagner wanting an unprecedented third term, DeSapio wanting to replace him and willing to depose him if necessary, Wagner running anyway and making bossism the issue—*his* issue, after eight years in which the reformers had associated him with DeSapio. When he did that, he put the new reform movement on the spot: Herbert Lehman and others had opposed his running for a third term, but if they now spurned his offer of an alliance against DeSapio or, worse, ran a candidate of their own in the primary who siphoned votes away from Wagner, they ran the risk of losing everything. Down in the Village, the title of a David McReynolds protest piece in the *Voice,* "Mr. Wagner, Go Home," adequately expressed the attitude of the community's activists after Washington Square Park and other incidents. But, at a meeting in late July, the VID decided to get behind him. Still, the community was split, with Jane Jacobs conspicuously accompanying DeSapio's candidate, state controller Arthur Levitt, on a walking tour of the Village in late August, seeking two things—revenge against Wagner for his "pious platitudes" while he continued to keep Moses on, and promises from Levitt against any bulldozing or highrise construction in the Village. On September 7, Wagner went into the primary a slight underdog.

Dan Wolf had figured out that if only fifteen voters per election district had switched their votes in 1959, DeSapio would have been beaten then. YOU AND 14 NEIGHBORS CAN DO IT, his headline implored. "It was here in Greenwich Village in a small room full of people that the battle for New York City was launched," he said, "and it is here where the first stage of the battle should symbolically come to an end with the political demise of Carmine DeSapio."

When the returns came in that night, Wagner had not only scored an upset over Levitt; he had routed him. And in Greenwich Village, the count for district leader was: James Lanigan, 5,972, 56 percent. Carmine DeSapio, 4,666, 44 percent.

Victory.

Mary Nichols was inside DeSapio's headquarters as he was being beaten. She wrote:

> Socialist Murray Kempton of the New York Post, sad-eyed, stood shoulder to shoulder with an equally depressed Rosemary McGrath, who heads the Village chapter of the extreme right-wing Young Americans for Freedom. Behind them was a female covey of native Village furies hysterically screeching: "The beatniks and Communists have taken over!" Up front in the plaque-bedecked Tamawa clubhouse, Carmine DeSapio was playing his last great scene with all the dignity and courtesy that had over the years earned him the title of "The Bishop".
>
> He smiled, a little wanly, as he repeated his words over and over again for the tape recorders of the various media. As each new microphone was thrust in front of his face, DeSapio would say: "The enrolled Democrats of the First Assembly District South have made their decision. In the final analysis, they are the real bosses."

Victory was total, but it was not final. That would take four years more, and by then the *Voice* would have become thoroughly embroiled in a new kind of politics, the kind that was to take the place of the old, ward-heeling structure of the Democratic Party and pass itself down into the 1970s, as the reformers secured bases all over the city, kept them, hit a high-water mark, were contained there, and then settled down to the business of preserving themselves as a permanent reform movement, an added wing of the New York Democratic Party, institutionalized, issue-oriented, often impossible to deal with, and describable with the tag usually hung on them when they were behaving at their political worst, "the West Side liberals." The old wing of the party had had its ethnics; this new one had the issues, or so it thought. The old one had relied on machines; the new one, on Movements. The old politicians cared about connections, these new ones about causes. Patronage had mattered to the old ones, but only purity seemed to matter to the new ones—and their fights over who had more of it were as ideological as they were internecine, and as insatiable as they were ideological.

Even before they had won, there was an example of what it was going to be like, when in the June 1960 primaries one of the original reformers, William Fitts Ryan, unseated an honest but regular Democrat, Ludwig Teller, from his congressional seat on the Upper West Side. Dan Wolf was pleased; Nat Hentoff, however, was not. "Bill Ryan's defeat of Ludwig Teller," he wrote in his column, "proved that the 'hacks' have no monopoly on half-truths and distortion. The gamy Ryan campaign reminded me of my youth in Boston in the time of James Michael Curley. Curley, at least, was not self-righteous."

Dan Wolf was so angry that Hentoff could be so ideologically picayune as to support a Tammany loyalist over an independent, and to use the column to say it, that he wrote a rebuttal. "Ludwig Teller, whom Mr. Hentoff supported, was part of the Tammany structure that has fastened on this city. He lent his clean, honest face to one of the most deeply corrupt political systems in the U.S. today. We are sorry that Mr. Hentoff chooses to consider one particular foot soldier of that conspiracy deserving of our gratitude. We cannot share his feeling."

His knuckles thoroughly rapped, Nat Hentoff was not content to be made the object of a Dan Wolf political lesson, so, starting an honored tradition among Reform Democrats and their supporters—the endless theoretical debate over whose credentials were holier, or more in order— he bounced right back the next week to give a discourse of his own, this one on "The Misplaced Innocence of the Village Voice."

He repeated his contention that Teller was "more qualified for Congress—morally and intellectually—than William Fitts Ryan," said "Mr. Ryan may vote differently than Richard Nixon, but he seems to be not dissimilar in other areas," and deplored "the cowboys-and-Indians emotionalism of 'reformers' such as the editor of the Voice."

A moral for future fights of this kind had already been established: When two reformers or reformer sympathizers argue, each must seek to tag the other with the opprobrium of being, regardless of appearances, basically a counterrevolutionary. Thus Wolf had categorized Teller (and, by extension, Hentoff) as an apologist for the machine, and Hentoff had categorized Ryan (and, by extension, Wolf) as, at least tactically, a reactionary. In an editor's note attached to the end of Hentoff's piece, Dan Wolf served notice he was most ready to continue the argument indefinitely:

> Only the most naive approach to politics can overlook the fact that the pro-organization Tammany leaders must give

their assent, silent or vocal, to a network of political and financial alliances that extends from East Harlem to the Dominican Republic. Any Tammany leader who doesn't know what's going on should get out of politics. . . . P.S. Frankly, Nat, where did you get the idea that the Ryan supporters are proposing him as a subject for canonization?

And that ended it, at least this time. But defeat for Carmine DeSapio did not finish him, not right away. Within a year the reformers had fallen to fighting among themselves and it looked as if Tammany was going to stage a comeback. James Lanigan, the leader they had just elected, quit the Village Independent Democrats in 1962. The VID found a new darling, lawyer Edward Koch, but when Koch took on Assemblyman William Passannante, a DeSapio loyalist, in the primary that fall, Passannante was renominated with 57 percent of the vote. In 1963, DeSapio was back after his old post again, and Lanigan did not even try to run. That left Koch to stop him, and, by 1,300 votes that September ("Last Hurrah for Tamawa! Village is Reform Country!" the *Voice* headlined it), he did. DeSapio sued, claiming voting irregularities, and won. A new primary was scheduled for June 1964. DeSapio campaigned hard, proposing to do something about congestion on Macdougal Street, to widen streets, to narrow sidewalks. It looked close: "The Last Hurrah or the Last Laugh?" asked the *Voice* headline.

In the issue of May 28, 1964, just before the primary, Dan Wolf wrote an editorial that made the case against DeSapio one more time and won him third place that year in the awards of the National Editorial Association:

> . . . For 12 years Carmine DeSapio ran Greenwich Village like an absentee landlord. . . . Homes were destroyed by real-estate speculators. People who were born and raised in Greenwich Village were driven away—his own people. . . .
>
> When DeSapio asks us for our vote, what is he giving us in exchange?—the various phrases coined by a third-rate advertising firm, mystical mumbling about "leadership." If we vote for this man we will only be getting what we deserve: the same old product with a slightly different package of promises, not one of which—we should know it by now—does he mean to keep. . . .

Koch won—by forty-one votes.

That August, at the Democratic National Convention, DeSapio was stripped of his last post, Democratic national committeeman. But he was still not politically dead. What remained of Tammany had fallen into the hands of the black boss J. Raymond Jones, who in 1965 floated plans to cut the Village in two with a redistricting. That did not come to pass, but Edward Koch had to give up his race for Manhattan councilman-at-large when DeSapio announced he was going to run for district leader again in the September primary. Koch beat him again, by 600 votes, and this "delivers the political death blow," Dan Wolf wrote. At last, he was right. DeSapio never ran for office again, and a little more than seven years later, he entered a federal penitentiary to begin serving a prison sentence for his part in the bribery scandal involving Mayor John Lindsay's water commissioner, James Marcus.

Carmine DeSapio did something for the men who had started the *Village Voice:* he made them giant killers. That, at least, was the reputation they acquired the night in September of 1961 when the man who had tried to boycott them out of existence went down to a defeat they had orchestrated if nothing else. Now they themselves became the center of attention for other news media, with Charles Collingwood coming down to the Village to do a show on the Village, its old newspaper the *Villager,* and its new newspaper, the one that had just helped to completely turn the city's political tables. On the night of November 16, 1961, there, on the CBS television network, were Edwin Fancher and Daniel Wolf, on camera, being interviewed by Collingwood, telling him their ideas about what the fights against Moses and DeSapio were all about and what they conceived their newspaper to be, ideas others had thought were crazy or, at best, impossible to bring off when they had started, ideas that had taken them over six years to successfully execute, but ideas that were working now.

6. WHEN HE HAD TAKEN THEM ON, THEY

had taken him on, and when they won, when the reformers in his district brought Carmine DeSapio down, the *Village Voice* became the paper of Reform Democratic politics just as it had become the paper of Off-Broadway and Washington Square Park. The complexion of Manhattan was changing, and the change, journalistically and demographically, was in the paper's favor.

But no paper is ever here to stay until it has a solid advertising base, and that was the other thing Carmine DeSapio had done for them: he made them go out and get one.

The fact was that ever since the beginning they had been unable to decide if this was a Village newspaper or not. To be sure, it was *about* the Village; it covered Village events with mostly Village writers. But precisely because there was no place else like the Village, its readership had never been just Villagers. That was evident, right from the start, in the addresses on letters to the editor—the Upper West Side, Brooklyn, even out-of-state. As near as they could figure it in those early years, one out of every five of their readers was from outside the dividing line of 14th Street. And the paper reflected that. The issue of April 18, 1956, announced that they were selling over "1500 copies on newsstands outside the Village" and that a special, separate uptown edition was being inaugurated. In May 1958 the paper announced it was on sale at two strategic uptown locations, 86th Street and Lexington Avenue in Yorkville, 137th Street and Broadway in West Harlem. And the issue of July 6, 1961, carried the notice that the paper was "now available on a large number of newsstands in most parts of Queens." But the economics of publishing are simple. The expense of putting out a newspaper can never be met by the money taken in from subscribers, or from readers who buy an issue at a newsstand, no matter how high the price of a copy goes. It must be defrayed by revenue derived from advertising. The more readers a publisher has, the more that publisher can charge advertisers, for the right to reach such a big audience. But if the readers are not there, then the publisher must do one of two things: offer low subscription rates to lure readers, and after them hopefully advertisers, too, or offer low advertising rates. Either way, the publisher can easily go out of business if the balance between advertising and readers is not juggled just right, and in time—that is, before the money runs out. Since all publishers of new papers perforce start out with no readers, that is the position they find themselves in, and if they do not have money that they can afford to lose, at least in the beginning,

112

either offering low rates or spending money to develop a base of advertisers and readers, they are, in the economic phraseology, "undercapitalized," and they are liable to go out of business very quickly. And the two founders of the *Village Voice,* Dan Wolf and Ed Fancher, were undercapitalized, to say the least.

According to the simple economics of publishing, therefore, their separate uptown edition was not economical, and after a few weeks they discontinued it. They had readers outside the Village, maybe, but not advertisers. They could not make up their minds what they wanted—"Greenwich Village is a state of mind," they would say, and they welcomed all the outside readers they could get. But they wanted it both ways—to have an outside readership and still be just "a Greenwich Village newspaper" when it came to going uptown and selling ads to support one—just as they had tried to have it both ways when they were critical of DeSapio at first. As it was, when DeSapio forced them to choose, one way or the other, whether to go out of business or to put him out of business, he freed them of both quandaries. They had wanted to be a community newspaper with a community ad base, but now, as the nature of the struggle and the dimensions of the boycott became clear to them, they had no choice. There was not enough advertising in the Village to support them, and there never would be. To survive, they would have to go uptown.

When they did, they discovered something. Books. Records. Theaters. Movies. Sportscars. Travel agencies. Boutiques. Gift shops. Specialty shops. Schools offering courses. A whole range of small, quality retailers. A whole slew of small businesses that did business citywide but had no advertising outlet till now. The *Villager* and the *West Side News* had not looked for them, and the rates of the *Times,* the *Herald-Tribune,* or the *New Yorker* were too steep for them, especially since the audiences of those publications were so big the shops had no way of knowing whom they would be reaching with an ad. But this new newspaper wanted them, offered them low rates, and got them. The reason Edwin Fancher could afford to offer them low rates was because he had so many of them advertising with him, and the reason he had so many of them advertising with him was because he also had so many of the readers they wanted. There was an audience out there, an audience interested in supporting Off-Broadway theater and saving Washington Square Park and cleaning up Tammany politics, an audience that could be described as an acquisitive intelligentsia. It was the audience Edwin Fancher had thought he could have in the very beginning, and now he had demonstrated that he had it. It was the audience such advertisers would want to reach. With the audience on the one hand, the advertisers on the other, and his paper as a conduit between them, Ed Fancher by 1961 had, though the figures did not bear it out just yet, the ideal editorial and advertising base to support a newspaper. He had the structure of a financial bonanza.

And he had it without the financial strings that are usually attached in journalism—dilution of the editorial product, self-censorship for fear of losing an advertiser the paper is dependent on. It was not just out of McCarthy-era political expediency that they disassociated themselves from the leftist press and did all they could to discourage the tag "radical" from being used against them; they genuinely *wanted* to *be* businessmen, precisely because that was the way, as they saw it, to guarantee the very brashness, the independence, the sheer difference to their newspaper that people, both those who liked it and those who didn't, misconstrued as leftism. They had both always, genuinely, been turned off by the Left, by the Communists, the Trotskyites, the socialists, the fronts, the fellow travelers, the hard-core types; and they were as disgusted with the doctrinaires now as they had ever been. Moreover, there were Left publications that, because they either could not or would not stain themselves with the capitalist exigencies of going out and getting advertising, were hypocritically dependent on the largess of millionaires to stay in business. *PM,* for instance, almost totally dependent on Marshall Field, did not attempt to sell ads until he had already lost interest in the paper, and by then it was too late. The point was not lost on Ed Fancher; even the *New Republic* and the *Nation* sent out letters to millionaires every Christmas, he said. They did not want to be dependent on anyone like that. Precisely because of the kind of paper they wanted to put out, they wanted advertisers, lots of them. If there were lots of advertisers, the paper would be beholden to no one of them in particular. If the paper was beholden to no one in particular, it could not be dictated to by any one. They could afford to offend whomever they wished, to tell whoever tried to dictate to them to go to hell and not have to worry whether or not they would go out of business for saying it. And they knew from experience now that it could come to that. So they tried to run their brash little paper like a business, and it was no contradiction. They did not do it to show how normal they were amid the prevailing patriotism of the 1950s, but because to be a money-making enterprise was to have the ultimate protection.

Except that, for seven full years, their paper was not a money-making enterprise. Between October of 1955 and December of 1962, the *Village Voice* lost nearly $60,000. Of that money, Edwin Fancher lost about half. Between 1955 and 1961, from the time he was thirty-one to the time he was thirty-seven, Fancher absorbed his losses and supported himself with his inheritance and his private practice. Dan Wolf, from the time he was forty to the time he was forty-six, was supported by the income brought in by his wife, Rhoda, a social worker. The two partners paid themselves $1,925 each to be editor and publisher their first year. The next year they had to cut back all the way to $450 a year each. The third year they inched up to $520, exactly $10 a week. By 1959 they were both up to $50 a week. Over the first six years the two partners, for their efforts, made a total of $18,000 in salary between them.

They tried everything. They gave out free sample copies in March of 1956. Everywhere they went, they would leave issues, even inside unlocked cars as they walked by. They experimented with the paper—shaving two inches off the bottom of the page in the issue of April 4, 1956, breaking it into two sections for a while in 1960 and 1961, rearranging the looks of it (Wilcock would say he remembered one seven-week stretch with seven totally different front pages on the *Voice),* moving to a new, Long Island printer—and to smaller pages with different type effective the week of February 23, 1961.

Nothing seemed to work. For seven years, they operated on the theory that they would not make it another two weeks. They made checks out to the staff every Friday, after the banks had closed, with instructions to please not cash them until the following Tuesday. In 1956, Ely Kushel, who had left his job with a large firm to teach at New York University, became their third accountant in less than a year of operation (Norman Mailer's father, Isaac "Barney" Mailer, had been the first). Kushel instituted a Daily Cash Report system, and prayed every day that Rose Ryan would take in enough cash downstairs to cover their bills due that day. Every month, Kushel prepared a written status report for them to read. For two reasons, he never used numbers at first—for one thing, numbers meant nothing to them, and the message wouldn't sink in; for another, if it ever had, they would have known just how bad off they really were. They were as naive about business as any two people he had ever met, and he never once told them how close to bankruptcy they were this whole time. Instead, he couched his message verbally, in metaphors, such as the one he usually led his reports off with: "The wolf is close to the door."

Normally, the process of bottoming out takes a paper five years, by which time it is either making money or out of business. It took the *Village Voice* two years longer than normal. While they waited for the process to complete itself, they picked up a motley crew. Joe Coleman was one.

Wacky, erratic, unpredictable, he was just the type of high-powered salesman they needed to put together an advertising department. He was also, they all agreed, nutty. Before he came to the paper, he had done promotional and marketing campaigns and comedy material for show business figures. When he came to the paper, he was full of ideas. "Selling nonpolitical rebellion" was one of them. He had the idea of special issues to generate ads, of parlaying an annual Off-Broadway awards ceremony and an annual Auto Rallye in the Village into theater and car ads, and his gimmicks, even with the embarrassment caused by a special Chinese New Year's section that had a Japan Air Lines ad saying "Visit Beautiful Peking," brought in a lot of money they might not otherwise have gotten. In his last quest for ads for the *Voice,* Coleman went as far as the famed opera house in Spoleto, Italy, for the 1958 summer opera festival. After he left the paper, he went to work for Huntington Hartford (once, wondering, "Why can't we get Huntington Hartford to advertise with us?" and refusing to believe that he could not get to talk to him on the phone, he had kept calling his way up through the entire A&P hierarchy until he got him) at *Show* Magazine, for Hugh Hefner at *Playboy,* for Bob Guccione at *Penthouse,* and finally for himself at his own ad agency. He was a crazy maniac, Ed Fancher described him many years later, but he kept the paper going. And he became the real-life archetype of the off-the-wall screwball in *Asphalt and Desire,* a novel by Fredric Morton, his brother-in-law, author of *The Rothschilds,* and a future contributor to the *Village Voice.*

Dan List was another one. When they hired him to be their distributor, he was doing the same thing for Howard Bennett's rival publication, *East.* Before that, he had been everything. After he arrived in the Village in 1949 from out of the navy, List led what he called "the usual Bohemian life"—nine months in the Village, three months in Provincetown. He was a sportscar dealer. He was a private detective. He worked part-time at the Café Figaro making espresso, along with a struggling actor named Steve McQueen. And, in the fall of 1957, when Jimmy Frankfort quit as Bennett's art director at *East* to resume cartooning in the *Voice,* he told them that List might be available. They had been looking for another distributor of their own since Norman Mailer had given up trying to do it himself and they had signed on with another commercial outfit, Periodical News.

Fancher, Wolf, and Tallmer took List out to lunch, at the Apollo Chop House, 9th Street and Sixth Avenue, bought him a Greek steak, and asked him. Yes, he said, if they could meet his conditions. He wanted three cents out of every dime they earned from every paper they sold. And, since his rent in a cellar on Perry Street was $55 a month, they had to give him a guarantee of $55 a week.

They hedged, thought it over for a week, and gave him what he wanted. On a Wednesday morning in the middle of October, he started out, the newspapers piled in the back of his Hillman station wagon and Norman Mailer's old index cards and route sheets in his hand. To be safe against their being called Communists, List, a man with a tremendous torso and a big belly, wore his navy cap while making deliveries and paid the $35 to get them into the Newsdealers Post of the American Legion. To make friends with the newsdealers, he hung around their stands and got them coffee, especially during the bitterest days of the DeSapio feud, when some of them tried to beg off and drop the paper, telling him what DeSapio would do to them if they didn't.

Eventually, there came a time when the paper got to be so thick each week, and had to reach so many readers at so many different newsstands, that Dan List gave up trying to do it all. He became a fleet operator, hiring his own freelance crew of drivers, renting different trucks each week (a precaution against a holdup on the streets; "the formula for doing business in New York is that nobody should know what you're doing," he said). As he did that, he became rich enough to deal in cars again. He began to buy up vintage automobiles and rent them out to film makers shooting period scenes in New York. *The Group* was the first major film he worked on, in 1965, and when he and his cars were late for shooting one day director Sidney Lumet demanded to know, "Where's Danny List and his Obsolete Fleet?" The name stuck. "The Obsolete Fleet" appeared in a long string of New York–shot, period-piece movies over the next decade; eventually List himself appeared on camera as an extra (a cabbie in *The Way We Were*) and co-produced a film, *The Lords of Flatbush*.

His love for all things automotive never stopped. Introduced to Jean Shepherd one evening at the Limelight Café soon after he had started at the *Voice* ("Oh, you're Jean Shepherd. I thought you were taller," he had reacted), he began co-hosting with Shepherd, every summer for nine years through 1965, the Village Auto Rallye, a procession of antique cars driven by their owners through the streets of the Village, sponsored by the *Voice*. And, for another nine years after 1965, he kept writing for the paper, as he had been doing since he started there, his column about cars and motorcycles, "Hubcaps."

They found Joe Coleman and Dan List. Whitey Lutz, on the other hand, found them. Herbert B. Lutz was his real name, and he was well-off himself. But his wife was even more wealthy, enormously so, and together they lived an unpretentious, middle-class lifestyle at their place on West 9th Street in the Village. On a day in 1956, when things were at their bleakest, this short, burly man walked into the office of the *Voice,* bought sixteen subscriptions, plunked down $32—one of the largest single sums of money they had seen since they started—and stayed around to talk. This paper is the greatest thing that has happened to New York since I can remember, he told them. My wife and I are just crazy about it. Won't you come over to our house sometime?

Dan Wolf didn't go, but Ed Fancher did, and met Lutz's wife. "If at any point," she told him over brunch, "you are short of money, let us know. We will be glad to help you."

Up to that point, neither Wolf nor Fancher had realized just how rich Whitey Lutz and his wife were. Afterwards, they found out. Whitey Lutz may not have been their angel, but he was certainly a godsend. He purchased subscriptions for his friends all over the world and for college libraries all around the country. For each of the next several summers, when ads dropped off, readers took vacations out of town, and revenue dropped almost to the danger point, he loaned them money to tide them over. And finally, this sugar daddy became a business partner; he bought Howard Bennett's 10 percent when Bennett left to found *East,* and invested his own money after that to help Fancher make up the $60,000 deficit run up over the first seven years.

It was their luck to be discovered by someone with the time and money on his hands that Whitey Lutz had. But Whitey Lutz did more than just dote on them; he indulged himself. He started to write in this paper that he was now supporting. He responded to Sy Krim's attack on the value systems of white jazz buffs, and after Niccolo Tucci had dropped the "Press of Freedom" column, Lutz revived it. Then, in 1960, when a new, unproduced playwright by the name of Edward Albee was trying to get a play he had written, called *Zoo Story,* onto the stage, Lutz obliged him; he and another man, Richard Barr, became Albee's backers and gave both the play, and its author, their first American production.

All through their organization, there were the free spirits, the original Village types, the flaky drifters with the fascinating case histories. They had poets selling the ads, artists doing the art work for them, dancers doing the dummies, actors taking orders over the phone and running messages in between scurrying out for auditions and callbacks. They had Maurice, the most famous paperboy in New York, as he was called around the office. An old, quite tall man with a flowing beard that made him look like Father Time, Maurice—he was known only as that the whole time they knew him—claimed to have been the press agent for Big Bill Thompson, mayor of Chicago in the twenties and thirties. Now, he lived in the streets and bars of the Village. He kept lockers around town, where he would store papers and magazines. And, every Wednesday morning, he would come by the offices of the *Voice,* pick up a load of papers left there for him, and sell them on the streets to support his lifestyle another week. Then there was Jackie, the derelict old lady Maurice took care of, who would never wash and never tell anyone where she lived, who wandered the streets of the West Village most of the time, except when she was permitted to sleep overnight on the ground floor of the *Voice* offices. She, too, got copies to sell.

And the janitor was a black man, a journeyman actor named Earl Jones, who in 1973, after fifteen-odd more years of struggling, played a small but important role opposite Robert Redford in *The Sting.* In those days, when Earl Jones was sick or took off or had an acting job, his place was taken by his son, struggling like the father to get a toehold in the acting profession. On those days, the offices, floors, toilets, and windows of the *Village Voice* were cleaned up by James Earl Jones.

★ ★ ★

On the second anniversary of his newspaper, in October of 1957, Dan Wolf wrote, "It is obvious to both the yea- and nay-sayers that *The Village Voice* begins its third year of publication stronger than at any time in the past." For seven years, those statements continued, always with that "we're-gonna-make-it" tone to them, gradually growing less defensive and defiant, more optimistic and self-confident. But for all of those seven years, regardless of whether it was one of those times when things were desperate or one of those times when things were getting better, one thing held true: this newspaper was their whole life, for all of them.

They worked sixteen-hour days usually, sometimes twenty hours, sometimes twenty-four, sometimes twenty-four two days in a row, and never fewer than six days a week, every week, for seven whole years. Jerry Tallmer would get into the office on Sunday mornings and work through the day and night, clearing all the copy, typing up fillers for the week. Then he would work all day Monday. *Then,* at four-thirty in the morning or so, he would take off, driving them in his car to the printer, first in New Jersey, later in Freeport, Long Island, staying there all night sometimes until the paper was ready and he could drive it home. And yet, when one Sunday Bill Manville came in, and Tallmer was there, all alone, working on copy in his tattered work shirt,

Manville just stood looking at him, and said, "You know, you have the best job in New York City." And Jerry Tallmer looked up at Manville, thought about it, and told him, "You're right."

Dan Wolf would get into the office between five and seven Monday mornings, work all through the day and night, too, and, on those weeks he went out to the printer, wouldn't see his wife Rhoda for nearly two whole days in a row. He and she postponed having their first child all through this period, until 1964, until they were finally, financially, out of the woods. Ed Fancher put in a full week at the office somehow. He was a workhorse, Howard Smith remembered, bundling papers and addressing labels until four in the morning one time. Nat Hentoff could recall taking a walk through Sheridan Square one Monday night and seeing the publisher of the *Village Voice* through the second-story window, pasting up his ad section for that week. He lived with the nickels and dimes, as Norman Mailer put it, in the early days, handling everyone's problems, having to cope with a new disaster every week. One week, Mailer remembered, Fancher had come in out of the rain to find that some newsstands had never gotten their papers that day. He listened. Then he wrapped up his raincoat like a basketball, threw it against the wall, and walked out again.

Over the course of these seven years, they formed a community. At the beginning, they were together all the time, Wolf, Fancher, Tallmer, Susan Ryan, Flo Ettenberg, John Wilcock, and others, at the office, at the printer, or at the Gallery Delicatessen on Seventh Avenue, where they liked to eat most of the time. Gradually, new characters came on the scene as old ones went, romantic liaisons were established and broken off, and the paper itself switched offices, in 1959, from the loft above Sutter's to two stories all by themselves over on the corner of Christopher Street and Seventh Avenue, right on Sheridan Square. There, a new writer, Jane Kramer, would watch the streets around Seventh, the ones that formed a triangle around the newspaper, fall into darkness, while inside the cluttered offices the bare lightbulbs burned on, and get strange surges of being young and powerful. She could remember the night John Kennedy broke the news of the Cuban missile crisis to the American people, how everyone connected with the paper—Dan, Ed, Stephanie Harrington, Mary Nichols—all instinctively came back to the office, and how it gave her the feeling that this newsroom of theirs was somehow at the center of everything.

★ ★ ★

It wasn't so much a well-managed organization, their accountant Ely Kushel said, as a well-unmanaged one. In August of 1961, they were looking for an ad director, and a woman named Alexandra Fendrick—nickname Sandy, turned thirty-nine and divorced, with two kids ages seven and fourteen to support—was looking for a job selling ads again, something she had done before for trade magazines. She had a job offer at *Backstage* and could have gone there, but she came in for an interview with Ed Fancher and wound up accepting less money—$80 a week plus 20 percent commission to start—from him. Once she had done that, Ed Fancher stood up, announced, "Goodbye, Sandy. I'm going to Mexico," walked right out of the office, and left this woman, who at that point pretty much knew her salary and nothing more about the place, in charge while he took a two-week vacation.

It was always like that there, but somehow it worked out, and under Sandy Fendrick, who stayed fourteen years and ran her end of things about as much by the book as they did, with about as much success, ads went up. The paper's classifieds section trailed only the *Times* itself in New York for length and placement power; they had already taken out their own first advertisement for themselves, designed by Bill Manville, *in* the *Times,* in November 1960. And, within a year, after DeSapio's defeat in the 1961 Democratic primaries, they got their first ad—from a local bank.

Another thing Ely Kushel had told them was that "once you break even, it's like you're printing money." By the late fall of 1962, they had, for all practical purposes, reached that point. They were just about breaking even.

"The wolf has moved away from the door," Kushel now began his monthly reports. There was no longer any doubt whether they would last, or for how long. Now it was just a question of when they would start to make money, and how much. It was a matter of waiting for it all to happen.

Circulation, from that disastrous beginning, had risen at a clip of 200 a month. It hit 3,000 by the end of 1955. It hit 5,000 by the end of 1956. The next year they raised the newsstand price to ten cents from five and subscriptions to $4 from $2. By December of 1958 circulation had hit 10,000. In 1959, they announced that it was 11,500 and rising by 100 a week, then 12,000, then, at year's end, 13,181. By the end of the *next* year, 1960, it was 16,578, and the issue of January 12, 1961, carried the following statement: "WE CHALLENGE anyone to dispute the following statement: '*The Village Voice* is the largest circulation community weekly newspaper in New York State.' " Circulation hit its high of 19,000 in early 1961 and at the end of 1962 it was resting at 17,000. Still, one out of every five readers came from outside the Village. They had subscribers all over the city, all over the country, in Alaska, in Canada too. In Europe—England, France, Sweden, Austria. In South America—Brazil, Peru, Paraguay, Chile. In Africa—Tanzania. In Asia—Ceylon, Burma. Not to mention Turkey in the Near East, Saudi Arabia in the Middle East, and Australia, all of them people seeking "other people just as much out of step as themselves," Ed Fancher gloated.

The paper was also an attention-getter by now. It was the subject of an article that appeared in the January 1958 issue of *Mademoiselle,* featuring a picture of founders Wolf, Fancher, and Tallmer, plus Jules Feiffer on a motor scooter and Dan Balaban on a Vespa, underneath the arch at Washington Square Park. There was a story in *Newsweek* ("A brash tabloid read by bankers as well as beatniks") in 1959, followed by other articles in smaller papers or trade magazines, and increasing mentions everywhere. The paper was also a launching pad for careers in books. Feiffer had his. Bill Manville had his. John Wilcock had the travel books, and *The Village Square,* a collection of his columns, published by Lyle Stuart. Robert Reisner, who wrote their early jazz criticism, had it collected and published as *The Jazz Titans* by Doubleday. Then, in 1962, Doubleday, on the occasion of the paper's seventh anniversary, published *The Village Voice Reader,* an anthology of the best writing in its infancy as selected and edited by Wolf and Fancher, with a foreword written by Wolf.

It was all in place now, except the profits. That took a little push.

★ ★ ★

The man who gave them that little push, who made the *Village Voice* into what it was going to be, has perhaps never received his fair share of credit for having done so. His name was and is Bertram Powers, and on December 7, 1962, Pearl Harbor Day, Bertram Powers was, as he is now, the head of New York Typographical Union Local No. 6. On that morning, Bertram Powers told his membership that negotiations with those New York daily newspapers where they had contracts running out had broken down. He told them to go out on strike. They did.

But Bertram Powers had not called just any strike this time. Because when those newspapers which Powers's union had *not* struck shut down in sympathy with those he *had* struck, a total and absolute blackout of printed news was imposed on the upwards of 20 million people of Metropolitan New York. And, just as the publishers in their united front decided to try and break Powers's union once and for all, he and his people decided to try and break them once and for all. So, instead of negotiating, each side decided to wait the other out. With people having nothing to read, the local television stations expanded their newscasts, trying to pick up the slack. The *Brooklyn Eagle,* dead since the mid-1950s, was revived. Long Island, suburban, and out-of-town newspapers were slapped down on the empty newsstand racks outside Grand Central Station, and snatched right up again by news-hungry commuters. Independent, temporary newspapers put together by mixtures of the different papers' staffs tried to get themselves out. In February, Dorothy Schiff, publisher of the *New York Post,* decided she could not take her losses anymore, and broke ranks. There were two predictions of possible stampedes accompanying her announcement—of advertisers to her, and of her fellow publishers to join her. Neither happened. February became March. In March, after the president of the United States personally upbraided him at a nationally televised press conference for his tactics and conduct, Bertram Powers came back to his membership with a settlement. And the membership rejected it. Another week followed, while Powers, publicly holding the bag now, called another vote on the same package and lobbied intensively to get it through this time. Finally, at the end of March, it passed. On April 1, 1963, the papers' presses started rolling again.

It had been 114 days—three months, three weeks, and three days—since they had been shut down. And, this time, things did not return to normal again after a strike. Because during those 114 days, the rules of the game in New York had been changed, for both sides, for good.

II.
THE CONCRETE...

7.

THERE HAD BEEN A ONE-DAY STRIKE OF the city's newspapers in December 1958. "Can you imagine calling a *strike* at a time like this—when honest to god *sex* might, at last, happen in a *comic* strip?" asked the man, an avid Mary Worth fan, of the woman in one of Feiffer's Typical Couple cartoons at the time. "Of course, I miss Walter Lippmann too," he says, suddenly reconsidering what he has said. "Well—we all do," she answers. The paper had also run a confessional article by Polly Kline of the *Daily News* describing what it was like to be out of work for a day. But this time, Miss Kline and her fellow writers were out of work for much more than a day, and the *Village Voice* did much more about it.

In the office, Dan Wolf, Arthur Sainer, John Wilcock, and whoever was there at the time maintained a constant vigil over the radio for the news bulletins that were their primary source of raw news, wrote it up, analyzed it, and did what nobody else in New York was doing—filled their paper with it. Immediately the paper bloated from twenty to thirty-two pages. All over the city, newsstand owners and operators, people who had never had any room for this *Village Voice* before, except maybe to hang it in the back of the booth or bury it underneath something else or keep it under the counter, began moving their copies of the paper right out front for the customers to see.

And very few of them ever moved it back again.

★ ★ ★

There were 17,000 people reading the *Voice* when the strike started. At its height, there were 40,000. When it was over, and all the dailies were back on the stands to read again, when the *Voice* had to give back its forefront space on the stands and the undivided attention of New York readers, the paper's circulation went back down again, as was to be expected. But not all the way. Readership steadied at 25,000. In the course of a three-month strike, the *Village Voice* had increased its audience by exactly half.

The strike sped up the process by which the paper had been getting stronger anyway. Still more readers meant still more advertisers, and for the first time, in January of 1963, Dan Wolf and Ed Fancher felt secure enough to start handing out checks to the writers who contributed to their paper. They were small at first—$5—but they grew. The strike sped up another process as well, a process that meant New York, for a variety of reasons—union settlements, the high cost of newsprint, loss of readers and advertisers to television and the suburbs—could not

127

much longer support, would not much longer be supporting, seven different daily newspapers. The morning *Mirror* was the first to go, in September 1963. Unable for years to show a profit, the paper had been virtually condemned to death by the duration of the 1962–63 strike and the high costs of settling it. Sentence took only five months to carry out.

Circulation of the *Voice* remained the same throughout 1964, while the paper was winning another "general excellence" award from the New York State Press Association, and then in 1965 began to move again. It was a seminal year for New Yorkers—the year their town was threatened by an acute water shortage, the year their Yankees' forty-year baseball dynasty came to a crashing end, the year their lights went out one night, all night. Most of all it was the year of John Lindsay, flashing his Kennedy good looks all over town, promising change and activism in City Hall, promising New Yorkers to clean up and rescue their city.

In September of 1965, just when Lindsay's campaign was ready to go into high gear after the finish of the Democratic primaries, just when the insurgent newcomer most needed to pick up the momentum and publicity that could only come from media exposure, Bertram Powers called another citywide strike of Typographical Union Local No. 6, and shut down every paper in town again. Every paper but one.

He left the pro-Lindsay *Village Voice* open for four crucial weeks, until the weekend of Columbus Day, when Powers settled with the papers and let them reopen again. This time, the effects on the paper were not measurable in simple circulation—on top of the incremental gains it had already been making, it moved up to 41,000 readers, and held them. They were rather measured in clout. The *Voice* had been a supporter of Lindsay ever since he had unseated an incumbent of his own party and gone on to win the so-called Silk Stocking District's seat in Congress in 1958. Its backing had come in especially handy the year before, 1964, when he had seemed to be in genuine danger from the Goldwater landslide and a particularly strong Democratic opponent, Mrs. Eleanor Clark French. So on November 2, 1965, when John Lindsay was elected mayor of New York with 47 percent of the vote in a three-way race, the *Village Voice* had a friend in City Hall, in more ways than one. John Lindsay read the election returns and returned compliments to his two friends at the *Voice,* publicly. "Fancher and Wolf are openly committed to their city," he said, and "their editorials in support of me in the last two campaigns have been as helpful as any I know of." Furthermore, he tapped Mary Perot Nichols, their reporter, his supporter, to come into his administration as a press aide in the

Parks Department under his dashing new appointee there, Thomas Hoving.

The costs of the second strike forced a weird shotgun wedding among the newspaper clans of Whitney, Hearst, and Scripps-Howard the following winter, Lindsay's first in office. New York gave up three very distinctive newspapers—Jock Whitney's morning *Herald-Tribune,* plus both afternoon chain newspapers, Hearst's *Journal-American* and Scripps-Howard's *World-Telegram & Sun*—in return for one schizoid mutant called the *World-Journal-Tribune.*

The *WJT,* as people tried to call the merger, meant to combine the established personalities of three separate newspapers, but never developed one of its own. This clumsy giant, built-in king of New York's afternoon readership, came across as an unintegrated amalgam of contradictory voices and competing interests. Besides that, it was cursed. It was only a few months old when Bertram Powers closed it down with a strike, and it had been open again only another few months when, on May 5, 1967, its three owners themselves closed it down again, this time for good.

All this while the *Village Voice* had been making steady progress and fresh inroads. When the *WJT* folded, its passing was covered by the paper, which by now had some 70,000 readers. A photo showed Pete Hamill, reporter for the *New York Post,* interviewing Jimmy Breslin, columnist for the *WJT,* while "looking on," as the caption put it, was the editor of the *WJT's* Sunday magazine section. The magazine was called *New York.* The editor's name was Clay Felker.

The death of the *World-Journal-Tribune* created a yawning gap in New York PM journalism, leaving the afternoon field entirely to Mrs. Dorothy Schiff and her *New York Post.* The *Post* was a paper that reflected the value systems of its owner—it was Jewish, liberal, Democratic, independent, and eccentric. The *Daily News* might be the nasty, right-wing, number-one tabloid in town, but in the *Post,* with its great battery of columnists—Murray Kempton, Max Lerner, James Wechsler, Mary McGrory, Hamill—Dorothy Schiff's hardy hard-core of good liberals could read, within reason, what they wanted to about the world.

But the paper most likely to succeed never did so. Dolly Schiff's *Post,* with the afternoon all to itself six days a week, moved up above 700,000 readers, and then just as surely went back down again, all the way, eventually, to 500,000. What the readers of New York did was to manifest their contentment with the *Times* every morning and the *Village Voice* every week. In the two years after the demise of the *WJT,* Ed Fancher and Dan Wolf's paper doubled its circulation outright. They had 90,000 readers by the end of 1967. By the summer of 1968 they had 113,000. By the summer of 1969 they had 126,000. By the end of 1969 they had 138,000. In the spring of 1968 alone, they picked up more readers—14,911—than they had in their first six years. By that spring, their paper had become so big—sixty-four pages, tabloid—that for the first time they gave it an index.

And in January of 1967, Dan Wolf and Ed Fancher's paper became the number-one-selling weekly newspaper in the United States, with a single-day circulation figure greater than that of 95 percent of the big city dailies in the country. Its readership in the Village was where it always had been—13,000—but layered upon them now was a brand-new readership, a full one out of every three coming from outside New York, and two-thirds of the New Yorkers coming from Manhattan Island. So "A Weekly Newspaper of Greenwich Village," which had already changed its subtitle from "A Weekly Newspaper Designed to Be Read," now changed it again, to "The"—not "A," but "The"—"Weekly Newspaper of New York." And, effective with the issue of May 8, 1969, it had a whole new logo, one in which *VOICE,* uppercase and upright, dominated *the village,* which ran lowercase and sideways.

Other people were writing about *it* now. "No matter how avant-garde you think you are," Hearst columnist Cholly Knickerbocker warned his following, "the *Village Voice* will give you an inferiority complex." In the 1964 play *Undercover Man,* an ingenue confesses to the young man who is seducing her, "Do you realize I'm one of the three people in Providence, Rhode Island who subscribe to the *Village Voice*? It makes me feel so Bohemian."

To Walter Winchell it was still "a Greenwich Village paper" and to Spiro Agnew, vice-president of the United States, its official title was "the *Greenwich Village Voice.*" To William F. Buckley, Jr., whose *National Review* was founded the same year, it was, first (1968), "a little New York Journal which energetically does its idealistic pushups once a week . . . [and whose] editors do it all with considerable panache . . . although the readership is confined largely to adolescents who blush with mischievous delight at seeing four-letter words in print," then (1970) "the constant companion and *fons et origo* of the bohemian smart set." To "Al Legro," writing in the *Long Island Entertainer* in 1967, it was "replete with self-conscious editorializing at every turn, inserted willy-nilly in every column and news story. If it were possible to transform a weather report into a press release for the Progressive Labor Party, the *Village Voice* would contrive it."

It should be read, wrote John Corry in a 1970 piece for *Harper's,* "not only for what it says but for what it is and for what it can tell us about our own slow return to the Dark Ages." Corry wondered if the sympathy of certain of the paper's writers for the Young Lords, a Puerto Rican street gang modeled after the Black Panthers, would hold up if they "had occupied a Riverside Drive club, or the beaches of East Hampton in August, or, say, the *Village Voice* itself." It served, along with the new *New York Review of Books,* as, quipped Tom Wolfe in *Esquire,* "the pulpit-voice of the Church of Good Liberals," and reading it would "confirm you in your supposition that it is really not worth going below 48th Street—ever."

Five years after its first article about the *Voice, Newsweek* ran another, in June of 1964. Ten years after its initial article about the paper, *Mademoiselle* returned to the subject, devoting a picture spread to it, showing various writers and editors (but not Dan Wolf) posing under the arch at Washington Square Park, in the issue of March 1968. *Time* did a feature on the paper in November 1966, and the *Wall Street Journal* did one in November 1967, complete with quote from co-founder (and still co-owner) Norman Mailer that the *Voice* was "the best-written paper in New York City, so probably the best-written in the U.S."

That was not all. Writers for other publications were not just writing *about* the *Village Voice* anymore; now they were beginning to write *like* it. Dan Wolf and his paper did not invent first-person participatory journalism, or the free-form, self-expression, personal-experience (and sometimes, just-too-damn-long) essay, but it did give a home to writers who could not write any other way, and who therefore could never have been published anywhere else until they got their chance at the *Voice.* Press critics variously thought they saw its style creeping into the pages of *Esquire, Harper's, New York* Magazine, *Ramparts,* even, claimed one of them, the *New Republic, Life,* and the *Saturday Evening Post.* Within the New York local press, it became a definite leavening influence on the feature pages of the *Times* and, before its death, of the *Herald-Tribune.* For the dailies it became, as confirmed ' by the writers who left it to go to work for them, a tip sheet for cityside news they had not yet fully reported or even uncovered. "We're a newspaper editor's paper," Mary Nichols boasted to *Editor & Publisher* in 1969. "Other papers take ideas from us." And "sometimes," she clucked, "the bigger papers screw up."

The paper's own in-house ads grew bolder, more pointed. It was the "House Organ of the Worldly," promising subscribers they were "sure to become incisive, searching, exquisitely funny, fluent, well balanced and touched with *weltschmertz.*" In 1963 it was selling itself as "America's Weekly Newspaper of Non-Conformity," with tag lines such as "SAVE YOURSELF! No one else is going to," or "For 4 bucks, You Can Live in Greenwich Village for a year," or "Now That You've Tried

Psychiatry, Self-Improvement, and Ceramics, try the *Village Voice.* It's cheaper." Now the pitches—still being thought up by Dan Wolf and Ed Fancher and their friends as before, not by any hired agency— became "Dissatisfaction Guaranteed or Your Money Back," or "This Christmas Make Someone You Love Nervous," or "Bar Humbug," or "Each Thursday the Establishment shudders a little bit," or "Every Thursday, we make the Establishment a little more paranoid."* Ultimately it was "Expect the Unexpected" and, in that gem at the expense of Punch Sulzberger's Gray Lady of 43rd Street, "Keep Ahead of the Times."

Just as important within the field of publishing itself, other publications took out ads of their own in the paper: the *Times* did. So did *Esquire,* the *New Republic,* the fledgling *New York* Magazine, out on its own now and not part of any newspaper anymore, and the embattled *New Yorker,* in need of younger readers in the late 1960s. For all sorts of advertising, in fact, the paper became a magnet. In the year 1965, it ran an average of 1,244 inches of advertising per issue; five years later, it was running an average of 3,349. In 1967, the year it switched over to offset printing, the paper was running between forty and forty-eight pages a week—and running six to seven pages a week of classifieds, running more than 1,200 separate, individual display and classified ads each week. It was doing so, publisher Edwin Fancher told the members of the New York State Press Association in an article written for their magazine that spring, by going after small ads that ran frequently rather than big ads that did not, thereby violating another cardinal precept of publishing. In 1968, having reached what was then its maximum size of eighty pages, the paper ran 1.7 million lines of display ads (62 percent of its income) and 460,000 lines of classifieds (another 18 percent). A typical issue of the *Village Voice* was two-thirds advertising.

Included in those classifieds, of course, as well as on the page 2 "community bulletin board," were the personals, the personals that had been such precursors in the fifties, that had only fermented with time:

> ". . . Murray. I still love you. John . . ."
> ". . . Vivian. Please call immediately. Let me know you are well. Worried sick. Will let you choose your life. Mother . . ."
> ". . . Rising young rock and roll critic announces engage-

---

*Originally the paper came out Thursdays; it switched to Wednesdays for a while in 1956, then back to Thursdays. Later, in the sixties, while still dated Thursday, it began to reach the streets on Wednesday mornings.

ment to rising young Barnard girl. Also he bought a dog . . ."

". . . I would like to contact cosmic visitors . . ."

". . . I desperately need 16,000 cancelled 5-cent George Washington stamps for an entertaining purpose too complicated to explain . . ."

". . . Veteran of three lunatic asylums wants to explore the possibility of book with gifted writer . . ."

". . . Michael Is . . ."

". . . Dear Prince: Would you forget your thinning hair, your troubled state and cardiac? Then try, for liberty from care, the pleasure of a midnight snack AH, a loaf of bread, a jug of wine and thou? Meet me at the Royal Roost, 28 Cornelia St., in their beautiful Cocktail Lounge. The Princess . . ."

". . . 'Kick a Puppy Today.' Later Pray for War. Stamp out Whooping Cranes and 27 more protests against Constituted authority and dogooding readerdigestion . . ."

". . . Wanted. Driver with full diplomatic immunity. Wanted to test fully modified 550 HP Corvette. Must have heavy foot and know speed . . ."

". . . JACKIE, ALL IS FORGIVEN, PLEASE COME HOME. LULU DANO . . ."

". . . Well, Oriental Prince, DID you have a happy, happy Tuesday? . . ."

". . . Hippies wanted for Psychedelic Gas-In at service station. Real LSD. Pot-type. Four males. Four females to pump gas. Good pay. All profits to an orphanage . . ."

". . . ROOM SERVICE—Bachelors, when it comes to your pad, do you turn the chicks off when you turn the lights on? . . ."

". . . Located on New York's most fashionable chic boulevard (W. 94 St.) this apartment offers you a sharing of the benefits of cross ventilation (you get cross—there's no ventilation), women (60 years old—cleans once a week), and stimulating conversation (Shaddup!) This ad won't be printed unless I say 'Share with male.' . . ."

". . . (LSD.) Looking—See D'hrama . . ."

". . . Dear Fatso Boom-Boom. We love you, Slum Goddess of the Upper East Side. Happy B.V.M. Day (signed) Rachel, Ginny, Georgia . . ."

(For this last one, the *Daily News*'s Charles McHarry, in his column "On the Town," offered "a free ear-piercing job to anyone, male or female, who can make sense out of" it.)

The advertising was pouring in by the late 1960s because by then the

Village Voice had tapped into a readership with a voracious, consuming interest in practically everything its editorial product had to offer, and with appreciable economic power to boot. The paper raised subscription rates to $5, but, except for a one-dollar discount to college students, it never needed to offer the traditional cut-rate subscriptions by which publishers temporarily beef up circulation—at the risk of increasing their mailing costs (for sending all those extra issues to all those new, discount subscribers) and aggravating their operating deficits. The reason it never had to do that was simply that it never had to carry more than 35,000 or so subscriptions; it had an audience that saved it overhead (and *truly* impressed advertisers) by buying seven out of every ten issues at a newsstand (for, as of May 1966, fifteen cents). At the beginning, the *Voice* had sought, as most beginning publications do, to achieve a standard base of readers in the standard way; in the mails, where otherwise dubious advertisers had a guarantee that the editorial product, and their ad along with it, would reach someone. In 1959, its circulation of 12,000 was in an exact 7 to 5 ratio, seven thousand in the mails, five thousand on the street. But Bertram Powers, with the first Great Newspaper Strike, had changed all that, and afterwards, on the sidewalks of New York, the *Village Voice* outsold *Time* and *Newsweek* both. It outsold the *New Yorker, New York,* and *Cue.* It outsold the *Atlantic* and *Harper's* and *Esquire* and the *Saturday Review.* It could guarantee its advertisers a tremendous reach with its audience (and charge them accordingly for the privilege) *without* the usual tradeoff of having to lose money sending copies to subscribers at home. From the money-making, publishing point of view, it was the best of both possible worlds, and no greater proof could be found for it than seeing the lineup of people in Sheridan Square, outside the paper's offices, every Wednesday or Thursday morning as the next issue of the paper came out, all of them waiting to be first on line for the listings of apartments for rent in the city, some of them with partners stationed across the street in phone booths ready to start making calls to landlords and agencies. In a city where the right apartment was more and more in demand, so was the *Voice,* because, more and more, that was where the right apartment was to be found.

At that point, the typical "trendmaker" *Voice* reader was thirty years of age, with a median family income of $18,771; three out of every ten were making $25,000 or more. Seven out of eight had gone to college, three out of seven did postgraduate work, four out of seven were "in professional, technical, or kindred occupations." Most drove Volkswagens or Fords or Chevrolets, most shopped at Bloomingdale's or Macy's or Alexander's and had a charge there, most had some kind of

Founding Father—Dan Wolf in the late 1950s. *(Photo by Gin Briggs)*

☆ ☆ ☆

Founding Father—Edwin Fancher, same era. *(Photo by Gene Dauber)*

Founding Father—Norman Mailer. *(Photo by Gene Dauber)*

☆ ☆ ☆

Present at the Creation—Jerry Tallmer, culture critic supreme, with Wolf by his side. *(Photo by Gene Dauber)*

Present at the Creation—John Wilcock, ''news editor,'' madcap columnist, vagabond, and irrepressible personality. Behind him, Washington Square Park and the South Village as they looked circa 1955. *(Photo by Gene Dauber)*

October 1955—at the first, Greenwich Avenue, office, Dan Wolf takes a call. *(Photo by Gene Dauber)*

October 1955—"publisher" Ed Fancher in conference. *(Photo by Gene Dauber)*

October 1955—Flo Ettenberg, among her other chores, makes coffee. *(Photo by Gene Dauber)*

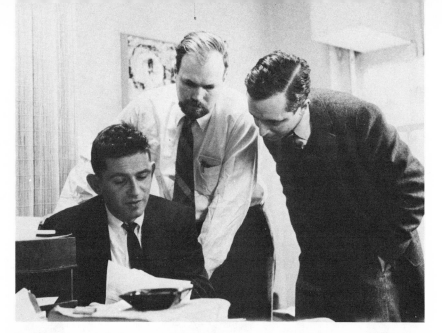

The founding triumvirate, working together in the early days—a rare photo. *(Photo by Gene Dauber)*

☆ ☆ ☆

Fancher, Tallmer, and Wolf outside their Sheridan Square headquarters, after their move in 1959. *(Photo by Daniel List)*

The first Obies, June 18, 1956: Best Actress Julie Bovasso, presenter Shelley Winters, Best Actor Jason Robards. *(Photo by Ben Schiff)*

☆ ☆ ☆

An Obie panel. At far left, nearest camera, Dan Wolf. At far right, John V. Lindsay, then the Silk Stocking congressman. To his right, Julie Harris and Ed Fancher. *(Photo by Gin Briggs)*

Jules Feiffer. *(Photo by Gin Briggs)*

☆ ☆ ☆

Mary Perot Nichols. *(Photo by Gin Briggs)*

Jean Shepherd, humorist, radio personality, and early *Voice* contributor, in his ''I, Libertine'' days. *(Photo by Gene Dauber)*

stock portfolio. They were, for the most part, indoor sportsmen—records, concerts, dance, theater, restaurants, movies. They did their social drinking by and large in the home, and they preferred seeing Europe to going skiing or camping. They looked at the *Voice,* on the average, for an hour, referred to it 3.4 times over the next week, and passed it on to 1.9 other people. Four out of five also read the *Times* every day; many, but not most, also read *Time, Newsweek, New York,* and the *New Yorker* every week. They were, Tom Wolfe teased, the "sandals-and-simplicity, educated, young-coupley mind at work."

There was irony in Wolfe's saying that, and historical inevitability too. Because, in the language of publishing, the audiences for the *Village Voice* and the *New Yorker,* of all things—the weekly magazine revered above all others for its reportage, its wit, and its *belles-lettres,* esteemed for its literary quality and envied for its upper-class sense of manners—were not all that different. They were, almost, a *New Yorker* audience in the making. Based on where they were coming from and where they were going—on life paths, class backgrounds, social aspirations, and purchasing power—it was logical to infer that, within a few years, they would reach *New Yorker* status and *New Yorker* affluence; they would be, as one out of five of them already were, *New Yorker* readers.

And in April of 1965 Tom Wolfe wrote for *New York,* which was then still the Sunday magazine section of the still-extant *Herald-Tribune,* a two-part profile of the *New Yorker,* where he tuned up the style of reportage he would use next to describe the exploits of Junior Johnson, race car driver, and of Ken Kesey, acidhead author, and, not least, to make himself famous as the first, and foremost, of the so-called New Journalists. He used the piece to do a number both on the magazine—he portrayed it as a place where a clan of "tiny mummies" worshipped their dead literary predecessors and practiced *omerta,* the Sicilian Mafia's law of silence, on all outsiders—and on its editor, the compulsive, almost fanatic recluse, William Shawn. Shawn, Wolfe revealed, was afraid of elevators. Shawn, Wolfe hypothesized, merging fact and fiction at some point only he and Shawn knew for sure, had been the original target for the kidnap-murderers Leopold and Loeb in Chicago in the twenties, not classmate Bobby Franks.

The article's two installments lured the literary elite of New York out into the open, those who thought the *New Yorker* and Shawn were the victims of sacrilege and those who thought they had it coming. Shawn himself broke his normal self-counsel in such matters (he was like Dan Wolf in this regard, only much more so) with an emotional letter to *New York* practically pleading for the second installment not to run, but did not himself clear up the subject any further. Whatever, throughout all the subsequent *Sturm und Drang* and threats of libel suits, Wolfe did get categorical backing from one man, *his* editor, the very uncircumspect Clay S. Felker.

8. DAN WOLF WAS AWARE OF THE PARAL-

lels between what he had created in 1955 and what Harold Ross had created in 1925, always wondering why it was the *New Yorker* never did one of its "Profiles" on the paper. And he himself resembled no one so much as Ross's hand-anointed acolyte and successor, William Shawn. Like Shawn, he was a combination recluse and editorial genius, with that same mandarin standoffishness toward *anybody else's* writers, with fatherly sympathy toward, and family loyalty from, his own. And none of them, no matter who they were or where, no matter what the depth or the duration or the denouement of their association with him had been, would, even years later, fail to repeat and agree, repeat and agree: *Dan Wolf was the central figure in the* Village Voice.

In the 1960s, after the *caporegime* of Jerry Tallmer, who had handled many of the duties of an editor in the beginning, and before the *caporegime* of Ross Wetzsteon, who took over many of the day-to-day details in the 1970s, in this the central period, Dan Wolf the central figure personally took charge.

And the paper took off.

★ ★ ★

They were no small-time operation anymore, not with 140,000 readers in 81 countries across the globe (including, the *Wall Street Journal* was meticulous enough to mention, one in Upper Volta, two in Togo, and four in Russia), but they still persisted in running it as one, after their very own half-assed fashion, doing everything so wrong that it came out right. And, because they were so unprofessional, they succeeded.

The place was indeed, as many said it was, run like a corner candy store. They had no company car, no corporate credit cards. From sheer force of habit, they still made out the checks Friday afternoons, a hangover from the days when they had thought they might go out of business at any time. They took ads at the last minute, which theoretically they weren't supposed to do, and didn't lay them out in the form of a pyramid, which theoretically they were. In fact when it came to layout, the *Voice* seemed a prime example of how *not* to do it: a dark crowded front page, stories squared off at jagged edges and jumped inside the paper back and forth, each jump the size of a part in a jigsaw puzzle. (The typical *Village Voice* piece started on page one, jumped to page 7, to page 57, to page 73, back to page 19, and finished on page 33.) In 1969, when they designed their new "VOICE" logo, it

137

was supposed to be blue lettering on a white background, but at the plant it got reversed, and when they saw it, they just left it that way.

They were, as many of them said they were, like a family. Or at least a community. Certainly, in their cramped two-story headquarters at Sheridan Square, it was impossible to feel otherwise. Everybody could see and hear and talk to everybody else at the other desks, and everybody had to troop past Dan Wolf's and Ed Fancher's office to get to the only john. Every Friday afternoon they packed into Dan Wolf's office for the weekly literary *salon,* where he and everybody else assembled there—*Voice* writers, friends of the paper, Village characters, city newsmakers—would hold forth on any subject of their choosing at any length. Every year everybody packed into Ed Fancher's railroad apartment on Christopher Street, where the beer was kept on ice in his kitchen bathtub, for the annual Christmas party. These parties became the stuff of legends, as well as major social events. Many times Mailer held literary court there, his listeners trailing from one end of the cattle car–crowded apartment to the other, hanging on his every word and crushing everybody else. One year Mailer actually got into a fistfight with one of the hangers-on in the coterie, a writer whose name people forgot, and who got the worst of the flurry, but who landed one lucky punch and gave Mailer a bloody nose before it was all over. Ely Kushel remembered coming up the stairs to the party that year, being passed by Mailer, going the other way, running down the stairs, clutching his nose, blood gushing out from behind his fingertips. Another year, the end of John Lindsay's first as mayor, His Honor himself showed up. And one time Maurice, their man of the streets, arrived—with, of all people, Odetta, the world-famous singer, as his date.

Eventually, the Family came to outgrow its home. And at this point they simply got lucky; there was no other way to put it. Just when Mary Nichols returned to the paper in 1968 and they had run out of space, the entire second floor of the apartment building next door became vacant. The paper was able to acquire the space, knock down the wall, and put Mary Nichols's office there, which as it happened put her directly above the writers' favorite bar, the Lion's Head, downstairs. And when even that space proved not to be enough, and it was imperative to give up Sheridan Square and find someplace else, they closed up one Saturday afternoon in April 1970 and moved everything into their new building on University Place in the East Village, just vacated by *Evergreen Review,* all in one weekend. When they did that, the paper not only got to keep its old phone number, but its new phones were already working by Monday morning when, so Ely Kushel said, they simply had no right to be, given what phone service was like in New York at that time. And when even *that* space was not enough, Kushel came across an ad in the NYU student newspaper placed by the dry cleaners on the bottom floor of their new building, and guessed right away—correctly—that business was bad. And they got *that* space.

At any rate, whether they were a Family, or whether they were a corner candy store, or whether they were a little of both, the *Village Voice,* on its editorial side as well as its business, certainly seemed to be the least professional, most disorganized journalistic operation in town. The trick was, though, that underneath the amateur veneer there was something else, a loyalty, that the other, more "professional" operations did not have, could never have. The people who worked for the *Village Voice,* on the editorial side as well as the business, would have done anything for it. And the man responsible for that state of affairs sat in the editor's chair.

★ ★ ★

"A new paper is here," he had written in the editorial of Vol. 1, No. 1, "and it is a painful business for an editor to write his first editorial." It was such pain, in fact, that this editor rarely did it. "The sense of power that comes with the anonymity of the editorial 'we' has not yet taken root." In fact, it never did. "The omniscience, the firm point of view, and the certainty that is so integral a part of the editor's armory is yet to be acquired." In fact, they never were.

This statement of no aims, as it were, turned out to be perhaps the most explicit credo ever put on paper by any editor starting a new publication. For what Dan Wolf was going to wind up doing, even if he did have to back into it a little bit, was nothing less than to rewrite the editor's creed entirely, to redefine it in action, existentially. And Dan Wolf was nothing if not a practitioner of existential phenomenology— the philosophy which holds that the only final answer is that there are no final answers, and that therefore everything is open to question, anytime. That was Dan Wolf all right, and in action he proved it, proved that it works.

Because he had never done anything like this before, and because he had no idea what it was he was doing at first, Dan Wolf at first had no idea that he was doing anything differently. But he was, as he soon found out.

The facts were that most American editors did not believe then, and do not believe now, as Dan Wolf did, in just "letting the writers write," and have never really let them do so. Most things that are published in America—virtually all of its newspapers, most of its magazines, and even some of its books—are still not, unfortunately, the result of the creative vision of a writer and of the writer's freedom to put that creative vision down on paper, regardless of whatever the First Amendment to the Constitution of the United States might say. On the contrary, most things published in America are published because an editor or a group of editors—a "committee"—decided in advance that they would be, and in what form they would be, and either found or told some writer to carry out their wishes and write it their way. There are exceptions to this rule, of course, but in practice most American publications still operate according to fixed formulas imposed and enforced from above by aggressive, interventionist editors who control their writers with red pencils that carefully map out what territory the writers are permitted to roam, and, if they so wish, arbitrarily permit no one to stray beyond. The struggle is constant, and in it only rarely do writers have the upper hand; in all too many cases, unknown to the great majority of readers, writers are "free" to write what they are assigned to write, and to say what they are edited to say, which, not surprisingly, quite often turns out to be exactly what the editor would have said if the editor had been the one doing the writing in the first place. Even at some of America's otherwise most reputable publications, it is neither unknown nor uncommon for writers—particularly freelancers—to pick up their articles and find them totally rewritten, without their consent, without their even seeing it, but with their name still on it. Against such cases as that, the only protection writers have is to be a favorite at the periodical or at the publishing house, or to have a track record of past literary and commercial success to bank on, or to have what Hunter S. Thompson once claimed he had with *Rolling Stone,* a contract prohibiting any changes in his prose without his consent. Or, best of all, writers can develop a close relationship with an editor who respects their copy and their right to write it their way.

Such editors are in the minority, but from this group have come the finest and most famous editors in American journalism and publishing, the ones who developed more and greater writers by going against the grain, by sensing talent and then letting it grow with their guidance present but their hands off. Maxwell Perkins was one such. Harold Ross, creator of the *New Yorker,* qualified for this group. So, very much, did William Shawn, his literary successor there.

And so did Daniel Wolf.

★ ★ ★

At Dan Wolf's paper, there was no matrix to be impressed upon the writers who came in, no in-house mold for them to fit. Here, the writers did not serve the editors; they were free to write what *they* wanted, not what the editor wanted them to write, not what they thought wouldn't get red-penciled. As a result Dan Wolf discovered and developed more first-rate writing talent while he was there than did any other American editor over a similar period of time at any other American publication, similar or otherwise.

He decided to do it that way, originally, because—and he freely admitted it—he didn't know what the hell an editor was supposed to do anyway. As far as he was concerned, the writing was either going to be good or it was going to be bad. If it was bad, there was nothing he could do to it that would do any good anyway, and if it was good, why should he change anything? He would just leave the writers alone, let them write whatever they wanted about whatever they wanted, encourage as many of them to write as possible, and somehow everything would work out all right.

That it did was not entirely by accident. Because Dan Wolf, like other editors, had *his* conception, too, of what he wanted his paper to be, and had expressed it in that first editorial. When he wrote about not having "the sense of power that comes with the anonymity of the editorial 'we' . . . the omniscience, the firm point of view, and the certainty," those were his concepts, and he meant it. As he went along, the vacuum he left at his paper was there out of calculation.

The paper was only a few issues old when his lack of editorial direction was becoming noticed enough that he felt he had to address himself to it. In a rare editorial entitled, appropriately enough, "Our Policy (?)," he began, "The editorial policy of *The Village Voice*—or the lack of such a policy—has been a source of some discussion among our friends, and even more so among our enemies."

> We think that it might clarify the situation to say that the *Voice* is not primarily interested in establishing a single journalistic or political program and hewing to it. . . . Our policy—designedly elastic, indeed often contradictory (at least to the superficial eye)—is to give voice to all the many divergent factors, pressure groups, attitudes, and conflicting personalities of the Village. We are a small paper and we have no illusion about our power to affect events. Therefore we believe our real function is to present every divergent view

which is ready to use our pages, and the only censorship we intend to exert is that our paper be as readable, as entertaining, and as provocative as the exigencies of time, resources, and talent can permit.

Wolf went on, "In this policy—or in this lack of policy—we believe that we are performing in a small way a deeply democratic function."

Every democracy depends for its health on the wide consciousness of its citizens. And we on the *Voice* are interested in anything which will enlarge understanding, even if at times private and long-contained hatreds break out in angry vituperative debate. The open presentation of antipathetic views is the health of the mind.

These were critical sentences, and the seed of everything that was to bear fruit at the *Voice* was contained in them. No editorial policy. No "political program," or, to put it another way, no party line. "To give voice to all." "To present every divergent view." "Angry vituperative debate." "The open presentation of antipathetic views." That was Dan Wolf, and that was the *Voice*.

If he said it once, he said it a thousand times: "This is a writer's paper," or variations on that theme. If they liked a piece, they accepted it, and that was it. There was as little copy editing as possible, and no copydesk, and never any of the scenes that took place at other publications when competing blocs of editors started arguing and casting votes on which articles to accept, reject, or change. There were not even any editorial conferences at all; "we think they're a waste of time," declared Edwin Fancher to *Editor & Publisher* when it did a story about the paper in 1969. And there were no assignments as such. Even after being at it for over ten years, Dan Wolf was still telling people that he didn't consider himself a professional, still didn't think that just having a newspaper to express his views made his views worth more than anybody else's. In 1968, when students and workers very nearly toppled the government in France, a reader in Paris they had never heard of named Martha Merrill started sending in manuscripts and photos describing the violence, and the paper simply ran them. They never met the writer, never heard from her again, and yet their coverage of the event turned out to be among the best that appeared in any American publication. Later that year, when the New York City school system was shut down by a prolonged strike that pitted black community groups against the largely Jewish teachers' union along racial lines, the paper ran pieces by Nat Hentoff supporting the community groups and by Michael Harrington defending the union alongside each other, without any comment of its own. Once, when Hentoff was visiting with the Neiman Fellows at Harvard University, a professor asked him, "How the hell is the reader supposed to know what to think when he's given so many different points of view?"

The fact that he conducted an orchestra of so many different drummers at the nation's first so-called alternative newspaper tended to obscure what Dan Wolf really had been from the start: middle-aged and middle-ground, a very conventional liberal and a whisper-quiet fighter. His own prose style, in the few editorials, articles, and reviews he ever did, was quite ordinary—plain, simple, direct, unaffected, with none of the spastic word bursts of his friend Mailer, who admired *him*. When, in a rare signed piece, he reviewed Rolf Hochhuth's 1964 play *The Deputy,* with its controversial premise linking Pope Pius XII to the wartime genocide of European Jews, he did so unfavorably, saying, "The play fails because of Hochhuth's devotion to literal truth, the most doubtful truth in art." When he defined his paper's politics once, he did so this way: "A passion for democracy, faith in reason and tolerance, and an implacable opposition to violence and dehumanization." That was all. He was never a participant. As he had not been a joiner and a signer in the thirties and forties, so he stood apart from the many Movements that swirled about him now. Neither he nor his friend Ed Fancher ever got arrested for refusing to take cover during the air-raid drills of the fifties, though a few of their writers, and their friend Mailer, did. Neither one of them ever met their chief antagonists of that time, Carmine DeSapio and Robert Moses, face to face. Their paper covered the ups and downs of Lenny Bruce and Bob Dylan and made cultural heroes out of them both, but neither of them ever saw either Bruce or Dylan perform. Their paper had some of the earliest, and the deepest, coverage of the drug culture of the late sixties, but neither one of them ever took LSD and neither had smoked dope since the fifties. Neither Wolf nor Fancher ever marched in a civil-rights or antiwar demonstration. In fact, for an editor, Wolf was not even well-connected into the literary scene. For all the comparisons between them, made by writers who wrote for both of them and by others as well, Daniel Wolf and the *New Yorker*'s William Shawn never met. And, months after a literary restaurant and saloon called Elaine's on the Upper East Side had become the most chic writer's eating and drinking hangout in town, when one of Wolf's writers, a critic named Dick Bruckenfeld, mentioned Elaine's to him in conversation, Wolf had never heard of the place.

Wolf was a shy man, too. In public matters, the shyness expressed itself in an intellectual divorce from the great events of his time and a genuine lack of interest in making contact with its greatest newsmakers that was known to go to extremes at times, as when one of his writers, Jack Newfield, became friendly with Robert Kennedy and decided to take Kennedy into the *Voice* offices one afternoon to meet the editor. When Wolf heard who was coming, he got out of his chair, made his way to a rear exit, closed the door behind him, walked halfway down the fire escape, and hid out there until Newfield and Kennedy had walked through the office looking for him, waited for him to come back, given up, and left. In the case of John Lindsay, Wolf had encouraged and supported him from the beginning, maybe even made the difference in getting him elected mayor, but all at a distance, never on a personal basis. Once he was elected, Lindsay sought to change that. One day when he was calling into the office and Wolf was trying to avoid talking with him, Wolf made a mistake, pressed the wrong button on his phone, and found himself trapped on the line with Lindsay. The mayor of New York invited the editor of the *Village Voice* to get together with him sometime, but the editor was only interested in getting the mayor off the phone. "What's your telephone number?" he said, offering to call him back. No sooner had he pronounced the words than Dan Wolf realized the total incongruity of asking the mayor of the City of New York for his telephone number.

And in private matters, he was straight to the point of being anal.

There was the morning one winter, in the Sheridan Square days, when he came by at four thirty, while it was still dark and freezing outside, to open up as usual, put his foot inside the door, and kicked Jackie, the rag woman who sold papers on the street for them, asleep there on the floor. There were "thieves" in her apartment, she had been complaining, and, because she trusted no one, she still refused to tell anyone at the paper where she lived, using their foyer to sleep instead, which they had been letting her do. Dan Wolf excused himself, put his coat on the rack, and went in to work, and Jackie got up, took it off the rack, and, using it for a blanket, went back to sleep again on the floor. Some time later, when Dan Wolf wanted to take a break and go home for breakfast, he came out, found her and his coat on the floor, excused himself again, got his coat back, and walked home—holding it at arm's length, though, going coatless himself in the bitter predawn cold just to avoid touching whatever might be on the coat now.

Another morning, Wolf came over to open up the office, and he was alone. At least, he thought he was alone, until he noticed that the layout table, on which they were supposed to do the dummies that day for the next issue, was down from its folded-up position, resting on one leg, and that on it he could make out two pairs of black buttocks moving up and down. As he kept staring at the sight, he realized that one pair belonged to the janitor, one of the successors to James Earl Jones in that job, that there was someone else with him, and that sexual congress was in session. He looked at them. They looked at him. Wolf moved first. "I'm sorry, excuse me," he said, and, averting his eyes from them, went upstairs to his desk, not coming down until the girl was gone. While he was up there, he thought about whether or not he should fire the man and decided that no, he couldn't do that. But, he told himself, if the table had collapsed and broken, and if we'd had nothing to do layout on today, then, *then* I'd have fired him.

In private company, at one of his weekly *salons* or at a tête-à-tête with one of the writers, he would relax, break down that reserve, show off with his tremendous wit. (He had, among other ways of being funny, an ability to take someone's name and twist it into a pun: Mary Perot Nichols into Mary Neurot Pickles, and so on.) But he kept carefully limited what company he would relax with. And only someone exactly like that could have made the whole thing work. If Dan Wolf had been like any of his writers, so different even from each other, the paper not only would not have been the same, it would not have been the *Voice*. Either some of their conflicting concerns would have had to be canceled out in favor of others, or the paper would have literally been torn apart by the competition. But by being so restrained and rational in his own lifestyle Dan Wolf guaranteed his writers the freedom to be flaky and revolutionary in theirs.

Thus, relativist, urbane, skeptical, detached, existential, libertarian Dan Wolf, without that much to say himself, editing the offbeat, avant-garde, freewheeling, existential, libertarian newspaper. Thus the Village voices, the editorial policy of not setting editorial policy.

Which was, it turned out, to set the most definitive editorial policy of all.

★ ★ ★

At first, he would lay out his paper strip by strip, uncut, with whatever was at hand. He didn't know what the hell he was doing *there,* either, he conceded. But as time went on, he knew exactly what he was doing, and he would spend hours doting on page one, or writing clever captions to go with the pictures, or fashioning phrases and making plays on words with the headlines and the titles of letters to the editor; the *Voice*'s were always the most witty in town. But if Dan Wolf was capable of spending hours doing something he wanted to do once he knew how to do it, he still didn't edit the copy very much, or very often. And he knew what he was doing there, too.

The fecklessness was all an act. To outsiders, to "professionals," he might seem to be a bump on a log, but Dan Wolf was foxier than that. He was always in control. His accomplishment was passive. He let it happen, and his genius was not to stop it. He gave his writers the opportunity to grow or to show they couldn't, room to roam limited, not by his red pencil, but by their own imagination. And he got more out of them by leaving them alone. They pushed themselves. He didn't push them.

"Go out and get your own assignment," he was apt to tell a beginner, and wait for an article to be dropped off "over the transom," literally, of their door. He would read it, looking for just one paragraph in there, the one paragraph that would tell him that here was a writer who looked at life a little differently, who was an original, an individual. That, and only that, was the essence of a writer to Dan Wolf. There were two kinds of writers, he thought, those who wrote out of expertise and those who wrote out of experience. He wanted the second kind. You didn't have to be a fantastic writer, he always thought, if you had something to say. It was what you had lived through that was important. That was one of the reasons he believed the professionals who came to him from other papers, already trained by someone else, did badly while the amateurs, or other people's rejects and misfits, did well, because the reporter's real-world, straight-facts sensibility was totally alien to the self-statement sensibility of people who suspended their defenses and declared themselves openly. That was why he often hired casually, on intuition, someone who had never been involved in journalism before.

Even with his established writers, Wolf wouldn't tell them what he wanted. "Oh, yeah, that sounds good. Go do it if you feel like it" was his standard response to their story ideas. He reacted that way, betraying so little of his true feelings, so that the writer, not knowing what he thought about it one way or the other, would not tell him what he wanted to hear, or, more to the point, would not tell him what the writer *thought* Dan Wolf wanted to hear. Dan Wolf wanted his writers to write what *they* wanted, not what they thought *he* wanted. When they did that, then he got out of them what he wanted, which was themselves. That was the way his psychology worked.

He even printed stuff of theirs that was awful, when he knew it and they knew it, as many people thought a lot of Jonas Mekas's columns were, as practically everybody thought practically everything written by Jill Johnston, the paper's dance critic–become–lesbian proselytizer, was, but Dan Wolf's attitude was that if the writer wanted to suffer from logorrhea, that was the writer's business. He indulged them, he let them go, even when they were at their worst, and instead of taking advantage, the great majority of them showed their gratitude by improving, rapidly and on their own. And, because he had never stepped in and stifled their originality, no matter what happened, Dan Wolf had writers who would rather have written for him than for anyone else. They trusted him. They had confidence in him.

And they told him everything.

★ ★ ★

"He edited people not copy," they all would say, over and over and over again, until they began to sound like the brainwashed army platoon in *The Manchurian Candidate*. It was another way of saying that he edited them before they ever wrote a word of their stories.

He was a psychoanalyst without portfolio, Mailer said, and no one could have put it any better, though one of his writers, Joe Flaherty, later tried, when he said that Wolf used to be locked up in his office like a priest in his confessional on a Saturday afternoon. He would get them alone, slink his slight, five-footish frame down into his chair, with its frayed leather and its sunken spring, light up on his corncob, and become the world's greatest listener. He would share in their thrills secondhand, vicariously, while they would sit down and talk out what they had done and learned in pursuit of their latest story with him. He became the receptacle and the backboard for their impressions, and the nursemaid of their neuroses, when that was necessary. He would never spike their enthusiasm for something by saying, as so many editors do, "That's not our kind of story, our readers aren't interested in that," by which they mean that *they* themselves aren't interested, and presume to know what is best for their readers. Dan Wolf's attitude—once again, exactly like William Shawn's stated policy at the *New Yorker*—was that he would publish what he pleased, and that sooner or later some readers or other of his would *get* interested in it, even if, especially if, it was a literally provocative article, one in violation of all their beliefs about some issue. In that, he showed an ultimate confidence in his own intuitive connection to the concerns of his audience far greater than that shown by most editors at most publications, with their force-fed formulas for readers and writers to follow. And it helped that his own range of interests spanned the breadth of all his writers. Because what was overlooked in his being such a canny conversationalist was that in these long, informal, exploratory sessions with him, he was scanning what was in their minds and slyly sizing up what was inside. A writer didn't have to have the same interests Dan Wolf did in order to get published by him; on the contrary, even when he was totally unin- terested in what they were into, he would want to see how interested *they* were in their own interests, and if it was genuine, if they were genuine, he published them. Above all, he wanted individuals. It was in these sessions where he found that out, where he earned his reputation for "editing people not copy," where he became Father to his Family.

They were one-way conversations and one-sided relationships, a lot of the time. Some of his writers, even some of those who had gone into intimate detail of their lives with him, would years later find themselves asking each other, and outsiders even, the most elementary questions, and seeking the simplest detail, of *his* life history. In these sessions, he told little of it. They were there to talk about *their* lives, not vice versa. Just as he knew enough to keep his distance from events outside, he knew how to keep his distance from them, too, when he had to. But he had his effect nonetheless.

Sardonic, sarcastic, and shrewd, suspicious of most people's motivations, with a sharp eye for when people were acting like fools, or in bad faith, he was able to detect when the writers didn't mean what they said, or had become enamored of someone who didn't. He could break down their pretensions, cool off their affected ardors, lay their clichés bare, and test the strength of their convictions, with a single, cynical "Do you *really* believe that?" When during the late sixties, one of his editors, Ross Wetzsteon, wanted the paper to cover the opening of an East Village Free Store, convinced that the hippies were finally going to get it together this time, Wolf advised him to wait a week. One week later, the store was closed and boarded up, and the word *LOVE* in front had been replaced by *HATE*. When he was dealing with Movement types, as many of his writers were, he knew just what to say to needle them, to keep them from going too far with their pet theories and their revolutionary nostrums. He let them know he had been around too long, and was too uninhibited intellectually, to be taken in by anyone's party line or groupthink or newspeak or doublethink, that he was a revisionist even when it came down to their Movement. In his own mind, he had achieved a true liberation they had not, but he continued to publish them, and they continued to write for him, knowing they were better off with someone like him as their editor. And when someone needed encouragement, he knew how to be supportive but still prod them, telling them, "This is pretty good," implying they could do better. Ed Fancher, the one with the *official* practice, once called his friend Wolf "the finest natural psychologist I've ever seen."

As with any family,* there were fights. Sometimes, in fact, the cross-fertilization of ideas at Dan Wolf's paper turned out to be more like a

---

*Often, it was more than a family, figuratively. It was family, literally. Besides Michael Harrington and Stephanie Gervis, joined together in wedlock, Dan Wolf found himself being sought out by, and accepting, more and more children (or spouses) of the already

cross-fire. The feud between his city editor, Mary Nichols, and his political-investigative reporter, Jack Newfield, was only the most celebrated. That one went on for years. Most went on for a few weeks, and were fortunately restricted to print, since, except for those on staff, most of the writers never met each other, except maybe at Christmas parties. Instead, they all met Dan Wolf—separately. And as in all families, the sons and the daughters eventually went away. Many left home for a year or two, five years in the case of their anti–Angry Young Man critic of the fifties, Charles Marowitz, but when they returned to New York their place at the paper was waiting for them if they wanted it. Most did. Some, however, did not, and most of them were in for a surprise when they chose not to.

Dan Wolf did indeed consider his paper to be a sort of experimental, freestyle laboratory of journalism, and it did indeed prove to be a vehicle of discovery. By the late sixties and early seventies, his writers had appeared in most of the country's major print media: the *Times, Life, Look,* the *Saturday Evening Post,* the *New Yorker, Saturday Review,* the *Nation,* the *New Republic, Partisan Review, Ramparts, More, Harper's, Esquire, New York, Playboy, Oui, Ms., Cosmopolitan, Vogue.* But there was an important distinction. Those Family members who branched out, but kept their old ties along with their new outlets, tended to thrive. Those who didn't tended not to. Some worried that Dan Wolf was no longer reading them. Some of them, as Steve Lerner and Michael Zwerin and Sally Kempton did, washed out of journalism altogether. And virtually all of them who graduated to more august but more structured institutions found themselves missing what they had had at the *Voice,* missing that feedback from the readers, that adhesive interest, that intense and immediate recognition of their name and association of it with what they had written before. The *Voice* Family was an extended family by now, an issue-oriented one in which letter-writers played a part by engaging the writers in dialogue. The point was not lost on his writers, and it was not lost on Dan Wolf: when Robert Christgau became the paper's resident rock music critic, Wolf told him, "We're going to miss you. You're one of the best letter-writers we've had."

established as the years passed. There was Sally (daughter of Murray) Kempton, and Mike (son of Murray) Kempton, and Steve (son of Arthur, Jr.) Schlesinger, and Mike (son of Dwight) MacDonald, and Susan (daughter of Paul) Goodman, and Steve (son of Max) Lerner, and Molly (Mrs. Andrew Sarris) Haskell, and Margot (Mrs. Nat) Hentoff, and ultimately in 1974, after Wolf departed, Mara (daughter of Margot Hentoff) Wolynski. Thus it seemed that even at the *Voice,* as at so many other publications in New York, connections weren't everything, but they helped.

★ ★ ★

Through it all, he was always in control. Through it all, he always kept his perspective. Through it all, almost until the end, he remained a superb judge of human character, with all of its double-edged complications. There was no order. There were no lines of authority. There were no star systems among the writers. There were no pecking orders. There was no pressure on them to produce. None of that would have been possible without the guarantee of freedom he gave them, and he gave them that guarantee just by being there.

There was a time, around 1969, when Michael Smith had become dissatisfied with the way the paper was being run. He was using drugs heavily during that period, and once when he typed ten whole pages on speed and turned in his copy in that condition, no one had said anything to him about it, except for Dan Wolf, who told him, "It's too smooth. Rough it up a little bit." That was too much even for Michael Smith in the state he was in, and one night before he left he typed up a memo to Dan Wolf spelling out all his dissatisfactions, telling him the paper was too loosely edited, leaving it in Wolf's typewriter.

In those days Wolf still came in at five in the morning on copy days, the days they got the next issue ready and sent it to the printer. The next day was copy day, and at seven when Michael Smith got in, Dan Wolf's answer was already waiting for him in *his* typewriter. It was short, reiterating what the paper was all about, and so simple that even before he was through reading it Michael Smith was wondering why he had ever written anything in the first place.

In it, there were those magic words again: "This is a writer's paper, not an editor's paper."

9. IT WAS THE 1960S, THE TIME OF THE

New Politics, the New Criticism, the New Journalism. And the *Village Voice* was in its ascendancy.

1963 . . . In January, the paper discloses that the Jefferson Market Courthouse will not be demolished after all; it will become a library. In May, it announces the Paris wedding of Stephanie Gervis and Michael Harrington. . . . In March, Wolf won't run a column by John Wilcock, about one of his old girlfriends; it is "too personal"; Wilcock invites readers to mail in for a copy . . .

. . . In October, Julian Beck and Judith Malina are arrested and their current Living Theatre show, *The Brig,* is shut down. They are charged with not paying taxes and "impeding Federal officers in performance of their duties." John Wilcock is there, too, and when challenged by the police because he has no press pass, he tells them, "Go ahead, arrest me," and they oblige him. In November, he is arrested again, this time with a photographer and an actress posing in the nude on Wall Street . . .

. . . The paper covers heavyweight boxing contender Cassius Clay's visit to a poets' conference, Bob Dylan's walkout on the Ed Sullivan Show when CBS bans his singing "Talkin' John Birch Society Blues" on the air, and Norman Mailer's appearance at Carnegie Hall in late May. . . . Reporter Susan Goodman covers the Village. . . . It is the year of the James Bond mystique, and Ken Sobol, their correspondent from the riots at Newport three years before, analyzes the secret agent as "a sado-masochist, an onanist, a voyeur, an anti-intellectual, a snob, a reckless driver, and all the other epithets he has been given. But above all he is a bumbler, a total failure by any reasonable standard."

. . . It is the year of Birmingham, tidewater mark of the civil-rights movement. In May, James Baldwin, Lena Horne, Kenneth Clark, Harry Belafonte, Lorraine Hansberry, other black intellectuals and artists, and a civil-rights worker named Jerome Smith who has just returned from the South, where he was beaten, corner Attorney General Robert Kennedy in his apartment on Central Park South and in a three-hour confrontation curse out the administration, white liberals in general, and him in particular. Lorraine Hansberry describes the scene to Diane Fisher, who writes the article "Miss Hansberry and Bobby K" in the *Voice.* . . . Arthur Sainer writes an open letter to Baldwin, debating his blanket condemnation of whites. . . . In September, former news editor Dan Balaban sends in correspondence from Prince Edward County, Virginia, where resistance to school integration

151

is taking place. "Superficial," Nat Hentoff calls it. . . . Balaban is not the only person Nat Hentoff is quarreling with in his support of the civil-rights struggle. After Jimmy Breslin writes a column in the *Herald-Tribune* putting down CORE, Hentoff writes one putting down Breslin, and Breslin writes a letter to the *Voice* putting down Hentoff—"who I do not know of," he says. That letter, in turn, draws a response from Theodore Bikel—actor, singer, Village resident, and *Voice* reader—putting down Breslin: "Mr. Breslin, you astound me. . . . Not only bad grammar but [your letter] speaks ill of your knowledge regarding matters of contemporary journalism." As for Hentoff, "Most whites of Breslin's age and background . . . are out of contact with the Negro social revolution," he decides. "Breslin is over his head in trying to write about most subjects outside the sports beat." . . . Feiffer's most barbed cartoon of the year, printed in the issue of May 23, shows JFK as vaudevillian, trooping and rhyming, backed by a choreographed chorus of "RHYTHM RHYTHM RHYTHM RHYTHM" sung by black-clad, briefcase-holding bureaucrats: "Life is full of ebbs and flows. I'd be a fool to oppose. Right's right. Wrong's wrong. Rhythm's rhythm. Go along. . . . Liberal program—easily wreckable. Unimportant—look impeccable. . . . Be amorphous, stay in office. Doing the Frontier Drag! OLE!" . . . And then came November.

"The absurdity of our lives has been exposed," writes Dan Wolf after the events of Dallas. Arthur Sainer does the article on Villagers' reaction. A follow-up piece asks: "Was Oswald in Village?" Feiffer's cartoon in the issue of January 2, 1964, is a contemporary madrigal tale: "One day into the country rode a handsome young prince. 'It's time to get moving again!' the prince declared. The country stirred in its sleep." But the prince dies. "And as the country prepared for sleep it hoped no one would ever ask it to move again. For it really did not want to kill any more princes."

★ ★ ★

When she came to New York, in the fall of 1962, Marlene Nadle had, by her own reckoning, read the *Village Voice* once. She had grown up, in Buffalo, New York, on the *New Yorker,* on Dorothy Parker and Wolcott Gibbs, then left, first to go to Africa with the American Friends Service Committee, later to go to New York. In the summer of 1963, when she was preparing to go down to Washington for the mass civil-rights march, she had quit her teaching position at New Rochelle High School, was getting her English degree at Columbia, and had never written anything professionally in her life. Nevertheless, she thought she would now, and she thought of the *Voice.*

When she called the paper up, she was told no, they had other people going down. She went anyway, introduced herself as a reporter for the *Village Voice,* came back, and, purely on intuition, began to write.

The march was on Wednesday, the 28th of August. By Friday afternoon she was in the office with the article, half typed, writing the other half of it out in longhand right there until she finished it. Dan Wolf came in and practically tripped over her as he tried to make his way upstairs. Someone explained to him who she was. Well, he said, he didn't know if he was interested in running such a piece, but he'd read it, and she followed him upstairs.

He read it. Then he called Michael Smith in and gave it to him to read. They both agreed; it was great, they told her. The next week, it ran on page one. Mailer noticed it and commented. *Esquire* quoted from it. And nothing else she ever wrote after that came as easily.

She drifted in and out of the *Voice* for years. In 1963, she took a job with the *World-Telegram* as a copy girl, and in 1965, the year she got the last interview Malcolm X ever gave and wrote it up in the *Voice,* she became a reporter across the river for the *Newark News,* a paper that once had to call up the *Voice* to ask who Tom Hayden was. (Hayden, one of the founders of Students for a Democratic Society, happened to be doing SDS organizing in Newark at the time.) There she did not get the chance to do interviews with Malcolm X or Tom Hayden, or any black militants or student radicals for that matter, or stories about the black community or the antiwar movement or any of the things she was into. By the time Newark broke out in riots, in the summer of 1967, she was gone, and covering it for the *Voice.*

That year she went off to Latin America, and stayed two years. She was in Bolivia when Che Guevara was killed, and covered it for the *Voice.* She got an interview with a member of Guevara's band, Marxist journalist Regis Debray, in his jail. And she interviewed a Marxist senator from Chile named Salvador Allende who was full of confidence that the democratic process would make him president of Chile. She went back again in 1972 and interviewed Allende, president for two years now, again. She found him changed—very somber, all his previous assurance and combativeness drained, a year before he was overthrown and killed in a *coup d'état.* She took these trips in between treks elsewhere—Thailand in 1972—and stays in New York, supporting herself working at the Public Library and writing for the *Voice.* That was where her relationship with Dan Wolf developed.

"So there's going to be a riot," she remembered him saying when she told him what was happening in Newark in July 1967. He was doing it to test her, she felt sure. The more she got into Movement politics, the more he teased her, needled her, doubted her, raised objections. When he did, she felt herself being forced to argue out all her positions with him, to clarify all her points. Before long, she found herself consciously writing to answer all his objections, writing for the most conservative *Voice* reader, not the one who already agreed with her views.

Their relationship continued along those lines, the paper helping her hang on to her $61, rent-controlled apartment on Bank Street in the Village whenever she took off for other parts, until in 1972 her father became deathly ill and she had to return to Buffalo. She was gone two years, and Dan Wolf was never her editor again.

★ ★ ★

Diane Fisher was different. She came by way of West Virginia, where the prophecy in her high-school yearbook had been that she would be the editor of a Greenwich Village newspaper. Out of college in 1958, she came to New York, a tall young woman with long, straight, streaked blond hair and strong, outdoorswoman features, and took a job as a secretary at the J. Walter Thompson advertising agency.

She had wanted to work for the *Village Voice,* and when she read an ad in the paper for a secretary, she applied for the job. But it didn't pay enough, and though they also had an opening for an ad salesman, she didn't get it—"Are you sure you could get out in the streets?" Dan Wolf had asked when he and Ed Fancher interviewed her. So she went to J. Walter Thompson and stayed there four years, living in the Village, getting more and more hip until the time came in 1962 when she decided that J. Walter Thompson was too square to stay there any longer. So she quit.

She called Fancher again. He didn't remember her, and no, he didn't have any openings right now, but, as it turned out, he needed some typing done for his clinic. She did it and, in October of 1962, had reason to call him again—for her money. He was sorry he'd forgotten, he said, and if she was interested they needed a receptionist at the paper. She began Halloween Day of 1962, and had been there five weeks when, one morning at the beginning of the newspaper strike, Dan Wolf stopped by her desk on his way in.

"You can write fillers, can't you?" he asked. Actually, fortunately for him, she could. She slugged some up, took them in, and he reacted, "You're a real pro, aren't you?" From that point on, Diane Fisher rose rapidly at the *Voice.* She did the story on the Lorraine Hansberry–Bobby Kennedy confrontation. When they introduced an entertainment calendar spread called "What's On," she was put in charge of it; it soon proved to be the best, most thorough entertainment guide in town. By 1964, she had the title "editorial assistant." Throughout the 1960s, her power grew at the paper she once called "the house organ of the world." Ed Fancher showed her how to do the ad dummy, and she took over the layout of classifieds. Soon she had nominal responsibility for all "the back of the book"—all movies, theater, art, music, and dancing—and for the layout of everything past pages one and three; Dan Wolf still did them.

She was not only responsible for the look of the paper; she was often the one held responsible for it, at least by those who hated its often admittedly raggedy-andy appearance. To that, it had to be said in her defense that she was only, always staying true to the *Voice* tradition of taking ads at the last minute and jumping, never cutting, stories. And, by the late sixties, she was writing again herself, doing music reviews, in the rock section she edited and called "Riffs," under the name of "Annie Fischer."

★ ★ ★

1964 . . . Thirty-eight New Yorkers ignore the screams of a woman named Kitty Genovese as she is stabbed to death. Feiffer has a comment. "Look out in the street, Charlie. Some lady's being chased by a guy with a rock," a woman standing by her window says. "Probably lovers. Don't get involved, Doris," advises her husband, not even looking up from his paper. It goes on like that until the victim is safely dead. Then she says, "Hey, look across the street, Charlie—Some guy's climbing out on the window ledge." This time he gets up and joins her at the window. They both begin shouting: "JUMP! JUMP!" . . . That summer, Feiffer introduces another permanent character: The Dancer. A lone, tiny girl dressed in black tights, she does improvisational dances to celebrate the times. "A dance to summer" is her first. "In this dance," she explains as she moves, "I symbolize the restlessness of new seasons. The desire to escape—from boredom. From responsibility. From cool men. From all inadequate pleasures. The desire to lift oneself out of the predictable. And never have to return." With that, she flies away. . . . Later in the year he comments on the presidential campaign between "Bang Bang Barry" and "Mr. President-of-all-the-people." . . . And in the issue of December 17, the *Voice* runs a letter attacking its drama critic, warning that "such casual disdain from so callow a cockroach" will no longer be tolerated. "To sum up," says the letter-writer, "Michael Smith is to be cashiered upon receipt of this instruction. His press card is to be burned. His typewriter is to be impounded. His air rifle and BBs are to be taken into protective custody." The letter is signed Mel Brooks. . . .

. . . In April, the World's Fair opens. Mary Nichols goes to inspect. A "large rathole in Flushing Meadow," she calls it. John Wilcock, on the other hand, contrary as usual, likes it. . . . The Village is changing. A picture spread in the issue of September 10 shows the new Lower East Side spots—the Annex, the Ninth Circle, Old Reliable, Stanley's, and Slug's—that, the paper declares, are "taking over the status of bohemia from Greenwich Village." A month later, after a sculptor is shot to death on Bedford Street and residents near Washington Square collect petitions protesting the noise and "flagrant solicitation of passers-by" there, police agree to assign more men to cover the park, which, writes Mary Nichols, is by now "alleged to be a gathering place for homosexuals and transvestites, both men and women, in recent months.". . . In April, a eulogy to A. J. Liebling, a book review by Alger Hiss, and the paper's first antiwar ad, "STOP MCNAMARA'S WAR" . . . In December, an essay by David McReynolds: "Vietnam is our Hungary" . . .

The year begins with what appears to be an official crackdown against the avant-garde. In January, a federal grand jury indicts Julian Beck and Judith Malina of the Living Theatre. They defend themselves at their trial—covered by the *Voice*—are cited for contempt, convicted, and return to the United States from abroad to be jailed in December. In March, seventy-two-year-old Mrs. Marion Tanner, the real-life model of Patrick Dennis's "Auntie Mame," is threatened with the foreclosure and auction of her Bank Street home for allegedly letting alcoholic strays stay there.

Throughout the spring, "unlicensed" artists are being arrested or having their places closed down by the city. "The current zeal of the City's Department of Licenses for the strict enforcement of licensing regulations against small avant-garde creative ventures," writes Stephanie Harrington in the March 26 *Voice*, "has so far resulted in the temporary closing of three Off-Broadway theatres, the suspension of poetry readings at Le Metro and a general malaise among culturally-minded New Yorkers as to what may be afoot. Already poet Allen Ginsberg is talking like Jane Jacobs." There is an artists' march on City Hall April 3. Ten weeks later, artists are still being arrested. . . .

The crackdown hits Jonas Mekas. During 1963 Mekas has become utterly infatuated with a new kind of underground film, the kind that will come to be called "camp"; his favorite, done by Jack Smith, one of the underground cinema's best-known actors, is entitled *Flaming Creatures*. Shot for $300 on an East Village rooftop, *Flaming Creatures* has no story line as such—only a cast of characters dressed up in elaborate costumes who expose their genitals to a Latin-beat soundtrack and engage in an orgy while an earthquake supposedly takes place. When an experimental film festival in Belgium bans *Flaming Creatures* from the competition, Mekas resigns from the jury of judges, gives a private screening in his hotel room for Jean-Luc Godard and Roman Polanski, among others, and takes over the festival projection booth in a brief abortive attempt to show the picture anyway. The authorities cut off his power and, in a scuffle, retake the booth. Mekas returns home to show *Flaming Creatures* in Greenwich Village. To avoid a "licensing" problem, he charges twenty-five cents admission to the Gramercy Arts Theatre and advertises the "Love-and-Kisses-to-Censors Film Society" as the film's official exhibitor. But, after three Monday night showings there, the theater owner receives a summons, forcing Mekas into the New Bowery Theatre on St. Marks Place, where, on the night of March 3, he (along with three others from his Film Makers' Cooperative) is arrested, and the film confiscated. Stephanie Harrington is at the scene; "Mayor Wagner and Governor Rockefeller have obviously learned something from the Russians," she reports. One week later, Mekas is arrested again, this time for showing Jean Genêt's homosexual love story, *Chant d'Amour*. The *Voice* publishes a plea for a defense fund for him and covers his legal difficulties, while characteristically running a statement by his former friend, the founder of Cinema 16, Amos Vogel, that "for the past year or so, friends and ideological sympathizers of Jonas Mekas, while applauding his pioneering, devotion and achievements, have watched with growing concern a progressive narrowing of his perspective, an inward-turning which threatens to limit his sensibilities." After letters in support of Genêt's film arrive from Jean-Paul Sartre and Simone de Beauvoir, among others, that charge against Mekas is dropped; but, despite the testimony of Susan Sontag, he is convicted on the other count (as reported in the June 18 issue), draws a six-month suspended sentence, appeals it all the way to the Supreme Court, and loses. . . . No matter. Mekas is soon turned on to other things, such as the new works of an unknown advertising artist who makes "films" of people kissing, sleeping, eating, and getting haircuts, often for hours on end. His name is Andy Warhol, and when Warhol shoots an eight-hour epic, *Empire*—eight straight hours of footage of the Empire State Building— in July 1964, Mekas is cameraman. "I think Andy Warhol is the most revolutionary of all filmmakers working today," he tells his readers. "He is opening to filmmakers a completely new and inexhaustible field of cinema reality. . . . What to some still looks like actionless nonsense, with the shift of our consciousness which is taking place, will become an endless variety and an endless excitement. . . . If all people could sit and watch the Empire State Building for eight hours and meditate upon it, there would be no more wars, no hate, no terror—there would be happiness regained upon earth." . . .

The crackdown also hits Lenny Bruce, only much harder, and Bruce does not recover. . . .

. . . The paper had always been a good vehicle for Bruce. His early New York appearances were advertised there; "the one-man show that induces violent boos from the square and glowing raves from the hip," one blurb about him said in 1960. "Bring your brains," it advised. He had fans there—John Wilcock, Nat Hentoff (who called him, in 1963, "the most radically original, creative, and vital comic" around). He was all that, and more—the most daring taboo-breaker ever seen in American comedy, the first totally uninhibited exponent of the new, black-humor consciousness. He was also, as events, covered closely in the *Voice* as nowhere else, were now to make clear, a very hung-up, very self-destructive man. . . .

. . . Bruce is in the middle of an extended engagement at the Café Au Go Go on Bleecker Street, when at ten o'clock on the night of April 3, just before going on for the Friday show, he is arrested backstage for having given an "indecent performance" the two previous nights. Howard Solomon, the café owner, is arrested too. The audience is given a refund. John Wilcock and other incensed supporters of Bruce hastily organize something called the Emergency Committee Against Harassment of Lenny Bruce. But Bruce, interviewed by Stephanie Harrington after his release on bail is, amazingly, not incensed at all—he is in favor of obscenity laws, and of prosecuting people for breaking them. "The local authorities won't believe it," she opens her piece, "but their best—perhaps only—friend since they busted Lenny Bruce . . . is Lenny Bruce."

> . . . A couple of hours spent with Bruce, however, can be a pretty incongruous couple of hours. First, tag along with him and his private-detective sidekick to the 5th Avenue apartment of a prominent civil libertarian, for whom they play the tapes of the shows for which Bruce was arrested. Sitting in a comfortable chair surrounded by wall-to-wall carpeting watching Bruce, in his light blue pants and white shoes and tan suede jacket, sitting stiffly in another comfortable chair, deadpan listening to himself on the machine. And then watching him get fidgety, though always attentive and polite, as the liberal lectures him on the history of the good fight against censorship in this country and explains that Bruce's language stems from an anal fixation, when all he really came for was some specific advice on his own case.

. . . There is no display of bitterness—against neither the police nor the law itself. In fact, Bruce displays more compassion for the police than just about anyone around the Village these days. "They die for less than $400 a month," he points out. "And they're ashamed of being cops. It's a shitty gig."

. . . As for the obscenity law, he says he thinks it's "correct. The whole issue," says Bruce, "is not that the state should keep its dirty hands off," as the liberal he visited had insisted. For Bruce "the key word is 'prurient.' Don't get people horny." And he says, insisting he is serious, that there should be a law against getting people aroused because "it's bad for our marriages." He says he's not for the repeal of obscenity laws because "most laws have been defined and tested under Constitutional law by men like Judge Black and some pretty other wise old cats. . . . Here's how wonderful the law is," he goes on, getting enthusiastic. "Even if [what you say] gets people horny, if it has some social importance it's not obscene."

. . . The only fear Lenny Bruce has is "of running out of carfare to the Supreme Court."

. . . John Wilcock, at least, thinks he sees the issue clearly. "What is an obscene performance?" he asks in his next column. "Apparently anything that offends the delicate susceptibilities of the local police. . . . Nobody is forced to listen to Lenny Bruce, even policemen."

. . . Wilcock himself has been acquitted of the charges pending against him, but not before a trial. The man most responsible for pressing it that far is an assistant district attorney named Richard Kuh. As Wilcock had informed his readers the previous December, on his first day in court "things were going very well. I had a strong impression that the judge was going to dismiss the case. And then suddenly Kuh came charging in. He took over for a young assistant District Attorney who was handling it. I don't know why; it seemed an awfully trivial case to involve someone that high up in the D.A.'s office." . . .

. . . The name of Richard Kuh has appeared in the *Village Voice* before, when he was one of the founders of the Village Independent Democrats. But times have changed. In the years since, Kuh has left the VID and joined the office of Manhattan district attorney Frank Hogan, the man Carmine DeSapio hand-picked to run for U.S. senator in 1958. And he is taking it upon himself, in 1963 and 1964, to take cases against people like John Wilcock . . . and Lenny Bruce. . . .

. . . Bruce's trial gets under way in July, and Kuh prosecutes it with a zeal above and beyond the call of duty. Watching Bruce's lawyers debate him, writes Stephanie Harrington in her piece "How Many Four-Letter Words Can a Prosecutor Use?" is "like reporting on a debate between Burt Lancaster and Abraham Lincoln."

> . . . When it's all over the court record may show that in the course of this trial Kuh has used the words he is prosecuting Bruce for using more than Bruce did in all the performances of his abbreviated New York run. . . . And then, of course, there is the defendant Bruce, who is beginning to look like the martyr the authorities are making of him. He usually wears a Nehru-like tunic and carries a black bag that contains the red flowpens he uses to write notes to his attorneys. He appreciates Kuh's dramatic sense and on good days gives him good reviews. One day he broke into Kuh's cross-examination of a witness to object to the manner in which the prosecutor was referring to a portion of a Bruce monologue. "Stop calling it the mezzuzah bit!" Bruce shouted half-rising. Kuh thereafter inserted the word "bit" at every opportunity when referring to sections of Bruce's monologues.

. . . Bruce, refusing to let them pursue a First Amendment defense and demanding the right to do his nightclub act in court, fires his lawyers. The judge, over Kuh's objections, grants Bruce a delay; at Kuh's insistence, though, he orders Bruce to undergo psychological testing. "It seems to me," Nat Hentoff comments, "that after all his years of service as an advocate of 'the people' in the courts, the least we can do for Richard Kuh is to give him a Rorshach test." . . .

. . . The trial resumes in November, and Bruce, frantic now in pleading his own defense, is silenced by the court for repeated outbursts. Stephanie Harrington reports it: "Please, he pleaded, permit him to present his monologue in court; all the judges had heard in the tape recordings and had read in the transcripts, he said, was a 'dirty show presented by the D.A.'; let him demonstrate, he begged, that his allegedly obscene gestures were not those of masturbation but those of benediction. 'I so much want to have the respect of this court,' he said."

. . . It does no good. He is convicted and cited for contempt. Broken and bankrupt, Bruce jumps bail, and the rest of his life is a quick downhill slide. An item in the paper in April 1965 tells readers that "while giving an imitation of 'Superjew', Lenny Bruce fell 40 feet out of a San Francisco hotel window Monday. The 38-year-old comedian broke his arm and suffered possible back injuries." In August 1966, Bruce dies in

Los Angeles of a drug overdose. "At his death," says the obit in the paper, written by Allen G. Schwartz, "he was an addict, a convict, and a fugitive." . . . In the *Voice* of February 22, 1968, Nat Hentoff's column has the news that the conviction of Howard Solomon, the café owner who had hired Bruce, has been reversed on appeal, complete with ruling that Bruce's act was not obscene. But, says Hentoff, "were Lenny Bruce alive today—Solomon's successful appeal notwithstanding—the comedian would still have had to serve the four-month sentence, since . . . the time for his appeal had expired. After that, he would have had to contend with the subsequent charge of bail-jumping. Only then could Lenny Bruce play New York again." . . .

. . . In late January, when New York's first school boycott takes place, Stephanie Harrington covers it for the *Voice*. . . . In February, the paper publishes the charge by the local NAACP head that a patrolman and a staffer of St. Vincent's Hospital in the Village beat him up. . . . In April, demonstrators disrupt opening day of the World's Fair with a "stall-in" on the highway approaches and a "sit-in" on the fairgrounds itself. Stephanie Harrington winds up covering, among other events, the arrest of her husband, Michael, along with yet another Harrington, the Reverend Donald—"the two Harringtons were to prove a source of helpless confusion to their jailers," she writes. . . . The publication of Baldwin's *Blues for Mister Charlie,* with its violently anti-white-liberal message, starts a debate in the pages of the *Voice;* the paper publishes a review of the book that the *Reporter* killed. . . . In August, the paper prints correspondent Lucille Komisar's account of the struggle by the Mississippi Freedom Democratic Party to get seated at the Democratic National Convention in Atlantic City. . . . It is the year of the so-called white backlash, and in a Feiffer cartoon, "Mr. Whitey Backlash" gives an interview: "In my opinion Negroes are going too far with their protests," he says. "May I quote you, Mr. Backlash?" asks the reporter. "No. This is off the record," he answers. "Then, sir, *on* the record you are *for* integration?" the reporter queries. "*On* the record," replies Backlash, "I'm even for *democracy, Sonny.*"

In the summer of 1964—Freedom Summer—Howard Moody of Judson Memorial Church, who had been active in the civil-rights movement, was on his way down to Mississippi, to visit a Freedom School in a town called Harmony. Before he left, he asked his friend Dan Wolf if he would like to go, and was flabbergasted when Wolf, who as far as Moody could tell had never been west of the Hudson except for World War II, said yes.

So the two men flew down to Jackson, Mississippi, in the first week of July 1964, rented a car at the airport, and started driving.

Harmony was an enclave where the blacks had owned and tilled the land themselves since Emancipation. When Wolf and Moody reached Carthage, they stopped to get directions. Wolf waited outside. Moody went inside a pool hall to make a phone call.

There were four rednecks inside the place with him when Moody entered, and, as he got into the booth, one of them came over and leaned up against it. Not wanting to reveal where he was going, Moody, a native-born Texan with a still-thick Southern accent, finished his conversation quickly, and calmly walked outside to the car, where Wolf was still waiting. He got back in and they kept driving, past town after town of empty stores and Confederate flags, passing, and being passed by, pickup truck after pickup truck loaded with rifles and shotguns on the road. Finally, they were low on gas, and Moody pulled into a station where he saw a black man painting the side of the building. He would ask *him* how to get to Harmony.

But when he went over to the man and asked him, the man kept painting. He must not have heard me, Moody thought, and asked again. The man went on painting, not even turning around. Moody excused himself and asked a third time. There was still no reaction. By this time, Moody knew what was happening, knew the man had heard him, knew why he wasn't answering, and knew what it would take to get him to answer. Moody didn't want to say it, but he went ahead and said it anyway: "Hey, BOY!"

This time the man turned around, and Moody got his directions.

They began driving again. They went through Philadelphia, where a search was under way for three civil-rights workers—Michael Schwerner, Andrew Goodman, and James Chaney—who had been reported missing there. By nightfall, they were in Meridian, and then it came over their car radio: that afternoon, about an hour before they had passed through the town, the dead bodies of Schwerner, Chaney, and Goodman had been dug up outside Philadelphia.

They made it to Harmony, met the people there, and attended a rally that night where Pete Seeger sang and Chaney's mother spoke. When they got home, Howard Moody wrote a short piece in the *Voice* that raised $5,600 for Harmony. Afterwards, Dan Wolf, who had been scheduled for a parachute drop onto the Japanese mainland eight days before the planned Allied invasion in 1945, remembered the thrill and fright of being inside a real police state, and the sight of the American flag, not as a symbol of the right, of reaction and counterrevolution, but as one of liberation, of the presence of the federal government against the Old Confederacy. Howard Moody remembered the sight of Dan Wolf, the cool, academic, New York intellectual suddenly thrust into the front lines, at a picnic the Harmony people threw for them, full of all that black Southern cuisine, excusing himself to go to the privy, and, taking one look at it, waiting until later.

★ ★ ★

Of all Dan Wolf's writers, the most committed, the most combative in all this, was Nat Hentoff. When blacks boycotted the public schools, he supported them. When the *New York Times* carried news reports of a black street gang called the "Blood Brothers," Hentoff attacked them for running an unverified story. When a black prisoner accused of murdering two white girls in their apartment on the Upper East Side recanted his confession, Hentoff quickly took up his cause in the column (the suspect, George Whitmore, was eventually cleared and another man found guilty). He proselytized for the black struggle in his columns—one typical title, "What Do They Want?"—and in his books.

Soon, he began to grate on other people who saw him, as one *Voice* correspondent did after covering a panel discussion at the Village Gate where Hentoff spoke, as a "jazz critic-cum-revolutionary." When his "race" novel, *Call the Keeper,* came out, it was panned in the *Voice.* Even Howard Moody was lukewarm in his review of Hentoff's other book on the subject, *The New Equality.* To those who didn't like him, Nat Hentoff came across as an insincere polemicist, the sort of self-righteous, strident, gullible, neurotic white black militant Tom Wolfe would later describe perfectly with the catchall words *radical chic* and *flakcatcher.* They could not abide what seemed to them to be his sensibility of excess, his grandstanding, his racial politics of almost suicidal self-hatred, his living in comfortable circumstances himself and sending his children to private school while telling others how to live and educate their children, his support of blacks who would strip less fortunate whites of what little they had.

Nat Hentoff didn't see it that way. He remembered his own poor, ethnic background growing up as a Jew in Irish Boston, his years as a shop steward and union organizer. His politics were, he said once, "libertarian socialism," and as far as he was concerned his being out front in support of radical blacks was just one more expression of it. He thought he knew as much about the working-class struggle as anybody else, and that he knew agitprop when he saw it. And, when he was criticized, he wasn't afraid to criticize back.

★ ★ ★

It was the last week of June 1964, and the Harlem riot was only three weeks away. In the Village, another one of those panel discussions was being held, three white liberals—author Charles Silberman, producer David Susskind, *New York Post* editor James Wechsler—and three radical black artists—actor Ossie Davis, actress Ruby Dee, playwright Lorraine Hansberry. Only this was not just another one of those panel discussions, according to the report in the *Village Voice* the next week.

Imagine three goldfish dropped into a fish tank filled with sharks. Or imagine Billy Budd mugged by the Emperor Jones. Then you might have some idea of the malevolent and paranoid violence . . . corrosive nihilism . . . [and] estrangement from reality . . .

The audience for this fratricidal Armageddon was about two-to-one white, but most of the whites appeared to be either self-flagellating kooks or east of ADA driftwood from the 1930s. . . . It was an audience that cheered from its guts— the way a fight crowd does at the first smear of blood—the mention of Malcolm X and Paul Robeson, and guffawed at references to Gandhi, Djilas, and Ralph Bunche.

. . . it is the kind of moral juggling of facts Soviet apologists are so expert at. . . . Their missiles equal our missiles. Budapest equals the Bay of Pigs. Djilas equals William Worthy. And so too does Congressman Dawson equal George Meany; Hulan Jack equals Bobby Baker; Malcolm X equals Governor Wallace; and Adam Clayton Powell equals Jimmy Hoffa.

. . . A majority of America's 40 million poor are not black, but are white. They are the skilled workers idled by automation; they are the hillbilly prisoners of Appalachia; they are the Bowery derelicts; they are the Italian, Jewish, and Irish victims of urban renewal; they are the millions of elderly; and they are the thousands of migrant farm laborers.

It is time Baldwin and the cultural Mau Maus to his left admitted that the enemy is not the white liberal. . . .

At this juncture, the greatest danger appears to be what Lenin once called "infantile leftism," a disease whose main symptom these days is an obsequious attitude toward any Negro holding a "Freedom Now" placard.

"One of the very worst reporting jobs I have ever seen in *The Voice*," wrote Hentoff, who had been there, two weeks later. The reporter, Jack Newfield, did not agree. The week after that, he disputed Hentoff's disputation of him. And the week after *that,* Hentoff wrote another disputation, this time of Newfield's disputation of his, Hentoff's, original disputation. A few weeks later, Dan Wolf took Jack Newfield out to lunch and hired him as an assistant editor.

Wolf received advice not to, and certainly at the time of his appointment there was little to recommend him. He had written a few articles freelance for the *Voice,* worked as an editor on the *West Side News* before it went out of business, been fired as a copy boy from the *New York Mirror,* and just failed his tryout as a reporter at the *New York Post.* Up to that point, most of Jack Newfield's life had been a failure, and there were those around him who thought it always would be. But Dan Wolf took a chance.

When Jack Newfield went to work for the *Village Voice* he was twenty-seven years old. His origins were lower-class, the poverty he had known in his boyhood desperate. He had been born in Brooklyn's Bedford-Stuyvesant ghetto, the only child of Jewish parents, the only white kid growing up on the block; he went to Boys' High, 90 percent black. When he was four, his father died, forcing his mother to go to work. When he went to Hunter College, he had to drop out, even though there was no tuition, and work for a year at Madison Square Garden, doing publicity for boxing events and the New York Rangers, before he could go back and get his degree. Along the way, Jack Newfield stopped believing in God, and started believing in left-wing politics.

He wanted to be a sportswriter, but his first job was as a copy boy with the old *New York Mirror.* That lasted until the night the wire service teletypes began to click with the first news of the American-sponsored invasion of Cuba. When he heard that, Newfield ripped the reports from the machine, stood there in the middle of the city room, and set them on fire.

That was the end of Jack Newfield at the *New York Mirror.* From there, he went to the neighborhood weekly, the *West Side News.* His first article in the *Voice,* "An Obit for Reform" Democrats, appeared on November 7, 1963. Finally, in the summer of 1964, he got a tryout at the *New York Post,* as a reporter and on the night rewrite desk. This time, he thought he was going to make it. But working for Dolly Schiff turned out to be, he said later, like playing third base for a last-place team in August. And the feeling was mutual. Jack Newfield failed his tryout.

Many of those who knew Jack Newfield from this period remembered the picture of a lonely, homely underachiever, a loser, grubby-looking, shabbily dressed, and insecure. But Dan Wolf knew what Jack Newfield's background was, and liked the fact that he had had to fight for everything in his life, that he was a hustler. So he hired him.

At that time, getting hired by the *Village Voice* was the best possible thing that could have happened to Jack Newfield, and Newfield knew it. But he also knew that, contrary to all appearances, it was not the only thing he had going for him in his life. Whatever else he might have, Jack Newfield had his political dedication. He was an activist. He was a part of the New Left, in fact he was under contract to write a book about it, titled *A Prophetic Minority,* which, published in 1966, became the first, and best, work about it.

Jack Newfield was a political animal, one with multiple motivations, and they were all apparent from the article he wrote that July, attacking the meeting Hentoff attended. The cut through the prevailing clichés of the Left. The writing from the gut about a multi-ethnic alliance of the poor all across America. And yet, at the same time, the implicit obeisance to the Left line by grounding even his criticism in a quote from Lenin. Jack Newfield's motivations were often more than multiple; sometimes they were simply contradictory.

He was into the New Left. He was also into the New Populism, which was not the same thing. He could not seem to make up his mind what he was, realist or revolutionary, and at times he seemed to want to have it both ways.

He had a wrong-righter's sensibility, a passion for all underdogs. But he was erratic and inconsistent. He would vent an old-fashioned, tough-minded, programmatic idealism one time, and embrace New Left groupthink the next. He could be an iconoclast or a sloganeer. He was an activist and he was a journalist; he was in the New Left and he was writing about it. He believed that change could come through electoral politics and the Democratic Party, and he didn't. He was enamored of Michael Harrington; later he became enamored of Tom Hayden at the time when Hayden was holding figures like Harrington and Irving Howe—older, more pragmatic, more moderate leftists—up to ridicule. Back and forth he went, and it was always hard to tell where he drew the line. As he gained notoriety and came to be quoted by the Establishment press—his verdict that the presidential campaign of Eugene McCarthy "has been run as if King Constantine was the manager" was picked up and rerun almost everywhere, it seemed, when he reached it prematurely in 1967—he would compare what he was doing to Orwell's covering the Loyalists in Spain, Camus's the Maquis in France, and Fanon's the rebels in Algeria. Yet he could still tell the *Los Angeles Times* in 1970 that "it's always a confirmation for me when *The Voice* gets attacked by the left." And, all in one interview he gave to *Newsweek* in 1968, he put down the Movement for its "hangup with the Che Guevara mystique," then said himself that "I prefer the Sierra Maestra to Camelot," said that "I'm not a guerrilla. I believe America is racist, the war is rotten. I don't want to write that on bathroom walls. Too many leftists enjoy being a cult," then summed up his own politics as "pro-pot, pro-riot, and pro-Cong."

With Jack Newfield, everything was political. That was the best way to account for his ups and downs and ins and outs. The causes were always changing, but he always had causes, and in his beginning years at the *Voice* they were Bob Dylan and his switch to folk-rock music, Tom Hayden and the SDS, Stokely Carmichael and SNCC, the New Left.

And Robert Kennedy.

★ ★ ★

     It seemed an odd coupling, considering that Newfield had gotten his first glimpse of Kennedy only the year before, shrieking at him across a picket line outside the Justice Department. But it was genuine. Jack Newfield thought he saw something in the public personality of Robert Kennedy, something raw, three-dimensional, existential, and up-front, that convinced him this was not just another politician. He liked him. Then he admired him. And, before it was all over, he had begun to hero-worship him. No one else would ever get that close again.

In the first week of September 1964, Robert Kennedy, having been already ruled out as a possible running mate for Lyndon Johnson that year, resigned from the president's cabinet, established residency in New York, accepted the Democratic nomination for United States senator, and began his campaign to unseat the popular Republican incumbent, Kenneth Keating, and overcome the "carpetbagger" issue being raised against him. That was only a few days before Jack Newfield began work at the *Village Voice*.

When Kennedy went on a campaign tour of the Village, Newfield was there, following him as he "evoked Beatlemania, laughter, and tears."

> "Where's Canarsie?" challenged a non-believer.
> "Somewhere over there," smiled Kennedy, pointing in the general direction of the Village Gate.

. . . Then Kennedy said he had to move on, and the crowd suddenly surged forward. Children and women struggled desperately to touch his sleeve and shake his hand. . . . ''Mommy, he touched me,'' a 10-year old screamed shrilly. . . . ''See you in the White House,'' yelled a passing Negro cab driver. The owner of the Sheridan Diner shouted, ''Want a cup of coffee?'' ''Sorry, I'm working,'' the candidate replied.

The rally at Sheridan Square was shorter, more enthusiastic, and spiced by hecklers.

''Go back to Boston, ya bum,'' roared a truck-driver voice. . . . ''I love you,'' shouted a young girl's voice.

. . . When the talk ended, the learned response was repeated. Kennedy walked back and forth on top of the three cars, and hundreds shoved, reached, and jumped to touch him, as if he were a faith healer who could fill the void left last November 22. . . .

A disheveled nymphet, clutching an autograph to her almost breasts, sighed, ''I'd rather have this than Ringo's.''

Behind her was the heavily lined face of an old woman, tears glistening in her eyes. ''God bless you, Kennedy,'' she said almost to herself.

Jack Newfield might have been impressed with Kennedy, but Nat Hentoff was not. "Multiply dangerous" was his verdict. Opinion on the Kennedy-Keating race at the *Voice* split along other lines, too. Dan Wolf did not endorse; "in the end in the voting booth, it will be our intuition of the man that will make the choice," he said. Mailer, on the other hand, did—with an essay, "Possibility of a Hero," declaring himself for Kennedy. "I wouldn't pretend to say Bobby Kennedy is not capable of marching at the front of a right-wing movement," Mailer wrote, but "I think Bobby Kennedy may be the only liberal about, early or late, who could be a popular general in a defense against the future powers of the Right Wing."

I have affection for Bobby Kennedy. I think something came into him with the death of his brother. I think Bobby Kennedy has come a pilgrim's distance from that punk who used to play Junior D.A. for Joe McCarthy and grabbed headlines by riding Jimmy Hoffa's back. Something compassionate, something witty, has come into his face. Something of sinew.

In the end, Kennedy won, and ran for president, as Jack Newfield for one had been imploring him to do, and lost his life in the attempt. When Robert Kennedy died, Jack Newfield went back to having no heroes again. He was still partisan, still engaged in the internecine warfare of the Left and the West Side reformers, and his copy was still liable to show it. Thus, in November 1969, at the time of the Vietnam Moratorium and the Mobilization March on Washington, Newfield suddenly turned on Allard Lowenstein, an early civil-rights activist in Mississippi and the brainstormer of the "Dump Johnson" movement in 1968, and attacked him. And in December 1971, after having been behind Edward Koch for years, he changed, and wrote, "I think Koch is trying to exploit people's understandable fears to further his own ambitions to be mayor." Koch, he even said, "began in politics as a member of Carmine DeSapio's club. In November of 1969, at Hunter College, he publicly red-baited the anti-war movement, and refused to support the biggest peace march of them all." Then, later, he went back to being a supporter of Koch again.

He was also still apt to subordinate his own point of view to the fortunes of the favorites he played, and, on occasion, covered for. The chief case in point was that of Bella Abzug. She had won a seat in Congress from the West Side in 1970, defeating the right-wing radio commentator Barry Farber in a race made close by the issue of whether she did, or did not, support the sale of jets to Israel. In 1972, when she lost her seat through redistricting, she ran a primary against William Fitts Ryan, the man who had been her political mentor, openly stating that she was challenging him instead of some other, more conservative incumbent because he was the easiest to beat, openly inviting women to vote for her just because she was a woman. Ryan won the primary. Ryan died of cancer. The party nominated Abzug for his seat. Ryan's still-fuming supporters, numbering Jack Newfield among them, rallied around his widow Priscilla, who received the Liberal Party's designation and contested Abzug in November. And on September 28, 1972, this letter to the editor, from Jack Newfield, appeared in the *Village Voice:* "I was there when Bella said at the VID in 1970 she was against the jets for Israel. And then I watched her deny she ever said it. And finally I lied, and denied she ever said it, so that she might defeat Barry Farber. I am now ashamed of all that."

But, gradually, a change came over Jack Newfield. In the years after the death of Robert Kennedy, he went from being an advocacy journalist to becoming an investigative reporter. He still made mistakes. In 1969, when his biography of Kennedy came out, Newfield quoted him as believing that Lyndon Johnson was having his telephones tapped, and in an interview cited Stephen Smith, Kennedy's brother-in-law, and Adam Walinsky, his speechwriter, as sources who confirmed the quote; they denied ever doing so. That same year, he wrote a piece for *Harper's* debunking Dolly Schiff of the *New York Post* and describing her recent offer of a column there to him; ten months afterward the magazine had to run an "Erratum: We are advised that there were a number of factual inaccuracies in an article about the New York *Post* by Jack Newfield in our September issue. We regret any harm that may have been done as a result of its publication." And in February 1972, Newfield, after a visit to a prison in upstate Dannemora, reported in the *Voice* that there were prisoners there who "have no beds and sleep on a concrete floor"; under cross-examination at the trial of a lawsuit involving the prison two weeks later, Newfield admitted that inmates had told him that, that he had not seen it for himself, and that it was "not factual."

But Dan Wolf appreciated what Jack Newfield was trying to do, and let him go his own way, let him make mistakes. And Jack Newfield appreciated the fact that Dan Wolf let him go, that he didn't have to worry about being fired for a mistake. So he stayed at the paper, until there came a time when he wasn't making mistakes anymore. He was going after lead-paint poisoning, and corrupt judges, and nursing home scandals, he was getting results, and he had become one of the best investigative reporters in the city, if not in the entire business.

Even then, a little trace of the old insecurity remained. In January 1975, after he had broken story after story over many weeks exposing inhuman conditions and systematized profiteering in the city's nursing home system, the paper wanted to nominate him for a Pulitzer Prize. A packet of material was prepared for submission and brought into him for his signature before it went out. Newfield refused to sign it.

He had a visitor with him at the time, who asked him, when the staff assistant had left with the unsigned packet and they were alone again, "How come you did that? Don't you want to get a Pulitzer?"

"Nah," he said. "They're fixed."

★ ★ ★

1965 . . . Murf the Surf, the thief who burgled the Metropolitan Museum of Art, is profiled in the paper by future *Esquire* writer Nora Ephron: "Murphy was, in a sort of pop-art way, the true 20th-century man." . . . A page-one obit for Lorraine Hansberry, dead of cancer at thirty-four in January . . . Another "general excellence" award from the state Press Association . . . Mailer constructs, and the paper runs a photograph of, a model for a geometrically designed, 3,000-foot-high "city in space." . . . When Tom Wolfe's two-part piece on William Shawn and the *New Yorker* comes out, Hentoff denounces the "gratuitous brutality of his gratuitously personal assault on William Shawn" and announces, "I shall appear no longer in the Tribune's *New York* under its present editorship . . . because I see no point in being an accomplice, however tacit, of a magazine that engages in thuggery.". . . In the July 15 *Voice,* letter-writer Neil Leonard asks, "Would any James Joyce devotees like to own the house in which Molly Bloom silently yielded her eternal yes? While making the Bloomsday pilgrimage in Dublin on the day it all happened, June 16, I was surprised to find Seven Eccles Street with a large 'For Sale' sign on it. Checking a bit, I learned that the house, an attached, run-down building in a rather slummy block, could be had for roughly $6000.". . . Washington Square Park is getting even rougher. In July, 1,180 signatures go on a neighborhood petition complaining that "groups have taken over large segments of the park, virtually making it their home . . . persistently engaging in offensive activity . . . noise . . . obscene language . . . drinking . . . staggering . . . littering . . . accosting . . . urinating . . . lying on benches" and "conspicuous lovemaking," making the park "unsuitable for children." . . . Newfield on Tom Hayden's SDS project in Newark, defending the switch of that "Brecht of the juke box," Bob Dylan, from folk to rock music, and describing the scene at Forest Hills as those two clashing groups of fans, the Mods and the Rockers, disrupt one of his performances.

> The Mods—folk purists, new leftists, and sensitive collegians . . . booed their former culture hero savagely after each of his amplified rock melodies. They chanted We want Dylan and shouted insults at him. Meanwhile, the Rockers, in frenzied kamikaze squadrons of six and eight leaped out of the stands after each song and raced for the stage . . . to touch their new found, sunken-eyed idol, while others seemed to prefer playing Keystone cops with pudgy stadium police, running zig-zag on the grass until captured in scenes reminiscent of the first Beatle movie.
>
> The factionalism within the teenage sub-culture seemed as fierce as that between Social Democrats and Stalinists.

. . . Jimmy Breslin and Nat Hentoff are at it again. Breslin writes a letter to the paper saying he was "quoted out of context" in one of Hentoff's columns. "It obviously is quoted this way in order to make some sort of a viewpoint stand up for the person doing the quoting. I am just a little bit tired," he says, of these amateur bastards doing things like this and from now on I think the best thing for all of us is for you to see to it that nothing of mine appears in your newspaper. Under any circumstances. I know the number of people who read *The Voice* is small and that it really doesn't matter, but I just prefer it this way. Apparently, you do not know what even basic responsibility amounts to. Therefore, you go your way, I go mine and let's leave it at that. I hold you personally responsible for insuring this request of mine.

. . . "For the record," answers Hentoff, "I will state Jimmy Breslin is not a pacifist. But he certainly is a professional."

. . . In April, Feiffer does a sendup of Westerns with a cartoon of a marshal dying in the arms of his loved one. "Why must it go on, Ben?" she asks him. "All this fightin', all this violence?" He answers her: "Someday there'll be a town here, Tessie—An' there'll be a church, an' there'll be a school, an' there'll be law—An' there'll be horseless carriages, an' there'll be factories, an' there'll be air pollution—An' there'll be alienation, an' there'll be drop-outs, an' there'll be violence. *That's* what we're fightin' for, Tessie. A heritage." . . . He takes off on Lyndon Johnson: "As your present president it is incumbent upon me to play a variety of roles in the course of a single day," says LBJ in the first panel of a strip that fall. "Policeman to the world," and he changes into a cop uniform. "Social worker to the poor," and he is dressed like a Salvation Army worker. "Lover of peace," and he is holding a guitar and placard. "Seeker of consensus," and he is a cowboy ready for a showdown. "Educator," and he is in cap and gown. "Civil rights leader," and he is black. "At the close of day what a relief it is to be able to git in my pajamas," he says, "and just be myself"—and he is "Superman." . . .

. . . Marlene Nadle interviews Malcolm X just before he is assassinated in February. . . . Howard Moody goes to Selma. Newfield joins him there for the march through Alabama that climaxes the civil-rights movement: "There were rabbis, junkies, schoolboys, actors, sharecroppers, intellectuals, maids, novelists, folksingers, and politicians." Newfield's articles on the Student Nonviolent Coordinating Committee draw praise from an unexpected source—Nat Hentoff: the "most penetrating analysis of the SNCC ethos and style I've seen anywhere. It also seemed to me Mr. Newfield's best piece yet, thereby presaging increasingly valuable reporting and interpretation by him in areas in which expert newsmen are so damned rare." . . . In September, Newfield interviews SNCC's Stokely Carmichael, "the happy warrior of the Movement. Last week, burdened by death, Carmichael sat in SNCC's New York office and remarked, 'I've just come back from my 17th funeral since I've started in the Movement. That's just too much killing, man.' " . . . Feiffer, in the strip, tweaks white guilt. "Do you see how I hate you, Whitey?" shrieks the black militant at the whites listening to him. *"You liberal reformers!! You crippled power structure! I scorn you, whitey! I revile you!"* Then, quietly, "That will be $1.50 a piece, gentlemen. Same time, next week?" he asks. "Oh, *please!"* they beg. . . .

. . . It is the year Lyndon Johnson escalates a guerrilla insurgency in South Vietnam that the United States is opposing with "advisers" into a full-scale war, America's longest, most unpopular, and first lost war. The antiwar movement is on in earnest, everywhere, and Feiffer is more *engagé* than he has ever been. In late April, an unseen presence gives a press briefing about "outside Northern agitators breeding discontent and revolution. These people in the South are my friends. A gentle breed. I know many of them—they don't want to fight us. It's these extremists from the North—streaming in, stirring up trouble." And then the punchline. "Without them, I assure you, there would be no problem in South Vietnam." . . .

. . . That summer, Adlai Stevenson drops dead on a London street. Hentoff describes only recently going to see the UN ambassador, a saint to liberals ever since the fifties, to urge him to quit and come out against the war:

> He received us—the delegation who had come in June to ask him to resign—with grace. . . . At first, he tried—loyally, some would say—to present again and to defend again the Administration's line. . . . Finally—though only intermittently—there were echoes of the Stevenson of the 1952 campaign . . .
>
> . . . At the end, he said—and I did not feel it to be rhetoric— "You honor me by coming. I do not have the chance often these days to have this kind of dialogue." Leaving, I was depressed. I had the sense of his impotence—and the sense of his knowing and caring deeply, hopelessly about the impotence. He could not resign. That was not the way he played the game. And because he could not—would not—change the rules, he had been trapped by them.

. . . Newfield, with a midnight sing-in for peace in September: "A SNCC worker, up from Mississippi for a week, surveyed the scene and commented, 'I'll tell you one thing, I wouldn't want to be governed by these kids.' But a reform Democrat was moved to remark, 'Isn't it beautiful to see so many young people against the war in Viet Nam? It shows a song can combat the irrationality of government.' " . . . In November, Michael Harrington deals with the question of the moment: "Does the Peace Movement Need the Communists?" His answer: no. . . . At Christmastime, Feiffer draws a Santa Claus who talks like LBJ: "And to you children *troubled* by war toys who've written me asking for advice, I am sending 150,000 elves to advise you. If escalation of advice is needed, I promise, it *will* be done! Santa Claus is on *your* side." . . .

. . . It is also the year John Lindsay makes his race for mayor, promising to "make our great city proud again." Mary Nichols is with him at his announcement—and follows him on the campaign trail. Newfield follows his efforts to court the Reform Democrats, and the chaos that exists in their party, which is, he writes, "atomized into countless antagonistic fragments, based on personalities, ethnicity, political philosophy, and opportunism"—as two reformers, Paul O'Dwyer and West Side Congressman William Fitts Ryan, both join what becomes a four-man race for the Democratic nomination against two regulars, City Controller Abraham Beame, and Wagner's own choice to succeed himself, the City Council president, Paul Screvane. . . . Screvane tries to make an issue out of infiltration by "subversives" into the city's Mobilization for Youth program. Newfield records an interview with "tall, handsome, intellectual Daniel Patrick Moynihan, candidate for City Council President on Paul R. Screvane's team [who] hunched forward and said earnestly, 'I happen to believe there is an international Communist conspiracy, and you can look like a damn fool if you don't admit the problem exists.' "* . . . In the primary, Wolf endorses Ryan, Beame wins, and the issue becomes: Will enough liberal Democrats vote Republican to elect Lindsay? . . . "I like Lindsay," says a Feiffer character. "But I can't vote for a Republican my liberal friends tell me. Because if a Republican wins in New York it will boost Republican stock throughout the country my liberal friends tell me. Thus putting Nixon in control of the party my liberal friends tell me. So I have to vote for Beame even if I think he'll be a terrible Mayor my liberal friends tell me. To make sure Nixon doesn't run

---

*Charged in particular with being a "subversive" was none other than Marc Schleifer, who in the fifties had rebutted the prevailing liberal viewpoints on advertising and nuclear disarmament in the *Voice.* In the years since then, he had maintained his contempt for liberalism, but from the other direction. He had flipped out politically,

against Johnson in '68 and win my liberal friends tell me." . . . But to Dan Wolf, in his endorsement, the issue is rather "Is New York capable of voting itself a fighting chance for survival as a great city or is it totally committed to its own doom? Lindsay is a man of possibility. Beame is a man of no possibility. Lindsay is a seeker, a man who values creativity. He is a fallible man, but an open man. . . . Many intelligent Democrats are . . . fearful of that word 'Republican.' They display an almost hysterical dedication to the one-party system."

. . . Mary Nichols's praise of Lindsay is higher: "He offers us the only chance for a renaissance in city living," she declares. "He has a vision of a civilized city. What we will have under Beame is at worst a nightmare of machine rule, at best, a repeat of the drab, drifting and uncreative regime of Robert F. Wagner." . . . When Lindsay wins, he offers her a job in the Parks Department under his new appointee there, Thomas Hoving. "Hoving To Write 'Finis' To Era of Robert Moses," her last article predicts.

★ ★ ★

As the year began, white liberals had a candidate to succeed James Baldwin as the foil they loved to fear: playwright LeRoi Jones. When, after the murder of Schwerner, Chaney, and Goodman in Mississippi, he sat on a panel at the Village Gate with its owner Art D'Lugoff, Cecil Taylor, and Nat Hentoff, he openly stated his refusal to mourn for the two dead whites. "The high points of the unSocratic dialogue," the *Voice* account reported, were

> LeRoi Jones proposing Mao Tse-tung for Mayor of New York; the Jewish D'Lugoff calling the Jewish Hentoff "anti-Semitic"; a Negro from the audience calling the Reverend Martin Luther King a "jackass"; another Negro in the audience calling for a "black SAC"; LeRoi Jones calling a white woman in the audience a "rotten fart" and Cecil Taylor repeatedly asking D'Lugoff for a job.

joined the ultra-Maoist Progressive Labor Party, gone to Cuba to interview Robert Williams (a black fugitive wanted in America for kidnapping), and at the time Screvane and Moynihan identified him as a "subversive" was running something called the Co-Existence Bagel Shop in the Village. In later years he underwent another incarnation—he took the name Suleiman Abdullah, moved himself and his family to the Middle East, and started working for a newspaper in the Arab quarter of Jerusalem. As for Daniel Patrick Moynihan, he recovered from his defeat for City Council president to serve, in that order, as Richard Nixon's domestic affairs adviser, U.S. ambassador to India and the United Nations, and United States senator from New York.

In early 1965, there was another one of these symposia, this one at the Village Vanguard, with Jones and Jonas Mekas and avant-garde artist Larry Rivers among others, and it went the same way.

In the audience that night was a twenty-nine-year-old woman named Vivian Gornick. She was a secretary, and she, like Marlene Nadle two years before, had never written anything professionally in her life. But that night she went home and began to write, and when she was through she dropped off what she had written at the *Village Voice.* The next week Dan Wolf published the piece—"An Ofay's Indirect Address To LeRoi Jones," he titled it—and called her up asking for more.

She could write now, but only erratically. For four years she submitted a piece every few months, until in 1969 she left New York, went on a trip through New Mexico and California, came back, went to see Dan Wolf, and told him she was ready for a staff job. "You're a neurotic Jewish girl," he teased her, "you only produce one piece a year"—but he hired her.

★ ★ ★

Paul Cowan was the son of two of America's better known, wealthy, Jewish, liberal parents. Both were born in Chicago, both inherited fortunes, both got their degrees at the University of Chicago, both produced radio shows in the city. His father, Louis, went on to direct the Voice of America during the Second World War, create such blockbuster television shows as *Stop the Music* and *The $64,000 Question,* and, in 1958, became president of the CBS television network. He held the job nine months, during which time the quiz-show rigging scandals broke. Though he was not involved, he resigned anyway in December 1958, charging Dr. Frank Stanton, then president of the company, with making it impossible for him to continue. In the years that followed, Louis Cowan remained active—with the Columbia Journalism School, Brandeis University, the Ford Foundation, and the American Jewish Committee, as a backer of *Partisan Review,* an originator of the National Book Awards, and the founder of Chilmark Press. His wife, Pauline, meanwhile, got active in civil rights early. She sat on the executive board of the National Council of Negro Women, and in the summer of 1964 went down to Mississippi, taking with her a band of well-off Northern women to see the South face to face.

Her son Paul was in Mississippi that summer, too, with a Freedom Project in Vicksburg, nearly completing a journey away from the liberalism of his parents.

Paul Cowan had been educated at Choate, where he remembered

hating the Protestant ethic of the school, being teased for his Jewishness there, and at Harvard, where he remembered being too timid to express his growing radicalism in the early sixties, where he dropped out at one point to wander as far away as England and Israel and work tutoring black youngsters in Maryland. His summer in Mississippi came while he was getting his own degree at the University of Chicago, which was how he met Allard Lowenstein. And in the winter of 1965 Lowenstein invited him to New York for the screening of a new film about blacks in the South, *Nothing but a Man.* That was how he met Jack Newfield.

Newfield urged him to do a piece for the *Voice,* and he did—an analysis of the way the media had covered civil-rights activity in Maryland ("Like foreigners at a baseball game, the reporters seem totally confused by what the participants are doing") that the *Voice* published in May. On the basis of that, and Jack Newfield's recommendation, Dan Wolf hired Paul Cowan for the staff.

He began the following fall, heavily under the influence of the prose of John Dos Passos and Edmund Wilson and the chords of Phil Ochs and Judy Collins, full of romantic illusions about writing journalism-of-Americana in the tradition of Woody Guthrie and Pete Seeger, or antiwar essays in the tradition of Albert Camus. But that was not what he turned out.

The reporting he did was perfectly creditable. He got an interview with General Lewis Hershey, national director of the draft. He did pieces on Lowenstein and the House Un-American Activities Committee's hearings on the Ku Klux Klan. He wrote about Chinatown and the cops of the Seventh Precinct. He was at loser Carmine DeSapio's headquarters on Primary Night, and at loser William F. Buckley's headquarters—Buckley ran a third-party spoiler race for mayor that year—on Election Night.

But it was just that—reporting. It was not what he wanted to do. And this would-be participatory journalist found it even more galling that in his whole time at the paper, he was never once able to bring himself to write in the first person, not even when he, a young man with draft problems who was against the war, wrote about General Hershey. Dan Wolf sensed something was wrong, too. He took Paul Cowan into his office and told him what he thought it was. Your stuff is stiff, he told him. You're writing like you're still at Harvard, still trying to impress intellectually intimidating people. Too many Harvard kids have it made too early, he went on. They stay in academics or government, in Cambridge or New York or Washington, all their lives. They never have to go outside their circle of friends and connections, never have to fight for anything, take risks, test themselves, do anything new after that. There are two kinds of people, he said, people who know life from books and people who know life from living. Go out, leave New York, get some experience, he advised him, do something you haven't done before, *then* come back and try to write.

Paul Cowan was stung by what Dan Wolf said, but he appreciated it, and didn't try to deny it. As it happened, their mutual agreement that he leave the paper coincided with something else—Paul Cowan had become very vulnerable to the draft. To avoid it, and to avoid faking a deferment or applying for a C.O., which he also didn't want to do, Paul Cowan went into the Peace Corps. He spent two years there, in Ecuador, and the experience crystallized all of Paul Cowan's dissatisfactions with his country. By the time he came out, after battling the agency from the inside, he saw it as another arm of American imperialism, his own country as a "sterile paradise," and himself as, and proud to be, an "un-American," which is what he called himself in his subsequent book on the affair. His radicalization was complete.

★ ★ ★

Susan Brownmiller was another writer Dan Wolf met through Jack Newfield. Before the *Voice,* she had been around—with *Coronet, Confessions,* and *Teen* magazines, with *Newsweek* as a researcher, and finally with a TV station in Philadelphia that had just fired her. She had, on the side, taken time out for civil-rights work in 1964, and, in the early sixties, before he ended a promising political career as an East Harlem state assemblyman with an abortive run for Congress and his obsession to uncover the "conspiracy" to assassinate John F. Kennedy, had worked in the political campaigns of Mark Lane. It was there she had first met Newfield, and now in 1965 Newfield urged her to write something for the paper, which she did—about a black police undercover agent named Ray Wood, who had infiltrated the group of black militants that had just been charged with plotting to dynamite the Statue of Liberty. She went in to see Dan Wolf and gave it to him personally: "I don't know if we want to run this at all," he told her, but he took it, read it, ran it, and asked her to do more, which she also did—covering soul singer James Brown's show at the Apollo, the crime fear in Washington Square Park, and Carmine DeSapio as he hit the campaign trail in pursuit of a political comeback—and Wolf put her on staff.

She stayed for a year, moved on to ABC News for two years, came back to the paper to freelance on and off for several more years, and then was off again, to do a book about rape this time, a book that took her four years to write, which came out in 1976 under the name *Against Our Will.*

★ ★ ★

Through Susan Brownmiller, Dan Wolf met Leticia Kent. In her case, it was by a kind of default; a friend of Brownmiller's interested in urban issues but unsure of her ability, she modestly submitted a piece dealing with traffic problems. "You're right," he told her. "You really can't write"—and he gave her the piece back. She then took it to the *New Republic* and sold it there. After that, he was convinced, and in 1966 hired her for the staff, to cover politics and the city, and do "Runnin' Scared" with Jack Newfield in Mary Nichols's absence, which she did for two years.

★ ★ ★

Ever since growing up in New Jersey, as a teenager recovering from polio and forced to stay in on Friday nights while her father's friends came over to watch the fights, Barbara Long had been into sports. And ever since she was five, she had been telling herself she was going to be a writer someday.

As it was, she was twenty-five, recovered from the polio, through with high school and college, living in New York on the Lower East Side, and working at a linotype shop, before she got started. Then, in September 1962, the publicity for the Liston-Patterson heavyweight title fight got her interested again. That week she went to see a middleweight contender named Joey Archer in a bout at Madison Square Garden. She identified with Archer. Soon she was a regular at Garden fights. And when, during the newspaper strike, she heard the *Village Voice* was planning to put out a literary supplement, she cast her bread upon the waters, as she put it. She wrote a ten-page critique of the work of her favorite author, Calder Willingham, and dropped it off at the paper, hoping that they would use it as the basis for someone else to write something.

Several months went by, and nothing was published—not by her, or anybody else. Then Barbara Long got a call from Ed Fancher, apologizing. We lost your piece, he told her, and we just found it again when we were moving some furniture. They were going to publish it, and they wanted her to write other things.

By 1965, she had been reviewing for them for two years, and she had also gotten to be good friends with Joey Archer. Starting with the pretext of doing a story on him, she was by now spending every Saturday at the gym with him instead of at the printer. One day he asked to see something she'd written, and she had to tell him she hadn't written anything yet. "Fighters fight, and writers write," he told her. About that same time Dan Wolf took her out to lunch and told her much the same thing.

"But I don't have anything to write about," she told him. Yes you do, he said. You have boxing. I don't know anything about boxing, and probably neither do you, but if you want to go ahead and write something about boxing, I'll publish it.

It so happened that at the end of that month, May 1965, the long-delayed heavyweight title rematch between Muhammad Ali and Sonny Liston finally came off, in Lewiston, Maine, and that Dick Schaap, sportswriter for the *Herald-Tribune,* invited her to a closed-circuit screening at the Hotel Astor with a lot of other writers, and that one minute into the fight Liston fell to his knees, dropped to the floor, and stayed down for the mandatory ten-count, and that none of the other writers there saw Ali throw a punch.

But Barbara Long had.

"A 6- to 10-inch overhand right," she called it. "The Lady Saw the Big Punch," Dan Wolf headlined her piece, in the next week's *Voice.* "A grand fight," she declared, "and I loved the minute of it."

She became an instant literary celebrity, the woman sportswriter, the only one who saw the punch. She wrote a piece a week for the *Voice* after that, for the next thirteen weeks. She wrote about Soupy Sales, the kiddie comedian whose double-entendre jokes had made an adult phenomenon out of his TV show, and Tom Wolfe, and Nelson Algren, the Chicago novelist, and a white comedian playing the Apollo Theatre on 125th Street. She wrote about pool hustling, and a sandlot pitcher named Big Deke, and she wrote about more fights:

> A riot? Not really. A bit of hanky panky. True, also, that, in a gesture of aesthetic activism only worthy of the highest possible praise from anyone with half an ear, they threw the console organ over the mezzanine railing onto the main floor below. Pushing and pummeling, a couple of arrests, a smidgeon of terrorism. All of that, certainly, but hardly a riot.

She quit her job. She was being offered assignments with *Sports Illustrated, Esquire, Vogue, Sport.* She had become an overnight sensation.

Dan Wolf, for one, thought it might be happening too soon, that maybe Barbara Long should have written some more for the *Village Voice.* Afterwards, she thought so too.

After all that instant success, things began to catch up with her. Jean Shepherd wrote a letter to the *Voice* attacking "her obvious desire of becoming a male," which was, Shepherd wrote, "almost as sad, maybe more so, than Norman Mailer's dreams and hopes of becoming a Renaissance Man Negro." *Sports Illustrated* killed her piece on Joey Archer. She did a piece for *Sport* about a flake halfback named Joe Don Looney who was cut before it could be run. She did a piece for the *New Yorker* about the Apollo Theatre which did not run. When the magazine gave her another assignment, to go out to Johnston City, Illinois, and cover a pool hustlers' convention, she couldn't write about it for eighteen months. When she did, the magazine didn't run that one, either. She was robbed in her apartment. She signed to do an "as told to" book, and when it was all written, the subject pulled out.

In 1970, after losing to champion Emile Griffith for the second time, Joey Archer retired. And Barbara Long came back to the *Village Voice.* That summer, she went to Spain, met the legendary El Cordobes, and did ten pieces about bullfighting. And that October, she went down to Atlanta to cover the prefight buildup as Ali ended three years of enforced retirement for draft resistance and stepped into the ring again.

★ ★ ★

1966 . . . Feiffer's tiny dancer is back with "a dance to 1966" and "a more *sophisticated* approach than my dances of previous years. It rejects the too easy alienation of my dance of '65. It eliminates the stylish disillusion of my dance of '64. It shuns the boastful nonconformity of my dance of '63. It denies the egoistic idealism of my dances of '62, '61, '60 and '59. This year's dance," she continues, "is strictly pragmatic. Realistic in its appraisal of the world, unsentimental in its summing up of my position in it. A dance to 1966"—and she starts to crawl. . . . In the issue of January 13, 1966, runs the most famous of all Feiffer's protest cartoons, the one of a demonstrator arguing with a bystander and delivering the punch line, "Mister, to *my* generation, *not* wanting to grow up is a sign of maturity." . . . Stephanie Harrington on the teachers' strike at St. John's University and on the "Joyous Pornographer," Ed Sanders. Later in the year, he is the lead singer of a bawdy new rock group, the Fugs. Five years later, he is the author of *The Family,* a book on Charles Manson. . . . Jonas Mekas compares Andy Warhol's new movie, *Chelsea Girls,* to Victor Hugo, James Joyce, and the "essence and blood of our culture, the Great Society." . . . Newfield on Tom Hayden's return from Hanoi. The paper reports the ten-day fast by Robert Nichols, Mary Nichols's estranged husband, to protest the use of herbicides in Vietnam. In April, Frances Fitzgerald, the future author of *Fire in the Lake,* is sending back reports from Indochina—to the *Voice:*

> This is the war in Viet Nam. This is the army making the war in Viet Nam. This is the colonel with the well-pressed suit who directs the army to make the war in Viet Nam. This is the woman who chews beetle nuts and who presses the suit of the well-dressed colonel who directs the army to make the war in Viet Nam. This is a Viet Cong guerrilla, the son of the woman who chews beetle nuts and presses the suit of the well-dressed colonel who directs the army to make the war in Viet Nam. This is the bomb that killed the child but missed the guerrilla, the son of the woman who chews beetle nuts and presses the suit of the well-dressed colonel who directs the army to make the war in Viet Nam.

. . . Gangs of teenagers are beginning to swarm over the Village every weekend, some of them literally attacking as they invade. On St. Patrick's Weekend, police try to enforce a curfew and seal off fourteen blocks without warning, but the crowds prevent them. Few know it yet, but the East Village Scene has begun. . . . In May, California correspondents send reports back to the *Voice* on Cesar Chavez's *La Huelga* in Delano and the disappearance of acidhead novelist Ken Kesey. . . . In August, Jeff Shero writes from Texas a profile of mass murderer Charles Whitman, after he guns down thirty-eight people from a tower in Austin. . . .

. . . "Robert Kennedy is changing," writes Newfield in February, "but not the way most people think."

> . . . He is not becoming the doctrinaire, mechanistic liberal, represented by Americans for Democratic Action and the Reform Democrats. . . . Kennedy's liberalism is something else, the product of a philosophical, detached mind that learned the absurdity of existence in Dallas in 1963. Staff members speak of Kennedy's lonely country walks and his long periods of self-absorbed introspection. One has the intuition that there are shafts of Kennedy's mind that dig deeper into the bedrock of meaning than is common among public men. It is hard to imagine Hubert Humphrey daydreaming about fate, or the absurd, or pain.

. . . By September, "pressure is building up for a drive by Robert F. Kennedy for the Presidency in '68," he reports. At the end of the year he puts it in "Runnin' Scared" when Kennedy, broken up by grief over the death of a nineteen-year-old constituent in Vietnam, cancels all appointments for the day and, unannounced, goes to the boy's funeral. But his affection does not extend to Bobby's adviser, and speechwriter to his dead brother John, Theodore Sorensen. "One comes away from an interview with Robert F. Kennedy thinking of Mailer, existential torment, spontaneity, and the curiosity of the man—the latent volcano beneath the ski bum exterior," he writes. "One comes away from an interview with Theodore Sorensen with images of wind-up robots, a mind sharpened by speed reading techniques, and Bartlett's quotations—stop-lights instead of go-lights." Another politician on his list of dislikes is Nelson Rockefeller. That fall, as Rockefeller is running for and winning a third term as governor of New York, Newfield writes about him that "there is an inherent conflict between the journalist and the politician, because one is trying to reveal and the other conceal. And in this on-going, unacknowledged duel, the politician has one built-in advantage: the guilt the reporter has to feel in having the bad manners to criticize a great man after taking his time and breaking bread with him. But, occasionally, the great man is such a faker, so unresponsive in his answers, that the reporter feels no guilt at all." At the same time he likes Rockefeller's fellow Republican, Mayor John Lindsay, describing him that fall as the "Young Mayor Versus Decaying City," as the man against the sea. But, while he is doing that, Carol Greitzer, Edward Koch's co-district leader in the Village, is writing in the *Voice* that "the honeymoon is clearly over" with the mayor. The first dissatisfaction among Lindsay's original supporters has set in . . .

. . . It is the year James Meredith is shot and wounded as he marches through Mississippi, and a march for Meredith turns into a struggle for control matching the older, established, integrationist, nonviolent leaders and their white liberal allies against younger, militant, separatist blacks. The militants win. That summer, Martin Luther King's open-housing crusade in Chicago and Cicero, Illinois, fails; Richard Goldstein reports on it for the *Voice*. The civil-rights movement is over. Black Power has begun. Newfield, in his article "Two Cheers For a Death Wish," describes what is happening.

> Black Power, the substitute for love, is the new thing that has entered the bruised history of the civil rights movement, existing alongside of King's dream of freedom and Wilkins' notion of integration.

. . . It is a mixture of agony, dignity, alienation, death wish, and aggression. It is generated by the same inevitable frustration that makes the victim take on the mask of the executioner, or the girl in the television ad scream, "Mother, I'd rather do it myself . . ."

It is healthy and purgative for the black man. But for a movement seeking majority support in a 90 per cent white land, a movement rooted in humanistic values and a chiliastic vision of brotherhood, it could be the final, doomed act of a Greek tragedy. SNCC declaring for separatism seems like the troubled Oedipus gouging out his own eyes.

At Selma, he recalls, they sang " 'We Love Everybody . . .' every time one of Sheriff Jim Clark's pot-bellied deputies came into view . . . under a halo of Gandhian agape"; when a Dixie flag was waving at them from the Alabama state capitol, "we sang 'America the Beautiful' in rebuttal, and made it sound like a revolutionary anthem." This time, "some of the SNCC types on the march entered Belzoni chanting, 'we want white blood!' "

. . . That summer, there is violence in the East New York section of Brooklyn. James Kempton is there for the *Voice:*

There was small-arms fire after the Negro boys had thrown their bricks and they scrambled down Warwick Street screaming, "The Man is shooting." One of them collapsed in a doorway at the corner of Dumont Avenue. He was moaning and when a priest turned him over he saw a gash across the forehead from a broken bottle. As a siren approached, his friends tried to hobble him away. Cops in blue helmets piled out of the squad car, and grabbed the wounded boy. Another boy started bouncing high on his toes, pointing at his head, yelling, "Hit ME, mother-fucker, hit ME!" A cop threw a loose nightstick at his legs knocking him off balance, then clobbered him at the base of the neck. After he went down shots rang from a roof. The police dropped to the pavement and drew pistols, peeking over the hood of their car.

. . . That October, Dr. Robert Spike, the civil-rights activist who was Howard Moody's predecessor at Judson Memorial Church, is beaten to death in Ohio. There is an obit for him in the paper and a service at Judson. . . . And that December, the paper publishes an extraordinary letter of disaffection with the Student Nonviolent Coordinating Committee and Stokely Carmichael, by a white former civil-rights worker:

. . . I'm out and I'm mad. Emotionally and intellectually I'm mad. It's the kind of anger one might feel in, say, a love relationship, when after entering honestly you find that your loved one's been balling with someone else, and what's worse, enjoying it. . . . It has turned its back on the concept of class struggle, negated the moral battle of good vs. evil, and indeed substituted a racism that even Malcolm X in his last few months had turned his back on.

The letter describes a beating he and a white girl, plus Carmichael and three other blacks, received that summer at the Newport Folk Festival—"[we] probably had the unique distinction of being the last whites beaten in SNCC."

After the beating all the SNCC workers were buzzing with strategy, we really had those bastard cops 'cause at that moment there were 60,000 SNCC fans all in one place and ready to go. Stokely was off by himself in a kind of mystical state. As the dawn started to come up it became apparent that whatever strategy was to emerge it would be Stokely's, for the whole consensus idea, the whole concept of participation and democratic decision making, had broken down. SNCC was a one-man show.

. . . Now, I feel for the other whites in SNCC, especially the white females. I identify with all those Bronx chippies that are getting conned out of their bodies and bread by some dark-skinned sharpie over at the Annex. I feel for all the white girls who did all the unglamorous work in offices throughout the country. I guess it's the same feeling that black SNCC workers got when they watched black women getting clubbed. That's a gut reaction.

. . . Personally I could accept SNCC's new direction if they showed that this concept of black power was going to be paid for by black money, but I don't think this will happen. I never understood why whites paid money to hear LeRoi Jones insult them. Perhaps I never shared their guilt. That's a sickness and that's sick money. It's that kind of dough that SNCC will probably go after and I don't think good things can come from an organization built on sick money.

The letter is signed, "Abbie Hoffman." . . .

. . . The next week, there is a follow-up. "I am writing this in exile," Hoffman says.

That is to say, I have a fear of dying because of threats made and because of what I have learned from talking to people on both sides of the issue. I am afraid and I'm not afraid to admit it. It's an unusual kind of fear. Not the same as the fear of dying on some dark road outside of McComb, Mississippi, but a fear of dying for the wrong reasons at the hands of one of my black brothers.

I talked for hours with my closest friend in SNCC who also happens to be white, about the article, SNCC, revolution, friendship, and when it was over, we left each other, each convinced that he was right, knowing that we could never speak to each other again.

. . . "A dance to 1967," says Feiffer's dancer at the end the year. "Establishing fresh approaches to the problems of poverty, crime in the streets, Vietnam, and civil rights. A dance to 1967"—and she winds up crouching on the floor, her head between her knees, gun in hand.

★ ★ ★

When he began to write for the *Village Voice,* Andrew Sarris was already thirty-two years old. He was still living in poverty, and had been almost since he could remember.

Things had not always been that way. He had been born, in 1928, into a well-to-do family of Greeks living in Brooklyn. But the Depression changed all that. His father's real-estate business went bankrupt. The family had to move eight times in six years. At one point they all had to sleep out on a beach for three days. At another they were living in a damp, uninsulated, cement-block house on the waterfront in Queens. And for a while they were operating the restaurant at a trolley terminal. They never forgot their patrician instincts—his father "hated the Left for presuming to level him with the masses" and "we were the only relief family to vote for Alf Landon in 1936," he remembered in his memoir of the experience. But though "it was the difference between being merely broke and being really poor," it was not enough. His father, out of work for ten years, tried his hand at a boat rental business and finally went to work as a dishwasher in the winter of 1941. Andrew Sarris grew up a sickly child, chronically underweight and, after two operations for mastoids, partly deaf. When he was fifteen, his father died of leukemia. Seventeen years later, in the summer of 1960, he was still living with his mother, in a small apartment, eking out an income with odd jobs here and there.

The summer of 1960 was a good time to be a film buff. The foreign film had finally found an *aesthete* audience in America. The New Wave was on its way over from France—Godard had started it the year before with *Breathless*. Auteurism—the school of criticism that saw film not as "movies" but as an art form, one in which every director left a signature on every work—was gaining influential adherents.

Andrew Sarris loved film. When he was a kid, his father would come home and describe to the family some movie "a friend" had just seen, always using that cover to hide the fact that it was he himself, frustrated in his search for any kind of work, who had been the one to go. By his late teens, Sarris was absorbed in the medium. In 1954, just out of the army, studying for a dramatic-arts degree at Columbia, he had met Jonas Mekas, and written for *Film Culture* almost from the beginning. So when, in the summer of '60, Mekas wanted to take a vacation, and needed someone to fill in writing his *Voice* movie column while he was gone, he chose Andrew Sarris.

The movie Sarris chose to review in Mekas's absence was *Psycho*, Alfred Hitchcock's new thriller about a homicidal maniac with a split personality. He more than liked it—he predicted it was going to become a classic: "Hitchcock is the most daring avant-garde film-maker in America today," and "besides making previous horror films look like variations of *Pollyanna, Psycho* is overlaid with a richly symbolic commentary on the modern world as a public swamp in which human feelings and passions are flushed down the drain."

The movie, and the review, had both been too much for Jerry Tallmer, and Tallmer said as much. But Andrew Sarris was right, as it turned out, and by 1963—with Tallmer gone, with Mekas getting more and more immersed in the underground cinema—he was appearing regularly, splitting the cinema beat with Mekas.

That suited Sarris fine, since he preferred the commercial cinema anyway—the Hollywood film, he felt, was at least as progressive, as innovative, as exciting as the underground. That was only one of the ways in which he differed with the sensibilities of the readers of the *Village Voice,* or with what he thought those sensibilities were. He thought of himself as a conventional mainstream critic. He believed in the value of entertainment for the mass audience. He had his standards—narrative, characterization, plot. He had his favorites, but his favorites were not always their favorites, and his politics was not always their politics. He did not like *Dr. Strangelove* in 1964 and he did not like *Hearts and Minds* in 1974. He was a Kennedy, liberal Democrat, he had traveled that distance and no more, and he was dubious about anybody who said they had, about the sincerity of New Left values and those who espoused them, it seemed to him, too eagerly.

In May of 1962, for instance, he wrote a humorous account for the paper of a birthday party, starring Frank Sinatra and Marilyn Monroe among others, thrown for John Kennedy at Madison Square Garden. But, he wrote in the same piece, "he is fighting as well as he can, and until the opposition nominates Albert Schweitzer, Bertrand Russell, Murray Kempton, or what erroneous legends have made of FDR, he is the purest liberal we are ever going to have."

The result was that he got it from both ends, at least in his own mind. He, with his aristocratic attitudes, was leading a marginal existence, living on scraps. For four or five years he would have gone almost anywhere else to write, but nobody wanted him, and he was under no illusions about it. For years, he was self-conscious that his colleagues in film criticism were refusing to accept him or to take him seriously, that he had a reputation as a "screwball" who worked for "an underground rag" that he had to live down.

But Dan Wolf and Ed Fancher protected him, so he said later, and the *Voice* made him. By appearing regularly, he learned his craft, learned how to spill his guts out on paper, to define himself, to write about movies his way. As his tone became confident, he came to respect himself, and others came to respect him.

In a profession enamored first of Bosley Crowther, with his priggish conservatism, and later of John Simon, with his polysyllabic egotism, Andrew Sarris was a breath of fresh air. He wrote film reviews for the common man. In them, he so systematically violated the standing rules against the use of the first person that, with his informal, intuitive style, he created an entirely new dimension of film criticism, one where the reviewer's own feelings and subjective moods came to equal the standard critical criteria. Above everything else, he was at all times overwhelmingly literate. After only a few years of appearing regularly in the *Village Voice,* Andrew Sarris had emerged, and earned his reputation, as the foremost, and most formidable, American exponent of auteurism.

He had also revealed himself to be a man of many more interests, and of a much wider range, than he might have seemed at first, as he proved in May of 1970. That month, after long being the doormats of the National Basketball Association, the New York Knickerbockers won the league championship for the first time, beating the Los Angeles Lakers and their center, Wilt Chamberlain, in the finals. For eleven years, Chamberlain, a seven-foot-plus leviathan, had been breaking every personal record in the books of the game. But only once had he been able to interrupt the dynasty of Bill Russell's Boston Celtics. Now, with Russell in retirement, he had lost again, to a team that had never been in the finals before, whose own center, Willis Reed, had literally limped onto the court with a painfully injured hip for the seventh and deciding game and inspired his teammates to a thorough thrashing of the full-strength Lakers, and Chamberlain, a moody man long since nominated as the Sonny Liston of the sport by the working press, seemed forever locked into the role of loser.

The next week, there appeared in the pages of the *Village Voice,* full of lucid analysis and energetic interpretation equal to the work of the most facile sportswriter, an article in defense of the career of Wilt Chamberlain, arguing the case that all those years Russell had been beating Chamberlain he had had the better team playing behind him, that Chamberlain's voluntary transformation in recent years from scoring machine to complete and selfless ball player had been all but ignored. That "even athletes who have slugged sportswriters have received more favorable press and media coverage than Wilt has. He is never given credit for exceptional performance or generous impulses. He is taken for granted as a brutal fact of nature." The article came from, of all people, Andrew Sarris, the paper's erstwhile film critic.

After all those prolonged hungry years, Andrew Sarris suddenly became a success in the 1960s. His work was published elsewhere. He began to teach, first at Yale, then at New York University. In 1969, he joined the faculty of Columbia University. That same year, he married Molly Haskell, a woman he had met when she worked for the French Film Office in New York and provided him with information for his reviews. And in the 1970s, while he was serving as chairman of the National Society of Film Critics, she was becoming a very formidable film critic in her own right, under her own name, doing for the feminist perspective in films what he had done for auteurism years before. And, like her husband, she was appearing in the pages of the *Village Voice,* every week.

★ ★ ★

He had "this crazy Saroyan idea that you had to be published before you were 30," but in October of 1966 Joe Flaherty was twenty-nine already and still had not been published.

He was a drifter, a well-read high-school dropout. He had been born, the son of immigrants, into an Irish enclave of Brooklyn, a neighborhood of double-decker two-family houses, stickball in the streets, wild wakes, and beer blasts for boys from the neighborhood who had made it good and passed the civil service test. When he was seven, the body of his murdered dockworker father had been fished out of the Gowanus Canal. In his teens, he had spent his time ingeniously crashing the movie theaters of Manhattan and falling in love with the detective novels of Mickey Spillane rather than attending either of the two schools—a Catholic prep school and a vocational high school—that he was forced to leave. He lost two jobs on Wall Street—one, on the floor of the exchange, for slipping upstairs the bogus news of a huge sale of General Motors stock that sent GM soaring on the Big Board, the other in a brokerage house for forgetting to cap the mimeograph machine one day and spraying ink over everybody in the office. He tried one blue-collar job after another—on a laundry truck, in an airplane parts factory, packing candy for A&P. He joined the army, and saw Germany. He went out to Los Angeles, and got married. He started to write, but all he got was rejection slips. He came back to New York, took a job on the docks, and was working as a stringer for his neighborhood newspaper, the *Park Slope News,* the night he was on his way home from work and came out of the subway to find a crowd gathered.

John Lindsay was coming, to speak in Grand Army Plaza on behalf of his beleaguered civilian review board, scheduled for extinction in a police-inspired referendum only a few weeks away. Joe Flaherty decided to stay, and worked his way through the crowd to get up close and hear him speak.

But he could not hear him speak, not with the volley of abuse being hurled his way by the crowd in general, and by one very fat, very loud organizer for the Conservative Party, right near Flaherty, in particular. As soon as Lindsay mounted the platform, the heckler began chanting, "Stop the civilian review board." Joe Flaherty had had enough. He whirled around. "If you don't shut the fuck up and let the fucking mayor speak," he told him, "I'm gonna slap you one right on the jaw." The man took one look at Joe Flaherty—burly, bearded, six-foot-plus, huge head, ham hands, longshoreman's rig—and shut up. The mayor of New York took one look at Joe Flaherty and winked. Lindsay finished his speech and went on his way. Joe Flaherty went home and started to write. About what had happened. About what he was thinking.

> They all stood there waiting for the helicopter to come down. You had the feeling some of them wouldn't have minded if it didn't make it on its own power . . .
>
> An Irish guy in a tweed sports jacket was instructing the crowd that a "yes" vote on the referendum was a vote for Lindsay. In a sentence he told what the Conservative Party in this city is all about.
>
> He was a big kid but not like his ancestors who worked the docks or the ones who wore shamrock-embroidered trunks

under the Garden lights on long-ago Friday nights. He had the weight, but it was going nowhere. His backside looked like a giant teardrop, probably from sitting too long on stools in the Knights of Columbus drinking 10-cent beer with his own kind to the tune of ''The Ballad of the Green Beret.'' . . . He said the Review Board was another offspring of Earl Warren's court and hadn't Warren ''banned school prayer''?

. . . You couldn't help thinking that the last time he saw the inside of a church was when he rifled the poor box when he was sixteen. . . .

A nice-looking kid in a blazer spotted Lindsay coming through the crowd and began to shout, ''Here comes the guy who's for social security raises, welfare, and unions.'' Here is this kid who never said ''en garde'' to his chin with a Wilkinson sword blade sounding like an honest-to-God John Paul Getty, crying creeping socialism and the whole lot . . .

. . . A woman in the rear of the crowd contorted her face into an anguished prune and began to recite a litany of hate at the mayor. ''You are for niggers, taxes, and filth, and you are through in this city.'' . . .

Much sport has been made of Lindsay's reference to New York as a ''fun city''; not enough attention has been paid to the validity of his statement. He's right; we have all the trappings of joy. We have a skyline that sends foreign visitors back to their homes with tales of a storied kingdom. Stand outside any office building in midtown, and the most gorgeous women in the world spin through revolving doors. On a summer afternoon you can go to the Big A and see Kelso and Gun Bow go head and head for a mile and a quarter in a rhymed couplet. Sit in the grass with a can of beer and watch the grace of two Puerto Rican teams playing softball. Their delight is expressed in their language, as quick and exciting as a young Ray Robinson's left jab. You can drink German beer in Luchow's on Sunday afternoon or belt boilermakers in Ireland's 32, or sip brandy after the theater in Shor's next to Gleason, Arcaro, and Graziano. You can put on a tie on Sunday and go to a museum and see anything from a brown and gold Rembrandt to a red and white Campbell's soup can. When the wife's lumpy mashed potatoes and overdone steak get you down, with a subway token and five bucks you can sample anything from flaming shish kebab to Indian curried lamb. And if you are looking for music, you just have to move up and down the scale of the city's streets. From the Met to

Arthur to Roseland to a dime-a-dance joint, from the Clancy
Brothers lamenting about "The Troubles" to Miriam Makeba
clicking her African magic . . .

What the hell has happened to us? New Yorkers have lost
their sense of style. . . . To hear the critics of this city you
would think we were something out of a Hogarth drawing.
Nothing but rape, drunkenness, and violence. . . . We have
all the intrigue of the Casbah, yet our souls are somewhere in
Levittown. . . .

He stayed up all night writing it, writing his heart out, and when he
handed it in his paper killed it, which is about what he expected. Joe
Flaherty thought no more about it for two weeks. And then one day he
got a call·at work from an old friend of his, congratulating him on the
great piece he had written for the *Village Voice* that week.

Joe Flaherty didn't think it was a very funny joke. For one thing, he
had already *read* that week's issue, and seen nothing in there by him.
"Read me something," he demanded over the phone. And, on the other
end of the line, his friend—who had not seen the piece before—began to
read it back to him, line by line.

He went out to the nearest newsstand and bought up every copy.
Sure enough, unbeknownst to Joe Flaherty, two editors on his paper
had liked his piece, submitted it to Dan Wolf, and signed his name to
the cover letter. Dan Wolf had not only run the piece, he had given it a
banner headline across the top of page one: "Why Has the Fun Fled
Fun City?" And Joe Flaherty had read through that week's issue
without even noticing it.

He read it now, though, every copy all the way through, at the
nearest bar he could find, with more tears rolling down his cheeks, and
more Irish whiskey pouring down his throat with every reading. Joe
Flaherty had been published, at last.

The next Monday he went straight to the *Voice* offices after work
and asked to see Wolf. He was still in his longshoreman's rig, and
guessed—correctly—later on that it appeared some burly Irishman had
come in to kill the editor. He wasn't in, the receptionist explained.
Flaherty left his name. "Joe Flaherty!" she said. "We've been trying to
get in touch with you. We didn't know where to send the check." All of
a sudden Dan Wolf was in.

Flaherty came upstairs and met him. They hit it off. How would you
like to go cover the police victory party on Election Night? Wolf asked.
So, the night the returns came in and the civilian review board
underwent death by referendum, Flaherty found himself in the Com-

modore Hotel, in a knock-down-drag-out fistfight with one surly cop, being hustled out of there just in time before being set upon by many others. That became his story. Then he covered the Bowery the night of the first freeze. Next he wrote a disparaging report on the progress of a welterweight boxer jointly owned by Norman Mailer, George Plimpton, and Pete Hamill. Hamill wrote a long letter responding to the article. Flaherty wrote a response to Hamill. It was a *bona fide* feud, the kind Literary New York loves. Next thing he knew, Joe Flaherty was being offered an assignment with the *New York Times* to do a profile for the Sunday magazine of a bookie he knew. He was off and running.

The tracks. The ring. The movies. The Church. The bars. That was where Joe Flaherty came from. That was what he knew. That was how he wrote, in an up-front, no-bullshit, tough-guy shorthand full of working-class wisecracks. He was a raconteur of rum and Romanism, a chronicler of Irish lowlife, a dispenser of dockworker and detective-novel wisdom, and he had no pretensions about being anything else. If other people did not care for his *persona* as the Jock Lush, they could take it or leave it. His *macho* was undeniable, but in an old-fashioned, romantic, positive sort of way, and his self-deprecation about his own manhood bordered on the hilarious. His politics were left of center, but with a small *l,* because, unlike so many others at the *Voice* who talked about the working class, Joe Flaherty *was* working-class. He had been there, and he never forgot it. Thus, when the feminist movement got underway with a day of marches and job actions in the summer of 1970, he wrote this rebuttal:

> What of those poor boobs of men who go out daily to work the docks, carry furniture, climb the high iron, and drive trucks, who mistakenly think they are doing it with the age-old hope that their sons and daughters won't be subjected to such drudgery, only to learn they have been exercising their chauvinism while they jailed their mates at home with the brooms and the kids? For shame, brothers, for not liberating your women for such higher purposes as liberating McSorley's and the men's bar at the Biltmore or picketing the Miss America contest or whistling at construction workers . . .
>
> Women rightfully want power, but what they fail to see is that most men are powerless. . . . If housework is a drudgery, it is no more so than the majority of work offered in this country. . . .

He did profiles of his friends, of George Kimball, the wacko one-eyed bartender, when he left the Village to run for sheriff in Kansas, and Saul Alinsky, the radical organizer, when he died. He covered the races. He covered the ring, never joining the crowded Ali cult. And, when Sonny Liston, the ferocious ex-con who had punched the great black-and-white-together hope, Floyd Patterson, out of the title, before in turn losing it to Ali, died suddenly, Flaherty alone among the sporting press tried to compose a sympathetic obituary:

> Well, the reader may justifiably say that the back of the hand is the only tribute a blackguard deserves. After all, the man was busted twenty times. He was a union goon, ran with the mob, cracked heads with the same niftiness a short-order cook prepares "two over light." . . . In short, Sonny was a badass nigger.
>
> Was he the bastard everyone says he was? To many, yes. To others, such as Claude Brown, he was the only man alive who could have quelled the Watts riots. I'm not pleading for his life-style—a bastard maybe, or, perhaps more fair, he did bastardly deeds. But he should be judged in context. He was better than the sport he practiced and the men who rule it. . . . And he was a lot better than the hucksters for sport who now so cavalierly dismiss his life.

He covered baseball, and the World Series. He covered football, and the Super Bowl, including one with so many fumbles, interceptions, and penalty flags that sitting through it, he wrote, "was like watching two sleazy stand-up comics trying to outdo each other. First, a slightly off-color joke, then a blue joke, a swish joke, a bathroom joke, and, finally, one dropping his pants for the final points on the applause meter." He covered politics, and the city. And if it was true that he sometimes cluttered his prose with one old-movie metaphor too many, or loaded it up with too much code decipherable only by another Irish Catholic, it was likewise true that he could at all times be counted on to be entertaining in an irreverent way that was all his own, and that at no time did he ever take himself too seriously.

"Do you *really* believe that?" Wolf would ask him when he would bring his copy in. To Flaherty, Wolf was "a gentleman," one of the highest compliments he could pay anyone, and every Friday morning when he went in to pick up his check at Sheridan Square he would stop by the editor's office and shoot the breeze till noontime. They would talk about the docks, his writing, anything at all, and Wolf would find things in him that he did not know anyone else but him could see. "Look, Flaherty," he would interrupt, "you've seen both sides. You've seen the workers and *their* bullshit. And you've seen the writers and *their* bullshit." Wolf saw the wild streak Flaherty knew was there, let him know he liked it, encouraged him to make use of it. After his writing had appeared regularly in the *Voice,* it began appearing elsewhere. In 1970 he went on the *Voice* staff; Joe Flaherty would never have to work the docks again.

Sports and politics were Flaherty's *fortes,* but they were not his only *fortes.* Years after he had established himself at the *Voice,* he developed another specialty—satire.

It began with an article by Merle Miller in the *New York Times Magazine* in early 1971, in which the author confessed his homosexuality and recounted years of agony in the closet. It continued with a two-part answer, "Heteros have problems too," by an Andrew Sarris in dead earnest, in the *Village Voice* early that February. But it did not conclude until a piece, "Asexuals Have Problems Too," by "Harold Nederland," was "submitted" and run by the *Voice* a few issues later.

> . . . What about us asexuals? Is there a Merle Miller or an Andrew Sarris around to champion our cause? You bet not.
>
> They must think it's a big thing to confess how many broads they've laid or boys they've buggered. Where is the man or woman with the courage to say the whole sex business leaves them feeling like a limp noodle? . . .
>
> Does anyone realize the early torment of an asexual? To have his father buy him a bike for Christmas, and when the salesman says, "A boy's or girl's model?" his father replies, "It doesn't matter." . . .
>
> And the social life of an asexual? I am continually invited to orgies to pour the vin rosé and roll the joints. (My friends call me a sexual lazy Susan.) When a friend's wife gets drunk early at a party, the husband not only asks me to take her home, but queries whether I would mind being sure she gets into her pajamas! And God, the agony of the family Thanksgiving dinner when someone says, "Pass the mashed potatoes to It."

It was by Flaherty, and it was "a very, very funny piece," said none other than Merle Miller, who had started the whole thing himself, in a letter to the paper. "And there aren't many of those in *The Voice* or any place else," he volunteered.

But there was one more at least, and it appeared in the *Village Voice* that summer, right after the Pentagon Papers crisis was over. This time, Flaherty used his own byline. "Last Friday I received a document that may or may not have national significance," he introduced himself, "from a longtime confidante, Lola, the hairdresser at the Hotel Pierre," which, to those who knew such things, just happened to be a spot frequently visited by Martha Mitchell, wife of the attorney general of the United States and the terror of the late-night toll call. Flaherty further averred that said "document had been left behind by . . . a middle-aged woman reeking of some unidentifiable odor who had come in for a bouffant tease and who fell asleep under the hair dryer while making a series of raucous phone calls" and "contained the minutes of a meeting that had taken place in a location called the Oval Room with five gentlemen in attendance, identified only by their first names and last initials."

Then, without further adieu, "What follows is for perversity or posterity, depending on the reader:"

> . . . SPIRO A.: The way I see '72, Chief, is a moral muscle maneuver between the lovers of law and the fanatics of ferment.
>
> JOHN M.: Save that shit for when you're on tour, Spiro. . . .
>
> RICHARD N.: Well, if we've got nothing positive going for us, who has an opinion on where we're the most vulnerable? (A collective silence, except for a voice unheard till now.)
>
> HENRY K.: It's ze var.
>
> RICHARD N.: The var? I mean, the war, Henry?
>
> HENRY K. (smiling knowingly): It's contagious, isn't it, mein Herr? . . .
>
> RICHARD N.: All right, Henry, the floor is yours.
>
> HENRY K.: Today ze floor, tomorrow . . .
>
> RONALD Z.: Do you mean, Henry, we should release the files and indict the opposition as warmongers?
>
> HENRY K.: Exactly. Though, mein God, forgive me, zey don't deserve zat esteemed title.
>
> SPIRO A.: A baffling but brilliant battle plan of colossal chicanery.
>
> JOHN M. (looking at Spiro A. with disgust): Jumping Jesus! . . . But it's illegal to release secret documents. After all, we're the party of law and order.
>
> HENRY K.: Exactly. After ze files are released and do zeir damage, ve go to court and try to suppress zem. To coin a phrase—a Yankee Reichstag.

SPIRO A.: Notwithstanding its nebulous nihilism, Chief, I would note that's a Nazi nifty.

HENRY K.: *Danke,* mein dolt. . . . Ze papers must reach ze New York *Times.*

SPIRO A.: What! That rag for the rich, the reformed, and the refined? Revolting!

HENRY K.: Precisely. Ve must feign ze fink is foreign to us. (Looking at Spiro) Mein God, vill someone alleviate zis alliterative ass from ze room before ve all suffer from syntactical symptoms? . . .

SPIRO A.: Sorry, Chief, but it just struck me. When the papers disappear, we can call them the Purloined Pentagon Papers.

RICHARD N. (rises and hugs him): You alliterative angel. (Spiro exits) . . .

HENRY K.: It's a shame, mein leader, ve couldn't have held zis meeting in a beer hall.

Joe Flaherty wrote those lines nearly three years before a set of documents called the White House Transcripts was made public. In this case, Life imitated Art imitating Life, but it was not nearly as funny.

★ ★ ★

1967 . . . Harlem's flamboyant congressman, Adam Clayton Powell, is unseated per order of his colleagues in the House of Representatives. Marlene Nadle writes this profile of him: "Adam Clayton Powell would make a great Broadway musical."

The swagger. The cigar. The beautiful girls. The boys from Bimini hymn-singing "Where He Leads Me, I Will Follow," while escorting Adam—in his Bermuda shorts—to a relaxed game of dominoes. Adam coming back with a few "Dominus vobiscums" and his favorite line, "I'm just a humble parish priest," while settling in next to his milk and Cutty Sark. Scenes of Adam: feet on desk, phone tucked jauntily against his ear, greeting LBJ with, "Hello, Baby!" Scenes of the Reverend Mr. Powell giving fiery sermons at the Abyssinian Baptist Church, then receiving his flock at the Red Rooster bar a short way up the block.

. . . In May, when the *World-Journal-Tribune* folds, she is there following Jimmy Breslin around on the last day:

Breslin . . . was passing through on his way to the bar. . . . [He] immediately got into an eyeball-to-eyeball confrontation with the uniformed guard whose spread-eagle body was blocking the door to the inner office. Thrusting his head forward like a fighting cock and speaking directly to the guard's left nostril, Breslin said, in a very controlled, very polite voice: "Do me a favor and take your fucking arm off the door."

The guard didn't budge.

Breslin, not used to being refused, tried again. "How would you like to be bashed in the nose?"

The guard didn't budge, he just pulled rank. Breslin backed off.

After all, what the hell is a newspaperman without a newspaper? Or even with one these days. Fat Jimmy walked away from a fight, maybe for the first time. He, like most of the W-J-T reporters that day, seemed drained of real anger, of all emotion, except, perhaps, disgust.

Hanging on to his yellow note pad, Breslin went up to the sixth-floor city room to join the other irrelevant men. As he moved among them, he kept muttering, "I should have gone to law school. I should have gone to law school."

. . . In July, when Newark blows, she is there.

. . . 3000 National Guardsmen in khaki fatigues and 375 state policemen in blue and gold patrolled beside the Newark city police. Each moved through the streets with his finger on the trigger of his gun. Some were more anxious than others to pull it, to knock off a black bastard, to get themselves a commie. It was open season on our bogeymen.

But there were others. A young, very blond, very scared Guardsman frantically waved down a police car to try to convince the cops to go after a looter, so he wouldn't have to do it. Another young Guardsman, a Negro, who was brought up in Newark's Central Ward—the black ghetto—was being torn by a double loyalty. He said he was just praying he wouldn't see anyone he knew.

And then there was Lt. James Hine. Hine, an advertising executive, could not quite get over the incongruity of fighting a battle alongside a laundromat. Even while he kept his .45 levelled at a two-story frame building on South Orange

Avenue, he kept shaking his head in amazement. ''What am I
doing here,'' he asked, ''just what the hell am I doing here?''

. . . And in October, when Che Guevara is caught and killed on a
guerrilla mission in Bolivia, she is there, too.

> The copter landed in a spot far from the swelling crowd,
> which, except for the press, was held back by soldiers with
> bayonets. . . . The corpse was hustled into a Chevrolet van
> which was pursued across the airport by journalists in jeeps.
> They passed crates of napalm and stopped in front of a small,
> three-sided shed that was to serve as a makeshift mortuary.
> A uniformed, stocky, blonde man in his 30s emerged from
> the van and shouted, ''Let's get the hell out of here.'' Later, he
> denied any knowledge of English. . . .
> The body was fingerprinted, then stripped of its clothes and
> washed down. Physicians, assisted by a beaming nun, pre-
> pared it for embalming. They incised the neck. The nun, still
> smiling, handed them forceps, scissors, and swabs. Report-
> ers, clinging to their vantage point, counted bullet holes; two
> in the neck and one in the thorax. There was also a wound in
> the abdomen. . . .
> Outside the shed, more soldiers held the crowd back with
> bayonets—but they couldn't quiet them. ''SHOW US CHE.
> SHOW US CHE,'' they shouted. When the doctors had
> finished, they dressed Che Guevara in his bloody uniform and
> raised him up on the stretcher for all to see.

. . . John Lindsay institutes a system whereby some aide stands by at
City Hall as "Mayor for the Night," and Leticia Kent covers Mary
Nichols's night. . . . Stephanie Harrington eulogizes the pacifist A. J.
Muste when he dies in February. . . . That month, in his last major
fight before his date with the draft, Ali, out for blood, pummels
challenger Ernie Terrell. "The Persecution of Ernie Terrell directed by
the Marquis de Sade as played by Muhammad Ali," Joe Flaherty
labels it. . . .
    . . . That May, Flaherty covers a prowar march uptown as it turns
into a riot. Newfield covers the opening of the Electric Circus in the
Village. That October, Newfield covers the March on the Pentagon to
stop the war. Leticia Kent covers the murders of Groovy and Linda
Fitzpatrick, a hippie and his runaway girlfriend, in the East Village. A
report arrives from Greece describing the right-wing regime that has

taken over there. . . . Feiffer, in the strip, on the war, with a mock newscast: "The Defense Department announced today that in addition to building a mined barrier across South Viet Nam it is also planning to build mined barriers across the White House, the State Department, and the Pentagon." On Black Power, with an impassive-looking brother—shades, Afro, and goatee—giving this monologue: "As a matter of racial pride we want to be called 'blacks.' Which has replaced the term 'Afro-American'—which replaced 'Negroes'—which replaced 'colored people'—which replaced 'darkies'—which replaced 'blacks.' " . . .

. . . Margot Hentoff, in her "Letter to New York" column, mocks the Left, decries the "general era of *mea culpa*," argues against legalizing abortion when Howard Moody writes an article for it, and when the film *Battle of Algiers* premieres, reviews the audience, sardonically:

> Its message was telegraphed loud and clear. Watch out, Baby, you can't stand in the way of the future. No matter what you fatcats do, the oppressed will inexorably rise.
>
> From the beginning, it was obvious that a number of parallels could be drawn between the French position in Algeria and our own policies both abroad and at home, between the rebels in the Casbah and our own nationalist leaders in our own "Arab quarters." And, as the film rolled on, the audience drew every one of them. Waves of applause broke out at scenes of terrorism against the French colonials, at individual acts of murder. At times, there were cheers. "Saigon next." A man shouted as the Algerians blew up a crowded cafe in the French quarter. "What do you people want?" a French officer asked on screen. The audience laughed in understanding and waited for the next bomb blast.
>
> They really loved the movie, those people in Philharmonic Hall, many of them dressed in dinner clothes and holding invitations to a post-performance champagne reception. If it was the intention of the festival's program committee to *epater* the bourgeoisie with its choice of an opening film, then it entirely misread the temper of the bourgeoisie. It doesn't *epater* these days, it just has fun. Has there ever before been such a time when the oppressors themselves sit and applaud their own symbolic murder?

. . . "Robert F. Kennedy's followers believe he must speak up now, or jeopardize his status as an alternative," Jack Newfield argues again at the beginning of the year. Jules Feiffer thinks so too. He draws a cartoon of two tiny RFK-look-alikes—"The Bobby Twins"—who face each other underneath parallel statements in each panel: "One is a Good Bobby. One is a Bad Bobby. The Good Bobby is a courageous reformer. The Bad Bobby makes deals. The Good Bobby sent Federal troops down South to enforce civil rights. The Bad Bobby appointed racist judges down South to enforce civil rights. The Good Bobby is a fervent civil libertarian. The Bad Bobby is a fervent wire tapper. The Good Bobby is ill at ease with liberals. The Bad Bobby is ill at ease with grown ups. If you want *one* Bobby to be your President you will have to take both . . . for Bobbies are widely noted for their family unity." In March, Newfield writes of "the change in Robert Kennedy since he discovered a world he never knew in 1960 in the hills of West Virginia. . . . The young man who grew up with cardinals, generals, big pols, and millionaires around the dinner table has become a hope—and possibly a hero—to radicals like poet Robert Lowell and columnist Murray Kempton." In April he predicts "a real possibility that the President will withdraw from the race. . . . My perception of LBJ is that, like Sonny Liston, he is a bully with a quitter's heart, that he will not run if he thinks he cannot win." But in June Kennedy daunts his supporters when he not only appears on the same dais with Johnson at a fund-raiser, but, as Leticia Kent acidly reports, "swelled the President's chest—with unequivocal praise. Kennedy said the President is the personification of 'greatness' as defined by Webster. . . . Unless there was a Trojan Horse somewhere, Johnson didn't mind. Bobby Kennedy and his dictionary were on the President's side." And Newfield finds a new object for his affections: John Lindsay. "The intangible, almost mystical bitch-goddess, Public Opinion, which is now making a slow, inexorable swing away from Robert F. Kennedy," he finds that spring, "is beginning to move toward the Mayor of New York."

> They still taunt him as "the niggers' Mayor" in Queens, but the mass media, the intellectual elite, the educated middle class—the opinion makers—have, after a dance of doubt, voted thumbs up on that ballsy boy scout. Especially away from satiated Manhattan—in Washington, D.C., and in California—political animals think more and more about Lindsay as a live horse for some future Presidency. His naive handling of the transit strike, his St. Paul's chapel rhetoric, his review-board defeat are receding from memory. What is most striking now is the carefully crafted image of the actor-liberal-glam-

orous Mayor, walking the squalid slums, joking with Johnny
Carson. It is the picture of a man slowly finding a national
constituency, a Jimmy Walker with character.

. . . "This sniper-filled summer of 1967 has stretched John Lindsay,"
he writes in September, after the longest hot summer of race rioting in
the cities. But still Newfield cannot forget or transfer his loyalty from
Kennedy. That month, "Runnin' Scared" carries an item that a poll
taken by the White House has shown Kennedy to be Johnson's most
potent running mate in 1968. "But despite the poll and the rumors,"
Newfield insists, "there is no chance that Senator Robert F. Kennedy
would run with Johnson. In fact, RFK intimates now think that the
odds are better that he would run against the President than with him.
One of these intimates said Kennedy is now 'rethinking all his options
for 1968,' after concluding six months ago that his only option was to
bite the bullet and campaign for Johnson. On the crucial issue of
Vietnam, Kennedy is further from the Administration than he has
been at any point since he entered the Senate." . . .

. . . Nevertheless Kennedy will not run, and the Dump-Johnson
forces go ahead without him. "Runnin' Scared" reports at the end of
August, "A small innocuous office called Concerned Democrats will
open next week with no publicity. Actually, it will be the headquarters
of a nationally-coordinated drive to defeat Lyndon B. Johnson in the
Democratic Presidential primaries next year." Two weeks later the
Village Independent Democrats vote "overwhelmingly" to oppose
LBJ's renomination in 1968, reversing a vote on a similar disendorse-
ment taken earlier in the year. And at the end of November, forced to
look elsewhere for a candidate, Allard Lowenstein's anti-Johnson
movement settles on Eugene McCarthy. Newfield has praise—"There is
something about Eugene McCarthy that makes one think that if a
bunch of tough kids were terrorizing the passengers in a subway car, he
would be the one improbable square to put down his book, get up, and
chase them onto the platform." But at year's end, having seen
McCarthy, a brittle and often difficult man, in action for only a month,
he is totally disgusted: "Let the unhappy, brutal truth come out.
Eugene McCarthy's campaign is a disaster. It has been run as if King
Constantine was the manager."

McCarthy's speeches are dull, vague, and without either
balls or poetry. He is lazy and vain. . . . Every professional
politician who has had any direct experience with McCarthy's
campaign has come away in desperation. It is so inept it

almost seems that only a paranoid view of his intentions can explain its failure.

. . . And after the Pentagon March, an ominous, prophetic open letter arrives at the *Voice* from antiwar organizer Jerry Rubin announcing that the violence that October weekend "marked the beginning of disruption as a leading strategy for the white peace movement."

> Johnson had to send his busy 82nd Airborne Division, veterans of the Dominican Republic and Detroit, to protect the Pentagon because he knew damn well that there were thousands of angry young people there who had come to tear that place up.
> And that's where it's at. We're angry. We're angry like Che. . . . We are going to screw up this society. We can force Johnson to bring the 82nd Airborne Division and 100,000 more troops to Chicago next August to protect the Democratic National Convention. With luck, Johnson will get himself nominated under military guard.

★ ★ ★

In the years since he had worked and written for Dan Wolf, Howard Smith had been around. He had been a photojournalist and cameraman, tried to become a producer of plays, motorcycled across America, and gone to Europe. Now he was back in the Village. His marriage had failed, he was working as a salvager and seller of antiques, he was unhappy with his life. He was also still seeing Dan Wolf once a week or so, and it was on one of these visits Wolf stopped by to tell him, "I'm thinking of starting a new column," and to ask him if he would be interested in doing it.

The column was to be a collection of short items full of slices of hip life—trivia, gossip, new fads, vital information. That was how Howard Smith saw it. That was how Dan Wolf saw it, except that Dan Wolf only saw it about every two or three weeks, when he wanted it every week. Because of that, Dan Wolf did something he rarely did with a writer: he lost his temper. "You write this column every week, not every two or three weeks," he ordered Howard Smith. "If you skip once more, it's not going to run again."

Howard Smith hated Dan Wolf for saying that, but he gave him a column every week for the next six months, until he realized that he was hooked. He'd never drop it now, he knew, and he knew that Wolf had been right.

Something happened to Howard Smith as a result of that column. "Scenes," he called it—appropriately, since other people began to read it to keep up on the latest trends in the counterculture scene. Then they took the next step—they began to call him directly. Helen Gurley Brown, editor of *Cosmopolitan,* when she was thinking of starting a youth magazine, was first. They met, they hit it off, and she introduced him to Dick Deems, an officer in the Hearst publishing organization, who eventually interceded on the paper's behalf when it was having distributor problems. When that happened, the *Voice* got on more newsstands everywhere, which boosted its growth, in this its heaviest growth period, still more, and Howard Smith was rewarded with the title of "assistant publisher."

He became a consultant to corporations seeking to penetrate the youth market. When ABC Radio established an FM outlet, Howard Smith, who had kept files on how to start a radio station since he was a teenager, went on the air. He had an interview show of his own—and guests like Mick Jagger, John Lennon, Frank Zappa, Jim Morrison, Janis Joplin, Xaviera Hollander, Dennis Hopper and Peter Fonda, John Lindsay, Buckminster Fuller, and Margaret Mead. He covered Woodstock with reports on the air every hour for five days. Finally Howard Smith got into what had remained his first love all along—film-making. At a screening for Andy Warhol's movie, *Trash,* in 1971, he was asked by movie distributor and theater owner Don Rugoff for a promotion quote. "A beautiful, funky movie," was what he came up with—and that was what Rugoff used, saying later, when *Trash* became a hit, that it was the quote, and not the movie, that had done it. Through Don Rugoff Howard Smith met an ex-huckster, ex-evangelist named Marjoe Gortner who was looking to make a movie of his life story. Through Don Rugoff, and through Max Palevsky (who had also helped finance, among other major ventures of the time, *Rolling Stone* and the presidential candidacy of George McGovern), he got the financial backing to produce and direct such a movie. And in March of 1973, Howard Smith found himself on stage in Santa Monica, California, accepting the Academy Award for Best Documentary for his movie, *Marjoe.*

Meanwhile, back at the *Village Voice,* he was still doing "Scenes." One day in 1970, in a column-related experiment, he took a braless girl in a very see-through dress around Manhattan, stopping off to gauge the reactions at various places. By that time, he had an assistant, a young graduate of Finch College in Manhattan, where she had been in the same class with Tricia Nixon, named Blair Sabol. With her he started, until he realized he was in over his head trying to do too many things at once, a fashion column. It was hip and irreverent, based on the premise that an industry, like fashion, claiming to create art ought to be judged critically, and after he dropped out she kept it going, with Stephanie Harrington, between them ranging so far afield that one feature in the spring of 1970 was a tongue-in-cheek commentary on the riot gear worn to demonstrations by *Voice* staff photographer Fred McDarrah.

★ ★ ★

Ever since she had come to the paper, Sally Kempton had been one of Dan Wolf's best reporters. Tall, blonde, the daughter of the respected *New York Post* columnist Murray Kempton, she had covered Carmine DeSapio's close-call defeat at his headquarters on Primary Night in June of 1964, and gone on from there—pieces on old radicals Irving Howe and I. F. Stone, on new freaks Jerry Rubin and Frank Zappa with his group the Mothers of Invention, on old *Voice* writer Bill Manville when he came back to New York and his novel came out. In 1967 she hit her creative peak.

In December of that year, a demonstration against the war outside the draft induction center on Whitehall Street at the tip of Lower Manhattan turned raucous, and arrests were made. Sally Kempton was covering it for the *Village Voice*. She began her report: "The Village Demonstration Piece, a sub-genre of the Village Street piece, is a rather elegant combination of visual description, overheard snatches of conversation, and notes on the outrages committed by TV news-cameramen, seasoned with quotes from the leaders of the various factions which inevitably arise during the course of any demonstration." But this piece, she made clear as she went along, was a little different. Halfway through the Whitehall Street fracas, Sally Kempton had changed from reporter into participant, and gotten herself arrested. She had become the parajournalist indeed.

But Sally Kempton was not one of those who eventually made it. She left the paper to freelance, and, while doing a piece for *Esquire* on the Arica sensitivity cult, became converted into one of its disciples. It was 1976 before she was published again anywhere in New York, and she never did reappear in the pages of the *Village Voice*.

★ ★ ★

Nineteen sixty-seven was the year Richard Goldstein hit his peak, too. He came to Dan Wolf by way of the Columbia School of Journalism, but not as one of its prodigies. When his mentors sent him out to do an interview with construction workers, his recollection was "Wow—I really shook." When he was sent to do a piece on radio station WMCA, he got it back with a note saying, "I don't know what this is, but you still owe us a story." And when he was sent to cover the United Nations, about which he knew nothing, he decided "it was like Kafka," and kept calling back in that nothing was happening. This, during the 1965 Indian-Pakistani war. Finally he sent in a story with a lead saying, "The crisis is like a creeping jungle vine." When he graduated, in May of 1966, he was convinced that he didn't want to be "a conventional reporter." A conventional reporter is one thing his teachers did not think he was in too much danger of becoming; one of them, Judith Crist, told him to cut his hair and learn how to spell if he ever expected to get a job.

Instead, Goldstein, just finished with a quickie book about the campus drug scene, presented himself to Dan Wolf in the summer of 1966, having decided to be a rock-and-roll critic. Which was fine, except that nobody knew what it was a rock-and-roll critic was supposed to do, least of all Dan Wolf. But for $20 an article, Wolf let Richie Goldstein go and write what he wanted.

Goldstein went, and he wrote. He was in Cicero, Illinois, that summer, filing reports on the defeat of Martin Luther King's non-violent open-housing crusade, asking "Has Black Power Killed Love Power?" He was in Eastern Europe that fall, reporting how teenagers' allegiance to the socialist paradises there was being weakened by Western music and American culture. He was in Monterey the next June for the first Pop Festival. He wrote about Andy Warhol, defending him. He wrote about the Rolling Stones, Marshall McLuhan, J. D. Salinger, Murray the K, the Bee Gees, the Velvet Underground ("Noise enough to make your ears sing back"), the League for Spiritual Discovery of Dr. Timothy Leary ("The doctor has until the first psychedelic Ban Roll-On commercial to do something about all this"), and "The Very Last Cowboy Saint," John Wayne (who "looms in the motion picture business like Mount Rushmore," he wrote about the Duke; "He's a bright young fellow, but we'd look funny going down Fifth Avenue together," said the Duke about him).

He became the paper's resident analyst of pop culture ("Pop Eye," he called his column), and everybody else's roving expert. With his peacoat, his tow head of blond hair, and his pixie looks, he cut a five-foot-four figure that was in demand on panels convened to discuss the phenomenon of "pop," was written about elsewhere, was relied on for his pronouncements about the latest. (Sample, fall 1966: "Judy Collins' transition from Joan Baez' kid sister to Barbra Streisand's chambermaid is regrettable. . . . The Blues Project aren't ugly enough to be freaky, mean enough to be hip, or cheeky enough to be teeny-fodder. . . . As serious musicians they lack the charisma we demand—and pay for—in our idols.") When he put down the Beatles' break-through album, *Sgt. Pepper's Lonely Hearts Club Band,* in the *Times,* as "an album of special effects, dazzling but ultimately fraudulent," it was an important rebuke—and it started a debate back and forth in the pages of the *Voice.*

He wrote about the Diggers in San Francisco. And, in October of 1967, when the hippie murders of Groovy and Linda blew the East Village "love" scene away, he wrote:

> . . . Events breed their own ritual. Maybe that is why the murder of James Leroy Hutchinson and Linda Fitzpatrick read like Act Three of an off-off-Broadway closet drama. The truest theatre of the '60s lies spiked across the city desk, slugged "slay."
>
> What happened at 169 Avenue B happens all the time. A man and his woman are hauled or lured down to the boiler room, where amid rags and ratsmell she is banged senseless, and both are stomped dead.
>
> Such crimes become incidents. We never hear about them unless the woman was pregnant, mutilated, or both. But Groovy and his girl were slaughtered right on page one of the *Daily News.*

As things turned out, the sixties didn't last, and neither did the hot flash with which Richard Goldstein's career had begun. In 1969, he left the *Village Voice* after a falling out with Dan Wolf. After that, he found himself stuck in a prolonged writer's block. His marriage broke up. Eventually, he started on the slow road back. He began to teach at the City College of New York. And he went to work for Clay Felker at *New York* Magazine working as a fellow critic of one of his old Columbia professors, Judith Crist.

★ ★ ★

As for Nat Hentoff, at least he proved in the year 1967 that the First Amendment was something he practiced in his own household. His wife began to write a column.

Margot Hentoff may not have been everything her husband was not, but she was certainly an interesting counterpoint to him. They did not so much agree in their opinions as intersect—occasionally. If he struck some as a theoretical bore, she struck them as an independent, and most entertaining, neoconservative, with an honesty about her that was refreshing: she was openly, frankly bourgeois, under no illusions about it. And, when she dissented from their dissents, as she frequently did, she made them think.

She was a freelance writer herself and had been in the letters column before, but the first piece in her own right appeared in the December 8, 1966, *Voice*. It was about the Village's fashionable, progressive, and exclusive Elizabeth Irwin High School, and the trouble her daughter was having there. Readers' reaction was predictable, given her husband's stated sentiments—"Why doesn't she send the child to public school where she can dream of movie stars all day and no one will push her too hard for subject matter?" asked Timothy Melvin, West 9th Street. "Tuition then could be sent to CORE." The school's reaction was also predictable; Margot Hentoff was asked to withdraw her daughter and, she wrote in a follow-up piece one year later, "they made me pay the full year's tuition before they would release her transcript, making that article the most expensive I ever wrote."

In that same piece, she was making up a list of "People I am not speaking to next year." On it were "Jimmy Breslin, because he once called my house at two in the morning and used obscene language. And it wasn't even me he wanted to speak to. . . . Two of my children, and Nat Hentoff. Maybe." And in her column, "Letter from New York," which by 1967 was running regularly, she frequently took positions which were not those associated with her husband.

As for the daughter, Margot Hentoff's by a first marriage, her name was Mara Wolynski. And in 1974, herself a freelance writer now, she wrote a piece for the *Voice*. In it she described growing up—and fighting—with her mother.

★ ★ ★

1968 . . . Jack Newfield is down on John Lindsay as the year begins: "There is something about the uptight White Knight which seems unrelievedly programmed. . . . He seems incapable, like those totally WASP characters in the fiction of John Updike and John Cheever, of making contact with his own deepest and truest feelings. He is forever Rock Hudson playing Mayor." And he writes, "Eugene McCarthy's presidential campaign has nearly collapsed." But still Bobby Kennedy will not make the race. Jules Feiffer draws "THE BOBBY TWINS EPISODE 2: IN WHICH THE GOOD BOBBY GOES ON 'FACE THE NATION' AND THE BAD BOBBY RESPONDS." The Good Bobby earnestly declares, "We're going in there and we're killing South Vietnamese. We're killing children, we're killing women—we're killing innocent people." The Bad Bobby follows that up with, "I will back the

Democratic candidate in 1968. I expect that will be President John-son." The Good Bobby rejoins, "I think we're going to have a difficult time explaining this to ourselves." A blank-faced Feiffer character recites: "An escalating war. Rising poverty. Rising racism. Riots in the ghettos. Crime in the streets. Drugs on the campus. A spreading disillusionment with electoral politics. In November in order to solve these problems—I can vote for Richard Nixon or Lyndon Johnson. In a free society there is always a choice." . . .

. . . But in February comes the Tet offensive. The *Voice* prints a report by correspondent Norm Fruchter, who spent the previous autumn in North Vietnam, that "no matter what we do, the Viet-namese will defeat us." In March McCarthy shocks Johnson in New Hampshire, running close behind with 42 percent of the vote. Finally, convulsively, Robert Kennedy gets into the race. Newfield files enthusi-astic reports from the field as his first campaign swing takes him through Kansas and California—"Robert Kennedy struck this Re-publican heartland soil like a spring tornado last Monday, leaving delirium in his wake. . . . Like the old Kansas City blues shouter, Joe Turner, used to sing, Robert Kennedy was rolling like a big wheel." Then, at month's end, LBJ himself withdraws from contention. . . .

. . . Four days later, Martin Luther King is assassinated. Joe Flaherty visits the saloons, first on Wall Street the day after the murder, where "the main offering seemed to be paranoia," and "any horror about the murder was tempered with selectivity. A middle-aged man in a gray suit who was holding forth at the end of the bar summed up the establishment theory about the assassination: 'It's a shame it had to be him instead of that son of a bitch LeRoi Jones.'" Then, on Saturday night after the murder, where "all the civility of the city seemed to be located on 125th Street in Harlem. . . .

> . . . Women shyly nodded greetings to the white face. Men who usually pass each other by lent their smiles and hellos as if they were passports to safety.
>
> . . . We all talked of the sadness of it. I was told to keep my money in my pocket, that the drinks were on my newfound brother. "Tonight we have to obey the memory of that man and all be brothers."
>
> When I finally said I had to leave, the young man tried to sum up Dr. King's love ethic. Perhaps it wasn't exactly what the Baptist minister was striving for, but when the words of saints descend into the streets, one can't grumble about translations. Putting his arm around me, the young man offered me one of the last things that remain the domain of the

poor, "I love you so much tonight, brother, if you stick with me, I'll see if I can set you up with a good piece of ass."

. . . At the end of April, there is student insurgency, and building takeover, and a bloody police raid at Columbia University. "You could tell something more than springtime was brewing at Columbia," writes Richie Goldstein, "by the crowds around the local Chock Full, jumping and gesturing with more than coffee in their veins."

> You could sense insurrection in the squads of police surrounding the campus like a Navy picket fence. You could see rebellion in the eyes peering from windows where they didn't belong. And you knew it was revolution for sure, from the trash.
>
> Don't underestimate the relationship between litter and liberty at Columbia. Until last Tuesday, April 23, the university was a clean dorm, where students paid rent, kept the house rules, and took exams. Then the rebels arrived, in an uneasy coalition of hip, black, and leftist militants. They wanted to make Columbia more like home. So they ransacked files, shoved furniture around, plastered walls with paint and placards. They scrawled on blackboards and doodled on desks. They raided the dean's offices (the psychological equivalent of robbing your mother's purse) and they claim to have found cigars, sherry, and a dirty book (the psychological equivalent of finding condoms in your father's wallet).

. . . Feiffer draws a sideburned, wide-eyed kid in his strip. "First we take over music. Then we take over fashion. Then we move into politics. We go into New Hampshire and force Kennedy to be a candidate. We go into Wisconsin and force Johnson to retire. Who needs drugs? I've got a reality high." But the euphoria of the McCarthy supporters—and Feiffer is one, running as a delegate to the national convention from New York—is shaken when Kennedy carries conservative Indiana and soundly whips McCarthy in Nebraska. Kennedy calls on McCarthy to quit the race. McCarthy refuses and implies he'll support Vice-President Hubert Humphrey (carrying Johnson's banner but shrewdly avoiding the primaries) rather than Kennedy, if it comes to that. The two liberal, antiwar senators are thus stuck in a personal feud, born of pride and awkward timing, that threatens to be mutually suicidal. And their supporters start to spill each other's ideological blood. . . .

Jack Newfield fires the first salvo in the *Voice* in mid-May: "What

candidate for President," he asks, "back during the plague of [Joseph]
McCarthy, drove the 'left-wingers' out of the Farmer-Labor Party,
voted to outlaw the Communist Party, and voted to cite dramatist
Arthur Miller for contempt of Congress? Bobby Kennedy? No. Eugene
McCarthy," a man "so emotionally removed from the underclass that
he has voted to exclude agricultural workers from minimum wage
protection and has voted to reduce rent supplements from $20 million
to $12 million," a man "so indifferent to the power of vested economic
interests that he has voted against cutting the oil depletion allowance,"
and yet a man "who has the near unanimous support of America's
liberal and intellectual elite from Kazin and Lowell to Simon and
Garfunkel." . . .

. . . This is only partially fair. Right as he is on the war, McCarthy
certainly, compared to Kennedy, represents the most elitist streak of
suburbanized, academic, cocktail-party liberalism on gut domestic
issues. But Robert Kennedy, in his *enfant terrible* right-wing phase,
had actually *worked* for Joseph McCarthy in the early fifties, while
Arthur Miller, contempt citation or no, was running now as a McCarthy delegate in Connecticut. And, moreover, when McCarthy had
begun campaigning, a certain writer for the *Village Voice* had compared him to St. Thomas More, had written that "he carries with him
not only the hopes of all those opposed to the war, but the faith of all
those who still believe that our representative democracy—despite the
power of the generals, despite the distortions of the news media, despite
the malapportionment of the Congress—can still work." That certain
writer had been Jack Newfield, and the next week Joe Flaherty quotes
those lines—just five months old—back to him in the course of a
roundhouse counterattack. "Newfield and his cohorts remind me of
Blanche DuBois," says Flaherty. "Overtly they are disgusted by power,
but subconsciously they find the pungent smell of a sweaty t-shirt too
powerful to resist in the bed they were always longing for." . . .

. . . Correspondence from France, where students and workers together are threatening to bring down the government . . . In New York,
both Newfield and Mailer are back in town. Mailer has just released his
first film, *Wild 90*—he placed an ad in the *Voice* in January offering
money back if viewers were dissatisfied—and now his second, *Beyond
the Law*, is ready. Newfield describes a day with him.

> At 5 p.m. Mailer the Drinker entered a small characterless
> bar across the street from the studio. Present were Jose Torres
> on crutches, with his brother and trainer, Pete Hamill and his
> brother, Farbar, and Tom Hayden, the revolutionary. Hayden
> began to discuss revolution with Mailer.

"I'm for Kennedy," said Mailer the Drinker, "because I'm not so sure I want a revolution. Some of those kids are awfully dumb." Hayden the Revolutionary said a vote for George Wallace would further his objective more than a vote for RFK . . .

At 6:30 p.m., Mailer the Rebel arrived at Dwight Macdonald's apartment on East 87th Street for a fund-raising party for the Columbia University student strikers. They wanted a piece of Mailer too.

. . . Then [Mark] Rudd, who faces six years in jail for his activities at Columbia, began to speak. Mailer the Rebel looked into his open, unfinished face.

Rudd said that the fires at Columbia last week were set by police provocateurs dressed as plainclothesmen after the students had left the buildings. Rudd also said that "plainclothesmen began the anti-cop slogans that started the violence on the sundial. They falsified evidence too."

Mailer the Rebel, nursing his fifth bourbon, interrupted to say, "I'm sure you're telling me the truth in general. About particulars, I don't know. I want the facts. What walls did you paint? What walls did the police paint? You've got to put the police on the defensive. I know that cops create evidence. They've done it to me. All cops are psychopathic liars. Your fight is to show that the people who run the country are full of shit. You've got to come up with the hard evidence of what the cops did. . . . If you win, then America will be a little different place."

Rudd then said something about needing money to pay for lawyers' fees.

Mailer the Rebel, punching his left palm with his right fist, interrupted, leaning forward in his six-button vest.

"Most lawyers are corrupt and filled with guilt. That's the liberal middle-class game, lawyers and fund-raising parties and more bureaucracy. Why don't you kids defend yourselves? If you're cool, and telling the truth, you're better off without lawyers. Let totalitarian America judge each one of your faces."

"We're too ugly," Rudd said, and Mailer mentally gave him that round.

Mailer the Celebrity, in a playful, puckish mood, was a few minutes early for the taping of the Merv Griffin television show. So, wearing his pancake makeup, he went off to Smith's proletarian bar on Eighth Avenue, for another drink. . . . Suddenly, a tall, hip Negro faggot approached Mailer, recognized him, and said he had gone to Choate.

Mailer the Celebrity looked at the man, who had a long knife scar on his face, thinking perhaps of Shago Martin or Sonny Liston, and offered to bet him $100 that he did not go to Choate. . . .

A little tight, Mailer walked out to face an audience that looked like it was bussed over from the Crimmins murder trial. Empty, pinched Queens faces. They were mindless television fanatics, and Mailer was quite aware that the last time he had been on Griffin's show, he criticized the Vietnam War and was booed by the Yahoo audience. But Mailer was up for this one; just before walking out, he had been throwing loving overhand rights that stopped just short of Pete Hamill's smiling face. "Not hitting you, Pete, takes something out of my character," he barked.

"Norman Mailer is one of the leading spectator sports in America," Griffin said, and Mailer swaggered out of the wings, hunching up his shoulders like Carmen Basilio coming to Ray Robinson.

They shook hands and Mailer the Celebrity announced, "My hands are cold because I've been holding drinks for the last two hours."

A current of panic shot through Griffin's all-American face, fearing that Mailer was wild drunk.

"How has the mood of the country changed since you were here last?" Griffin asked, sounding like a Sunday robot-panelist.

"The instances of faggotry have gone up in the country," Mailer said.

"That means more smoking, folks," quipped Griffin.

Griffin then asked Mailer about the Presidential election.

"If Humphrey runs against Rockefeller, I will take the year off and go to Coney Island. . . . Humphrey may slip through because he is a whale who moves like a snake on the way to the hog trough."

Mailer then tossed off passing references to the film "Marty" and Machiavelli, which the Yahoo audience did not seem to understand.

"Is this the idiot row?" Mailer barked. . . .

Suddenly, stand-up comic Morey Amsterdam, a walking file

of one-liners, said, "I've come here to learn something, and I'm still waiting."

The audience, finding its spokesman at last, cheered wildly.

Mailer, quite sober by now, then revealed his secret weapon—self-depreciation. "Morey," he said, "once again you've inherited the problem of a landslide." . . .

. . . Howard Smith on "The Shot that Shattered the Velvet Underground," the near-fatal wounding of Andy Warhol . . . And then, Los Angeles. Pete Hamill has been writing a column for the *Voice* since quitting *Newsday*, literally titled "In Transit," while he shuttles back and forth between New York, the Irish coastal village of Howth where he is at work on a novel, and the campaign in California, where he is writing speeches for Kennedy. Early in May, after the Battle of Columbia, he reminisces about how, as a high-school dropout just out of the navy fifteen years before, he applied there, and the school rejected him. In the middle of the month, he leaves the campaign, bitterly describing how it is being run by California boss Jess Unruh's men. "They all had neat suits," he writes. "And they all had neat hair, and they all had crisp shirts with button-down collars. And they were all pricks." But he relents, and is back in the Ambassador Hotel the night of Kennedy's victory in the primary, as Bobby gives his last victory speech.

Then a pimply messenger arrived from the secret filthy heart of America. He was curly haired, wearing a pale blue sweatshirt and bluejeans, and he was planted with his right foot forward and his right arm straight out and he was firing a gun. . . . We knew then that America had struck again. . . . I saw Kennedy lurch against the ice machine, and then sag, and then fall forward slowly, to be grabbed by someone, and I knew that he was dead. . . . Kennedy's face had a kind of sweet acceptance to it, the eyes understanding that it had come to him, the way it had come to so many others before him. The price of the attempt at excellence was death. You saw a flicker of that understanding on his face, as his life seeped out of a hole in the back of the skull, to spread like a spilled wine across the scummy concrete floor.

. . . The Jack Ruby in me was rising up, white, bright, with a singing sound in the ears, and I wanted to damage that insane little bastard they were holding, I wanted to break his face, to rip away flesh, to hear bone break as I pumped punches into that pimpled skin. . . . Just one punch. Just one for Dallas. Just one for Medgar Evers, just one for Martin Luther King. Just one punch. Just one. One. Kennedy was lying on the floor, with black rosary beads in his hand, and blood on his fingers . . .

. . . Rosey Grier [was] holding the gunman by the neck, choking the life out of him. "Rosey, Rosey, don't kill him. We want him alive. Don't kill him, Rosey, don't kill him."

"Kill the bastard, kill that son of a bitch bastard," a Mexican busboy yelled.

"Don't kill him, Rosey."

"Where's the doctor? Where in Christ's name is the doctor?"

Grier decided not to kill the gunman. They had him up on a serving table at the far end of the pantry, as far as they could get him from Kennedy. Jimmy Breslin and I were standing up on the table, peering into the gunman's face. His eyes were rolling around, and then stopping, and then rolling around again. The eyes contained pain, fright, entrapment, and a strange kind of bitter endurance. I didn't want to hit him anymore.

. . . I sat there drinking rum until I was drunk enough to forget that pimpled face cranking off the rounds into the body of a man who was a friend of mine.

. . . Feiffer draws a couple in bed, her hair in curlers, watching television, switching channels. "Make your move, Ringo! Bang!" Switch. "Eat lead, you lousy stoolie! BANG!" Switch. "Die you cruddy Jap! RATATATTAT!" Switch. "Get a doctor! Senator Kennedy's been shot!" Switch. "My sonic gun will finish you off, space man! ZAP!" Switch off. " 'Night, honey." "Sweet dreams, dear." . . .

. . . Steve Lerner, son of Max, *New York Post* columnist, joins the staff. He writes about his unsuccessful tryout to be in Michelangelo Antonioni's new film, slated to star young amateurs and be called *Zabriskie Point,* about John Lindsay's Give-a-Damn program, about the troubles of the Liberation News Service. . . . Paul Cowan is back writing for the paper again; he follows a George Wallace rally in Boston. . . . David McReynolds is in Prague as Soviet tanks roll in to crush the Czechoslovakian experiment in "human socialism." . . . Hamill and Newfield are in Miami as the Republicans nominate Nixon. . . . Then Newfield, Cowan, and Lerner are in Chicago for the Democratic conclave that anoints Humphrey and turns into a four-day horror show when Mayor Richard Daley and his minions make a mockery of the proceedings on the convention floor while his police force goes berserk out on the streets. Newfield describes it:

> At the southwest entrance to the Hilton, a skinny, long-haired kid of about seventeen skidded down on the sidewalk, and four overweight cops leaped on him, chopping strokes on his head. His hair flew from the force of the blows. A dozen small rivulets of blood began to cascade down the kid's temple and onto the sidewalk. He was not crying or screaming, but crawling in a stupor toward the gutter. When he saw a photographer take a picture, he made a V sign with his fingers.
>
> A doctor in a white uniform and Red Cross arm band began to run toward the kid, but two other cops caught him from behind and knocked him down. One of them jammed his knee into the doctor's throat and began clubbing his rib cage. The doctor squirmed away, but the cops followed him, swinging hard, sometimes missing.
>
> A few feet away a phalanx of police charged into a group of women, reporters, and young McCarthy activists standing idly against the window of the Hilton Hotel's Haymarket Inn. The terrified people began to go down under the unexpected police charge when the plate glass window shattered, and the people tumbled backward through the glass. The police then climbed through the broken window and began to beat people, some of whom had been drinking quietly in the hotel bar . . .
>
> Demonstrators, reporters, McCarthy workers, doctors, all began to stagger into the Hilton lobby, blood streaming from face and head wounds. The lobby smelled from tear gas, and stink bombs dropped by the Yippies. A few people began to direct the wounded to a makeshift hospital on the fifteenth floor, the McCarthy staff headquarters . . .
>
> The defiant kids began a slow, orderly retreat back up Michigan Avenue. They did not run. They did not panic. They did not fight back. As they fell back they helped pick up fallen comrades who were beaten or gassed. Suddenly, a plainclothesman dressed as a soldier moved out of the shadows and knocked one kid down with an overhand punch. The kid squatted on the pavement of Michigan Avenue, trying to cover his face, while the Chicago plainclothesman punched him with savage accuracy. Thud, thud, thud. Blotches of

blood spread over the kid's face. Two photographers moved in. Several police formed a closed circle around the beating to prevent pictures. One of the policemen then squirted Chemical Mace at the photographers, who dispersed. The plainclothesman melted into the line of police.

. . . The fall campaign—Humphrey and Nixon and Wallace—gets under way. When Wallace brings his show to town for a rally in Madison Square Garden, Joe Flaherty goes:

> . . . Then they brought on Wallace. For about fifteen minutes the Garden exploded with clapping, whistling, foot stamping, and shouting. . . . There were the Italians who had left their sanctuaries in Bay Ridge and Staten Island with the Blessed Mother standing sentry on their lawns. There were the young Irish kids who shot baskets at netless hoops on the blacktop schoolyards of Our Lady of Something or Another. . . . And . . . the innocent, untouchable girls of our boyhood. Their faces now prematurely old with hate and their legs grown heavy with too many children. The same girls you tried to maneuver against banisters with their mothers a flight away. . . .
>
> As they left the Garden, they performed the most primitive ritual of the evening. They gathered in groups, as they made their way toward their homes, like men in a time when fire was not yet discovered, gathered to protect themselves against the eternal black night they live in.

. . . On Election Eve, Pete Hamill urges other dissident Democrats to reluctantly vote for Humphrey, Chicago notwithstanding, if only to prevent the election of Nixon:

> In the end, one thought is unacceptable. That is, to wake up every morning for the next four years—almost 1500 mornings—and reach for the cigarettes and the coffee and remember again that Richard Nixon is the President of the United States.
>
> That is the experience I don't think any of us can survive. . . . You could be looking at a field ripe with summer, and suddenly remember those shifting eyes, counting the house, with the plastic teeth moving in the formless mouth, and the jowls quivering with an attempt at righteousness. . . .

Nixon would almost certainly try to re-cast America in the image of the Eisenhower years, and he would almost certainly fail. . . . And when Nixon does not see things happening according to his plans, he panics. Underneath, Nixon is what the fight managers call a dog. . . . [And] when the Eastland types start calling us all down to Washington, we had better have someone on the Supreme Court to help us. There are at least four openings on that court coming due in the next four years; Nixon won't appoint anyone who would free you and me from a contempt of Congress conviction.

. . . It is accurate about what is to come, but it is not enough, not even at the *Voice,* where Dan Wolf, in his editorial "For President," says simply, "Your guess is as good as ours," and at year's end, after Nixon's win, a picture page of 1968 displays Daley—"ARCHITECT OF DEMOCRATIC DISASTER"—and Jerry Rubin, Yippie leader—"ANOTHER ARCHITECT OF DEMOCRATIC DISASTER"—and Abbie Hoffman, Rubin's fellow Yippie—"THIRD ARCHITECT." . . .

. . . In October Richard Goldstein is there as Julian Beck's Living Theatre and the Lower East Side Motherfuckers disrupt a benefit for the Columbia strikers being held inside Bill Graham's Fillmore East. . . . That fall, the experiment in school decentralization breaks down over "community control" of the Ocean Hill–Brownsville district and a citywide teachers' strike is called. In one issue of the paper, Nat Hentoff, an uncritical supporter of the community forces, debates the pros and cons of the strike with Michael Harrington. In December, reporter Joe Pilati, covering the scene for the *Voice,* has his nose broken during one incident there. . . . Mary Nichols, back from the Lindsay administration to be assistant editor, wonders aloud, "Is District Attorney Frank Hogan sitting on the indictment of former Tammany Chief Carmine DeSapio?" and at year's end reports, finally, his indictment—by United States Attorney Robert Morgenthau. . . . Howard Smith on the closing of that local landmark, the Café Figaro, after thirteen years as the Village's premier coffee house . . . "A dance to the New Year," announces Feiffer's dancer on the eve of 1969. "In this dance I salute the return to traditional values. Traditional family ties. Traditional respect for authority. Traditional economics. Traditional apathy. A dance to 1959."

★ ★ ★

Besides Mary Nichols, there was Robin Reisig, a veteran of Alabama where she had worked for the *Southern Courier,* and Mary Breasted, who broke into print with an investigative piece on the Tudor City residential development in mid-Manhattan. Both came to the paper from the Columbia Journalism School. Both began writing for it in 1968. Both became protégées of sorts of Mary Nichols as investigative reporters, helping her cover the city beat—politics, corruption, drugs, the courts. There was Annette Kuhn, the young German-born assistant to Mary Nichols in the Parks Department, who had begun attending Dan Wolf's Friday afternoon *salons* with her, and who finally followed her to the paper to do a column, "Culture Shock," on the art world.

There was Alan Weitz; a Hunter College dropout at seventeen, he joined the paper as a mailroom worker in 1967 and gradually worked his way up, over the next seven years, to be an assistant editor under Mary Nichols. And there was Ross Wetzsteon; hired as a part-time proofreader in 1964, within a few years he was editing theater and books, writing about drugs and culture. There was the temperamental Fred McDarrah, photojournalist, former entrepreneur of "Rent-a-Beatnik," and letter-writer to the *Village Voice* in the early days, before he became its staff photographer. There was John Perrault, its regular art critic, and Deborah Jowett, its regular dance critic. There was, on a paper that, for all its public hand-wringing over White Guilt and Black Power, never had a black editor or a black staff writer, the occasional music criticism of composer Carman Moore and the occasional column by novelist Charles Wright, the only two blacks to write regularly for it over the years. There was Michael Zwerin, still corresponding from abroad, writing about jazz, or the drag that life in the Soviet Union had become, or his sex life in London, or whatever. When the notorious call girl from the Profumo scandal, Christine Keeler, compiled her memoirs, Michael Zwerin edited them. And when the sensational Sunday tabloid *News of the World* published them, the paper and its new owner, an Australian publishing emperor named Rupert Murdoch who had just embarked on an intercontinental campaign of newspaper acquisitions, both received a vote of censure from the British Press Council.

And there was Don McNeill.

10. SOMETHING WAS HAPPENING ON THE
streets of the Village.

After 1965, there were no more summertime Auto Rallyes; it was getting too violent, Danny List gave as his reason. And by the following spring, it was starting, on the corner of Bleecker and Macdougal, on Saturday nights. It was an invasion: Bikers. Cheap wine. Violence against locals. At first it appeared to be gangs from Brooklyn or teenyboppers from the suburbs; "I've lived in the Village for 18 years, but these kids make me feel like a tourist," Ed Fancher told *Newsweek* when it did a story on the phenomenon. Finally, in mid-March, the police decided to do something. Units of the Tactical Patrol Force were sent in to seal off fourteen entire blocks and to enforce a 4 A.M. closing time for the bars inside the perimeter. When they tried to deploy, an angry, spontaneous crowd, 1,000 strong, thwarted them. "This weekend," David Gurin wrote for the *Voice,* "was only the beginning of a long spring and summer which will certainly deepen the misery of local residents, and will probably bring violence to resident and visitor alike."

> Young heads have already been bloodied, usually by gangs of 10 or so (with plenty of neutral or approving bystanders) who have chosen a single youth with a Rolling Stone haircut on whom to demonstrate their strong feelings about the connotations of long hair.

It was not that, but it was something just as momentous. What was happening was that after all those years as a special place, zoned off from the world above 14th Street, the rest of America was becoming a little more like Greenwich Village—and Greenwich Village was becoming more and more like the rest of America. In the upheaval that was to follow—from the first ferment to the last torment—there would be a kind of entropy. Little Greenwich Villages would spring up all over, in Cambridge and Berkeley, in Georgetown and Madison, in Ann Arbor and Austin, and Greenwich Village, in turn, would lose its separate identity. It would pay the ultimate price—it would lose its specialness.

East of Washington Square, nothing could stop it, an entire migration of runaways trekking in from all points, pouring into those red-brick, straight-lined, row-housed blocks that used to be called the Lower East Side, that would from now on be known as the "East Village," just as those who lived there would be called not "Beatniks" but "hippies." By that summer, Michael Harrington wrote that a walk through the area was "like attending a huge Halloween party. The streets were alive with frontiersmen and guerrillas and painters from the 1830s. There were bearded homosexuals aggressively holding hands, girls with long, straight hair walking barefoot on filthy sidewalks to prove their organic oneness with nature, and teen-agers panhandling or sitting and staring blankly, strung out on drugs."

That fall of 1966, Don McNeill started to write for the *Village Voice*.

★ ★ ★

He came from a newspaper family, born December 21, 1944, in Tacoma, Washington. His father had been lost at sea on submarine duty, and his mother, a stringer for the *New York Times*, had remarried, to an Associated Press bureau chief, and relocated, to Alaska, when he decided to drop out of the University of Washington at the start of his senior year, drifted clear across the continent, and took a loft on the Lower East Side. He arrived in town a conservative kid—he admitted to Dan Wolf later that he had worked for Kenneth Keating against Robert Kennedy that fall. He lived for two years on money from home, sometimes taking friends to uptown hotels for overnight stays, taking some courses at NYU, and then he presented himself to Dan Wolf. By the end of 1966, he had done his first articles on the HUAC hearings in Washington which Jerry Rubin disrupted Yippies-style by appearing in a 1776 Revolutionary War outfit, on a Nazi rally in Yorkville, the closing of the City Lights bookstore in San Francisco, and the civilian review board rally in Park Slope where Joe Flaherty made his debut.

Joe Flaherty remembered a sweet kid—sweet, that was the word many of his contemporaries and co-workers came up with to describe him—who was a lot better than the movement he covered. He was Candide, Howard Smith said, the true innocent. He was also not a very good writer, at least not yet.

The problem, as Dan Wolf saw it, was that he had to give up his journalist's background, to stop writing straight prose and hard news. That was why his stuff was so run-of-the-mill. But Dan Wolf never said as much to Don McNeill's face. He liked him too much. He admired this young man for what he had, his eager yet honest exterior, his ability to open up to so much experience and still assimilate it all. He was so self-effacing and yet he had so many interests. He could go into and out of the scene at will. He was having a good time, yet he still had good judgment. What he had to do, Dan Wolf decided, was to learn how to write his beliefs on paper. He was afraid to at first, Wolf knew. He was experimenting, with drugs, with his life, with his writing, with himself. But Wolf knew he could do it, and planned to let him learn it himself, at his own pace. He, Wolf, would listen, and let him go his own way.

That was not what Don McNeill wanted, at least not at first. He was still straight, still insecure, and didn't know how to read this aloofness of Wolf's. He asked Howard Smith to go for a walk with him one night, and while they walked, said, in his soft tones, "Howard, I'm shy. I don't know how to say this. But I think I'm about to be fired. Am I?"

"Of course not," Howard Smith replied. "That's just Dan's way. He just wants you to be self-motivated, that's all. Look, I'm telling you that Dan likes you a lot." Don't worry, he reassured him.

In time, Don McNeill stopped worrying, and started writing, the way he was born to write, coming into direct contact with himself, writing about what he was living, living what he was writing. He wrote about his scene. The druggies. The dealers. The Diggers. The flower children. The *Hare Krishna* types. He wrote about its dark side. The junkies. The bikers. The ripoff artists. He wrote about his friends. Ed Sanders. Allen Ginsberg. Paul Williams, editor of *Crawdaddy*. Abbie Hoffman, out of SNCC now, into the Yippies. And Captain Joe Fink, the "good cop" commander of the Ninth Precinct. He wrote about *their* friends. The Group Image, the East Village Street band. Country Joe and the Fish. Herbert Huncke, the "oldest living junkie in New York." He was free and in control of what he wanted to say now, getting sharp shafts of cutting insight, never proselytizing for his scene but always understanding it, and reproducing it all on paper in quick, easy turns of phrase. Thus, he wrote: "Hippies are not as dependent upon parents' bankbooks as *The New Yorker* cartoons would have you believe. . . . With each stage, the road back to middle-class serenity becomes longer and more cluttered." And, when hippies tried to counter Armed Forces Day 1967 with Flower Power Day: "A nice picnic but a lousy protest."

He was there when the scene hit its peak: Easter Sunday, 1967. The Central Park Be-In.

> It was a feast for the senses: the beauty of the colors, clothes, and shrines, the sounds and the rhythms, at once familiar, the smell of flowers and frankincense, the taste of jellybeans . . .
>
> People climbed into trees and made animal calls, and were answered by calls from other trees. Two men stripped naked, and were gently persuaded to reclothe as the police appeared. Herds of people rushed together from encampments on the hills to converge en masse on the great mud of the meadow.

> They joined hands to form great circles, hundreds of yards in
> diameter, and broke to hurtle to the center in a joyous,
> crushing, multiembracing pigpile. Chains of people careened
> through the crowds at full run. Their energy seemed inex-
> haustible.
>   The password was "LOVE" and it was sung, chanted,
> painted across the foreheads, and spelled out on costumes.

He was with Allen Ginsberg when Ginsberg testified before a Senate
Committee on the use of LSD, telling the senators how he had prayed
for Lyndon Johnson's recovery from a gall-bladder operation while
tripping his brains out on the Big Sur. He followed East Village denizen
Louis Abolafia as Abolafia ran for president on the "What have I got to
hide?" platform and distributed flyers of himself standing nude but for
a hat over his equator ("Louis Abolafia has balls, even if he does hide
them with his hat"). He covered the opening of the Hudson Street
Ashram, the East Coast headquarters of Timothy Leary's League for
Spiritual Discovery (LSD). He was with the Diggers when they planted
a tree in St. Mark's Place. He wrote about the dealers (" 'It's something
to write home to Mother about,' said a youth from Connecticut after a
successful exchange") and the users, and the drugs they all tried, Don
McNeill included. The grass. The speed. The acid. The new discovery,
STP (Serenity Tranquility Peace), that was to take LSD's place. Even,
for some of them, the smack. And he wrote, with mixed emotions,
about his neighborhood (it "has the bleak air of postwar Europe," he
admitted), and its inhabitants:

> The transient rut is not a creative one. It is a fertilizing, pre-
> creative experience for a few. It is an interim for a few. For
> more, it is a long road down, laced with drugs, especially
> amphetamine. Many dig the descent; oblivion can be seduc-
> tive. There is a fascination in being strung out for days on
> amphetamine, a fascination in Rolling Stone echoes, a fas-
> cination in the communal chaos of the Lower East Side, as far
> removed from Westchester as is India. If you wade in too
> deep, you may learn that the East Side undertow is no
> myth . . .
>   . . . In a time of infectious war and domestic insurgency,
> America is losing its youth to a mysterious, invisible, and
> invincible Pied Piper. The American white middle class is in
> the realm of last resorts. . . .
>   There has never been a generation so detached from their

parents. All of the practical binds are gone. It has been decades since the average middle-class family needed their adolescent children for anything more than dish-washing, baby-sitting, and lawn-mowing. For the parents, the postwar ties were emotional ones; for the children, the ties were material. Now the children, by rejecting the parents' material values, also throw off the need of support. The society has reached such a point of affluence that a resourceful kid can live off its waste. A kid who lacks resources can live off his peers, who are, more often than not, willing to sustain him. Every commune carries a few.

He kept growing, kept getting better all the time, and they grew closer, Wolf and McNeill, these two sensitive men, the one young, with his short hair, his light undergrowth of beard, and his leather jacket, the other old. Don McNeill wrote home, "I always knew in my heart I'd find a newspaper to love and I've found it."

But the scene he wrote about couldn't last. Even in the beginning, he had noticed the combustibility of the ethnic mixture there:

They are worlds apart, the hippie and the Puerto Rican. Add other worlds and other blocks on the East Side, the trim, stark Ukrainian neighborhood just west of Tompkins Square, the dwindling congregations of tiny synagogues. The hippies are unique in that they may borrow freely from all the other cultures. They may buy groceries at the supermarket, bread at the kosher bakery, late-night soda at the *bodega*. And, to the bewilderment of their neighbors, the hippies contribute a culture of their own to the scene. Starting with ominous dress and long hair, and extending to stores for books, beads, and psychedelic props, boutiques are opening in long-vacant storefronts—all on the same streets, alternating in the same apartments. The worlds continually overlap without touching.

And finally, on Memorial Day 1967, it happened. The first fighting.

The Ukrainians had had enough.
"Hare Krishna" may be a song of love for the Lord Krishna, but it's a little esoteric for a Ukrainian grandmother who wants to sit in peace and talk about the old country. A daffodil is an empty gesture to an old man who can get no sleep at night. In the late afternoon on Memorial Day, the Flower People were

out in force, complete with kirtan and bongoes, and some of the Ukrainians bitched to the park foreman.

The park foreman had had enough.

Tompkins Square had been a peaceful, if boring, park before the hippies came, and he had heard enough gripes from the Ukrainians to write a book. Moreover, the hippies were playing musical instruments, and sitting on the grass at that, both in violation of park regulations. He walked over to the Ninth Precinct Station to make a complaint.

You can't ignore a formal complaint, so a couple of cops went over to the park and told the hippies to shut up and get off the grass. The kids laughed, and kept singing. The cops ordered them to leave. "They laughed at us," Patrolman John Rodd explained. "That's when the trouble started."

The cops had had enough.

A call went out for reinforcements, and three sergeants and fifteen patrolmen were sent to the park. By this time, the hippies had also been reinforced, and where there were once twenty hippies singing, there were now two hundred. The Tactical Patrol Force was summoned, and thirty-five radio cars and seventy riot-trained cops rushed to the scene. Again, they ordered the crowd to disperse.

The hippies had had enough.

They had been having a nice time, and Frank Wise had brought some groceries to pass around, and if they can't smoke grass in the park they can damn well sit on the grass and praise the Lord. They locked their arms and kept singing. And the cops started to pry them apart and carry them off to paddy wagons.

And Frank Wise had had enough.

Frank Wise is no kid. He is thirty-seven, working on a doctoral thesis, and his wife and infant child sat nearby as he rose to protest. "My God," he said, his arms outstretched as police dragged his friends away. "Where is this happening? This is America." A nightstick flew, and Frank Wise was covered with blood. More cops waded in, more nightsticks flew, and Wise became a martyr.

Bystanders wept, and everyone human should have gasped, my God, what has impatience wrought?

That October, McNeill was in California, as the Haight-Ashbury people tried to hold a "Death of Hippie" festival, before the scene, and the dream, went into its final self-destruct phase.

There's not much reason now to go to Haight Street unless
it's to cop. The street itself has a layer of grease and dirt which
is common on busy sidewalks in New York but rare in San
Francisco, a film that comes from bits of lunch, garbage, and
spilled Coke ground into the cement by the heels of Haight
strollers. It is not a pleasant place to sit, yet hundreds do,
huddled in doorways or stretched out on the sidewalk, in torn
blankets and bare feet, bored voices begging for spare
change, selling two-bit psychedelic newspapers that were
current in the spring, and dealing, dealing, dealing. The
dealing is my strongest impression of Haight Street. The
housewives with their Brownie cameras miss the best part of
the show . . .
The elders now harbor hopes that San Francisco will indeed
become a "free city." If any city can, it can, but it must be
born, not made. The hippie was made but the community
called Haight-Ashbury was born, and it was a virgin birth—an
evolutionary experiment and experience. It was beautiful, I am
told, in the golden age before the Human Be-In which awoke
the media to the precious copy lying untapped on the south
side of Golden Gate Park. "Were you here a year ago?"
people ask. If you were, then you know. . . .
Saturday, the *Chronicle* reverently reported that the Hippie
was dead, but by Monday they were back in business again,
with their daily quota of copy from the Haight. The banner
remained strung across Haight Street for a week, as a re-
minder, and the Psychedelic Shop was closed and boarded
up, and the parking meters were cleaned of the white paint.
But the kids still panhandled and sold newspapers and
lounged in the doorways, and the occasional tourist still
gawked from behind the locked doors of his car. Nothing had
changed. It was all the same.

And by January 1968, back in New York, he was writing, "The
hippies are dead and the Diggers may be dying. A year ago, neither
word had yet appeared in *The New York Times.*"

In twelve months the Lower East Side went through
changes unprecedented in its constantly changing history.
Many will be hard to forget: the Be-Ins, the Sweep-Ins, the
Smoke-Ins, the free music, the free dope, the Free Store; the
Diggers, the dealers, the deaths. Others are already forgot-
ten. . . . The True Light Beavers, a small band of intergalactic

nomads who built shrines of garbage and wore True Light
Beaver tee-shirts, issued one handbill declaring "There are no
problems, there are only things to be done," and immediately
disbanded.

Love to the True Light Beavers.

The East Village scene was going fast. Bikers took over the Cooper
Square Free Store. The Diggers experiment collapsed. The street
demonstrations started turning ugly, and the police started turning
violent in trying to contain them. Finally, on Friday night, March 22, it
all came to a head. The Yippies swarmed all over Grand Central
Terminal to celebrate spring, seized the information booth, and literally turned back the hands of time on the clocks. The cops counterattacked.

I was standing close to the cops when they started to clear
the entrance, shoving people into the terminal or out into the
street, where more cops were waiting in formation. I ran
around the corner to the Vanderbilt Avenue entrance, and
came to the balcony that overlooked the terminal in time to see
a wedge of blue slice into the crowd, nightsticks swinging,
until they came to the information booth, where they paused.
The kids slid off the roof and the crowd recoiled. The police
surrounded the information booth and, in seconds, now
reinforced, charged the crowd again, forcing the demonstrators back into the huge corridor which led to the subway. The
crowd simply made a U-turn in a connecting corridor and
flowed back into the terminal, and the cops went wild.

Now another formation of cops charged toward the stairs
where I was standing, and I made for the street again,
rounded the corner, and returned to the 42nd Street entrance,
which was now entirely filled with police. I pinned on my press
credentials and began to move through the police lines. My
credentials were checked twice, and I was allowed to pass. At
that point, I was stopped a third time by two uniformed cops.
They looked at my credentials, cursed *The Voice,* grabbed my
arms behind my back, and, joined by two others, rushed me
back toward the street, deliberately ramming my head into the
closed glass doors, which cracked with the impact.

Don McNeill took five stitches, and did two typical things. Next
morning he called up Nat Hentoff to read him what he had written so
far and, when he got to the bottom of the ninth paragraph and there

happened to mention that he himself had been a victim of the police brutality, Hentoff interrupted, "Move that up to the front. That's not self-serving." Which Don McNeill did not do. And when the piece was finished, Don McNeill rebuked, along with the city, the Yippies too for "a failure in planning . . . that borders on gross incompetence and irresponsibility."

All in all, "it was a pointless confrontation," he wrote, "and somehow it seemed to be a prophecy of Chicago." Which indeed it was.

Don McNeill was going to go to Chicago for the *Voice,* and in the months intervening he marked time. He did more features; when he attended a Black Panther rally where Bobby Seale ranted and raved a jetstream's worth of the most homicidal hatred at his white audience, he reported Seale's words straight, allowing himself just one sardonic comment at the end: "The least you can say about white skin is that it seems to be pretty thick." He and Allen Ginsberg started doing research into marijuana, and into political influence on the drug culture. He set up an interview with Abbie Hoffman where they would test the limits of his professional journalism and their personal friendship. He started making plans for that "careful" book he was going to write on the Lower East Side. And he rented, along with some friends, a lakeside cottage for the summer in upstate Monroe, New York.

Late in the afternoon of Saturday, August 10, 1968, Don McNeill decided to go for a swim before dinner. He made it out to the raft. Then he dove off. A ten-year-old boy watched him dive, saw him hit the water, saw him bob up once screaming "Help," and go back down under the surface again. The boy ran to tell his father. His father didn't believe him. By the time the boy was able to convince his father to come down to the lake, there was only one thing left to do, and that was to fish out the drowned, dead body of Don McNeill.

Dan Wolf was spending a summer weekend with his family on Fire Island when he got the call from Leticia Kent, who was first to get the news. He came right back to New York, to greet Don McNeill's mother and stepfather at the old Fifth Avenue Hotel when they got into the city.

The next week, in the *Village Voice,* "We have had a death in the family," explained Tish Kent to readers in an obituary, and a Dan Wolf obviously broken up with grief wrote these lines on the editor's page:

> On Tuesday morning at 11, I should have been waiting for Don McNeill to turn in his copy, late, as it always was. This Tuesday at 11 I helped carry his casket into Saint Mark's-in-

the-Bouwerie. One cannot easily bury the dead when the dead is 23. Don was probably the most talented, the best of us and certainly the best loved. The world is not full of gentle people, and when one of them goes the loss is singular.

For some, this is an easier world to leave than to live in, but for Don, who quietly engaged every part of it, everything was always beginning. In the exhibitionist apocalypses he wrote about and lived through, he kept his privacy, his individuality, his quiet. And symbolically, when he died he was swimming alone; there was no one to rescue him.

There were eulogies. From Richie Goldstein. From Newfield. From Hentoff. And from his poet friend Ed Sanders, these lines:

I kiss your hand, fair brother
I cry for you, for us
When the lines shift to fill
the bright gap at the barricades.

Years later, Dan Wolf would avoid the subject of whether or not Don McNeill was the best writer he had ever had. Perhaps it was that, with all of his promise, there was no telling how good Don McNeill might have become. But what was certainly true was that there was no young writer who had ever shown more promise, or to whom Dan Wolf had ever gotten closer, and that in all his years as editor of the *Village Voice,* no event ever hurt Dan Wolf more than when Don McNeill left it.

11.

TOWARD THE END OF HIS BOOK *Growing Up Absurd,* written at the dawn of the sixties, social critic Paul Goodman praised England's Angry Young Men. They "specialized in piercing the fraudulent speech of public spokesmen and in trying to force them to put up or shut up," he said. "They have learned to cry out 'shame!' " And he predicted that "when a million Americans—and not only young men—can learn to do this, we shall have a most salutary change."

In the 1960s, there were a million, and more.

★ ★ ★

If you were different now, you were not taking off. You were taking over. That was the difference. The value systems that had made Greenwich Village a place to retreat to at one time were not in retreat any longer. They were on the move, all over America, sweeping everything before them. The Revolution was at hand. America would never be the same again. Neither would the Village. And both places, before it was all over, would be more than a little sorry the whole thing had ever happened.

The word *counterculture* was always a misnomer; there had been no culture to counter in the first place. *It* became the culture, the only culture. And it happened just like that, overnight, without a fight. The old order, it seemed, couldn't wait to surrender and put on its love beads. The Establishment encouraged, even welcomed, the breakdown of its own social mores. The result was a sort of Fave New World, a world in which even businessmen turned on, and designed entire new industries to cater to, and revolve around, the consumptive tastes of the triumphant young and free.

On their way to a victory they never planned, something happened to the values of the Beats and the Bohemians. An entire sensibility was being lost. It was the season of self-righteous stridency. A militant army was on the march. This army relieved Beat of its post, and stationed Hip in its place. It discharged the cafés, and assigned their function to the concert. And to a generation of middle-aged, set-back types like Dan Wolf, it gave the command, in an alien, alienated voice, to get on or get off the bus. Its message was, as Godard put it in the mouth of one of his characters on film, that the only way to be an intellectual revolutionary was to give up being an intellectual.

Dan Wolf's paper had been out there, on the fringes, long enough now to have established the precedent, and the paternity, for other "different" papers. It had also established itself enough by now to come under revisionist attack and economic competition from several of them. And Dan Wolf, for the first time, was old enough to feel it, to feel his age. For years, the paper had been running as a promotion Feiffer's image of a Beatnik, shades and sandals on, lighting up as he sits at his coffee-house table, *Voice* in hand, describing, feature by feature, how he goes through the paper every week, and how "then I write my letter accusing everyone of going Establishment." Now it was no longer an advertising gimmick, no longer an in-house joke.

★ ★ ★

Several things about this counterculture struck Dan Wolf as strange. The loss of standards, for one thing. The Bohemians had believed in suffering with one's life for one's art; the Beats had put their lives ahead of their art. But both had believed in art itself, and had operated according to codes. The hippies, to him, seemed to think that living one's life was the same thing as art. He liked to use as an example the acceptance of Barbra Streisand as "beautiful." Once, there had been a certain Platonic idea of what constituted beauty in a woman; now that, and all the old criteria, was being discarded. In every area, the idea was afoot that people could be and do whatever they wanted. In everything, what had been considered deviant behavior was now considered the norm. He saw it as a mass failure of nerve on the part of the rest of society; the whole thing had all come too fast, too easily.

With him, the big thing had been to keep your individuality. Now the thing was to be a part of something bigger than yourself, to join some movement, some collective, some commune, some committee, to be a member of some overwhelming "we." That was not his sensibility, he knew, and it was not the only point he had in uncommon with these people. In a rare interview he gave at the time, he referred to "the inexorable aging process. That's the one thing you can't escape," and worried about the effect the youth cult was going to have: "Don't trust anyone over 30 and all the rest of it. It'll be a burden when they grow up. Because they *will* grow up, and they'll see the younger kids behind them, and they'll say these kids aren't doing it right anymore, the way *we* did. It's true for every generation, sure. But it'll be especially hard for these people because they've made such a big thing about youth-is-right and age-is-wrong."

It was that very "youthquake" that spawned the new publications in the sixties that either laid claim to the *Voice's* pedigree or took aim at the audience it had proven was there.

The first was the *Los Angeles Free Press,* founded by Art Kunkin, dedicated by him, in its first issue, the week of May 25, 1964, *en hommage* to the *Voice.* It was a self-proclaimed, conscious, admiring imitator. As the decade wore on, other "alternative weeklies," or "underground newspapers"—those became the neologisms for them—surfaced in other cities, following, or trying to follow, the same kind of format. There was the *Different Drummer* in Philadelphia, the *Fifth Estate* in Detroit, the *Berkeley Barb,* the *San Francisco Bay Guardian,* the *Boston Phoenix, View from the Bottom* in New Haven, and the *Independent Press* in Harrisburg. Then there were the rock magazines—AKA "fanzines"—*Crawdaddy, Rolling Stone, Fusion, Zoo World.* There were the Young Left outlets—*Ramparts, Win, Hard Times.* There was the *Great Speckled Bird,* the Liberation News Service, the Underground Press Syndicate.

And there was the *East Village Other.* There was *Rat.* There was *Evergreen.*

★ ★ ★

The East Village scene, which presented Dan Wolf with Don McNeill, also presented him with rivalries coming at him from awkward angles—from farther left politically, from farther out culturally, from inside his home base, the Village. For just as Wolf and Edwin Fancher had conceived that the influx of the late forties and early fifties could be used to break the *Villager's* monopoly, so now the immigrations on the East Side convinced other entrepreneurs that the *Voice,* too, could lose its primacy, and deserved to.

In 1957, when he was nineteen, Walter Bowart had flipped a coin in his hometown of Enid, Oklahoma, to see if he would go east or west, to New York or California. It came down east. Eight years later, he was painting and tending bar in New Jersey when his friend, the poet Ishmael Reed, asked him for help in starting up a newspaper.* Reed couldn't use Bowart's ideas, but did get him in touch with a poet friend, Allen Katzman. And those two, Bowart and Katzman, now carried it on. Bowart chipped in $1,000 of his own money. They scraped up another $4,000 from friends. They took offices at 147 Avenue A, corner of 10th Street. And, on October 1, 1965, not quite the tenth anniversary of the premiere of the *Village Voice,* they launched, with the same initial circulation of 2,500 the *Voice* had had, the *East Village Other*—the other village, the other voice.

---

*Something that Bowart had thought of doing before. From the *Village Voice,* July 23, 1958: "WRITERS-ARTISTS with avante-garde ideas to gamble on new shoestring publication. Paid on acceptance. We make money. You make money. Write, or interview in person after 6 p.m. W. H. Bowart, 100 Bedford St., N.Y.C."

The front page of Vol. 1, No. 1 was a headline, repeated all the way down the page: "TO COMMEMORATE THE GLORIOUS NEWSPAPER STRIKE THE HERETOFORE UNDERGROUND 'OTHER' EXPANDS ITS PATAREALISM." *Patarealism,* typically, was a word they made up. "PATAREALISM IS THE HISSING SOUND YOUR FLESH MAKES AS YOU BURN TO DEATH FOR A _____," said a message scrawled in black magic marker on the office walls. "The *East Village Other* is much more interested in reporting events before they happen than afterwards," said another. There was a wall poster of Prince Kar-Mi, "presenting mysteries of the spirit world and demonstrations of occult powers by a series of astounding feats that have no counterpart on earth," and written into the prince's mouth, cartoon-style, were the words, "Shit, man, I read all about it in *EVO.*" On the doors were painted—naturally—*LOV* and *JOY.*

The paper was literally swimming in the psychedelic revolution—acidhead graphics, "postlinear" prose. "High on the Range," a recipe column by "Panama Rose," offering tips on how to make such dishes as "marijuana balls." Its comic strip, drawn by art director Bill Beckman, featured the adventures of "Captain High, Weird Outlandish Wonder" (capital letters W-O-W), the hero "who never comes down" (only his feet showed) and foiled his nemesis, Inspector Nodding-Act, by intercepting the police radio band and diving to the location of the next dope bust to warn the doomed druggies in time. And there was more. Tuli Kupferberg of the Fugs, writing for them. A crossword, Hipuzzle. Plus "Poor Paranoid's Almanac," "A Guide for the Arrested," nude spreads of the "Slum Goddess of the Month," and "Swinger Services" classifieds (". . . Frenchman, graduate student, writer, will happily share his East Village apt. with swinging chick. Excellent for learning more about French ways"). There was political commentary on the level of a front-page cartoon showing Lyndon Johnson in a Nazi uniform with dollar bills where his swastika armbands ought to be, and reader dialogue on the level of "Dear Sir: Your newspaper is below the intellectual level of my 14-year-old son. . . ." "Dear Madam: If our newspaper is below the intellectual level of your 14-year-old son, it must be below your intellectual level also. . . ."

It had a lot of things, and it may have had one or two things the *Voice* did not have, but it was not cool. And, if it was not explicitly at war with the *Voice* at first, it was so after Walter Bowart's interview with Seymour Krim, published in the *Herald-Tribune* on December 27, 1965.

Just as New York has replaced Paris as the cultural center of the world, the East Village has become the true Montmartre of what real estate agents call Greenwich Village. . . .

The Voice is a very good paper, possibly not as good as the Christian Science Monitor. But they're getting conservative by the minute. . . .

When we make important decisions we consult 'I Ching,' the 2,500-year-old Chinese Book of Changes that was used by Confucius and Lao Tzu. Do you think the Voice could ever be as East-oriented as the East Village Other?

And by February 1, circulation having increased to 7,000, the *East Village Other* was ready to go from being a monthly to a biweekly, with a new editor—John Wilcock.

In addition to his column at the *Voice,* which he had never stopped, John Wilcock, since the beginning of *EVO,* had been writing a column for them, too. Now he went further, investing $1,100 of his own money and stepping up his own involvement as the paper stepped up its competition. When he did that, Dan Wolf and Ed Fancher did something they had been meaning to do for years.

They had not gotten along with him, not since the beginning, but, typically, they had not been able to bring themselves to fire him, and he had not taken it on himself to quit. They had simply coexisted with him, uneasily, limiting his connection to the paper as much as possible, denying him a desk at the office, but never actually getting around to dropping his column.

This was different now, though, and when Ed Fancher heard that John Wilcock had been going around the Village telling people that the *Voice* was a dying newspaper and that *EVO* was "the wave of the future," he called him into his office and told him he could not stay at the *Voice* if he was going to "promote them and slander us," and edit a rival newspaper. (Neither he nor Wolf knew about the $1,100 investment yet, though they found out later.) The next week, at the end of "the 529th Village Square," John Wilcock informed his readers that "after 10 years the editors have decided they want to drop my column and I have agreed with this decision. . . . This has never been a happy place for me to work," and "although I was one of its founders"—a claim Wolf and Fancher let him make in print, though it would never cease to irk them—"I have never had any financial interest in it or any say in its policy. . . . My fights with the paper have become more frequent." With that he was off to *EVO,* throwing himself into the enterprise with as much *élan* as he had manifested at the early *Voice.*

★ ★ ★

By 1969, the circulation of the *Village Voice* had continued to rise, to 138,000; but *EVO* had reached a third of that. That same year, after the *Voice,* which had also rejected an ad for Al Goldstein's *Screw* Magazine, rejected one for a homosexual dating service, a gay-rights group staged the first demonstration ever held outside, *against* the *Village Voice.*

That was also the same year Grove Press's *Evergreen Review* published, at the end of the year, a revisionist history of the paper written by New Left pundit J. Kirk Sale. Sale quoted Wilcock ridiculing his days at the *Voice* ("They wouldn't even let me print the name of the Fugs at first, they said 'That's just Wilcock trying to be dirty again.' ") He quoted Jeff Shero, editor of the underground humor magazine *Rat* (also East Village–based, and one might have thought more logical competition for Yippie Paul Krassner's *Realist*) and a one-time *Voice* contributor, putting the paper down: "I read it from time to time, but I don't really think it's relevant to anything I'm concerned with. The writers there aren't interested in change. . . . I think what's happened is the *Voice* has grown old, along with its readers. Sure, it still gets 100,000 people reading it, but they're the same people who used to read it, most of them, only they're getting older."

He blind-quoted a Lindsay aide saying, "The *Voice* isn't as important as it once was, five years ago, even three. . . . It doesn't have the same local sources." He blind-quoted a staffer that "two years ago, even last year maybe, there was a crusade. But not now. Now it's more like a lament." Thanks to a longstanding friendship with Stephanie Harrington, he got an interview with Dan Wolf, and revealed, shades of Tom Wolfe with William Shawn, that Dan Wolf was either fifty-two or fifty-three (he was fifty-four, actually) and that he was hard of hearing (correct; even after an operation on his ear in the seventies, he still couldn't hear very well, and refused to use a hearing aid). It was the paper of the "bo-libs," he wrote. Bohemian, liberal. "Bohemian, not hip, yip, digger or beat; liberal, not radical, revolutionary, love-cultured or anarchistic. The bo-lib, born into the Lost Generation, is getting to be an old man."

"Now it speaks for those whose revolutions have become doubts," said Sale about the paper, "whose hatreds have become merely distrusts, whose passions have become tempered interests. You've come a long way, baby, but you got stuck there."

★ ★ ★

All this had to pass, and it did. Bowart said, after a few months of Wilcock, "We needed some professionalism. Now maybe we've got too much," and Wilcock was off again, first to start his own *Other Scenes* (when he tried to take out an ad for it in the *Voice,* Sandy Fendrick made him pay cash—in advance), then around the world again. As the East Village idyll finally collapsed into a sleazy combat zone, *EVO*s circulation dipped by 7,000 in 1970 and it folded in 1971, the same year Bill Graham closed up his Fillmore East on Second Avenue after three years of operation; the same year a pack of pathological feminist media collectivists took over Jeff Shero's *Rat,* ran him out, and ran it into the ground in short order, attaining notoriety in the meantime only by running open letters from fugitive terrorists Susan Saxe, Katharine Power, and Jane Alpert; the same year, only a few months after vacating its offices in the building on University Place in the East Village that the *Voice* took over, *Evergreen* folded.

As the 1970s wore on, it became apparent that most of the ersatz, out-of-town *Voices* had failed to develop the sophisticated, diversified balance, the pool of writing talent, or the supportive readership to keep from tilting toward bankruptcy (Art Kunkin lost control of the *Los Angeles Free Press* in 1972 to a pro-Nixon businessman), Maoist politics, or sexual kinkiness. The latter, reflected in personal classified ads, was a field out of which the *Voice* eventually pulled entirely, and left to others who took it up—as the *Berkeley Barb* ("White guy turns on to blood, seeks more of same"), the *Boston Phoenix* ("Ladies, I can lick your problem"), and Cambridge's *The Real Paper* ("F-CK A CHINK! Imaginative, hung and handsome oriental super-stud into those subtleties of the East right up there for some freelance sex"), among others, did. Of all the imitators, the closest, and the most credible competitors, both came from Greater Boston, where a massive base of college-age readers proved able to support not one but two alternative papers, the *Phoenix* and *The Real Paper.* Both papers featured enough talent to almost bridge the gap with New York–caliber writing. Both, especially before 1974, had far more professional layout and graphics.

But the pattern was otherwise, and in the realm of the rock magazines it merely repeated itself. Thus, in 1974, even as *Rolling Stone* had come so far toward a rich respectability as to lure and land Richard Goodwin (even if only temporarily) to write for it about Washington politics, two other ex-fanzines—*Fusion* and *Zoo World*—went out of business. Looking back from the vantage point and climate of the 1970s, the accomplishments of the *Voice,* and of *Rolling Stone,* appeared to have been in socializing the mass media, in opening up access to them, rather than in fathering a race of imitators. It had entered the mainstream, and Dan Wolf, for the first time in his life, had been made to feel like an old man in the process.

12. 1969. . . AS THE NEW YEAR BEGINS, NAT

Hentoff ends his column, lamenting, "I was becoming more contentious than is good for self-knowledge." A week later he has changed his mind and resumed writing again. . . . Susan Brownmiller, back with the paper, on her trip to Pennsylvania to meet a seventy-nine-year-old abortionist, "the legendary Dr. Robert Douglas Spencer," and on the militant, feminist Redstockings . . .

. . . It is the season of disruption. Old leftist I. F. Stone is speaking at NYU when even he is confronted with a claque of New Left detractors. Nick Browne reports what happens.

A plague on all their houses was the message. Big power was not solely a capitalist problem. . . . In what society were reforms given a large audience? . . . If we tear down the structure of American society, what are we going to replace it with?

Shouts from the rear: "Cuba!"

"Listen, Cuba is only excused by our repression, much as I admire Fidel. . . . Communism is a technique for taking surplus capital out of the bellies of the working class." . . .

They had heard this before and didn't like it. He put down Marcuse. The hissing increased like a Sunnyside fight mob urging the fighters to mix it up.

He pointed out that in this capitalist country he was free to stand and talk. Free discussion was a reality.

From the hall: "But you can't make any changes!"

Large applause.

And Stone, weary as a cardinal: "Listen, if you brought about change you'd have to put three quarters of the population in concentration camps to reconcile them to that change."

That stopped them for a moment.

. . . Three weeks later, it happens again, to a culture symposium at the Friends Meeting Hall. Robert Pasolli gives the paper this report:

It was disruption pure and simple, although Steven Ben Israel, principal disrupter, called it at one point "a high seminar in brain damage repair." Julian Beck and Judith Malina, the heads of the radical theatre just back in New York,

238

sat calmly on the dais, along with fellow panelists Robert Brustein, Paul Goodman, and mediator Nat Hentoff, as members of the troupe romped, cavorted, and otherwise mocked the intellectual elite who had gathered for one of their exercises in civilized discourse.

Israel joined the issue within minutes of Brustein's opening remarks. Brustein was reading from notes, reasoning carefully and amiably, reiterating his well-known preference for high art. When he said that "art should be done by supremely gifted individuals," Israel yelled from halfway back in the hall, "We're all supremely gifted individuals." Brustein: "I dispute that." Israel: "Up against the wall." . . .

The last podium event before complete chaos was the advent of Norman Mailer, to whom the assembly reacted as if pulling a trump card. Mailer went to the dais, took a mike, and asked for quiet. There was a lot of applause, then he got his quiet. (Somebody near me said, "Shhh, God is speaking," in a tone which was more admiring than ironic.) Mailer assumed what looked like a cross between a barricades pose and a send-up of a barricades pose, but that might be his regular stance, and said some things about the French revolution. These were short observations, which he interspersed with long pauses for assessment if not for effect. During one of these, Israel yelled, "Mailer, you should have sent up your suit," and started jumping around on a pew. . . .

. . . It is too much for Feiffer, and in a famous strip that runs the week of May 22, 1969, he draws the moustached face of a smug student radical bragging, "I occupy buildings—raid files—scream obscenities—throw rocks—and call cops pigs—in an attempt to humanize this brutalized society." It is too much for Pete Hamill, too. At the beginning of the year, he offers the Left some rules of conduct to follow:

> . . . An absolute cleaning up of the language. . . . A black racist should be called a black racist. If George Wallace is a white racist, then Rap Brown is a black racist. . . .
>
> . . . Liberals in general, and intellectuals in particular, should cease functioning as excuse-makers for people who hate them. If Rap Brown calls me a honky or a racist bastard, I have no obligation to make excuses for him; my only obligation is to laugh at him, or to belt him. I certainly have no obligation to say: yeah, Rap, oh you're beautiful, Rap, oh please lash me

again, Rap, baby, give it to me some more while I make out the check. The liberals who put up with this sort of racist crap are masochist jellyfish. . . .

. . . *We should finally admit that no serious change in this country will ever be effected through Assholism.* Abbie Hoffman and Jerry Rubin and the Yippie kids who hang around them can be funny at times, and brave. But basically they are assholes. . . .

. . . *We should make some small start toward relieving the paranoia of the cops.* . . . Someone has to prove to me that you change them by calling them "pig" or by shooting random members of the force in the back from ambush . . .

. . . *We should stop the Romantic Revolutionaries every time they call for blood.* . . .

I remember one brave revolutionary in Chicago, who wanted to broadcast a tape recording from a loudspeaker on a high floor of the Chicago Hilton. The tape would tell the kids in Grant Park that the revolutionary was in the hotel, that they should storm the place and join him. Naturally, the kids would have been slaughtered by Daley's thugs and the National Guard. Naturally, this is what the revolutionary wanted. . . . Personally I'm tired of the sight of blood. I've seen enough blood in the last few years to last me a lifetime; some of the blood I saw last year ran right through America, and the wounds haven't stopped hemorrhaging.

. . . Hamill keeps it up, writing for the paper from the scene of Protestant-Catholic warfare in Northern Ireland, making the case for Herman Badillo to be the first Puerto Rican mayor in New York, and then suddenly, so suddenly Wolf and Fancher profess to learn of it for the first time only when they see his first column there, he is back with his old paper, the *Post.* . . . Newfield on the-makings-of-presidents author Theodore White, "The Groupie of the Power Elite" . . . Ross Wetzsteon at the police bust of the play *Che!* . . . Coverage of the arrest of twenty-one Black Panthers for conspiracy . . . The Easter Sunday Be-In has come a long way backwards in two years. Spectator Lenny Kaye writes what happens to a girl who strips naked in 1969:

She took off her clothes about 5 p.m., a little spaced out but sort of happy. The crowds immediately gathered (as they had each time someone took off their clothes). The photographers began snapping away and people began pushing into her. And more, and more, and she accepted them and God knows

to what she was sacrificing herself and the crowds moved in,
pinching and feeling and shoving and laughing and acting as
if they had never seen a girl, without her clothes, much less
touch one.

. . . 1969 is an election year, too, time to reelect John Lindsay or elect
someone new. And one of the candidates running in the Democratic
primary is none other than Norman Mailer. He is campaigning on ideas
that are new, strange, and different—making New York City the fifty-
first state, subdividing it into independent neighborhoods, banning
motor vehicles from Manhattan. He is supported by a battery of
writer-advisers (not to mention Jules Feiffer: "I'm for Norman because—because—because," sighs one of his characters). He has as his
candidate for City Council president none other than Jimmy Breslin.
And in the April 3 *Voice,* the candidate for mayor, calling the city he
hopes to govern "a cancer and leprosy ward that has infected the rest of
the country," and his running mate, saying of their prospective
opponents, "Those clowns haven't said anything right in 45 years.
They're a bunch of bums!" announce that "a series of strategy
meetings will be held this week." Out of those meetings comes yet
another addition to the campaign—campaign manager Joe Flaherty.
Three weeks later, Flaherty explains how it happened.

> . . . I arrived at Mailer's house and found a number of other
> writers, including myself, taking notes, all having purple wet
> dreams about next year's National Book Award for Arts and
> Letters. . . . Like all such evenings attended by polemicists, it
> resembled the building of the Tower of Babel. Right winger
> Noel Parmentel wanted Mailer to run alone on the ticket;
> others wanted him to run with Jimmy Breslin in an attempt to
> appeal to the working class. Another group was pushing for a
> Black Panther for comptroller, and still another wanted a
> woman on the ticket to run on the platform of female rights.
> Along about now I was wishing that Carmine DeSapio would
> enter the room and restore some decent totalitarian clubhouse
> order.
> Besides all this, the evening was taking on a carnival
> atmosphere. Ice cubes were tinkling in glasses like the Bells of
> St. Mary's and the ideas being put forth were getting more
> bizarre with every chime. Mailer finally took the floor, present-
> ing a surrealistic platform with his baroque pointing and
> jabbing, Jimmy Cagney style. His running mate, Jimmy
> Breslin, sat in a chair, growling his ideas on the issues: ''When

we get on tv with them, we'll just tell them they're full of shit''
and ''fuck them and their Mickey Mouse issues—the city is
lost'' and ''I wouldn't even let Norman *debate* those fuckin'
bandits; he'd get arrested for consorting.'' By now my notes
resembled passages from ''Finnegans Wake.'' . . .

As radical as the program sounded, it made complete sense
to me, and I also realized there wasn't a politician in New York
who would dare run on such ideas. Mailer was now my
man . . .

But the thing that intrigued me about Mailer was that he
carried the idea of community control to its smallest unit—
man itself. When someone suggested the idea of replacing the
water in toilets with chemicals to remove the waste, Mailer
refused, noting that man is losing contact with himself and
''should be able to smell his own shit.'' Programs for the poor
were repugnant to him because they place man in slots
negating his chance: ''to forge the destiny of his soul.'' In
short, he is still naive enough to think our soul possesses the
grace to manage our own lives.

. . . In the primary, Mailer, who (naturally) receives the (naturally)
qualified endorsement of his old friend Dan Wolf ("He has become an
irritating, occasionally infuriating, but creative national asset and
should be nurtured"), places fourth in a field of five. It is a victory of
sorts; he does not finish last. But John Lindsay, meanwhile, in the
Republican primary, fails to finish first . . .

. . . Lindsay is in trouble. With Jews over Ocean Hill–Brownsville
and the school strike; Newfield records his hard time with a Jewish
audience that February ("A man leaped up to shout 'liar' with such
violence that his yarmulka fell off"). In Queens, where snow crews fail
to remove a blizzard and leave the borough's inhabitants trapped for
over twenty-four hours that winter. With liberal Democrats who broke
ranks to support him in 1965, and whom he has paid back by, in the case
of Edward Koch, campaigning against them for Congress. Mary
Nichols, for one, takes him to task. "Fusion is a dead issue at Gracie
Mansion," she writes. "Mayor Lindsay, I hope you avoid—at least for a
few weeks—those St. Paul's School chapel speeches. . . . Mr. Clean, you
had better come off that high moral perch." When he announces for
reelection in the spring, Pete Hamill laments: "This year, John Lindsay
must run as one of them."

. . . He is in trouble with the GOP rank-and-file, too; he loses the
primary to an archconservative state senator, John Marchi, and his

hopes for reelection rest on the third-party Liberal line in a three-way race with Marchi and the Democratic winner, City Controller Mario Procaccino, a crude machine hack. "John V. Lindsay faces the most difficult problem of his career," writes Mary Nichols, his disaffected supporter, in the primary's aftermath. "It is whether he can become humble and learn from experience. It may be that he has an inherent character defect and cannot." But he can, and does, at least for the election, reassembling a liberal coalition free of Republican patronage debts in time to head off the gaffe-prone Procaccino. Wolf endorses him again—"he is aware that he must experiment to keep the city alive, that the death of a city is not the quick death of a thrombosis but the slow death of cancer. He does not have the temperament of a mourner at the wake." And Joe Flaherty produces a fanciful diary of "Mayor" Procaccino's first day in office: "Over the sounds of the piped-in Muzak, one can hear the laborers laying linoleum in the East Wing. . . . 11:30 a.m.—The mayor announced a citywide contest to rename Gracie Mansion, because the 'real people'—the 'little guy' who makes this town tick—thinks 'Gracie' sounds too faggy." . . . In November, Lindsay wins a second term. . . .

. . . It is the year of the Vietnam Moratorium, and of the Nixon administration's first attempts to suppress dissent and intimidate the news media. That fall, as his tiny dancer returns to perform "A dance to —", she is interrupted by Attorney General John Mitchell, who begins interrogating her, "On or about September 28, 1969 did you or did you not perform in this cartoon a 'dance' or so-called 'Dance to Autumn'? And in this cartoon did you or did you not encourage, through bodily movement and gesture, demonstrations against the war in Vietnam? And subsequent to this cartoon did or did not such demonstrations, in fact, take place? This cartoon was in violation of Title 18, United States Code, Section 2101."

. . . That summer, Steve Lerner is at Woodstock as

> Stoned silly most of the time, more than half a million freaks from all over the country made the painful pilgrimage to Max Yasgur's 600-acre farm to play in the mud. Many of the long-hairs were the only hippies on their block, or in their home town, and the mass rally served as a confirmation of their lifestyle after months of sitting alone counting their psyche-delic beads.

. . . Later, in December, there is coverage of the would-be Woodstock that wasn't—the Rolling Stones concert in Altamont, California, where a gun-waving fan is knifed to death by rampaging Hell's Angels bodyguards. . . . Vivian Gornick goes to Jack Kerouac's funeral, Mary Nichols goes to Carmine DeSapio's trial. . . . Michael Zwerin interviews George Harrison in London and Mike McDonald writes about the incredible climb to the top—from ninth place to the World Series in one year—of the New York Mets.

★ ★ ★

In the early morning hours of June 28, 1969, the New York City police staged yet another raid against yet another gay bar in the West Village, the Stonewall Inn. But things did not work out quite as expected this time. This time, when they were told to disperse, the homosexuals fought back. They regrouped out in the street and stormed the place, trapping the police inside, throwing bricks and bottles and garbage, finally setting fire to the club. And they were back the next night, and again the night after that, to demonstrate.

The gay liberation movement had begun, and the Stonewall was its Lexington and Concord. And the *Village Voice* was there—Howard Smith on the inside with the police, Lucian Truscott on the outside with the gays. Except that Truscott, a new Dan Wolf discovery, a West Point cadet writing for the *Voice* while on leave from the Academy, did not call them "gays." He called them "the forces of faggotry," a term that had always been acceptable when used by *Village Voice* writers in the past, but not anymore. That gave the new, militant gays a score to settle with the *Village Voice*. And when, while Ed Fancher was on vacation, a gay dating service went in to place an ad, and Rose Ryan refused to accept any ad with the word *gay* in it, they had another.

One afternoon in late November, Howard Smith was looking out at the paper from the window of his office across the street. The office was something the paper was paying for, so that if someone came in to see him, he could be buzzed by phone, pick up his binoculars, see who it was, and tell the desk whether he was in or not. But this day, Howard Smith looked out and saw four pickets, carrying signs, outside the *Voice* building, protesting *Village Voice* discrimination against gays. And this time he did the calling.

Dan Wolf was out, but Ed Fancher was in. He knew what was happening, knew what had brought it on, and instead of doing anything about it was settling in for a long siege. He explained what Rose Ryan had done. "And now they want to see me to countermand the order."

"Well, are you going to do it?" Smith wanted to know.

"I can't *now*," said Ed Fancher. "If I give in to this demand, they'll do it every week."

"Are you aware of what's going on outside your window?" Howard Smith shot back. "Times have changed, Ed. Fifteen minutes ago there were four of them. Now there are eight. See them," he urged, and at length Fancher agreed to—a delegation of three or four of them, though, not the whole group. They, in turn, agreed to that. Howard Smith, meanwhile, got on the phone and called up Michael Smith, who was going through a homosexual period at the time, to ask him to be there. He agreed, and a few minutes later, they entered the building, past a real crowd now, perhaps two dozen pickets, and went upstairs to have their confrontation.

Three spokesmen for the group came into Ed Fancher's office. To begin, the publisher offered them a concession: the word *gay* could now appear in ads for the *Village Voice*. But they were no longer interested in that. Instead, as such Movement delegations of the late sixties were wont to do, they now had other demands. They told Fancher, at one time or another during the harangue that followed, that they wanted free ad space in his paper, a gay community news section, a gay editorial slant, and gay writers hired on staff. To none of this would Fancher give in, and when he did not, the group only became more inflamed. "You have no gay writers!" one of them screamed. To that, Howard Smith had an answer. "Yes, we do," he said. "Oh, yeah, who?" he was asked. "Him," he said, pointing to Michael Smith. His questioner, taken a little aback, turned to Michael Smith and asked him was he gay, and Michael Smith said yes he was, and that round went to the men from the *Village Voice*. Finally, after they had calmly sat through it all, Howard Smith decided enough was enough, and that he would try to gain tactical advantage by deliberately losing *his* temper. He picked on one of their points and began to scream, *"That's handing you the newspaper!"* It seemed to work. At any rate, it was their guests who now calmed down, and when they left, it was agreed among all parties that the *Village Voice* would now take gay ads, and that the gay rights group would not attempt to make any further demands telling the *Voice* what it could print.

But the issue of sex—any kind—in the paper would come up again, and when it did their reaction would be typically inconsistent. When, that same year, they began to get complaints from the Chemical Bank, where they had placed the paper's account, about the four-letter words they were running in their newspaper, and the bank withdrew its ads in protest, Dan Wolf and Ed Fancher walked into Chemical one day, withdrew all their assets, walked over to Manufacturers Hanover, and redeposited everything with them; two years later, the partners, after running them for years until they had grown by leaps and bounds, tried to rid their paper of ads for unlicensed massage parlors, and artist

Larry Rivers was refused an ad for his new book, *Tits,* because of the title. Eventually Wolf and Fancher came to be grateful for the rise of *Screw,* the sleazo sex magazine of Al Goldstein's they had once refused an ad for, back before the gay issue ever came up, because it took the personal sexual classifieds away from them.

★ ★ ★

Nineteen sixty-nine was the year of the Chemical Bank incident. It was the year of the gay demonstration, making them feel as besieged and harried as many a college administrator of the time, which is initially just how Edwin Fancher had wanted to react. It was the year of the height of *EVO*'s success, and of J. Kirk Sale's harsh piece in *Evergreen,* both making them feel that maybe they were out of it now, that maybe time, and things, had passed them by. It was the year they decided they wanted to move out of their old offices on Sheridan Square, the Sheridan Square that had begun to remind Dan Wolf of the Grand Guignol, what with people with painted faces coming out after dark. It was the year after the death of Don McNeill.

It was a time to feel old. It was a time to feel tired. It was a time to feel mortal.

★ ★ ★

In the summer of 1968, Dan Wolf took a call at work from R. Peter Straus, communications capitalist, owner of New York radio station WMCA, and fairly well-known supporter of fairly liberal causes. Straus said he had something he wanted to discuss, and would Wolf want to get together to talk about it. Wolf agreed.

What Straus had in mind was either buying or starting a paper or papers in the suburbs around Washington, D.C., perhaps as a cooperative venture with the *Voice.* He wanted to know what Dan Wolf thought about the idea.

Dan Wolf's reaction was that he had no reaction, but he agreed to go down to Washington and take a look around. He reported back to Straus that the only kind of paper they could have put out would have been a kind of Washington version of the *Villager,* which obviously he was not interested in doing. But now Straus came back at him with other ideas—maybe a new afternoon paper in New York, or an expanded *Voice.* And he wanted to know if there was an opportunity to invest in the paper.

That would depend, Dan Wolf told him, on our getting to know one another better, but Mailer needs money, I think. Why not contact him, see if you can buy some of his stock, and we'll see how things work out from there?

Peter Straus followed Dan Wolf's advice. On August 21, 1968, the sale of 5 percent of stock belonging to Norman Mailer was duly announced. Meanwhile, Fancher, Wolf, and an assistant of Straus's were sitting down to discuss other ideas—book-publishing ventures, travel clubs. One of the possibilities they explored, at least to consider it: that R. Peter Straus would purchase 51 percent, majority control, of the *Village Voice*. And while that was going on, they agreed, or thought they had agreed, on something else—the hiring of Mary Nichols.

For the better part of three years now she had been doing public relations for the Parks Department. She was eager to return, but in the intervening years she had gotten a divorce from her husband, Robert. There was no way, not with a family to support, she could afford to return at her old salary, and no way the *Voice* could meet her new one. But, they thought, if she split her duties—part-time city editor at the *Voice,* part-time radio commentator on WMCA—and they split her $395 salary between them, it could work out. Mary Nichols was agreeable to that. And so, it seemed to them, was R. Peter Straus. So Mary Nichols quit her job, and started work at the *Voice,* and had a meeting with R. Peter Straus where he offered her $75 a week.

It was only a part-time job, Straus explained, and he couldn't very well share the costs fifty-fifty. When he heard that, Dan Wolf decided that if he was going to have to pay her $320 a week, he may as well take care of the whole thing himself. (Thus, he *could* meet her old salary, it seemed, if he had to.) He also decided that R. Peter Straus was not someone he could work with. The assistant who had carried on the discussions about investing and expanding with them soon afterwards left Straus's employ, and they did not pursue it after that.

But the idea had been planted in Dan Wolf's head now, and in the succeeding months he began to articulate it more and more to his friend Ed Fancher. "What if one of us gets hit by a truck?" he would ask. If one of us dies or is incapacitated, what would happen to this paper? What would it be worth?

The fear of being wiped out was only a part of what was on Dan Wolf's mind. The other was that he was bone-weary. He was fifty-four years old. He had been forty years old before he had accomplished anything with his life, and for the last fourteen years he had been working sixty, seventy hours a week to keep it going. He and his wife had waited until he was forty-nine, and she was thirty-eight, to have their first child, John, born to them in 1964, at which time he had worked himself up to $80 a week. Now, they had another child, a daughter, Margaret, and Dan Wolf's newspaper was going to show a profit of $264,000 for the fiscal year ending July 31, 1969, and for the first time in his life he was living well.

But he wanted to make sure it was going to continue that way, and he was afraid that if he could not separate himself from his work grind at the paper now he never would. He wanted to set himself up, to provide for his family, now, not later, when it might be too late. He was, after all, a product of the Depression, and in the back of his mind was the thought that things might never be going as good again as they are now.

He kept thinking and talking that way until the early months of 1969, when he and Jack Newfield were talking, and the subject turned to Bobby Kennedy, and Newfield told a story about a time in Kennedy's East Side apartment when he and the other disciples had been assembled, how in the middle of the meeting Kennedy had started to read poetry aloud and then stared off into space, how everybody there had been in a state of mind-blown reverence, how he himself had gone, "Wow," out loud, until one of Kennedy's aides came over and whispered in his ear, cautioning him, telling him not to get too taken in by the scene, not to take it too seriously.

That aide's name was Carter Burden, and you really ought to meet him, Newfield suggested: he's not like most of the people who surrounded Bobby. He's different. He's going to go places.

Dan Wolf had heard about Carter Burden, and what he had heard—from Mary Nichols, from his friend, Congressman Ed Koch—had been favorable. And Dan Wolf knew that Jack Newfield had very little use for most conventional politicians. But in this case Jack Newfield was very impressed, and Dan Wolf was impressed that Jack Newfield was impressed. He asked Newfield to set up a meeting, just the two of them, for drinks sometime. Newfield did.

They met at a bar on the Upper East Side of town, and Carter Burden came only three minutes late. Which, as Dan Wolf discovered later, was practically a compliment.

Carter Burden. Harvard '63. Columbia Law '66. Great-grandson of Cornelius Vanderbilt. Great-nephew of Douglas Fairbanks, Sr. Husband of Amanda Mortimer, who as it happened was the stepdaughter of William S. Paley, who as it happened was the board chairman of CBS. A kid who had money, and power, and pedigree, and had had them all since birth. The epitome of the well-connected WASP. The Beautiful Person, Ivy League edition. Those were the facts about Carter Burden. And so far, the facts were all Dan Wolf knew.

But he was not a right-wing Republican, as Wolf would have expected based on his background. And he was not a *Women's Wear Daily* playboy, which is the image Dan Wolf had of him. Instead, Wolf found himself in the company of a smart young man with a nice personality, an omnivorous reader, a thinker of enormous intelligence, sensitivity, and perception. He was charmed.

They talked in philosophical terms, about politics, his career, his life, the *Voice*. Carter Burden asked who owned it, and Dan Wolf told him— Ed Fancher and I own 35 percent each, Norman Mailer owns 15 percent, Whitey Lutz 10 percent, and Peter Straus 5 percent. Burden wondered why Peter Straus was interested, and Wolf told him it had been up in the air at one time whether Straus was going to buy a bigger chunk of it, but no longer. Then he said, "Ultimately, we will sell. You just don't go on forever. But it's not something you sell to anyone."

"If you ever consider selling *The Voice*," Carter Burden said, "or even selling part of it, I wish you'd let me know. I'd be interested."

Dan Wolf asked him, "Do you really mean that?"

And Carter Burden said, "Yes."

That was the end of that for the time being. The two men went on to talk of other things. Then they parted. But the next day Dan Wolf told Ed Fancher what Carter Burden had said, and renewed his arguments: One of us would find it awfully difficult to run the paper without the other. We need to find a buyer. Now.

Ed Fancher was not convinced they needed to, but he realized that his was a very different financial situation from Dan Wolf's. For one thing, he was still a bachelor. For another, he had a family trust fund coming to him, and had always had his practice, so he had never known outright poverty the way Wolf had. A sale, besides realizing some money right now from their investment, might enable them to expand. And Dan Wolf importuned him; Carter Burden seemed to be someone they could live with, someone they could trust, someone they could rely on to take over the *Voice* and run it as they had wished after they were gone. He seemed to be interested in keeping the *Voice* as it was, unlike Capital Cities Broadcasting, which, they had heard from a third party, might be interested, and in a position to offer more money. So Fancher told his friend, sometime that spring, to go ahead, to start negotiations for the sale. Before he did, he asked Wolf how much he thought he would want for the paper.

Just like that, Wolf was ready. $3.2 million, split between them, in exchange for 51 percent control, he said. For him, $1.6 million would guarantee that he had a million dollars left over after taxes, and that was what he wanted. Ed Fancher said, Sounds OK to me. And that was how it was done—no appraisal, no consultants coming in and telling them how much everything was worth. Dan Wolf placed a call to Carter Burden, and told him they were ready to talk.

Ed Fancher met Burden over lunch one day late that spring. Other lunches followed. They all got to know each other. And now Ed Fancher, too, was convinced it was the right move. The main reason was they simply liked him. This was not, as Fancher put it, like selling a brick. This was their baby, and if they were going to sell, it had to be to somebody they could work—and work out a succession—with, somebody they could count on to maintain the tradition they had started. It wasn't just money. Everything they knew about Carter Burden they liked; everything they had heard about him was good; every impression he had made on them was favorable. And Burden was anxious for them to stay on at the *Voice,* to keep on running it just the way they had been. Over one of these lunches then, it was agreed: Carter Burden would buy 51 percent control for $3.2 million, with his central demand being that they continue to run the paper. That June, as Carter Burden prepared to go into a primary for nomination to a seat on the City Council, a profile of him and his wife Amanda, by reporter Mary Breasted (noting that she "was rated among the best-dressed women of the world while she was at Wellesley," and that he, a *magna cum laude* at Harvard, "did about as well at Columbia Law School"), appeared, followed by an editorial endorsement from Dan Wolf (in which Wolf revealed to the readers of the *Village Voice* that Burden was many things—"the best representative of the 'new politics' running in the primary," "concerned about the human condition," "personally engaged in the causes he espouses," a man with "a far-ranging mind" who was "in the process of defining himself in the crucible of politics"—all that, but *not* the fact that he was a prospective buyer of the newspaper they were reading). And that summer, Ed Fancher went off on vacation, leaving it with Dan Wolf and the lawyers to work out all the details in his absence before he returned.

But when he returned, in August, all the details had not been worked out.

The first snag was hit when Carter Burden's lawyers advised that, for tax purposes, the deal must be for 80 percent of the stock, not 51. When he heard that, Edwin Fancher was upset. He and Dan Wolf had already given some thought to possibly buying up some of Mailer's or Lutz's stock when the deal was over with, so that they would be left with more than 19 percent between them. But that was something they wanted to consider later, as an option. Now they *had* to do it, right away, to avoid being written out of the paper altogether, to swing the deal at all in fact. It would have to be a complicated package now, and it would be for a lot more stock than they had been prepared originally to give up, and Ed Fancher was annoyed. For the first time, he gave serious thought to the possibility of breaking the deal off, but he did not. Then the president of Union News called him up, to remind him that when Union News had agreed to put its 5,000 or so copies of the *Voice* on its stands it had retained the option of someday distributing the papers itself instead of letting Dan List do it, and to tell him that it was now exercising its option. A few days after that a man who identified himself as Willie Levine, their "new distributor," walked into their offices downstairs, introduced himself to circulation manager Carole Rogers, and demanded a contract from the paper for him. Now, it so happened that Willie Levine was the brother-in-law of Henry Garfinkle, owner of Union News, which Fancher already knew. It also so happened that he was under federal indictment in Boston, and the subject of a continuing series of articles on organized crime appearing in the *Wall Street Journal*. So Fancher stalled until he finally received another call from the president of Union News threatening him, "Look, either you take Willie Levine as your distributor or you're off the stands."

"OK," said Edwin Fancher. "We're off the stands." And he promptly called his prospective buyer up to tell him what had been done, confident he had done the right thing in refusing to get mixed up with a character of the caliber of Willie Levine, certain that his new-owner-to-be would think so too.

But, to his surprise, Carter Burden only wanted to talk about Fancher's "raping the assets," and sent word through his negotiators that he was, in fact, very displeased with what Fancher had done.* And then, on a day when they had told Wolf's and Fancher's lawyer, Louis Hoynes, that they were too busy to see him, two of Burden's attorneys came down to inspect the premises they wanted at 80 University Place. Wolf and Fancher considered the move essential and had said so— relations between the overcrowded classified staff and Rose Ryan had deteriorated to the point where they had been given notice by the New York Newspaper Guild of an attempt to unionize their part-time workers. But Burden's lawyers recommended against it, at least for a while, by which time the property might well be gone, and there was another hitch.

But the deal went ahead, and in the fall of that year Dan Wolf and Ed Fancher made the journey to Provincetown, Massachusetts, to see Norman Mailer. They outlined the details, as they had already done over the phone before they came up, and Mailer told them that he really didn't want to sell any of his *Voice* stock, that he had always wanted to leave it as a gift to his children, but that as a friend, if they needed it, this was his offer: he would give up 5 percent of his stock for

---

*In the end, Ed Fancher won his battle. After six weeks of continuing exposures in the *Wall Street Journal*, Union News sent word to him through an intermediary it was willing to revert to the original agreement—to distribute the papers itself, rather than farm them out to any "independent" such as Willie Levine.

$100,000, 10 percent for $280,000, and all 15 percent for $500,000. Next day, on their way to see Whitey Lutz, they considered his offer: he was asking about $30,000 more for 10 percent than they had been prepared to give, but Mailer was Mailer, and they knew him well enough by now, so they decided to take him up on his offer for that percentage at that price. That night they reached Manchester, Massachusetts, and stayed over with Whitey Lutz and his wife there. Lutz listened, and got back to them through his lawyer—he and his wife would sell all but one of their 10 percent for $9,000. Then they took R. Peter Straus out to lunch, and he told them what he wanted—$100,000 for his 5 percent— once again, about $30,000 more than they wanted to spend, but they took it.

In January 1970, they drew up the agreement, finally. Carter Burden, in the end, paid Dan Wolf and Ed Fancher an even $3 million, not $3.2 million, roughly $43 a share for 28 percent each of their stock. At the same time he bought up the stock Mailer and Lutz and Straus had put on the block, to give him his total of 80 percent. To do all this, he did not purchase any stock himself—instead he formed a holding company, Taurus Communications, 70 percent owned by Carter Burden, to buy it for him. The other 30 percent in Taurus was to be in the possession of one Bartle Bull, the man for whom it was named (*Taurus* being Latin for "bull"), the man who had met Carter Burden at Harvard, introduced him to his wife Amanda, and just managed his successful campaign for city councilman.* He had met Dan Wolf and Ed Fancher over dinner one evening at La Grenouille, and then came in on the negotiations representing Burden; in fact, he had been one of the two lawyers who had gone down to survey 80 University Place and advised Burden to hold off taking space there.

A couple of times during the bargaining Burden had said to his old friend Bull, "You don't seem very responsive," meaning about the deal Burden had planned. Which was true. And when, besides the guarantee on its loans to him, Manufacturers Hanover, Burden's bank, wanted someone representing him there at the paper to protect the investment, Bartle Bull agreed to do it, to put $100,000 of his own money into Taurus Communications and become its namesake. But first he went out to lunch with Carter Burden at the restaurant in the CBS Building

---

*With, once again, the support of Dan Wolf: "Carter Burden, at 28, has already a substantial biography of commitment. As an aide to the late Senator Robert F. Kennedy, working daily in Bedford-Stuyvesant, he learned what must have been unbelievable to anyone from his background. The thrust of his campaign indicated that he learned it well and that he will be a courageous spokesman for the people he represents rather than the captive of special interests." (From the *Voice*, October 30, 1969.)

and told him his misgivings. "Haven't you ever seen *The Treasure of Sierra Madre?*" he asked his friend.

"What do you mean?" Burden asked him.

"Problems develop when you start sharing money together," Bull spelled it out.

"What are you talking about? We've just been through this campaign together," was Burden's reply.

"The trouble with mixing friendship and money, Carter," Bull answered, "is that you can screw up the friendship."

Despite his misgivings, Bartle Bull went along, and when, a few days before the signing, Carter Burden asked Dan Wolf and Ed Fancher whether they would mind if Bartle came into the picture and went to work down at the *Voice* with them, maybe they could teach him a little about the business and he could help out in some way, they said fine. Dan Wolf, for one, thought Carter should know what was happening with his investment. And so Bartle Bull came on board, with the vague title of "vice-president and general counsel," and with duties that were left undefined.

What was not left undefined, however, was that Dan Wolf and Ed Fancher were to have total editorial control. Carter Burden was very specific on that, so specific he held up the agreement until the terms of their employment contract made it absolutely, emphatically clear that he could not exercise any editorial authority, and could not therefore be held responsible for editorial policy. He wanted Wolf and Fancher to continue on the exact same basis as they had before, and toward that end offered them ten-year employment contracts. They did not want that much, and negotiated him down to five years. But the contract was not terminal; at the end of five years it could be either renegotiated or renewed. Under its terms Dan Wolf and Ed Fancher were to receive $80,000 now, with the rest of their money to come in five annual installments, plus interest, plus annual salaries of $62,000 for Wolf and $42,000 for Fancher (based on a scale of two-thirds of his time spent as publisher, the rest as psychologist), which was about what they were already making, plus bonuses if earnings reached certain levels. And, besides all that, he gave them a new shareholders' agreement, to replace the old one, with all of its references to special arrangements with Howard Bennett they had wanted to get rid of, one that stated simply, in what seemed to them to be ironclad terms, that in the event Carter Burden chose to sell any of his stock they had the right of first refusal on it.

The agreement was signed and announced on January 23, 1970. Fancher refused to discuss details for the media, but did say that he foresaw an expansion by the *Voice* into international circulation and book publishing. Bartle Bull promised, "The *Village Voice* will cover Burden as candidly as it always has."

At that moment, Daniel Wolf and Edwin Fancher were convinced that they had it all. They had taken a paper from nothing, starved with it, turned it into a bonanza, and now, fifteen years later, they had sold it in such a way as to set themselves up financially for the rest of their lives. And they still had their livelihood: the paper was still theirs to run, for as long as they wanted it. They had their money. They had their editorial freedom. They had their security. And now they looked forward to getting to know their new owner Carter Burden much better, convinced they had made the ideal sale to the ideal guy.

They hadn't.

The fact was that, for the first time in his life, Dan Wolf's Distant Early Warning system, his psychoanalytical antenna, had failed him. For Carter Burden was not what he seemed to be, not at all, and there would come a time when Dan Wolf, and Edwin Fancher too, would regret ever having seen anything in him, regret *not* having seen through him.

Perhaps it was the circumstances of Carter Burden's birth that had done it to him, the fact that he had never *had* to earn or work for anything a day in his life, the fact that his own fate had never been on the line in anything he had ever done, that had made him the way he was. But something had done it. For, in the clutch, Carter Burden acted as if he did not have to account for his actions the way other people had to, that he could just do whatever he pleased and not even have to consider the effects of what he was doing on other people. This streak, this weakness, was lying there in Carter Burden's character, and, in time, it came out.

As the seventies wore on, the glamour in Carter Burden's varnish began to wear off. His political career did not pan out—he did not go on to higher office. Neither did his marriage; he and his wife, the Beautiful Couple, split up. And, in his publishing career, it was even worse.

He was nonfunctional. That was the word Dan Wolf came up with to describe him, and eventually even his old friend Bartle Bull agreed with it. He had to be nursemaided, coddled, pushed, prodded, and cajoled just to get him through an ordinary business day. He thought nothing of keeping people waiting for hours, or even failing to keep his appointments at all, and if other people were stood up or had their schedules wrecked by him, that was their problem, not his.

He was willful, and he was wimpy. He was supine, and he was sneaky. He had been spoiled. He could not handle tension, or scenes, or any kind of interpersonal difficulties. He was a model of disgrace under pressure. He was about as weak as it is possible for a man to be and still be considered a man. And, in time, he would move on from breaking his dates to breaking his word. In his relations with his business partners, Carter Burden resembled a natty little sportscar with four shifts—postpone, ignore, avoid, and sell. He was a dangerous dandy.

But, by the time they would find all this out, it would be too late for Dan Wolf and Ed Fancher to do anything about it.

And now they had sold him their newspaper.

III.
. . . AND THE CLAY

13. WHEN CARTER BURDEN BOUGHT THE

Voice, and insisted that his interest in it was purely financial, there were those who doubted that, particularly, among the writers, Jack Newfield and Joe Flaherty. But the staff as a whole was remarkably quiescent about the fact that they were now suddenly under the control of someone who was, after all, an ambitious politician. Flaherty, for one, tested the limits early; soon after the sale, he covered a Democratic state convention where Burden was, and made a point of referring to him as a "groupie" (of Arthur Goldberg, a candidate for governor), "an ingenue to the resort's tennis pro" (the conclave was held at Grossinger's), and, wrongly, as an "Assemblyman" (which mistake got into the paper). He wanted to see if it would get through, and it did.* A year later, Burden passed another, more public, test.

In March of 1971, Noel Parmentel, one of the paper's few right-wing contributors over the years ("I want to give Red China a seat in the United Nations—ours," he had said in 1963) had a fourteen-page, two-part series published in the *Voice.* It was entitled "Portnoy in Tall Cotton," its subject was Henry Kissinger, and its focus was "mainly a speculation into whether a public trust could become a public thrust." To that end, Parmentel spared nothing of Kissinger's—not his supposed Jewish complex, not his sex life, not his power drive. Kissinger, Parmentel explained, was a man "forever sniffing about the corridors of power," and "as autocratic in his demands for a good press as was ever that other little German *doktor,* Joseph Paul Goebbels. . . . Many White House observers behave as obscenely obsequiously to Kissinger as Kissinger does to his betters. . . . It's 'Doctor' Kissinger this and 'Doctor' Kissinger that. . . . He revels in this title glory as much as any Great Neck dentist ever did."

The article "goes on endlessly on the theme that Henry Kissinger is physically revolting and that therefore the notion that he could be attractive to women is a Portnoyan fantasy," conservative columnist William F. Buckley, Jr., informed his readers soon afterwards. "Offhand I would say that five thousand words of the series are devoted to this extraordinary theme. Most of the balance is devoted to an

---

*Flaherty had interviewed Burden prior to the sale for a possible article, which he subsequently did not write. Burden, he wrote later in an unpublished reminiscence, "spent most of the time taking notes on what I thought about the city. Flattering, to be sure, but when a millionaire who is out to save a city careening toward bankruptcy takes notes from a man whose economics never got beyond the tooth fairy . . . one is not impressed."

extended ribbing of Kissinger's Jewishness, on and on and on about how he's ashamed of it, how he is really nothing more than a social climbing little kraut whose Prussian instincts serve him well in his capacity as cold-war enthusiast. Then a few thousand words of anonymous slander, allegedly by ex-professors, associates, friends, all of whom, seriously, sound exactly like Parmentel, and that is it." The piece was, Buckley wrote, "the sort of thing that used to appear in *Confidential,* and gets excused by the intellectuals if the victim is an associate of Richard Nixon," and its author was "an amusing verbal brawler who is probably the most tasteless polemicist in America."

But that was not why Buckley had written his column, because he went on to reveal that, in the aftermath of the article, he had actually written a letter of complaint to Carter Burden, councilman of the City of New York and chief stockholder in the *Village Voice,* and received a reply, from which he now quoted. "It would be a grave disservice," Burden had written Buckley, "to the integrity of the paper and its staff if I were to presume that mere ownership of stock gives me a special right to protest its policies. That is not to say that I do not recognize the responsibility which is inherent in any stock ownership—I fully accept responsibility," he insisted, but it was for the writers "to write what they choose," not for him to censor or disapprove. "So," Buckley interpreted Burden's comments, "it comes down to: If I can make a buck by publishing an article that trades in antisemitism, sex-talk and slander, I consider it my 'responsibility' to do so." Of Burden, whom he described as "a young and ambitious millionaire, a Roman Catholic aristocrat . . . who has his eyes on higher office and could certainly count on the aid of the New York Establishment, in which he is a heavy stockholder," yet whose purchase of the *Voice* had "shattered the swingers, as if the Holy See had bought controlling interest in *Playboy,*" he predicted: "That young man will go far."

As it turned out, Carter Burden was right: it was "mere ownership of stock" to him, nothing more. Bill Buckley was right, too: Carter Burden did go far, though not in the direction people expected. And, because it was "mere ownership of stock," politicization of the *Village Voice,* by Carter Burden or anyone else, was not what happened to the paper in the 1970s. Something else instead did.

In April of 1970, the initial doubts of its new owners overcome, the *Village Voice* moved its headquarters away from its home of eleven years, to a narrow, five-story structure halfway between Washington and Union Squares, on the corner of University Place and 11th Street. There, they finally had the room they needed. But something was missing. At the old place, they had all been together, out there in the open, totally accessible to whoever might come in off the street. In the new one, street level was taken up with classified; the writers were all on another floor, the fourth, walled off from each other in their own separate offices and cubicles; Dan Wolf's and Ed Fancher's office was on yet another floor, the fifth. Travel between the two floors—traffic between writers and editors—was practical only by using the back stairs, and people downstairs could come up only via the front elevator; the days when anyone could just wander in off the street to see someone were gone. The public was cut off from them, and they were cut off from each other. It was a setup ideal for the creation of cabals and cliques, for plotting and "Politburos," as Joe Flaherty called them, and they began occurring now as never before in the paper's history.

In March of 1970, the paper raised its price to twenty cents an issue. That was only the start of a new profit drive ordered by its absentee owner, who, for the five years that Fancher and Wolf were scheduled to remain at their posts, was going to be in debt not only to them but to the bank for an unpaid principal. The drive continued—the price went up to twenty-five cents in May 1973, thirty-five cents outside the city— and extended into other areas. Subscriptions were $6 a year, then $7, then $8.50. The rates for ads increased, and, once the paper had switched printers, escaping its ceiling of 80 pages and ballooning to 132 pages in size by 1974, so did the number of them. This drive to squeeze maximum profit out of the *Voice* probably came just in time, because in the new decade the *Village Voice* gave every sign that it had found as much of its natural constituency as it was ever going to. Circulation reached its peak of 151,000 in the spring of 1971, slipped back down after that, and lingered between 140,000 and 150,000 for the next three years. Nor did its owners diversify into the international circulation and the book publishing Edwin Fancher had said they would start at the time of the sale of the paper, as the tenets of growth capitalism dictated they should do. But, for the time being, it was no matter; the audience they had was capable of being milked far more than it already was in support of the *Voice,* overhead was low, any problems they might have were years off, and profits actually reached a high of fourteen cents on the dollar in 1973.

In December of 1970, the paper and its Family having grown so big, the *Village Voice* Christmas party had to be held in the Judson Memorial Church, courtesy of Howard Moody. (A year later, even Judson could not hold everyone who was coming; the party had to be switched to the premises of the paper itself.) On his way over there in a cab, Michael Harrington noticed that the old San Remo had become a Howard Johnson's.

And, he might have added, the old *Village Voice* building, on Sheridan Square, had become a Burger Towne.

The process of assimilation, of entropy, of the Village that had begun in the 1960s was complete in the 1970s. But before it had finally burned itself out, literally, with hard drugs and high explosives, the great counterculture surge had half mutated, half devastated Greenwich Village.

When the Village became the place to be, it became chic and groovy to be there, and when it became the scene everybody wanted to make, there was no room for everybody, so room was made. For all their victories of the late fifties, the Jane Jacobses had been fighting on the wrong front. In the 1960s, real-estate developers got hold of Greenwich Village, and before they let go, its face was changed forever. Modern, bland-skinned highrises went up, literally overshadowing its row-housed streets, multiplying the numbers of people on them, pricing out of the neighborhood its original people, its original flavor, its originality. The 1970s was the time in Greenwich Village of the high-rises and the high crime, of the solidly entrenched, newly aggressive gay community and the end of rent control. It remained an enclave, but a far more affluent one, and it had to yield some of its hegemony as a hideaway to Brooklyn Heights and SoHo. In 1969, shortly after pleading guilty to a reduced charge of disorderly conduct for seizing the stage and ripping up the stenographic records of a public hearing on the proposed Lower Manhattan Expressway, shortly after her teenage sons had been declared 1-A by their draft board, Jane Jacobs left New York, permanently, and settled across the border in Toronto, Canada, a city where many of her most progressive ideas were already in practice. Even Village theater lost some of its creative edge; in the 1970s, Off-Broadway, Off-Off-Broadway, and the Obies all became institutionalized. And the Becks were off to such distant locales as Venice and, supposedly to be close to a working-class community, Pittsburgh, to ply their trade there.

As for Dan Wolf and Ed Fancher, their lifestyles changed accordingly, too. In 1970, Edwin Fancher finally got married, and, after ten years at it, gave up his post at a Village psychiatric clinic to go totally into private practice. Both men took some of their newly come-by money and used it to buy apartments in a stately Fifth Avenue prewar building, where the elevator made a stop right in the living room of Fancher's penthouse suite, where the two men were connected via intercom with one another's apartments, where they both now settled back and became family men (Fancher and his wife having two children of their own). And, at the *Village Voice,* Dan Wolf became less and less visible.

It was not as if he was no longer there; he was, and when, after he was gone, one of the writers who broke in there in the seventies, Phil Tracy, would be quoted in a magazine article that by the time he got to the paper "Wolf had already quit. He'd just be there to have lunch, sign the paychecks and talk," Wolf was stung. As far as he was concerned, he was as much the editor as ever; but in the 1970s Dan Wolf, enjoying himself in a way he never had in his whole life, was not working at it anymore. He was delegating authority, he was removing himself from the day-to-day operation of the paper, and he had more or less chosen a successor. The man he had chosen, the man he was delegating authority and day-to-day decision making to, was Ross Wetzsteon. Their relationship went something like this: Dan Wolf would stay in his office, and let Ross Wetzsteon solve all the problems, and when Ross Wetzsteon had a problem he could not solve he would bring it to Dan Wolf, who would solve it for him. There were those on the paper who thought the only reason Ross Wetzsteon was ever able to solve *any* problems, or handle *any* of the responsibilities, was that he always had Dan Wolf behind him, to turn to at all times, and subsequent events would tend to vindicate their judgment. But the fact remained that in the early seventies Dan Wolf had become about as *emeritus* as any editor ever gets, that he was now the paper's Godfather, and that the man who was now his *capo* was named Ross Wetzsteon.

It was not as if *nothing* was happening at the paper. For instance, when the prisoners in New York City's jail, the Tombs, staged a riot in October of 1970, one prisoner by the name of Ricardo deLeon gave a manuscript describing the events from the inside to Mary Breasted, their reporter there, and she in turn gave it to Wolf. A local prosecutor from the office of District Attorney Frank Hogan called him up demanding to know whether he in fact had said manuscript in his possession, and Dan Wolf, as he put it later, for some reason decided to tell the truth, said yes, was ordered by Appellate Judge Harold Birns to turn said manuscript over to the court as evidence, and very nearly became the first journalist in the United States in the 1970s to go to jail for asserting his right to keep his sources of information secret.* And in January of 1972, when Tony Scaduto's book about Bob Dylan was published, and the *New York Times* reviewed it favorably, one of Dylan's friends, the man called "One-Legged Terry" (because he was), wrote an attack on it, and asked the *Voice* to publish it. The *Voice* refused (an attack against the *Times* should, they felt, be in the *Times),*

---

*No, he did not go. Wolf's lawyers filed an appeal to the order, and the case was later dropped.

and Howard Smith found himself facing, for the second time in as many years, a horde of would-be invaders.

He was upstairs in his office when the call came in from the receptionists downstairs. Five people with sound and camera equipment, identifying themselves only as "video artists," had just barged past them and boarded the elevator in an ugly mood. He immediately got on the phone to the fifth floor, where they locked their doors, and very shortly he could hear a commotion where the fourth-floor receptionist's desk was. They had arrived, screaming about their First Amendment rights and how the people at the *Village Voice* were all Fascists in the pay of the philistines, filming people telling them to get out. Howard Smith saw One-Legged Terry leading them, and he knew then why they were there. Then he saw who was standing next to him, looking very uncomfortable about the whole thing, holding out a microphone and tape recorder.

It was Dylan.

All Howard Smith could think of was, *I always wanted to meet him. What a bad situation to meet him in. But I can't kiss ass. I'm going to do what I have to do.* After listening for a little while, and listening to them say the only way he was going to get them out of the building was by throwing them out, Howard Smith bluffed. He told them, "Look, this is private property, but I don't believe in physical violence. So I'm going to call on those Fascist pigs, whose job it is to keep civilians from beating each other up, and you're going to end up in court. I'm going to turn my back, right now, I'm going to go in my office, and I'm going to call the police." And he proceeded to turn around and do precisely that, while one of them stood in the doorway watching him do it. It worked. They lingered, while Terry and some of the others kept insisting, "I don't believe he called," but, by the time the patrol car had arrived, they had dispersed.

The very next night, Howard Smith was walking along Houston and Macdougal Streets when, once again, he met Bob Dylan. Dylan was there, walking his dog, and came up to him. He wanted to apologize, he told Howard Smith. "I was embarrassed. If I had known what they were going to do, I wouldn't have gone along with it." And Bob Dylan told Howard Smith he was sorry.

They still had their reader dialogue, too:

> The other day while I was riding on the IRT Lexington Avenue line during a hot rush-hour evening, a fat woman standing next to me farted rather loudly. I turned my head the other way and a man sneezed in my face.

Dear Sir: Who are these Johnny-come-latelys of the "new journalism," Whelton and Newfield? We did it first. Never mind Lenny's party—what about that shindig at Cana? Who else could have thought up that water-into-wine shtick? And "working-class backgrounds"—what about that carpenter gambit we used? And talk about tripping—check the Book of Revelations.

—Matthew, Mark, Luke and John
The Original Eyewitness News Team
Cloud Nine

I read *The Voice* every week, cover-to-cover, every article, even the ones I don't understand. How come there's never anything in *The Voice* about seltzer? I like seltzer. Is *The Voice* anti-seltzer?

Dear Sir: Help—Name Withheld! Brooklyn.

I'm probably one in two million, but this is the first opportunity in my whole long life of 15 years to be able to write a newspaper; or anyone for that matter. Aren't the pictures on the front page of your October 22 edition reversed? I hope I haven't missed some kind of inner meaning! Love your paper any way you do it.

(Yes, you're right.—Editor.)

But one thing they did not have, not all through this period, and that was the relationship they had hoped for with their new owner, Carter Burden. They did not complain—it was, after all, the ideal situation, to have sold the paper and yet not to have the owner around all the time, breathing down your neck—but they never could quite figure it out either. Because, after the sale, except for a few Christmas parties here and a few social occasions there, they almost never saw anything of Carter Burden again.

Until it was already too late.

★ ★ ★

1970 . . . Richard Nixon is tearing the country apart. In Chicago, the conspiracy trial of eight militants draws to a close with one defendant, Bobby Seale, bound and gagged in his seat for the "crime" of trying to defend his own case, and huge contempt sentences heaped on the other defendants and their lawyers. Feiffer draws a caricature of Julius Hoffman, the vicious, senile judge who presided:

"The first defendant called me a Fascist. He shall be hung by the neck until dead. The second defendant called me a liar. He shall be thrown to the lions. The third and fourth defendants compared me to a baby. Their tongues shall be ripped out. The fifth defendant asserted I was bigoted. He shall be drawn and quartered. The sixth and seventh defendants accused this court of acting illegally. They shall be shot at sunrise. The execution of these sentences will be delayed until the jury returns with its verdict." In the issue of March 12, page one is a picture spread of an explosion that took place the previous Friday morning, just one block away from the designated new headquarters of the *Village Voice,* that wiped out the entire brownstone building at 18 West 11th Street and all of its inhabitants—members of the Weather Underground, using it for a bomb factory. It includes a shot of the man who lived next door, and had been rousted out of bed, Dustin Hoffman. . . . Then, all in the first week of May, Nixon orders the invasion of Cambodia, Ohio National Guardsmen wound and murder demonstrating students on the campus of Kent State University, and on Wall Street, while cordons of police stand idly by and businessmen on their lunch hour applaud, a peace rally is attacked by mobs of hardhat construction workers. Joe Flaherty is aghast:

> . . . It came as no surprise that the most rampant brutality happened on a Friday—payday, which means early boozing and 90-proof patriotism. And the Wall Street workers cheered them on, showering them with capitalism's sperm, ticker tape. . . .
>
> But the most tragic placard in sight at these demonstrations was one proclaiming "God Bless the Establishment."
>
> . . . the same beloved Establishment that rapes the quality of their daily lives by channeling their tax dollars into *Terry and the Pirates* adventures, building highways they'll never use, and granting tax exemptions to fat cats who sneer at them. Whatever happened to their built-in shit detectors that told them the only way to win the Congressional Medal was to come home in a box. . . .

. . . Feiffer begins to chronicle the adventures of "Dick n' Pat."

"No, I can't arrest them, Mrs. Mitchell," he has Nixon saying over the phone. "No, I'd like to but I can't arrest them yet. Maybe in my second term I can arrest them but no, not in my first term. No, I don't think I'm overcautious, but I can't put Congress in jail." Another strip finds Vice-President Agnew confronting a towheaded youngster. "What's it going to be—anarchy or repression?" he asks. "What do I get if I pick anarchy?" asks the boy. "You get lawlessness, you get riots, you get strikes, you get guerrilla warfare," answers Agnew. "What do I get if I pick repression?" the boy asks. "You get law and order, you get police brutality, you get apartheid, you get detention camps," answers Agnew. "What do I get if I pick peace and an end to poverty and racism?" asks the boy. "You get ignored," Agnew tells him. "So what's it going to be—anarchy or repression?"

. . . That fall, Nixon sends Agnew out on the campaign trail to engage in the most Orwellian character assassinations ever heard in American politics. In New York Agnew even lets it be known that Nixon is supporting the Conservative Party maverick James Buckley, brother of columnist William, over the GOP's own nominee, the man Nelson Rockefeller had picked to fill out Bobby Kennedy's term, Charles Goodell. In mid-October, Newfield writes an "Open Letter to John Lindsay":

> Dear John, Something very deep and very ugly is going on in America. Spiro Agnew is spreading a poison we are going to spend a generation seeking an antidote for. He is doing it with a White House plane, and with Nixon's speechwriters, and he is getting away with it.
>
> And you have been quiet. You seconded his nomination in 1968. You are not up for election this year, and this gives you a certain freedom. But the only time you ever refer to Agnew is by inference, at Goodell rallies, or at the Liberal Party dinner in Manhattan.
>
> But you have to go into the heartland of this wounded dinosaur of a country, you have to go to Colorado, or Oklahoma, or Maryland (Yes, Spiro's back yard), and stand up and attack and expose Agnew. You have to do it with a hundred facts. You have to do to him what Ed Murrow did to Joe McCarthy. . . . If you pretend to have any claim on the allegiance of people like myself, then go out now to Middle America, yes, risk a little bit of your future, go out of Manhattan, and stand up and say it straight. Before it's too late.

. . . Lindsay attacks Agnew, but only once, in New York, and while he breaks party ranks to oppose Rockefeller for another term, he stays inside them to support Goodell, who, doomed to lose anyway, stays in the race, finishes a distant third, and prevents the Democratic nominee from defeating Buckley.

★ ★ ★

Nineteen seventy was the year of the women's movement. There were articles indicative of the new, so-called "raised
consciousness" in the *Voice*—articles with titles such as "Combat in
the Erogenous Zone."* August 26 was a day of marches, rallies, and job
actions by women. And just prior to the 26th, there was a fund-raising
party on the Long Island estate of feminist sympathizer Ethel Scull.
Congresswoman Patsy Mink was there, media people were there, Gloria
Steinem was there, and then in the middle of the press conference, a
very tall, very braless woman took off her shirt, took off her pants, and,
clad only in her panties, dove straight into the swimming pool.

Jill Johnston was her name, she was a writer for the *Village Voice,*
and she had not always been that way. Back in 1959, when she had
written her first dance review, she had been a very straight, twenty-
nine-year-old woman, and a very conventional, pretty good reviewer of
progressive dance. She kept it up, and by the early sixties had a regular
column with the paper, called "Dance Journal."

And then, in 1965, something happened. Most people would call it a
nervous breakdown, and Jill Johnston was, in fact, confined to New
York's Bellevue Hospital for a time. But Jill Johnston insisted on
calling it a "breakthrough," and came out of the hospital claiming to
have had a number of visions while there—one of which was that she
stop trying to be a judge of other people's work, and simply make her
life a work of her own.

Which she now proceeded to do. When Jill Johnston came out of the
hospital and resumed her column, a few things had changed. For one
thing, it was not criticism anymore. For another thing, it was not about
dance anymore. And, for another, it was not even *prose* any more.

As Jill Johnston said, "telling it like it is means telling it like it was
and how it is now that it isn't what it was to the is now people." Her
column started out like this without capitalization but with punctuation and then there wasnt even any punctuation anymore not even for
contractions like that one and jill johnston was just writing about
anything that popped into her head anything at all like how her day
went and what she did and what female lover she had just taken up
with and where she was going and this and that and nobody but her

---

*In a previous era, the newspaper had exhibited its share of the "old" consciousness.
From the *Village Voice,* November 24, 1956: "FEMALE MODELS. Must be attractive and
have good figure for PHOTOGRAPHY. PART-TIME MODELS. Pretty, female, good figure, no
experience necessary for glamor pin-up photography."

most loyal devoted fanatic followers could get through it let alone stand it and it drove everybody else at the paper crazy especially the people who had to quote unquote edit her but she did it anyway

It was a song of herself, by herself, for herself, about herself, and of interest to nobody but herself, and it was the feature everybody loved to skip, but Jill Johnston had her fans, and most of them read the paper *only* for her, so Dan Wolf did a typical thing. He let her keep her column, and its title, and its position, and simply, quietly moved in Deborah Jowett next to her with a *real* dance column. Once, Diane Fisher, nominally her editor, told her, "Jill, this is not a literary magazine," and once Dan Wolf bumped into her in the hallway and asked her, "Who gave you permission to write your autobiography?" But by the time Wolf had even asked her that question she had already been *writing* her autobiography for four years, and after he had asked it and she had told him simply, no one, there was no change in the situation. She just kept flowing along, year after year, turning in ream upon unreadable ream of her lesbian logorrhea, and they never touched it, not even when Jill Johnston's own mother wrote the paper offering to pay them *not* to run it anymore.

A kind of self-appointed court scribe to Bulldike Nation, she did not merely practice the lesbian lifestyle, or simply advocate it; she proselytized for it, militantly (sample title of one of her columns: "Ladies and Genitals"), and on the subjects of men and sex, Jill Johnston possessed some mighty strange ideas, such as that "every woman who remains in sexual relation to man is defeated every time she does it with the man because each single experience for every woman is a reenactment of the primal one in which she was invaded and separated and fashioned into a receptacle for the passage of the invader. . . . Feminists who still sleep with men are delivering their most vital energies to the oppressor," ideas that became even more remarkable upon reflection that, first, if followed to the letter they would result in the extinction of the entire human race within one generation, and that, second, they were almost word-for-word the exact same sentiments uttered by the character of General Jack D. Ripper in the movie *Dr. Strangelove* as he blew up the world in order to protect "our precious bodily fluids."

There were all sorts of Jill Johnston stories. She was afraid of elevators, and so petrified to go up in one that, at the new offices, Ross Wetzsteon would get calls from the front desk to go all the way down or meet her on the back stairs just to pick up her stories. And when, on the night of April 26, 1973, carrying on in the tradition she had established at Ethel Scull's in August of 1970, she walked past two policemen on her way into the Guggenheim Museum, "making obscene gestures and speaking in obscene language," and repeated the exact same procedure with the same two policemen on her way out again thirty minutes later, Jill Johnston found herself being taken to the 23rd Precinct station-house and booked for harassment of police officers. Almost everyone had a Jill Johnston story, it seemed, and some of them, or at least the wish to hear one, traveled widely, as Jack Newfield discovered the night he fulfilled a speaking engagement in upstate New York. He finished his talk, opened the floor up to questions, readied himself to be asked about Bobby Kennedy, the war, or the New Left, and his first questioner wanted to know: "What's Jill Johnston really like?"

★ ★ ★

Nineteen seventy was the year their other lowercase commentator, Joel Oppenheimer, began appearing regularly in the paper, too, though the similarities stopped there.

Joel Oppenheimer had come to New York City in 1953, when he was twenty-three, and stayed there ever since—living in the East Village, the West Village, even, for a while in the late fifties, in the Bronx—except for the time he had spent in North Carolina, with the Black Mountain poets. He was an accomplished poet himself—five books of it to his credit, plus some short stories, plus a play. He knew about publishing from the other end as well—he had worked with his hands, as a production man at print shops and ad agencies. And he had taught others what he knew—as the poet-in-residence at City College, and running the poetry project workshops at St. Mark's Church on the Lower East Side, where he had met Seymour Krim and Clark Whelton, one past and one present writer for the *Village Voice*. He had also been a Lion's Head regular for years, and when, in 1969, Philip Roth's autoerotic novel *Portnoy's Complaint* was published, creating some-what of a literary stir with its frank talk about male masturbation, Joel Oppenheimer wanted to write an answer. He tried reading it out loud to his friends in the pub, and they urged him to take it next door to the *Voice*.

Joel Oppenheimer wasn't sure. He was a poet, after all, and they were a newspaper, and he didn't expect that they'd want to publish anything of his. But there was a guy there named Ross, one of his friends told him. Bring it to him. So Joel Oppenheimer dropped it off, addressed it to Ross Wetzsteon, and in the issue of March 6, 1969, the *Village Voice* published "Oppenheimer's Kvetch," a kind of book review:

Neither Alexander Portnoy, Philip Roth, Sandra Hochman, nor James Wechsler can possibly know more about Jewish jerking off than I do. . . . I even know young Jews who jerk off right-handed (Freud having pointed out somewhere that the vast majority of Jews jerk off left-handed due to overwhelming guilt). . . .

I'm glad he wrote the book, but I wish I wasn't being bombarded with it. As a matter of fact, I'm considering incorporating j.o.e.l.—jews owed every leeway—whose main function will be to sue Philip Roth and his publishers, in order to pay, pro-rated of course, all Jews of the male persuasion over the age of 30 a reasonable percentage of the take. After all, didn't we have it all, and talk interminably about it, between ourselves, to ourselves, to our shrinkers, to our shiksas, to everybody but our mothers?

He closed with a poem he had written years before, "Blonde Ladies' Sonnet" (". . . I, like all men, was born to haul/ass after beautiful women. . . . I am warm passionate Jew, blood/running/hot all through me . . ."). After that, he wrote several other pieces, dropped them off, and they, too, got published.

Several months went by this way, and Joel Oppenheimer was embarrassed. He brought himself into the paper to meet Ross Wetzsteon. "Look," he started to offer, "if it's an intrusion . . ."

"It's no intrusion," Ross Wetzsteon reassured him. "I wish you'd intrude every week."

That was just what Joel Oppenheimer needed to hear, and their relationship went on from there, Wetzsteon supporting and encouraging Oppenheimer, Oppenheimer grateful for his support and encouragement. Soon, Joel Oppenheimer was appearing practically every week and commenting, e e cummings–style, on practically everything. Like Jill Johnston, he eschewed capital letters; but unlike Jill Johnston, he retained all the other standard punctuation so that he was always easy to read. He was unlike Jill Johnston in another respect too: he was funny. No matter what he was writing on—baseball and the Mets, his family, himself, life in New York—he loaded his stuff up with wit, and irony, and the right outrageous comment at the right time. Eventually, the paper invested him with the title "poetry editor."

But of all the things on Joel Oppenheimer's mind, sex was never very far. Nor was mere poetry his only artistic interest in that regard; in the issue of February 5, 1970, approaching his first anniversary with the *Village Voice,* there appeared in the paper a photograph of Joel Oppenheimer, pants down, back to the camera, making mock pelvic thrusts at a chicken he held in his hand, all as part of "a very brief but

poignant love scene," the cutline said, from his forthcoming film debut
in an underground epic entitled *End of the Road.* And in July 1973, in
one of his rare excursions into upper case, Joel Oppenheimer's total
output for the week was as follows:

> On a certain night in the month of June, 197–, passersby in
> the neighborhood of my desk might have noticed nine men in
> black robes tinkering with the mechanism of my typewriter.
> What follows is the best I have been able to do since their
> attentions.
> The luscious pink-tipped mounds of white flesh danced
> before my eyes, as my hot lance pierced to her very core. Her
> eyes flashed, whether with anger or passion I could not tell,
> but, indeed, her heart beat faster under my not so tender
> ministrations.

Joel Oppenheimer was different from the others in that it had been
Ross Wetzsteon who had brought him along, typical of more and more
of the writers who were to follow him to the paper, while his contact
with Dan Wolf was minimal. But Ron Rosenbaum came to the paper in
the old way.

★ ★ ★

He was twenty-three years old when Dan Wolf met him, late in the
summer of 1969, at a party thrown for Nassau County Executive
Eugene Nickerson on Long Island, and Dan Wolf knew that as soon as
they were both back in the city, Ron Rosenbaum was going to call him
up and ask for a job.

Rosenbaum was a Yale graduate ('68) and a Carnegie fellow; he had
passed up further study in English, though, to go full-time into
newspaper work, first with a paper out on the Island, the *Suffolk Sun*
(for whom he covered the Chicago Democratic Convention in 1968),
then, through an ad he had read in the *Village Voice,* as assistant
editor for the summer on the *Fire Island News*—where, as he put it, his
job consisted of writing half the paper, and where Rhoda Wolf,
vacationing out there with her family, came across his work and
mentioned it to her husband.

Sure enough, Dan Wolf was right. Ten days after the party, he
received a call at the *Voice.* It was from Rosenbaum, and he referred
him to Mary Nichols, who hired him.

There was never any explicit endorsement of the proposition, certainly none from Dan Wolf, who dismissed the subject out of hand if it
was ever raised in his presence, but a consensus did emerge, among his

colleagues in the 1970s, that Ron Rosenbaum was the most talented writer discovered by Dan Wolf after the death of Don McNeill. Certainly there was an ease, a fecundity, a graceful glibness to his writing that no one else seemed to have.

He started out covering local subjects—a profile of the emerging, artists-oriented SoHo neighborhood just below the Village, a piece about Westbeth, the old telephone company building that was being renovated into a residence for writers and artists. He went to Washington to cover the end-the-war march in November 1969 and to New Haven to cover the Free-Bobby-Seale march in May 1970. He covered John Lindsay as he campaigned for mayor in 1969 among Brooklyn's increasingly anti-black Jews, Kenneth Gibson's triumphant election as the first black mayor of Newark in June of 1970, Democrat Arthur Goldberg's futile race against incumbent Nelson Rockefeller for governor of New York a few months later ("Like Paul McCartney before him, Arthur Goldberg has had to wage an uphill campaign to prove he is, in fact, alive"), and the last, desperate hours of George McGovern's doomed run for the presidency in 1972, brilliantly cross-cutting in his article between snatches of anecdotes from the last week of the botched campaign and what came over his car radio as he twiddled the dial driving through South Dakota on his way to McGovern's Election Night defeat party. He could generate his own humor, too, as he proved on a couple of occasions, one being the summer of 1973, when he took a break from investigative reporting on such heavy topics as the Watergate break-in, the assassination of John Kennedy, and the police bust of Abbie Hoffman for selling cocaine, to tell his readers about a place called Junior's, in Brooklyn, extol the virtues of "The best cheesecake in New York," and explain how he knew that it was, in fact, that:

> . . . I believe I have, as far as appreciating cheesecake goes, a certain gift I would describe as the equivalent in the world of tastebuds to the gift of absolute pitch in the world of music. I am perfectly attuned to every resonance. It is a modest gift— some people make movies and others conduct symphonies with a perfection I could not hope to aspire to—but in its own realm my gift is just as absolute. I don't have high standards. I *am* the standard.
>
> So it is from this perspective that I urge you to get your ass down to the corner of Flatbush and DeKalb and try out Junior's cheesecake. This is no longer a matter of argument or persuasion. If you don't agree with me, I'm afraid there's something wrong with your mouth.

And two years earlier, in July 1971, Ron Rosenbaum was responsible, singlehandedly, for perpetrating perhaps the most effective torpedo job ever done on anyone, or anything, in the *Voice*. The subject was Troy Donahue, that washed-up Warner Brothers TV star of the early sixties with the surfer-boy looks and the wooden acting technique, at the start of a media hype campaign for his "comeback" starring role in a *roman à clef* movie about the Charles Manson Family. Rosenbaum's account went like this:

> "Believe me, you won't believe Troy when you see him," the press agent tells me. "He's a bearded hippie! And believe me, *he is fantastic in this picture*. He plays Charles Manson! Actually we can't call him Charles Manson because of the legal thing, but it's the Charles Manson story. Troy is this sex and drug crazed Jesus-type cult leader of a hippie commune who kills a pregnant actress and her Hollywood friends. You see the parallel?" . . .
>
> The press agent sets a date for the Top of the Sixes and promises to send me Troy's "bio." He tells me I will recognize him, the agent, "because I wear wild shirts and wide ties. But I guarantee you won't recognize Troy." . . .
>
> Troy is dressed in white. White sneakers, white Levis, white t-shirt, white Levi jacket. A silver crucifix and some other trinkets hang from a chain around his neck. . . . There are gray hairs scattered through Troy's blond beard, and tiny red crinkles of visible veins on his cheeks. Troy is 35.
>
> I'll never forget Troy's first words to me, when he stepped over his motorcycle helmet to greet me at his table at the Top of the Sixes. This is a literal transcription:
>
> "Hey brother. Dig the scene. Dig the scene. Wow man. Dig the scene."
>
> If I had any doubts left that Troy was in fact a bearded hippie, he set them at rest when he twisted the conventional handshake I had offered into an interesting version of the Movement "power" grip, and concluded the greeting by saying, "Yeah. Dig the scene." Just us hippies together . . .
>
> We begin to talk about Charles Manson.
>
> "I knew the dude," Troy tells me. . . . What was his secret, I asked.
>
> "It was his cock," says Troy.
>
> "His cock?"

"His cock."

Before I could ask Troy for more details the press agent interrupts.

" . . . Troy's performance is going to shock people. I think it's an Oscar performance although the Academy would never have the guts to give it to him." . . .

"I would make a prediction right now," producer Bob Roberts declares in the silence that follows. "I would predict there would be more murders. This Manson thing will be just the beginning. This movie is not about an isolated incident, it's about what's to come. And there *will* be more murders."

The press agent looks over at me nervously, then back at the producer: "Bob, maybe you shouldn't predict murders. Maybe you should change that to tragedies." He turns to me. "Say that Bob feels that this is a movie about a tragedy which may not, let's see, which may not be the last of its kind."

"But I think there will be *murders* too," says Bob a little disconsolately. "I'm willing to be quoted as predicting murders."

"I just don't think it's a good idea," says the press agent.

"Shut up! You don't know anything," Troy tells the press agent.

"That's nice," the press agent says with some dignity. There is an embarrassed silence at the table.

"Oh hey man, I'm just kidding. Here." Troy reaches for the press agent's hand, takes it into a firm "power" grip, looks him in the eye. "Brothers. Right?" The press agent nods dubiously.

Troy gets back on the subject of Charles Manson and begins explaining how Manson either was or wasn't just like Hitler.

"So I said to David Frost, I said, 'Did Hitler do it? I mean did he? He didn't. Man, Hitler didn't do it. You know what I mean?' And Frost looks at me and says: 'He didn't do it?' And I said, 'No man, he didn't do it, did he?' It blew Frost's mind. All he could say was 'He *didn't* do it?' "

Troy looks at me. "But the thing is he really *did* do it. Can you dig it? He *did* do it . . .

★ ★ ★

"I took acid man. I took acid and I met The Man. I met The *Man*. And The Man said cool it."

"Cool it?"

"Cool it. That's what he said. I was with these doctors, and
. . . now you know some people take 250, 350 mikes and
play around and think they did acid. But I did acid. I was with
these doctors in Miami and I was standing by this metal railing
watching the ocean and all of a sudden there was a thun-
derstorm man, like the end of the world. And lightning, man.
So I'm holding on and this lightning hits the railing, comes
right along to me and right through me. I should have been
fried, man. Then I knew. Cool it. That's what the Man was
saying. Cool it." . . .

The press agent takes out some glossy pictures. . . . "And
here's Troy before. You could use these as before and after
pictures."

"Yeah, but that's bullshit," says Troy. "That 'before and
after' thing is bullshit. I was always the way I am now. See that
picture of me with my hands in my pockets, looking so clean
cut? You know what I've got in my pocket. You know what?"

I shake my head no.

Troy gives me a sly look, puts two fingers up to his mouth,
and takes an imaginary drag on an imaginary joint. "You
know what I'm talking about now? That's right," he says with
satisfaction.

Our conversation is interrupted by three elderly ladies who
have come over from a nearby table to ask for Troy's autograph.

"I can't believe it. The women still recognize him everywhere," the press agent says.

Troy flirts graciously with the ladies who say they want the
autographs for their nieces and granddaughters. When they
leave to return to their table, Troy turns to me.

"Crazy. Aren't they great. Wow. Look at those heavy legs."
He smacks his lips. "Wouldn't you like to mow their
lawns?" . . .

"Well, I'm off on my cycle now man. Wish I had one of
these"—he takes a final drag on his imaginary joint . . .

"The whole thing's going to be very big. This picture.
Listen," says the press agent, "one thing you might want to
mention in your story is that the company that's distributing
this picture is a publicly owned company. It's traded over the
counter. That's kind of interesting, you know, you might want
to work that into the story when you mention that TransWorld
Attractions Corporation is producing and distributing Troy's

movie. You know. That it's publicly owned. Something like
that. I'll tell you it's only selling for maybe a buck a share now,
right Bob? But when this picture is released . . . Of course it
wouldn't be ethical for me to tell you to buy . . ."

"But I could tell him, couldn't I?" chuckles the producer.

The next week there appeared in the *Village Voice* a letter from the
producer, obliquely stating, "I would like to compliment the reporter-
writer Ron Rosenbaum for his remarkable memory—considering he
took sparse notes—but more on his fluid writing style, which Troy
Donahue, by the way, found most amusing reading."

His contemporaries were amazed at him, in more ways than one. He
could write fast, and long, driving himself to stay awake for extended
periods of time to finish something, and with such seemingly easy force,
that they were dazzled by him. At other times he appeared to some of
them to be a bit dazzled himself, and certainly acted that way. With his
long, red beard hanging all the way off his face and his inflamed eyes, he
struck some as a Dostoyevskian figure; but to others, who caught him
at different times, the eyes were simply spacey, the look on his face
more demonic than anything else.

He awed them, but at times it seemed that wasn't enough. It was as if
he had to terrorize them too.

Suffice it to say that Ron Rosenbaum's writing skills were in a far
more developed state than his emotional maturity was. Certainly no
one who ever wrote for Dan Wolf, with the exception of Norman
Mailer, was more prone to waste his otherwise prolific energy on
personality clashes of his own making.

His behavior was periodically liable to descend to the level of a
spoiled brat with a limited attention span. He had an animus in him, a
snideness, and he lost friends and made enemies when he got into snits
with them over nothing. He was given to playing bizarre pranks on
other people, and making aimless threats and accusations, almost for
sport, like a vindictive kid trying on a new toy fright mask.

These proved to be unfortunate traits, because while there was no
one who professed to be more loyal to Dan Wolf than Ron Rosenbaum,
when it later came down to acting, constructively and together, in
order to save what Wolf had created, no loyalist of his did more to
derail, disrupt, and demoralize any attempts to do so, or to offend and
antagonize potential allies, than did Ron Rosenbaum. When it
counted most, all the others could count on him for was seeing plots in
everything, casting aspersions on everyone but himself, making plans
he never followed through on, and blowing hot and cold at all times.

★ ★ ★

1971 . . . Paul Cowan on coal miners, Clark Whelton on the end of rent control in New York . . . Marlene Nadle from Chile, and a front-page picture spread showing Pete Hamill, Norman Mailer, and Budd Schulberg, all at the Fight, Ali-Frazier, March 8, 1971 . . . Vietnam veterans milling in Washington to protest the war stage a mock "search-and-destroy" raid. Robin Reisig is there: "A man in dirty green was shouting at me in a language I didn't understand. 'Dung lai!' Someone said he was asking for my identification. I said I didn't have any. So he shot me." Writes ex-GI John Hamill, Pete's brother: "Winning the war for the GI in Vietnam is the 707 home." Nat Hentoff, in his column, passes along this information: "Just before the deadline for this issue, I received what I consider reliable information that the New York *Times* has a breakthrough unpublished story concerning the White House, the President, and Southeast Asia. The story is the result of intensive team reporting by some of that paper's most diligent and experienced men. Is the story going to be published?" he poses the question. "Or are there still *Times* executives and editors who might hold back such a story 'in the national interest'?" The story, of course, is the Pentagon Papers, and when the *Times* goes ahead with it three weeks later the Nixon administration precipitates a constitutional crisis over its publication. How Nat Hentoff gets his information, he never tells. . . .

. . . Crime and drugs and danger in the Village: in the issue of April 15, the paper publishes the account of Mel Kramer as he successfully buys heroin on the corner of West 3rd and Macdougal. . . . Ads for runaways, placed by worried parents in the *Voice* . . . A Feiffer hippie is stopped on the street by a black robber and, while the gunman strips him of his watch, his peace medallion, his wallet, his transistor radio, and finally his guitar, pleads: "Hey brother, you don't want to rip me off. Free Huey . . . Free Angela . . . Free Attica . . . Free all political prisoners . . . Right on! All power to the—POLICE!"

. . . In the fall, Hentoff uses the column to criticize the paper for its decision not to take advertising for Larry Rivers's book *Tits*. . . . Nick Browne reports from Belfast. . . . At the end of November, the paper reports the death of Mike Kempton—Murray Kempton's son and a former *Voice* reporter—and his wife in a car accident. . . .

. . . The male-female dialogue continues. In the spring, Susan

Brownmiller writes a humorous but bitter account of "a long and systematic continuum of humiliation"—namely, being goosed by men—on the occasion of her having been, right on the streets of the Village, for what she hopes is the last time. In the fall, "S," an unidentified woman, describes, in explicit sexual detail, how "in the course of a year, I experienced nine impotent men," and recounts her night with the "civilized rapist," 240-pound "Jerry." From across the ocean comes the reply, by Michael Zwerin: "Having written of successes with women," he says, "I lie unless I also document the failures." And he confesses one such—"We rolled around, The Lady and I, straining, a failure. It was a lady I'd been courting, she turned me on. Yet there we were and nothing was happening. After long enough I stopped coaxing and went down. I love going down. But she pushed my head away and said: 'No substitutes.'" Feiffer retells the tale of Eden: "God made man in his image. Man took one look at his image and fell in love. God got word that man was becoming too conceited and made woman. Woman took one look at man and said, '*That*'s made in God's image?' and instantly became idolatrous. Man took one look at woman and said, 'Now that there are two of us I am less than one.' So they went their separate ways and never saw each other again. Moral: We are surrounded by imposters."

★ ★ ★

Howard Blum's first article appeared in the *Village Voice* in October 1967, when he was eighteen. He was studying at the London School of Economics, and the same Saturday night of the march on the Pentagon there was an attack on the U.S. Embassy in Grosvenor Square which he witnessed. He mailed a description of the event to New York, and got back his answer—a check, and a tearsheet of the article as it appeared in the *Voice*.

He had always wanted to write for the *Voice*, and when he got back home he did again, this time about Riverdale, the upper-crust Bronx neighborhood where he had grown up. It was not a pleasant portrait, and the *Riverdale Press* denounced it. After that Howard Blum (pronounced "bloom") was off to California (to get his master's at Stanford), and corresponded to the paper from there. In 1971 he returned home again, wrote some more for the *Voice*, and eventually went on staff.

A lot of his early writing was egotistical; that was what he would call it years later, looking back on the days when he had been "a kid running around with a *Voice* press card." Not all his pieces were accepted. But he didn't mind. He stayed around. He was learning, he was having fun, and, most important, he was getting to know Dan Wolf.

Dan Wolf was getting to know him, too. He was a quiet one, with nondescript features and short black hair, and he was really quite modest, compared to some of those he worked with. He was as intense as they were, but his intensity expressed itself in a serious, low-key, sensitive strain. He was self-effacing. Above all, he was forthright; that proved, at a later date, to be his most distinguishing characteristic. And Dan Wolf liked what he saw in this young man; he had a steady, straight reliability about him, all the reporter's instincts that had traditionally been missing on the paper. He was a different type, and Wolf encouraged him.

They became so close that Howard Blum actually credited Dan Wolf with molding his personality, with a power to shape him and his thoughts no one ever had, or would have again. Whatever was wrong in Howard Blum's writing, he felt sure Dan Wolf had picked it up; because Wolf never touched his writing, they only talked about him, and he could feel himself getting better.

He wrote about the spreading "welfare hotels" around the Village and New York, and first-person reminiscences about the city. He went off to Europe, filing reports from Paris ("Tomorrow is Rosh Hashanah and I wish I were home") and Istanbul. Then he returned home, and did his first truly great reporting.

It was early 1973, and there was a new phenomenon out on the streets of the city: older, predatory homosexuals scooping up young, docile boys wherever there were runaways to be found, then raping them, or pimping for them, or worse. There was a new name for it too: chickenhawk. Howard Blum wrote:

> Boys are for sale in this city. 12-year-old boys are selling themselves for $10 at Times Square. Pimps are selling teenagers for $50 every night at 53rd Street and 3rd Avenue. Lonely runaways are met at the Port Authority Bus Terminal by pimps, lured away by the promise of a free meal, and then beaten into prostitution. Boys, kept high on ups and heroin, are exhibited in a 10th Street restaurant; ask and you'll be told their price. And for $100, a call service will deliver the type of boy of your choice. . . .
>
> This is a world of chickenhawks, those men who enjoy sex with boys not much older than 16, and their chickens, those boys who out of desire, fear, or panic submit. . . . The high-spending chickenhawks include a well-known professional athlete, a TV newscaster, a high church official, and numerous

actors. . . . The word has spread around the South Bronx that money can be made by allowing yourself to be used by an old man in a movie.

And in September 1974, doing a piece on old Communist Party survivors of the McCarthy purges, he captured the pathos of one old victim completely:

> The interview is going nowhere. Immediately he sets the ground rules. His name cannot be used. The tape recorder must be shut off. There can be no mention of the names of his wife or daughter.
>
> All I can do is agree. The morning has been wasted. . . . I ask my questions and he gives his answers, but always adds, "Maybe you shouldn't mention that. I'd really appreciate if you left that part out. You know, I wouldn't want to get my daughter in trouble."
>
> I wind up the interview very quickly. "Oh, don't go yet. You just came. Let's talk some more. Do you want a Coke or something?"
>
> I talk with him a little longer. Finally he explodes: "What is it with you kids today? You know, my daughter, she's married. She has a son. A child I've never seen. She tells me she doesn't want the kid to grow up with an FBI file. My own grandson and I've never seen him. She tells me not to visit; I'd only be followed, her husband would lose his job. She tells me not to call, that they listen in, they'd find out where she's living and bother her child."
>
> Suddenly he starts to cry, uncontrollably. "I write her sometimes. She never answers. She says she doesn't want her child to be punished for what I've done. She says she doesn't want her son to pay the way she had to. They tormented her at school. They . . . " He cries and cries, unembarrassed. He grabs my wrist, a father talking to a son. "She could never understand I only did what I had to do. I didn't want her to be punished. I only did what was right." He cries and he cries.

He was a good writer. He was also a good man. When the crunch came, and so many of his colleagues were taking one copout after another, or zigzagging their way around searching after some sort of refuge, Howard Blum was one disciple of Dan Wolf's to act with a consistent rectitude. He said what he meant, and he meant what he said, and he did so without playing any games.

★ ★ ★

His grandfather had been a general, and fought with Patton himself in Sicily. His father was a colonel, and he came from one of America's more illustrious military families. But Lucian K. Truscott IV was cut from the mold a little differently.

Even as a teenager, living on an army base in Kansas, he kept a copy of the *Village Voice* on the wall of his quarters. And, in the late 1960s, when Lucian K. Truscott moved east, and became a full-fledged cadet at the United States Military Academy in West Point, he moved up another notch at the paper too, and began to write for it.

He wrote letters to the editor for two years, and poems, and he and Dan Wolf corresponded. Then one day in December 1967 Lucian Truscott received in his mail, from Dan Wolf and Ed Fancher, an invitation to the *Village Voice* Christmas party. It was being held that day. Lucian Truscott rousted up a buddy of his, they both got leave, took the train to New York, and arrived at Ed Fancher's apartment in time for the party, in full military uniform.

They were, needless to say, an unusual sight, with their short hair and their military bearing and their arguments, here at the height of the Vietnam War, in support of it. But the war was an abstraction to Lucian Truscott; in other ways, ways that counted to him, he was in rebellion himself. He was in the military, but he was not *of* it, and he seemed to have fewer problems mingling in the world of the *Voice* people than some of them had with him mingling *in* it. Dan Wolf could see that, could see where young Truscott was coming from and where he was going, and he was amused. Lucian Truscott spent other leaves in New York, talking for long hours in Wolf's office, and writing other things for the *Voice*—on the Electric Circus, on evangelist Billy Graham playing the Garden, and, of course, the famous Stonewall Inn incident. Wolf appreciated the young man. He was a straight-ahead person; that was the way Wolf described him. If he has an itch, he scratches it. He says what's on his mind. Wolf liked him for that, found it refreshing, and could tell that, with all of his military *macho,* Lucian Truscott was a figure in transit, making a personal journey far longer, and over much more difficult terrain, than many of the New Leftists at the paper who scoffed at him had ever had to make to get to be where *they* were. He enjoyed him, he encouraged him, and he exposed him to a world of freedom at the *Voice,* a world that to Lucian Truscott was new and different.

The glory years—*Time* Magazine comes to the office. Left to right: Diane Fisher, Jack Newfield, Ed Fancher, Stephanie Harrington, Howard Smith, and Dan Wolf. *(Photo by David Gahr)*

☆ ☆ ☆

Under the Arch at Washington Square, members of the Family assemble, 1968. Standing, left to right: Howard Smith, dance critic Deborah Jowitt, Michael Zwerin, Joe Flaherty, Dan List, Margot Hentoff, Michael Harrington, Nat Hentoff, jazz critic Carman Moore, Jonas Mekas. Kneeling, left to right: art critic John Perrault, Ross Wetzsteon. *(Photo by Duane Michals)*

"Himself at Churchill Downs covering the Derby for the *Voice*. Such elegance! This will kill my longshore image."—Joe Flaherty, 1977. *(Photo by Jeanine Johnson)*

☆ ☆ ☆

Don McNeill, the protégé, before his death in 1968. *(Photo by Diane Dorr-Dorynek)*

1969—then-Congressman Edward Koch, City Councilman candidate (and *Voice* owner-to-be) Carter Burden, and Burden's campaign manager Bartle Bull, campaigning on Manhattan's East Side. *(Photo by Belinda Breese Bull)*

☆ ☆ ☆

Bartle Bull in 1972. *(Photo by Belinda Breese Bull)*

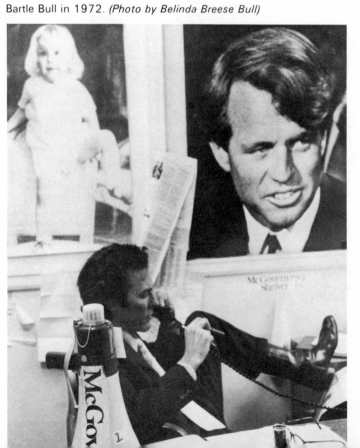

One of the Men Alone—Howard Blum. *(Photo by Gwyn Metz)*

☆ ☆ ☆

Man Alone—Clark Whelton. *(Photo by Dick Frank)*

Man Alone—Ron Rosenbaum. *(Photo by Janie Eisenberg)*

Paul Cowan. *(Photo by Rachel Cowan)*

☆ ☆ ☆

Lucian K. Truscott IV, with shopping bag. *(Photo by Carol Troy)*

Alexander Cockburn, in a pensive moment, January 1977. *(Photo by Janie Eisenberg)*

☆ ☆ ☆

Karen Durbin, editor, talks at staff meeting called to discuss the Murdoch takeover, January 1977. *(Photo by Janie Eisenberg)*

The Man Who Fell to Earth: Clay S. Felker, founder, *New York* Magazine; "editor-in-chief," the *Village Voice,* 1975–77. *(Photo by Alfred Whalen, courtesy UPI)*

☆ ☆ ☆

The Face of the Future—Rupert Murdoch. *(Photo by Mark Sennet, Camera Five)*

Inevitably, the conflict with his *own* world, with the background and environment he had known since birth, had to come, and it did, late in 1969, at Fort Carson, Colorado. Truscott had been shipped there, with his second lieutenant's commission, out of West Point, and from there he continued, while on active duty, to correspond with the *Voice*. He sent back an account of leading a platoon for the first time—"It was then that I realized I hadn't done shit in my life. I had not held men's lives in my hand as I held them right then." And, when Fort Carson was the scene of demonstrations, he put on his journalist's hat again to describe it:

> They came in bunches of five and six, some struggling against the gusting wind with banners and signs proclaiming support for the anti-war movement within the military, demanding improved military conditions within the stockade and increased rights for the Army enlisted man. More than 100 strong, they made the turn off four-laned Route 115 and headed for the main gate to the post. An article in the Denver Post the day before had advertised their intent, and the Fort Carson authorities were prepared. A line of concertina barbed wire and a small phalanx of MPs met the protesters a short distance from the gate. The MPs were silent, stony-faced; the protesters noisy and unsure of themselves. The confrontation was underway.

Then Lucian Truscott did a couple of articles that put the military in a bad light, or so it thought. He wrote about the taking of drugs by soldiers. His superiors had been keeping an eye on him for some time; they were aware that he might not quite measure up to be military material in the end—this writing for a radical hippie underground newspaper in New York was, after all, most unlieutenantlike—and, after the drug articles, Lucian Truscott was called in and read the riot act: he could either resign his commission, now, or he could be dishonorably discharged. Lucian Truscott chose the first.

He came back to New York in the summer of 1970, and Mary Nichols put him "in charge of seeing that the reporters room doesn't keep degenerating into a pig pen and that all typewriters stay in good repair," as her internal memo read. Then he went on staff. In the next year, he covered the court-martial of Lt. William Calley for the My Lai Massacre, and rock impresario Bill Graham's closing of the Fillmore East. He grew his hair long, and the paper made an amusing "before-and-after" picture contrast, using two shots of him, as an in-house ad.

He lived in a houseboat docked at a pier in Manhattan. And he began to live the life of the New Journalist—a status about which he kidded himself when a high-school student sought to interview him in that regard:

> Friday morning I woke up, and the first thing I thought about was the interview with that kid. What does a New Journalist wear, I wondered aloud. I mean, what is this kid going to think of me? A suggestion was made that I should wear a t-shirt with "Strike" imprinted on the front, a tightly clenched and viciously determined-looking fist on the back. I considered it. The advantages of such a t-shirt were obvious. The interviewer would immediately know I am committed; upon turning my back on him, he would be made aware of the fact that I am *tough*, that I mean *business*. You don't fuck around with a New Journalist, by god, and a strike / fist t-shirt would get that message across with fervor.
>
> I ended up wearing an old pair of corduroys and a shirt I've had since high school. The kid came up to my cubicle at *The Voice*. He was scared. Very scared. I immediately put him at ease with a few reassuring comments along the lines of how I had never been interviewed before. He relaxed.
>
> "You know," he said, smiling for the first time, "I tried to get Tom Wicker first, but he was too busy, and then I tried to get Jack Newfield, but I couldn't get through to him, so I settled for you. I thought you would be older or something. You know, I mean, I didn't think you'd have long hair and that you'd look like you do. My teacher told me you had been a battalion commander in Viet Nam and that you were a colonel."
>
> "Wicker and Newfield, huh?" (The effects of being told that I was third behind Wicker and Newfield were fighting to show through my otherwise cool facade—did this kid have any idea how heavy this was for me? He couldn't, he just couldn't.) "Then what was that stuff about 'young radical writer' in your letter."
>
> "Oh, that. I'm not really sure what I thought, I guess."

Time went on, and Lucian Truscott's hair was short again, and he was living on the Lower East Side, in a building the junkies took over, apartment by apartment, and things were not so funny anymore. He was living in the midst of drugs and murder now, one night he was arrested for carrying a concealed weapon (a sword-cane), and he wrote about that, too:

> It is said the middle class riots by moving away, and that's right. But I would take it a step further. The middle class moves away when it gets pissed and scared. I got pissed, because I got arrested when the streets were crawling with junkies I had had to pull that sword on. And scared, man how I was scared! I'm middle class, and I moved. And I won't go back, not for love or money or principle will I go back . . .
>
> When it came down to it, down to five apartments empty out of seven, down to jumping every time I heard the wall creak, down to hating the sound of the words "Avenue B," I split. I went to New Jersey,* and I wallowed in the freedom, I wallowed in the fresh air of not having to be afraid of getting mugged, or "ripped off," as it was said. There was no romance on Avenue B. There was no humor in the sign which read "No nodding." There was no satisfaction in living in the midst of filth and squalor and junk and degradation and crime, when in fact I didn't have to. There was only fear, and though she is often a comely seductress, she never fails to make a lousy lover.

The military bearing, in a way, never really left him; he simply transferred it. He was built like a tank, squat, with a gruff, blunt, four-letter exterior. Other people said they were happy; Lucian Truscott would say he was "as happy as a pig in shit," and that was different. But he knew who he was, and he never lost that directness of his that had attracted Dan Wolf to him in the first place. Dan Wolf had pegged Lucian Truscott right, and he proved to be someone to be counted on.

★ ★ ★

There was a pattern to the selection process Dan Wolf used with young writers in the seventies. They were men, they were intense individuals, they tended to be loners, and they tended to be iconoclasts, beyond the ideology of the sixties into a post–New Left sensibility. The Men Alone, they might have been labeled. Ron Rosenbaum was one such. Howard Blum was another. Lucian Truscott, of course, was one. And so, certainly, was Clark Whelton.

---

*It should be said here that Lucian Truscott moved back, a year later, to a loft on the edge of the SoHo district.

He was a New Englander by birth and background—born and raised in Wethersfield, Connecticut, graduated from Bates College in Maine—and he had been reading the paper off and on since the year he got out of school. Eight years later, in 1966, at twenty-nine, Clark Whelton was teaching at a boys' school in New Jersey, married with two young children, and trying to write fiction, when he decided to give it all up, move to the city, and try to make his living there as a writer.

He couldn't make it, not at first, and he and his family came close to the brink of starvation. Between 1966, when he began the first of eight years as live-in superintendent of the building at Avenue B and 4th Street, and 1970, the average income of him and his wife, put together, was $3,500 a year. What money they had went for food and rent. They saved nothing, and when there wasn't enough milk to go around, their kids got it and they didn't.

He was on unemployment for a year. He worked on the waterfront, moving furniture, driving trucks, and finally as a projectionist in underground movie houses. He enrolled in the St. Mark's Church writers' workshop taught by Joel Oppenheimer and Sy Krim, and worked on his fiction—plays, short stories, novels. And one poem, on the occasion of Truman Capote's throwing a masked-ball party for himself at the Plaza Hotel to celebrate the publication of *In Cold Blood*. It struck Clark Whelton as lurid that the Beautiful People should be celebrating that way, when the father of the family that had been murdered by the subjects of Capote's book—a man named Herbert Klutter, his head blown off at close range—had had to be buried with his face masked in cotton, and had hated alcohol and tobacco all his life. So he wrote "The Ghost of Herbert Klutter at the Plaza," imagining Klutter's reactions as he moved among the party-goers, submitted it to the *Village Voice,* and the *Voice,* in its issue of December 8, 1966, published it.

He kept writing over the next year—a chapter in a book about Adam Clayton Powell being put together by poet Ishmael Reed, articles in *Win,* the radical pacifists' magazine, on the New York antiwar demonstrations—but it wasn't enough. Clark Whelton was down at one point to $50.

Then, fire broke out in the same building on his street where, a few months before, a Puerto Rican had been held captive and tortured by a gang of bikers and hippies. The fire department came, put out the blaze, knocked out the windows on one floor doing it, left the scene. And later that night a junkie came back to that same building, which he had been using to shoot up in until he had been caught and thrown out of there, and set fire to it again, and with the open windows the flames shot into the apartment of the Puerto Rican family above. Four of them died, painfully—Clark Whelton could hear them screaming, came out and could see them burning—and he wrote "Born to Be Burned," an account of it, which the *Village Voice* again published. Then the New York garbage strike of February 1968 piled refuse a dozen feet high on some of the city's streets, and gave Clark Whelton inspiration for another piece ("Garbage is big business. Garbage is politics. But last week on the Lower East Side, garbage was food for rats and food for political thought"), and once again the *Voice* published it. By this time he was wondering, Is this all it takes to be published in the *Village Voice?* But he was also thinking, not counting his poem of long before, *That's two-for-two I've gotten published so far. I'd better stop now.*

Yet he did not stop. He slipped more pieces under the door, and more of them ran on the front page, and in May, after his report from Washington on the disastrous fate of the Poor People's Campaign, Martin Luther King's last project, he had his first phone conversation with Dan Wolf—he had been unwilling to pester them with phone calls up to then. He also did a piece for *Eye* Magazine, on why Bobby Kennedy would not get elected president, and before the article could appear Kennedy was assassinated. While the magazine and he were arguing over what, if any, kill fee he was to be paid for it, Clark Whelton's money ran out.

At just that time, he had done another piece for the *Voice,* one on a visit to Yippie headquarters where preparations for the Democratic convention in Chicago were under way, and on the morning of the following week that the *Voice* came out Clark Whelton slipped out of the projector's booth at his movie house to go to a newsstand and buy a copy. He peeked; he was afraid to look. And at first glance his reaction was *Shit, somebody else did it.* But then he looked, saw that the byline was, in fact, his, and jumped three feet in the air. He had passed a test. He had known what it was like to be broke, and he had survived. He was convinced now, for the first time in his life, that he could support himself with his writing. He left the projector running, and never went back.

The *Voice's* check of $50 got him through July, and *Charlie* Magazine, on the basis of the Yippie article, offered him a $300 assignment to do a piece about "revolutionary students." Next the magazine offered to send him to Europe to report on the revolutionary student movements there. Clark Whelton had been right.

One Monday night before he left, the thought occurred to him that he had not written for the *Voice* for a while. Just then, he heard over the radio that city teachers were taking their strike vote on the Ocean Hill–Brownsville issue that very night, only a few blocks away, at the meeting hall of the Maritime Union. Though he was by no means a trained reporter, Clark Whelton went over and took notes on the meeting. As it turned out, the *Village Voice* had had no one at the meeting, so the next week its lead story on the schools crisis was by Clark Whelton. "The teachers came out to vote Monday night . . . to democratically decide whether or not one million New York City school children could attend class the following day," it began. When he got a follow-up call from Mary Nichols suggesting that they "stay on" the situation, Clark Whelton had figured out how the *Village Voice* got most of its stories—by waiting for people to come forward and *do* them.

He went off to Europe; he was inside the American Embassy in Paris as the returns of Nixon's defeat of Humphrey came in, and he was in Prague to send back a report to the *Voice* after the Soviets had crushed the Czechoslovakian experiment in liberalization. Then he was back, to do other pieces—he followed a group of American diplomats around as the U.S. Information Agency took them on a tour of the Fillmore East, complete with a performance by the Joshua Light Show, to reacclimate them to American life after their service abroad, did a piece on the closing of the Café Figaro, and was in Hyannisport to gauge the reactions among Teddy Kennedy's constituents as the news of Chappaquiddick came in—and he stayed on the course he had chosen, at the paper he had chosen. In 1969 he turned down a job paying $17,000 with *Newsweek*. He turned down a full-time job with New York State consumer advocate Betty Furness, for whom he had been writing speeches. And, in April 1971, he turned down a job, paying more, with Clay Felker of *New York* Magazine, to take a job, the same week, with the *Village Voice,* on staff.

With his gaunt, reedy frame, his rapid-fire speech, and the sometimes stark stare of his eyes, he did not seem the type to possess a sense of humor, but Clark Whelton was a master of puns, joke-telling, and trivia, sports or otherwise—mental contests of any sort. He and Ron Rosenbaum would play a game, sometimes with a third party, usually with each other, a game they called "Blanding Out," the purpose of which was to start a conversation, and prolong it for as long as possible, without any of them once using any means of expression other than a cliché. For several years in a row beginning in 1971, he gave out year-end "awards" for such "articles" as "Robert Moses Admits Eating Pizza—Link to Mafia Confirmed, by Mary Perot Nichols." And, early in 1972, when the brouhaha began over the authenticity of Clifford Irving's hoax "biography" of Howard Hughes, Whelton commented with excerpts from a supposed Hughes biography of his own:

Howard Hughes is on the "F" train. He paces back and forth, jotting down numbers in a small leather-bound notebook. His disguise is ingenious, but imperfect.

"Thinking of buying the subway system?" I ask. He is annoyed, but wastes no time with denials.

"I'm thinking of selling it," he says. "But first I want to be sure that my improvement is being implemented." Perceiving my question, he continues: "The workers who constructed this car were raised from birth on organic food."

We get off at 34th Street and walk into Nedick's. Howard Hughes orders artichokes faucis au maigre, caneton rouennais, pointes d'asperges a la sauce verte, and mousse aux marrons. I have a frank, fries, and an orange drink. Howard Hughes cautions the chef on cleanliness.

"Why do you suppose they're so interested in me?" he says. He smacks his lips when he chews. Juice trickles from the corner of his mouth, runs down his chin, and vanishes beneath a loose corner of his beard.

"How's your hot dog?" he asks.

I vow not to let him pick up my tab, but he doesn't offer.

We cross 6th Avenue. Howard Hughes curses the automobile exhaust in the air. I look back.

"I own it," he says.

"You don't know what I'm looking at."

Howard Hughes smiles. On the corner, Scientologists are selling certainty. They step aside. . . .

I walk into Nedick's. The black waitress spirals a damp cloth across the counter, staring past me while I make up my mind. I order potage aux bouquets, gigot de mouton roti, champignons au fromage, and tarte alsacienne.

"Shove it up your ass," the waitress says.

Howard Hughes calls at midnight. "Don't ever try that again," he warns. His voice is tense and angry. I lean back against my pillow.

"You're old," I tell him. "Your time is short."

I hear him breathing. "Life is lived laterally, not lengthwise," he says.

Howard Hughes approaches me in the park. He is not disguised.

"You are to have complete and absolute freedom," he says. "All secrets may be revealed. Without exception."

"Freedom is not granted," I tell him. "It is taken."

"Ah, but they know this," Howard Hughes says. "They know that what they need can only be taken from where it is."

I sit down on a bench. Howard Hughes picks up a stick, kicks aside the dead leaves, and scratches the outline of his book into the earth.

Whelton was also an inveterate dog-hater, who had already gone on record to declare his wish to rid Manhattan of them, and received bags of dog shit mailed to him at the *Voice* by way of answer. And so, in the spring of 1972, when he learned from a friend that dog meat was in fact a Chinese delicacy, that, in Chinatown, Chinese who knew the right code words from the menu were ordering it, and that the whole thing was kept a secret to avoid offending Occidentals, Clark Whelton decided to go public with his information, in an article entitled "Dobermans Are Delicious," featuring the recipe (actually just substituting the word "Doberman" for "pork") for "sweet 'n sour Doberman."

He didn't expect to be taken quite seriously, but then he was not totally kidding either—after all, he asked in it, "How many chances do we get to eliminate hunger and pollution at the same time?" And on May 20, two days after the article appeared, the Chinese American Restaurant Association of Greater New York filed an $11 million lawsuit against the *Village Voice* charging defamation of reputation and loss of business. Four days after that, the *Voice* lawyers, the restaurants' lawyers, and a State Supreme Court Justice all had to sit down for lunch at the New Pine Garden restaurant on Chatham Square in Chinatown, and the *Village Voice* had to admit that the article, with its quotation therein of "H. R. Wong, a local restaurateur," was "satiric" and "regrettable," and promise to give equal space to a retraction and apology before the suit was withdrawn.

But Clark Whelton was more than just a funny man. He was serious, so serious in the blunt truth he spoke about certain things that eventually the paper nearly ruptured over his right to express them.

When they had first moved to New York, he and his wife had gone the radical route. He had not just written about peace marches; he had been in many. He had written an entire unpublished play on an antiwar theme. And he lived in a radical atmosphere—the offices of the left-wing *Guardian* and of *Rat* were on the same block, and only two doors away, so close he could hear her as she looked in vain for her dog one night, lived a woman named Jane Alpert, and her boyfriend Sam Melville—both of them tried and convicted in 1970 for Weatherpeople bombings.* He had been as idealistic as anybody else in the beginning.

But, over the course of five years, Clark Whelton changed.

For one thing, he noticed how his neighborhood was changing. In the beginning, the Poles and Ukrainians had been there, harassing them at every turn, painting "Kill Hippies" and "Cut Your Hair or We'll Cut Your Balls Off" on the sides of buildings. It wasn't until they had moved away that he began to miss them. Then he saw what was happening. The tough white kids who had kept the block safe were getting strung out. Their parents were moving away. Blacks and Puerto Ricans were moving in. The people who had threatened them in the beginning were also the people who kept the streets safe, and now that they were gone, those streets were not safe anymore. Groovy and Linda Fitzpatrick were murdered only six blocks away in the fall of 1967. There were other murders, and bikers, and junkies, and fires, and crime, and fear. While all this was happening, Clark Whelton and his family were starving—and, to his surprise, surviving. He, like anyone raised in the middle class, had always been afraid of poverty. But now he was living in it, *beneath* the level of poverty itself, and a funny thing had happened: he'd discovered it hadn't killed him. He had gotten by. So could others.

Clark Whelton had learned the hard way, on the front lines, that "peace and love" were not enough, that black was not necessarily beautiful, and that poor was no excuse. And while he was learning this, he was losing friends who were retiring to Vermont communes in order to protect their delicate ideology from coming into contact with the consequences of its failure. He was encountering other ideologues, who invariably lived on the Upper West Side or in the West Village, who were saying, it seemed to him, that the middle class was *the enemy,* when it had been his middle-class standards that had gotten him *through,* when they were only *talking* the lifestyle he was already *living.* They glorified what happened in a ghetto, Clark Whelton decided, because they could afford to.

Clark Whelton grew disenchanted with the depravity, and the dope, and the parasitism, and the violence, and the hypocrisy. He became disgusted with it. And finally he turned on it with a fury he had once reserved for poverty and racism and the war. He had come full circle.

---

*Sam Melville was sentenced to Attica State Prison. Jane Alpert jumped bail, to surrender to authorities later, in 1974.

Now he hated the New Left, and all it stood for, and the smug orthodoxy of established liberalism that coexisted with it, even encouraged it, and when he thought he saw at least two such ideologues working at the same paper as he did, he was not afraid to say so.

Throughout 1971 and 1972, he was on the cutting edge of a neoconservative counterattack in the pages of the *Voice*. When, in early February 1972, policemen Gregory Foster and Rocco Laurie, one white, the other black, were killed by a band of murderers calling itself the Black Liberation Army who set them up, shot them in the back, and then blasted the dead men's genitals off at point blank range, he cursed the perverted *zeitgeist* that had made it possible:

> The next morning the snow had stopped but the blood was still there. The kids coming up the avenue on the way to school stepped around it. The people on the bus stood up in their seats to get a better view. Dogs crossed the street to sniff cautiously at the red slush, then trotted away. Two cops were dead. Shot in the back at point-blank range, ripped by a total of 14 bullets while they tried to find the owner of a double-parked car. Two cops were dead, and if you hurried, if you got to the corner of 11th Street and B before the thin winter sun came up from behind the tenements and melted the snow on the avenue, you could see their blood. You could see where they died. Where was that again? Eleventh and B. You know the block, that's where Groovy and Linda were beaten to death with a brick four and a half years ago. Well, it's just four doors north, right on the corner. Right in the middle of what some people still call the East Village, right in the center of what used to be the hippest part of the hippest neighborhood in the city. Right on a corner where you could always score a little acid, buy a little grass, put in an order for Moroccan hash, then go back home and smoke yourself into a dream of peace and love. The Puerto Rican kids call it *''la esquina de los tecatos,''* the corner of the junkies, but what the hell, that's all right because by getting into drugs people put themselves outside the society which oppresses them. Drugs are revolution. Drugs are freedom. And when the junkies come to crack open your apartment door and carry everything you have off in pillowcases, well, you have to understand that it is your own fault, because by not dedicating every moment of your life to overthrowing a corrupt and oppressive society which drives poor people into drugs, you are in fact *encouraging* the very

junkies who rip you off. Can you dig that? Of course you can dig it, I know you can dig it. And can you dig that the reason the streets are filthy in the East Village, and the reason people throw their garbage out the window, is because the streets around Rockefeller Center are clean and the people on Park Avenue have servants to bring their garbage downstairs for them? I *know* you can dig that. It's so clear. It's so simple.

"Greenwich Village—lovely, liberal Greenwich Village of the charming streets and historic brownstones—is poised on the edge of disaster," he wrote in March of 1971.

. . . Narcotics pushers now work the parks with seeming immunity. The welfare hotels still practice their profitable profession of concentrating the most desperate and miserable cases in New York in the places where they can be helped least. Drug freaks and high pressure panhandlers huddle on the corners along Sixth Avenue. Spoiled, arrogant teenagers from the suburbs, who use the Village as a vomitorium for all the hatred they've been forced to swallow by other people in other places, roar through Sheridan Square in daddy's Buick, looking for another after-hours club and another source of drug information when they find that the Haven is full. Addicts from Harlem take the "A" train down to the Village because heroin is cheaper on Waverly Place than on 125th Street, and the women in Washington Square are easy to intimidate with accusations of racial prejudice. Burglars, muggers, and stick-up teams have learned that any neighborhood which will tolerate all of the above has got to be ripe for the picking. And so, while real estate speculators and other drooling scavengers of social decay wait in the wings, Greenwich Village is being picked. Block by block.

And it wasn't just the Village. In late 1971, the Lindsay administration was trying to force three low-income, highrise housing projects on Jewish, middle-class, low-rise Forest Hills, Queens. Clark Whelton was there.

When Mayor Lindsay gets around to writing Poor John's Almanac, one of the little sayings certain to be included is: any block worth busting is worth busting right. The annotated edition will explain that this means *think big*. Don't just settle

for chasing out the middle-class families. Break up the entire
neighborhood. Turn Brownsville into World War III and the
South Bronx into an open sore. Stick a string of welfare hotels
into Greenwich Village and knock down a community of self-
built homes in Corona. And if someone points out that these
changes have made life worse, not better, in the area, then
stencil him with words like ''racist'' or ''bigot'' and open fire
on another neighborhood.

These were not opinions designed to go down easily. Congressman
Herman Badillo wrote in to dispute Whelton's arguments against the
Forest Hills project. When a radical school principal named Luis
Fuentes was involved in a dispute with teachers and parents over the
policies he was pursuing in his experimental Intermediate School 201,
he, too, quarreled with Whelton in print for siding with those seeking
(successfully, as it turned out) his ouster. But Whelton was adamant:
"At some point," he wrote in rebuttal of Fuentes, "the victims run out
of excuses for their failure and are faced with the miserable possibility
that perhaps they deserve what they get. If all people are created
equal," he wanted to know, "why do some go to the top while others
remain behind?"

It was strong stuff, and it badly needed saying, but it was precisely
what certain people at the *Village Voice* did not want to be told, and
when Clark Whelton spoke his mind on the Attica prison rebellion, and
who in his opinion was *really* responsible for the thirty-eight people
killed there, the trouble really started.

14. BY 1971, THE REVOLUTION HAD NOT

worked out, and the evidence was everywhere. The Screamer Left and the Bomber Left had had their day, and there were bodies in Greenwich Village and at the University of Wisconsin to show for it. Nixon was more in control than ever; there were dead bodies in Kent State and Southeast Asia, not to mention tens of thousands of spectacularly unconstitutional mass arrests in the streets of Washington, D.C., during Mayday of 1971, to show for *that*.

For all of the frenzy, the activity, and the rhetoric that had gone down since it had first coalesced into a movement, the New Left had accomplished only one thing, the only thing it ever would accomplish— it had made the world a worse place to be.

It, and its intellectual progeny, and the social side effects they created, had fallen far short of actually delivering on the utopian, romantic promises of "participatory democracy," "raised consciousness," and "power to the people" they had made. Instead, the only legacy left behind was an insidious moral valuelessness, transmitted into the mainstream of the body politic, a mass-marketed doublethink and newspeak that now, with the politicization of practically everything, made certain crucial segments of Black America, and Young White America, too intimidated or inflamed or neurotic even to identify the parasites in their own midst. It was "violence" and "destruction" that were fashionable and attention-getting. It was a "revolution" run by the spoiled children of the affluent new middle class, for the benefit of that middle class, that sought the protection of that middle class—and its liberalism—to carry itself out. And it was run by "revolutionaries" whose ultimate goal was not the overthrow of the government but getting themselves on the six o'clock news. It had been a media event, nothing more, one more manifestation of America's decadence in the electronic age, and it had been bankrupt from the beginning, only it had not been politically possible—"cool"—to say so in the heady Black Power Summer of '66 or the Love Summer of '67 or the Chicago Summer of '68 or the Moratorium Summer of '69 or the Kent-Cambodia Summer of '70.

But it was possible now, and it was inevitable, if the *Village Voice* were to stay true to its traditions, that if Clark Whelton had not said so, someone else would have had to come along who would have; all he was doing was telling truths that were as obvious as they were long overdue.

But no matter to some. The fact remained that Clark Whelton was

295

making himself unpopular in certain circles, was telling a certain constituency what it didn't want to hear, and more important, what they would have preferred not be printed in the *Village Voice*, traditions or no.

★ ★ ★

On Thursday morning, September 9, 1971, at Attica State Prison in upstate New York, the prisoners in Cellblock D staged a well-planned uprising. It came off with precision. Soon, D Yard was sealed off, and the guards were hostages. For four days, they stayed that way, knives at their throats, while a mediation committee shuttled between the prison and the assembled forces of the state outside, and Governor Nelson Rockefeller refused to come to negotiate himself until Monday, September 13, when state troopers and National Guardsmen, on Rockefeller's order, shot their way back in. When they did, thirty-eight people died—twenty-eight prisoners, killed by guardsmen; one hostage, killed by prisoners; nine hostages, killed not by prisoners but by their would-be rescuers, the Guardsmen.

The total casualty count, and the number of dead hostages, was known right away. It took another twenty-four hours for the whole truth—that it was the governor's men, not the convicts, who had killed all but one of the hostages—to come out.

The first news—containing the casualty counts but not the full explanation for them—reached the *Village Voice* just as it was on deadline, and reached Clark Whelton's ears just as he was already in a rage at statements he had heard by William Kunstler, member of the mediation committee, over radio station WBAI in New York the night before, statements, some made by Kunstler himself, some attributed by him to Black Panther Bobby Seale, that seemed to be egging the prisoners on without telling them what was bound to happen to them, and now that he had heard these incomplete, fragmentary news reports the only thing Clark Whelton could think was that these so-called radicals Seale and Kunstler were responsible. They had led the prisoners on, then they had split and left the men they had excited to face the bullets alone. He told Ross Wetzsteon what he wanted to write, and that he wanted the WBAI tapes. Ross Wetzsteon told him there wasn't time, to go ahead with what he had and get the documentation later. And so Clark Whelton wrote:

> There are three treatments for cancer—radiation, chemotherapy, and surgery. All three poison or mutilate the body and may even kill the patient before the cancer does. But the most skillful of physicians can only try one of these three

scourges if he wants to attempt a cure. As destructive as they are, there's nothing else.

The State Prison in Attica, New York, is nothing but a different kind of cancer. The police attack on rebellious inmates there was ugly and bloody, but as destructive as it was, was there anything else?

. . . In the 1960s, American practitioners of radical politics expanded the theory of the alibi into an illusion of collective innocence. . . . For a while it seemed as though it might work out, that flowers, goodness, righteous thinking, and political showmanship might actually be an antidote to the toxic effects of government. Even the advent of Weatherman bomb tactics, Panther militancy, and the auto-hypnosis of "armed love" somehow kept alive the illusion that the cure for society's ills was only a matter of doing away with the doctors who kept society sick.

The explosion of blood and violence at Attica has ended that illusion and stripped away the insulating alibis that kept it intact. In assessing the blame for the sordid murders at Attica, no person or group will bear a heavier burden of guilt than the contemptible '60s radicals who in their role as members of the mediating committee tacitly encouraged the prison inmates to go on thinking they were political prisoners engaged in a struggle of conscience instead of civil criminals engaged in a struggle against their keepers. Sixties radicals like William Kunstler—who have no experience with the realities of governing other men—should have known that amnesty could not possibly be granted by Governor Rockefeller or anyone else. By sticking with the radical theory, the pathetic and intoxicating '60s rhetoric which insists that radical believers are innocent victims of a fascist government, they pushed the prisoners deeper into delusion. By stating that unlimited quantities of time were available for negotiating, Kunstler demonstrated his perhaps willful ignorance of basic government which must consider the effect that a siege has on other prisons and on the rest of the population.

The state had to act. Five days of talking is an extraordinary length of time for the negotiations to have continued. By not arguing against the political fantasies of the prisoners, the '60s radicals on the mediating committee were leading them, and the hostages, to inevitable death and a useful place in the propaganda pantheon of the left. . . .

The prisoners of Attica formed a government during the five

days they controlled cellblock D. Armed with the ideas of '60s radicalism, they put some of them into practice. Among their first decisions was a death threat against their hostages. . . . An early demand of the Attica prisoners was transportation by plane to a ''non-imperialist'' country. Nothing could symbolize the over-the-rainbow dreamworld of '60s radicalism better than this request. Where did the prisoners think they were going to go? To North Korea? To China? To Cuba, Russia, Albania, police states all? . . . To persist in the floating innocence of '60s radicalism is to delay and deform any chance at social progress.

It was a fair piece, for all its uncompromising language, and it would stand the test of time. But, right then, there were two things wrong with it. The first, over which Clark Whelton had no control, was that it was written before the news came in about how the hostages had died, which not only lifted the chastened mood of the Left but meant that the audience that read Clark Whelton's remarks did so in a context and atmosphere totally different from the one he had written them in. The second, which he knew he would have to correct right away, was that he had made all his charges about "60s radicalism" without once even referring to the WBAI tapes, or using them as documentation. He went out now, got hold of them, and wrote a piece for the next week that not only criticized Rockefeller (his "responsibility for the slaughter of Attica is clear and unmistakable") but corroborated his original charges in convincing detail.

By then, however, there was something else in the paper concerning his original article, too, a letter that went:

> Clark Whelton's article blaming '''60s radicals'' for the Attica Massacre was disgraceful. It was written in haste by a man whose knowledge of the intricate negotiations at Attica seems to have been inadequate. His one concrete point is an unjust criticism of William Kunstler. It is based on prejudices, not information. It contradicts the testimony of Tom Wicker and Herman Badillo, who served with Kunstler on the negotiating committee and agree he did good work in extremely difficult circumstances. The committee members understood that Kunstler was there as the lawyer for the citizens in Cellblock D.
>
> There are criticisms to be made of the political line that defines all prisoners as political prisoners; criticisms to be

made of people who talk but don't act. Clark didn't make them with any precision. He didn't argue. He ranted.

The principal blame for the Attica Massacre rests with Nelson Rockefeller. He is responsible for the murders—guards and inmates. In a just society he'd be impeached, tried in criminal courts, and given a life sentence in a real rehabilitation center.

The letter was signed by three other writers for the *Village Voice.* One of them was Jack Newfield, who had stated his opinion on the matter the previous week—"The citizens of cellblock D should be thought of as a nation, just like the hippies at Woodstock. And as a nation, they were more just and less violent than the larger nation outside. . . . In the end, the nation inside Attica turned out to contain the human beings, and the nation outside the walls was the one run by the animals." The second name was that of David Gelber, a freelancer. And the third was Paul Cowan.

★ ★ ★

When Paul Cowan came out of the Peace Corps in late 1967, he had completed the journey that sent him in there, or, at least, become the person he was going to be.

Over the next few years, he finally came into his own as a writer. His style blossomed into an original one blending the techniques of human interest and investigative reporting, rich with multiple gifts—of being able to turn saturation reporting into instant, contemporary oral history, of being able to submerge himself in the community he was covering and come out with reportage sensitive to all the different hues, gradations, and complications therein, of being able to convey the many different flavors of Americana everywhere he went. Though he had never been one himself, he had the ability to identify with, and capture the pathos of, America's forgotten people.

Those were qualities that served him well when he interviewed in depth the jurors who sat in a judgment they could not reach in the Harrisburg conspiracy trial, or when he visited the site of fundamentalist upheaval over the introduction of progressive textbooks into a West Virginia school system:

The battle in Kanawha is a cultural revolution, in the strictest sense of the term: an effort by the rural working class to wrest schools—the means of production of their children—away from the permissive technocrats who now control them.

It is a holy war between people who depend on books and people who depend on the Book. . . .

I have rarely covered a story that left me feeling as emotionally conflicted as this one has, for it seems to me that some of the pro-textbook people—the Northern educators and bureaucrats who devised them, not the local people who adopted them—are involved in a kind of cultural imperialism. But some of the protestors, who may be able to gain control of the country through the courts, through elections, and through threats of violence, are capable of outright totalitarianism.

I know that the people who designed the textbooks believe that the children of fundamentalists (and, to a lesser extent, of the white working class in general) have to be freed from the narrow-minded influence of their parents in order to become functioning members of 21st century America. But is it ethical or prudent, to confront them with textbooks they regard as blasphemous, to use their classrooms as "testing grounds," to train their teachers to be "change agents"? To me that is, quite literally, a way of telling kids "we have to destroy your culture in order to save you." I've interviewed some curriculum reformers and textbook authors, and it's clear that they see the "creekers" in the same derisive terms H. L. Mencken used during the Scopes trial . . .

Their intentions are probably benign, but isn't their policy a fresh example of the arrogance of power? You can invite a person into your culture. But I don't believe you can impose your culture on another person without risking unforeseeable psychological harm.

And, again, when he mingled with the aging, unassimilated, poor Jews still living on New York's Lower East Side:

During my weeks on the Lower East Side I began to feel some ethnic loyalties I never knew I possessed. Yet I also realized that, in real life, I represented many of the things the people I met there were complaining about. I have always lived in an assimilated environment, I married a Gentile without feeling a trace of emotional conflict. I knew very little about my religious heritage. During the past decade I've worked with blacks in the civil rights movement and Latins in the Peace Corps but, except for a six-month stay in Israel, I

have never worked with or written about dispossessed Jews—
or even realized that they existed in America.

. . . Many of them would regard my ideas and activities as a
form of betrayal. And the more I learned about their problems
the more unsettling that contradiction became. . . .

They feel as if they've been abandoned by uptown liberal
Jewish intellectuals, politicians, and philanthropists who,
they think, care more about blacks and Puerto Ricans than
about the nagging problems of the Jewish slums. And, worse
than that, abandoned by their own children. Many successful
young people who have escaped the neighborhood haven't
sent their parents money or even mail in years. And many of
those who still help out do so with visible annoyance . . .

One night I went to a small basement shul near the Forward
building on East Broadway with a man in his early 60s, a cab
driver who had only become religious as he realized that death
was approaching. I was always uncomfortable going to these
synagogues. I kept worrying that some elderly Orthodox man
would realize I didn't know the rituals, and wheel at me and
denounce me as an imposter. So I'd rock back and forth a
little, faking a daven; I'd try to remember to turn the prayer
book's pages backward, following the Hebrew text; I'd mutter
a few moaning sounds hoping that whoever heard me would
hear my barely audible creaks as the appropriate prayer.

. . . There was a fervor to the ceremony that left me
unexpectedly moved, though I could only understand the
tiniest portion of what was going on. Yet there was something
ghostly about the fervor. The shul, the ceremony, belonged to
the aged: I was the only person there under 60. . . . The
people I was meeting were part of a generation that was still in
the desert.

Over those same years, though, Paul Cowan was doing something
else as well—he was making a permanent place for himself in the office
politics of the *Village Voice*. For if there was something admirable
about his writing, watching him strain to drop the clichés of the New
Left as he learned about America, there was something pathetic about
it, too, because it was obvious that it was a struggle, that he really
believed all those clichés in the first place. He once remarked, later,
that he thought his writing had come into its own only very gradually,
when he stopped writing as if his old compatriots in the Movement
were looking over his shoulder all the time. Chances were that Paul

Cowan had not come nearly as far a distance as he thought he had, and not nearly far enough for a great many of the people who worked with him.

He himself said it all, when he wrote at the end of his Peace Corps memoir how, when he heard the news that the Viet Cong had attacked the American Embassy in Saigon, he got rushes of being there with the attackers, fighting alongside of "my government's enemy, the people." That one statement summed up why it was that the antiwar movement, as well as the war itself, had left a curse of its own upon America. For while there were always too few Americans opposed to the war in Vietnam, there were always too many opposed to it simply because it was a war their own country was fighting. An entire sector of a new generation, including some of its supposed "best and brightest," came to maturity blissfully, sometimes willfully, ignorant of their country's overwhelming contribution of good, in an incredibly short time, to the human race, and casually convinced that the society of which they were members was the most brutal and repressive in the world, people who saw the war not as a violation of American fixed principles, but as their logical extension. It was a slippery, facile anti-Americanism—held and espoused by, of all people, Americans. It was a mentality that subscribed to the old Russian proverb "The enemy of my enemy is my friend," and Paul Cowan, as he served notice with that passage of writing, bought it whole.

To those he turned off, he represented the epitome of the phenomenon of radical chic—rich, white left-wingers propagating the idea that Americans should loathe themselves. He struck them as patronizing and condescending, the apotheosis of the affected Movement type, dispensing dogma and doubletalk, full of jejune gibberish from the latest Left line, a mouther of revolutionary platitudes and nostrums, and a leader of a superficially revolutionary lifestyle. They mocked him for his incessant use of the groupthink "Jack and I" when he talked, and for his use of the cross-legged lotus position, on the floor, when he sat.

The facts were, however horrified Paul Cowan might be by them, that he and Jack Newfield did spend a great deal of time together, did think alike, did cite each other as support for their own opinions, and were both rich. Paul Cowan, the recipient by birth of not one but two great fortunes, who dressed in the plainest possible clothes and sometimes had to borrow small amounts of money from other people, lived in an apartment building on the Upper West Side that was very, very nice, with a doorman who was very, very Negro. And Jack Newfield had by this time married money, in the person of the accomplished and independently wealthy photojournalist Jane Eisenberg, so for the first time in his life *he* was well off. The facts were also that when Clark Whelton began writing his counterrevolutionary heresies in the *Village Voice* and telling anyone who would listen that groupthink was bullshit, that you see life differently when you live on the Lower East Side instead of in some uptown doorman building, that some people who lived where liberalism was in style and where they were personally safe from crime just didn't want to be told what wasn't fashionable, there was little doubt whom he had in mind, and both he and they knew it.

★ ★ ★

In the week after his article on Attica came out, nothing was said to Clark Whelton directly by any of them—Newfield, Cowan, Gelber—or by those who agreed with them, about it. Nothing had to be. It was what was *not* said that mattered. They did not confront Whelton directly. That was not their style. Instead, they withdrew to their offices, collectively drew up a statement, took it upstairs, and got it published. And, otherwise, they avoided contact with him. Clark Whelton, meanwhile, knew what was going on, knew what was being said and written about him at the other end of the hall, and he felt the tension. Finally, after several days of it, of whispers and statements and meetings and rumors and terse passages through hallways, Ross Wetzsteon called people into his office to clear the air. Mary Nichols was there, and Mary Breasted, and Alan Weitz (who had worked his way up to an editor's job by now), and Newfield,* and Cowan. There, feelings came out in the open. Newfield told Wetzsteon he had heard that he, Wetzsteon, had told others that if it had been up to him he would have killed Whelton's piece in advance. Ross Wetzsteon denied telling anyone that, and both Mary Breasted and Mary Nichols backed him up on that. Then Mary Breasted, Mary Nichols's protégée, and Jack Newfield went at each other, and she told him she believed that if, in fact, it *had* been up to him, Newfield, he *would* have killed it, just to prevent that anti-New Left viewpoint from ever getting in the paper. Cowan interrupted, "Do you have anything against me too, Mary? If you're harboring feelings about me behind my back, I wish you'd tell me what they were." And she replied, "Yes, Paul, I do, but I don't think you want to hear it," but he did, so she told him. "I

---

*Jack Newfield denies any knowledge either of this meeting or his statements at it. The account rendered here is a composite, and a consensus, based on the recollections of those who *do* remember it.

can't stand your whole goodie-goodie manner," she said, and recited a list of all the faults implied in his various personal mannerisms. Jack Newfield and Mary Nichols began to say things to each other, and just as quickly stopped before it flared up. Then they all broke up, and when they did Jack Newfield made everyone laugh with a cryptic comment: "Maybe Carter Burden will be the one thing to unite us." And on her way out, Mary Breasted was called back in by Ross Wetzsteon, who told her, "Thank you for saying that to Paul. We've all been meaning to say that to him."

One thing the meeting could not resolve, because he was not there, but one reason why it had had to be called in the first place, one thing pressing on the minds of Newfield and Gelber and Cowan and the rest of those at the paper who thought the way they did, was their nagging fear that Clark Whelton's pieces, and especially his piece on Attica, had found their way into the paper because Dan Wolf wanted them there, that Wolf had turned silently against them, into a closet conservative, and they had to find out.

They never did find out, because Dan Wolf kept his silence. But it was true.

The facts were that Dan Wolf agreed with Clark Whelton, about issues in general and about Attica in particular, and wanted him to go right on saying what he was saying. The fact was that Dan Wolf, while he might not have become a so-called neoconservative—he did not use that label, or any others—had had it. He had had enough of the New Left, and the Movement, and cause politics, and radical chic. He was fed up with the Revolution, and what it had done to the country, and what it had done even to his own neighborhood.

It was an attitude that had been coming on gradually. Even in 1964, in Mississippi, something about the kids' commitment had disturbed him. There might be nothing in the world more important to them than the blacks now, he thought, but they won't be back. They'll go back home, up North, and they'll get off the train or the bus or the plane, and the blacks will be left behind, on the front lines, and when this stops being an event, a place to be, a sexy cause, they won't be here. Later, when Tom Hayden was organizing for SDS across the river in Newark, a sixth sense told him that Hayden was not going to stay there, that the wheel was going to turn someday. Now, it had, and old friends who saw less and less of him as they became more involved, like Howard Moody, could feel and see, on the few occasions when they would run into him and talk, just how conservative he had become. Dan Wolf had transferred his doubts. In the beginning, there had been one self-righteous ideology, militant Americanism, and he had opposed it, and some people had misread him because he had. Now, there was another self-righteous ideology, and he was as turned off by that one as he had been by the first.

Those were the doubts they had about him on the Left, and they were justified, though, typically, he never once explicitly said so, not even to Whelton. And, at the end of November, when Clark Whelton was in the paper again, ranting against yet another good liberal goal, the housing project in Forest Hills, and Paul Cowan was going out there himself, to do the saturation interviewing and the serious reporting he thought Clark Whelton was not doing, those doubts were surfacing again.

★ ★ ★

There was more to Jack Newfield's and Mary Breasted's exchange at the meeting held in Ross Wetzsteon's office than what was said there. And the issue of Clark Whelton's articles was only one of the fronts on which the staff of the *Village Voice* was splitting apart in that fall of 1971. There was also the Mary Nichols-Jack Newfield feud.

When Mary Perot Nichols left the Lindsay administration to go back to the *Voice* in the summer of 1968, it was without illusions anymore. Forty-two now, divorced, on her own, she resumed her lifestyle, entertaining friends at Thursday night *salons* in her LaGuardia Place highrise, with its panorama of the city, and, back at the office, going about her routine of jawboning over the phone with her sources and hatcheting her enemies in her column.

And one of those enemies now was John Vliet Lindsay.

She had supported him from the beginning, admired him always, and eagerly gone to work for his administration. But something had happened to John Lindsay as mayor, and for Mary Nichols it was summed up in his attitude toward the Lower Manhattan Expressway. It had been a pet project of Robert Moses, Mary Nichols's *bête noire,* for many years, and in 1965, with the support of outgoing Mayor Wagner, Moses had actually attempted to start work on a part of it, but opposition from then-candidate Lindsay, plus a citizens' group lawsuit, had stopped him. And then, once he was in office, Mayor John Lindsay had turned around and begun to give the same reasons for justifying the project all the other mayors had given, and had tried to ram it through, if anything, even harder than they had, and, when he broke his word, Mary Nichols broke with John Lindsay.

Some politicians know how to betray you with class, she said later; not John Lindsay. But it was more than that. It was a whole attitude, of prissy patrician elitism followed by, in practice, the worst kinds of deal-making with the worst forces in the city. She came to loathe her immediate boss, Lindsay's hot-shot whiz-kid parks commissioner Thomas Hoving. And she came to think that the mayor himself, the man she had thought was going to trigger a renaissance in her city, was nothing but a bum.

In one of her first articles after returning, she alluded to her "usual disgruntled attitude toward the city administration." And then, as she covered the case of Lindsay's water commissioner, James Marcus, whose confessions of bribe-taking ultimately led to the prosecution and conviction of Carmine DeSapio, she became more caustic. "I am convinced the man's schizophrenic," she announced in her column of June 11, 1970. One week later, in the wake of disclosures of massive police corruption by police officers Frank Serpico and David Durk (the latter a friend of hers), she chided that "while the Mayor is traveling to Denver and Berkeley, sounding the note of civility against the Nixon-Mitchell brand of repression, here in New York City where he has the power to make changes in the New York City Police Department, little is done." And that November, after Lindsay's diehard support of Republican Charles Goodell and Democrat Richard Ottinger's narrow miss at staving off James Buckley, she wrote bitterly, "Another small shift to Ottinger would have done it. Instead, Lindsay continued to play quid pro quo politics (you endorsed me so I'll endorse you) until the end, as if this were the highest morality. None of Lindsay's *talk*, about re-ordering national priorities and the perils of Agnewism means as much as what he might have *done* to prevent New York from getting its first Conservative senator." The next year, she wrote off his experiment closing Fifth Avenue to all traffic but bikes as "little more than a media con."

"Bob Wagner: Where are you now that we need you?" she wrote in April of that year. She called Richard Aurelio, his chief aide, "Lindsay's chief thug-in-residence." And after Attica, she wrote, "While Lindsay public relations men have been running around planting in columns and at TV stations the notion that Lindsay is ever so much superior to Governor Rockefeller on the prison issue (David Garth personally called one high network executive on this), prison officials under Lindsay's Corrections Commissioner George McGrath are busy making a mockery of the reforms he promised."

John Lindsay was her favorite target, but he was not the only one. There was Pete Hamill, for instance. He once suggested, in the *Voice*, that gambling be legalized in New York and that racketeer Meyer Lansky be brought in to run it; she got on him for that. Pete also had a thing for Brooklyn machine Democrats; he had once defended Assembly leader Stanley Steingut in the paper and hung around quite a bit with Kings County boss Meade Esposito. She got on him for that, too. (In the December 21, 1972, *Voice:* "Pete is helping Meade write his autobiography, which you can almost bet won't have too much in it about the days when he was a bail-bondsman for the mob.") There was Murray Kempton, columnist for the *Post.* Once, when she had attacked Tony Scotto, the longshoremen's union official and oft-accused member of organized crime, Kempton (as well as, on civil libertarian grounds, Nat Hentoff) had defended him in the *Voice;* he later claimed that his endorsement of New York Attorney General Louis Lefkowitz for reelection in 1970 was kept out of the paper, by her.

And there was Jack Newfield.

They should not have been all that far apart, really; they had many of the same targets—organized crime, corrupt judges, and, especially, Nelson Rockefeller. Newfield once told a group of Columbia University journalism students that "Nelson Rockefeller is my white whale"; she once wrote that trying to get the goods on him was "like the proverbial flea crawling up the leg of an elephant with intentions of rape." But they never got along, right from the very beginning, when she left for the Parks Department and he took over "Runnin' Scared," and she called to give him a tip that David Rockefeller, manager of the family fortune and head of the Chase Manhattan Bank, was trying to get an alternative-urban-architecture show banned from the Museum of Modern Art.

She accused him of telling Barry Gotterher, Lindsay's aide and Newfield's friend, that she was not only the source of the leak, but that she *wrote* the item. Newfield simply denied any knowledge of the incident, and, when asked, would explain his animus for her with the words: "She's just not a pro."

He meant it, too. Once he even went on a radio talk show—on WMCA, Peter Straus's station, of all places—and called her "the Stanley Steingut of journalism." And she, reviewing his book about corruption in the city's criminal justice system for the *West Side Literary Review,* wrote:

> Let me state my bias at the outset. For any reader who does not know, Jack Newfield and I have enjoyed (endured?) a journalistic feud for some years. Sometimes our feuding has been carried on in the pages of *The Village Voice* and once it even broke into *The New York Times.* We feud because our definitions of the function of a journalist diverge sharply. I

believe that the *primary* function of a journalist is to tell the
truth. Jack Newfield (I am only stating my opinion and he may
not agree) believes that the function of a journalist is to write
and speak propaganda for the person or cause he happens to
be enamored of at the moment.

He was not as bad as all that; he was, something she would only
rarely concede, genuinely committed to what he was doing. And she,
which she would sometimes concede, had her favorites too, friends and
sources she got close to and looked out for—such as Ed Koch, the
congressman, Bob Morgenthau, the United States attorney, and Alex
Rose, the Liberal Party boss. But he was, as it continued to bust up,
writing less and less about the New Left and focusing more and more of
his attention on the left wing of the Democratic Party. And, as he was
doing that, he was trying to play West Side liberal politics at the same
time he was trying to report objectively on it, which was a contradiction in terms.

The Jack Newfield of the 1970s, describing his politics, would say
that he was *not* a revolutionary, that he was a democratic leftist, that
he believed in incremental change, and that he had all along. Instead of
blanket indictments of the system, he was choosing specific targets
within it now, and going after them, such as the series on lead-paint
poisoning of ghetto children that ultimately goaded the Lindsay
administration into a $3 million program against it, and his pieces on
political connections in the judiciary, culminating in his cover story for
New York Magazine in the fall of 1972, "The Ten Worst Judges in New
York," and conditions in the city's jails—which was where he first
clashed with Mary Breasted.

When prisoners had rioted in the Tombs in October of 1970, she
covered it. Later, Newfield got on the beat, with stories about beatings
of prisoners after the uprising was over. She claimed she approached
him about inaccuracies in his stories, and that he turned away without
even listening to her, and decided for herself that Newfield was just a
social climber who didn't care about issues, only about meeting people,
which was just what her mentor thought. So when she said what she
did to him up in Ross Wetzsteon's office after the Attica flare-up Mary
Nichols didn't say anything. She didn't have to. Mary Breasted was
saying for her just what she would have said herself.

They coexisted, uneasily, occupying adjacent offices, often working
on the same stories, typing away next to each other on Monday
afternoons against deadline, sometimes writing about the same enemies, sometimes writing about each other, and when they were done,

bringing them upstairs, separately, without a word. Through it all, they maintained the least possible contact, exchanged the minimum of pleasantries, talked with each other as little as they could. And once, when they did, about Rockefeller, and her comments wound up in a story done for *New York* that Jack Newfield had researched in *Voice* files, Mary Nichols scribbled him this note:

> *3/9/70*
>
> *Dear Jack,*
> *I'd appreciate it if you didn't quote a conversation with me without notice that I'm being interviewed for another publication.*
> *Further, I think you're writ [sic] that Rockefeller piece for N.Y. Magazine was despicably disloyal.*
> *And to use our morgue was a piece of chutzpah beyond understanding.*
> *But then, you aren't a very sensitive fellow.*
> *Mary Nichols*

They each had their defenders. He was the more committed, she was the more approachable, and Dan Wolf sometimes tried to referee between the two. He admired her for her tough-mindedness, but, when it came to Newfield, he sometimes felt she was being too hard, and tried more than once to explain him to her.

She was tough-minded. She was tough-talking, too, tough in every way, a literally tough broad, and, though she once called Murray Kempton a "male chauvinist," no feminist. She thought like a man, she fought like a man, she had made it as men's equal in a male world on their terms, and she had no apologies to offer anyone for that fact, so that when a feminist contingent *did* form at the paper, they did not look to her for guidance or sympathy. She went about her duties, spinning the Wheelodex in her office to decide whom to call next and yakking with them in her deep-pitched Shelley Winters voice, with the gleeful, unbridled enthusiasm of a cheerleader, and it was difficult not to like her, unless one was intimidated by her. Which some were, because she could bellow with the best of them. One who found that out was Alexander Cockburn, the English writer who came to the paper in 1972, and who, one day when she had ordered the transcript of a CBS-TV show on the Rockefeller family sent to her at the office, was downstairs when the package arrived. He took the liberty of opening it up, and, seeing what was in it, took it up to the fifth floor to run off Xeroxes of its contents for himself. Quite a few minutes later, an irate

Mary Nichols, after waiting for the material—she needed it for next week's column—calling down to the desk, and learning of its whereabouts, marched up to the fifth floor, and in front of everyone, ripped the Xeroxes out of his hand, snatched the rest of the package away from him, and bawled him out in such a tone, screaming, from the minute she got out of the elevator, *"What are you doing stealing my mail, you rotten son-of-a-bitch,"* that Alex Cockburn, the type who fancied himself capable of the right quip at any time, stood there, speechless, and as chastened as a little boy. Another time, when she came out of her office heading for the elevator and noticed her editorial assistant, James Wolcott, sitting at his desk staring off into space, and asked him what he was doing, and he replied, "Meditating," she shot back, "Go meditate on unemployment," fired him on the spot, and stepped onto the elevator.*

Like Dan Wolf, Mary Nichols had turned into something of a neoconservative by this time, though it was less of a secret in her case. She had gone on record, in conversations with various friends of hers, how the successful battle over folk singers' rights in Washington Square Park had been the beginning of the end for Greenwich Village, and how the location of a welfare center on 14th Street had made things worse. She, who sent her kids to private schools, used to ask Nat Hentoff how he could support his various causes in the public schools when he did the same thing too. And, that fall, when Clark Whelton was reopening wounds with his salvos about Forest Hills, Mary Nichols chose the same time to reopen her feud with Newfield. Defending *New York Post* reporter Allan Wolper, whom Newfield had attacked in his column, she wrote, of Newfield's attack, "I am ashamed that this newspaper published it."

> It would appear that Newfield is an advocate of conformist journalism. Whatever Jack thinks is the party line of the moment is what everybody in the trade, seemingly, ought to follow. It is noticeable to those listening to the late night talk shows that Newfield—for whatever reasons—is warming up to the Presidential aspirations of Mayor Lindsay. He hasn't put many of these new opinions into print yet—perhaps he feels his readers will notice a too rapid switch in his line.
>
> I myself date the new Newfield politics to about the time he

---

*It did not stick. Wolcott was rehired for another post at the paper and later, became a staff writer.

was one of two New York City reporters who attended the New Hampshire wedding of Lindsay's assistant, Jay Kriegel (which happened to be the weekend of the Attica riot).* While Jack may have thought he was invited only because of his charm and good looks, I think he was invited because the Lindsay crowd thought they could use him. And they have. I think the Wolper hatchet job was nothing less than a political contract—whether explicitly or implicitly. The people at City Hall wanted to get Wolper, and Newfield was their instrument.

Nor was the Jack Newfield–Mary Nichols feud the only other source of dissension at the paper.

★ ★ ★

Every genius has a blind spot. Dan Wolf's was money. It was not as if he was a cheap man. On the contrary, he had it in him to be extraordinarily generous to those close to him when he knew they needed it, picking up tabs, loaning them money, even, as he did for some of the writers, arranging to have their places sublet when they took off and left town for long periods. It was not as if he was a hard-bitten man, believing that others should suffer as he had suffered. But he *had* always underpaid his writers, unavoidably in the early years, deliberately later on, and by now it had reached the point where Dan Wolf was dangerously out of touch.

In the beginning, they had paid nothing, because they had had nothing to give, and that had not been the point of writing for the *Village Voice* anyway in those days. But, starting in 1963, the paper had started to make money, and they had started to pay. It was only a little at first, but even then, when Jane Kramer had been offered a job at the *New Yorker,* she claimed he had offered her a raise to get her to stay (which he denied doing), and she thought to herself, *Goddammit, the money was there.* Through the sixties, the fees and salaries had inched up. When Barbara Long had attracted the attention of the town with her pieces about boxing and other things in the summer of 1965, it was for $20 a piece. When Joe Flaherty had burst on the scene with *his* pieces about boxing and other things a year later, it was for $15 a piece at first, then gradually $30, $50, and $75, until, after his first

---

*A misconception that gained wide currency around the *Voice*—even Dan Wolf believed it—and that affected events to come. In reality, Jack Newfield had attended the wedding, in New Hampshire, of Lindsay aide Jay Kriegel the weekend *after* the Attica uprising—and then only because, he said, his wife and the bride were friends.

child and (he claimed) threatening to leave the paper, he went on staff in 1970. About four years earlier, going on staff had meant about $100 a week. In 1970, it meant $125. A year later, that was still all it meant. The standard freelance fee was $75 to $100. And the columnists ranged only from about $100 to as low as $60.

Which was just not enough. Even faithful Mary Nichols, who, thanks to the mixed-up communications with R. Peter Straus in 1968, had been the only one to be truly paid well by them, declared, for public consumption, "Civil Service pays better than the *Voice.*" And even she took them to task for never, in all their years there, setting up a pension plan for their employees, which was another thing they admitted they should have done, but just never got around to doing.

In the early days, the way they had paid had always jibed with the circumstances they were in. But now, with the Burden deal, it was obvious that was no longer the case. Now, they obviously had it to give, and they were still refusing to, and their refusal to do so had gone long past the point of being reasonable. It had gone, in fact, to the point of being stubborn. On one occasion, Nat Hentoff had called up Ed Fancher to demand a $10 raise, and Fancher had refused to give it to him, and Hentoff had said, "All right then, I quit," and Fancher had let him. And it was *Hentoff* who had had to call back, apologize, and rescind his resignation—without getting the $10. Another old one who had become disaffected was Jules Feiffer. He had waited, all through the sixties, for a raise from them for his cartoon—not that he needed one, what with the syndication of his strip and other ventures, but he wanted one symbolically anyway—and thought he was going to get it on the occasion of his tenth anniversary with the paper. When it didn't come, he said nothing; he felt it was up to *them* to bring it up. But when the fifteenth anniversary came and went, in October of 1971, and there was still no raise, he decided, "OK, they don't care about sentiment." He went in, saw Dan Wolf, and blurted out that his feelings were hurt by the fact that, after all he had done for the paper, he had never gotten a raise there. Dan Wolf, he recalled, looked at him, seeming to be absolutely stunned, and said it had never crossed his mind. And Jules Feiffer got his raise.

They had their reasons for doing as they did, reasons that were not uncompelling. It had been their risk at the beginning, and their risk alone. Several times, when things were at their worst, they had approached rich young men for capital and backing, and each time they had been refused. Now that their vision had withstood everything, and stood at last to make a profit, it was they who deserved to make a profit from it. They didn't pay well, but they offered total freedom to anyone who would take it, including the freedom to show themselves off, be discovered, and move up in the world elsewhere. The paper was meant to be a laboratory, a proving ground, and they had no objections if someone used it to make the best possible deal on the outside and move on.* And the facts, cruel as they now might be for the writers who sought to organize the *Voice* to face, were that all but a handful of young, aspiring American freelance writers worked for compensation at least as little as what the *Village Voice* paid, and were heavily edited to boot. Exploited as those writers might feel and like to describe themselves, they were a privileged sect, and their complaints had to be considered in context: the paper had made them, they hadn't made the paper, and if they had not been writing for it, many other, unpublished, writers would have been, who were at least as good as they were.

★ ★ ★

There was an undercurrent to the resentment that fall. It concerned who did and didn't get to go "on staff," and it came by and large from women. For the first time, the *Voice* had a feminist contingent, and for the first time the accusation was being heard around there that Dan Wolf was a sexist.

It had to be one of the most ridiculous things ever said about him. Whatever else he did, Dan Wolf exploited men and women without regard to sex. In fact, if any generalization were to be made about his track record, and Ed Fancher's, it would have to be that they *preferred* to hire women for positions of power and responsibility. Head of advertising was Sandy Fendrick, a woman, making, with all her commissions, well over $60,000 a year, more than either Fancher or Wolf. Head of classified was Rose Ryan, a woman, who created problems for them by *not* being able to get along with her staff, who were also women. Head of circulation was Carole Rogers, a woman. Virtually all the staff on the business side, advertising, classified, and circulation, all the *support* positions, all the people who got the writers' words out on the street for people to read, were women. But, like a lot of writers who know basically little about the newspaper business, these writers assumed that the only people necessary for getting out a newspaper were themselves.

On the editorial side, of all the women who wrote for him, none was on staff; but of all the men who wrote for him, only four were. Of the

---

*Which was part of the reason why, while Jules Feiffer resented them, they resented Jules Feiffer, who, they felt, had successfully pursued the status of a celebrity, and had the break the *Voice* had given him to thank for it, and never showed his gratitude.

two associate editors, one, Diane Fisher, was a woman. Mary Nichols was city editor, making twice what anyone else was making, with male writers—Ron Rosenbaum, Lucian Truscott, Howard Blum, Clark Whelton—who worked under her. And these feminists had remarkably little rapport with her. That the presence of these women editors did not fill their appetite for mathematical, feminist equality was only because Dan Wolf, under his scheme of things, didn't give *any* of his editors that much power over *any* of his writers.

He had always hired women, and published them, without discrimination. But a lot of the women who wrote for him wrote themselves out, or produced only fitfully, and his attitude was that that wasn't his fault. If a woman wrote for him and then moved on, as Susan Brownmiller and Barbara Long and Sally Kempton and Jane Kramer had, either because she had run out of things to say or because of a more attractive deal elsewhere, that was fine with him; that was what the *Voice* was all about. On the other hand, there were women such as Stephanie Harrington and Diane Fisher and Mary Nichols, women who had stayed with him, and achieved, and it was conspicuous now that they had little contact with, and gave no aid or comfort to, those women who belittled Dan Wolf as an exploiter and a manipulator of their sex. Because, brutally put, along with the just gripes against Dan Wolf there were being insinuated some unjust ones, and this one was being circulated by women who had always been underachievers, were then, and always would be, as a way to rationalize their underachievement.

★ ★ ★

It was true; for most of them, being exploited by Dan Wolf was the best thing that had ever happened to them. But it was also true that, at least where it came to money, the writers had a case, and it could not go on this way.

He just could not understand that he was no longer poor; he seemed to think he still was, and acted it. Nor did he seem able to understand why his writers were. Bohemia, the Greenwich Village of Dan Wolf's youth, was dead. A cruel, warping inflation had exploded the Manhattan real-estate market, particularly in the Village. Dan Wolf's writers, over the years, had served to glamorize the Village; and now, especially the young ones among them, they couldn't afford to live there. The $16-to-$26-a-month walk-up of the late forties and early fifties had permitted Dan Wolf and his friends, with only a little part-time clerical employment or whatever, to eke out a living. But those days were gone, and so were those rents. With the building boom in highrises around

Manhattan, and the lifting of rent controls on all vacant apartments, the standard writer's garret was no longer $20. It was more like $200, and the price of every other living essential, from food to the Con Ed bill to subway tokens, had been distorted too. And, if they didn't like it there at the *Voice*, there were fewer and fewer "other places" to go to. The publishing industry, having failed to anticipate the omnipresence of television, the decline of fiction, and the rise in the cost of paper and postage, was in a state of violent contraction. Outlets—from the other undergrounds all the way up to *Life, Look,* the *Saturday Evening Post,* and four New York dailies—were drying up. As that was happening, more and more young people were pouring into New York all the time, wanting to live in the city, wanting to be a New Journalist, wanting to see if they could write for the *Village Voice,* more of such people than there could ever be space for. Dan Wolf's writers, once again, had tended to glamorize the mission of being a New York journalist; but they had not succeeded in increasing the rewards for such work, and that only served to decrease their confidence in themselves while it increased the peril of the financial position they were in.

Against all that background, Jack Newfield approached Dan Wolf in late November of 1971 and asked him for a raise, from the $200 a week he was already making to $225. He had other reasons than need for asking; he knew that Mary Nichols was making twice as much money as he was. And Dan Wolf had more than one reason for refusing. Only the week before, Newfield had reported that a citizens' group was trying to contest the license of WPIX-TV, a local channel owned by the *Daily News*—but had not put in his story that Mrs. Ronnie Eldridge, well-connected maven to the West Side liberals, was one of them. Wolf wrote him a memo:

11/19/71

Jack—

Apropos of what we talked about the other day (re sweetheart stories), I want to state a further reaction of mine to your piece on WPIX.

It was disingenuous of you to attack the News for not running the whole WPIX story and then for you to refer to the people who are trying to take over WPIX as simply a group of "private citizens." Ronnie Eldridge is a "power broker" between the Lindsay and Kennedy camps. That's how she was described by someone who has great affection for her, and I don't think you'd deny it for a minute. Beyond that, she has been a very central and political and highly-paid public official.

The plebes have a right to know such relevant facts. Would
you have been as chary about mentioning names if a group of
conservatives that included a Buckley had been trying to take
over a station? Wouldn't that have been the story's lead?
Dan

There was another thing on Dan Wolf's mind, too. For some time,
Jack Newfield had been contributing articles to *New York* Magazine,
among other ways of supplementing his *Voice* income, and Wolf
considered Clay Felker's magazine to be a rival of theirs. So, as far as he
was concerned, if that was the way it was going to be, if Jack Newfield
was going to shill for his friends in his news articles and devote his
excess energy to writing for Felker, then let him go. He gave Jack
Newfield the standard speech, that the *Voice* was never meant to be a
permanent place for anyone, and suggested that if he didn't like it
there, perhaps it was time to move on.

And Jack Newfield (though, later on, he would concede the rightness
of Wolf's remarks in that memo) decided, as long as that was the way it
was going to be, if Clark Whelton was going to go on with his red-
baiting articles under the protection of Mary Nichols and she was
going to get a privileged money deal from Dan Wolf, then he would do
something about it. He told others on the staff what had happened,
and he circulated the call among them for a meeting.

★ ★ ★

They met, on the last Sunday in November, just as the
paper was publishing Clark Whelton's new outrages on Forest Hills,
and Mary Nichols's latest assault on Newfield. The meeting was held
in Paul Cowan's apartment on Riverside Drive, and nothing could have
galled Dan Wolf more, when he found out, than that Cowan had been
the host of such a meeting, Cowan who was at least as rich as those
young men who had left them hanging for money in the early years. It
galled him in general that some of those who were now the most
strenuous exponents of the "exploited writers," namely Cowan and
Newfield, had wealth, while some of those sticking with him, like Clark
Whelton, really needed it.

Some stuck with Dan Wolf because there were other issues involved,
and, as those issues became involved, both at that meeting held in Paul
Cowan's place and later, it became apparent the staff of the *Village
Voice* was going to prove incapable of "organizing" to do much of
anything. To start with, they did not know one another very well, the
product of years of individualistic ways and associations with Dan

Wolf. And, beyond that, they simply did not like each other that much. There were too many feuds, and petty hatreds, and schizoid cliques—"Politburos." It had been that way for some time, but this first attempt at a mass meeting first made it manifest.

Should they form a union? Was the paper moving to the right, with Clark Whelton's articles under Mary Nichols's protection, and what could they do to stop it? Was Dan Wolf the enemy? Or was Jack just using them to get back at Dan and Mary because he hadn't gotten *his* raise, and was a radical chic faction trying to use the issues of "pay" and "the union" in order to take over editorial control of the paper? All of that was swirling around in people's heads, and none of it was resolved.

Clark Whelton, Lucian Truscott, Ron Rosenbaum, and Howard Blum—the men alone, Dan Wolf's and Mary Nichols's boys—were not there. They were all close to Wolf, either didn't need the money or preferred to ask him for it themselves, and wanted no part of a group attempt to *force* him to pay more, or to do anything else. Mary Nichols, though she agreed that Wolf and Fancher should pay the writers more, wanted no part of Jack Newfield, counted herself as management, and stayed away. But Mary Breasted was there. And, when she came, Jack Newfield regarded her as more than just a shill for Mary Nichols. He called her "a labor spy for Carter Burden."

Naturally, since in this situation Burden was management, was "Capital," Jack Newfield was understandably down on him, for the moment at least. But that is not what he meant. Mary Breasted, as Jack Newfield and a few others at the paper knew, had recently, since the split-up of Councilman Carter Burden and his wife Amanda, begun to date him, and it had gotten serious. That made her privileged, in a way; at least she *had* contact with him, which not even the editor and publisher could claim. But such was the level of *Village Voice* politics that, six months later, when Mary Breasted departed New York for a prolonged period to write "What New York Does To Its Writers," a treatise about the city's "literary-journalistic court, with all its passing fads and quick causes and popularity shuffles," two of the fawners she cited were Jack Newfield (incorrectly), for going to Jay Kriegel's New Hampshire wedding rather than Attica, and Nat Hentoff (correctly), for advocating community control of public schools while putting his own kids into private ones. The next week, there were letters from Newfield—and from Margot Hentoff, who pointedly dropped the name of Councilman Carter Burden in hers.

Andrew Sarris, a little suspicious that many of the others were at Cowan's only to find out what everyone was making, was there. So was

Cowan's brother Geoff, a Washington lawyer and occasional contributor to the paper. So was a labor lawyer. So was Jules Feiffer. So were both Hentoffs. So, though he was officially on sabbatical to write a novel, was Joe Flaherty. All in all, about fifty of them came, staff writers, regular contributors, columnists, and hanger-on freelancers, and though they agreed on little else, they did agree to pick a delegation to go see Dan Wolf and present some demands to him. This statement was written up later:

PROPOSALS BY A GROUP OF FREE-LANCE WRITERS, REVIEWERS, AND COLUMNISTS FOR THE VILLAGE VOICE

Fees

Present fees for free-lance articles, according to our understanding, range from $75 to $100 to $125

We propose that for writers who are regular contributors to the Voice, the basic fee for a free-lance article be $150.

For articles requiring an added dimension of time and research, the fee be $200 in addition to expenses. (When an article falls into this second category is to be decided, of course, between the editor and the writer.)

In the event a writer believes that the kind of article he wants to work on will require much more extensive time and research, he would negotiate that fee, and expenses, with an editor. Provided, of course, the editor first agrees that the article should be undertaken.

Columns

We propose a basic fee of $100 for regular columnists

In the case of columns that involve, by their nature, investigative reporting—and the research thereby entailed—we propose a fee of $150. For example, Ellen Frankfurt [sic]*, Geoff Cowan, Nat Hentoff, Jill Johnston*

Reviews

With regard to such regular reviewers—who are also columnists—as Andrew Sarris, Michael Smith, John Lahr, etc., we are not empowered to negotiate for them but do feel they ought to receive more, certainly the basic fee of $100 mentioned above.

Theatre reviewers now receive, we understand, $50 for the first play in a review and $25 for the second. We propose those rates be raised to $80 and $45.

Film reviewers, we understand, now receive $60 per film piece, regardless of how many films are included. We propose the basic rate for a film piece be raised to $70 with $25 added for each additional film reviewed.

Book review fees are now $60; we propose they be raised to $75.

Television reviews and reviews for the Riffs *sections are now $50, and we propose that they remain at that figure since we feel the rates are fair.*

Health Insurance

We would ask management to find out if there are ways by which regular contributors, who are not on staff, can be covered by a health and hospitalization plan.

To encourage a sense of being an organic part of this newspaper, which is important to all of us, we propose that we try having regular meetings, monthly meetings, which could be attended by anyone who wanted to come—management, editors, staff writers, other contributors.

The intent of these meetings would be to provide an exchange of views, suggestions, questions, etc. The goal is not *at all to try to shape the* Voice *in any one or another ideological direction. We all agree that the* Voice*'s most fundamental value is that it is an open paper, and we all want it to remain open to all views. We would like to continue to meet with each other—which we could do by ourselves—but we also want to have informal contact with editors and management in a context that will encompass the* Voice *as a whole because it is the paper as a whole we feel attached to.*

The statement itself was a reflection of how difficult it was to bridge the deep ideological and personal gaps within the "family." For while the first part, the part about fees and perquisites and health care, reflected a rough consensus among all those delegated to go see Dan Wolf, that last part, the call for monthly meetings, did not. It was the wish of Paul Cowan and Jack Newfield and their wing of the writers, such as David Gelber, an occasional contributor, and Ellen Frankfort, a health columnist, who were on the committee with them. It was not the wish of Mary Breasted, who was in this thing for more money, not so that those people, under the guise of "participation" and "community" and "democracy," could gang up on Clark Whelton, or maybe even Mary Nichols. And certainly neither that part, nor the exhortations at the end about the paper being "important to all of us" and their feeling "attached" to it, were what Joe Flaherty, ex-dockworker, had in mind about labor negotiating.

That was Class C Mobile, he said. *You get paid top dollar for your work. You make management pay through the teeth, and you make 'em terrified to fuck with your copy. This is an adversary relationship, not some guru circle-jerk*—by which Joe Flaherty meant Paul Cowan. He could not understand this love-hate relationship some of them seemed to have with Wolf. *That's not how you negotiate,* he would say.

There was an even worse split when Lucian K. Truscott IV, ex-cadet at the United States Military Academy, found his name on one of the petitions circulating around the office, cornered David Gelber—whose cocky radical-chic sensibility was getting on the nerves even of other people who agreed with him—among the writers' cubicles on the fourth floor, and growled, "Who the hell put my name on this list?"

"It was a group decision," Gelber tried to explain. "We thought you wouldn't mind supporting the points of the writers. What are you going to do, hit me?"

"Next time," Lucian Truscott warned, "I'm going to take you out and wipe the streets with you."

The night before they were to see Dan Wolf, the committee of nine met at Mary Breasted's place. There, theater critic Dick Bruckenfeld urged Newfield not to go with them the next day; he had spoken to Dan that afternoon, he said, and Jack's presence would be a red flag. Newfield agreed, took himself off the committee, and the next afternoon seven *Village Voice* writers trooped into the office of Dan Wolf for a confrontation unprecedented in the history of the newspaper. Cowan was with them, and Gelber, and Ellen Frankfort, and Bruckenfeld, and Robin Reisig and Mary Breasted, two of the regular, but nonstaff, writers. And Nat Hentoff. The eighth member, Joe Flaherty, was late.

The conference was a mismatch, right from the very beginning. For one thing, they were divided, among themselves, and in their feelings toward him. Wolf had no such problem. He was seething, and just waiting for the right opportunity to show it. He was seething that this scene was taking place at all, that it had come down to this, to have a group of his own writers come into his office to present him with demands, seething at the gall of these people, these radicals who couldn't get their way up to Attica, these peripheral hangers-on like David Gelber, trying to freeze themselves in, trying to *make* him freeze them in. And he had been briefed on what their proposals were. He knew how he was going to react. They didn't.

Hentoff, the old unionist, the ex-shop steward, opened the meeting, coolly, stressing that no matter what he might have heard, they only had the good of the paper in mind by coming. Dan Wolf riposted by reading them a list, name by name, of all the writers who wrote for the *Village Voice,* but whose stories got held, and thrown in with the overset, so that *theirs* could run right away.

They fell back, and the meeting descended to the personal. *None of you came to me when I was personally hard up,* Wolf complained. *I've printed stories of yours that weren't very good just because I wanted to avoid hurting your feelings.* They complained back, how they really loved the paper, how he didn't understand, how he wasn't available to them anymore, and went into individual sob stories, just in time for Joe Flaherty to arrive, hear this, and decide that this was not what he had been called away from the Lion's Head, missing a perfectly good afternoon of sitting around placing bets on the horses, for. He took the floor, and, once more, in his Raymond Chandler way, told the rest of the writers in there with him that love and relationships were not negotiable issues, that pay and health insurance and guaranteed kill fees were, that they should stick to them, give the man a set of demands, then get out and wait for his reply. That was the way it was done, he explained to them. And then he asked Dan Wolf if he had anything to drink.

It so happened Wolf had some bourbon on hand, and rounds were now passed, in cups. The atmosphere changed. Wolf kept emphasizing that the *Voice* was never meant to be a parking place for life, something to be frozen into, that there was no reason they should not expect to move on eventually, and they kept emphasizing that they should be rewarded for having been so loyal to the paper, and he kept saying, *Freezing you in means freezing out everyone else.* But he did something he had never done before: he conceded the pay was too low, and promised to raise it. Then someone brought up the demand for editorial meetings, the item he was sure they thought would be the easy one to go down. Dan Wolf, figuring in advance that if he did it now, they'd back off, blew his stack. He brought his fist down, pounded the desk, and exploded: "That I will never have. Never. You want to have your meetings, *you* have them. You only want them to dominate other people anyway. But as long as I am here, there will be no meetings to discuss editorial policy." He could see the shock register on their faces; they had not expected that from him. But they had underestimated him; Wolf knew that it was its independence, its individuality, its total commitment to openness, the fact that its writers could come in and say whatever they wanted without fear of being controlled by anyone, the fact that it had never *had* any "direction," that had made the *Voice* what it was. When they wanted to call meetings to *discuss* what directions it *would* take, therefore, they were tampering with the very life and soul of his newspaper. And that he would not abide. Money he could give them. His newspaper he would not give them.

The subject returned to money, and things calmed back down; there was even a little camaraderie going. Then Ellen Frankfort made the mistake of asking whether he would throw open the books to show them just how much money the paper was making.

That did it, as far as Dan Wolf was concerned. It was bad enough to him that David Gelber, a fringe figure, had entered his office as part of a "writers' delegation" to see him; but Ellen Frankfort was even more peripheral than David Gelber was. Of her he knew little, except that Ross Wetzsteon had been running her column for the better part of two years and that, one evening that summer in Provincetown, Rhoda Wolf had had occasion to spend an evening in her company, reporting back to her husband that this short, blue-eyed blonde was a guttersnipe and a character assassin and a dangerous one to be watched out for. He didn't know her. But he knew he didn't like her. And, after what she had just said, he knew he wasn't about to tolerate her telling him what to do. Without raising his voice, he looked straight at her, for the first time all day. "Who in the hell are you?" he asked. "And what are you even *doing* here? I don't even know why we publish you; you're one of the worst writers we have. And our books are none of your fucking business."

The meeting went on a little longer, but that was it for the day. Further proposals were exchanged. At one point, Flaherty told Wolf he thought $200 would be a fair price for a freelance piece, and Wolf counter-offered that that was OK with him, so long as they knew, if he was going to be paying that kind of money, it was going to be like other publications—they might not run every week, and he was going to edit them a lot tighter. When Flaherty brought back that reply, he encountered panic; that was more than they were worth, they didn't want to be edited that way. Eventually—to his credit, said Hentoff—Dan Wolf wound up offering the writers more than they had asked for in that initial set of demands. Between the end of 1971 and the middle of 1974, staff salaries for *Village Voice* writers went up from $125 to $225—and more of them went on staff. Most freelance pieces went for $125. Blue Cross–Blue Shield benefits were extended. There was no union. There were no editorial meetings. And there was no more trouble. Jack Newfield got his raise, contingent on a cutback in his pieces for *New York* Magazine. Ellen Frankfort kept writing her health column for another year or so, then left to write books and had revenge of sorts with one, an acid memoir of her time at the *Voice*. And the *New York Times* ran a news story in its Sunday editions recapitulating the entire episode. Mary Nichols, reached for comment, laid the whole thing to an attempt by Jack Newfield and his friends—"liberal groupies"—to accomplish a Left takeover at the paper, and delivered her opinion that Newfield was seeking to ingratiate himself with Lindsay so he could write a book about the mayor's upcoming presidential campaign. Jack Newfield, for the record, called John Lindsay "a fool" and Mary Perot Nichols "a mental case," and in his year-end "My Back Pages" column publicly wished her "a terrible New Year."

So Dan Wolf paid his writers more, and did it without having to give in to the dangers of editing by committee and groupthink. But something else was lost. Because it was as Dan Wolf had said—when the writers got their money, they stayed put, and when they stayed put, they closed the paper off. Perhaps, if Dan Wolf had not waited so long to pay them competitive fees and salaries, and had done it without having to be pushed, before there was any attempt at "organizing," they might not have noticed how suddenly, relatively, well-off they were, and perhaps not felt the attendant need to stay. But if he was wrong to pay so low for so long, Dan Wolf was right about one thing. Between the beginning of 1972 and the middle of 1974, there was less turnover at the *Village Voice* than there had ever been. The New Journalists of the sixties became, more and more, the careerists of the seventies. Before they had complained that they could not make a living at it. Now that they could, they did, and wrote that way— because it was a job, not necessarily because they had something to say. The paper was cut off from the kind of new blood who might have had something more original to say about the state of the mid-seventies than the incumbents did. The files of the *Village Voice* were replete, in 1972 and 1973, with applications for employment and inquiries about story ideas, and also with the terse, routine turndowns patented by other, inaccessible publications—"Unfortunately we don't have any staff jobs available at this time . . . Sorry, but we are absolutely jammed with too much copy now." For the first time, not every unsolicited manuscript that came in—and there were a lot more than fifty a week now—was being read. It had ceased to be the place of opportunity.

There was one other aftereffect of the battle between Dan Wolf and some of his writers. For the first time since there had been one, his "Family" had fractured, right out in the open, into Balkanized sects of divided loyalties, hostile to one another. To some of them, they no longer worked for "Dan and Ed" but for "management." And none of them would ever be able to act as one again.

Which, before too long, they would need to do.

15. *1972* . . . JACK NEWFIELD, ON THE PRI-

mary trail in Florida, rails against Hubert Humphrey and is down, again, on John Lindsay:

> Hubert Humphrey has dyed his gray hair, has bought some neat suits and shirts, and is acting like everyone in the country has amnesia about 57,000 dead in Viet Nam. . . .
>
> . . . [His radio commercials say] "Hubert Humphrey will stop the flow of your tax dollars to lazy welfare chiselers." . . . Humphrey should be doing charity work in the wards of VA hospitals. . . .
>
> . . . On the day he announced for President in Miami . . . Lindsay said Castro was uncivilized, that he was exporting revolution to the rest of the hemisphere, and that he was against normalizing relations with Cuba, "until there is some sign Cuba is ready to re-join the family of nations."
>
> A few days later I called a friend of mine who works for Lindsay to complain about the attack on Cuba. The friend told me: "Don't worry, Jack. We've given John a new position on Castro."

. . . In July, Newfield is back in Florida, as a delegate, when George McGovern is nominated. He is at his best describing the shabby performance of the "New Politics":

> At the most basic human level, the reformer leaders behaved like parodies of hacks. . . . One night a bunch of us were sitting in [Matthew] Troy's room watching Doug Ireland eat a midnight steak. Suddenly a reformer from the 23rd District delegation walked in with three prostitutes. He offered them around the room. There were no takers. The next morning this same reformer was up in the caucus denouncing sexism and male chauvinism. . . .
>
> At the Tuesday caucus it was demanded that all of our delegation's 95 gallery passes be turned over to Ralph Abernathy and Beulah Sanders of the National Welfare Rights Organization. This struck the guilty and paternalistic liberals as a wonderful idea. It helped them forget their maids. One after another the affluent delegates from Westchester and Nassau got up to support the motion. . . .

. . . As soon as the vote was over, I watched delegates who had voted to give their passes away rush to the podium and try to make private deals to retrieve their own personal passes. . . . A few hours later, Abernathy's aides could be seen in front of the convention hall, selling our gallery passes for $20 apiece.

In the last hour of the convention Teddy Kennedy spoke. As he spoke Pete Hamill put his arm around me and pointed to the picture of Robert Kennedy hanging from the ceiling of the hall, framed perfectly by the bobbing standards of Massachusetts and California. A few feet away, Frank Mankiewicz and Ronnie Eldridge were locked in a sobbing embrace, united by a memory of Bobby.

We wished at that moment it was Bobby we were nominating. But it wasn't.

That November, Flaherty is even more critical of the McGovernites. Sent by them into Queens with a sound truck, two days before the election, he remarks, "Even St. Patrick was given more time to purge the snakes." . . . An old scar resurfaces when Clark Whelton reports on an incident in Brooklyn where a school bus bearing black youngsters is stoned and the occupants attacked with pipes. He gives the white residents' side—that the blacks on the bus had been taunting and attacking them. . . . A week later, there is a letter to the editor from Jack Newfield, saying, "I am looking forward to Clark Whelton's article defending slavery on the grounds that Africans littered a lot during the 14th century."

★ ★ ★

He "never saw the Greenwich Village Dylan described on the liner notes for Peter, Paul & Mary's second album. It died before I ever got around to leaving Innwood," Phil Tracy remembered.

The Village was rumored to be full of queers and women who would fuck if you asked them nicely. It was hard to say which group frightened me more. I was 21, a virgin, and scared to death there might be some flaw in my masculine character, so I spent a great deal of time walking around the Village. . . . The beer was cheap, and from one of the cushioned booths we could ogle girls from Queens while they ogled us. . . . If someone who actually lived in the Village had tumbled down the stairs by accident, he or she would no doubt wonder how they had been mysteriously transported to the outskirts of Sunset Park. It was lots of fun (if only in retrospect) but it had nothing to do with the Village.

My first real link to the Village was the Lion's Head. I started hanging out there hoping to strike up a conversation with Pete Hamill or Joe Flaherty. I wanted to ask them how one became a famous writer. Fortunately, I never worked up a sufficient amount of courage to walk over and start talking to them. But gradually I began to fit into the Lion's Head crowd. To this day, I shudder to think what I must have looked like.

Eventually, he "recognized it was the worst possible place to go if you were serious about your ambition," so Phil Tracy, the chunky, wise-cracking Irishman with the good nature and the high-pitched voice, product of Innwood and Manhattan College, went on to do other things. He joined the Young Christian Students, wrote for the *National Catholic Reporter,* was busted as part of a civil-rights demonstration down South in August of 1962. He did public relations for the United Fund, and was an officer in the city's welfare workers union. He worked in the campaigns of Robert Kennedy, Paul O'Dwyer, Herman Badillo, and, when he was running abortively for City Council president, five years before he became governor, Hugh Carey. He covered Woodstock for *Commonweal.* He took off for San Francisco for a year, spending six months in a commune. And he began writing for the *Village Voice.*

It was the fall of 1970, and antiwar demonstrations were planned for downtown Portland, Oregon, site of an American Legion convention. To head the kids off, Oregon Governor Tom McCall came up with the ultimate co-optation: he staged a rock concert outside the city. And it worked, as Tracy described in a missive to the *Voice:* "The only casualties recorded in the confrontation between the American Legion and the People's Army Jamboree in Portland last week were a couple of myths and one elderly lady who suffered heat stroke."

Soon, he was back in New York, where Mary Nichols took an interest in him. He wanted to cover politics, and she wanted someone up in Albany to cover state government. Soon, he was up there, saying things, in his column "Albany Anagrams," about the legislators, and their governor, that they were not used to reading, such as his comments about Nelson Rockefeller's pet project, the Albany Mall: "To build Rocky's brainchild on the shifting sands of Albany they had to excavate some 2.7 million cubic yards of clay and quicksand and sink 22,000 concrete piles to support the monstrosity. As one observer noted, that trick alone makes Khufu, builder of the Great Pyramid, look like a home improvement contractor." But then, "when you compare it with the waste and corruption that accompanied the building of the state Capitol the Mall begins to look like a Spartan training camp."

And, when the legislature was out of session, he had all New York City to write about, such as the time, in 1972, when Bella Abzug tried to unseat her political mentor, William Fitts Ryan, in the Democratic primary. "With Ryan it's the older men," he wrote.

> They come up to him and say things like "I hope you beat that dame," "You gotta beat that broad," "Good luck Bill, I hope you beat that woman. We don't need any more of them down there." While it wouldn't be fair to say Ryan encourages such talk, it wouldn't be honest to say he discourages it either. Just like any politician on the stump, he takes his support where he finds it and the devil take the hindmost. . . .

Two months later, winner Ryan lost the bout with cancer that was obviously killing him during the campaign. "Death is a singularly unsentimental occurrence," Tracy wrote, "especially when it's mixed with the passing of power. So they waked Bill Ryan Monday night, and after paying the briefest of tributes to his memory, the reformers honored him in their highest fashion by starting a fight over his job."

★ ★ ★

Fred Morton was a successful author—*The Roths-childs*—long before he began his column for the *Voice*. He had known Dan Wolf and Ed Fancher since the fifties; Fancher had been the one who moved Morton's wife Marcia out of her family's Bronx home to the Village. (Her brother was Joe Coleman, their advertising manager.) He had written for them before—a piece on his first novel appearing in paperback, a review of Bellow's *Mr. Sammler's Planet*. But, in 1971, in love with the free-form debate and the reader dialogue of the *Voice* and looking for a way to break out of his own writing mold, he came to them and asked to do a column.

"Morton Rampant," it was called, and the title was apt, because his impressionistic vignettes ran in all directions. He wrote about his fellow Jews—and their shift to Richard Nixon. He wrote about his native Austria—chronicling a visit back there in 1972, he described, one week, having dinner with the chancellor, and the next, having lunch with his estranged radical son. He wrote about politics—an interview with George McGovern after his win in the New York primary, and a portrait of a fading, bitching hero of 1968, Eugene McCarthy, as he baited a drunken Edward Albee at a cocktail party. He wrote, at the height of all the hype over it in early 1973, about *Last Tango in Paris*—casually mentioning in the last line, that, of course, he had not actually *seen* it. He wrote about New York street life, and escalating paranoia—about getting mugged himself. About waiting ten minutes at his local fish store while the owners and a customer exchanged tales of black street crime until he stalked out, slammed—and smashed—the door. And, using the name "M.," about the day he took a plane flight, and made a friendship with a fellow passenger while their plane developed engine trouble and was forced to land again, only to discover, when it came time for a black airport official to handle their bags, that his newfound friend was a racist:

> He walked over to the next line while M., instead of just shrugging and walking those five little paces too, stayed in his place. He did mentally ask his feet what the hell they thought they were doing, standing pat like that—abolishing racism in the United States? or perhaps just pampering a liberal-whitey conscience? But the feet simply couldn't be moved. In fact they turned away a little so that M. didn't have to look at Neighbor on the other line. But he heard him all right.
> *"I shoulda known from the hair,"* the gravelly voice said softly, bitterly, from the other line.
> And M. could think of no retort, nothing bitter or persuasive. Almost immediately his turn came and he zipped his airline bag open, he hissed it open at the god-damn black who had robbed him of a buddy.

★ ★ ★

Arthur Bell came to the *Voice* in 1970, from Random House, where he had been publicity director for children's books, with two pledges in mind—never to wear a tie again, and never to engage in office politics. Both pledges proved tough to keep, especially, where he was going, the second.

He took Mary Nichols out to lunch one day that summer. He had a reason. He was in the newly formed Gay Activist Alliance, and he wanted to know whether the *Voice*—this was a year after Stonewall Inn, less than a year after the paper had been picketed—would be willing to give coverage to the gay movement. Which it did—coverage by Arthur Bell.

Carrying on in a long tradition of participant journalists at the paper, he was full-time homosexual activist, part-time writer for the *Voice*, starting with his first pieces, an account of a sit-in at Nelson Rockefeller's New York offices and a profile of Spiro Agnew's son Randy, whose living arrangements—he had divorced his wife, was living with another man, and was widely rumored to be gay—were causing momentary embarrassment to his right-wing father. Arthur Bell kept writing, focusing more and more on corrupt underworld influence behind the gay bar scene—he accompanied Strike Force raids on some suspected of being fronts for organized crime—and he kept proselytizing.

On April 10, 1972, he was arrested for a sit-in at the *Daily News;* Mary Nichols had to write the judge on that one, requesting a postponement since "at present Mr. Bell is on assignment in California, honoring a commitment made long in advance of his April 10th arrest and the recent scheduling of his May 1st court appearance."* And, one night that summer, he came home and stepped into the adventure that became the basis for the film *Dog Day Afternoon.*

> Tuesday, Aug. 22. Home about 10 pm. A message from a friend on my cassette phone unit. "Just heard a couple of homosexuals are holding up a bank in Brooklyn and they're holding people hostages. Thought you'd be interested. Bye."
> I made a couple of quick calls and got through to the CBS local newsroom: "Yes, two men have been holding seven hostages at gunpoint since 3 this afternoon at a Chase Manhattan branch in Brooklyn. We have the bank's phone number." I called. "Hello, this is Arthur Bell for *The Village Voice.* Can you tell me what's happening?" The voice at the other end said, "Arthur, am I glad it's you. This is Littlejohn." "Littlejohn, what the hell are you doing down there?" "I'm one of the robbers." "Jesus Christ!"

"Littlejohn" was John Wotjowicz, member of the Gay Activist Alliance, and after talking with him Arthur Bell was very quickly back on the phone again. He called Mary Nichols. She called her friend, police lieutenant David Durk, and got his wife. She, in turn, got her husband just as he was about to go on Barry Farber's radio show. Durk, in turn, got a police escort for himself, and Nichols, and Bell, which went screaming through the night down the Belt Parkway into Brooklyn. There, for the last five and a half hours of a siege that ended

---

*Charge dropped after a year's good behavior.

in the death of Littlejohn's partner Sal Natuarale, Arthur Bell mingled with the assembled gays. He talked with Ernie, the homosexual wife of Littlejohn whose sex-change operation was the stated purpose of the robbery, and with others, and while he was there he learned that the man who had supplied Littlejohn and Sal with the guns had been Mike Umbers, the same Mike Umbers who had been the target of several police raids of after-hours clubs, whom the *Voice* had identified as involved in the West Village porno trade, and who had threatened to sue the paper for being so identified.

Two nights later, Arthur Bell was chairing a gay activists' symposium on whether or not the bank robbery had been a revolutionary act, when a young man named Gary Badger walked in, pleading for money for a proper burial for his dead friend Sal Natuarale. Bell, who had gotten one confirmation for the Umbers information already, took Badger up to the roof and questioned him. Badger, too, confirmed it. Then it was Arthur Bell's turn to go on the Barry Farber show, and he was off to the studios, keeping that information, for now, to himself.

At seven thirty the next morning, he got a call from Gary Badger. "I've just been shot at twice at the Morton Street pier," Badger told him, frantic. Once again, Arthur Bell called up Mary Nichols, who got Alan Weitz, who got his car, and as the three of them put Badger in the back seat Badger's roommate rushed out of the apartment on Barrow Street to tell them, "There's just been a bomb scare at the *Village Voice.*"

They drove down 12th Street, and as they got closer to the *Voice* building they could see close to 100 people, plus fire trucks, outside. Weitz parked the car, walked over, and came back to tell them it was true: there had been a bomb scare—two, in fact. The occupants of the car took off to FBI headquarters, where Badger told his story, and where Bell told *his,* after phoning in the item to his friend Nicholas Gage at the *Times,* hoping its printing would serve as life insurance.

Then they split up. Mary Nichols's secretary took Gary Badger home with her for safekeeping. Arthur Bell went off with a friend, Mary Nichols offering him her place for the night. She and Mary Breasted went off to her favorite bar in Hoboken, and when she returned at 2 A.M. she saw a lump asleep in one of the bedrooms. She assumed it was Arthur Bell. When she woke up in the morning, she found otherwise. The lump was her daughter Kerstin, back from a trip to Europe. "What are you doing here?" she asked. "I just got back," she was told. "Well, I'm leaving town," Mary Nichols told her daughter. "I'm too scared to stay here"—and with that she was off to spend the weekend at a friend's house in Pennsylvania.

Two years later, Arthur Bell was in the chambers of the New York City Council one spring night when, thanks to lobbying by Catholic and firefighter groups, and a last-minute reversal of position by Queens's tough-talking, beefy Matthew Troy, the proposed citywide gay civil-rights bill failed again. Bell was so incensed, especially by Troy's going back on what Bell perceived to be his word, that when Troy was being interviewed by TV newsman Gabe Pressman outside the chamber doors he interrupted. "Take a walk," Troy told him. But Arthur Bell did not take a walk. Instead, he lifted up his foot and drove it hard and straight into the rear end of the councilman from Queens, who whirled around to give him, he recalled, a very feminine slap across the face. It was like Rosalind Russell and Paulette Goddard in *The Women,* he exulted, and police had to separate them.

Eventually, Bell drifted away from writing about underworld figures to writing about show business ones—which proved to be at least as dangerous. "Remember the old days when a contract was a seven-year deal Lana Turner signed with Louis B. Mayer?" he wrote. "Times have changed, and nowadays a contract is more likely to be what a 'maligned' name in the news claims to have put out on an inter-viewer"—as he claimed Ryan O'Neal did when he committed the capital offense of mentioning the surgical scar O'Neal had down his back. Bell even had a semi-threatening letter sent to him at the *Voice* by Burt Reynolds himself. But he kept right on; "Barry White preaching 'love unlimited' made me yearn for a weekend with Adolf Hitler," he wrote in a report on New York's disco scene.

★ ★ ★

Nineteen seventy-two was also the year that Alex Cockburn arrived at the *Voice.*

He was thirty-two, coming across the Atlantic from London, where he had worked for the *New Statesman,* the *New Left Review,* the *Times Literary Supplement,* and, as editor, for the ill-fated, radical *Seven Days.* His father was Claud Cockburn, distinguished journalist of the British Left and biographer of Evelyn Waugh, and it was through his family, who had rented a summer cottage on the Irish coast near the, one rented by the family of Bartle Bull's wife Belinda, that he had a connection at the *Voice.* It was not much—Bull once called him "an admiral in the British sponge fleet," and the feeling was mutual—but Alex Cockburn made the most of it. He had an ability to ingratiate himself that was literally incredible, and it proved to be his stock in trade.

Despite their feelings toward each other, he wangled an invitation to lunch from Bartle, where he met Dan Wolf. And there, Wolf was charmed. Cockburn had style, he had manners, he was, like Wolf himself, an easy conversationalist, with a gift for the suave, witty, flip comment. He was slick, he was glib, he was facile—all qualities that could cut both ways, as Dan Wolf should have seen but didn't. For only the second time in his life—and the first, Carter Burden, was not yet apparent—Dan Wolf had completely misread someone.

Cockburn kept hanging around until he had Wolf won over. They had been discussing bringing someone in to run the book-publishing division that had been on the boards ever since Burden had bought the paper, and now Dan Wolf suggested to his colleagues that Alex Cockburn was the man to run it. They had been looking for someone to do a regular column of press criticism, too, and Alex Cockburn eagerly took up that assignment as well. Still later he got another column, "Surplus Value," in which, along with colleague James Ridgeway, he dispensed his Marxist economic theories in between dispensing his elegantly phrased quips. Wolf was clearly enamored of his new acquisition. At one literary party he brought Cockburn to, he ran into one of his earliest protégées at the *Voice*. He introduced them. "I discovered her," he said to Cockburn. "And I discovered you." And he said it proudly.

But in over two years of operation, the *Village Voice* books division produced only one book. It was by Alex Cockburn, about chess.

That was perhaps the best metaphor for Alex Cockburn's whole career at the *Voice,* maybe even his entire life. Later, after his behavior patterns had long since established themselves, assessing the reasons Cockburn acted as he did, and his own inability to judge the man's character right away, Dan Wolf could only wonder whether it was the contradiction in Alex Cockburn's background—the British upper-class mores he was raised amidst contrasted with the low income the family was always forced to live on, given the circumstances of the life his father led—whether Alex Cockburn had seen the same thing happening to him all over again with the failure of *Seven Days,* whether he had come to America to make it big for once, to not be on the losing side of anything anymore. Certainly, it fit the way he acted. Certainly, no one ever got closer to Dan Wolf who used him more.

"The normal mental picture most people even dimly aware of *The Village Voice* have of its employees," he wrote once, "is—so far as I can tell—of a bedraggled layabout, ill attired, and almost certainly under the influence of some powerful narcotic." That was not for Alexander Cockburn. When the time came to act according to the principles laid down in his own anti-capitalist column, Alex Cockburn always had one extra, perfectly dialectical reason for sitting right where he was and coming up with even more nostrums for a new, even more plutocratic owner—and the time came, in Alex Cockburn's case, not once but twice. The gospel he adhered to in the theory of his columns might be "From each according to his ability, to each according to his need," but the one he followed in the practice of real life was called "Looking Out for Number One." When he had the choice, Alex Cockburn chose—and the parties meant more to him than the Party did.

That was Alex Cockburn, and many of his fellow journalists, who recognized him for what he was, were justifiably wary about saying so, since he was known, in his "Press Clips" column, to make attacks that were savage, personal—and, often, damn funny too.

★ ★ ★

1973 . . . On Saturday, January 27, a Vietnam truce is declared. For Americans, at least, the war is over. A disgusted Phil Tracy goes around a town where no demonstrations are taking place and where prayers for peace are being said by Cardinal Cooke, "who in war had blessed the troops and whose predecessor had blessed the warplanes." . . . John Lindsay announces he will not run for reelection, clearing the way for his sixty-seven-year-old controller, clubhouse Democrat Abe Beame. On Primary Eve, Mary Nichols writes, "I started out to write a nostalgia piece about the John Lindsay I once knew—you know, the one who was fresh when everyone else was tired. . . . But in the last week of his reign, John Lindsay went out into a few school neighborhoods to do his old number of walking through and touching the hands of the populace. . . . And it made me want to puke." Of Beame, that "nightmare of machine rule" she had seen eight years before, she writes: "The election of Abe Beame as mayor may not be the worst thing that has happened to this city." . . .

. . . That February, Norman Mailer turns fifty—and throws a party for himself. Lucian Truscott is there as Mailer, in a lair of feminists, tells a joke about a divorced couple who accidentally meet in a restaurant:

> '' 'Darling, you're looking wonderful,' he says. 'And you're being splendid,' says the wife, who was recently remarried to a much younger man. 'Darling, I have a question to ask: How does your young husband like sticking it up your worn out old pussy?' 'He likes it fine,' she replies, 'once he gets past the worn out part.' ''
>
> The Laughter: Hisses, boos, some scattered giggles, snickers, guffaws. ''This is terrible,'' says an irate woman. ''He shouldn't be allowed to get away with that. A woman

would never get away with shit like that." . . . Mailer didn't either.

In all the crush, Mailer tries to explain why he has invited them all there—he wants to form a "People's FBI and CIA." Truscott continues:

> . . . I approached Mailer with the idea that his "notion" would have been more interestingly delivered, and most probably better-received at a Lion's Club luncheon in Effingham, Illinois, than thrown in the gaping maw of The Big Yawn. . . . A crush of people pressed between us, and I began edging away. Suddenly his hand snaked through them and gripped me firmly by the arm. "Come back here," he growled. "I'm not finished talking to you. You're not supposed to walk away from your commanding officer like that. I'll bet you never tried that at West Point." I had to admit I hadn't.

Soon, Truscott is writing about West Point again—with a reminiscence of his days there under Commandant Alexander Haig when Haig becomes White House chief of staff. That Nixon move fails to halt the spread of Watergate, and Truscott spends the next year on the investigative reporting trail of Bebe Rebozo. Rosenbaum looks into, among other things, the conspiracy theories surrounding John Kennedy's assassination. . . . At year's end, Clark Whelton and Nat Hentoff are in agreement, both defending the right of geneticist William Shockley to speak his racial theories on campus.

There were new features—columns on TV, Kids, and Food. There were new faces: critic John Lahr, son of the great comic actor Bert; Anna Mayo, on environmental issues; Brian van der Horst, ex-marine biologist, ex-record industry executive, ex-film critic and freelance writer, as co-writer of "Scenes." There was Robert Christgau on rock, and, after he left to go to *Newsday,* Geoff Stokes—veteran of the civil-rights movement, New York political campaigns, and the Lindsay administration*—to do the same thing.

And there was trouble.

---

*And of the same archconservative Jesuit university attended by the author of this book. Just prior to his graduation, in 1961, Geoffrey Stokes was told not to attend the ceremonies—on the grounds that he had grown a beard.

16. HE HAD THE BULL LOGO EVERYWHERE—

on his car, his belt buckles, even on statues he kept in his office. His efforts at socializing among the writers, such as at their summertime softball games, were few and awkward. Several of the writers held him in open contempt. Ron Rosenbaum was quoted calling him a "rich brat," Jack Newfield called him a "clown," and to Howard Smith he was "a pompous ass with a broomstick up his ass." His reputation preceded him at the paper to such an extent that it even penetrated one writer's subconscious. Drama critic Arthur Sainer had a dream, in which he was fired. And when he asked why, Bartle Bull told him: "Because you keep eating sandwiches, and your posture is terrible."

In later years especially, once he had acquired the self-confidence of being in charge of his own publication and responsible only to himself, Bartle Bull visibly mellowed into an easygoing, cordial, and gregarious man. And he had his moments then, moments when he could be warm and friendly. But those were few and far between, because Bartle Bull had been sent down to the *Voice* by his friend Carter Burden with explicit instructions to get three things—money, money, and more money. Animus from the writers was only one of the pressures he was under.

He grated; that was how Dan Wolf put it, and he would count himself one of only two people, the other being George Dillehay, the mild-mannered, Southern-drawling business assistant Bull hired, who liked him. And Wolf knew why: because he was such an authoritarian.

In his years at the *Village Voice,* Bartle Bull did things that were tactless and rude. He was brusque and bumptious, officious and abrasive and arrogant. He was snippy. He was nasty. Negative feelings had developed about him around the building only a few days after he got there. Trying to cope with this new situation, he just didn't fit in. He just could not make friends, it seemed, he could not help being snide, and most people at the *Voice* worried about what would ever happen to the paper if he took over.

He was aware of the resentment and tried all he could to cool it by avoiding undue contact with people, because, in a friendly sort of way, his business partners, Dan Wolf and Ed Fancher, let him know just how all-pervasive it was, and, in a friendly sort of way, he took that to be their way of driving a wedge against him with the staff, which, in a friendly sort of way, is what it was. He would joke about it with them, and remark, as if a little surprised by it himself, how well the three of them, at least, got on together. But they did not always get on. There were episodes of tension, and by 1973 there was more than that.

★ ★ ★

He was four years older than Carter Burden, having been born in 1938, in Britain, his mother an expatriate American, his father a Tory M.P. who fought in Egypt and never fully recovered from the wounds he received there before dying in 1950. He was shipped out of the country in 1941, to escape the bombing, to America, and wound up staying on in his new country. There, early in life, he developed two acute interests. One, thanks to his grandmother Bertha Baur, former suffragette and Republican National Committeewoman, who took him with her to Chicago for the Eisenhower-Taft convention in 1952, was politics. But young Bartle was cut from the mold a little differently—he was a Democrat, at ten the only one in his private-school class to support Harry Truman for president, three years later the only one to support the firing of MacArthur. The other was newspapers. When he was ten, he not only supported Truman, he wrote entire articles about the election campaign, and read the *New York Times* cover to cover, every day.

He went on to Harvard, in the same class as *Voice* critic Julius Novick, a couple of years ahead of Paul Cowan, and worked three years on the *Crimson,* as literary and then as sports editor. An article he wrote correctly predicting that the 1958 elections would result in a solid triumph for the Conservatives over Labour, and not the close call the British themselves were expecting, had been circulated and read at Oxford before his arrival for postgraduate study there, and set him up well. Harvard Law followed, where Bartle Bull first met Carter Burden.

He was entering his second year, and Carter Burden his senior year as an undergraduate, one day in September 1962, when they sat down at the Pamplona Coffee Shop, and Carter Burden remarked he was disappointed there were no new girls around this year.

"Stanley Mortimer's got a sister at Wellesley," Bartle Bull suggested, then had an idea. He called up Amanda Mortimer, sister of his classmate Stanley, and invited her to the A.D. Club for what was supposed to be a surprise dinner party for her brother. Of course, there was none; only a blind date set up for her when young Carter Burden arrived to pick her up. Carter and Amanda were married out on Long Island in the summer of 1964.

Bartle Bull graduated from law school that June to enter the conservative Wall Street law firm of Cadwallader, Wickersham, and Taft, where his most exciting task was handling the copyrights of the Eugene O'Neill estate, and where he soon became restless. He went to Hattiesburg, Mississippi, where, as he was registering black voters in the basement of a church, the rednecks outside were firing off rifles into the air and armed blacks had to stand guard in the parking lot, and where he brought suit against the local mayor and police chief when they had him arrested for "driving without a Mississippi license." And he went to Bedford-Stuyvesant to volunteer as part of Bobby Kennedy's project there, as did Carter Burden, both of them then going on to Kennedy's presidential campaign.

Bull was the Greater New York coordinator for that campaign, and he was the manager of Carter Burden's successful 1969 drive for a seat on the City Council, in which his candidate won all 155 election districts, a fact in which Bartle Bull took special pride, since the district spanned both Spanish Harlem and the rich, white, generally Republican Upper East Side. And then, at the request of his friend, he gave up his law practice to become a full-time newspaper executive, come down to the *Village Voice,* and look after this new investment.

He arrived a few days after the sale and set up an office, as "vice-president and general counsel," since it wasn't clear yet what, if anything, he would be doing, and it was by no means certain what Carter Burden *wanted* him to do. Ed Fancher suggested that title, which was dropped after a while because Bull didn't want it, and Fancher also wrote him a memo, five pages long, and presented the reasons to him verbally too, suggesting that he take over circulation, an area they felt needed more attention than Ed Fancher could give it right then in the way of promotion, and where they felt he might get to know something about the business. They involved him in other things—the move to University Place that spring, the Tuesday morning ad department meetings that Ed Fancher held. That June, he negotiated a new contract with their printer, the Patent Trader of Mount Kisco, New York. He was helpful; they were pleased. He branched out into other things. At the suggestion of Dan Wolf, he started a column, called "Ecofreaks," which showed that he could write very well indeed. And he became host of the weekly talk show which the *Voice* began broadcasting over cable television in Manhattan.

They did, as Bartle Bull said, get along. But that was personal. In business, there was room for only one publisher, and Bartle Bull and Ed Fancher had staked out the same territory.

He went straight from Wall Street to 11th Street, Ely Kushel, their accountant, said, and there was always a problem of sensibilities with Bartle. Dan Wolf could remember, and delighted in retelling, the incident, not long after his arrival, when one of their advertising salesmen underwent a periodic psychotic epsiode and the police had had to be called, the look on Bartle Bull's face as he came out of his office to watch one of his best ad salesmen being led past him in handcuffs.*

Howard Smith was only the most vocal. Smith offered the paper Marjoe Gortner's autobiography as part of its new books division; Dan Wolf was willing to part with a $5,000 advance each to Marjoe and a co-author; but Bull, Smith said, reacted, "Marjoe? He should pay us to do a book about his life just to make him famous," and the *Voice* passed the book up, as it did *Rock Dreams*, a collection of sketches of rock stars by the Belgian artist Paellart with text by rock critic Nik Cohn, which Smith had come across in Paris. In both instances, Smith claimed, it was Bull's opposition that scuttled the projects. And, according to Smith, Bull kept making demeaning cracks about his film of *Marjoe* until the 1972 Christmas party, after it was already out and successful, when he approached Bull to start up a conversation, and Bartle, going, "All right, all right, I know what you're going to say, you were right, you were right," walked away from him.

Bartle Bull, of course, denied acting any such way at all—the decisions not to publish the books were mutual between him and Dan and Ed, and he probably had just meant to get away from Howard Smith at that packed party. Likewise he denied Howard Smith's version when, in the fall of 1973, Smith was unable to cover a Hell's Angels boat ride as the bikers had asked him to. Howard Blum went in Smith's place, wrote an article putting the bikers down, and they called up the paper threatening to kill both him *and* Blum. A conference was arranged for them with Ross Wetzsteon and Ed Fancher, and, Smith claimed, Bartle, informed of their coming, had ducked out, only to come up to him the next day, after things had gone all right, asking if Howard could get the bikers on Bull's next TV show.

"You upper-class snob," Howard Smith said he told him, and whether the story was true or not, what was definitely true was that by the fall of 1973 a lot more people at the *Voice* felt that way about Bartle Bull than just Howard Smith. By the fall of 1973, even Ed Fancher, after coexisting with him for four years, was becoming exasperated.

To Fancher the problem was that Bartle Bull was erratic, that there were times when he'd be there every day and times when he would vanish for three months, as he did in the fall of 1972 to direct George McGovern's campaign in New York State, only to come back for a couple of weeks and take off again on a European vacation, while he,

---

*Bull, in turn, felt he had been around himself, more than Wolf for one had, and insisted he was not nonplussed by this incident at all.

especially after he quit the Washington Square Institute for Psychotherapy in December of 1970, was spending well over forty hours there, including weekends—that, and that from time to time Bull would usurp authority that was his as publisher.*

To Bartle Bull the problem was that thanks to the gentle nature of the acquisition, the two men had become spoiled, living in the best of both possible worlds, having sold their publication without losing it, that now they were resisting necessary change, that Dan Wolf was using his ability to manipulate people to do it—and that Ed Fancher was just not a good businessman, and Bull wanted his job.

★ ★ ★

They knew he was there under instructions to maximize profit, to take in as much revenue as possible, and sought all they could to accommodate him. But there were limits.

They had never, for instance, taken ads for astrologers, personal counselors, or encounter groups. Psychotherapist Ed Fancher was unalterably opposed to them, and whenever one would appear in the paper he would complain about it, and point out that they were illegal. Bartle Bull would say he understood, that it was Fancher's profession, that he *had* to say that, that he *couldn't* take them, and would kid him about it—but they were not taken, except by occasional accident.

They had, however, always taken, since the early days, ads for models and masseurs and masseuses (such as "for the ultimate in massage," in January 1964). And that, literally as well as figuratively, now became the rub.

In 1970, Edwin Fancher, to satisfy the wishes of those parlor entrepreneurs who were duly licensed by the state, put "Unlicensed Massage" in a separate category of the classified, behind "Licensed," with restrictions on the kind of language and the number of ads per customer. But in the next year, regardless, ads for unlicensed massage parlors in the *Village Voice* exploded, until they took up two full pages, and more. And Ed Fancher began getting two kinds of complaints from his ad department downstairs. One concerned the type of customer they were getting—swarthy, ugly-looking Mafiosi types who were walking in, plunking down ads for ten parlors at a time, and paying cash for them. The other concerned Bartle Bull himself, who, Fancher was told, was coming around, pushing them to take as many of the ads as they could get.

*Bull's side of this was that he was managing to come in mornings during that time, when Fancher happened not to be there.

That his partner was going around him, making incursions into an area he felt was his as publisher, annoyed Edwin Fancher, but he did not act, not right away. Instead, he presented the arguments to Bartle Bull why the *Voice* should discontinue the ads—that a modest number of them, especially in the old days when they came in on their own and they weren't all whorehouses, were all right, but now that they were whorehourses and Mafia whorehouses at that, it was going to discredit the paper if they were not stopped.

To that Bartle Bull countered that nothing had been proven against them yet, and belittled his business partner for suddenly turning puritanical, unilaterally changing paper policy after all these years without consulting his majority partners, its new owners, in such a way as to diminish its assets. That was true, of course; they *were* turning more conservative, or at least respectable, or at least were eager to *seem* that way. This was two years after they had refused ads for *Screw* and gay dating services; it was the same year they would reject Larry Rivers's *Tits*. They didn't need the money anymore, not that kind of money, not that badly. But Bartle Bull, as he now made clear on behalf of Carter Burden, did need it. Which was his second reason for why the ads should continue. Which they did, until the last week of April 1971, when the *Daily News* revealed the unlicensed parlors, once and for all, to be what they were—chronic fronts for prostitution.

The night after the *News* story hit, confirming his worst fears about possible damage to his newspaper, Edwin Fancher sat down and typed out to his partners a memo that, in its obvious hastiness and unusually bad spelling, reflected just how upset he was:

> *Thursday nite 4 / 29 / 71*
>
> *Dan,*
> *Bartle,*
>
> *I just got around to reading the full story in the N.Y. News on the masseur parlors, and thinking about the implications for us.*
>
> *Firstly, I think it is clear that we cann't pretend that we don't know that we're advertising whore houses in our classified masseur columns. . . .*
>
> *I think we have to examin the potential danger of continuing to accept this kind of advertising for ourselves and for The Voice. It puts all of us individually under the clowd of knowingly profiting from the promotion of prostitution. This has implications for me as a psychologist, and certainly for Bartle as a lawyer and as General Council of the Voice. . . . I*

think it could be most embarassing to Carter, however. We have seen that Big Bill Buckly is after him,* and I believe it would be just like Buckly to hit him on this kind of thing. Carter can rightly say that enither he nor Taurus have editorial control of the Voice and hence cann't censor what is printed. But there is no such aragnement over advertising acceptance. The sleeper in this issue is the fact that many of these operations are probably operated by the Mafia. The classified girls know when a big bruiser pulls out a wad and pays $450 cash for a bunch of ads. It could be a very nasty charge that the crusading Voice takes this kind of money.

And, lastly, I think I must remind you that both Rose [Ryan] and Sandy [Fendrick] feel that this kind of advertising is harmful to building healthy advertising. Certainly publicity like the News article, won't make the agencies eager to place their class advertising in the same paper. The banks and national accounts will be most adversly affected.

I have not wanted to push this issue of the unlicensed masseur ads, because I know how Bartle feels about them. But, I think the issue is potentially quite dangerous, and, at least, requires some cool thought.

Ed F.

Bartle Bull was not only unmoved; he told Fancher to his face that he had seen Carter, and that Burden agreed with him, Bull: ads for unlicensed massage parlors should continue to run. He also sat down and typed out to his colleagues a memo that lowered the boom on them with a bluntness of language they had not yet heard from their business partners in general, or from him in particular:

Gentlemen—

In response to Ed's suggestions for revising classified policy for model and massage ads, I thought I would set out my thinking in this area. Frankly, I am somewhat disturbed by the continuing pressure for conservative changes in advertising policies. I think we should settle such matters among ourselves and then support a consistent policy, rather than going to people in the advertising departments with different policies. Out of respect for professional sensibilities I have not raised the issue of encounter ads, or even astrology ads. I do

*This was shortly after Buckley's public complaint about Noel Parmentel's Kissinger article.

not think new ownership could have been more restrained in terms of instituting new policies and in abstaining from the traditional effort to place new people in key jobs. Relying greatly on your judgment in terms of staffing relationships, I have not urged a single new advertising policy and have not sought to replace a single key person. But I do feel that I am entitled to resist changes *that in my judgment may reduce the value of the paper as a business. My thoughts:*

1. These ads are a recognized, accepted and integral part of the Voice, considerably pre-dating Taurus. In general they are read for humor and amusement. Our readers and advertisers know they are there and generally like them. (Some history: The Voice has carried model and massage ads since 1956 (longer than most classified categories), including in that year ads for "athletic" and "experienced" male models, "pin-up models", females with "good figures"; key words like "Swedish" and "private studio" were used in Voice massage ads in the 1950's; "Frank Buonecare", for example, has advertised since at least 1962; ads reading "for the ultimate, call Betty" have run since at least 1966; "Magic Fingers" and "Richard French" have run since at least 1967; 1969 saw "Kenny, Anytime" and, "Girls for Exploitation Movies.")

2. In the interest of good will I have already accepted more restrictive standards of acceptable language, fewer ads, and less conspicuous presentation by a break-up into two sections.

3. None of the 5 law firms that have represented Voice interests in the last two years has recommended that we restrict these ads.

4. While Voice policy has grown more conservative, other publications, the law, and standards of taste in general, have grown more permissive, thereby reducing the Voice's exposure.

5. In over a year of attending weekly display advertising meetings and listening repeatedly to each salesman's explanations of advertiser resistance, I have never heard one complaint about massage ads. (They do complain about dirty pictures and language in the editorial sections.)

6. Our classified section has grown dramatically during the period of the growth of the massage ads. It is precisely during this period that we have secured such new, conservative accounts as Peck & Peck and Bloomingdale's. Nor has it affected the display ads we get from synagogues and from

Catholic, Quaker, Presbyterian, Episcopalian and Unitarian Churches.

7. I don't understand the argument that "we may be attacked", specifically by the Daily News or Bill Buckley. They are not our constituency. Our constituents are our readers and advertisers, and potential individuals of broadly similar outlook. The Voice has been attacked many times, and we all understand that Voice policies are not to be influenced by Carter's politics.

8. Conservative change is being urged on a business-judgment, not moralistic basis, yet these high-rate ads are among our most profitable, taking, I believe, less than 10% of our general classified space and bringing in more than 10% of our general classified income.

9. I do not see sufficient basis for the argument that, because of the Daily News story indicating that some masseuses are prostitutes, 'we could get away with it in the past but we can't get away with them now.'

10. If things do get rough with women's lib, with the law or in some other way (I'm surprised we aren't deluged with many complaints about these ads), we can then moderate or change the policy as necessary. On the women's lib aspect, which I think is potentially a real problem, two points are that many of these advertisers are men, and many women feel that women are entitled to earn money any way they please.

He closed with a warning to them about Rosetta Reitz, their new classified ad manager and intended eventual successor to Rose Ryan, who, an outspoken feminist, had raised particular complaints about the ads. "It seems to me that it is inappropriate for Rosetta, after only a few days in the classified department, to be a material element in this discussion," Bull said pointedly. "If her attitudes in this or other areas are going to inhibit her from carrying out the policies that we determine, she should not have responsibility in that department, and her position must be based on this understanding. If she has personal views that prevent her from carrying out Voice advertising policies, which were clearly known to her in advance, she should have raised this issue before taking this job."

Twenty-four hours after he had received Bull's memo, left for him at the paper, Edwin Fancher responded with one of his own,

Bartle,
When I accepted a five year contract as Publisher of The

Voice (and, remember, Dan and I had suggested a three year contract), I assumed that I would continue with the duties and responsibilities of that position. One such responsibility by tradition, and possibly by law, also, is for advertising acceptance policy.

I recognized that you and I have had a disagreement on the acceptance of Model and Masseur ads. I might point out that all the knowledgeable experts on The Voice, Rose, Sandy, and Dan Wolf disagree with your point of view on this, and believe that your policy will ultimately be harmful to The Village Voice as a business. But, maybe we're all wrong, and anyway, a new owner has a right to make policy. That is why on two occasions I suggested that you take over the responsibility for advertising acceptance from me, and I indicated that I would not interfer [sic] with you. I felt that you did not want to do this. Therefore, I told you that I intended to cut back on these ads in a systematic way until they were less prominant [sic].

I want to repeat my offer here, and make it very clear. If you will put your name on the mast head with the title Vice President In Charge of Advertising, or write me a letter on Taurus stationery indicating that you will henceforth be in complete charge of advertising acceptance policy, I will not complain about any advertising that you may want to accept. This means you can accept encounter groups, hypnosis, models, etc., etc. Your letter will be shown to the department heads in question, so that they will know where responsibility lies.

One more word about Rosetta. It has always been our philosophy that employees, and particilary [sic] department heads, (or in Rosetta's case, someone being groomed to be a department head) should feel free to express their opinion. The Voice has been successful by encouraging initiative and independence in department heads. Rosetta does have strong opinions on this issue, but she acted to limit these ads only on my personal instructions, not on her own initiative.

But, I repeat again, my offer to turn full responsibility for all advertising acceptance policy over to you in the ways I outlined above, so that there will be no misunderstanding about where responsibility lies.

Ed Fancher

At the same time Fancher—belatedly, he felt—moved to reassert his authority downstairs. He issued new regulations, stating that the

Voice would accept no new unlicensed massage ads and permit none that dropped out to come back in, with an eye toward whittling them down by attrition. These directives Bartle Bull did not challenge.

He did not, of course, want or take any such title as "vice-president in charge of advertising," but he *did* take a new title when that formality, the Village Voice Company, consisting of Dan Wolf and Ed Fancher and, since 1970, Bartle Bull too, held its annual meeting at the end of July 1971—president of the *Village Voice.*

Dan Wolf held it, and offered it to him, and discussed his reasons with Ed Fancher beforehand—that part of Bartle's problem was that he had no real title or defined powers, that giving him this might at least solve *some* of the problem, and that, especially after the massage parlors, it might serve as some sort of consolation prize. Ed Fancher went along, and Bartle Bull, looking, Fancher thought, a bit flabbergasted by the offer, accepted.

That made a kind of peace settlement. But the same week they met and gave Bartle the title, the *New York Times* got onto the story, with a bylined piece by reporter Fred Ferretti quoting, among others, Mary Perot Nichols ("I've noticed those ads and the dreadful people bringing them in. . . . It makes me very uncomfortable to think the *The Voice* might be in part subsidized by organized crime") and Councilman Carter Burden (who said he had "heard absolutely nothing about" any problem at the paper. "I think I would have gotten some vague feedback. . . . People have said to me 'How could you run that stuff,' " but "I've stayed out of it"). The following month, four operators in Queens—who, the story in the *New York Post* noted conspicuously, "advertised in the *Village Voice*"—were arrested for running a prostitution ring. And a year later, when a girl who answered a model ad in the *Voice* went to WNEW-TV and complained she had been told she would have to massage nude men, Edwin Fancher found himself on the phone under interrogation from station reporter Christopher Jones, who informed him, midway through the grilling, that none other than Councilman Carter Burden had introduced legislation in the City Council to give the city regulatory powers to crack down on such parlors, the very parlors he wanted taking out unlimited advertising in his newspaper only the year before—a fact of which Fancher, to his embarrassment and consternation, had not been aware.

As time passed, the number of ads went down, until by the spring of 1974 they were gone altogether. But, by that time, other points of contention had arisen.

★ ★ ★

In 1973, their contract with Patent Trader was up, and the plant, under new ownership, was seeking to renegotiate it with a steep increase. They decided to find another printer.

They came across a small print shop called Textmasters, around the corner on 10th Street, run by a man named Cornell Fay, who, Dan Wolf surmised, was on his way out of business. At Wolf's initiative, they called back and made him an offer: the *Village Voice* would take Textmasters over, and he would run it as their subsidiary, composing the paper every week. Fay agreed. They made arrangements for the paper to be run off in Connecticut at the presses of the *New Britain Herald,* and a long-term deal to buy newsprint, and began negotiating a contract with Fay.

Up to this point, the three partners, Wolf, Fancher, and Bull, were in agreement. But now Bartle Bull began acting alone. He kept his partners out of it, leaving instructions that they were to direct all inquiries for Textmasters through him and his assistant, George Dillehay, and at Textmasters that no one there was to talk with anyone at the *Voice* but *him,* as Dan Wolf found out one day when, standing in Bartle's office on the fifth floor, he asked one of Fay's aides whether they had dummying tables ready or not, and the aide hesitated, saying, "I don't know if I'm allowed to say anything about it."

Wolf persisted, and got his answer, and later spoke to Bartle Bull about it. Bull was apologetic, saying, "Of course when I told them that, I didn't mean you or Ed," but apparently he had *not* specified that, and it was clear to Wolf that Textmasters was not in any position to do the paper yet, while the time was drawing near for them to leave Patent Trader.

Ed Fancher, meanwhile, was furious, that after eighteen years in the business his partner was freezing him out, furious at another encroachment upon his authority as publisher. But he said nothing—he was, after all, in favor of the idea, as was Dan Wolf, and he knew how much it meant to Bartle to run *some*thing his way—not even when Bull brought back a contract that Ed Fancher didn't think was the best. But when it was obvious they would have to stay on after their contract was up at Patent Trader, finally Ed Fancher did say something.

The plant offered to continue working on the paper an additional twelve issues without a contract, from mid-October 1973 to mid-January 1974. Bartle Bull counter-offered that they do it for an additional four weeks instead of twelve. The printer refused, not wanting, they said, to lay off workers just prior to Christmas. And so

Bartle Bull refused their terms altogether: the *Village Voice* would leave Patent Trader after the issue of October 17, 1973, as originally planned.

Ed Fancher, at this point, told him he was making a mistake, to take Patent Trader's terms and give Textmasters enough time to get set up. A printing consultant Bull brought in from Philadelphia said the same thing. But Bull overruled them, insisted that Textmasters was ready, refused Dan Wolf's suggestion that some *Voice* staff work over at Fay's shop to make sure he got the paper out all right, let go, against their wishes, Dick Bell, the production assistant who had worked as their man at Patent Trader, and plunged ahead. Effective with the issue of October 24, 1973, the *Village Voice,* at its wholly owned subsidiary, Textmasters, Inc., began to print itself.

Textmasters was *not* ready to put the paper out yet. After the first week, when Dan Wolf and Bartle Bull had to stay up most of the night overseeing it, the job had to be farmed out to Weiss Brothers, their pre-1964 printer in Newark, and to several other plants, all at different locations. There was chaos. There were cost overruns. There were that many more mistakes and typos and ragged edges in a paper that, even in the best of times, could not afford to have any more. In the winter of 1973–74 the *Village Voice,* a paper not noted for its good looks in the first place, looked even worse than usual.

But there was more than one reason for that.

★ ★ ★

The Textmasters problem was one. The 71-percent solution was the other.

All newspapers, and magazines too, have to get money from somewhere. To get it, they choose different routes. At one extreme are those periodicals that accept little or no advertising, and rely almost totally on a dedicated hard core of reader support; as a result, their price per copy is quite high, which tends to *keep* a small audience small, and these publications tend to make little or no money. At the other extreme are those publications that are *basically* advertising vehicles, where there is little or no journalism, and what there is is packed in around the ads. These are known in publishing as "shoppers," and, because they have so little reader interest in them, they often have to be so-called "controlled circulation"—that is, mailed free to every household in a given area—in order to attract advertisers into using it as a medium.

The *Village Voice* had what its founding owners thought was a nice balance between the two. In the early days, when the paper had been small, the ad ratio had been between 45 and 55 percent. In later years, as the paper got thicker, they decided to raise it. They considered 66 percent to be the ideal ratio for the paper, and 68 percent to be about as high as they could go, though, if a rush of ads came in at the last minute or it was Christmastime, they would consider going over. As it was, they were high, far higher than most similar or competitive publications, higher than everyone in New York but the *Daily News*.

Bartle Bull thought they should go higher, and said so several times. He had reasons: the whole point of going beyond eighty-page papers, as they were doing with their new printers, which meant extra bundles to distribute them in, more newsprint, and more money spent, was to run more *ad* pages, which would more than pay for themselves; the paper ran enough editorial copy already. And, Carter Burden needed the money. So papers should be tight. That meant, if the ads came in, bigger papers with more ads in them. It also meant, if the ads did *not* come in, smaller papers with, if necessary, some stories *not* in them. Which was the problem, as Diane Fisher tried to explain in an in-house memo in early 1973:

> *I can understand wanting to run up the ad ratio in a large paper, but we have geared up our editorial operation to be able to fill those 100-page-plus papers, no matter what ratio we are faced with, and when the amount of space suddenly shrinks we are faced with commitments (for example, 150 inches of Centerfold, automatically, no matter what the size of the paper) that must be kept. The regular writers aren't faucets which can be turned on on Monday afternoon after we find out we need copy, and turned off otherwise. And once these regular columns, which we still are adding, go in a small paper there's next to nothing left for even topical news stories, let alone our ever-expanding overset. If we cut back on the columns, on the other hand, we'll be stuck with wide-open big papers when they happen, and nothing to fill them without wiping out our back-up overset. I think it's really unfair to insist on jamming up under-100-page papers, where the ratio may not be as profitable, but the editorial space is considerably less, ratio or not.*

And there the matter rested, until November 30, 1973, five weeks into the Textmasters quagmire, when Bartle Bull sent a memo around the office, stating, "Although it makes things tougher for everybody, I'm afraid it is imperative that we continue to run tight papers in the 69–71% range."

Bull used the word *continue* because, "incidentally," as he put it, "since 1970 we have run 43 papers in the 69–74% range, of which 26 were in the 70–74% range." And he listed a series of reasons why it was now going to be essential, indefinitely, including a sudden shortage of Canadian paper.

Ed Fancher—a little shocked by reading that memo, as was Dan Wolf—had a talk with Bartle Bull, told him he appreciated his reasons for wanting to do what he did, and that, since this was the Christmas season anyway, he would go along with it for the month of December. What would happen when December, and the Canadian paper shortage, were over, was left unresolved. So was the issue of just who was in charge, and who was going to be making policy at the paper.

Five weeks went by, and Ed Fancher sent Bartle Bull a memo, dated New Year's Day, 1974.

> *Since your memo . . . we have run five consecutive issues with 70 or 71% advertising, so I think it is time to review the results.*
>
> *Firstly, the policy has been a success in two regards. It has reduced our paper consumption enormously. . . . Secondly, it has maximized our profit picture by keeping our costs at rock bottom. Since Display and classified sales were $45,000 above last year in November, and will probably be about $61,000 above last December, we should have made up for some of our short term mistakes on composition costs due to the delay in getting Fay set up completely.*
>
> *In other regards, however, the policy has had some very negative effects. I have met with great annoyance and bitterness about it in all segments of the staff. The editors hate it because it makes it very difficult to dummy properly, and calls the wrath of writers down on their heads for this. One writer asked me if "you guys are aware of the rage this is causing down on the fourth floor?" The dummy people feel under terrible pressure from everyone to do what they feel is almost impossible. Particularly since we now have so many full pages without ads, such as centerfold, page 3, book page, plus weekly request from editorial for one, or usually two additional pages without ads, their job becomes horendous [sic]. Even the display salesmen complained to me last week that their advertisers are beginning to complain about being ganged up on pages, and asked when we can stop "junking up" the paper. One of the writers even commented that if we can't*

[sic] *get paper, we should do what the Wall St. Journal did,
and limit our ads.*

*What I think the staff is reflecting is a feeling that with such
a high ad ratio, the gestalt of the paper is subtly changed and it
almost suggests the appearance of a "shopper". What I am
really worried about is that there may be readers who feel this
way, that a sense of dissatisfaction with the paper can set in,
which might be suble* [sic] *and hard to detect, but very real in
the long run.*

*I also think that we must keep in mind that the 65% to 68%
ad formula is generally considered extremely high amoung* [sic]
*newspapers. Rolling Stone runs 29% to 53%, and New York
Review of Books often runs under 40% advertising. . . .*

*In any event, it is my opinion that it is in the best interests of
The Voice to revert to our traditional formula beginning with
the new year.*

Bartle Bull's response was to come back with documentation, charts
and graphs and tables, month by month, issue by issue back through
the year 1965, to show that the previous owners of the *Village Voice,*
Daniel Wolf and Edwin Fancher, had run *their* share of plus-68-percent
papers in their time, and that the year they had run the most was 1969,
the year before it was sold to its new owners, the year when it was on
the block. And he made his new policy, the new policy he had
enunciated on his own and merely informed his partners of, stick.
Throughout the winter and spring, the percentage of ads tapered off—
by a point or so, to around 70—but the complaints about it did not. As
late as April, the dispute was still going on, and Bartle Bull was writing
his partners this memo:

*1. During our paper crunch last Nov–Dec . . . I ran tight
papers, up to but never over 71%. I have never run a paper over
71%. Since 1969 Ed ran 13 papers over 71%.*

*2. So far there have been 15 issues in 1974. I have not run
one paper over 70% in 1974. The average for these weeks is
67.7%. For the first 15 weeks of 1969 (last year before
Taurus) it was 68.5%, and the papers were 30 pages smaller.
Of the 15 weeks, I have run tighter papers 4 weeks, Ed ran
tighter papers 10 weeks.*

*3. I presume we are running tighter papers than Ed ran in
more recent years, although never as tight as his really tight
ones.*

The point was inarguable: they *had* run issues of over-68-percent advertising in the past. But what Bartle Bull did not mention in his arguments, and the statistics he marshalled to back them up, was that a 48-page or a 64-page or an 80-page paper with 71 percent advertising, such as they had run, *looks* a lot different from a 96-page or a 104-page or a 120-page paper with that much advertising in it, such as they were running. In a short, "tight" paper, the "news hole"—the amount of space allocated for stories in the layout dummies—is at least more compact. In a longer, "tight" paper, the news hole—expanded, but not as much as the space for ads is—must perforce be broken up that much more as the paper, and the reader's eye, goes along. In the *Village Voice,* that meant stories that jumped only once before now jumped two or three or more times, and instead of jumping for only a few pages they jumped perhaps dozens—this, in a paper that had no margin for aesthetic error to begin with.

And there *were,* as Ed Fancher said, unhappy people. Diane Fisher was unhappy. So was Ross Wetzsteon. So was Sandy Fendrick. So was Dan Wolf, especially after the Monday afternoon when Bartle came in the office, Sandy Fendrick told him she had enough to go eight extra pages over what they'd planned for that week, he said fine, and then she called Wolf back upstairs at five o'clock to tell him she had lost the ads and wanted to go back down to the smaller paper.

She asked Wolf if it was OK, and Wolf told her to do what Bartle said, and she said, "I can't," so he said, "Talk to him, then," and she said, "I can't, he's gone," and now Wolf was annoyed, annoyed that with his *diktats* this situation was arising at all, doubly annoyed that he wasn't even around to resolve it. Do the smaller paper, he finally told her, and called in Ross Wetzsteon, who had to cut editorial, and told him, "Bartle's given her the figure. Let *him* justify it. I'm not going to take the responsibility. He's given her a rigid schedule, let her follow it, and it can be his problem, and *when* it is maybe he'll begin to understand what's going on around here." But when Bull came in the following morning and asked what had happened, Wolf simply told him, and did not press the matter further.

They were not the only ones who were unhappy, either. Jack Newfield was exasperated that the stories he had written were jumped all over and made to look terrible. He and Paul Cowan bumped into Fancher on the street, and the two of them said they were so displeased with the way the paper looked, and the prospect of Bull taking over, that they just might decide to form a union. Ed Fancher told them that the idea of starting a union just because they didn't like the possibility of Bartle Bull running things was ridiculous, but when Newfield asked him if he was going to stay on or not, Edwin Fancher had to admit he didn't know. Other writers came to him and made the same complaint. Those who knew the deal they had worked out asked the same thing. Edwin Fancher, into the fifth and final year of his employment contract, with relations vis à vis his partner Bartle Bull openly deteriorating, still had to admit he didn't know.

And, when he finally got his first word, it was not encouraging.

★ ★ ★

He had come to them in 1964, thirty-two years old, out of Cornell, where he had spent four years, out of the army, where he had spent six, out of the world of freelance writing, where he had started out for the men's magazines—*Cavalier, Playboy*—and was still trying to make a living when he became their printing-day proofreader, for $50 a week. Over the next ten years, Ross Wetzsteon rose at the paper, steadily, until by 1974 he was almost at the top—almost, but not quite.

When he had first come there, Dan Wolf had looked him over, with his eyeglasses, his ragged, Rasputin-long beard, his brown paper lunch bag, his plain old Sears clothes, and had read him as one of life's borderline cases, out of a sheltered background, living a basically sheltered existence, and yet exposing himself to a rarefied, potentially frightening atmosphere. He wondered about him a little. But there was no doubt that he was competent, and reliable, and as time went on Ross Wetzsteon acquired more and more duties—and power. He went from being a proofreader to being a copy editor, and, in August 1965, his first bylined article, about the politics of the Lower East Side Anti-Poverty Board, appeared. From there he turned to writing and editing features, and in the summer of 1967 Dan Wolf, Ed Fancher, and Diane Fisher flew up to Vermont, where Ross Wetzsteon was on vacation in a small cottage with his quiet wife and little girl, to offer him the job of associate editor, the same title Diane Fisher had. He accepted.

They had equal titles, and because she had been there longer they considered her theoretically superior to him at first, but that did not last. As time went on, it was Ross who read the copy and talked to the writers and came to be considered the principal assistant, until by late 1969, when in the course of the negotiations with Burden and Bull, he was asked the inevitable question "What would happen if you got hit by a truck tomorrow?" Dan Wolf had an answer: Ross Wetzsteon was ready to take over tomorrow, if necessary. And after the sale, it was Ross who acquired the title "executive editor" (there being no "managing" editor at the *Voice,* there being nothing to "manage"), who was elevated to the three-man "Editorial Board" that was specified as part of their 1970 employment contract (but that never met), who evaluated the manuscripts and dealt with the writers and made all the day-to-day decisions on freelance material and next week's issue. And he did so with Wolf's consent; explicitly, if not by words then by actions, Dan Wolf in the 1970s had designated him as the successor.

With his always-nicely-arranged, compulsively neat desk, his always-sharpened pencils, and his tendency to be doing deep knee-bends in his office when they went by, Ross Wetzsteon struck some of the writers as being a little strange, but he was generally well-liked. And he was well-qualified for the position he held. He was calm, open, and wise, with a personality and temperament that was outwardly gentle, soft-spoken, and unflappable—when Mary Breasted, subbing for Mary Nichols on vacation, approached him on deadline to say that one of the writers was still tripping on mescaline from a party at her house the previous weekend and would be unable to do his story, he just said, "Is that all?"—and a commitment to the First Amendment totally in synch with what they had established. He was also, on the technical side, a very good editor, with a gift for witty, ironic heads that was the equal of Dan Wolf's—"Oh Dada, Poor Dada, MOMA's Hanging You"—and a quiet skill at working with writers. His style was not *not* to edit them, but rather to talk, gain their confidence, exchange artistic visions, and then, if changes were needed, suggest ones they wished they had thought of all along. Even some of those who did not like him personally wanted to be edited by him.

Ross Wetzsteon idolized Dan Wolf, openly, calling him, for quotation, "the single most important person in my life." And as executive editor and heir apparent, he was entitled to pay the expenses of the writers who worked for him directly.

One day in late 1973, Wetzsteon came into Dan Wolf's office to tell him he had assigned a woman named Marilyn Webb to cover the Guru Maharaj Ji religious cult on its tour down South for the *Voice*. Wolf said he didn't know very much about her, that he wasn't impressed with what he *did* know, and that a story like that would normally be given to Ron Rosenbaum. "But she really wants to do it," Ross Wetzsteon explained.

"It's going to be enormously expensive," Wolf complained, "and in that case, I want our own person to do it, somebody I have confidence in."

"She wants to do it anyway, and all she wants for expenses is $150," said Wetzsteon. "She can't do it for $150," Wolf objected.

"Yes, she can," Ross Wetzsteon persisted. "She's made her own arrangements; she's going down on the group's own train. And, besides, she *really* wants to do it." Since he felt so strongly, and it had been her idea, not Rosenbaum's, Dan Wolf went along, thinking it was set: she would be paid $600, $200 each for a three-part series, with any expenses to be in the fee.

But Marilyn Webb came back to New York and began submitting expenses for a lot more than $150 and demanding a lot more than $600 for her fee. When she wasn't paid she showed up in Ross's office, and when he avoided her she went down to the fourth floor and told people she was being cheated. After a couple of weeks of that one of the writers came to Dan Wolf and told him, "She wants to see you."

Dan Wolf didn't want to have to deal with her; it was Ross's problem, he said. But when it became apparent that Ross would not see her and she would not go away, he saw her, and she presented him with letters from Ross Wetzsteon, and other written documentation, all of it indicating to Dan Wolf that Ross had been telling him one thing and Marilyn Webb another, that Ross had apparently agreed to give her the money and bury her fee in future expense accounts.

To read it was a shock. Dan Wolf had always trusted Ross Wetzsteon, would never have noticed anything was wrong, and he was very disturbed. He scheduled another meeting in his office, with both Marilyn Webb and Ross Wetzsteon present, where they confronted each other, and she called him a liar and began once more to produce her evidence, and this time, especially when he heard how weak Ross's defense was—"Marilyn, I think you misunderstood. I think you didn't understand what I was doing"—and saw her break down in tears, he was certain she was telling the truth, which meant that Ross Wetzsteon had been lying to her and lying to him. He asked Ross to leave, went to Bartle, told him the situation, and said, "We have to give her the money; it's our obligation. Whether I said it or not, he said it, and he was representing the paper when he did," and the *Village Voice* settled with Marilyn Webb all of the nearly $1,000 it owed her.

Then Ely Kushel, making a spot check through the books, came across figures that did not jibe to him, and reported back that it seemed people were being paid for articles they never wrote—by Ross Wetzsteon. This report, coming as it did on the heels of the Marilyn Webb incident, touched off a full-scale crisis inside the business circles of the *Village Voice*. Ross Wetzsteon's files were audited by Kushel, and his expenses checked out, line by line, by Dan Wolf and Bartle Bull and Bull's assistant, George Dillehay, together. In this case, Ross Wetzsteon passed his test; for every question they asked him, he had an answer. Mostly, the sheets just reflected the paper's new policy of paying on acceptance of an article, not publication. But to have been brought before such a procedure at all was a tremendous indignity, and if that incident and its aftermath were not enough to finish off Ross

Wetzsteon's friendship with Dan Wolf, or to cripple whatever chances remained of an orderly succession between the two, what Dan Wolf now began hearing from his staff did. At first, he had gotten feedback that they believed Marilyn Webb's story. Now he was told other things.

Early in 1973, there appeared, for several weeks running, poetry in the *Village Voice*. They had almost never done that, and when light verse by a woman named Ruth Batcheler began to run Dan Wolf thought it unusual, but not so unusual he thought to question why. He might not be impressed, but it was evident to him that Ross Wetzsteon was, and he deferred to Wetzsteon's judgment in such matters.

One night around the time of the Marilyn Webb incident, Howard Smith was driving Dan Wolf somewhere, and brought it up. "Do you know about Ruth Batcheler?"he asked.

"What about her?" was Dan Wolf's reply.

"He's been fucking her, that's what. *That's* why her poetry got in the paper." Then Smith blurted out all the details, how word had gotten around the fourth floor that Ross Wetzsteon was running a casting couch up in his office, trying to sleep with the women who worked with him, and rewarding those who did, how he himself had gone to Ross and Ross had not denied it, how he had lectured Ross to stop, how alienation had spread all among the writers.

This was the first Dan Wolf had heard of anything like this, and his mind was blown. He would have to confront Ross Wetzsteon with *this,* too, now. When he did, Ross acted sheepish, and defended himself by saying he had slept with only two women he had published, Ruth Batcheler being one and Ellen Frankfort, just once, the other, but at least to that extent he had to admit it was true. He couldn't help it, he said; he was a sucker for light verse. And it wouldn't happen again, he promised. Not long after that, Ruth Batcheler became the poetess-in-residence at *Screw* Magazine, debuted her efforts there with a long poem, complete with two-page illustrated spread, giving intimate detail about her affair with a man who had a long beard, and a copy of the magazine made its way around the offices of the *Voice*. Dan Wolf began to hear other stories about Ross Wetzsteon, some of them about his sexual proclivities and some of them not. This time Wetzsteon told Wolf that he had been going through a particularly lonely and depressing period (he was divorcing his wife, and separated from his little daughter), that he was in psychotherapy now (which Wolf knew; Ross's father had committed suicide during his Montana boyhood, he had not been told the truth until his mid-twenties, and it had caused him problems, which he kept no secret), and that from now on things were going to be different. Dan Wolf told him he hoped so.

★ ★ ★

The two men pretty much stopped talking to one another, except when necessary, and any dreams Ross Wetzsteon had of succeeding to the editorship of the *Village Voice* as long as Dan Wolf was around were ruined, and he knew it. In the fall of 1973, before any of these incidents, he had had a job opportunity elsewhere, and gone to Bull to ask if Bartle would have any "problems" with his succeeding Dan. He had been told that no such problems existed, that they had no one else in mind, and had said if that was the case he hoped Bull would let Dan know. Now, at least according to Wolf (Wetzsteon denied it), he came to Wolf himself, said if Wolf went he did not think he could handle things all by himself, and asked Dan to stay on.

But in his heart he felt about Wolf the same way Bartle Bull felt about Edwin Fancher—that *he* was doing all the work, that *he* was running things, that Dan was tired and didn't feel like doing anything, that if only Dan would go things would work out all right. Now he saw, or thought he saw, that Dan would not go, and was prepared to be devious and manipulative in defense of his staying, and Ross Wetzsteon began to resent and detest his former mentor. That was a conclusion, if not an attitude, also being reached—separately, but concurrently—by his putative partner Bartle Bull. Wetzsteon remembered that, after one of the meetings called to discuss his fate in the wake of the Marilyn Webb incident, Dan Wolf came in to tell him, "I covered up for you really well at that meeting," followed by Bartle Bull, who told him, "He spent the whole lunch telling me what a pathological liar you were." Bull did not remember it exactly that way, but to him Wolf was certainly going all-out to discredit Ross Wetzsteon.

And so, as the year 1973 came to an end, Bartle Bull went out to lunch with Councilman Carter Burden, told him what was going on at the *Voice,* and came back with a decision on what to do. He went into Dan Wolf's office and formally asked him to stay on when his contract was up.

Wolf asked, "What about Ed Fancher?" and Bartle Bull replied, "Well, Ed has his practice anyway." He didn't really think Fancher would *want* to stay on. Dan Wolf said he didn't think he would want to stay unless Fancher was staying too. Bartle Bull urged him to think it over. Wolf said he would, and told his partner what had been said. Fancher now offered to bow out, telling Wolf not to say no just because he wasn't being included. But Wolf went back and told Bartle Bull that Ed Fancher was his friend, that he'd been doing this for eighteen years with him, that he couldn't go on doing it without him, and if that was the case he would have to turn down Bartle Bull's offer. Bartle Bull looked unhappy, said he was sorry Dan Wolf felt that way, hoped he would reconsider, and the offer was not raised again.

Right afterwards, when he was upstairs complaining once again about the way the paper looked thanks to Bartle Bull, Jack Newfield asked Dan Wolf, "What's going to happen to this paper if Bartle takes over?" and Wolf didn't have an answer.

"Well, is your contract going to be extended?" Newfield wanted to know. Dan Wolf said he didn't know, that he didn't even know if he *wanted* it extended, that he hadn't done anything about it. "Why not?" Newfield asked. "Because I really haven't made up my mind," Wolf told him.

It was true. For once in his life, Dan Wolf, who had made a career out of being decisively passive, was simply being indecisive. He had run out of things to do, and he did not know what he wanted to do next.

He had been a nobody for so long that he found it impossible to consider himself important now, and yet he knew that many people *did* consider him important, were counting on him. This so-called "centrifugal force" at the *Voice,* as he knew everybody, even Ross Wetzsteon and Bartle Bull, considered him to be, now knew just how easily things could blow apart at the very center there. He knew Ross Wetzsteon had delusions of grandeur, though he didn't know if Ross still wanted his job, or would accept it; he didn't know how far Ross's power drive carried. But he knew that people didn't want to work under Ross, and that he would have to stay in his job if it meant Ross taking over. About that, he had mixed feelings; he no longer had the will or the energy to devote the time to his paper that he once had, he had had it in a way, and he was anxious that he not get locked in now or he would never be doing anything different to his grave. But if his going was going to put other people in a bad position, then he owed it to them to try to stay, at least for a while. So he was ambivalent. He was heading into a fight, he knew it, and he didn't know how it was going to end, but he knew he wasn't ready for one.

While Dan Wolf was thinking this, Ed Fancher was having his problems with Bartle Bull, problems of authority and management of the business, problems that only begged the question of whether their contracts were going to be renewed, and on what terms, and when. There was only one man to complain to about it, just as there was only one man who could renegotiate their contracts: Carter Burden. And they both now knew that.

So, when Jack Newfield urged him to get in touch with Burden, Dan Wolf said he would.

★ ★ ★

But he didn't, not at first. Newfield came up again, wanting to know if he had done anything yet. This time Wolf promised to call him sometime after the holidays. When they came and went and he *still* hadn't done it, Newfield finally asked, "Well, then, do you object if *I* get in touch with Carter?" and Wolf said, "You can do anything you please, but Carter's a very difficult man to get a hold of," and he warned Newfield *not* to discuss his affairs with Carter, *not* to bring up the subject of a new contract for him, and *not* to blow up too much against Bartle, because Burden after all was Bartle's friend. Newfield, after trying several times, did manage to have dinner with Burden. When he did, Burden seemed surprised at his insistence on a meeting at all. Newfield came back reporting that he had been very careful not to bring up the subject of Dan's contract or Bartle's personality and that the upshot was he had urged Carter to get in touch with him, Dan, and that Carter had said he would, the next week. Which Burden did not do. Wolf dropped him a note suggesting that they meet for a drink to discuss things. Which got no answer. So then, after more prodding by Newfield and a few others, he placed a series of calls to Jane Low, Carter Burden's secretary, and at last a dinner was set up, with Wolf and Carter Burden and Burden's latest girlfriend, Susan Thompson, in attendance, at La Petite Ferme, a small restaurant in the Village.

This was January 1974. The two men had had almost no contact since the day the contract had been signed four years before. Wolf told him about the troubles at the *Voice*—the difficulties with Bartle, his autocratic and high-handed manner, how he had botched Textmasters, how his 71-percent ad ratio was causing everyone problems. Burden took it upon himself to say he knew Bartle Bull could be disagreeable, but it was he, Burden, who had been pressing to get income out of the *Voice,* that the money had not been coming through as he had hoped. Wolf said if he wanted to find out about the business he really ought to talk to Ed Fancher; as far as Wolf knew, the paper was doing fine. Burden agreed, and said he would get in touch with Fancher immediately. Dan Wolf stressed that if he were to stay, it would have to be with Fancher or not at all. Carter Burden seemed to indicate he did not consider that an unreasonable request. Then the subject turned to Carter Burden's plans. Burden said he was looking to sell some of his stock to take some of the financial pressure off him, but that he would not be selling the *Voice* in any case, and the evening was left with a kind of consensus: Burden conceding that Bartle could be a difficult guy to work with, promising to speak to Fancher, Wolf passing that message on.

Edwin Fancher had spoken to Carter Burden in the past four years even less than Dan Wolf had—just a few words at a party. He now placed numerous calls with Burden's secretary, and he was not called back. But in the meantime, Dan Wolf had called him, too, and got through, and told Burden once again that if he wanted to talk about the business side he had to talk to Fancher. Carter Burden had apologized and said how terribly busy he was and asked if they could talk over the phone right there. Against his better judgment—he was not a phone person; besides being hard of hearing he preferred to do business face to face—Wolf had said yes, and suddenly Burden had mentioned getting rid of Bartle Bull. He didn't know if that could be done, he said, which Dan Wolf found strange, considering no one had proposed it. Still more phone calls to Jane Low followed, all asking for another face-to-face meeting, until finally one was arranged, for the night of March 18, 1974, in the River House, Carter Burden's East Side residence.

★ ★ ★

When, during the course of their negotiations with him, Carter Burden had switched signals, suddenly seeking to make it a deal for 80-percent control, with a holding company to buy it for him, and with them to be paid off in installments while he took out bank loans to pay them their balance, it was presented to them purely as a tax advantage: he would borrow money, and write off the interest to the bank as a business expense. At no time was it presented in terms of Carter Burden needing the money and not being able to pay them their lump sum right away. But early in 1971, after the first year had gone by and their first stock dividends had duly been paid, Edwin Fancher noticed something. Carter Burden—or rather, "Taurus Communications," through which he was acting—was beginning to withdraw money from the company. The "advances to the parent company in excess of income taxes," or "retained earnings," as they were called, would come at the initiation of Bartle Bull or of Roy Figueroa, the accountant at the company of Carter Burden's uncle, William A. M. Burden, would be signed by Ely Kushel, and would have to be cosigned by either him or Wolf, so they knew what was going on, even if they did not know what it meant at first. But, as time went on, a pattern to these withdrawals emerged. The sum outstanding from the paper's cash reserves would grow and grow until just before July 31, the end of their fiscal year, when all but a little of it would be suddenly redeposited in time for the yearly audit, then almost immediately withdrawn again, to grow until the next year. Ed Fancher, after a while, began to figure out what was going on: that Carter Burden was dipping into the paper's cash reserves to liquidate his bank obligations, keeping the money out to play with and spend as he went along, that, just prior to the end of the fiscal year, he was arranging *another* loan, for almost the entire outstanding amount, paying back *that* loan within twenty-four or forty-eight hours at little or no interest, and then resuming his ways.* He could also figure out what was happening to the interests of the minority partners: that, when it came time to declare a dividend, with all this money still out, the profit picture, and therefore the dividends, were both less than they should have been. In 1970, all profit was declared as dividend. In 1971, with more growth, Taurus simply declared the same dividend, $3 a share, as the year before. In 1972, with more growth again, the dividend was still $3. And in 1973, with still more growth, it was still $3.

Ed Fancher approached Ely Kushel about it several times. Kushel told him it was common practice, where one company owned so much of another, and they should take out a little advance against dividends themselves, just for protection, which they both did. Beyond that, Kushel told him, there was not much they could do. He told Dan Wolf about it several times, but Wolf, no money man, yessed him off, listening without comprehending. And he knew from talking to Bartle Bull that Taurus—Carter—was always short of cash, so he let it ride. But he didn't like it.

When he came back from vacation in the summer of 1973, having skipped the formality of the "Board of Directors meeting," to find that, for the third year in a row, dividends had not gone up, Ed Fancher went to Ely Kushel again and complained. Once again Kushel told him there was nothing he could do about it short of complaining to Carter Burden personally, and now Fancher knew he would have to do just that. But other problems intervened—Textmasters, the 71-percent hassle, the whole issue of Bartle in general—all overshadowed by the question of whether or not there was to be a new contract, all matters which would be moot if there was none. And in the spring of 1974, as they waited to hear from Carter Burden, the sum of money outstanding from the *Village Voice*, which had begun with $31,000 withdrawn in 1971, had reached a total of $778,000.

When he had met with Carter Burden in January, Dan Wolf had not known this. Fancher had tried to explain it to him several times in the

*As Fancher so testified in depositions for his lawsuit against Burden in 1975.

past, but it had not sunk in. Now Fancher tried again, told him just how much money was involved, and this time he got through. Now Wolf understood for the first time that this was not just another advance against dividends Carter Burden was taking, but practically all the excess money in the company, and he was as alarmed as his partner. They resolved to bring it up to Carter at the River House, and to let Fancher do the talking.

They met. They sat down. And Carter Burden promptly threw them off balance. "Look, we can't get rid of Bartle," he began. "I've checked. My lawyers tell me he can't be gotten out. He's really locked in there." This was the second time he had said that, and the second time he had caught them off guard with it. As Ed Fancher now tried to make clear, they liked Bartle Bull, they had always gotten along with him in the past, before this dispute over Textmasters and this 71-percent thing, and they were asking only to have things go back to the way they were before, not to get rid of him.

"Now, look, Carter," Fancher began. "My contract is up at the end of the year. So is Dan's. And there is no question in my mind that you are under absolutely no obligation to renew it. But, if you *do* want to renew it, there are two conditions that would have to be met in order for me to continue." One, he said, there would have to be a clear delineation of authority between him and Bull, spelling out once and for all exactly who was to do what, and that Burden would have to be party to it. And two, this practice of milking the company, draining it of revenue by borrowing from cash reserves, without paying interest, without raising the dividends to his fellow stockholders, and without offering the minority owners their fair share of the $778,000 he was keeping out, would have to stop.

This was the first time either of them had mentioned this question to their business partner. Burden stood up, grew red in the face, and promptly threw a fit. *"Your stock?* Your stock? Listen, as far as your stock is concerned, my lawyers tell me your stock is worthless. That it's worth absolutely *nothing!"*

He had never spoken to them that way before. Wolf, who had a few vodkas in him, stood up too, and, quietly, said, "Well, Carter, if that's the way you feel about us, there's only one thing to say. This is war. Who do you think you are, saying our stock is worthless? You have no right to say that. You don't give a shit about the *Voice;* you never did. The only thing you care about is your political career. And, Carter, I can embarrass you and your political career. And I will, because if it's a war you want, Carter, then I'll fight."

Burden calmed down first. The red-hot look left his face. "Hey, look,

I didn't mean that," he apologized. "Come on. Let's sit down and talk about something else." For the next two hours their discussion ranged over many things. Ed Fancher brought up the feeling against Bartle at the *Voice,* and the possibility, based on what Newfield and Cowan had said, of a union there. "Well, why the hell did you ever make him president in the first place?" Burden asked. "That wasn't my idea; you didn't even *talk* to me about it. That's what gave him the idea he had more authority than any of us thought he should have." They made the point that it had been a psychological thing, after the massage parlor episode, to give him a title and make him happy. "Well, it's your own fault then," said Burden. "And, incidentally, Ed, you were right about taking those massage parlor ads."

Ed Fancher brought up flexible terms for their renewal. It would have to be for at least two years, but it didn't have to be for five. He offered, for $15,000 a year more, to stop his practice and raise his workweek from 28½ hours to full time. He reiterated that any money taken out of the corporation should be only in dividends so that the minority partners could get their share. And he stressed that the lines of authority that had worked for three and a half years, before Bartle had begun acting up, were good ones. They ought to be continued, reinstituted, and reinforced. With none of this did Carter Burden seem to be in disagreement.

Then Ed Fancher brought up a rumor they had heard from Jack Newfield, that he, Burden, was thinking of selling the *Voice* to *New York* Magazine. Not so, said Burden. He said what he had said before. That he had bank loans and other pressures on him. That he was looking to sell a part of his stock, but in no way all of it, not the *Voice* itself. And did they know of any buyers interested in coming in?

They went to the door. "Well, we've had a good meeting," Carter Burden said. "I think we understand a lot more now. Obviously, what the three of us have to do now is meet with Bartle, right away, say these things to his face, and thrash it out among the four of us. Let's get together this week," he suggested, and said he'd set up the appointment with Bull himself. Fancher and Wolf offered to keep the time open on their calendars.

But they did not meet, not that week, not the next week, not the week after that, while a litany of broken dates, canceled appointments and unreturned phone calls was tersely recorded by Edwin Fancher in his date book:

April 1—Meeting with Carter Burden cancelled. Tried to reach Carter.

April 2—Cancelled by CB.
April 11—2 p.m. Cancelled by him.
April 15—Monday. Meeting with Carter Burden cancelled.
Carter Burden ill.
April 26—4 p.m. meeting with Carter Burden cancelled.

Finally, six weeks later, the four of them met for lunch at La Cocotte Restaurant on East 60th Street in Manhattan, and any notions Edwin Fancher may have had about one big knock-down, drag-out session to settle the whole thing were quickly dispelled when Carter Burden arrived late, with his chauffeur right behind him, continually interrupting, "Mr. Burden, you have a meeting of women to go to on the other side of town." There was barely enough time for Fancher to repeat the points he had made before about the dividends. Burden said nothing to that. Bull said nothing at all. When the subject of rumors of a sale to *New York* came up, Burden simply said what *he* had said before. And that was it. Time to go. They would all have to meet again soon.

Wolf and Fancher had come away from the River House meeting heartened that good lines of communication had been set up at last, that they had finally gotten their message across. They came away from this one feeling that for some reason they were being given the run-around. In the weeks that followed, there were no more meetings. There *were* more phone calls that went unreturned and more appointments that went unkept, and there was a lot of talk between Fancher and Wolf as to why. There was even talk with Bartle Bull about it too, now; he struck them as sincerely trying to set up a meeting, and getting the run-around just like them. And there were many more questions from the writers as to what they were going to do, all of which they had to answer by saying they didn't know. Mary Nichols called Carter Burden's office to inquire. She got no call back. Ron Rosenbaum called Carter Burden's office. He got no call back. Richard Lewisohn, a businessman friend of Fancher's, called him to say he heard the *Voice* was up for sale, and Fancher said no, only that Carter Burden was looking for a new investor. Would he be interested? Maybe, Lewisohn said. He joined Fancher for lunch, met Dan Wolf, and afterwards placed several calls to Burden's office. He got no call back. Meanwhile, Ely Kushel was getting pressed by a Burden family financier for monthly statements more detailed and complex than the usual ones. When he asked, he was told they were to obtain additional bank financing. Ed Fancher recorded five more weeks of frustrated waiting in his notebook:

April 29—Noon meeting with Carter Burden, La Cocotte Restaurant. Carter came late. Carter Burden's chauffeur kept coming in, "Mr. Burden, Mr. Burden," Left before got anywhere. Unsatisfactory. Agreed to meet again soon.
May 20—Called Carter Burden. Didn't get a call back.
May 22—Wednesday. Got call from friend [Lewisohn]. "I hear from the grapevine that the Voice is up for sale." Repeated offer. "Well, yes, I might be interested depending on price." Tried to reach Carter. Called Jane Low. "Look, Carter hasn't called me back. I'm not calling about what he thinks. All I'm asking for is 3 minutes on the phone. I don't want to see him, don't want to meet with him, just 3 minutes."
May 23—Thursday. Told BB other investor interested in VV. He said he'd get CB to call me.
May 28—Tuesday. Dinner with Carter Burden, Dan Wolf, and Bartle Bull. But Carter sick, 2:45. Postponed till Friday.
May 31—Friday. Friday out too. Meeting postponed again. CB meeting postponed till next week.
June 4—Tuesday night. Left for day. Dan called. Carter would like to meet with us at Brook Club.

The message had come from Bartle Bull, who had been informed only ten days before what was up.

★ ★ ★

Strain had been showing in the relationship for some time. In 1972, Bartle Bull, try as he did, was unable to get his friend, Councilman Carter Burden, to work for George McGovern for president. In 1973, Bartle Bull was not campaign manager for the reelection bid of Carter Burden. And now, in the spring of 1974, after four and a half years at the *Village Voice,* faithfully carrying out Carter Burden's wishes, dutifully executing all his demands, obediently applying his pressure, Bartle Bull realized that he had deliberately made himself an unpleasant figure to most of the people he was in contact with. He was tiring of his role as nothing but a support resource to the career ambitions of another man. He was beginning to have ideas and ambitions of his own. He wanted to be publisher of the *Village Voice,* he wanted his friend to make him that and get it over with, and he could not see what was taking him so long.

He *could* see, though, that he very likely no longer qualified for the title "Carter Burden's best friend," that he had been eclipsed by a new, much slicker rival, well-connected in both New York and Washington (where he had served Mayor John Lindsay as the city's official lobbyist), named Peter Tufo. Bull had been watching Tufo for some time, knew Burden was becoming enamored of him, and he did not like it. He did not like Peter Tufo. He did not trust Peter Tufo. And he knew Tufo was giving Carter Burden advice to unload the *Village Voice,* telling him the *Voice* embarrassed him, that he shouldn't be carrying that much debt, that he ought to divest himself of it. So when, in the last week of May, Bull and Burden met for lunch, and Burden belatedly informed his friend what was up, and the terms of the deal he had been busy making, negotiated—naturally—by his newfound friend Peter Tufo, all an incredulous Bartle Bull could say was "Why didn't you tell me?" And Carter Burden told him, "Because you'd have opposed it."

Burden explained the deal to Bull almost the same way he explained it to Wolf and Fancher ten days later: this was a deal for a new investor, nothing more. We get more cash for less stock. We have the bank loan off us now. And, plus, this is the best way to deal with the Dan-and-Ed problem.

His level of annual income was more than handsome enough to suit all but a handful of people in the United States of America for the rest of their lives, but Carter Burden considered himself to be in financial trouble. And he was, at least more so than he had ever been, or let his business partners, Wolf and Fancher, know he was. To the existing credit crunch of his bank loans had been added, in recent months, the extra burden of heavy alimony for his now-divorced wife Amanda, and the decline of his stock portfolio as the economy began its post-oil-embargo nosedive. Carter Burden was being squeezed, and he felt it. He had to, in the parlance of financial circles, "get liquid," and, so he believed, he had to do it in a hurry. As his money worries had been mounting, Carter Burden had seen his investment in the *Village Voice* slipping. It was still netting ten cents on the dollar, phenomenal for publishing; but in the fiscal year before that it had been closer to fourteen. Ad lineage (and income) had been down for the fall of 1973, just before Christmas, and for the spring of 1974. As it had become clear in his own mind that this property of his was never going to produce the amount of money he needed to have, he was getting reports from Bartle Bull, reports that changes would have to be made in the structure of the place but that the two men were resisting change, that Ed Fancher was hopeless managerially and would have to be replaced, that the transition ought to be graceful and gradual, but that Dan Wolf, with his ability to play people like a violin, was capable of making a transition impossible, and, with his indirect intrigues, was already setting him, Bull, up. And, when he met with them at River House, and heard Dan Wolf threaten his political career, Carter Burden decided that Bartle Bull was right, that the *Voice* was a snake pit, that he could now go out and do what he was about to do in good conscience.

So at nine thirty the next morning, June 5, 1974, Daniel Wolf and Edwin Fancher, assuming Carter Burden wanted to meet with them to discuss the possibility of Fancher's friend Lewisohn buying in, journeyed uptown to the Brook Club on East 44th Street, and there met Carter Burden and Bartle Bull. They all sat down, and ordered, and then Carter Burden turned to them and launched into what he had to say: "Dan, Ed, at two o'clock this morning the *Village Voice* was merged with *New York* Magazine."

17.

THE COMPARISONS WITH LORD BEAVER-

brook and Henry Luce were always made too easily. That was not it. The true *persona* of Clay Felker was not some right-wing, blueblood fat cat. It was not, in fact, anyone out of real life at all. It was from television, of all places, that it came, from the central character of the long-since-syndicated smash series, *The Name of the Game*—Glenn Howard.

Glenn Howard. Cool, classy, dapper, polished Glenn Howard. Single, swinging, good-living Glenn Howard, the socially alert, politically with-it publishing magnate who, through dry wit and aggressive trading, somehow survives every episode of intrigue in a world full of swindlers, secret agents, and horny secretaries. There was never any doubt, to those who saw the show, and him in action, too, that, given the financial empire to work with that "Glenn Howard" has, and given actor Gene Barry's (full head of) hair and (trim) waist lines, Clay Felker could step out of any script, the very model in motion. Nor, somehow, did it seem necessary to actually *see* a copy of "Howard Publications' " *Crime* and *People* to know that, off-screen, they looked, read, and *felt* just like *New York* Magazine. Clay Felker and Glenn Howard, Glenn Howard and Clay Felker. Felker, Howard. Howard, Felker. Howard Felker. Howard Glenn. Glenn Felker. Glenn Clay, Clay Glenn. Clay Howard, Howard Clay.

ZOWIE!

★ ★ ★

Clay S. Felker. *"S"* for "Schuette," as in "sooty," a name he, needless to say, did not use. Born, St. Louis, Missouri, October 2, 1925—not 1928, as he later tried to have people believe. It was a journalistic family—his father, Carl, had been managing editor of the *Sporting News,* his mother, Cora, had been a women's editor—but middle-class, not rich—his father, after many years of service for the *Sporting News,* got a pension, but no stock, a fact Clay Felker never forgot. Raised in suburban Webster Groves. At eight, produced his first newspaper. Graduated, Webster Groves High, 1942. Graduated, with time out for stints in the United States Navy and, as a statistician for the old New York Giants, Duke University, Class of '51. Editor of the *Chronicle* while there. Met Peter Maas, who wrote for him there and elsewhere. Met Leslie Aldridge there, too, who wrote for him and married him. (Marriage ended in divorce. Second marriage, to Pamela Tiffin, Hollywood starlet, likewise ended in divorce, 1969.)

A reporter, 1951–57, for *Life,* covering Washington and sports. Moved to New York. Moved, 1957, over to *Esquire* to be feature editor. Ghost-wrote such how-to-do-it articles as "Esquire's Liquor Intelligencer," "The Compleat Evader," and "The Compacht Yacht." Gave, 1960, Norman Mailer the idea to go to Los Angeles and cover the nomination of John Kennedy at the Democratic National Convention, and a slice of journalistic history was made. (Also, about the same time, intro-duced Mailer to the woman who was to become his fifth wife.) Contested Harold Hayes for editorship of the magazine, 1962. Lost, and left. Joined Viking Press as a consulting editor. Hooked on, a year later, with Jock Whitney, who wanted his *Herald-Tribune* to come out with a lively, colorful, pungently written Sunday magazine to compete with the *Times* and the *News,* and wanted Felker to edit it. Working title: *New York.*

New York, under Felker, turned out to be the outstanding success story of the *Trib* in its later years, running against the tide of its decline and eventual death. It was, with Jimmy Breslin and Peter Maas and Gloria Steinem and George "Adam Smith" Goodman and Tom Wolfe (his articles on Junior Johnson, Ken Kesey, and William Shawn all appeared under its aegis) among those on board, a literary as well as a commercial success. It survived the merger into the *World-Journal-Tribune,* and, when even *that* did not survive, it still went on.

Clay Felker had been expecting May 2, 1967, before it happened. He took his *W-J-T* severance pay—$6,575—and bought all rights to the *New York* logo, the breezy, script face "NEW YORK" designed by his friend and editorial assistant, Milton Glaser. Then he went out to get himself some money. At forty-two years of age, with his latest horse just shot out from under him, Clay Felker was through working for other people. He would never again be someone else's employee, not if he could help it.

He went to Armand Erpf, a Wall Street financier whom he knew. Erpf, a suave septuagenarian, was taken with Felker, and with his idea for a smart-looking, self-supporting urban service magazine aimed at New York's free-spending, high-living, new money class. He took Felker around on his party circuit, introduced Clay to his moneymen friends, and set out assembling a syndicate.

He put his own money in. He got other wealthy friends and contacts to do so—Edgar Bronfman, board chairman of Seagrams, and the two John Loebs, Sr. and Jr., of the investment banking house of Loeb, Rhoades, and others. By October of 1967 he had raised $1.1 million.

But there were restrictions on that money. Armand Erpf's people might be impressed with what they had seen of Clay Felker, so far, but they were not yet impressed that he had any business sense, and they wanted controls. There had to be directors from the financial community—A. Robert Towbin, of C. E. Unterberg, Towbin, agreed to be one, and to invest some of his own money. So did Alan J. Patricof, head of his own business consulting–venture capitalist firm. Armand Erpf had to be chairman of the corporation. And Clay Felker could not be publisher.

To those conditions, Clay Felker, having little choice in the matter, said yes. But he never ceased to think of himself as a businessman first and foremost, never stopped wanting to run his own show someday.

He would keep his mouth shut at business meetings like a child being sent to prep school, Bob Towbin recalled. Towbin had met Felker before, back in 1963, through George Goodman (the businessman who used "Adam Smith" as his *nom de plume),* when he had still been at the *Tribune,* and been sounding out business people even then about starting up his own magazine. Nothing had come of it at the time, but later, when Towbin had seen that Felker had been promoted within the *Trib* hierachy and stayed with *New York* after all, he had remembered, and kept it in mind that Felker was a man who might need watching.

He had nominees for the publisher's job—all flunkies of his, Towbin said they were—but the board looked elsewhere. It was Alan Patricof who brought up the name of George Hirsch, former executive with Time-Life International, young (still in his thirties), and, as his avocation, an accomplished distance runner (he had finished in the top quarter of the Boston Marathon). Hirsch looked good to the board, and they picked him.

The first skeleton staff was hired. Milton Glaser came aboard as art director and Judith Crist as movie critic. A studio was acquired on East 32nd Street and converted into offices. The first direct-mail solicitation, for charter subscribers, went out, and, in April 1968, so did the first issue.

Which was, Clay Felker would concede later, "before it was ready." The magazine was going to be all about "New York and good writing," said its prospectus, and in the early issues of *New York* there *was* good writing—Gloria Steinem on John Lindsay walking the streets of Harlem the night of Martin King's murder, on Gene McCarthy and Richard Nixon campaigning for president; Tom Wolfe on the etiquette of street fighting; Breslin on Joe Namath and Robert Kennedy. But there was also an editorial identity crisis, an ungainly dichotomy between the Black Power fist that adorned one cover and the chic *dolce vita* value systems glorified inside on the ad and service pages. Something had to give. And, expecially after the magazine ran a nude spread of Andy Warhol's model Viva, something did.

The first issue, 132 pages long, ran 64 pages of ads. The second, 68 pages long, ran 12. For the rest of 1968, the average number of ad pages was 9. For the rest of 1968, *New York* Magazine lost $2 million. With funds running dangerously low, the investor-directors organized an emergency second financing in November of that year that brought in another $1.6 million, saved the magazine, and resulted in Alan Patricof, who had been especially effective raising funds, being made president of the company. The next year, Erpf arranged the purchase of a conference center in upstate Tarrytown, New York, as a money-making instrument, and the company successfully went public, at $10 a share to start—attracting such a motley group of small investors as (among others) Edwin Fancher, publisher of the *Village Voice* (100 shares), Daniel Wolf, editor (600), and Frank Sinatra, singer. And, when an article by Nicholas Pileggi about the torture of apartment hunting drew unprecedented reader response, Clay Felker had found his editorial formula: "We as journalists looked too long and too lovingly at the hippies, yippies, protesters and rock groups," he decided. "They are no longer, to use the cliché, relevant. What *is* relevant is that you can go broke on $80,000 a year, that you can't get an apartment, that there are new pressures on marriage, and new ways to make money." From that point on, said one of his editors, "we're editing the magazine for the people Clay had lunch with today, for the people I had lunch with yesterday, for the people we see all the time." The short, violent shakedown cruise of Clay Felker and his magazine was over. The long, violent *rest* of the cruise was about to begin.

★ ★ ★

American magazines will never be the same, thanks to Clay Felker. In only a few years, he totally changed what they were about—their structure, their content, even their purpose. He wrought a revolution in his industry. He set its pace. He was its envy.

Through his sidekick and editorial partner Milton Glaser, he left a permanent visual legacy—breezy, blazing, slick-looking covers, eye-catching graphics, liberal use of color, artful use of white space, and, not least, those tantalizing toplines that teased with their knowledge of just "how" and "why" everything was done. And inside his magazine, Clay Felker patented a style, a style that told his readers just what they wanted to hear about—which was, according to him, "how the power game is played," and, even more important, "who are the winners."

"This is the Rome, the Athens, the Paris of its time," Clay Felker said of his city, and he and his audience lived it up accordingly. Clay's People were the ones who trafficked in the world of limos and discos and

Sunday brunches, who went to the right art exhibits and the right opening nights and the right fashion shows and the right preview screenings and the right parties, and who knew just what to discuss there—Nelson Rockefeller's latest blunder and Teddy Kennedy's latest scandal and Diane von Furstenberg's latest line, movie stars and meditation, open marriage and commodity futures and snorting coke. The basic *New York* reader, it seemed from reading the magazine, was expected to be able to pick up the latest Pucci (or Gucci) at Bloomingdale's (or Saks), have sex with their psychiatrist, swing on over to Sotheby Parke Bernet to get in a bid at the auction, rustle up a table for dinner at Elaine's (or Nicola's), dance the Hustle at Wednesday's, be seen at Regine's, get picked up by a whip-wielding bisexual at Maxwell's Plum, stop by P. J. Clarke's for a late hamburger, and decide between the Hamptons or Fire Island for the summer—all in a twenty-four-hour period.

It was shlock, of course. It was a show, put on for an audience of *arrivistes* who lived in penis envy of their *New Yorker* counterparts, who had to be *seen* acting rich in order to be sure they were. But, when it worked, there was nobody better at it than Clay Felker, the man who invented it. And, when he decided he needed more of them, Clay Felker would let would-be readers in on just what they were missing:

Is it true that you had to ask ''What?'' when your very best friend mentioned omnisexuality—the new look in discotheques? . . .

Is it true that you haven't yet had a primal scream when others in therapy screamed long ago, and are now into silent meditation? . . .

If you sometimes wish that once—just once—it was *you* who had heard it first, and who were standing there in the center of the room with Jackie, Ari, Punch, Truman, Abe, Birgit, Lenny, Mick, Liza, Yoko. Rocky, Hermione, Raquel, Tennessee, Teddy, Rudi, Stacy, Barbra, Billie Jean, and all the rest hanging on your every word . . .

. . . *the enclosed card can be of help* . . . *It gets you a trial subscription to NEW YORK* . . .

. . . Is it totally safe now to pour California, or do some snobs still insist on French? . . . Where's the ''must'' place for lunching these days? What's the new executive garb . . . Where to find the best coffee, the right weight-loss club, TM, pizza, the best buys in wine, the right real-estate agent in

Putnam County, nearby campsites, ice cream, gardening supplies, antiques, dog trainers . . .

Bisexuality—Judy Klemesrud on how it's showing up in fashion, in hairstyles, in bars, and in bed . . .

What it's like to find yourself naked on a New York Street . . .

How to write a pornographic book . . .

What it's like to lose your husband to voyeurism . . .

Can adultery save your marriage? . . .

Office politics: Where you stand is where you sit . . .

What your bed sheets tell about you . . .

How, when, and why to fire your shrink . . .

He did not give much in interviews, if he gave an interview at all, but Clay Felker did reveal himself once, perhaps more of himself, and what he was about, than he had planned to, in an article he wrote for the prestigious *Antioch Review*. It was called "Life Cycles in the Age of Magazines." Referring back to the practices of his former employer, *Esquire,* Felker said that new magazines must, as it did, "employ a subtle, sophisticated formula for a literate and active, Upwardly Mobile audience. . . . Print must be for the educated and affluent élite, providing something that cannot be put on the home TV set."

Print for the élite: that was it. And so Clay Felker titillated his audience with tales of money and power and sex—"classy trash," one of his best writers, Richard Reeves, called it. He fed them a steady editorial diet, equal parts de rigueur, savoir faire, avant garde, bon vivant, and nouveau riche. He told them, every year, who New York's Ten Most Powerful People were, and the salaries 100 of its best-known celebrities were making. And he prettied up his package with an editing style that employed adverbs, question marks, and exclamation points the way Helen Gurley Brown used parentheses in *Cosmopolitan,* and for much the same purpose—the come-on.

The fact that those cover come-ons promised what was impossible to deliver on the inside pages was not the only objection to be made on journalistic grounds against Clay Felker's *New York.* Some of the objections cut deeper. They questioned whether what appeared in his magazine qualified as journalism at all.

It was not as if Clay Felker was all bad. Certainly, there were those far worse than he was—case in point, his main competition in the field of city service magazines, Herbert Lipson *(Philadelphia, Boston),* a man with a truly black track record of revolving-door editors, publication-promised-but-never-paid-for stories, and staged, phony cover shots. And when he was good, Clay Felker could be very, very good. He published the marvelous political reportage of Richard Reeves, the superb investigative reporting of Nicholas Pileggi, the cultural criticism of Judith Crist and John Simon, the financial coverage of Andrew Tobias and Dan Dorfman. He published "Adam Smith" and David Halberstam and Gloria Steinem, Tom Wolfe's "Radical Chic," Jack Newfield's "The Ten Worst Judges in New York" (a story idea he thought up), and pieces that skewered Nelson Rockefeller and Henry Kissinger well before the bloom had fallen off their rose with the rest of the media. He pioneered with such regular columns as "Best Bets," "The Urban Strategist," "The Passionate Shopper," and "The Underground Gourmet," the new wave of bargain basement-*cum*-urban survival-*cum*-consumer protection features in magazines.

But when he was bad, it was as Felker himself wrote in *Antioch Review* when he said, "In magazines in which status is the chief incentive, the articles may be shorter, or rehashed from other material with which the writer is already familiar. The form will often be that of an essay which can be written off the top of the head." There were stories that appeared in *New York* Magazine, about sensitive subjects such as adultery and street gangs and sex criminals in suburbia and psychiatrists who seduce their patients, stories that deserved serious treatment, but that, to the unjaundiced eye, appeared to be deliberately superficial, or poorly researched, or sensationalized. And, in several spectacular instances, it went even beyond that.

In 1971, *New York Times* reporter Fred Ferretti sued the magazine, claiming that an article he had written for it had appeared, using his language, under the byline of Jimmy Breslin. Four years later, *New York* settled out of court, the magazine and Breslin printing an apology.

On the third anniversary of the Chappaquiddick incident, *New York* ran a piece, complete with aerial photography, entitled "The Perfect Alibi That Teddy Overlooked," claiming that a sandspit connecting the island to the rest of Martha's Vineyard would have been Edward Kennedy's perfect cover story for his actions the night Mary Jo Kopechne drowned. One month later, the magazine had to run a letter from writer Jim Roy, conceding that said sandspit was not there yet in July 1969. "My research was, alas, remiss, and the story is in error," he wrote. "My apologies."

That same summer, a piece by author Albert Goldman, "I Have Seen the Future—And It's Fire Island," described a "surf-pounded isle, where the ordinary costume is a bikini and the ordinary mattress is a beach and the invitation of the thick, dark, sensuously enveloping night is ACTION! . . . Orgy is a grand old tradition on Fire Island." To complaints about its accuracy, Goldman replied that his "article was intended as a broad-scale picture (built up, like star photography, from dozens of discrete but superimposed impressions) of a region where I have resided, on and off, for thirteen years." Then an editor for the *Fire Island News* did a piece of his own, for [*MORE*] Magazine, exposing Goldman's methodology—he had visited Fire Island only five of the previous thirteen summers, and for less than twenty-four hours in 1972, the year he was writing his supposedly authoritative piece, his piece had already been written *before* he came out, his inexperienced, nonjournalist girlfriend had done what little "interviewing" there was, and, taken as a whole, "Goldman's story was a piece of unlabeled fiction." In the article, *New York* executive editor Byron Dobell was quoted as saying he didn't "give a damn how Goldman got his information or who his informants were," that the piece was "clearly an impressionistic piece with no pretense to objectivity," and that "of course I wish morality and truth to triumph, but in the meantime let's at least have art."

In 1971, Gail Sheehy wrote a series for the magazine, the basis for her book *Hustling,* describing the world of New York City's prostitutes. One piece described a hooker "Redpants" and her pimp "Sugarman," who appeared from the article to be real people. But, as it turned out, "Redpants" and "Sugarman" were "composites," based on notes she had taken in her interviews, *plus details fictionalized from out of her imagination.* Exposed by the *Wall Street Journal,* Clay Felker told the paper that, in such cases, "We are going to be more careful in the future about alerting the reader."

In 1973, Aaron Latham wrote a profile for the magazine of Sally Quinn as she left the *Washington Post* for New York and the *CBS Morning News.* Quinn, a friend of Latham's, cooperated, and did not suspect anything until she was asked to pose, in a nightie, in bed, as "The Girl You Want to Wake Up With Every Morning." When the article appeared, her worst fears were realized. Her friend Latham had relentlessly depicted her as a dizzy chippie ("At a Washington dinner party, Sally Quinn was the center of attention as she verbally measured many of the town's most prominent politicians. Her conversation was a Gallup Poll of penis sizes").

That same summer Latham did another profile of another friend, Gay Talese, in another unguarded moment, following Talese, at work on a long-awaited, much-obsessed-with book about sex in America, around a nude health spa. "An Evening in the Nude with Gay Talese," when it appeared ("Amy reached out and took hold of Gay's penis as calmly as if it had been a pool cue. . . . 'I'm going to tear it off,' she said"), publicly finished the subject's friendship with the author, and very nearly his own, rocked marriage as well. It caused David Halberstam temporarily to withdraw from contributing to the magazine in protest on behalf of his wounded friend, Talese. But it caused Clay Felker no grief at all. "The Talese and Quinn pieces were magnificent," he told an interviewer in 1975. "Those articles were a mistake only in the sense that they gave our enemies, wherever they may be, a club to beat up on us with."

But the Talese and Quinn pieces were not magnificent. They were hatchet jobs, made meaner by the fact that the subjects did not realize what Latham intended to do with the side of themselves they were showing him, and more incestuous by the specter of one journalist humiliating and cannibalizing another for the sake, not of news, but of literary gossip.

But that was Clay Felker. He was a packager, a promoter, not a publisher. In fact, had his own magazine been scrutinized by one of his consumer service features, it would have had to be included under "Consumer Beware"—and when the two professional journals of press criticism, [MORE] and the Columbia Journalism Review, examined him, both found him ethically wanting. Even at his best, he was still putting out the kind of issue he did one week in the late summer of 1975, when an earnest plea by labor mediator Theodore Kheel* advocating regional government for Metropolitan New York appeared in his magazine, in between something called the "Diet Soda Taste-Off" and a slavishly name-dropping report on what the literati were doing in the Hamptons this summer (mostly, it appeared, drinking, talking about one another, and giving interviews to New York Magazine). By any rational yardstick, there was no escaping the conclusion that Clay Felker's magazine was never anything more than a very exciting piece of junk—and that he, try as he might, was never anything more than a Little Citizen Kane Who Couldn't.

★ ★ ★

He also wrote, "The vitality of a magazine depends not on great publishing organizations, precision editorial formulas, vivid promotion, or high-powered salesmen but on the vitality of one man's editorial dream." He also said, many times, "I edit by what interests me." Whatever else it was, New York Magazine was not a "writers'

---

*Kheel was more than just a labor mediator. He was a personal friend of Clay Felker's, lawyer for New York Magazine Company, and, since 1974, one of its board of directors.

newspaper." It was an editors' magazine, where the writers reflected the point of view of the editors, and the editors reflected the point of view of Clay Felker.

His personality imposed itself on everyone and everything. It was his magazine, and the magazine was his life. It, and what was going to go into it next week, were all he ever talked about. He had a single-minded, monomaniac's determination to make it with this vehicle of his, this time. Every cocktail party he attended, every dinner he sat down to, every get-together he threw at his duplex on East 57th Street, just off Sutton Place, was a reconnaissance patrol. He was constantly on the prowl for information, quizzing his hosts and guests, on the lookout for some new trend he could put between the covers of his magazine, notorious for interrupting the sleep of his writers with late night–early morning phone calls, badgering, importuning, interrogating: "Who's hot? What's in?" "Stars" were what he was interested in. "Stars" were what he had at his magazine—not writers. He made a "star," perhaps the biggest one in his galaxy, out of his steady girlfriend, Gail Sheehy. And, long before the Latham piece, he promised to do the same for Sally Quinn—in a line she, going him one better, repeated on the Dick Cavett show and used as the title of her book about her CBS experience. He was an impresario, a producer, and he lived a style of life accordingly, a lifestyle that, with its conspicuous consumption and compulsive partygoing, might have been deduced as the efforts of a Midwestern Outsider with an inferiority complex trying just a little too hard to get himself accepted in the Big City.

He was also, with his paunch, his vanishing head of brown-going-on-white hair, and his face that could turn beet-red in a flash whenever he decided to get angry, what seemed to be a prime candidate for a heart attack. Except that Clay Felker never got heart attacks. He gave them.

His temper was legendary. He could erupt like a shot, as if jump-started by some defective cable transmitting berserk energy all through his nervous system, shriek and holler and bellow and bark, and then, just like that, it would all be over. His tantrums came, blew themselves out, and went. One person who found that out was Clark Whelton, one day in April of 1971 when, having just been offered a chance to go on staff at the *Village Voice* for $150 a week, he received a phone call from Felker, offering him a contributing editorship at *New York* for $300. He'd been reading Whelton's stuff in the *Voice,* he said. He liked it. "But people don't take the *Voice* seriously. You've got no future there. Come here. You'll be closely edited here. I'll do for you what I did for Gloria Steinem. I'll make you a star"—that line again. And then, just as Whelton was thinking maybe he didn't *want* to be closely edited, that he wasn't sure he *wanted* what was going to happen to him here, he heard, on the other end of the line, an art director approach Clay Felker with a question about next week's cover, and heard the editor of *New York* Magazine begin to scream that *RED SELLS, RED IS VISIBLE, EVERY WEEK IT'S RED, NOW I WANT RED ON THAT COVER,* and then turn back to finish, normal as could be, his conversation. Clark Whelton said he'd need twenty-four hours to think about it, and called back the next day: he was going to the *Voice.* Felker's reaction: "You're crazy. You're being ripped off."

Whelton was not all they competed for. They competed for ads, especially after the *Voice* began seriously looking for national advertising, for readers—about one in three *Voice* readers also read *New York* Magazine—and, on a purely prestige basis, for the bragging rights around town to having started the New Journalism. Edwin Fancher and Daniel Wolf did not know much about Clay Felker—Wolf knew him not at all, Fancher had met him only once at a cocktail party—but neither had any respect for the editorial product he put out; "empty" was Wolf's verdict. But then neither went so far as to sell their stock in it, either; and, if they did not care for him, other people did, and still others, no matter how he may have offended them on one occasion, took care not to let it rupture the relationship permanently. Clay Felker could publish awful stuff about someone, or someone close to them, and still retain their friendship, or be able to start it up again later. Thus, despite all the dreadful things his writer Aaron Latham had written about her writer Sally Quinn, he remained the very good friend of Mrs. Katharine Graham, publisher of the *Washington Post* and chairman of the board of the *Washington Post* Company. And, even though his writer Julie Baumgold had done a denigrating profile of Carter and Amanda Burden, *après le divorce,* lines of communication with the councilman remained open.

★ ★ ★

Nineteen seventy-one was the year *New York* Magazine, after its shaky start, broke even. It was also the year the tenuous power relationships that got it that far came undone.

The year began with Jimmy Breslin, founding contributor, making trouble. The magazine was "boring, static, predictable, and nominally written," he said. "Too dilettantish for me." That, and he wanted more stock in it. "I put my complaints in private for months, but nothing happened," he told *Women's Wear Daily*—so he started going public. And then, on February 1, 1971—just as, according to board member Bob Towbin, he had agreed to Breslin's demand that Clay Felker must go—Armand Erpf keeled over at his desk on Wall Street and died.

Also according to Bob Towbin, he called Felker at the magazine as soon as he got the news. "Yes, I just heard," Felker told him. "I want to see you this afternoon." So the two men had lunch. And, over lunch, Clay Felker said, "Bob, now that Armand's dead, there's something I want you to know. I've got to be made chairman of the board and chief executive officer of the company."

Armand Erpf's body was barely cold yet. Robert Towbin was aghast. But he kept his feelings, his feelings that this was a cruel and a self-destructive man whose presence he was in, to himself, and just said, "Clay, let me give you a little advice. Don't say a word to the others on the board of what you just said to me. I'll call them." And he did, polling them on their sentiment. Their answer was no—sort of. Alan Patricof, not Felker, took Armand Erpf's title as chairman. But Clay got some of what he wanted—he took Patricof's title of president. Soon he had more.

Within a few weeks, Breslin, after calling mass meetings of the writers and otherwise threatening action, walked out on the magazine—and took only Peter Maas with him. It was "by mutual consent because Mr. Breslin was too busy with other things to contribute articles to *New York*," the magazine's official statement said. It was "a tempest in a teapot," Clay Felker said. By that summer, George Hirsch was out too.

They had had only one substantial disagreement—Hirsch wanted a *Life*-size magazine, Felker wanted *Time*-size, and Felker won—but Clay Felker had never wanted George Hirsch there in the first place, and now that Armand Erpf was gone his days were numbered. George Hirsch knew it, knew he could not keep up with Felker's incessant, implicit ultimata to the board that he be given total control or else, knew he could never keep up with every demand and accusation and complaint Felker had to make about him and his alleged interference, knew he could not compete with their presumption about Clay's indispensability, and could feel his support among them ebbing away. He was right. That summer, Hirsch concluded his position was untenable and resigned. Clay Felker took his title.*

Now he was almost everything—editor, publisher, president of the company. Now it was Clay Felker's show, indisputably. And in the next two years, with him in total control, *New York* continued to sail—to nearly 400,000 circulation, to ninth place (and eventually seventh) in total ad pages among American magazines, to profits of $401,000 on over $9.7 million in sales. That was four cents on the dollar, and that

---

*In 1973, George Hirsch, as publisher, launched *New Times* Magazine.

was remarkable for a magazine still only five years old, but it should have been more, and would have been but for three things. One, *New York* had not found, as most magazines do not, a way out of the seasonal cycle of advertising revenue. It still made all its profit in the spring and fall quarters, and still lost money in the winter and summer. Two, as many magazines that try to establish a significant advertising base do, it had deliberately sought to build up a circulation of subscribers through the mails (eight out of nine copies went to readers that way). Such subscriptions cost magazines money to maintain, especially if they try to bloat the numbers by offering discounts, as *New York* did. And three, Clay Felker liked to spend money, especially if it was other people's.

He just was not a businessman. He simply could not live within his means, and he would not have known what an accurate budget projection was if he had tripped over one. That was not readily apparent yet to the outside world, but it was to his partners, who had the thankless task of trying to restrain him. And, far from being restrained, Clay Felker wanted to expand.

The pilot issue of Gloria Steinem's *Ms.* was market-tested as a *New York* insert; but she eventually published her magazine independently. *Couples,* another insert, devoted to the state of the sexes in America, did not make it. Paris and London versions of *New York* were considered, and dropped. Finally, Clay Felker thought he had it: he announced, in May 1973, the acquisition of *Los Angeles* Magazine for $500,000—and then, almost immediately, when there arose some dispute over the magazine's true circulation figures, the deal was off again, and fell through.

But still he did not give up the idea of expansion, of establishing the outposts of empire. For, as he had written in his *Antioch Review* piece, "there appears to be an almost inexorable life-cycle of American magazines that follows the pattern of humans. A clamorous youth eager to be noticed; vigorous, productive middle-age marked by an easy-to-define editorial line; a long slow decline, in which efforts at revival are sporadic and tragically doomed." And when wild-card factors began to enter the picture—a tripling of paper costs in the next five years, the chilling effect of new U.S. postal rates—Clay Felker could anticipate that a glossy, weekly, localized magazine like *New York* was only going to be able to go so far. If he wanted to go national, he would have to have something else.

And there was always the *Village Voice.*

★ ★ ★

He and Carter Burden had talked about a possible deal between them involving their two publications long before June 5, 1974—eighteen months before, in fact. As early as December 1972 Felker had come to Alan Patricof with the possibility of buying the *Village Voice*. It was Felker who had taken the initiative when he heard rumors Burden was looking to sell, and who kept it up, despite the dubiousness of his board chairman, all through 1973—over dinners in the city, out at the Hamptons during the summer. "We've just started to make money. Isn't it too soon?" Patricof wondered. No, said Clay Felker. *Newspapers make economic sense. And we can't make* New York *national. The magazine business is going down the tubes. We've got to diversify.* Then Patricof questioned the pricetag Felker was willing to pay Burden: $8 million, straight cash. "Clay, there's no way you can pay these guys that kind of money," Patricof told him. In his view, the deal had to be cash *and stock*—and the board backed him up. As late as December 1973, the magazine's directors were officially against buying the *Voice*.

But Clay Felker persisted, and in his capacity as chief executive officer, went ahead and appointed Felix Rohatyn, member of Lazard, Freres, a man who within the year would be using his gift for financial *legerdemain* in various eleventh-hour attempts to rescue the City of New York from bankruptcy, to negotiate for him with Peter Tufo, acting on behalf of Carter Burden. By the last week of April, fully several days before Burden sat down with his erstwhile best friend and two business partners for the meeting at La Cocotte Restaurant that struck them as so curiously unproductive, the discussions had reached the sensitive stage, and remained so for the next six weeks while details were hacked out. By the middle of May, Clay Felker was bringing Carter Burden over to Robert Towbin's house in the Hamptons for Towbin to meet him and have a look at the tentative agreement.

Towbin, a little annoyed that Clay had gone ahead on his own, looked the papers over closely. "Clay, from my point of view, this is a great deal," he advised him. "But mark my words: I don't think we ought to do it.

"Look, Clay," he explained, "as much as we fight, this is your magazine. You can do anything you want with it." But he had looked over all the statements, seen how the *Voice* was run, and he said, "If you buy this, Clay, you're going to be getting into bed with business types, who have financial statements, who have their own investment advisers. I don't think you ought to do it. But if you really *want* to," he relented, "then I'll vote for it."

Clay Felker really wanted to, and Bob Towbin voted for it. But first there was the matter of Clay Felker's contract. At this stage of developments, Felker introduced the point that Carter Burden wanted him to have a long-term contract—and that he, with his new added duties, would have to have more money, more stock, more bonuses, and more perks. There was some bucking to that on the board*—after all, Clay had gotten 30 percent of the corporation to start with in 1968, and had kept 30 percent while they diluted their own holdings for the second financing, so he could give stock away to friends of his like Goodman and Breslin and Glaser—but Clay Felker got his way again. Alan Patricof was appointed to negotiate new contracts with him and Glaser, the magazine's incorporation charter with the State of Delaware was amended to permit the creation of new stock, and hands were shaken all over on the deal at 10 P.M. the night of Tuesday, June 4. It took four more hours for the lawyers to draw up the documents to be signed, and then it was done.

Officially, it was neither a sale nor a merger; it was a transfer of stock. Taurus Communications retained its identity, but was absorbed as a wholly owned subsidiary into a reorganized *New York* Magazine Company. The company—NYM Co. for short—agreed to absorb a stated total of $2.5 million in Taurus's bank debts,† to fulfill its obligations to Wolf, Fancher, and the others, and, for $800,000 cash, to give it 603,000-odd shares of stock, representing 34-percent control, in the company (prorated, individually, according to their ratio of Taurus ownership, so that Carter Burden received roughly $560,000, 425,000 shares, and 24 percent, and Bartle Bull roughly $240,000, 178,000 shares, and 10 percent). Clay Felker and Milton Glaser got new, five-year employment contracts. Felker got a raise from $80,000 to $120,000 (just short of the $125,000 he wanted), with bonuses if growth reached 7 percent per year (since his own projections called for 8.75-percent growth, he only had to meet 80 percent of his own promised levels to collect). In addition, the company made cash loans, at $2 a share each, to Felker, to buy 75,000 shares ($150,000), and Glaser, to buy 25,000 ($50,000). Finally, the board itself was reconstituted. Carter Burden

---

*Which, with Erpf's death and subsequent additions to it, now consisted of Felker, Glaser, Patricof, and Towbin; James Q. Wilson, Harvard government professor, expert on the criminal justice system, and friend of Felker's; and Thomas Kempner, general partner in Loeb, Rhoades and friend of Patricof's and Towbin's.

†Which figure remains one of the great unresolved discrepancies in this entire episode. In other releases describing the arrangement, the debt is listed as $1.8 million. Edwin Fancher, for one, was convinced the difference was due to Carter Burden's $778,000 in outstanding money being included in the first, higher figure, and though that seemed likely, none of the participants in the deal was subsequently able to explain it, one way or the other.

became vice-chairman. Bartle Bull became a director. So did *New York Magazine* counsel Theodore Kheel. And so, with 250 shares, did Peter Tufo. Carter Burden and Clay Felker entered into an agreement, under which the two men would vote, via a complicated formula, for each other's future nominees to the board, and have the rights of first refusal on any sale of each other's stock,* which agreement was not to expire until December 31, 1979. But there was a catch.

The catch was that if the company went one full year—not one full calendar year, but for example, the fall quarter of one year followed by the first three quarters of the next—without showing a profit in any one quarter, the agreement was invalidated. But naturally, since *New York Magazine* was already showing a profit two quarters every year, and the *Village Voice* always showed a profit, no one expected that to happen. No one. Naturally.

★ ★ ★

That summer, at a "Management Seminar" symposium, reflecting on how he had handled the Jimmy Breslin showdown three years before and how he had just handled the other showdown he was now going to cause, Clay Felker would say, "Editorial revolts . . . have to do with the basic root of all disagreements, which is money and control, except that when you're dealing with intelligent young journalists who came out of civil-rights movements and the peace movements, they are clever enough now to always cloak money issues and control issues in the rhetoric of independence and editorial integrity, which makes it much harder to deal with."

It was a slogan he lived by. It was going to make a marvelous epitaph.

---

*A crucial, subsequent Catch-22—Patricof wanted the *company* to have first refusal on Burden's stock; Felker demanded, and got, an extraordinary *personal* right of first refusal.

18. WHEN CARTER BURDEN DROPPED HIS

little bombshell on them over breakfast at the Brook Club the morning of June 5, Dan Wolf and Edwin Fancher went into shock.

They had nothing to say. There was nothing they could say. After all these years with their newspaper, working it up from nothing until it was one of the most important forces in American journalism and they were living in comfort they had never dreamed possible, they were being told, matter-of-factly, by someone they had trusted explicitly, that it, and they, had been delivered into the hands of someone else. It was the absolute worst thing that could have happened. It was just what they had been most afraid of, and now it had come to pass. It was just what Carter Burden had said to them was *not* going to happen, and it was happening. They might lose their jobs. Worse, they might even lose their newspaper. And at that moment there didn't appear to be a goddamn thing in the world they could do about it.

And to *Felker*. Dan Wolf could feel the disgust in him rising as he listened to Carter Burden drone smoothly on that this was just a business merger, that *New York* Magazine has certain strengths we can use, strengths like promotion, circulation, and marketing, but that there was every intention of keeping the publications separate, that Bartle and I have 34 percent of them according to this deal, that we'll be in control no matter what, and that you two will receive an offer to buy out your stock if you want it.

Finally, Wolf managed to get out that they considered *New York* Magazine to be their chief competitor. And he told Carter Burden he was shocked.

Bartle Bull, who struck them as acting nervous, who had let Carter do all the talking thus far and avoided eye contact with them, now spoke up to say that he was getting a new, two-year contract to continue as president of the *Voice*. Edwin Fancher then added, "What will our role be?"

That remained to be seen, Carter Burden said. They couldn't be sure. Francher pressed him: "Well, does that mean we're out, then?" Burden said, "No, not necessarily. We just have to see how things work out." Then he went on to describe the financial details, said he would have to go right back after breakfast to put the finishing touches on the press release, and asked to meet with the staff as soon as possible to explain it to them personally.

They finished breakfast. Carter Burden went his way, and the other three hailed a cab. By now, it had sunk in what had happened, and as

383

they stepped inside Dan Wolf turned to his partner, Ed Fancher, and said, "I don't know how I'm going to tell them now. How am I going to handle this?" That was what upset him more than anything else. At fifty-nine years of age, after nineteen years of it, he could stand going— but there were other people, who felt they needed him, and what about them?

The three of them talked little on the way downtown. When they got out, Fancher went over to see his patients. Wolf went in and told everyone—writers and editors, whoever was there. Bartle Bull called in his assistant, George Dillehay. "Sounds interesting," Dillehay reacted. "I think it's going to be good," Bull said. Then the four—Dillehay, Bull, Wolf, and Fancher, who rejoined them—went out to a Village restaurant, the Dardanelles, for lunch. They all seemed a little tense, a little drained, George Dillehay remembered of his lunch partners that day, and when it came to talking about Clay Felker, and what life was going to be like under him, they tried to find only optimistic things to say.

When they finally got alone that day, Dan Wolf and Ed Fancher began to discuss what they should do now. They knew that they had been screwed, that their contractual right of first refusal had been violated,* but they decided to wait, to see what Burden would have to say, see what it would be like working with Felker, to make the best out of the situation for the time being. They had not called Burden on the right of first refusal that morning to his face, and, with their thoughts collected, they did not call him on it now.

★ ★ ★

In these crucial first forty-eight hours, Clay Felker made no direct contact downtown himself. Instead, he stayed right where he was and made soothing public statements.

Privately, he was making contingency plans to put out the paper from the offices of *New York* and hire a whole new staff if there were any kind of mass staff walkout—shades of *l'affaire* Breslin. And he had problems of his own. Richard Reeves, his star political writer, was restive about the deal, implying he would leave the magazine when his contract was up because of Carter Burden's presence on his board of

---

*Of course, there are two sides to every legal story; and had the subsequent lawsuit gone all the way to trial, this is one of the points that would have had to be adjudicated. Obviously, Carter Burden had signed a document with his business partners in 1970 giving them first refusal on any sale of the newspaper he might make to any putative new owner, and just as obviously, the paper now had a new owner—without any first refusal being offered to them. But for legal purposes, Carter Burden could claim he had not "sold" it—only exchanged his stock in it for stock in something else—and the *New York* agreement certainly seemed designed in such a way as to circumvent that "first refusal" clause.

directors. "How can I [write about him] when he owns a piece of what I write?" he was quoted in *Time*. And, he told [*MORE*], "someday he and Clay are going to have a real showdown."

But to do nothing, for now, proved the right thing. Clay Felker stayed behind while Carter Burden went to talk to them instead. That solved one important problem for him. Hardly anybody blamed him for what happened after that.

★ ★ ★

It had been on her door a long time. Someone had once, for a joke, taken a photo from a cover of the *New York Times* Sunday magazine, one that went with its inside story of Carter and Amanda Burden, showing the Happy Couple in happier days, and inserted into Carter's mouth, cartoon-balloon-style, the words "I've got a surprise for you, Mary. I've just sold the *Voice* to Tony Scotto."

It had hung there ever since. But now that it was a real surprise, the joke did not seem so funny anymore.

★ ★ ★

Beginning with lunch the first day, the Family had begun to gather in groups to discuss what to do—and got nowhere.

They just could not get it together. They could not agree on any plan of action. They could not even, apparently, speak the same language. After all these years of being disorganized on purpose, they could not organize now. That was just not the nature of being a writer for the *Voice,* and it was evident from that first day it was not going to change at this late date.

Some were still angry at Dan and Ed over the money issue, and blamed *them* for what had happened. Most wanted Dan and Ed to stay, and to get a guarantee that they would—but some wanted that strictly as protection for themselves, not out of any love for the two men. Not all of them were against Felker either—Flaherty and New-field, to name two, had been happy writing for him. So the writers, with their crisscrossing, divided loyalties, did nothing, and the thought had already begun to dawn on at least some of them that, if worse came to worst, and Dan and Ed *were* fired, they might do nothing then, too. They had a place for themselves at the *Voice,* an outlet, as they called it, and some of them had nothing else. What would they do if they didn't have that?

It was, thus, a limp and fractious group that poured into Mary Perot Nichols's apartment high above LaGuardia Place in the South Village that Thursday night, June 6, a day and a half after first hearing of the takeover, to hear Councilman Carter Burden explain it face to face. It was the meeting Burden had asked for, that Wolf had arranged at his request, and Wolf had thought it was with the understanding they would both try to keep things as cool as possible. Which only made him that much more surprised, and ticked off, to hear Carter Burden open the meeting by attacking him.

Right from the start, Burden was saying things about Wolf, in front of his staff, that Wolf interpreted as a deliberate attempt to turn the meeting against him. In fact, the very first thing Burden said was a lie: that Dan had come and *asked* him to make a deal for the *Voice*.

"That's not true and you know it," Dan Wolf shot back, amazed. Carter Burden simply retracted the statement, moved on, and resumed the attack from another direction. He was in this situation, he said, because he'd had to pay so much money to Wolf and Fancher that now he was strapped. And then, without anyone asking, he told everyone just how much he was paying them. He gave their salary figures, which had not been given out before. And he gave the figure for the original sale—except he gave it wrong, counting all the accrued interest he had *preferred* to pay them, and giving it as $3.7 million, not $3 million. He mentioned the figure a couple of more times, Wolf asked him to please clarify that, Burden mumbled something and started to go on, and then Dan Wolf spoke up and said that just wasn't true.

What Carter Burden was saying bothered Dan Wolf; but what he was leaving unsaid between the lines bothered him more. To Dan Wolf, the implication was clear: *They sold you out when they sold to me. What are you defending them for?*

Other people got that feeling, too, and contested the figures he was using. When he repeated a statement that had appeared in that morning's *New York Times*—that, as part of the transaction, *New York* Magazine Co. "assumed about $2.5 million in debt owed by The Voice"—Howard Smith called him on it—it was *his* debt, not the *Voice*'s. Howard Smith also confronted him with a list of items—editorial integrity, renewal of Dan's and Ed's contracts—that the staff had drawn up and wanted assurances on. That infuriated Carter Burden; he wanted a Xerox.

And thus the meeting proceeded, always bordering on acrimony, Alan Weitz taking notes.

> *Present were Dan, Ed, Carter, Bartle, Mary, Ross, Jack, Paul, Alan, Ron, Clark, Howard S., Howard B., Audrey, Lucian, Diane, Fred**

---

*Wolf, Fancher, Burden, Bull, Mary Nichols, Ross Wetzsteon, Jack Newfield, Paul

Carter began and talked for 5 to 10 minutes. Tone was hostile from the beginning. Said he resented the fact that we were upset with the merger and apparently had no faith in his judgement [sic]. *Mad about statement in the Times that staffers were urged not to discuss merger.*[*] *Mad about talk that he had avoided us for weeks. Alan said he had called Times when the paper hit the stands to say the statement was erroneous. Ron said he had left three messages for Carter with Jane Low* [sic], *sect. Carter said he got 3 confused or incomprehensible messages. Ron said they were very clear— he was speaking for staff members and they all wanted a meeting. Ron said Alan was present when one call was made.*

Carter sketched the the [sic] *agreement made between Cartel* [sic] */ Bartle and Wolf / Fancher in 1970 when 80% of the Voice was acquired by Taurus. Said Wolf and Fancher received $3.7 million. First time most members of staff had ever heard what exact figure was. Never felt they needed to know. Dan visibly annoyed. Carter mentioned figure 2 or 3 more times. Clark later told Carter he thought this was "an attempt to drive a wedge between us and Dan and Ed." My own feeling at the time was Carter was trying to tell us they were millionaires, had been taken care of, and shouldn't be of such concern to us. I also had a suspicion the 3.7 figure worked out to much less. And that perhaps Dan and Ed were still owed money.*

Carter appealed for our trust, saying, "You've had four years of living with me"—an attempt to show he had stuck to his word about not interfering. Said Felker owns 9% of stock, while "We have the most significant position on the board. 34%." [†] *Admitted it was "not the ideal position" and there was "no question a new partner was involved." Said Felker was in an "impotent position" regarding NY Magazine because the board was so divided. Said it was "implicit in Taurus' mind and NY Magazine's" that the same editorial position continue in VV and NYM.*

Asked what would happen if they wanted to bring in new

Cowan, Alan Weitz, Ron Rosenbaum, Clark Whelton, Howard Smith, Howard Blum, theater editor Audrey Berman, Lucian Truscott, Diane Fisher, Fred McDarrah.

[*]The story in the *Times* had inaccurately reported that "staff members of The Voice were urged yesterday by the management not to dolscuss [sic] tne merger with outsiders."

[†]He went further than that, according to many others present; he said, "Well, my ex-father-in-law Bill Paley only owns 8 percent of CBS, and there's no question who's boss there."

editor and publisher when Dan and Ed's contracts were up
Carter said, "theoretically they could do that . . . I cannot
make a promise on that [Dan and Ed staying]. Asked how he
personally felt about their staying he said: "I am in favor of it. I
have to see how it works out." Used the word "chemistry" a
few times. Asked if he wanted to break the contract, Carter
said "I certainly do not."

Carter said "I'm just as fucking loyal to The Voice as Dan
and Ed." Said there were "certain issues we've had discussions on, certain points we're in disagreement on." Bartle
said, "The truth and legal reality [of editorial control] is that
they sold it 4½ years ago." And "We had the ability to
terminate the contract."*

Carter said Felker agreed that the future lies with newspapers not magazines. Said the new corporation has the
"resources to increase circulation, to pay people more." Said
Felker had "no detailed plan" and "Felker's paranoid he's
being taken over by us." Carter said the "Village Voice is going
to be exactly what it is. Hopefully it can be improved (within its
tradition)." And, "Felker cannot put anyone on the board I
don't agree with."

Carter on editorial independence of Voice: "I give you my
word and assurance of that." On Felker: "I don't think he
belongs in the VV. And I think he knows that."

Bartle said Felker wanted [Ted] Kheel on board. Carter said
Peter Tufo negotiated for him. On Kheel's board position said,
"I didn't get out-maneuvered." On Tuffo [sic]: "He is my
agent. Felker is not that crazy about him." Bartle says Tufo
"will vote like Carter tells him to vote."

Carter: "I don't think anything bad's going to happen to the
Voice." And said, "it makes a stronger entity to have companies together." Said there will be "money to expand . . . we
had a half-assed book operation, couldn't put any money into it
. . . they've got expertise in marketing, production, distribution . . . good talent that we've lacked." Said "money is going
to be poured into The Voice."

Carter said the quote from Felker in the Times about no clean
sweep was a "disastrous statement."

---

*He did more; he produced the letter Ed Fancher had written in 1971, at the height of
the massage parlor conflict, reminding him that "Dan and I had suggested a three-year
contract" back in 1970, and offered that as evidence they had been considering leaving
anyway.

> *Carter admitted, "I knew goddamn well coming here I couldn't give you satisfaction." On independence of the Voice said: "I will go down fighting and I don't expect to lose." On Dan and Ed said: "I can't give you an employment contract today . . . unresolved issue as far as contract goes . . . expect they will [get them]."*
>
> *Carter on NY Mag: "Good for what it is . . . think VV is more important. Will last longer in long run." But "VV got a little stale lately."*
>
> *Carter on Victor Kovner retaining his job: "You don't have to worry about that." Said Tufo wanted his job but Bartle objected, wanted Kovner.**
>
> *. . . Bartle, 2 or 3 times, said Ross had always been mentioned by Dan as his successor.*
>
> *. . . I think every person spoke up at some time, except Ross. After the meeting Ross went up to Ron and, in a reference to Ron's phone calls, said, "He [Carter] could have gotten garbled messages. You know how things are at The Voice." Ron was furious and said "What are you, his messenger boy?" Ross was shaken up and left.*

Dan Wolf had taken Carter Burden's speech, both what he said and the way he said it, to be a hostile act, and he could not figure out why Burden had done it; but when after the meeting people came up to him and asked him if he still trusted Carter Burden he told them yes. Because, strangely enough, he still did.

But other people did not, and later, when their judgment had been vindicated, there would appear something called the "Wall of Shame" at the *Village Voice*. It was the wall on the fourth floor, where the elevator let passengers out into the writers' cubicles area, and on it would appear, periodically, one graffito or another aphorizing one more grim aspect of life there under their new, changed situation. The major decoration on this wall was a poster advertising a new album by pop singer Randy Edelman. The album was called "Prime Cuts," and the poster showed Edelman leaning on a supermarket window, against a background of price billings. Except that not all the prices were from the album cover, or from any supermarket. "CARTER'S LITTLE

---

*Exactly true; Kovner had been handling the paper's legal work for years. He was good—the *Voice*, for all its controversies, had not lost a libel suit yet. And he was popular with the writers, who felt he backed them up on tough stories. Tufo *did* want his job, and Bull *did* object. Eager to keep Tufo out of the *Voice*, Bull persuaded Burden he could not very well have his own personal lawyer as the paper's general counsel if he wished to keep his distance from it, and the matter was dropped.

LIVER 69¢," for example, had been written in, as had "CARTER BURDEN'S WORD 2¢ 1¢ Can't give it away free," as had "VOCAL PROMISES, incl. FREE LIES."

The choice of an album cover by Edelman on which to pen these sentiments was prematurely appropriate, for in a subsequent album he would record two songs, one describing the bitter story of the "Uptown, up-tempo woman" and the "Downtown, downbeat guy" who move in together and have a desperately unhappy affair, the other a remake of the British sixties hit, "Concrete and Clay." To those who knew the songs, and the situation, the metaphor and the irony were too rich to be ignored.

★ ★ ★

Thus, in January 1975, seven months later, when he was writing a spoof about the Ultimate Disaster Flick, Clark Whelton fantasized this scenario—"A Boeing 747 has been hijacked by a gang of kidnappers who are holding a New York City Councilman for ransom. Unless their demand of 5000 pounds of sugar is met, they are threatening to release the councilman unharmed"—there was little doubt whom he had in mind. Other *Voice* writers were already finding the humorous aspects in the situation. Jack Newfield wrote that he looked forward to doing a story on "The Favorite Recipes of the Ten Worst Bisexual Judges in New York." Alex Cockburn, hearing of the takeover on his way to catch a plane out of town, picked up on that idea and dashed off this:

> There are great possibilities in the co-existence of the two magazines under one umbrella. Writers here are eagerly starting new projects symbolic of the change: Recipes of the 10 Worst Bisexual Judges, How Jews Talk to Their Gay Plants, the 50 Lowest Salaries in New York, Best Dog Runs, Renovate Your Brownstone Into a Welfare Hotel. To speak for myself: this column has always fearlessly attacked the weak and defended the strong. For a sycophant such as myself there is something dizzying yet exhilarating at the thought of so many new asses to kiss.

Cockburn made his plane and missed the meeting that followed. Many of those who knew him took that as his way of being sarcastic. When he returned, they learned otherwise.

★ ★ ★

Five days went by, and Dan Wolf and Ed Fancher had their first meeting with Clay Felker. It came at the Players Club, off Gramercy Park, for lunch on Tuesday, June 11. Carter Burden, Bartle Bull, and Milton Glaser were there too.

Carter opened the meeting by prodding Felker to say something about his thoughts as far as the *Voice* was concerned. Felker responded with a little set speech, how all of them were indebted to Wolf and Fancher for having created this newspaper, how they had made a gigantic contribution to journalism, how they had some of the best writers in the country writing for it, how much he respected it, how he only wanted to help it get greater circulation and promotion if he could, that's all.

Dan Wolf was not impressed, and changed the subject. He wanted to know, he said, whether or not they were going to continue. It was entirely up to him, Felker, he realized; he just wanted to know. If the decision was made to retain them, they could talk about a new contract; but first, he said, we just want to know this. And if he *did* decide to retain them, there were two things he should know before offering them a new contract. One, Ed Fancher will have to run the business side, and two, I'll have to have absolute editorial control, just like I've had with Carter for the last four years.

Clay Felker didn't use the word *chemistry,* but he did say that "we'll have to see how things work out." Wolf couldn't understand why he was hedging and pressed him for an early decision. And he told him he really ought to come down to the *Voice* right away to meet the staff. There were problems down there with the *New York* takeover, he said. Most of the staff, he said, have always been a little suspicious of, a little *contemptuous* of, *New York* Magazine. They regard it, he said, as a place where the editors are always telling the writers what to do, where quotes and stories are made up. And, Dan Wolf made clear as he went along, he agreed with that assessment. He wasn't sure if he used the word *vulgar* or not, but he knew he came pretty close, and when he did Clay Felker, far from putting up a fight about his choice of words, maintained a very unsurprised, unoffended silence.

When he had the floor again, Felker stressed that he wanted to keep his role limited. There will be no direct control, he said. I will keep away from the *Voice.* The ideal relationship between the *Voice* and *New York* should be peripheral—two totally separate entities, with no cross-fertilization, except for, as he said, promotion and circulation—and that was the relationship he wanted to have. As for meeting the staff, I can't right now, he said. I'm very tired. I'm going to be on vacation till the Fourth of July. I'll meet with them then.

I don't think you should wait that long, Dan Wolf advised him. There's a lot of uncertainty down there about the future, about the paper and your intentions. Don't worry, said Clay Felker. "There's plenty of time. And your contracts are good until January."

They talked about other things. Felker said he'd like to improve the paper's graphics; Milton Glaser spoke up and said if he could help in any way, he'd be glad to come down, but not interfere. Felker also asked them not to give any raises for the time being, until he had a chance to come down and get acquainted with the operation; Fred McDarrah, their photographer, had written them a rambling, belligerent letter demanding one. And then Dan Wolf brought up something he was pretty sure they already knew. There had been criticism by *Voice* people of some new *New York* board members—Mary Nichols of Tufo, and lately, Jack Newfield of Kheel, in a piece that made connections between the stands he took on transportation bond issues and the holdings he had in New York banks, a piece about which Kheel had been furious—and now, he wanted them to know, a freelance writer had come to them with certain allegations about Kheel's dealings with the labor union that had put a prefab housing project in Rochester, New York. Mary Nichols was working on it with the writer, who was checking it out, and if it checked out he would run it. He and he alone would make the decision, and he would not tolerate any interference on it.*

They listened, and said nothing, and after three hours, the meeting broke up. Ed Fancher would describe it later as "an uncomfortable luncheon."

★ ★ ★

A week went by. Fancher wrote letters to the lawyers for Whitey Lutz and Norman Mailer, giving all the details he knew. He and Wolf asked Bartle Bull for more details, but Bull was unable to supply them; his papers were at home and he hadn't read them, he said, and he struck Fancher and Wolf by the way he said it as being depressed and unhappy. He also wanted them to know he'd said what he did at Mary Nichols's house that night because he felt he *had* to defend Carter in that situation. Meantime, Fancher gave Whitey Lutz a call. It's still very unclear what the terms of the sale are, he told him, we're still very much up in the air, and we don't know what to do about the

---

*The allegations eventually did *not* check out, not to the satisfaction of Mary Nichols and Dan Wolf, who decided not to run the piece.

right-of-first-refusal issue. The two men discussed how they might go about counter-offering Felker for Burden's stock, if they decided to try to exercise that right now. He didn't know how he could counter-offer 600,000 shares of unregistered stock at a figure-per-share they were still trying to find out, and he didn't know who Carter owed money to, nor how much he owed them, but at least, he, Lutz, could guarantee that figure of $2.5 million in loans. They also talked about their other option, which was being bought out as Carter Burden had said they would be.

Norman Mailer called Wolf to find out what was happening. Clay Felker called him, too, twice, from what Wolf assumed was long-distance, on vacation. Wolf's and Fancher's lawyer, Louis Hoynes, was in touch with Theodore Kheel, lawyer for *New York* Magazine. So was the freelance writer who was working on the story about Kheel, making an unsuccessful attempt at an interview by telephone. Dan Wolf knew this, so when he got a call from Clay Felker's secretary the afternoon of Tuesday, June 18, he was sure what it was for.

"Clay wants to meet with you this afternoon at five," the secretary said. "Is that all right?"

"Certainly," said Dan Wolf, wondering what had happened to Clay Felker's vacation.

Five came, and Felker arrived, on time, his administrative assistant Jane Maxwell with him, and immediately on entering Dan Wolf's office said, "I want a meeting with the staff. Right now. I've waited too long."

Wolf was a little flustered. "But they're not here now," he told Felker.

"What do you mean, they're not here now? It's five o'clock."

"Most of them are gone."

"I don't care. I want a meeting with them," snapped Felker.

Wolf was firm. "Mr. Felker, you'll recall it was us who wanted you to have a meeting with the staff. And when you agreed, you agreed to meet with the whole staff. Now, at five o'clock, you're not going to get many of them. And that's not what the staff wants."

Felker abated. "Well, all right then. But I still want a meeting. Tomorrow."

Wolf wasn't sure there would be many more available on Wednesday, and suggested Thursday, but Clay Felker was already on his way out the door. Wolf called after him that Norman Mailer had telephoned that day, wanting to know what was going to happen to his stock. "Well, Kheel has called your lawyer," said Felker, turning around. "We're going to make you the same offer we made Taurus. Cash, or cash and stock. I hope you'll agree to accept some stock." And with that, he was gone.

As it turned out, Wednesday was *not* a good day. Dan Wolf and Ed

Fancher got in touch with Howard Smith and some of the other staff members; quite a few were out of town, and quite a few of those in town were peeved at the short notice. Since Ed Fancher was going to be at the same place Felker was that night—a publication party for *All the President's Men* authors Carl Bernstein and Bob Woodward—it was Fancher who told him. All right, Thursday, Felker agreed. But he was definitely not pleased.

★ ★ ★

He toured the building the next day, anyway, meeting a few of the writers, and on Thursday afternoon, June 20, he was back. And this time, they were there, cramming into Ed Fancher's office— Sarris and Gornick and Whelton and Reisig and Rosenbaum and Newfield and Cowan and Truscott and Blum and Mary Nichols and Ross Wetzsteon and Howard Smith, all of them practically, staffers and contributors alike. Fred McDarrah scurried around, getting good angles, taking pictures. Ed Fancher was off to one side, sitting behind his desk. Bartle Bull was off to the other, leaning against the opened door, George Dillehay standing beside him. Next to Dillehay, in the opening of another, side door, stood Carter Burden, his business jacket off, his tie still on. And next to him, almost out of sight, almost out of earshot, as he was wont to be in such situations, stood Dan Wolf.

Beside Fancher's desk, in front of them all, sat Clay Felker. Andrew Sarris, nearest the desk, facing Felker, spoke first.

He spoke for several minutes, and when he was through everyone would remember with what eloquence he had spoken, though no one could remember exactly what he said. There were good and bad things in the *Voice,* Sarris conceded, but freedom to write was the important thing; that was what had made the *Voice* what it was. And if that were lost, there would be nothing left. That, he went on, had been the problem with the *Saturday Review* people;* they had changed so much they lost their original base.

He finished, coming on, in his own wry estimation, like Demosthenes or the Declaration of Independence, and when he was through, he sat back, and Clay Felker started right in with what he had come there to say. Andrew Sarris, looking at him, thought, *He didn't even flinch. The ball game is over.*

Look, no one here is going to be fired, Felker said. As for Dan and Ed,

---

*Sarris was referring here to magazine entrepreneurs John Veronis and Nicholas Charney, who, fresh from their success with *Psychology Today,* bought into Norman Cousins's *Saturday Review,* took over and forced Cousins out, radically changed the magazine into four separate weeklies, moved it to San Francisco from New York, and ran it aground in 1973—with the wreckage taken over by Norman Cousins again.

we'll just have to wait and see. They have a contract now. As to whether or not they get a new one, that depends on how things work out between us. When the time comes to make that decision, it will be up to me to make it as chief executive officer of the corporation. And, as chief executive officer, I have to retain ultimate editorial authority. That's not something I can give away, he said. But maybe we can work something out.

There. He had said it. He was the boss. And nobody had bucked him.

As for the *Voice,* his goal was to support what it is and to expand it, not transform it, he said. He respected it very much, and would not try to alter its basic character. But there would have to be *some* changes. We've made a study, he said. The *Voice* will not survive, the way it is going, another two or three years. Something has to be done. And we can do that.

Ed Fancher heard that and started sputtering. He looked at Carter Burden and Bartle Bull and waited for them to say something. When they didn't, he interrupted, loud enough for all to hear. "Just a minute. I want everyone here to know that what Clay Felker said is not true, and they shouldn't believe it. In fact, just the opposite is true. The *Voice* has made more money than *New York* Magazine every year that *New York* has been in existence."

Neither Bartle Bull nor Carter Burden took up that tack, but Howard Smith did. Clay Felker simply went right on insisting, "This place is run like it's a weekly newspaper with 10,000 circulation—like a college paper. Like a country store."

He handled other complaints. Vivian Gornick told him, "We feel like a conquered province here." Lucian Truscott picked a fight with him when he said he had the impression no writers' stories were ever turned down at the *Voice.*

"Oh, yeah?" Truscott said. "Well, it so happens Dan Wolf has rejected articles of mine that he didn't think were any good."

Felker seemed surprised. "Well, we reject articles at *New York* Magazine, too, but not in so many words. The story just dies."

"Yeah, well here at the *Voice* editors don't lie to writers," Truscott came back at him.

Then Howard Smith brought up an idea he and Carter Burden had talked about enthusiastically that night in Mary Nichols's place, an idea Burden had cited as one of the real advantages of the merger—the kind of diversification, like book publishing, which the *Voice* had been unable to do. He asked Felker if the corporation would now be diversifying, expecting to hear good things.

"Diversification," Clay Felker said, glad somebody had brought it up. "I want to put that to rest right now. Diversification is out. Book publishing is a disaster, a quagmire. That's a harebrained idea of yours, Howard."

Smith was speechless. He looked to Carter Burden. Burden kept his mouth shut and puffed on his pipe a little harder.

There was another such incident before the meeting broke up. Carter Burden was describing once again to the writers how the stock deal worked, how he and Bartle Bull could vote their stock together and use it to protect them if necessary. "Don't mislead them, Carter," Clay Felker interrupted, quietly, and Carter Burden went silent.

When the meeting was over, Howard Smith felt strangely optimistic. It might work, he thought. We can get the writers on TV shows, get national ads. It might be a radical change on the business side, but not anywhere else.

Others were not so sure. They felt as Clark Whelton did, who told the reporter from the *Times* what, in his estimation, had taken place: "We tried to tell Felker that he was smoking in the refueling area, and he tried to tell us that he was smoking very, very good cigars."

★ ★ ★

Nearly three weeks went by. One of Fancher's investment advisers, John Gold, was in touch with Robert Towbin to inquire about *New York* Magazine's financial performance. Gold called him back with this message, recorded in his diary: "John Gold called Towbin's firm. They said 20 cents dividend this year. Earnings are 50 to 60 cents a share." And with this message, too: "Board expected a fuss from the writers but key writers will stay and will blow over."

There were other meetings—Felker, Jack Thomas, his marketing director, and Kenneth Fadner, his business vice-president, with Bartle Bull and Sandy Fendrick and Ely Kushel, to discuss the business. There was another lunch—Dan Wolf with Carter Burden and Bartle Bull, where Wolf told Burden he just couldn't see himself working with Felker, that he was just so revolted by him, that the man was just such a packager who didn't care anything about writing or journalism, and where Burden told Wolf that he understood how he felt, but he hoped things would work out—and repeated that old line, "You never know when a truck will come along and run you down, Dan."

They gave their terms for a contract. Dan Wolf was willing to take a 50-percent pay cut in order to get complete editorial control but, on the advice of his lawyers, asked instead for a three-year renewal at the same salary. Ed Fancher asked for three years at salary parity with Bartle— $70,000. His friend Dan Wolf thought he was making a mistake. Days went by with no word of a counter-offer. Every day people came into his office and asked Dan Wolf what was happening with his contract, and he had to tell them he didn't know. Howard Smith began getting phone calls from friends he had in publishing, telling him he was crazy to believe Felker, that there was no way he was going to keep Wolf and Fancher. And on Saturday, July 6, Ross Wetzsteon, who had rented a summer place in East Hampton, got a call from Clay Felker, whose own place was not far away, inviting him over for lunch. Lunch lasted seven hours.

Milton Glaser was there, and Aaron Latham, and so, as usual, was Gail Sheehy. They all sat around and talked about the *Voice,* and Felker asked him a lot of questions, which Wetzsteon answered. They did not talk about replacing anybody, but Felker did ask him what Dan Wolf did at the paper, and Ross Wetzsteon told him, basically nothing.

He told Clark Whelton about their conversation the following Monday, and Whelton was appalled to hear what he had done. "That's not true and you know it," Whelton told him. But this time Clay Felker was not within earshot. And the next day, Tuesday, July 9, Dan Wolf got a call at the office from Felker.

Fancher was on holiday upstate, so Felker asked Wolf to meet him alone. We're having a meeting of the Board of Directors late this afternoon, he said, but I ought to be free about seven. Can you meet me in the lounge of the Barclay Hotel about then? Wolf said he could.

Felker came at eight, though, not seven, so Wolf killed the time in between with a few drinks at the bar. When he finally did get there, he was in a hurry. Before they had even sat down the words were already out of his mouth.

We had a meeting today, and came to this conclusion, he said. *We think it would be a good idea to give Ross and Bartle their heads for a while. They need a chance to run things on their own. Your presence and Ed's are just a little too powerful. Your personalities are too strong. You inhibit them. As long as you're there, Ross can never take over. We think you should step aside.*

It did not take long for it to register in Dan Wolf's mind that he had just been fired.* *This is what I'd like you to do,* Clay Felker was continuing. *Don't go down to the* Voice *for about two or three months. After that, I'd like to talk to you about being a consultant.*

At that moment, Dan Wolf felt no sense of defeat. He felt no fear, no regret, no shame, no bitterness at anyone, no rage for revenge. He felt

---

*At the board meeting just concluded, Felker had asked for, and gotten unanimously, authorization to do whatever was necessary at the *Voice,* including firing Wolf and Fancher *if it became necessary;* no one had thought, as Bartle Bull put it later, that he was going to do it in twenty minutes.

only relief. He had been reprieved. His ordeal was over. He had wondered how long he was going to be stuck in this situation, and now he knew. He wasn't going to have to put up with it, with Felker, any longer. He was out. He felt happy. He felt free. He could stop hiding his true emotions now. He could say just what was on his mind.

"You don't have any intention of making me a consultant," he said.

"No, I do, I really do," Felker answered. "I'm serious."

"I doubt it."

Well, look, I really have to get uptown now, Felker said. I think you'd better get in touch with Ed Fancher and tell him this yourself, Wolf said. I will, Felker said. They walked outside, Felker hailed a cab for himself, and opened the door. He turned around to say good-bye. But Dan Wolf had one more thing to say to him first. And he leaned forward and said it:

"You're a very neurotic man, Mr. Felker, and someday the same thing is going to happen to you."

To that, Clay Felker said nothing, except good night. He shut the door of his cab, and it took off into the New York night.

★ ★ ★

Later that night, Dan Wolf called Ed Fancher and told him what had happened. As Fancher put it in his diary: "Dan called me at Gypsy Trailer Club to say that he had seen Felker for drinks this evening after the Board of Directors of New York Magazine met. Felker told him he was appointing Ross Wetzsteon as executive editor and he wanted Dan to remain as a consultant perhaps even after the contract is over. He is also making Bartle chief of all business functions and wants me to also be a consultant. So we are both fired."

The next day, he came into the city, early, and met Felker for coffee in the Village. There, Felker told him basically the same thing: Stay away for a couple of months. Give Bartle and Ross a chance to establish their authority. In the meantime, you and Dan can go on masthead as founding publisher and editor, if you want.

We'll think about it, said Ed Fancher. "Why'd you fire us?" he asked.

"I just thought it would be best," said Clay Felker.

"Were we uncooperative?" Fancher wanted to know.

"No, not at all. I just thought it would be best if you stepped aside so Bartle and Ross could take over."

"What about that buyout offer you mentioned?"

"Oh, that," Felker said. "Have Louis Hoynes call me directly on that instead of Kheel. I don't think it's a good idea for Kheel to be handling it."

And so it was left. Except that later that same day, someone from

[*MORE*] called him wanting to know if it was true he and Wolf had each demanded three-year contracts at $70,000 each, and Fancher knew the contents of their letter had been leaked. Then the offer to buy them out never came. So on July 19, Ed Fancher invited Bartle Bull over to his apartment to, as he recorded it in his diary, "read the riot act" to him.

Look, we're going to sue you unless you make us the offer we were promised, Fancher threatened. Bull was sympathetic. He was trying to get Carter Burden to move on it, he explained, but Carter was out in the Hamptons. More time passed, until August 14, when Clay Felker personally wrote Willkie, Farr, and Gallagher, their law firm, to tell them now was not "an appropriate time . . . to make an offer to purchase" their minority stock.

They discussed with each other and with Whitey Lutz the possibilities of putting together a package big enough to exercise their right of first refusal. But it was hopeless. It had been a *fait accompli.* Their lawyers advised them they would have had to chain themselves to their desks that first day for the right of first refusal to be effective now. And that only begged the question of taking on Felker anyway. Either they were going to sue him or they weren't.

So, on September 18, there was filed in New York State Supreme Court a lawsuit, plaintiffs being Daniel Wolf, Edwin Fancher, Norman Mailer, and Herbert B. Lutz, minority stockholders of the *Village Voice,* against *New York* Magazine, the *Voice,* Taurus Communications, Clay S. Felker, Councilman Carter Burden, and Bartle Bull. The suit charged defendants with having "willfully and knowingly interfered with and violated plaintiffs' contractual rights," with "conspiring" against and having "misled" them by "fraudulent" means, with breach of "fiduciary duty" and the written "shareholders' agreement," with taking "actions not in the best interests of the Voice," and asked $1.5 million in compensatory and punitive damages each. Specifically, Felker was charged with having, for personal gain, sought to enhance *New York*'s competitive position at the expense of the *Voice,* and with having assured the minority shareholders of an equal offer for their stock when he "had no intention of making such an offer"; Burden and Bull were accused of getting a "premium" price for their stock, with violating the right of first refusal, and with having "advanced without proper corporate authority . . . substantial sums properly belonging to The *Voice.*"

Plaintiffs did not seek that control of the paper be returned to them. They sought only money, which is what the Board of Directors of *New York* Magazine Company took away from them on October 7, when they stripped Fancher and Wolf of their remaining fifteen weeks' salary.

On January 23, 1975, the day their contracts were to have expired anyway, the week the 1,000th issue of the newspaper he had started hit the stands, Dan Wolf found himself in Peter Tufo's law offices giving a deposition as part of pretrial discovery proceedings.

★ ★ ★

When they heard what had happened that night in July, Dan Wolf's loyalists began calling in and stopping by. All of them asked what they should do, and to all he gave the same advice: *Don't walk out. Stay at the paper. Hold on to your jobs.*

That was what bothered him the most—people left behind he couldn't protect. He didn't want to see them lose their jobs now on account of him. So he told them he didn't know what he was going to do, that they should stay put and not do anything. Starting the next day, Fancher told them the same thing.

It was a gesture on their part that saved face all around, for even their most diehard supporters at that moment were having problems equating their duties to "Dan and Ed" with their own careers, and there would have been a lot less than solidarity if they had called for any kind of action. Not all the Family could be counted as loyalists anymore, between newer writers who did not know Wolf well and those still smoldering over the money fight and the older ones who professed to see a synthesis in it all—Hentoff, for one, and Flaherty, for another, who translated *Realpolitik* into streetese for everyone: "Hey. They sold the fuckin' candy store."

Flaherty, in a gesture he thought would be appreciated, sent both men a bottle of champagne, a stunt that struck Dan Wolf as tasteless and permanently offended him. But that was not what hurt Dan Wolf the most in the few days after he was fired. What Alex Cockburn did, or rather did not do, was. Cockburn let two weeks go by before even trying to call Wolf at home. When he did, and got Rhoda Wolf, because Dan was out, he left no message and never called back. Nor, by that time, was Wolf even tempted to call him—he had already been getting reports back from the paper, reports that Alex Cockburn had found a new object for his flattery. So Alex Cockburn and Dan Wolf, a man who had given him a start in a new country, openly proclaimed him a protégé, and thought they had become close friends in the process, never spoke to one another again.

The next week the announcement, though not the reasons for it, appeared in the paper, along with this "staff" statement, a kind of retroactive Apostles' Creed:

Dan Wolf and Ed Fancher did something very few people do in a lifetime: they created a new idea. That idea is the *Village Voice*. . . . In time, Wolf fashioned a new concept in journalism. He let the writers write. He edited sensibilities not copy. He shared with writers his remarkable psychological perceptions. He tempered their enthusiasm with skepticism and a sense of history. And he printed articles he personally disagreed with. Most important, Dan and Ed cherished individuality. They recognized and understood that people produce at different tempos and in different voices. They created an environment of total freedom.

Over the years other publications imitated *The Voice*. None succeeded in capturing the essence of this newspaper. Because for 19 years its soul was Dan Wolf and Ed Fancher. We are their children.

But aside from that, and from some mention by Cockburn, there was nothing. On July 22, Clay Felker gave raises to everybody—base staff pay from $225 to $300, the going article fee from $125 to $200. And he had no walkout on his hands.

★ ★ ★

Also that same July night, Ross Wetzsteon and Clay Felker got together, at Felker's request. "Sit down," Felker told him. "I'd like to read you a press release." Which he then preceeded to do, all about how Clay Felker has just announced that Dan Wolf and Ed Fancher are to remain as consultants and that Ross Wetzsteon will assume the duties of editor, and how "Mr. Wetzsteon's appointment assures the continuation of the independence, vigor, and integrity of the journalism and commentary that have always characterized the *Village Voice*."

He looked up from what he was reading. And Ross Wetzsteon said, "Thank you very much for your confidence." Months later, in an interview, he would be asked what if, at that moment, he had *not* wanted the job. He answered, "Obviously, if at that point I had decided I didn't want it, he could have recalled it. . . ." But Ross Wetzsteon did want it.

And now, at last, he had it.

★ ★ ★

Starting that night, and for the next thirty months, the *Village Voice* was under the journalistic equivalent of a military occupation. When it came, Ross Wetzsteon, the other editors, and all the writers proved incapable of doing anything to stop it. They had their meetings, to be sure, meetings at Mary Nichols's place while she was away, where they all worried aloud about their editorial freedom and who there was a spy, where they decided to draft another one of their statements and send another one of their delegations to see Ross, where they left behind their cigarette butts and, in Jill Johnston's case, a handprint on the wall to be cleaned up by Mary Nichols's daughter after they had gone. And they had their statement, written up by Howard Blum and Alexander Cockburn and Paul Cowan. Six of them— those three plus Hentoff, Marlene Nadle, and Robin Reisig—met with Ross, where he told them, "Look, we'll give Felker 20 percent, and keep 80 percent of the old *Voice*." And, after two such meetings with him, the group disbanded. There was no organized resistance put up after that—only the occasional sniping from the rear that never stopped.

All through the summer and fall of 1974, it was Felker, Felker, Felker. Fancher's and Wolf's names were removed from the masthead the issue of August 22. He was everywhere, signing Pete Hamill to a contract when Hamill finally gave up his *New York Post* column for good, throwing a huge gala for him at the Village Gate, smoothing things out when old friend Dolly Schiff sued Newfield and Cockburn over the way they reported her dismissal of writer Al Aronowitz (Newfield agreed to cover the arbitrator's decision, eventually favorable to her, and the case was dropped out of court), backing up Mary Nichols in her exposés of oilman-turned-would-be-newspaper-publisher John Shaheen. He let all sorts of rumors fly—the *Voice* was going to go national, with regional sections or separate editions in new cities or one big biweekly "Best of the *Voice*" for nationwide distribution besides the regular weekly issues in New York, he was going to hire *Rolling Stone*'s deposed managing editor John Walsh, he was going to take on Jann Wenner, publisher of *Stone,* in a coast-to-coast circulation war.

On the business side, he raised the ante, considerably—classified to $2 a line, commercial display ads to $8, subscriptions, in one jump, from $8.50 to $15,* the newsstand price, in two jumps, from twenty-five cents to thirty-five, in August, and from thirty-five to fifty, in December. He began bringing in his own people—the dreaded Jane Maxwell as general

---

*Which was more than the rates then being offered by *New York* Magazine, a point Fancher and Wolf raised in their lawsuit.

manager, Steve Blacker as associate publisher for marketing, Bill Ryan as "vice-president—finance," David Shanks as circulation director. Select Magazines, Inc., *New York*'s distributor, took over out-of-town distribution of the *Voice*. A national ad staff, with offices in Los Angeles, Chicago, and Detroit, was set up.

And in editorial, he did the same thing. In came Milton Glaser to design a "new look" for the paper. A strip began running down the side of the first page in August, telling readers what was inside, and by fall stories were off the front page altogether. The words of the day were "all-art covers." The word was "readability." That meant wider, and fewer, columns on a page. It meant no more jumps, lots of white space, blocked-off ad sections, Corona and Bodoni type throughout the paper. Gil Eisner, who had done similar jobs for *Life, Esquire, Crawdaddy,* and *New York,* came in as art director. To complement the cartooning of Feiffer, Felker moved in Edward Sorel, whose savage topical carica-tures on page 3 were, if anything, better than Feiffer, and, in the midsection, Stan Mack, Clarence Brown, and Jan Faust, whose strips were grossly derivative of R. Crumb on his worst days. From *New York* he brought down Judy Daniels—quiet, competent, a loyal worker of his for six years—as managing editor. He also brought down, to do the book section he had once been able to handle in his off-hours from the *Times,* Eliot Fremont-Smith, who in the intervening years had made his way to *New York* by way of the Little Brown Publishing Company and the ill-fated Charney-Veronis regime at *Saturday Review,* and Richie Goldstein, back to the paper he had left, under unhappy circum-stances, five years before. He brought in other editors—Diane Straus and Robert Christgau. She was the daughter of R. Peter Straus, the broadcasting owner Wolf and Fancher had once, briefly, been partners with. He was the rock critic who had been writing for the paper before he had moved to *Newsday* at the end of 1971, a man after Felker's heart—cocky, pushy, and prolific.* Another editor, Karen Durbin, also came in. The only one not personally picked by Felker, she came recommended by Jack Newfield and Geoff Stokes, who knew her from her freelancing (some for the *Voice*), her activities in the antiwar and women's movements, and her press work for John Lindsay's environ-

---

*And, not unlike Felker, the sort of editor who enforced his opinions as absolutes—as one freelance writer found out who wrote in suggesting a profile on a singer Christgau, as it happened, did not like. "To be blunt," said his reply *in toto,* "I think Billy Joel is a self-pitying phony who has already done somewhat better than he deserves, and have no interest in a feature on him. This may seem unduly prejudiced to you, but that's the way editorial judgment works. Sorry." There was probably no more succinct statement of how the *Village Voice,* following the events of 1974, went about forfeiting its birthright.

mental protection commissioner, Jerome Kretchmer. Finally, to inaugurate his national connection, Clay Felker hired a West Coast editor, Jon Carroll.

★ ★ ★

It was not the *Village Voice* that needed to go national; it was Clay Felker who needed to. For the changes he was making and the plans he had in mind, a brand-new publication would have done as nicely; but a brand-new publication would have incurred a puddle of red ink, at least initially, and by using the *Voice* he avoided that. The *Voice* in 1974 was a publication in economic trouble; but it faced only the prospect of a shrinking profit structure, not the threat of imminent collapse Clay Felker had said it did in his meeting with the staff on June 20, 1974. The financial future of *New York,* as Felker already knew when he made that statement, was far shakier, though that was still being disguised by the statistics coming in from the magazine's upward, "growth" phase.

Clay Felker was operating like a quack doctor whose diagnosis was hardening of the arteries and whose cure was to surgically take the patient's heart out. As the paper's Manhattan slant went, so might the four out of nine readers who came from there. As the paper mounted out-of-town circulation drives, it would incur costs for trucking, mailing, and distribution, overhead it had always been exempted from in the days when seven out of nine readers had walked up to a newsstand and bought it there. As its rates went up, in pursuit of big national advertisers, its original base of local, medium-size shops might be driven elsewhere. The *Voice* was in danger of diluting, possibly even poisoning, the special formula on which it had nursed.

But Clay Felker could not be told that. His mind was made up, his decisions were carried out, and his goals were set. "What's On," the paper's culture calendar, was taken off the back page in the fall, and put near the classified, also moved, deep into the interior, so that both could be stripped and replated for the national edition, which would come, according to schedule, in September of 1975. By then, according to Clay Felker's master plan, the *Village Voice* would have a circulation of 250,000.*

With the removal of "What's On" to the inside, the loyal reader who read the paper in one sitting, first page to last, now had to start with the end of Sarris's and other critics' articles, or use mirrors. The new,

---

*At the time he took over the *Village Voice,* in the spring of 1974, its circulation stood at 144,000.

"slick" layout was easier on the eye, to be sure; the old chase sequences in the stories were out. But Milton Glaser would defend his approach by telling critics, "It's silly to pretend all week that you've just come out," and use that as a justification for having cover art, not stories, on a front page. Which was no answer to two things—that one cover sitting out on a newsstand looks no less stale after seven days there than two or three stories with headlines do, and that there are some weeks when there is no "cover" story.

And when those weeks came, and there was no one story that rated being put above all others on the cover, the *Village Voice* began to do something it had never done before. It began to plug stories out of all proportion to their newsworthiness. It began to overpromise to its readers. And on the inside, putting every story in a left-to-right two-page spread, the paper found itself using screaming, banner headlines on stories whether they rated them or not, often as high as 84-point, often accompanied by tacky art work (such as the head of a current newsmaker superimposed on the reproduction of a nineteenth-century Thomas Nast cartoon). It was LOUD. It was HYPE. It was conduct unbecoming the *Village Voice*. And, one week in November, it reached its absolute nadir, when Milton Glaser used as the cover shot a picture taken at a "Surrealist Party" thrown by an illustrator friend of his, showing a fey, divine-deco, drag-royalty couple, beneath the headline, PARTYING OUR WAY TO HARD TIMES.

The changes were being felt. In mid-August, after Richard Nixon's resignation, Clark Whelton wrote a piece concluding that Ted Kennedy, in the post-Watergate morality, would never be able to run for president himself now because of Chappaquiddick. The paper published Whelton's piece all right; but on the cover there was something called "The Great American Soap Opera," a photo spread advertising his article. On one side, there was a picture of Susan and Betty Ford, taken the morning of Gerald Ford's oath of office; "an image of suburban WASP America," the caption read. "Matching the mass marketeers' world of detergents, freeze-dried coffee, and other Heartland products, Betty Ford sips coffee with a neighbor and her daughter the day dad became President." On the other, a snapshot of Joan Kennedy, with the cutline: "An image of faded glamour. No magic of yesteryear could look more tired than the wounded features of Joan Kennedy congratulating Leonard Bernstein at Tanglewood. Can this match Betty Ford's homey suburban kitsch as a style for '76?"

Clark Whelton's piece had not even *mentioned* the name of Joan Kennedy, let alone Betty Ford. He wrote Felker a note, telling him how disappointed he was. He learned later it was Felker himself who had written those lines. And on the "Wall of Shame" up went little blurbs for "Freeze-Dried Heartland Products."

Then came "the Wednesday afternoon Valium sessions," as Andrew Sarris called them. In the *Village Voice,* where articles had never been cut to fit space before, articles were now being cut—sometimes ham-handedly, sometimes to the author's discovery only *after* the paper had come out and some vital part was missing. The solution was supposed to be that writers would keep within a word ceiling in the future, but that had never been done before at the *Village Voice,* either. For the first time in the paper's history, *editors* were thinking up ideas for stories and *finding* writers to do them. And the kind of articles they were assigning, as well as the kind of articles they were holding out of the paper to make room for what they assigned, said something about the point of view of those editors, and what had happened to the *Village Voice* now that they had imposed their point of view on it. Theater critic Julius Novick put it best, with his crack that the week the paper held out his review of Bertolt Brecht's *Good Woman of Setzuan* to run an article on the Man Who Electrolyzes Cher's Mustache, he knew priorities had changed.

Probably no event was more symbolic of the change than the arrival, that summer, of Richard Goldstein to be an editor there.

Five years before, he had left, in a fight over money; years later, his life in pieces, he had come back looking for a job, and been told, he said,* by Dan Wolf, "Richard, this is a business. Why don't you go work for Felker?"

The words stung Goldstein. He could still recall the time, having done four or five installments of "Pop Eye" so far, he was working on another, in the office, at six A.M. on copy day, when Wolf came in, as usual, stopped by his typewriter to tell him, "The column's going real well," and how that had raised his morale so. Now, with this remark, he decided this was a man who could very easily mix cruelty with compassion, and was no longer owed any awe or loyalty from him. He had always thought of *New York* Magazine as "the evil world" and the *Voice* as his "cloister," but now he took Dan Wolf's goading advice, and went to Felker. He was not sorry he did. In the three years that followed, Clay Felker made him—the word applied—a star. He became a kind of resident culture analyst—and a red flag at the *Voice,* both to those who knew him when and despised what he had become, and to

---

*As for Dan Wolf, he denies this incident ever happened, and the quote Goldstein attributed to him.

those who knew him only from his writing and despised him as the epitome of Felker *shlock*.

His reputation preceded him at the paper, then, and Richard Goldstein returned the animus in full. His first week back there, he had to stay late to finish a feature he was doing on Bruce Lee, the kung-fu movie star. He had no office of his own yet. But he knew where there was an empty one he could use. He went down the hall to Dan Wolf's old office, which Wolf had just cleared out only a day or two before. He went inside. He turned on the lights, went over to the clean desk top, and put his typewriter down. Then he got into the chair behind the desk, and sat back. He was in the captured capital of the enemy, which is what he had come to think of Dan Wolf by now. He was using the desk, and sitting in the chair, of the man who had snubbed him, the man who was now out on his ass. At that moment, savoring the scene, Richard Goldstein felt a feeling of triumph surging all through him.

★ ★ ★

He began by getting the silent treatment from the old *Voice* people, especially Rosenbaum, with whom he had once been very friendly. Then, one night, a picture Richard Goldstein had posed for, bare ass to the camera, as a cover photo for a now-defunct counterculture magazine, *Us,* was gotten hold of, Xeroxed, and, by morning, distributed all over the offices of the *Village Voice.* Its caption: THE FACE OF THE FUTURE.

To clear the air, he went downstairs to the cubicle of Lucian Truscott. "I want to have a little talk," he said. When Goldstein had been writing his *Voice* column and Truscott had been a West Point cadet who admired it, they had been close. Goldstein had had Truscott up to his Riverside Drive apartment, had taken him to Fillmore concerts. But then Goldstein had left the *Voice,* gone to work for *Us,* told Truscott the underground press was going to replace the *Voice,* and when *Us* had collapsed, gone to work for *New York,* where Truscott and Rosenbaum and the others knew he had not written much, where they had heard he bad-mouthed the *Voice.* Now he was here, and Truscott, among others, was galled.

Okay, Truscott said, so Goldstein, standing in his doorway, started talking. About how now that Clay had taken over, things were going to change, editing was going to be tighter, layout was going to be different . . .

"Do you see this ad? Do you see this ad?" Truscott, rising out of his chair, was interrupting already, holding one of the paper's old "THE VILLAGE VOICE IS A WRITER'S NEWSPAPER" ads (that listed, down the line, "RICHARD GOLDSTEIN, who writes on everything from him to hype," even though he had not written for them in years) in his hand. "This is a newspaper for *writers,*" he said vehemently. "What are you going to do now—are you going to pull this ad out of the paper? Or are you going to continue to mislead *Voice* readers that this is a writer's paper when in fact what you're telling me is that it's now an *editor's* paper? Huh? What are you going to do now?"

I was a writer when you were a fucking cadet, Richard Goldstein was thinking just at that moment. He didn't say that. He said, "You're acting just like a sergeant would act in basic training," instead. "Every time I say something you say I act militaristic," Truscott blew back. "That's the oldest cliché in the book, calling me *macho.*"

"Well, you are *macho.*"

"Fuck you."

The peace conference was over. "All right," Goldstein announced, "This is the way it's going to be. There's going to be tighter editing around here, and *you* in particular are going to get it. You've needed it for years."

"Get the fuck out of my office," Lucian Truscott said. "I never want to see you down here again. You've got a lot of fucking nerve marching around here after diddlying around at *New York* Magazine for four years." Goldstein stalked back upstairs.

Lucian Truscott was right; it had been a writer's newspaper. And Richard Goldstein was right; things were going to change. Nowhere was that more evident than on the fifth floor, where things had always been slow and quiet, unless one or more of the writers were up there to talk, where now every wall but one was gutted to make one big roomful of open cubicles.

It made space for all the editors, artists, and other support personnel Clay Felker was bringing in. It also was the exact same office plan Clay Felker had at *New York* Magazine, an office plan denying privacy to everybody, an office plan that permitted him to see and hear everyone whenever he wanted, and *be* seen and heard *by* them whenever he wanted *that.*

"Publisher" Bartle Bull was at least asked, nicely, by Felker, if he would mind a move downstairs to the third floor. Ross Wetzsteon, "editor," walked into his office and found George Dillehay and a contractor there, already at work on Clay Felker's orders, doing the specs for its demolition.

In the eight months he held the honorary title of "editor," probably the only act of significance Ross Wetzsteon got to carry out was the firing of Diane Fisher. It was something he had wanted to do for a long time—the two of them had never gotten along—and that she had been expecting ever since the firing of Dan and Ed, while two months went by, she was stripped of duty after duty, and the new contingent of Felker people complained she was uncooperative. She entered the hospital for two days in late September for some scheduled surgery, and by the time she got out word had been passed to her, by way of Alan Weitz and Dick Bell, the former *Voice* production man she had been seeing and who picked her up at the hospital, that she was through. Bell drove her to the *Voice*. Ross met her there. He knew he was going to fire her. She knew he was going to fire her. He knew she knew. "Look, there's no easy or tactful way to say this," he started. "Cut the crap and give me my severance pay," she said.

Fred Morton came in to see Wetzsteon, right after the *New York* takeover, just prior to his annual European vacation. "Heil Clay!" he remembered Wetzsteon's mock salute, and Ross telling him how upset everyone was there, and asking Morton if he knew anyone who could give him a job. Then Morton got a letter in Europe from Wetzsteon, after the firing of Dan and Ed, saying that things were changing rapidly and he would explain more when Morton returned in September. But when Morton *did* return, Ross reassured him that "no, I'm not unhappy," that all this was "terribly exicting," and that "you're one of the few people we won't have to ask to write shorter." So Fred Morton submitted two columns, which were not run.

He was surprised they were not; that had never happened to him before. Then a letter from Ross Wetzsteon came, telling him his first piece had not run because Ross had been unable to get in touch with him over changes he wanted to make and so had had to kill the entire piece. Fred Morton was angry.

He was angry because he had been at home, and had an answering service, and Ross Wetzsteon had lied to him. He called Wetzsteon back, and found him evasive. Then his second column ran, delayed a week and not listed in the index, and he called again to tell Ross Wetzsteon, "This is unendurable." Ross Wetzsteon agreed it was "terrible, but you don't have to be so touchy about it," and seemed to Fred Morton to be in a state of nervous agitation.

Morton did not write for the paper again. He bumped into Wetzsteon at the paper's Christmas party, and Ross told him, "Things are settling down, we must have lunch," and Fred Morton said, "Call me," but Wetzsteon didn't, and afterwards Morton didn't think he ever really intended to, which was true.

Fred Morton and Diane Fisher were the first two to go. Many more would follow.

★ ★ ★

1974, 1975 . . . On Election Eve, the *Voice* publishes an unusual open letter of endorsement of U.S. Senator Jacob Javits against his Democratic opponent, ex-Attorney General Ramsey Clark—from Norman Mailer, who happens to be suing the paper the letter appears in. . . . Clark Whelton on what it was like to live three doors down from Jane Alpert and the late Sam Melville on Avenue B and East 4th Street, as the fugitive feminist finally gives herself up . . . Ron Rosenbaum probing the cocaine bust of Abbie Hoffman . . . Howard Blum on a day with the New York Police Department bomb squad, when Puerto Rican terrorists blast Fraunces Tavern in Lower Manhattan . . . Mary Nichols covering Nelson Rockefeller's vice-presidential confirmation hearings . . . Paul Cowan in West Virginia, covering the school textbooks controversy there . . . Lucian Truscott roving the Middle East, coming back by way of Holland with an open letter from ex–New York cop Frank Serpico describing the new life he leads there . . . Phil Tracy, nine months before Nelson Rockefeller's prize anti-corruption prosecutor is first ordered fired, gives, in "From Supercop to Superflop," the first public debunking of Maurice Nadjari. . . . Jack Newfield, zeroing in on Rabbi Bernard Bergman, the chain of horror-show nursing homes he runs, and the political influence he has bought . . . John Hamill, on his service as a GI in Vietnam now that Saigon is falling . . . Pete Hamill, nominating Michael Harrington for president, and incurring the wrath of an old *Post* colleague when, urging new Governor Hugh Carey to do something about the nursing homes mess, he writes, "Be an Irishman. Be on the side of the victims. . . . Go in there and wipe those rat bastards right off the face of the earth." . . . "I had hoped that the spectacle of Daniel Patrick Moynihan would by now have loosened the grip of that notion and freed us all to think of the Irish as the finks the essential story of their rise in our society has instructed us that they are," replies Murray Kempton in a letter to the editor. Written mainly to settle an old personal score from *Post* days, it starts a mini-replay of old *Voice* literary brouhahas, draws irate counter-mail from disaffected ex-fans charging him with bigotry, and a lengthy defense from Joe Flaherty. . . . Flaherty on the Wilbur Mills–Fanne Foxe–Washington Tidal Basin incident . . . Jill Johnston, writing with capitals and punctuation, yet, interviewing stripper Foxe in Boston . . . Clark Whelton and Lucian Truscott with a "memo" of who Gerald Ford really ought to consider for his vice-president: "Fanne Foxe. Advantages: Fanne. Disadvantages: Foxe . . . Frank Serpico. Advantages: Honest. Disadvantages: Honest . . . Richard Nixon. Advantages:

Crusading Congressman, exposed Jerry Voorhis and Helen Gahagan Douglas, nailed Alger Hiss, Ike's active and popular vice-president for eight years, braved howling mob in Caracas, bested Khrushchev in Moscow kitchen debate, courageous comeback from narrow defeat in 1960, far-sighted statesman who ended Vietnam War, brought about detente with Soviet Union and opened new paths of peace with People's Republic of China. Disadvantages: Phlebitis." . . .

. . . But there is not much more than that. And, in the issue of Christmas Week, there is the column of Andrew Sarris. Ostensibly, it is about the dismissal of his colleague, Stuart Byron, by the *Real Paper*, to make room for its political writer, Andrew Kopkind, to turn to film. But Sarris moves closer to home:

> Our lives hang by a thread, as Pavese once said, and in these difficult times our jobs hang by even less that that . . . Byron insists on covering the beat, Kopkind prefers to cover the scene. Unfortunately, most publishers and editors prefer the scene to the beat. What they don't realize is that a beat well-covered eventually becomes the scene. . . . In the *Voice* itself I can't turn a page without bumping into a thinly disguised movie review from an unlikely source, usually left field. . . . No one wants to be pegged or cubby-holed, the film critic least of all . . . [but] as the editor of the movie department at the *Voice*, I must report that the scene is beginning to squeeze the beat. Of course, I know as well as anyone that Jackie Onassis and Fannie Foxe will sell more papers than Carl Dreyer and Fritz Lang. A touch of tits and ass doesn't hurt in the slightest. Quite the contrary. The thing is to find a culturally legitimate excuse. . . .

It was personally meant for Goldstein, who had exasperated Sarris in the early months, and whom he proceeded to lecture in print for holding freelancer Bill Paul's review of *Earthquake* until his own, "feel" piece on Disaster Movies was ready, and then for displaying ignorance of cinema history in it. Goldstein grumbled—"more people than Sarris should review movies," he complained to one journalist— but the article was printed.

It was the first publicly expressed criticism, timid and limited as it was, of the way things were going under the new regime. And it was only part of the problem. To any outside observer, it was obvious by early 1975 that the *Village Voice* was publishing less, not of quantity but of *substance*, than it had ever published before. More and more the paper was running features that were show reviews or culture criticism or personality profiles or celebrity interviews. Of course, it was an outward manifestation of Clay Felker's "star" mentality, a sensibility that was now indisputably in control. But, more subliminally and more important, the *Village Voice* had stopped making trends that others would follow. It had begun *itself* to follow trends. It was covering—reacting to—events. It was publishing stuff that everyone else in publishing published. It had ceased to be the paper where a new writer could always be discovered, or a new idea always discussed.

★ ★ ★

The crew of editors that came in under Clay Felker—Goldstein, Christgau, Durbin in particular—came there with ideas of how the *Village Voice* should be changed, ideas they tended to explain in the Movement rhetoric they were used to using with each other, ideas they knew were anathema to many of the people downstairs. What they did *not* know, not at first, was that Clay Felker had not brought them in there to have their own ideas, but to execute *his* ideas. And so they found themselves in the middle—suspected and despised downstairs, rebelling against him upstairs. They found themselves, to use Movement lingo, inside a participatory police state.

The problem was that Clay Felker would come down to his new acquisition on Wednesdays for a lunchtime editorial meeting—and editorial meetings were one of the innovations at the *Village Voice* under the new regime, held at least once a week—where the contents and the cover of the next week's issue would be decided upon, and then would come down again on Monday afternoon, with Milton Glaser, charging through the fifth floor, raging and storming about how this story and that picture were not right, how the cover was awful, how everything had to be changed, forcing them to tear up all their plans and start all over again at the last minute.

That was not the way they had thought things were going to be. They began to dread living under the gun with Clay. They began answering him back. And when they did *that,* Clay Felker went into some of the best vein-popping numbers he ever did.

It started with the PARTYING OUR WAY TO HARD TIMES cover. At first, Goldstein would not write the article to go with it (which was another *Voice* first—writing a lead story in the office on copy day to go with a cover shot selected beforehand).

"Goddamnit, Goldstein, you shit, why don't you write that article?" Felker finally barked at him, and, this time, Goldstein complied. But there were other incidents. Felker, on more than one occasion, came in

proposing cover shots which professional models had posed for. He denounced an Off-Broadway picture spread—"these pictures have no depth, no momentum, no character." When Karen Durbin questioned his judgment once, he turned on her: "You're a visual idiot. What do you know?" He threw other screaming shit fits, howling and wailing and bellowing so that everyone on the entire floor could hear him, once standing right by an embarrassed Goldstein, who was trying to carry on a transcontinental telephone conversation with, of all people, Roy Rogers at the time. After Goldstein had worked with writer Greil Marcus, scaling a 25,000-word epic about Elvis Presley down to a manageable 5,000 words, and devised a last-page layout with which to jump the article back inside the paper, Felker walked in, took one look at it, and shrieked, *"This page is SHIT."*

"Bullshit!" said Goldstein, refusing to change it. "It is *not* shit! And I'm not going to feel guilty about it!" They were all fighting him now, even his "own" people. But there was no stopping him. He went up to Robert Christgau one time, saying, "There aren't enough stars in the paper. What's hot?" and looking through the latest copy of *Variety* until he came across an ad for the hit Jamaican movie, *The Harder They Come,* starring *reggae* singer Jimmy Cliff. "This guy Jimmy Cliff. Can we do a feature on him?"

"No," said Christgau.

"Why not?"

"Because he's not going to be a star," Christgau said.

"Why not? Why not?" Felker was poking his finger at him.

"Because he doesn't have enough *talent,* that's why," Christgau told him, watching a look of horror cross Felker's face.

And then Clay Felker walked in the office, in January of 1975, and announced, "There will be no more lowercase sentences in the paper."

It was an order he had tried to give two months before, but had been talked out of at the time. A compromise had been reached; Jill Johnston would do one feature a month, regular capitalization, in exchange for keeping her column as it was before, though at a shorter length. But now he could not be dissuaded. The order stood: For Jill Johnston. For Joel Oppenheimer. For everybody.

Felker called up Oppenheimer himself, at home, and reached him just as he was making dinner for his children; he and his wife Helen had separated only twenty-four hours before. Oppenheimer had already been cut back to once every other week, but this was much worse. Here he was, forty-five, a single father with no fallback position or emotional support behind him. He knew he could not say, "Fuck you," which he wanted to do. He had to listen.

Felker waited for Oppenheimer to say something. "Is something wrong?" he asked. "Yeah," said the poet. "I've never published a word in upper and lower case." Felker went on to tell him it was arrogance to write his way, how it showed contempt for his readers, and Joel Oppenheimer just said, "Well, I'll have to think about it," leaving open the possibility he would leave the paper rather than submit.

As it happened, each week one of the writers was being invited to the Wednesday editorial conferences and this was Joel Oppenheimer's turn. Oppenheimer didn't know if he should come now, but was persuaded to and, thanks to the backing he got from the other editors and his own knowledge of printing, was able to make points—"I write short paragraphs, the tightest ones on the paper, and I use commas when I have the option not to use them"—that Felker, and Milton Glaser especially, who was visibly impressed with how much he knew, could not deny. Felker changed the subject. "Clay, excuse me," Joel Oppenheimer interrupted. "Did I win or did I lose?" Felker did not give him a direct answer that day, but by Friday the word came that he could continue to write the way he had. And Joel Oppenheimer went out and bought the editors a chocolate cake.

Jill Johnston, however, did not have it so easily. Just for agreeing to the previous compromise, she reported back to her editor, Karen Durbin, her friends were telling her, "Well, Jill, he's put you in girdle and high heels, he's made a girl of you." And now this—Jill Johnston's columns began to bear references to a "mr steel the capitalist," who wanted to capitalize her work.

She was in Massachusetts most of the time, so communication was by phone. But even that presented its problems, seeing as it was Clay Felker, big-city hot-shot publisher, talking on one end of the line, and Jill Johnston, madcap free-spirit lesbian, talking on the other. "She doesn't want me to have any authority," he could complain to Karen Durbin, who acted as their go-between. "He doesn't want me to have room to breathe," she would tell Durbin. "She's just using me," Felker would tell her. "He doesn't really want to run me," Johnston would tell her. After one conversation that winter, supposedly for him to explain the new policy to her, he came off the line saying, "She's crazy. She's absolutely crazy. She just tied me in knots. I gave in. What else could I do? Run the goddamn column! She's impossible. I can't fight with her anymore. She's just too much."

But did you reach an agreement? Karen Durbin wanted to know. "An agreement? I don't know," he said. "We'll have to work something out. She's vanquished me."

But as soon as Karen Durbin got on the line with Jill Johnston, she began getting a different version. "He's crazy. He wants to run everything. He's the man."

But he says you've won, Karen Durbin told her.

"Won?" replied Jill Johnston. "There's no way to win against the man." And so the situation remained. The paper began printing her column with periods, but no graphs or caps, and she began "an extended essay with the working title what is journalism and if you know what journalism is what is literature?—dealing with the history of my origins and attachment and formation as a writer in relation to the village voice."

But the ugliest of the confrontations came that April, over an article Judith Coburn wrote.

A freelancer who had covered the war for the *Voice* years before, she got a go-ahead for a piece on the politics of Operation Babylift, the eleventh-hour mass airlift of Vietnamese infants out of encircled Saigon, and at 5 P.M. on Monday afternoon, April 7, it was ready to run.

That was when Felker came in, barnstorming as usual, hastily read the piece, and declared, "This is Communist propaganda."

What was Communist propaganda? he was asked. This thing here in the beginning about the aid, he said, pointing to an early sentence: "And in Saigon, U.S. Ambassador Graham Martin was reported to have made the argument to top Saigon officials that the airlift was helping shift American public opinion in favor of the Thieu government." That's not true, he said. That aid request will never pass. We have to say that somewhere. We have to add graphs saying the aid won't pass.

Judith Coburn was not willing to do that, and Karen Durbin, her editor, backed her up. "I AM THE EDITOR!"* he exploded. *"You people here think I can't read English!"* And he was blasting off again, sputtering, quaking, stopping all work on the fifth floor while terrified people turned around to watch him, his face turning so scarlet and his manner so violent that Judith Coburn actually worried he was going to hit her, and wished to herself she could just crawl under a desk until it was all over.

He began scribbling and crossing out on her manuscript. She said she wanted her article back. He said we have to do it—it's a matter of truth and honesty in journalism.

Alan Weitz, one of the old loyalists, made an associate editor by Felker the previous summer and silent this whole time, chose this

---

*True. In March, he had stopped pretending and put himself at the top of a new, redesigned logo as "editor in chief."

moment to say some things he had been meaning to tell Clay Felker for a long time. "How can you talk about truth and honesty in journalism," he asked, "when every week in *New York* Magazine there's an exaggeration or a distortion? You've always made stories out to be more than they are, and now you're trying to do the same thing to the *Voice.*"

Felker looked incredulous. "Why can't I get my way?" he begged someone to tell him. *"Why am I being thwarted?"*

"Because you don't know how to be civil," Alan Weitz told him.

Typical of *Village Voice* anecdotes, there were three differing versions as to who typed up the compromise sentence, the one labeling Ambassador Martin's notion "highly doubtful," that saved the day—depending on the one telling the story, it was Karen Durbin, Ross Wetzsteon, or Eliot Fremont-Smith. At any rate, the minor, almost trivial change sufficed; it satisfied Felker, it satisfied Coburn, it set him to apologizing all around before leaving.

But the scene he had caused that day cost him Alan Weitz, a young man whose editorial abilities he admired. Weitz went out to a three-hour lunch with Judy Daniels, explained he had worked for the *Voice* for eight years and could not participate in what was happening to it any longer, and turned in his resignation. And, in the aftermath of the incident, when Coburn and the editors proposed an Indochina War retrospective picture spread, Felker shot it down. "Who cares about Cambodia?" he told the editorial meeting. (That was another thing new at the *Voice;* article ideas being dismissed out of hand on the grounds that our-readers-don't-want-to-read-about-that.) *"Time* and *Newsweek* have pictures of Cambodia." So they did; and Alexander Cockburn's column examined their coverage—using, as illustration, the cover of *Newsweek,* complete with subscription label that indicated where the copy being used came from—"NEW YORK MAGAZINE. 755 SECOND AVE. NY NY.")

After these battles had gone on for months, Felker invited them up to his place for a Wednesday lunch that was supposed to settle all problems. There, the salaried chef from the built-in kitchen at the new headquarters Clay Felker had taken over for his magazine in late 1974, just a few months after the *Voice* deal, prepared a meal of roast goose (or duck, or rabbit, depending on whose recollection it was) for them in the corporate dining room, and Milton Glaser presented a slide show that, as they pieced it together afterwards, had something to do with "subliminal graphic design" in "the post-print age" and "the tribal identity of magazine readers."

That's just it, some of them tried to point out. *As you increase the base, you're alienating the tribe.* Jack Newfield, who as a "senior editor"—a title Felker invented when he came in—was entitled to be there, and who, despite friendship for Felker, was already publicly comparing what he was doing to Lyndon Johnson and South Vietnam, spoke up. He was concerned, he said, the *Voice* was being "colonized" by *New York,* and "trivialized" by personality pieces.

Clay Felker used that old line again—"The *Voice* was dying when I bought it."

Jack Newfield had an answer: "There's more than one way to kill a newspaper."

★ ★ ★

In the same issue of April 14, 1975, that Judy Coburn's "The War of the Babies" ran, there was another article, by Blair Sabol, a onetime staff writer just moved back from the West Coast. It began with a description of getting a phone call from Linda McCartney, wife of ex-Beatle Paul, the afternoon following Linda's marijuana bust in Los Angeles, "for the first time in eight years."

> Did she need money . . . no, she wanted to go shopping in Beverly Hills. Now you must understand the last time I knew Linda was in her groping groupie days. I met her on an interview with Warren Beatty after his Bonnie and Clyde success when he was into giving nonverbal explanations and Linda was into photographing stars with little or no film in her camera. I remember how impressed I was with her come-on hard-on talents as she got in front of Mr. B in a miniskirt and her legs in a full wide-angle split for at least six rolls of Ectachrome. Warren ended up ushering me out of his Delmonico's suite within 30 minutes and kept Linda for two days.

From there, Sabol went on how "her pictures turned out to be mediocre to poor," and that since "the eventual McCartney score . . . Linda considers herself very much the rock star," with an "affected Liverpudlian accent." Her piece then included an account of a recent L.A. party where she mistook Helen Reddy for a waitress, where Tatum O'Neal "stormed off angrily to break in on her father, who was dirty digging it with a black model," and where "I followed Dylan onto the dance floor. . . . He turned in my direction for a full 16 measures, and yes friends, I DANCED WITH BOB DYLAN!!"

The Sabol piece "could well have run in the old *Voice,*" wrote Nat Hentoff in his column three weeks later. "Dan Wolf enjoys gossip and the long needle as much as Clay Felker. But in the old *Voice,* the piece would not have gotten nearly the prominence the new management gave it—two full pages up front, with three photographs." And the day it came out, "my older daughter called to ask if I were now writing for the *National Enquirer."*

"The same indignant question, 'What the hell's going on at *The Voice?'* invariably erupts these nights when I talk at colleges, no matter what the alleged subject of the evening," he went on. There is discontent, moreover, among some writers and editors at *The Voice.* . . . When the new management first arrived, there was considerable apprehension. Now there is knowledge. . . ."

> . . . *Voice* journalism—with exceptions every issue—is becoming increasingly formularized to fit the overall circus barker tone of the paper. . . . I would no longer advise a young writer that *The Voice* is a desirable place to break in. You could burn out fast. . . . Gone are the unpredictable, unfashionable, sometimes rambling, often idiosyncratic (but not *'streamlined'*) pieces that were integral to the old *Voice.* This latter kind of writing (which, God knows, could be boring but occasionally was marvelously beguiling) usually cannot be assigned. It gropes into the light from one particular writer's grumbling obsession. . . .
>
> This is not to say . . . that every issue of the old *Voice* was so resplendent in its authenticity that it had to be read all the way through before life could continue. . . . There are writers who are authentic *schmucks,* and the old *Voice* printed a goodly number of them. But it *was* handmade, and the writer's sensibility powered the paper. Dan Wolf respected writers. Not in their persons, necessarily, or he would have paid them a lot better. But he did respect their work. . . . [Clay Felker sees them] as Balanchine sees dancers—they exist to be bent to fit, and so they are interchangeable. . . .

It was the strongest, most direct attack yet. But they were still not united, and the article showed why. In the case of Sarris's initial complaint, for instance, he had cited not only Richard Goldstein, but Margot Hentoff too—wife of Nat, and someone so critical of Felker she stopped contributing to the paper—as among those poaching on his territory. Now, Hentoff singled out Blair Sabol, no lackey of Felker, simply because he had never liked her—and despite the fact that his own stepdaughter, Mara Wolynski, had written a very similar piece for the paper four months earlier, describing model Margaux Hemingway, Ernest's granddaughter, and her boyfriend, hamburger chain heir Errol Wetson, in terms at least as loathsome.

★ ★ ★

The idea of starting a union was Ron Rosenbaum's. He had been spending long afternoons in Howard Smith's office, expounding his conspiracy theory of how Felker had bought the *Voice* to destroy it, listening to Smith lament how under Dan and Ed the *Voice* had been a benevolent corporation interested in people's feelings, but how now under Felker it had turned into just another impersonal, growth-minded one. Then one day he came in, all fired up to do it.

Howard Smith had always gotten along with Ron Rosenbaum, but was under no illusions. He knew Rosenbaum's interest in this project was liable to disappear overnight, leaving other people to hold the bag. Look, he warned, I'm making a movie. "I haven't got the time to do much work on this. You're going to have to do it."

"Are you kidding?" Smith had never seen Rosenbaum this excited. "Why don't you think I'll do it?"

"Ron," said Smith, "you don't know what it's like. Once you get committed to this . . ."

"I will never back out!" Rosenbaum yelled. "Never! Never! I'll follow through!"

Okay, Howard Smith went along. They took their first step, deciding who to affiliate with—since Smith's lawyers were counsel for the Newspaper Guild, they went there rather than District 65 of the Distributive Workers of America, the publishing employees' union. They got other people to join them: Jeanne Oliver, a production assistant and Smith's current girlfriend. Pegi Goodman, an editorial assistant, and Ann Cummings, who worked in advertising. Nat Hentoff and Paul Cowan. On May 7, six days after being formally notified by the Guild that the attempt was under way, Clay Felker received a list of five names on the "Organizing Committee," and therefore untouchable from being fired without cause at least until the attempt had failed. Smith's name was on the list, and Oliver's, and Cummings's, and Goodman's, and Hentoff's.

But not Ron Rosenbaum's.

They were just about to mail out their first open letter, when Rosenbaum started vacillating—"I never promised to do all the work. I never said I had the time." And, he told Smith, "I'm working on something so big for *New Times* that when the *Voice* finds out about it, all hell will break loose. I might get fired. I might have legal problems."

He backed out of putting his name on the committee. And on May 7, he came into Howard Smith's office to announce he was going to quit that day.

May 7 was a Wednesday, a day, Ron Rosenbaum knew, when Clay Felker would be in the office about noon for the weekly editorial meeting. He waited. Then he went upstairs.

He found Felker talking, in the office Ross Wetzsteon had been moved to, with Wetzsteon and Ken Auletta,* a new writer. His latest paycheck was in his hand as he strode across the room, attracting the attention of Felker, who stood there and stared as he stopped, said, "There's no amount of money that can make me work for the piece of shit you've turned this paper into," tore the check into little pieces, dropped them on the floor, and walked out again.

Clay Felker looked to Ken Auletta and asked, "Who was that?"

When the next issue of *New Times* featured an interview of Abbie Hoffman, on the run and gone underground since his cocaine bust, by Ron Rosenbaum, Clay Felker began telling people—in one case, an audience of journalists at the Deadline Club—that Rosenbaum had stayed on the payroll for a year, deliberately not producing, and used *Voice* expense money to do the Hoffman story. That was not so—while Rosenbaum had not exactly burned himself out in the last year, he had written as much as any contributing editor to *New York* did, and not only Alan Weitz, his editor, but Judy Daniels, Felker's loyalist, specifically contradicted Felker's charge about the expense money—and no one seemed to believe it except Felker.

And yet Ron Rosenbaum, after he quit, told the *SoHo Weekly News,* "I decided I didn't want to do it for the embarrassing, shrill and vulgar paper the *Voice* had become"—which certainly seemed to be the tacit statement of a man who had, in fact, started out to do the Hoffman story for the *Voice.* And, months later, when Felker's and his accounts of the affair had both been published, he on at least one occasion

---

*Auletta was about the closest Felker came to "discovering" a new writer at the *Voice.* His career had been mostly in politics, in the service of Howard Samuels—in the Commerce Department when Samuels was secretary and Lyndon Johnson was president, in New York City's Off-Track Betting Corporation, and in two Democratic primary campaigns for governor. After the second losing try, in 1974, Auletta had, for two weeks, been a political columnist for the *New York Post,* until, his first column not having run, he demanded an audience with the publisher, Dolly Schiff, where she told him, first, that he had used *likely* twice in one paragraph, and second, that as a former political aide, should he really be writing a column on politics? "That's a fair question, but you should have asked it before you hired me," he replied, and went off to freelance. Felker had taken him out to dinner, with Gail Sheehy and Jack Newfield, in December and offered him a job then, but Auletta had put him off. After a few articles for the *Voice,* though, he had reconsidered and come on staff.

refused to give an interview and threatened to sue if the reporter did not agree, in advance, to censor any mention of what Felker had said about him.

Ron Rosenbaum had gone out spectacularly. But he had not helped other people by what he did, nor by the way he did it. And not for the last time.

★ ★ ★

The organizers began trying to get signatures on union cards calling for an election. Others joined the committee—Marlene Nadle, theater critics Arthur Sainer and Dick Bruckenfeld, photographer Abner Symons, production assistant Dick West. They began issuing statements and wrote flyers. Hentoff, Cowan, Smith and Oliver bought shares of *New York* stock, entitling them to attend the May 30 stockholders' meeting. Hentoff and Smith showed up, leafleting people as they went inside. They did the same thing outside the Obie Awards, which Felker had moved uptown to Lincoln Center.

"All of this publicity, much of it inaccurate," Clay Felker told *Media Industry Newsletter,* "washes away quickly." But, in explaining why he could not afford to have a union come in there, he had to admit two things—that the *Voice* had shown a profit of only $46,000 for the first quarter of 1975, compared to $255,000 the year before, and that circulation was down.

He claimed it was 140,000, down 4,000 in a year, and filed that figure with the Audit Bureau of Circulation. To his stockholders, he gave hyperbole: "Since we acquired control of *The Village Voice* in June 1974 its circulation had held steady at an average of approximately 150,000 copies weekly." Neither statement was true. As checks of the ABC figures showed, the paper had begun, for the first time, counting even the bleak early days, to "grace" subscriptions—that is, continue them for a time after a subscriber had let one expire without renewal. Not counting them, it was really down to 134,000. And documents, slipped anonymously to Howard Smith and Jeanne Oliver by someone in circulation, showed that for the first week of June, not counting graces, it had actually slipped to 129,000—a drop of *15,000!* Felker's reaction, when that figure was made public, was to have Bill Ryan, the financial vice-president he had installed at the *Voice,* come up to Howard Smith at the *Voice* baseball game and tell him management regarded the documents in their possession as stolen property.

But Felker counterattacked. He began showing up at department meetings—not just editorial but business, advertising, circulation, clerical, too, since the union was trying to organize all of them, and when he did they began showing up to debate him. He threw Howard Smith out of one meeting, but he did not throw out Jeanne Oliver, and the tall, thin, deliberately spoken blonde, on her way to law school, surprised him with her ability to keep up, detail for detail. He alternated between being benevolent—he didn't know these problems existed, just give him time—and potentially avenging—you know what happens when a union comes in, I might have to put in time clocks, I might even have to shut the paper down. His department heads took workers aside to find out what the problems were. He hastily promulgated a "Personnel Policy Manual" to explain how *Voice* workers could already get sick leaves and hearings for their grievances. He quickly came up with a medical plan to co-opt what the union might offer. And wherever he went, he played on the latent fear of unions.

And he won, because once again the writers of the *Village Voice* failed to get it together. Several expressed misgivings about what would happen to freelancers under unionization, and claimed Smith and the others took a what-do-you-care attitude; but they held a meeting, just for freelancers, and none came. Jack Newfield remembered that Howard Smith had opposed *him* when he sought to organize people in 1971, so he refused to help Howard Smith now. Some, at a mass meeting at the NYU Loeb Student Center, and later, complained to Howard Smith about "gangster" union officials and having to be in the same union with classified and clerical workers. As for Alex Cockburn, they knew he had, in the year since Felker got there, become his biggest *Voice* "star," invited to Clay's parties, privy to his late-night phone calls, and they knew Cockburn was loving it, just as he had loved sucking up to Dan Wolf when Wolf was the one to suck up to. He couldn't sign the union card, he explained to them at first, because he felt support for the union was strictly out of hatred for Felker, and maybe Felker's methods weren't so bad, maybe they would do something for the *Voice*. Maybe, Jeanne Oliver said, but conditions are bad right now, and we don't have a say in anything, and you're supposed to be a Marxist. All right, he finally agreed—or at least, promised to sign the union card if they promised never to tell Felker he did so. And the men alone who were left—Whelton, Blum, Truscott—once again refused to join something. They had other plans.

That summer, Jeanne Oliver's mother became fatally ill, and she had to return home. All meetings and attempts to organize stopped. The Newspaper Guild had set a goal of 70 percent signatures before trying an election, to make a massive show of force and be sure of winning beforehand, though by law they needed only 30. They failed to get even that.

★ ★ ★

Spring-summer 1975 . . . Howard Blum on undercover cops, tracking down dope pushers in Harlem and professional arsonists in the South Bronx . . . But when the police cancel another undercover operation—Project Cleveland—in the garment district, David Durk, an old friend of the *Voice,* leaks the details to Jack Newfield. They get printed, and Durk gets transferred. . . . Mary Nichols profiling Frank Church, the Idaho senator probing the CIA . . . Paul Cowan on Tom Hayden, the onetime Chicago 7 conspiracy defendant, running for the Senate in California . . . Karen Durbin, interviewing Mick Jagger as the Stones tour America, making the mistake of wondering out loud if "Midnight Rambler" is not a *macho* song:

> Seeing as how we'd degenerated to the level of five-year-olds in a sandbox I prepared to retreat to a friendlier line of questioning. Too late. No matter what I asked about anything, the answers came out in grudging monosyllables. So I put on my adult reporter face and said, "Well, thanks very much," and he put on his adult performer face and said, "My pleasure," and there you have some irony.

. . . And Ken Auletta, as Nelson Rockefeller turns a grilling before the state panel investigating the Bergman nursing homes scandal into a stump performance:

> Thursday's hearing ended as it had begun, with Rockefeller walking to the platform and shaking hands and offering a little personal touch to each commission member. He and the chairman chatted. . . . He asked commission member Peter Berle how his mother was. One by one he gripped the hand of each commissioner and staff member. Then he darted back across the table seeking another staff member, because "I didn't say good-bye to her."
> The host was thanking everyone for coming. . . .
> Then the vice president bounced down the flight of marble stairs, heading a parade of staffers and secret servicemen. He thanked another cop, walked over, and patted the arms and hands of the women at the switchboard desk, the cop at the inside door, the four young girls beside the front entrance. He said, "Thanks for the job you're doing" to the helmeted cop at the curb beside the Lincoln limousine, pressed closer, reached

out and touched the people crowding the sidewalk, waved and blew kisses to citizens across the street, recognized and said hello to a rabbi, and shouted to no one in particular as he entered his car, "This is still a great city. The greatest."

He was off to another campaign stop. This time, the grand jury.

There were also, for the first time in many years, personal, sexual classified ads. There were two articles, in the June 16 issue, debating the pros and cons of being circumcised. There was the cover story of the July 14 issue, supposedly the bitter autobiography of a psychiatrist who had failed, lost a homosexual patient to suicide, misdiagnosed a neurologically disturbed boy, given in to temptation and had intercourse with a patient, given up.

The article had been submitted, over the transom, by a "Robert Ashby," and neither Judy Daniels nor Diane Straus, who handled it, had thought to check out its factuality—until it had already been published, and the *New York Post* had gotten onto the story that perhaps it was a phony. Three weeks later, the *Voice* had to run this statement, bordered, one column, on the inside: "After investigating the controversy that 'Confessions of a Disillusioned Therapist' (*Voice,* July 14) produced among therapists, we find that we were taken. Richard Ashby is not a Ph.D., as he claimed in his article," nor had he gone to the New School and Columbia as he claimed. And when the home phone number he had given was called, his roommate had answered and explained that Ashby, suffering from "personal problems," had left New York. "He has not been heard from since," the statement said.

It had taken exactly one year from the firing of Dan Wolf and Ed Fancher for the *Village Voice* to descend to the level of "Redpants and Sugarman."

★ ★ ★

They had been leaving one by one. Now they began leaving in droves.

Clay Felker and Ely Kushel had little use for each other from the beginning. Kushel knew that a part-time accountant was not Felker's idea of a business operation, and one time Felker so aggravated him, swaggering through the department en route elsewhere, he had spoken up, "Listen, the next time you come in here, you say hello to everyone here." Twice he tried to resign, but agreed to stay on until Felker could get people of his own in to take over. At the end of 1974, he was gone.

"There's a place for you," Felker had told George Dillehay at their first breakfast meeting, but it was not to be in circulation, which he had been running since Carole Rogers's departure the year before. "George," Felker told him after taking a look at his books, "you're a nice guy, but you're not a circulation director." Dillehay had not tried to fight it, but he did once question the wisdom of one of Felker's ideas. That was a mistake. "Boy," said Felker, whirling around on him, "I'll tell you this once and just once. I know what I'm doing."

George Dillehay did not try to offer any more suggestions after that. In fact, he began to consider it a good day if he could go home to his wife and report that Felker had not come in or been heard from that day. By the middle of April, when an opportunity came up to work for a publisher of children's magazines, he took it.

Even before then, Dillehay had been walking by Steve Blacker, the "associate publisher" Felker had brought in, and overheard him telling a salesman, "There's a guy here named Bartle Bull, who won't be here much longer."

He had never been "publisher"; that was a cruel joke at his expense. Felker had never ordered him around; he had simply, from the day he moved his offices, given orders around him. He was cut off and cut out. Felker bad-mouthed him to the other *New York* Magazine company directors. Felker dismantled Textmasters, his baby, and sold its equipment to Patent Trader, in January of 1975. And, as Bartle Bull found out only afterwards, Felker went skiing over Christmas with Carter Burden in Sun Valley, Idaho.

What Felker was doing to him was galling, but when he realized just how much his best friend had let him down, the greening of Bartle Bull was under way. After years of fronting for another man, at great psychological expense to himself, he began taking matters into his own hands, and in many ways it appeared to be the best thing that had ever happened to him.

He decided to jump before he was pushed—just in time, too, since in the departmental meetings during the union drive Felker was using him as a scapegoat, saying such ominous things as "I haven't been here, I've trusted everything to Bartle." He knew Dennis Smith, the New York City firefighter and author, and they both believed that a magazine aimed at firefighters and their families would work on the market. That spring, he quietly lined up Wall Street investors. And, late one Saturday afternoon in May, he came over to Carter Burden's apartment to tell him he was getting out.

The visit turned out to last seven hours, and was adjourned around the corner to P. J. Clarke's for dinner while Burden tried to talk him out of it. "Who's going to fight with Felker for me?" he asked at one point.

"That's your problem," Bartle Bull answered. "You got into bed with him, you sleep with him. I can't ask you to do a better job with my career than you did with your own." And, before the night was over, he had told Carter Burden, "I can't go tiger-hunting with you, Carter."

"Why not? Because I'd shoot you in the back?"

"No. But I might need you, and when I'd turn around, you wouldn't be there."

Bull left the paper, but not the corporation; the board, on which he had plenty of friends, even if they were not Felker's, voted him $40,000 as termination on his contract. And while he resigned as publisher, he remained as president until May 30, 1976, with $35,000 in consulting fees to be paid him until December 31, 1976.

Felker's people moved to clean the rest of the house. Sandy Fendrick returned from vacation to be told by Steve Blacker that she could stay only if she accepted a one-third cut in salary, the loss of all her accounts except entertainment ads, and the taking away of her title, "display advertising director." She quit. Rosetta Reitz left. Even Maurice, the bearded bum, was told, one Wednesday night when he stopped by for his weekly allotment of papers to sell, that he wasn't going to get the *Voice* anymore. The paper printed a statement claiming it had all been a mistake and pleading with him to come back, but Maurice would not go back.

Nor was Maurice the only eccentric the paper lost that summer, by choice or design. In the issue of July 7, Jonas Mekas wrote this:

> The long pages of long articles on third-rate Hollywood stars and fifth-rate Hollywood movies will continue in this paper, and other papers and who cares! Somewhere somebody has to make money and you can't make money with Ecstasy or Beauty or Poetry.
>
> The adventure and the excitement have gone out of this paper for me. I am a free man now, with no power of the Press. I can go on to other business. And I am going with clear and good consciousness. I gave my 15 years.
>
> . . . This is my last column.

Shortly thereafter, Mekas began appearing again—in the *SoHo Weekly News*. Art critic John Perrault also left the *Voice* and joined *SoHo*. And Jill Johnston, who had been telling the story of her life and gotten as far as the 1970 swimming pool incident, ended one column,

"This will be continued here or elsewhere at some point," and never continued it.

Lucian Truscott, meanwhile, had several of his ideas and manuscripts rejected. Another piece, on the New York disco scene, became the object of a three-way committee-editing job between Karen Durbin, his editor, Goldstein, who felt something should be added about the gay scene, and Christgau, who wanted to kill it altogether. "This is a fucking outrage," he snarled at one point. "That was very gracious," said she. "Yeah, well, nothing's fucking gracious about this place," said he. Finally, he gave up. "I'm fucking sick and tired of this," he told her. "Write anything you want." And he left.

One piece of his that had run all right was about the Vinnell Corporation, a California-based military firm that had been sending mercenaries to train Saudi Arabian troops. But when he went out to Los Angeles to write two follow-up pieces on Vinnell, they did not run. And when, before the scene about the disco piece, Judy Daniels took him out for a drink and asked, "Lucian, we've noticed that you're not really happy. What's wrong?" he used the occasion to ask her what had happened to them.

"Well," she said, "nobody made a decision to do anything. They just sort of evaporated."

"Evaporated?" He was incensed all over again. "That's the first time in my life I've been told something that I wrote *evaporated.* What do you think my typewriter prints—little teacups full of water?"

Lucian Truscott took a few days, figured out what the signals meant, and wrote the following, military-style:

25 July 1975

Memo for:Clay Felker
Judy Daniels
interested parties
From: Lucian K. Truscott IV

1. This is to serve notice that two weeks hence, on Friday, 8 August 1975, I intend to leave the staff of the Village Voice. I wish to accept my final paycheck on that date, as well as payment for accrued leave I have coming.

2. I have come to my decision independent of any recent disagreements I've had with others at the Voice. My decision to leave the Voice is a personal one, reached after a great deal of thought, based primarily on my feelings that it's time I moved on. August 8 will make it five years almost to the day since I started working full-time at the Voice. I've never spent five years on one payroll in my life, other than that of the U.S. Government. I've got that old Army itch to move on.

3. Recent events have influenced my decision. In the past few weeks I have been able to place with other publications (most notably, the New Yorker and Harpers [sic] Magazine) articles which were unacceptable to the Voice either when presented as proposals or as finished manuscripts. This struck me as odd, especially in the former instance. The Voice always used to be the place to which one turned when an idea for a piece was not greeted enthusiastically elsewhere. In at least three instances, the opposite seems to be the case. This appears to me a signal event.

4. In addition, over the past several months, there were at least six pieces I suggested doing for the Voice which were turned down, as proposals, quite abruptly. After this happened, I found myself gradually tailoring my ideas along the lines of what I think might be acceptable to the new operating sensibility and format of the Voice. The tendency is to gravitate toward areas one knows from experience the new editorial staff at the Voice will greet with enthusiasm. This was discouraging to me. In the past, experiences I have had and ideas which resulted from them have given birth to perceptions which simmered along until they eventually thickened into articles. I am uncomfortable with the present circumstance, where one is encouraged to try matching pre-conceived notions of editors with ideas and experiences which are acceptable to the growing number of editorial personnel who affect each story printed in the Voice. Dealing with this system, if that is what it can be called (at present, it is a defacto situation) has for me been like trying to fill a half-dozen buckets full of water by carrying teaspoons of water to each in turn after a 20 yard dash. Inevitably this leads to one bucket or another getting slighted.

5. I have always been less a reporter, more a wordsmith. I've never been able to sit down and whack up a story on order. I am thoroughly incompatible with an editorial policy which asks the writer to try pleasing all (or most) of the editors, all of the time. And as I've said repeatedly in the past, I am in disagreement with the new policy at the Voice whereby editors attempt to second-guess the wishes of the reader and deliver him or her what he or she allegedly wants to read. All of the aforementioned are problems I've had with the way the Voice is presently being run, and all have contributed, in varying degrees, to my decision to move on.

Two months later, a gunman took over a West Village bank and held hostages, and Truscott, according to the story he told on a radio show, was standing outside, his old press pass visible, when a homicide detective, fiftyish-looking, approached him and said, "Oh, gee, you work for the *Voice.*"

"Not any longer," Truscott told him.

"I've been a subscriber for five years," said the detective. "Boy, the *Voice* has sure gone to hell under Felker, hasn't it?"

Lucian Truscott's name was gone from the masthead as of the August 18 issue. Clark Whelton's was gone a week later.

He had been brooding all winter and spring and summer, thinking about doing it, and now that most of his friends were gone he needed no more persuasion. He told Judy Daniels, and wrote Clay Felker a note, telling him that the editorial direction of the paper was now clear, and he could no longer be a part of it. He went back to freelancing, and began learning once again what it was like to run low on money. After him, at the end of the month, there was one more disgruntled departure—of Robin Reisig, to take a job up in Cambridge with the *Real Paper.*

Ross Wetzsteon was not fired. He was not forced to quit. He was humiliated worse than that. From Day One of his "editorship," Clay Felker humbled him simply by being Clay Felker, by running around, issuing orders, directing everything—and totally ignoring him.

He had it worse than Bartle Bull. His impotence was something Clay Felker demonstrated constantly, openly. And Bull had no staff downstairs to protect, bitching at him because he could not handle Felker and was therefore betraying them. *If only Bartle and I had been able to take over and run things our way,* he thought. *Then, things would have worked out all right.* But that was not to be. By the late spring, after he had been demoted to "executive editor" beneath "editor-in-chief" Clay Felker, he knew it had never been intended to be, that he had been picked for the job because he could not stand up to Felker, and that Felker knew it. The pressure became too much, and Ross Wetzsteon became immobilized. He could not edit any longer. He could not function. He showed up to work, but he could not work.

One day, something snapped. Julius Novick was with him in his office, and they were talking, and there was one minor provocation too many—afterwards neither of them could remember what it was. But it got Ross Wetzsteon to rise out of his chair, plant his feet by the window, and ram his right hand through the glass.

Blood and shards all over his fingers, he walked to a nearby emergency room, had his wound dressed, and felt better that day than he had in months. Later that month, Ross Wetzsteon checked into a hospital for a few days of complete rest, and came out, if not a changed, at least a cured man to become, in a new *Voice* reorganization, the chief theater critic—which was, he learned to his relief, what he had always *really* wanted to be.

★ ★ ★

It had been Dan Wolf's prediction all along that when it was Carter Burden's turn to give a deposition, an offer would be made to settle with them out of court. Sure enough, when the time came, so did the offer. The settlement—$485,000 for all of the minority's 20 percent—was reached April 11, and announced in the next issue of the paper.

They were free now to start a paper of their own, and their loyalists were waiting for them to do so. But they were not so sure they wanted to, and because they were not, an episode of miscommunication followed that disenchanted some of the members of the Family closest to them.

Ed Fancher, at least, was eager enough. But Dan Wolf was a good deal less so. He was, after all, nine years older—he was sixty now—and he was willing to give up time, energy, and money only if it was to help *somebody else* who was going to do the work. That was the way he felt. That was the message he thought he was giving. But that was not the message other people were receiving, and every time he did *anything* to move the idea of a new paper along, he raised their expectations that much higher, until they were too high.

The first meeting held to discuss it was in late April, in Ed Fancher's office. Wolf was there, and Diane Fisher, and Alan Weitz, who had just left, and Howard Smith and Ron Rosenbaum, who were still talking about a union, and Truscott and Whelton and Blum, and right away apprehensions set in when Fancher opened up by saying, "We're meeting here today because Howard Blum asked for us to meet."

"What do you mean, Howard Blum?" Smith interrupted him excitedly. "I thought *you* wanted us to meet."

"Well, there's no question I'm interested, of course," Ed Fancher explained, and the meeting went on. Other meetings followed. Diane Fisher designed a dummy. They discussed titles—*The Week* was a popular one. So, especially to Dan Wolf, was the one Alex Cockburn's paper in London had used, *Seven Days.** When Nat Hentoff's piece on

---

*As did David Dellinger in a new radical publication he was getting off the ground. Hearing that, they had to scrap the idea.

the new regime, with its mention that Dan Wolf had not paid writers well, appeared, Wolf called him up. "You wouldn't want to get ripped off twice, would you?" he asked. Wolf met with Hentoff, and Paul Cowan and Jack Newfield, to discuss money—were they willing to go in on this with him, either with money of their own or money they could get others to put up?

But the closer he got to being committed, the more Dan Wolf realized how little he wanted to do it. The closer he came to having to work with Newfield and Cowan and Hentoff again, the more he came to realize the things about them he couldn't stand—that Jack was an operator, Paul was totally self-involved, and that Nat, while a nice guy, was a pain in the ass, a pompous leftist who had been writing the same stuff for years.

There were other problems to be considered—Would Dan List agree to leave the *Voice* and distribute the new paper? Would the Mary Nichols wing of the old staff be able to get along with the Jack Newfield wing of the old staff? Would Ron Rosenbaum be able to get along with anybody?—problems that were not solved at meetings Clark Whelton, Alan Weitz, and Lucian Truscott had with Cowan and Newfield that summer. They came back claiming that those two, while expressing alienation from Felker, were pressing their old 1971 demands for editorial conferences again, plus Newfield wanted guarantees—"Felker's given me the best deal of my life. Why should I leave that for a risky enterprise? Can you give me a better one?"—plus, at any new paper he, Newfield, would have to be above Mary Perot Nichols in rank.

One Friday in mid-August, a luncheon was scheduled for Gene's Restaurant, down the street from Wolf's and Fancher's place, where all these things were to be talked out—until, just beforehand, Alex Weitz came to Wolf to tell him Jack Newfield had gone to see Felker the night before.

Jack Newfield had not gone to see Clay Felker for the reason Dan Wolf and Alan Weitz thought—to tell him everything, play both ends against the middle, and get himself a better deal. He had gone to see him, among other things, to save Nat Hentoff's job.

Felker had been giving off vibrations that Hentoff's column was "too serious," and, whether that or what Hentoff had written back in April or the union drive was the real reason, the fact remained that once the union drive had officially failed Nat Hentoff could be fired again, and it seemed to many upstairs that he would be, very shortly. Hentoff knew it, and had not asked anyone to intervene in his behalf. Newfield had done so on his own—but could not very well say so here.

Because Nat Hentoff was going to be at this lunch, as was Margot, and Paul Cowan, and Alan Weitz and Dan and Ed. So Jack Newfield, with his wife, joined them, sat down, and was completely unprepared for what happened next.

"Jack, I want to know something," Dan Wolf started in. Newfield waited. "Why did you go to see Felker right at the point when we're discussing putting out a new paper?"

Newfield fumbled for words and protested it wasn't what Wolf thought. The others at the table—those who did not know what was going on, anyway—could not believe what they were hearing. This was supposed to have been a meeting to discuss ways to get a paper out. What was Dan Wolf doing?

Wolf repeated his question. Newfield tried to explain the meeting with Felker had been scheduled before, that it was no secret. Why would he betray them like that?

Because, Wolf responded, "You wanted to improve your situation at the *Voice,* didn't you, Jack? Well, if that's the way it's going to be, why are we even meeting then?"

The more Newfield said, the more that made it worse—particularly when he said, at least the way Wolf's side at the table heard him, that, if there were going to be a new paper, he would have to be political editor, with power over Mary Nichols.

"You'll both have the right to suggest stories, like at the *Voice,*" Wolf said curtly. "You'll have a column, she'll have a column. But that's the end of the game anyway. I'm not going to do it now."

Jack Newfield had never seen Dan Wolf act like this. Paul Cowan demanded he apologize. Wolf refused. Margot Hentoff chided him, "Are we ganging up on you, Dan?" "Margot," he smiled back at her, "I have utter faith in you. You have no loyalty to anything. Any group you're a part of won't stay together very long." They both laughed at that.

Newfield went back to the *Voice,* muttering to people there about how insulting and irrational Dan had been. But Dan Wolf had had an objective—he had wanted to torpedo any chance for a new paper, at least one that Jack Newfield would want to be a part of. And he had succeeded. Before that lunch, Jack Newfield had made up his mind, or so he said, to leave Felker and go with Wolf. After that, there was no chance.

At the very same time that scene had been taking place, there had been another one going on, only about 100 yards away, which meant almost as surely there would be no new newspaper.

Karen Durbin and Richard Goldstein and Robert Christgau had not been approached about joining it, but Durbin and Goldstein, at least, had been seriously thinking of quitting all summer. The Monday afternoon disruptions had never stopped, and in fact, while Newfield had gone up to *New York* the night before, Karen Durbin had gone up, too, to make one more try at getting Clay Felker to leave them in peace on deadline.

The next day, she and Charles Whitin, an editorial assistant, were sitting down having lunch at the ZZZ Coffee Shop, right down the street from Gene's, when Ron Rosenbaum walked in and saw them.

She knew him, but not well. He came over to the table, so close he stood over them. Then he said, "I hear you don't think the way I left was a good gesture. I hear you think it was cheap."

She was a little taken aback, but it was true, and she said so. "Yes, I do, Ron. I think to accept thirty-eight paychecks from Clay Felker and then to tear up the thirty-ninth is cheap indeed. I think Alan Weitz left with a great deal more dignity. He made a moral point. You did not. I think you made an ugly gesture, but one with no meaning."

Rosenbaum glared at her. "You know," he said, "I despise what you're doing. I think you're dancing on the grave of something fine. You're collaborating in the destruction of a great newspaper. You and Goldstein and Christgau. You're like the Vichy French. I don't believe you really fight Clay. You're just like teacher's pets. You titillate him."

Nor was he through. "I think you're immoral and corrupt, and I think your writing shows it. You're the kind of writer who'd write an article like 'Can a Feminist Love the Nazis?' "

He went on that way, for a few more minutes, and when he left Karen Durbin was riled, not so much by what he had said as the way he had acted so cool when he had said it. She remarked on that to Whitin. "He wasn't so cool," Whitin said. "The whole time he was talking to you, his hand was jerking so much that he kept bashing me in the leg with his book."

That was not the last time Ron Rosenbaum compulsively turned off someone who might have made common cause against Felker. When Paul Cowan accepted an assignment to cover the Portuguese revolution, Rosenbaum called him up to hector him, "Here you're such a guardian of morality and you're going to Portugal for Clay Felker." Then word got back to Howard Blum that he, too, was a "Nazi collaborator." Eventually, even Dan Wolf and Mary Nichols, Rosenbaum's original benefactors, gave up on him and his rambunctious attitude.

Talk about the new newspaper did not die out right away; meetings went on. But by the fall of that year, when they began to bicker over who was to be editor, the dream fell apart completely.

Alan Weitz had perhaps been more excited to start this new paper than anyone else, because, as he understood it, he was to be editor. That was Alan Weitz's understanding of what Dan Wolf wanted. It was not Dan Wolf's.

Wolf had envisioned making Weitz editor only under a setup that would have him, Wolf, as honorary editor overhead—not unlike the arrangement with Ross Wetzsteon in the years 1970-74. At least, that was what Wolf began saying when others at the meeting—Clark Whelton, Mary Nichols, Lucian Truscott—began expressing objections to putting Weitz in charge, and doubts as to whether he could handle the job. Then Wolf reversed course, and nominated Whelton to be editor, which brought objections from Howard Smith, who started fighting with Mary Nichols, and left both Weitz and Whelton sorely disillusioned. There was no more talk of starting a new paper after that.

★ ★ ★

If Jack Newfield and Paul Cowan had entertained any lingering desires of leaving the *Voice* for the "new paper" after what happened at Gene's Restaurant, they were certainly persuaded to stay when, at the end of August, Clay Felker gave everybody what they wanted: a new editor.

He had asked Tom Morgan once before, in May, but Morgan, deep into his memoirs of four years as John Lindsay's press secretary, had turned him down. In August though, he asked again, and this time Morgan, 60,000 words into it and coming to realize it would never be finished, said yes.

Tom Morgan had dreamed of coming to New York all during his Minnesota childhood, and the day after graduation from college in 1949 he was on a train. He lived in the Village, worked for Adlai Stevenson, and became a prolific freelance magazine writer—for, among other places, *Esquire,* where his editor was Clay Felker. Books he also wrote, and a novel, and a screenplay, and finally, in 1969, wanting a change, he went to City Hall to represent John Lindsay, in which capacity he was both praised and damned, on occasion, by the *Village Voice.*

He professed respect for the newspaper, for its reporting on New York in general and for Jack Newfield in particular, but when he had left office with Lindsay to become a corporate vice-president at *New York,* and Felker had asked him one day, "The corporation's thinking about buying the *Village Voice.* What do you think?" his opinion was that the *Voice* had been a great sixties paper, but now, like the rest of the alternatives, it seemed to have run its course—which was probably exactly what Clay Felker wanted to hear. That summer, his presence in the *New York* hierarchy had been one of the things that most worried such old Lindsayphobes as Mary Nichols. But now he was here.

And, from the beginning, he was a welcome relief. He came in, issuing only two orders—that all headlines have verbs from now on, and that all stories deliver on what the headlines advertised, though whether he considered *New York* Magazine to be an offender on that score was something he would not discuss—and seeming to exercise the authority he claimed he had. The Monday afternoon conniptions ceased. Clay Felker came by only rarely, though whether that was because he was totally satisfied, or had decided to keep hands off, or was simply too preoccupied with his latest creation, *New West,* a California version of *New York,* was not clear. And, though it had only one way to go after that summer of '75, though the paper, perhaps reflective of Morgan's own background as a straight and a pol, tended, especially during the city's fiscal crisis and the fight over continued free tuition at the City University, to run inside articles by political types of interest only to other political types, the *Village Voice* did manage, under Tom Morgan, to turn out a slightly better journalistic product.

But not all was sweetness and light while he was there. And the most unpleasant thing that happened came right at the beginning, at his initiative, as if he provoked it just to get it over with.

He was not just the former press secretary of one man whom Mary Nichols hated. He was also, since his 1974 marriage to the former Mary Rockefeller Strawbridge, daughter of former Governor Nelson Rockefeller, the son-in-law of another. What he now proceeded to do could not be explained simply as the action of a Rockefeller lackey—after all, many of the releases and statements he issued in Lindsay's last years had themselves been slashing attacks on Rockefeller, and he printed articles, by Ken Auletta and Jack Newfield and others, far more critical of him than the ones Mary Nichols happened to be writing now. But he had, over the years, built up a liking for Jack Newfield, and an inability to abide her, and he acted on it.

Mary Nichols went to Maine that summer to work on a book about the history of Greenwich Village. In her absence, "Runnin' Scared" was given to Ken Auletta. When she returned, she and he were informed that he would continue to do it. Mary Nichols turned in her first article for Morgan on Common Cause, the self-styled "citizens' lobby" she had been denouncing as a Rockefeller family front. The article ran—but references she put into it at the end, about how her probing the Rockefeller–Common Cause connection might be the reason she had lost "Runnin' Scared," did not. Then she wrote a piece about the Urban Development Corporation, a Rockefeller fiasco in state government whose default in early 1975 had prefigured the New York City bond panic, claiming that its board chairman, George Woods, a former director of the *New York Times* Corporation, had stifled the *Times*'s UDC coverage. Morgan sent her a memo saying he'd like more focus to the piece. She rewrote it, stressing the *Times* angle over the UDC one. Then, on Friday, October 24, he called her secretary, Mary Ann Lacy, and left word that she should meet with him—in her office, away from everybody else—that afternoon. Mary Nichols knew what was coming. She took three Valiums.

He came down. She was waiting for him. He threw her story on the desk. "Mary," he said, "I don't think you and I are going to get along here. See Jane Maxwell about your severance pay."

On his way out, he turned. "I'm not an animal," he told her. "If you need help getting a job, let me know." And she told him, "Tom, I know this must hurt you as much as it does me."

Lucian Truscott learned of it just after he and Clark Whelton had finished taping an interview for WBAI-FM about the *Voice;* only a few nights before he had thrown a party in his Houston Street loft, to celebrate the twentieth anniversary of the founding of the paper, and 500 people had come. He added a statement to the tape about it and hastily dashed off five letters—to Andrew Sarris and Molly Haskell, Jack Newfield, Paul Cowan ("Who will be the next person to go, Paul? I'd really like to know what you're going to do this time."), Morgan ("This letter is to let you know how contemptible I think you are. . . . I have never been so glad about anything in my life, as I am glad that I resigned from your paper"), and Felker himself (. . . "I hold you at a new level of low regard. . . . You are a little man, Clay Felker, and you've shown the world just how little you are by your firing of Mary Nichols"). He demanded the others do something. But the only one left to do something, it seemed, was Howard Blum, who called up Judy Daniels and sent a note to Tom Morgan to tell them he no longer wanted to be part of a paper that had fired Mary Nichols.

The next week, the *SoHo Weekly News* ran the piece Mary Nichols was fired over. And the *Villager** ran a piece, "Let Us Now Praise Mary Nichols," by Clark Whelton:

> . . . If Mary Nichols and the independent spirit of the old
> *Voice* had not joined forces, this community would be a much

*One of the small ironies in this entire situation was that the *Villager* had come under new ownership and was, by 1975, a brash, hip street sheet not unlike the early *Village Voice*.

different place today. A four-lane highway would probably slice through the center of Washington Square, and what remained of Soho would be dominated by a noisy, foul-smelling concrete gash known as the Lower Manhattan Expressway. The far West Village might well have been razed and its rough charm replaced by the sterility of 40-story glass towers. The Village might never have received the protection of the Landmarks Commission and the old Women's House of Detention might still be around in some new hideous incarnation.

. . . Now Mary Perot Nichols has been silenced, not by her outside enemies but by her own paper. Or perhaps by both.

But not everyone was so nice. "Nichols' pieces were often inaccurate, full of unguided missiles," Pete Hamill told the *Villager*. And "she was fast and loose on the civil liberties of people if they were Italians." According to Jack Newfield in the same article, she was fired only "because she wasn't writing good stuff in the last few years and had developed serial obsessions," and her being sacked "strengthens the radicalization of the paper." She was, he claimed, "part of the right wing of the *Voice*," with "a paranoid conspiratorial idea that Rocky runs" it. And Jane Maxwell offered Mary Nichols, an employee of fifteen years' standing, severance pay of eleven weeks. A meeting in Tom Morgan's office, where he was twice interrupted by phone calls from "the family"—the Rockefeller one, not the *Voice* one—failed to resolve that issue. So, the following January, Mary Nichols filed a $6 million libel-and-slander suit in New York State Supreme Court against Morgan, Hamill, Newfield, and the *Villager*.*

There were other unpleasant incidents. In March, the decision was made to remove Gil Eisner as art director by Felker and Glaser and replace him with their new appointee, George Delmerico. Morgan concurred, and left it to Glaser to communicate, which he did, tactlessly, on the run on a Friday. Morgan apologized at a staff meeting for the way it had been handled, and Eisner remained as a senior editor, doing art work but no administration. In May, Howard Blum won Columbia University's Meyer Berger Award for journalism about New York City. Morgan had written warm recommendations to go with the

---

*The suit was making its way through the New York courts in 1978. In November 1976, Mary Nichols took a job as an investigative columnist with the *Boston Herald-American*, then left that paper to become communications director for the city's mayor, Kevin White, then returned to New York to run the city's radio and TV stations for her friend Mayor Ed Koch.

submissions by Hamill and Newfield for the award. Blum, who had already quit, got a very short, cursory one. Two days after winning, Blum got a call at home from Morgan congratulating him.

Blum was not pleased that his ex-editor had waited two full days to call him, nor with the grudging recommendation Morgan had given, and said so. Morgan, it turned out, had some hurt feelings on his mind, too—Blum had left the paper without talking to him—and had thought he was being magnanimous in giving a recommendation at all, and so they left it. But, except for occasional incidents, calm was restored to the *Village Voice* under Tom Morgan, at least on the surface.

On the surface.

If there was one flaw in Tom Morgan, it was a penchant for company-man *macho.*Thus, in an interview, he would dutifully recite the latest propaganda figures of how well the *Voice* was doing, expecting his listener not to know how little those bloated figures were worth. He would retell the decision to publish, in February 1976, the suppressed report of CIA activities compiled by a House committee: "I got on the phone with Clay and I said, 'I don't know what's going to happen to us, but I want you to know at this moment that I'm proud to be working with you.' " And he would say, for the record, what a wonderful man Clay Felker was, when in fact, Clay Felker was treating him not so wonderfully.

The Monday conniptions had never stopped; they had merely been transferred to the telephone, where Tom Morgan, acting his best as a buffer between Clay and the staff, had to take them all alone. In April of 1976, Jack Newfield wrote a piece about Felix Rohatyn, Felker's financier friend. The artists came up with a caricature of Rohatyn as Edgar Bergen, manipulting a "Charlie McCarthy" Abe Beame. Felker called up the art department, and ordered it held up while he tried to have it killed. Morgan had to threaten to quit to keep it in. Felker accused him of "bad faith"—but did not test the issue of the editorial freedom guaranteed in Morgan's contract, as Morgan now reminded him it was. In August, Newfield wrote another anti-Rohatyn piece. This time, Felker called Morgan from the West Coast: "Why do you have to print that?"

"That's a legitimate piece by one of my staff members," Morgan replied, trying to make his defense as high-sounding as possible.

Well, Felker said, it was "irresponsible. They can't do that to my buddy. I'm going to write a response"—which Morgan and Newfield spent the next week waiting for, and which never came.

Then, in September, Morgan and his editors agreed on an endorsement of Bella Abzug in the Democratic Senatorial primary. Felker, a supporter of Daniel Patrick Moynihan for the same nomination, stepped in, and, using the one contractual device open to him, a clause giving him and Morgan mutual vetoes over each other's endorsement preferences, ordered it killed.

That was it, as far as Tom Morgan was concerned. He had just passed fifty, and been nourishing a desire to be his own publisher anyway—a desire his new marriage had certainly made possible. It had been a brutal time with Felker—he had come in to the *Voice* hoping to attract a citywide liberal audience, and had spent more and more of his time fighting with Felker every ten minutes, listening to him bitch how Richie Goldstein ought to be fired and the articles ought to be like *New West*'s. He decided to get out right away. On September 23, 1976, his resignation was announced. He had lasted as editor thirteen months.*

His place was taken by Marianne Partridge, thirty-one, who had come to the *Voice* as managing editor in July (after the departure of Judy Daniels, with Felker's blessing, to start up a new magazine for working women) from *Rolling Stone,* where she had been East Coast editor. When she had told Jann Wenner she was leaving, he had screamed, "You fucking whore!" and given her the rest of the day to clear out. As it was, in going from Wenner to Felker, Marianne Partridge was going from the proverbial frying pan into the proverbial fire. At year's end, Clay Felker told her that the last eighteen issues of the *Village Voice*—the ones put out in the four and a half months she had been there—were "the worst in the history of the newspaper."

★ ★ ★

1975, 1976 . . . Paul Cowan reporting from Portugal on Communists and socialists, and from Chicago on Nazis . . . Jack Newfield exposing a scheme by Off-Track Betting and major corporations to take Madison Square Garden off the city's tax rolls, revealing that Senator Jacob Javits's wife Marion is a paid ($67,500) lobbyist for the government of Iran, connecting a New York State sports cartel to the Arizona Mafiosi reporter Don Bolles was after when he was blown up in his car . . . In the issue of February 16, to inaugurate the national edition of the *Voice,* the cover blares: "THE REPORT ON THE CIA THAT PRESIDENT FORD DOESN'T WANT YOU TO READ"; the paper prints, having obtained its copy from CBS reporter Daniel Schorr, the report, ordered suppressed by the full House of Representatives, of a select committee to investigate the Central Intelligence Agency. . . . Timothy Crouse, once of *Rolling Stone,* joins the staff, to cover crime and

---

*Morgan and *The Nation* subsequently announced a deal for him to buy the magazine, which fell through. He later obtained funding for *Politicks,* a new magazine of his own.

justice. . . . Clark Whelton, freelancing, on a fatal riot in Washington Square Park . . . Jill Johnston, writing again, from Tennessee—fully punctuated . . . Nat Hentoff pans Ellen Frankfort's *Voice* book, and pays for it:

> In a recent issue of the *Columbia Journalism Review,* I wrote—with Ellen Frankfort's book on *The Voice* as a basing point—an essay on the history of this newspaper. I was critical of certain journalistic practices of both the "old" and the "new" *Voice,* coming down somewhat harder on the latter, though not without hope for what might come. At the time, I was negotiating for a staff position here, having served more than a Biblical apprenticeship, certainly long enough to be judged on competency or lack of it. Because of that essay, however, I was informed by the editor of *The Voice* that I had not manifested the degree of loyalty and of shared values which are most fundamentally required of staff writers. Hence, this Benedict Arnold would not be on staff.

There were also interviews and profiles and criticism of stars, stars, stars. Gould and Carson and Parton and Redford. Streisand and Carlin and Nicholson and McCartney. Stallone and Capote and Jackson Browne and Tom Jones. Jerry Lewis and John Wayne and Frank Perdue and Mel Brooks. Robert Altman and Jeanne Moreau and Henny Youngman. Critic Richard Gilman attacking critic Pauline Kael. Endless articles on sexism and feminism and the women's movement. Recycled articles, covering subjects already or simultaneously covered by *New Times* and *Rolling Stone,* on the Beach Boys' comeback and the country music–Jimmy Carter connection, as the three publications became increasingly homogenized. Those telltale "How" and "What" headlines, or ones that talked down to *Voice* readers as if they were simpletons ("Supreme Court on consensual sodomy sets back liberty") or asked asinine, facetious questions ("Is *Star Trek* Taking Us on A Trip to 1984?" . . . "Is *Hearts of the West* Anti-Semitic?"). Covers that were blotchy, crammed eyesores, hoary, gaudy, and gross-looking.

Special inserts. "VOICE CLASSIFIED PULLS" ads all over the city, in subway stations, at bus stops. Radio spots—"It's a great new *Voice.*" One-hundred-sixty-page issues, a record. 162,000 readers, also a record. Record ad revenue, too.

But the thicker it got, the quicker it could be read. And behind those numbers, real economic decay had set in. The ad "YOU'RE PAYING

DOUBLE FOR EVERYTHING ELSE—WHY NOT BUY US FOR HALF PRICE?" was the tipoff. Clay Felker had doubled the newsstand price—and in late 1976, raised it still higher, to sixty cents—so he could encourage mail subscribers, at cost to himself, to take the paper at a discount that was *equal to the newsstand price of the paper when he bought it.* Ed Fancher, the amateur publisher, would never have dreamed of committing such kamikaze capitalism. Ad lineage was down, not up. And with all the "pros" he brought in, all of them dutifully reciting the line that the paper would have gone under if they weren't there, he had drastically increased his overhead. The bottom line of *New York* Magazine Company's figures showed that the *Village Voice,* which had made, before taxes, $1,087,000 in 1973, the last year before Clay Felker got there, had made only $622,000 before taxes in 1976,* his second full year running it. He had taken over a publication that was supposedly dying, and he had reduced its profitability by almost half.

Another ad brazenly proclaimed, THE FOX IN THE ESTABLISHMENT'S CHICKEN COOP. "In *The Voice* you learn what's real and what's fake . . ." but the fact was that the *Voice* was now itself a fake.

Clay Felker had taken over a paper in 1974 that was unique, populated by a community of writers who constantly agreed to disagree and who were edited, if that was the word, by a man who simply loved good writing for its own sake. By the end of 1976, Felker, whatever his own politics might be, had discovered that New Left rhetoric was a commodity that could be bought and peddled just like any other, and that was what he had done. For the first time in its history, it was possible to predict, in advance, what position the *Village Voice* would take on anything. The paper that had never had an editorial line now had one, a smug, institutionalized hippie leftism. The paper that had always been open to every point of view was now cravenly jingoistic. Clay Felker had taken the most ambitious, the most experimental, the most exciting American newspaper of its generation, and he had built a monument to vulgarity with it.

There were little epiphanies everywhere. R. Crumb, a hero to Zap Comix readers of the sixties, actually revived "Mr. Natural" for the *Voice* in 1976—but, after a few forlorn months that showed just how dated it was, he gave it up. Joe Flaherty's writing had never seemed so cluttered and indecipherable. Then there was Pete Hamill. Once, he had been good for a gutsy, blunt, street-wise populism—but that was before he had sold scripts to Hollywood, lived with Shirley MacLaine, and become a Clay Felker star. Now he was good only for leftover

---

*According to projections he himself had made at the time of the *Voice* takeover, it should have been making $1.2 million by then.

Movement babytalk and a curious kind of raised-consciousness, post-*macho macho.* He wrote an article for the paper about why America must go socialist—and datelined it Las Vegas. His solution to the fiscal crisis was for New York to secede from the rest of America; "Up the Republic!" he began signing off his articles. He did a piece idolizing one Pedro Albizu Campos as "probably the greatest Puerto Rican of his generation"; Campos, by Hamill's own admission, was a terrorist who had served time in jail for various assassination conspiracies, including the one against President Harry S Truman in 1950. He wrote a bizarre article somehow all about the end of *machismo,* Ernest Hemingway, and why Nikita Khrushchev was the real hero of the Cuban missile crisis. It was sad; Hamill, who could have been a contender, had settled for being the Burt Reynolds of the New Journalism. He was writing like Mickey Spillane at a teach-in.

As for Alex Cockburn, he conducted an almost pathetic vendetta against Jimmy Carter almost from the moment Carter—"The Nashville Candidate," "The Southern Nixon"—became a credible contender for the presidency, broken only to wage attacks against California Governor Jerry Brown when Brown entered the primaries. And in the issue of May 3, 1976, the sensibility of the new *Voice* expressed itself when a fine piece by Ken Auletta on why political journalists act just like politicians, which surely would have made page one of the old *Voice,* was shunted off to page 10, so the cover could show Edward Kennedy, clad Captain America-style, bursting through a circus drum, beneath the headline, "Afraid of Carter? Tired of Hubert? HERE COMES TEDDY!"

The piece was by Cockburn (his associate, James Ridgeway, received co-author credit), and any savvy observer of American politics knew by that time that such a "scenario," as Cockburn put it, was not even remotely in the cards for 1976. But Teddy Kennedy supposedly sold newspapers, even if there was no news about him, as this article had none, and the decision to run that cover had been made *seven weeks in advance.* Four weeks later, when its total implausibility could no longer be denied, the headline ran "Can Jimmy Carter really be stopped? Did Teddy goof?" Not "Did We Goof?"

★ ★ ★

Perhaps the Dan Schorr affair said it all.

He was covering the CIA story in January 1976 when the House voted not to release the Pike Committee's report on the agency's misdeeds and mistakes. His network decided a few on-the-air references to what was in the material was enough, and CBS reporter Daniel Schorr found himself with what he believed—correctly, it turned out—

was the only complete copy of the report outside the hands of the legislative and executive branches, looking for an outlet to release it to.

He got in touch with his CBS colleague, Fred Graham, a trustee of the Reporters Committee for Freedom of the Press. Graham got him in touch with a lawyer who had helped the Reporters Committee win a recent case, named Peter Tufo. On the night of Thursday, February 5, Tufo called Schorr. He had made some inquiries, he said. So far nothing. But he did have one firm offer—from Clay Felker.

He would publish the full text, Schorr understood Tufo to be saying, and make a "substantial contribution" to the Reporters Committee— Schorr had wanted the Committee to get, and it had agreed to receive, any royalties from a paperback edition of the report.

Dan Schorr's reaction was, "Oh, no."

"I've got to think about that," he said. "It's just too awful." What Dan Schorr meant was that the previous spring Clay Felker had published not one but two derogatory profiles of him—one in *New York* in June, the other, the worse offender to Schorr, by Washington freelancer Ann Pincus in May, in the *Voice.**

"Think about it," Tufo advised him. "But the offer is valid only until tomorrow. Felker has to have the document tomorrow afternoon."

The next morning, Dan Schorr called Peter Tufo back with his answer: Felker could have the document. But he, Dan Schorr, would not write an introduction to it, as he had planned, and would not announce himself as the one releasing the report. Not for Felker.

That afternoon, when Aaron Latham came into the *New York* offices, Clay Felker took him aside and said, "We have a Pentagon Papers situation here."

"Operation Swordfish," Felker dubbed it. Latham Xeroxed a copy to write an introduction to, and the other copy of the 338-page report was sent to *New York*'s typesetters. The next Wednesday, in *New York* magazine type, with an introduction by a *New York* writer, a twenty-four-page insert, featuring portions of the report, was the cover attraction for the first edition of Clay Felker's national *Voice.*

When the contents of the Pike Report were disclosed, things looked very bad for Dan Schorr. He was identified as the one who passed the document on, and roundly denounced by other journalists, even those on the Reporters Committee, for the way he had acted—for trying to "sell" secrets, for not identifying himself with the disclosure, and, worse, for apparently attempting to slough off the onus on his

---

*From "Hope and Chutzpah in the Newsroom," May 26, 1975: "One of Schorr's greatest assets is his ability to sell a story, to convince the editors and subsequently the public that his story is important. The question is: is it?"

colleague Leslie Stahl as the one responsible. The House Ethics Committee was empaneled to look into the leak of the Pike Report, and to subpoena Schorr if necessary to find out who gave it to him. CBS suspended him.

For Clay Felker, however, things could not have looked better. He denied ever having offered money for the Pike Report, and Peter Tufo denied ever having acted as an intermediary between him and Schorr; he had been representing, without fee, the Reporters Committee, Tufo said. For its part, the Reporters Committee said it no longer wanted any money as part of the deal. And the first edition of the national *Voice,* intended as a biweekly "best of the *Voice*" for distribution "west of Pittsburgh," sold well—its press run was 80,000 copies.

But seven months later, having written his article in defense of himself for Felker's archrival *Rolling Stone,* Dan Schorr appeared before the committee, made a noble declaration in support of the First Amendment and in defiance of the committee's order that he reveal his sources, and faced its members down without getting a contempt citation. And the *Village Voice,* besides an editorial by Morgan and the good wishes of Cockburn in the press column, printed an extraordinary analysis of the event by Geoff Stokes* who said, among other things, that Felker, Latham, and *New York* editorial director Sheldon Zalaznick had, by answering questions back in February "as to the physical condition of the report . . . provided the investigators with important evidence in their search for Schorr's source."

Three weeks before that, after only twelve issues, after he had just torn up the fourth, writers' floor to put in cubicles to supposedly accommodate "the national staff," Clay Felker had to terminate the operations of the *Village Voice'*s national edition. Circulation had steadily declined since that first issue. In six months, it had lost $195,800.

★ ★ ★

        In the fall of 1976, Australian super-publisher Rupert Murdoch, who had transferred his base of operations to London in the late sixties and thence to New York in the mid-seventies, tried to buy the failing, respected London *Observer,* but was outbid by Robert Anderson of Atlantic Richfield Company. Commenting, Alex Cockburn said, "No doubt the British ruling class had rogered him again. His opportunity will, I imagine, soon recur."

Sooner than anybody thought.

_____

*Which Felker, to his credit, published.

19. ALAN PATRICOF, THE MAN WHO WOUND

up taking Felker on more than anyone else, used to rationalize it with World War II metaphors: *Somebody has to stand up to Hitler.* Actually, what had been signed in the early morning hours of June 5, 1974, was the Nazi-Soviet 1939 nonaggression pact of New York journalism, and Clay Felker had been the one to spend the next two years lining his best generals up against the wall and having them shot, gobbling up his smaller neighbors while leaving open all the natural invasion routes into Mother Russia, and then assuming that somehow, because he had signed something, it couldn't happen to him.

But it did happen to him, and when it did, Clay Felker did a very strange and ironic thing. He began to complain that his magazines' "independence" and "integrity" were being destroyed. He began to claim that his idea for a publication was being stolen. He asserted that he had a "right of first refusal" on the stock of Councilman Carter Burden, and that his right was being violated.

As he sowed, he reaped. It was as simple as that.

★ ★ ★

He ridiculed Wolf and Fancher for the way their business was run like a candy store. But he ran his own businesses like a discount house—offer cut-rate prices, move the merchandise, hold nothing in inventory, keep the profit margin low, and use whatever money is at hand to open up a new outlet and do it all over again. That mentality can work as well as it did for E. J. Korvette's—or as badly as it did for W. T. Grant's. In Clay Felker's case, he could have had it all. But he had to expand. And he had to fight.

★ ★ ★

It was in March 1975, after one of their Sun Valley skiing trips, that Clay Felker and Carter Burden tried their little *putsch.*

A *putsch* is what Bartle Bull called it, when Burden came back and told him what he had agreed to: voting with Felker to oust Alan Patricof and Robert Towbin from the board, and replace them with one nominee each of their own. "This is a mistake, Carter," Bull warned. "He's going to go after these guys today, me tomorrow, and you the day after that. What are you going to do then?" Bull told him he would not vote for it. Nevertheless, Ted Kheel tried to arrange breakfast the next morning with the two men scheduled to be voted out at the directors' meeting that afternoon.

Patricof could come neither to the breakfast nor to the meeting; he was in Chicago on business. But Kheel got Towbin to come, to the Regency Hotel, and backed into what he had to say: "Clay and I think there should be a black and a woman on the board."

"Good idea," said Towbin.

"And we want you and Alan to resign. You have a conflict of interest."

Towbin paused. "Ted, I'm going to try to be calm," he said. "But I have stock in a lot of things. You tell Clay that if he tries to get me off the board, I'll destroy him."

Breakfast was over. Towbin called Patricof in Chicago and told him what was up. Patricof got on a plane back. He called Carter Burden, told him he was not going to submit, and offered to buy out his stock. And he called the other businessman board member, Thomas Kempner of Loeb, Rhoades, telling him to get John Loeb, Sr., whom Felker held in awe if only for his name, to call Felker—which Loeb did.

By the time Patricof had gotten back to New York and the board meeting, two new members had been voted on the board—Gordon Davis, black, a lawyer, a friend of Peter Tufo's, and a progressive-minded member of the City Planning Commission,* and Joan Glynn, a Revlon director, and not only a woman but the one who by reputation went out with Clay Felker when Gail Sheehy did not. No one had been voted off. And Clay Felker was telling Bob Towbin it was all "like a husband and wife having a fight."

When the meeting was over, Patricof, Milton Glaser, and Felker went off into a corner, supposedly to talk things out. But Felker flared up: "You fucked me, Patricof. You fucked me back in the beginning. You fucked me with George Hirsch. You cheated me on my *Voice* contract.† You fucked me when I tried to get rid of Bartle. You undermine my management of the company by asking too many questions about the budget." It was pure vitriol. Patricof announced he was through listening to this abuse, and walked away.

The changes were announced to the assembled stockholders at the annual meeting that spring. So was the resignation of board member Bartle Bull, whom Felker had been bad-mouthing to Patricof and others on the board as "a restraint on me," as publisher of the *Village Voice*.§ And so was the first of what had to be some very disconcerting

---

*And, as of 1978, New York City's parks commissioner.

†A reference to yet another bizarre corporate maneuver Felker had pulled: the previous spring, barely two weeks after the *Voice* deal had been concluded, he had asked his business partners on the board if the price he had to pay for his NYM Co. stock could be reduced from $2 a share. A contract being a contract, they had naturally refused.

§Bull was not the only NYM Inc. publisher to resign that spring; in March, when he

news to the stockholders of *New York* Magazine Company.

Midyear earnings per share, which had been twenty cents the year before, just before the merger, were down to nine cents. The company, which had lost $85,000 in the first, "bad" quarter the year before, had lost $131,000 this year.

It was news that continued at year's end. Though, for the second year in a row, NYM Inc. managed to pay a ten-cent dividend, earnings per share, which had been thirty-six cents for 1973, and thirty-two cents for 1974, were down to thirty. Ad space in *New York* was down 7 percent for the year. The *Voice* lost eight display ad pages, and its classified was down for the second year in a row. Clay Felker had all sorts of reasons for why this was happening—the sale of Tarrytown Conference Center the year before (to get cash up for the *Voice* deal), the cost of the *Voice* deal, the cost of settling the *Voice* suit, the cost of remaking the *Voice,* the recession, all the reasons except the real ones.

He was overspending. Revenue was at an all-time high, but he was swelling the numbers by charging everybody—readers and advertisers alike—more, and expenses were more than keeping pace with whatever transfusions came in. In his projections, he was continually underestimating his expenses and overstating his income. His company had strapped itself for cash—it had $1,808,000 in hand at the end of one year, '73, and only $864,000 in hand the next.

And the trend continued—though ad space picked up in both the *Voice* and *New York* in 1976, midyear earnings per share went down another penny. It was time to reassess and reevaluate. But Clay Felker didn't want to do that. He wanted a new magazine. And he wanted a new contract.

★ ★ ★

"It will maintain the same high journalistic standards in quality of writing and excellence of graphics that have made *New York* Magazine one of the most successful publications introduced in the last decade," said the statement that announced the launching of *New West* Magazine on January 22, 1976. The decision to start a West Coast slick magazine had been taken by the board the previous October. And the first issue, after a mass (433,000 homes) prospectus mailing and a test newsstand copy, was ready by the last week of April.

It was all done in high Clay Felker style . . . "The California Woman: Psychological Penalties of Being Locked into Paradise" . . . "New York or California—Where's the Power Now?" . . . "Best Burrito in L.A." . . .

---

took the "editor-in-chief" title at the *Voice* as well as *New York,* Clay Felker gave up the title of publisher of *New York,* which his associate Jack Thomas took over.

"Rating San Francisco's Legendary Restaurants" . . . "62 Stars Who Saved Hollywood" . . . "Succulents are the Sexiest Plants: Learn to Love Them" . . . "Best Fettucini Alfredo in Southern California." The first issue, 172 pages long, ran 93 pages of advertising and went to 133,000 charter subscribers. It was "one of the most successful magazine introductions in publishing history," said the company's midyear statement. "A STAR IS BORN," read the cover illustration on the annual report, showing the words *New West Magazine* imprinted on the wet pavement outside Grauman's Chinese Theatre.

It was done in the high Clay Felker style in other ways, too. Those 133,000 charter subscribers were lured with bargain subscription rates of $6 and $7. He quickly reached a total readership of 240,000, nearly twice what was planned; but to get them he spent $2 million on an R. H. Donnelley "sweepstakes" mailing of "money-saving coupons" to "residents" all over California, not to mention another $100,000 on radio and television; and then, *because* he had so many readers, he began putting out two separate editions of the magazine, one for Los Angeles, another for San Francisco. He leased two Alfa-Romeos, at company expense, for his transferred *New York* editors to use. He bought, also at company expense, the "city room of the *Washington Post*"—desks, chairs, typewriters, other equipment—from Warner Brothers when the shooting of *All the President's Men* was completed. And so *New West* Magazine, which had been budgeted for a little under $2 million, cost $4 million. And it lost, not the $500,000 Clay Felker had told his board of directors it was going to lose, but $2.3 million.

These figures Clay Felker did not tell his board right away, just as when a *Village Voice* reader survey that had been promised for release in June 1976 came up with the finding that much of the paper's traditional audience had been alienated,* he ordered it suppressed, just as, in the six-months report for 1976, dated nearly a month *after* he had had to abort it, Clay Felker told the stockholders only, "In 1976 we have begun the testing of a national edition of THE VILLAGE VOICE. Results of the test are not as yet conclusive." But some figures not even

---

*Sample sentiments—"As your price increases, your quality decreases. I have read your paper for 10 years (faithfully), but recently I only purchase it out of boredom." . . . "Please watch out! N.Y. Mag is too smart-ass and VV is getting close." . . . "If I miss a few issues, I don't feel guilty now." . . . "Your theatre section has gone steadily downhill." . . . "You seem to have forgotten the middle word of your title . . . I only buy it every other week. I steal it on the off week." . . . "Soon an article on what my towels say about me? . . . Dreadful tragedy." . . . "Cut this Reno Sweeney, Peter Allen shit. FUCK FELKERISM!"—and many, many more.

he could cover. That same six-months report tried to state the net midyear income as $143,500, down only $20,000 from the year before. But, in the small print, Felker had to admit that "extraordinary income of $372,700" from a onetime accounting procedural change was being counted as part of that figure, and that, "prior to income from this accounting change, the company experienced a net loss of $229,200."

★ ★ ★

In December of 1975, a year and a half into a contract that was supposed to last Clay Felker till the end of 1979, Alan Patricof got the call, from Clay, demanding a new contract.

"Look," he said, "I'm starving. I'm underpaid. I'm in debt. I can't make it. If you want to continue as chairman, you better support me on this. I'm holding you *personally* responsible to get it for me. You've never done anything for me before. Now's the time to show me you're on my side."

As Alan Patricof tried to explain, he wasn't on the salary committee. But Bob Towbin was,* and Felker now began to work on him.

Towbin, like Patricof, knew that Clay Felker had always felt he was underpaid, and exploited because he didn't own more of the company. But, to the business people, it was not their fault that Clay had chosen to give his original 30 percent of the stock away (while they diluted the relative strength of their own shares when they undertook a second financing), any more than it was their fault Clay had been unable to collect his bonuses because of the unrealistic targets he himself had set. Nevertheless, Towbin now tried to mollify him. "Clay," he said, "I told you this once before. Don't talk about this with anybody. First, sit down and figure out what your requirements are. Then come back to me and tell me what you need. And let me caution you about another thing. If you're going to start a magazine on the West Coast, which is going to cost money, it'd be better not to start it if your demands prove excessive." He thought they had an agreement: Clay Felker would let Bob Towbin bring this up to the board when he thought the time was right, and not force the issue. And Clay Felker thought Bob Towbin was his friend.

He came up to him at an Academy Awards party they were both attending in Los Angeles in March, and put his arm around him. "You understand me," he said. "You and me. We're both businessmen." He went on and on like that. He would not stop. His voice became louder.

*Along with Kheel and Thomas Kempner.

Tears appeared in his eyes as he was talking. The rest of the party came to a halt as people turned around to stare at him and tried to figure out what to do—leave, or stay. Bob Towbin became embarrassed, for himself and the position he was in, for Clay and the way he was letting his guard down, and for the others there who were witnessing this performance. Finally, Clay left. The next morning, Towbin got a call, as if nothing had happened—all about his plans for *New West* and the new contract he wanted *

And he wanted a lot, a $2 million package over five years: $150,000 a year; a sign-up bonus of $150,000; a buy-back, at "fair market value," of the stock he had gotten on loan in 1974, and 150,000 new shares of stock issued in his name, for free this time; a trust fund to be set up and paid out to'him at the end of the contract; the company to buy outright his Manhattan duplex, in order that he could pay off *another* loan he owed elsewhere; and exactly half the financial terms given to him to be given to Milton Glaser.

Towbin recommended acceptance—"we can always fire him with cause; maybe it's buying him off," he put it to the other board members—but he encountered resistance, especially, for the first time, from Carter Burden. Burden had come away from the *putsch* of a year before with the feeling that Clay Felker had suckered him, that perhaps there was more to the relationship between Clay Felker and his board members than Felker was telling him. He now came out against it—"If you give him this one, you're going to have to give him the next one"— and, especially when they learned that Towbin had been out to attend the Oscars with Clay, all the other board members felt Towbin had been conned by Felker. Which Towbin himself thought at the next meeting when, explicitly against his instructions, Clay Felker brought up the issue of his contract and forced a vote on it. The vote, of course, was no, and Towbin, furious with Felker, realizing his own effectiveness was at an end, gave up his seat on the committee, his place taken by Carter Burden. On June 15, a counter-offer was made to Felker— $125,000 a year, plus $3,000 for "financial counseling," plus $30,000 for every year *New York* and the *Voice* matched their pretax earnings of 1975, plus a bonus of $30,000 for the year he missed in 1975, plus lower interest on his 1974 stock loan, plus a "put" on his apartment,† plus incentive bonuses, all of it retroactive to the first of the year.

---

*An almost exact replica of this incident had taken place with Alan Patricof in Felker's New York place several weeks before. In fairness to Felker, this was uncharacteristic conduct for him; he was, if anything, strictly a social drinker.

†That is, "if you will take up residency in California and no longer charge the corporation for your living expenses while on the West Coast," the company would buy his New York co-op and absorb whatever loss there might be in selling it later.

Felker was not satisfied with that, and tried to counter-offer the counter-offer. He hired Ted Kheel and another consultant, for $25,000 each, at company expense, to advise him. Yet another consultant was called in to try to reach a compromise package. And all summer long, whenever the subject of *New West*'s cost overruns would come up, or seem to be about to, Clay Felker would stall, or offer whole new figures, or steer the agenda back to his new contract, until some of his partners became convinced that he was hiding something, that he wanted that contract first before he told them just how bad it was.

Finally, in September, with Felker and Glaser ready to make yet another proposal, the full explanation had to be made: that "expenses have increased as a result of higher costs to replace expired subscriptions and a greater number of subscribers serviced," and that, as a result, a "substantial operating loss" had resulted. When he and the other members were told just how substantial, Bob Towbin, for the first time since 1969, was concerned about the company's ability to survive. He spoke up. "I'm now against the contract," he said. "Nobody's told us we're up for over $4 million on this thing. And I insist we get a bank loan."

The company did not do that, not right away—for the time being, it sold off preferred stock to raise cash. But other things were done. Kenneth Fadner, Felker's financial vice-president, was instructed to come up with a "worst case analysis" on NYM Inc.'s financial position. A joint statement, "signed"* by Felker and Patricof, went out to stockholders, informing them that *New West*'s losses would "offset all of the profit generated" for the year, though "we look forward to a return to profitability of the overall company in 1977."

And, privately, still other steps were taken.

★ ★ ★

The railing against Patricof by Felker had been getting wilder and more repetitious, but not until he went out to the Hamptons that summer, and was told by friends what Felker was doing—making the cocktail-party circuit, denigrating him in the most violent language—did the chairman of the company have any idea that it had gone outside board meetings. When he heard that, Alan Patricof decided that this time Clay Felker had gone too far.

He began meeting with each board member, individually, over

---

*Officially "signed," but not actually; for this statement, which included the lie told to stockholders that the national *Village Voice* was still being tested and had not in fact already folded, Felker put the print of Patricof's name on it without showing it to him, and sent it out. Patricof later wrote Felker a letter of complaint to that effect.

breakfast,* sounding them out, confiding his own concerns, asking them what should be done. Then he brought them all together for a meeting at Carter Burden's place in the River House in September, where the decision was made to form an "executive committee," one that could meet more frequently than the full board, get to the magazine two or three days a week, oversee Clay's spending—and to force it on him even if he quit.

That he might quit was something they had to consider; he had threatened it before, and it had been hanging over the contract negotiations all along. Now, he threatened it again.

It bothered him as much that Alan Patricof was on the committee† as that he was not, or so he said. "I have to be on that committee. If you want my resignation, you have it. Alan Patricof doesn't know anything about publishing. Alan Patricof has ruined this company. Alan Patricof"—and he was off again, absolutely out of control this time, uglier than he had ever been, so bad that Milton Glaser even—"Oh, Clay, not again!"—tried to get him to stop.

Kheel moved to amend the resolution, then to table it. Finally, saying "it's more important to me to have the executive committee," and that "I think Clay will regret having said the things he has said here today," Alan Patricof voluntarily took himself off the committee.§ The motion then passed, 8 to 0 with three abstentions (Felker, Glaser and Kheel), and the committee—just the two of them now, Burden and Davis—began going down to the magazine.

They began going over the books, too, and for the first time learned the full dimensions of the expense-account existence Clay Felker was living. *New York* Magazine Company was not only paying for a gym at its Second Avenue offices, and for a staff dining room that had been redecorated repeatedly, but for "Felipe, Executive Chef," who was on the payroll for $25,000 a year, as was Kheel, as was the other consultant Felker had brought in over his contract. They further discovered—no one had known it before—that two leased Alfa-Romeos were being written off on the company, as was the set equipment of *All the*

---

*These meetings were not, as Clay Felker later tried to claim through Gail Sheehy, who got an article published giving his official version of the affair, "clandestine." Clay (and Milton Glaser and Ted Kheel) was not invited to them, but his friends Mary Joan Glynn and James Q. Wilson were; Glynn and Patricof had lunch, Wilson and Patricof managed to speak on the phone during breaks in their conflicting schedules. And while neither Glynn nor Wilson was invited to the River House meeting, both voted for the resolution that came out of it.

†Along with Carter Burden and Gordon Davis.

§He also privately consulted a lawyer about the possibility of suing Felker for slander.

President's Men, as was Berta, the woman who cooked and cleaned and answered the phone at Felker's 57th Street co-op. In November, Burden communicated to Felker, in writing, the bad news—that after "in-depth discussion of the current status of, and future plans for, *New West,* the Executive Committee is not at this time authorizing any increase in maximum cumulative cash investment." In plain English, no more money would be spent on Clay Felker's West Coast baby.

By the month of December, the real year-end loss for *New York* Magazine Company had been projected—$566,000. The company borrowed $750,000 from the Chemical Bank of New York to pay its December bills. The stock, which had once been worth $10 a share, was down to $2, sometimes dipping as low as $1.75. And *Media Industry Newsletter* was confidently predicting, "Look for Warner Communications to acquire *New York* Magazine Company. Felix Rohatyn brings together two of his chums, *New York*'s Clay Felker and Warner's Steve Ross, adds Carter Burden and Bartle Bull . . . [who are] said to be ready for buyout."

The item—Ross of Warners had been going out with Amanda Burden, and that gave it some credence—was wrong, but there was something to it. What had happened was that late that fall, Bartle Bull had had lunch with an old friend of his, Dan Wolf, where the subject of a possible buy-back of the *Village Voice* had come up, and that afterwards Ed Fancher had inquired at Warners about a possible mutual interest in buying it. And when Clay Felker issued a statement, on December 2, saying that "I wish to state authoritatively and unequivocally that New York Magazine Company is not for sale," that was far from the truth, and he knew it.

Alan Patricof, for one, had decided that autumn that the only solution was for a buyer to be found. If that meant Clay found one and bought them out, that was fine with Patricof; just as long as this situation did not continue. There were interested parties: Bob Guccione, publisher of *Penthouse,* was one. And, in November, there were two serious overtures made to Patricof, by representatives of the Pritzker family fortune and the Marshall Field publishing ogranization; but when he sent the Pritzker man on to talk to Felker, the report back to him was that they were no longer interested. This only compounded the situation to Patricof—Clay was not only turning off his board members now, he was turning off potential buyers, and if he did that what was anybody going to do? On December 3, at a party at "21" with Kheel, he confided his feelings in the matter. "I'd like to see Clay find a situation he'll be happy with, and people he'll be compatible with," he said. "Do you mind if I tell that to Clay?" Kheel asked him. "No, of course not," said Patricof, figuring that was the best way to get a message through to Clay, whom he already knew was holding meetings with Rupert Murdoch.

★ ★ ★

Sir Keith Murdoch was perhaps the first great popular Australian journalist, the man who circumvented British censorship to report the truth about the disastrous military expedition at Gallipoli in 1915. But, though he was running the country's largest newspaper group when he died, he never got control, or even especially wealthy, in the process. And his son Rupert, born in 1931, though he went to the best schools—Geelong Grammar, Oxford—was shunned as "Red Rupert" when he ran, unsuccessfully, for an Oxford political club.

So when Sir Keith died in 1953, and young Rupert was called home from London, where he was serving as a subeditor on Lord Beaverbrook's *Daily Express,* and a Brisbane newspaper had to be sold off to pay debts, all that was left was the family's majority interest in the *Adelaide News* and *Sunday Mail,* plus a radio station in Broken Hill. But, from small beginnings, the empire known as News Ltd. was born.

When his crosstown rival in Adelaide offered to buy him out, Murdoch put the offer on page one, along with an editorial attacking the evils of newspaper monopoly. When a local aborigine was accused of murder, Murdoch came to his defense, and was actually tried—and acquitted—for seditious libel for doing so. Young Rupert proved capable of handling himself in a circulation war in a country where circulation wars were often settled in the old-fashioned way. In 1956, he bought a Sunday paper in Perth. In 1960, he bought the *Sydney Daily Mirror,* and took on the local *Sun;* when he outbid his competitors for a printing plant and they sent a street gang to occupy the site, he rounded up a gang of his own and had the building recaptured. He kept expanding—into Darwin, into a chain of suburban newspapers, into a partnership with Australian television magnate Frank Packer. In 1964, he founded the country's first "national" newspaper, the *Australian.* It was, and is, his most serious newspaper, and the only one that lost money. And in the 1970s Rupert Murdoch was willing to use it to drive from office a man he had tried to put in only three years before.

He had helped make Gough Whitlam Labour's first prime minister of Australia in twenty-three years, with a secret $90,000 campaign contribution and favorable press coverage in 1972; but in 1975, having decided Whitlam was an incompetent, he broke him. During the election campaign that year, he ran embarrassing stories (including a few he wrote himself, under the byline "A Special Correspondent"), killed favorable ones, wrote vociferous anti-Whitlam editorials, and forced twenty-two of his best journalists out on strike in protest. But he got his wish: Whitlam lost.

In 1968, only thirty-seven years old and already reputedly worth $50 million, he took his act back to the mother country. He beat M. P. Robert Maxwell to the six-million-Sunday-circulation *News of the World* that year, and to the failing left-wing tabloid daily, the *London Sun,* the next. And he treated Britishers to the brand of journalism he had perfected Down Under.

It was a brand of journalism full of "news" about killer bees, naked ladies, and homicidal maniacs. Its specialty was the subhuman interest story: TERROR VICTIM FLEEING . . . POLICE DRUNK, LOOTING . . . GANG BANG JUDGE SAYS 'I BOOBED' . . . SEX OUTRAGE IN SCHOOL LUNCHBREAK . . . GREEN MONKEY DISEASE SHOCK . . . POLICE SNIPERS IN WILD BEACH SHOTGUN SIEGE . . . TORTURE PETS WITH HOT FORK . . . I LIVED WITH CHARLES' GIRL . . . MCMAHON CONFESSES I LUST TOO . . . SAVOY HORROR ARSON CHARGE . . . WIFE IN THE BATH MURDER . . . THUGS ROB EX-MAYOR, BEAT DOG . . . THE 11 FACES OF A SEX FIEND WHO MUST BE FOUND BEFORE HE KILLS . . . and always, always the notorious page-3 "promotions" with voluptuously photographed, virtually nude, very nubile young women. It was, as the British said, "Boobs and bums." Or, as the Americans would say, "Tits and ass." Or, as the satirical magazine *Private Eye did* say, "Rupert 'Thanks for the Mammary' Murdoch." It was just this side of pornography.

News of the World, which had been no prize to begin with, kept right on going strong with three censures from the British Press Council in its first six years under Murdoch,* and the *Sun* more than quadrupled its circulation to 3.5 million—but it had its side effects, a few of them lethal. In 1971, for the second time in eight years, Rupert Murdoch's penchant to publish the diaries of teenage girls with overactive imaginations was later overshadowed by a suicide.† And, the previous fall, two brothers, attempting to kidnap Murdoch's wife Anna,§ mistakenly abducted the wife of one of his lieutenants, and murdered her.

---

*For publishing Christine Keeler's memoirs, for printing a story about one of the Great Train Robbers on the lam in Brazil, and for catching—and photographing—Lord Lambton, peer of the realm, in bed with a prostitute.

†The first time, in Australia in 1964, a fourteen-year-old girl and her boyfriend were expelled from school. The boy hanged himself. The second time, a fifteen-year-old girl dancing in the chorus of a BBC pop music show, and supposedly having sex with the show's executives, committed suicide. In both cases, the girls were certified virgins.

§Whom he met and married in 1967 when she was a reporter for him in Sydney.

The kidnap-murder incident, combined with the generally low opinion of him on Fleet Street as a panderer from the outback, made Murdoch, a stay-at-home anyway, even more of one over the next two years. Meanwhile, he set his eyes westward, on America.

He looked at the *Washington Star,* settled for acquiring the *San Antonio News* and *Express,* made the *News* over in his image ("A divorced epileptic, who told police she was buried alive in a bathtub full of wet cement and later hanged upside down in the nude, left San Antonio for good this weekend. The tiny, half-blind woman, suffering from diabetes, recounted for the *News* a bizarre horror story filled with rape, torture and starvation"), and moved across the ocean to a Fifth Avenue residence in New York City. Early in 1974 he brought out the *National Star,* which, after a disastrous beginning, bottomed out, dropped the "national" from its name, and settled for competing with such publications as *Midnight, National Enquirer,* and the *Tattler* for the audience of emotionally unfulfilled American housewifes. And he set about getting to know people. People such as Katharine Graham of the *Washington Post*—he attended parties at her house. Clay Felker of *New York* Magazine—they had houses near one another in the Hamptons and talked publishing frequently. Dolly Schiff of the *New York Post*—they lunched frequently and stayed in touch. And Councilman Carter Burden, with whom he had a lunch in early 1974, where, for exploratory purposes, the sale to him of the *Village Voice* was discussed.

With his unprepossessing looks, conservative dress, and soft, high voice, Murdoch the man cut no Felker figure. Nor did he have anywhere near as much personality—he was no more extroverted than he had to be, and kept whatever emotions he felt in check and to himself. All that was known about him in America, really, was that he had a reputation for getting what he wanted, for being ruthless with competitors, for sacking his help, sometimes without warning after long service and with casual cruelty, that he rarely evinced interest in anything he could not own at least 51 percent of. And that, after making his millions—$100 million, more or less, from eighty-seven newspapers, eleven magazines, and seven TV and radio stations—he was looking for "cachet."* He wanted, after all these years, and all those stories about ax murders and sex deviants, to become respectable. He tried, and lost, for the London *Observer* in the fall of 1976—but no sooner was that

---

*Perhaps his classiest property was London Weekend Television, the outfit that produced *Upstairs, Downstairs*—but that was one of the few things he owned only minority interest in.

over with than the announcement was made, after the closing editions of the *New York Post* for Friday, November 19, that the paper had been sold to him, by Dolly Schiff, for roughly $30 million.

That weekend, Murdoch let the *Voice* have a scoop—an exclusive interview with Alexander Cockburn on his plans for the *Post* (which the paper, in a parody of his headlining style, billed, "EXCLUSIVE . . . RUPERT MURDOCH TELLS ALL"). And he accepted Clay Felker's invitation to a Saturday night dinner at Elaine's.

Gail Sheehy was there, with Clay, and Pete Hamill* and Shirley MacLaine were there, together, he telling Murdoch what he should do with the paper, she telling him what Australia should do with China, and Felix Rohatyn was there. The talk ranged over many things, mostly publishing, and in a cab on the way back home Clay Felker asked Rupert Murdoch if they could meet. He was having trouble with his board, he said. Could they get together and talk?

Nine days later—Monday, November 29—Rupert Murdoch came up to the *New York* dining room for an executive lunch, where Felker told him everything—who was on the board, whom he was having fights with, how he wanted to buy Burden's stock, how he was thinking of picking up stakes and moving out to California. Murdoch said he and his investment man, Stanley Shuman, might be able to work something out. They both agreed, when one of them brought it up, that of course they could never work together—but Rupert Murdoch did not have that in mind.

Ten days later—Thursday, December 9—Shuman, Murdoch, and Felker met again, this time at Murdoch's corporate offices on Third Avenue. He had been thinking about what they talked about, Murdoch said, and this is what he had come up with: he would buy *New York* Magazine Company. Clay would move to L.A. Murdoch would sell *New West* to him. Or, if Clay and Milton could not raise the money to buy it, he would loan it to them, with editorial control until the debt was paid off.

Faced for the first time with someone actually following through on all his idle talk about a sale, about getting out of the company, about getting out of New York, Clay Felker hesitated. He said he'd need a couple of days to think it over, called back, and said he was no longer interested. Which was too bad, because Rupert Murdoch now was. If Clay Felker would not sell him the company, somebody else would. It was not as if he did not know who to go to now, thanks to Clay. And it

---

*Who was to leave Felker shortly and resume a column with Murdoch's new rival, the *Daily News*.

was not as if, after spending $30 million on the *Post* deal, he did not have a little cash left over.

★ ★ ★

On Monday night, December 13, Alan Patricof, at their request, stopped by to see Murdoch and Shuman at Murdoch's apartment. They had informed him initially of their interest, and given him the details the week before of their dickering with Clay. Now they informed him of their turndown, and discussed with him the mechanics of making a deal without Clay—the timing, the price, the tender offer.* Patricof told them what he had told everyone else who was interested: the only way to buy the company was to buy Carter Burden's stock, the only way Carter Burden's stock would be sold was if Peter Tufo was behind it, and Bartle Bull would have to be dealt with separately from Burden. He also told them $6 a share wouldn't do; if they were truly serious, they would offer $7.

On Friday, December 17, at the *New York* Christmas party, Peter Tufo came up to Clay Felker and asked, "You don't want to work for Rupert Murdoch, do you?" Felker, dancing so hard he eventually sprained his knee, laughed him off. Tufo then proceeded to go out to dinner with Princess Lee Radziwill, his steady date, Stanley Shuman, and Rupert Murdoch, at posh Parioli Romanssimo, and tentatively, verbally agree to a sale of Carter Burden's stock for $7 a share.

On Wednesday, December 22, Tufo came over to Clay Felker's for lunch and told him, for the first time, of the offer. Felker swore he would never work for Murdoch, that he would counter-offer. Tufo tried to get him to change his mind, then agreed to give him a chance to match it. Felker at once phoned Murdoch to remind him he still had a right of first refusal, and was going to fight. Then he called up Felix Rohatyn, who, as investment banker for the *Washington Post* among others, recommended he get back-up assurances from Katharine Graham. He did, and left town for Nassau, as a guest of David Frost, for the holidays.

One week later, with Felker and Burden having spoken via a bad Sun Valley–Nassau phone connection and then again once Felker was back in New York, and the stock having ballooned to $5 a share amid heavy trading, *New York* Magazine Company suspended all over-the-counter trading, officially conceding that "serious discussions are in progress

---

*That is, the offer that must be made to all shareholders—at the same price—in order to make a public company private, as Murdoch wanted to do in this case.

which could lead to a sale of a significant amount of the company's stock." By the next day, Katharine Graham was agreeing to give Clay Felker an employment contract, loan him enough money to match Murdoch's bid for Burden's stock, and, against continually varying conditions brought up by Peter Tufo, who was dealing with them in New York while phoning his client out in Idaho for further instructions, cover Burden against any possible indemnities if the whole thing collapsed. Late that afternoon, they thought they had a deal, and Felker and Graham, both exhausted, went out to dine at Le Madrigal with Richard Reeves. But early that evening Tufo called Felix Rohatyn back with one more condition: Murdoch was willing to make Carter Burden chairman of the board of the new company. Was Katharine Graham willing to do the same? Rohatyn doubted it, but also doubted to Tufo that Murdoch's offer meant much.

At one thirty that morning, Clay Felker got a phone call from Sun Valley, Idaho. It was Carter Burden, and he was testy, wanting to know about the details of Clay's prospective deal with the *Washington Post*. "You aren't buying those shares, the *Washington Post* is," he said. "I'm not going to sell to you now."

Clay Felker roared at Burden—how he *had* to accept the *Washington Post* offer, how people had heard Tufo make the verbal agreement and everybody knew verbal agreements were binding, how he was going to sue him if he didn't, how he and writers like Richard Reeves were going to ruin him if he didn't, how there were going to be no more magazines left if Murdoch took over, how everybody in New York journalism was going to be hating him, going to be after him for this.

Carter Burden hung up.

He then picked up the phone and redialed. He got Peter Tufo, whom he told not to accept any check from Felix Rohatyn signed by Katharine Graham in the morning.

One was offered—raising the ante to $7.50 per share—but Tufo duly rejected it. And all day long, on this last business day of the year, Katharine Graham and Felix Rohatyn and Clay Felker and their entourage waited in the offices of *Newsweek* for a call from Carter Burden that never came.

A split now arose among the anti-Felker members on the board. Robert Towbin, though he had known since that fall that Stan Shuman was working for Rupert Murdoch, and had solicited his interest in buying *New York* a couple of times, professed to find out that the takeover was under way only when Milton Glaser asked him over the phone if it was true Carter Burden was selling his stock to Murdoch. As the man who considered himself to be the magazine's investment banker, he was furious at Murdoch for going around him, and at his partners for going along without telling him. He phoned Felix Rohatyn on December 31, while Rohatyn, apologizing for not having contacted him before, was waiting out Carter Burden in vain. "If Mrs. Graham wants to bid $8.25, that'll hold things up till Monday," Towbin told him. "Then the board can decide." He didn't know about $8.25, but she was willing to go to $8, Rohatyn thought. Towbin sent a telegram out to Sun Valley saying he could get $8.25 from the *Post* for everyone anyway, and that he had discussed it with other directors. When he heard that, Alan Patricof was furious at Towbin for interfering and suspected that he really wanted to get a commission on the deal.

On that Friday, the 31st, Rupert Murdoch had made his first appearance in the *New York Post* newsroom as publisher, telling his assembled employees, "Forget everything you've read about me." Then Stanley Shuman came into town from Florida, and the two of them sat down with Patricof. He told them what Towbin had done, told them Felix Rohatyn had said the *Washington Post* would go to $8, and recommended they go to $8.25. Early the next morning, New Year's Day, Tufo and Shuman picked up Murdoch at his upstate New York retreat. Then the three men got in Murdoch's private jet for a 2,000-mile flight to Sun Valley, Idaho.

That afternoon, something else went out from New York to Sun Valley—a telegram from Clay Felker's lawyers, informing Carter Burden that a temporary restraining order had been obtained against any sale of his stock. That evening, going ahead anyway, Rupert Murdoch pushed a check for $3,507,916.50—425,202 shares, at $8.25 a share—across a restaurant dinner table to Carter Burden.

On Sunday, January 2, the rest of the coup fell into place, even as the first writers' mobilization was getting under way. On Saturday, a telegram, signed by Marianne Partridge, Jack Newfield, and Ken Auletta among others, had been sent out to Burden, asking for "the chance to discuss possible ownership and management changes with you or the entire board" on Monday. The next day, Auletta,* Edward Sorel, Judy Daniels, and a slew of the now-galvanized *New York* people put their names on a statement saying that "Carter Burden and other directors have chosen to threaten the leadership of Mr. Felker by selling out to Rupert Murdoch, an Australian publisher with no ties to New York City or California, and whose standards, as reflected in most of his publications, are incompatible with" them. Among Felker's accom-

---

*Who was on the staff of both *New York* and the *Voice*.

plishments cited by the statement: he "has strengthened the *Village Voice.*" That same day, Marianne Patridge and the *Voice* senior editors, who had to have known better, issued a public statement of their own, containing the following, ridiculous passage:

> There is something called *The Voice* tradition. At its essence is editorial integrity and independence. Clay Felker respects this tradition and we at *The Voice* respect Clay Felker. Above all else we are a writers' paper. Clay Felker has published articles he has disagreed with. He has protected writers from external intervention. This is a rare quality to find in a publisher anywhere in the world.

But that afternoon, even as Ken Auletta, Richard Reeves, and the other *New York* writers who embarked on a last-minute phone-call campaign claimed, apparently with some merit, they were getting assurances from two board members that they would hold off and meet with Clay's writers before deciding what to do, Murdoch's lawyer Howard Squadron was collecting signatures and pledges good for another 24 percent of the stock—from Bartle Bull, from Alan Patricof, from George Hirsch, and, literally while Reeves was on the phone with him and getting what sounded to Reeves like an agreement not to, from Thomas Kempner. By eight o'clock that night, Rupert Murdoch was back in town, in possession of 48 percent of the stock of *New York* Magazine Corporation, and Stanley Shuman was asking Robert Towbin for a meeting.

Towbin had told Auletta that afternoon that, since Felker and the writers both wanted the *Post,* he would vote for the *Post* if the bid was the same. But at six, Tom Kempner had called him to say, "It's all over." Murdoch had not only paid them $8.25, more than matching the *Washington Post;* he had protected them on the upside, that is to say, promised in advance to better any *future* counter-offer, whatever that offer might be. It was, indeed, all over, and Bob Towbin knew it. He could refuse to put Murdoch over the top, but then he knew that any combination of five or six others would be enough to, and that he would have antagonized Murdoch forever, for nothing. So, annoyed at the way he had been left out of the action and put into a position where he would have to go back on his word to Auletta, he showed up at Murdoch's Fifth Avenue place, calling Rohatyn and Felker first to tell them what was up. Murdoch was there, and Shuman, and Squadron, his lawyer, and Carter Burden, his new friend.

Towbin stalled; he had to call his lawyer, he said, and had a few changes made in the deal. Then, still stalling, he called his daughter, and asked her if there were any messages. There was one. It was from Katharine Graham, asking him to call her at home.

He went inside, into Murdoch's library, and dialed the number, leaving the others outside, still waiting. Katharine Graham picked up the other end. Bob Towbin introduced himself. "This is the situation, Mrs. Graham," and he outlined it to her. "If you say no, I won't put him over the top. If you tell me you'll pay more than $8.25, I have a reason not to. But I wouldn't pay more for it if I were you; in my opinion, the price of this stock is out of hand already. And, frankly, Mrs. Graham, if I don't do it somebody else will. This company's going to be sold, Mrs. Graham, and there's only one reason why its being sold—and that's because of Clay Felker. And I think you know it."

When she spoke, she sounded resigned. Was there anything she could do? she wanted to know. No, he told her. "I guess you're right," she said. "Thank you for calling."

He came outside. "That was Mrs. Graham," he announced, and Rupert Murdoch shot him a look. "I'll sign." And the champagne was broken out.

By signing over 12,000 shares in his own name, plus another 20,000 in the name of his house's clients, Robert Towbin gave Rupert Murdoch exactly 904,010 of the 1.8 million shares of *New York* Magazine Company—exactly 50.02-percent control. Murdoch made the announcement later that night, and, sounding very much like a recording from the recent past, said that of course Felker's publications "should have their own identities," that "I hope very much that he will continue to contribute his editorial genius," that he was "very conscious of the feelings of the writers and editors," and that it was only "natural that they should feel a little uncertain." For his part, Clay Felker, sounding no less like a recording, said, "I intend to preserve the integrity of our publications."

On that Sunday night, the corporate war was over. Rupert Murdoch had captured Clay Felker's capital city, and that was that. Clay Felker had started a process, a process of corporate intrigue in New York journalism, that now, according to the way those things worked, was going to work its way by finishing him off. He had stormed into the *Village Voice* like a bull in a china shop, wrecking other people's dreams and practically everything else in sight at the publication, until now, thanks to the very means he had chosen to mount that invasion— an alliance with Councilman Carter Burden—he had bulled his way into the arena, alone, with an even bigger bull than himself.

That was what had happened. But for the next five, final days, Clay

Felker, refusing to recognize the inevitable, managed to prolong the countdown, get the best surrender terms any defeated general ever got, and generate one last great whirlwind of publicity doing so.

On Monday, he issued a desperate, defiant statement to all staffers— "I intend to fight and fight as hard as I can . . . and I expect to win"— coupled with the strange warning that "it is improper to discuss the work of the company with anyone except me." That afternoon, the *New York* staff assembled, voted to ask the board to delay any sale for at least ten days, and picked a delegation to address the board meeting scheduled for that night. They were already too late: across town, at Howard Squadron's office, the checks were ready—for Bartle Bull and George Hirsch, for John Loeb, Sr. and Jr., and Edgar Bronfman, for Alan Patricof and Bartle Bull and Thomas Kempner and all their clients. They had all unloaded on Clay Felker, all in one weekend. To buy what he wanted, in this case, figured to cost Rupert Murdoch $15 million before it was all over. He had paid off the bulk of the investment within twenty-four hours.

That night, a six-hour board meeting of *New York* Magazine Corporation took place at Ted Kheel's law offices. Accounts of it were predictably partisan, but about one thing all parties did agree—the coolest customer in the room, a man who supposedly had not slept for forty-one hours, was Rupert Murdoch. He showed up. He presented the board with documentation that he now owned majority control of the company. The board voted, 6 to 5 with one abstention,* to remove Mary Joan Glynn and James Q. Wilson, and replace them with Rupert Murdoch and Stanley Shuman. Murdoch was seated. Theodore Kheel, who had been rising in his chair and announcing that, as company counsel, he was protesting the legality of everything they had done so far, protested this too. "In that case, Mr. Kheel," said Murdoch matter-of-factly, "I would recommend that we go one step further, and hire a new counsel." That vote, with Murdoch and Shuman on board, was 8 to 3.

Byron Dobell, Richard Reeves, and Ken Auletta were admitted to speak. Auletta put Towbin on the spot about what he had said regarding the *Washington Post.* Towbin, knowing it was true, tried to hedge. "You fucking liar!" screamed Felker at him, according to most accounts. "You fucking liar!" screamed Towbin at Felker, according to

---

*Burden, Bull, Tufo, Patricof, Towbin, and Kempner in favor; Felker, Glaser, Kheel, Glynn, and Wilson against; and Gordon Davis, who owned no stock, and had not been in on the *coup* over the weekend, abstaining. Davis counted himself out as a conscientious objector to the strategy being pursued by his friend Tufo & Co., and before the wild meeting was over had turned in his resignation.

Towbin's. "You don't know what Clay has tried to extract from us in the way of contracts," Carter Burden told them. "He tried to sell this company to Murdoch himself, so what are you so upset about?"

"Carter, that's a lie and you know it's a lie. I went to Murdoch as a friend for his counsel. Rupert, isn't that true?" Murdoch affirmed that it was he, not Clay, who had made the only official offer.

"Clay threatened me that 'Reeves will do you in,'" Burden said.

"Why don't you tell the truth?" Felker raged. "You asked me for a commitment to be publisher! I wasn't willing to give you a tin hat marked 'Publisher,' and he was. And I wasn't willing to do that because you're nothing but an incompetent dilettante!"

It was royal *chutzpah*—Clay Felker acting as if he had just discovered that Carter Burden was a sniveling, untrustworthy little man capable of selling out on a business partner, as if he had not known that on June 5, 1974, when in the early morning hours Carter Burden had done exactly the same thing, with him. (If anything, Carter Burden was acting more honorably this time; he at least had given Felker some notice, and had not talked about "chemistry.") But Bartle Bull, at least, had a memory: every time Felker got up and expressed outrage over being undone, or robbed of his publications, he was there with the perfect answer: "What did you do to the *Village Voice?*"

Before the writers left, Clay told Murdoch, "Rupert, you and I talked about this over lunch that day and agreed we could never work together, right?" Murdoch said he understood they had been talking about them both being publishers. "We could work together if I were publisher and you were editor."

"Clay, I think you're an editorial genius. I want you to stay and run the magazine." He asked if they could get out of there and settle this thing themselves, together. He asked if he could meet with the staff, would that help, but the representatives there said no. Then Clay Felker offered to meet with him if his staff, the next day, said to—which, in the event, they did not.

★ ★ ★

At one o'clock Wednesday afternoon, the scene of the drama shifted for the first time to the *Village Voice,* where the writers had not been noticeably up in arms.* It soon became apparent why.

---

*Something noted with bitter derision by Richard Reeves on Friday morning of that week when, standing outside the offices of his own magazine in the rain, supposedly on strike, he said, "We're supposed to be the corporate capitalist types, and they're supposed to be the anti-Establishment weekly. We're out on strike, and they're still holding meetings to decide."

Felker got up on a table, spoke and answered questions for a half hour or so, then left. Ken Auletta spoke. Then Paul Cowan presented a "statement of general principles" he had written up. And Auletta asked that Rupert Murdoch be identified by name in the statement.

Jack Newfield and Karen Durbin were among those who agreed with Auletta. But Geoff Stokes, and Howard Smith, and Nat Hentoff, and Alex Cockburn* were now among those who spoke up and did not.

"What's the difference who owns us, one millionaire or another?" Stokes asked. "Look, Clay's no saint," Auletta tried to explain, "but he doesn't come down here and censor your copy. He's not around that much. You've got a tolerable situation and replacing it with somebody you don't know. And what do you do if Rupert Murdoch agrees with that statement?" The compromise statement, eventually approved unanimously, spoke of "irreducible characteristics" of the *Voice*, "the abolition of which would destroy its identity and would be intolerable to us"†—but it named no enemy by name and promised no specific action. Clay Felker had come to the staff of the *Village Voice* to ask them for help. And they had helped, sort of—they had thrown him a giant puff ball.

There were separate meetings that night, where each department attempted to define what an "incursion" would be, and what job action they were prepared to take, and named two people each to sit on an all-paper committee. There was also discussion on what to do if *New York* Magazine went out on strike the next day, and there was no consensus. Too many people remembered what had happened to Dan and Ed, or considered it *New York* Magazine's fight. Of course, there were those

---

*Cockburn was showing his usual genius for knowing just how far to commit himself to anyone or anything. The week before, in a hysterically funny "predictions for 1977" column co-written with Newfield and James Ridgeway, he had teased Murdoch: "JANUARY . . . According to news leaks in the *National Star* Richard Nixon is telling David Frost he was 'set up' for Watergate by Ben Stein and Jeb Magruder, but says he is not bitter. . . . FEBRUARY . . . Rupert Murdoch announces new team for *New York Post*. Dino DeLaurentiis named as editor-in-chief, Evel Knievel as sports editor, Martin Abend as chief of editorial page. . . . OCTOBER . . . Rupert Murdoch fires Dino DeLaurentiis from the *New York Post*, DeLaurentiis is replaced by Norman Lear. . . . NOVEMBER . . . Killer bees appear in Los Angeles, kill Burt Reynolds. . . . DECEMBER . . . John Dean becomes editor of the *New York Post*." In the current issue, his column had discussed the takeover, and identified Felker as "a kind friend to this writer," but had not directly attacked Murdoch, only Burden and Bull—"two outstanding arguments for 100 per cent inheritance tax." Plus that, he had been going out with Katharine Graham's daughter. Say what you will, the man got around.

†It also said: "It appears that the ownership of *The Voice* will change. We as a staff would oppose the operation of our publication by any individual or organization which would not respect the principles of independence that have survived at *The Voice* thus far, and are prepared to act in defense of these principles."

who felt that, whatever Clay's faults, he was better than Murdoch, and at least they had finally been able to find a way to live with him, but when they found out the next morning what he had done, all their support went.

He had said, the previous afternoon, he was looking for another buyer, and that "it's someone who would be acceptable to you," though he would not say just who. On Thursday morning, the early editions of the *Daily News* said who: Sir James Goldsmith, chairman of multinational Cavenham, Ltd., a man who had, like Murdoch, been outbid for the *Observer* in October, who was just as foreign as Murdoch, and considerably more reactionary—he had filed 100 writs of libel in a single year against *Private Eye*, plus a criminal libel suit against its editor personally, in an obvious attempt to run the British humor magazine out of business. Uptown, supporters such as Richard Reeves were troubled to learn that—would Goldsmith be willing to drop the libel actions, Reeves wondered—but even more so by what else Clay Felker had to tell them that morning: his lawyers, poring over his contract, had finally, the night before, found the loophole that nullified the right of first refusal after four consecutive losing quarters. Carter Burden had known what he was doing: he had danced and delayed with Felker and Rohatyn and Kay Graham until midnight New Year's Eve for a reason. Clay Felker's case had collapsed.

At eleven o'clock that morning, with nothing left to do, the entire staff of *New York* went out on strike, leaving the issue due at the printer the next day undone—and incapable of being done, according to Felker and Glaser, who, in their own legal interests (since the magazine stood to lose $250,000 by not coming out), formally walked around the building before pronouncing that sentence. Rupert Murdoch sent his own printing people over, Bartle Bull himself and other people from *Firehouse* Magazine worked on paste-up all night, and Alan Patricof dunned people on the phone until he had determined where some missing editorial material was. The issue got to the printer on time, at six thirty the next morning, Friday. And by then, Clay Felker's white flag was halfway up the pole.

The federal judge who had issued his restraining order earlier in the week had done so on the assumption that face-to-face meetings between Felker and Murdoch would take place, and put off hearing a full court case on a permanent order pending several delays; at last he ordered Felker to meet Murdoch by five o'clock Thursday afternoon, which he did. The meeting lasted two hours, broke up, and resumed later, with lawyers. Clay Felker was giving up.

All day long Friday, a couple of hours at a time, the scheduled hearing at Federal Court on Foley Square in Lower Manhattan was postponed. *New York* Magazine was empty. The *Voice* was silent and tense—only the production department had wanted to walk out the day before, and then only symbolically—with people whispering and speculating upstairs and in their offices and on the stairs, about what it all meant, and most of them agreeing: Felker must be through. Outside, the rain kept up, making everything slushy, and Rupert Murdoch's *New York Post* headlined the news that Frank Sinatra's mother was dead in a plane crash. Alex Cockburn went downtown, gave up waiting for court to convene, and left. Bartle Bull stopped by, briefly. So did an Australian TV film crew—not one of Murdoch's—that had flown 7,000 miles to cover the event. Finally, at 5 o'clock, a phalanx of lawyers descended on the room. Judge Thomas P. Greisa came out of his chambers. And a small battery of news media filed into the jury box. Diane Fisher, an old *Voice* loyalist, sat in the almost-empty audience, next to Lucian Truscott's current girlfriend. Gil Eisner sat and doodled portraits of the participants. And Howard Squadron stood up and said, "We are able to report, Your Honor, that the agreement has now been reached."

Clay Felker was going to get, from Rupert Murdoch, a $1.8 million package—two years' severance pay at his current $120,000 a year, plus the offer of $8.25 for his 180,000 shares along with all the other stockholders, plus a year to pay off his $250,000 debt to the company, plus the lawyers' fees of $70,000 he had run up that week, plus a release from his noncompete clause,* plus two-year employment contract guarantees for the managing editors at each of his three publications, plus the same guarantees for ten other writers or editors to be selected. From Clay Felker, Rupert Murdoch was going to get his resignation, and Milton Glaser's.

Not quite simultaneously, Clay Felker stepped into a restaurant-bar called Chicago, across the street from the offices of *New York,* where his staff was assembled, stood on a chair, and said, "I want to announce that Milton and I are leaving," an opening line which bummed his faithful listeners out. He ended with, "Rupert Murdoch and I disagree on the meaning of friendship, of human values and the meaning of journalism, and that's what it's all about. Now I'm going to go out and start the best magazine I can." Then he stepped down, made his way through the crush of people and television lights, and was gone, leaving

---

*His old contract forbade him to work for any competing publication in any city where any of his properties appeared; according to this settlement, he simply could not go to work for *Los Angeles* or *Cue.*

his loyalists to wake him in his absence. About the same time, on the fifth floor of the *Village Voice,* Marianne Partridge called a staff meeting and read the terms of the settlement to the people gathered there. They listened—Jack Newfield and Richard Goldstein and Karen Durbin and Howard Smith and all the others who were there. They did not react. There was nothing left to react with. For the second time in thirty-one months the *Village Voice* had been the object of a successful, outside, corporate takeover. The first time it had not proved able to resist, and the second time, though it was the reason, it had not only not resisted, it had not even been at the center of the action. It had been simply passed by. And so, since there was nothing more to be said, they all simply went home. History had repeated itself. The circle had come full.

★ ★ ★

In the beginning, two men had had an idea, an idea for a paper that no one had ever put out before, a paper where writers could write what they wanted for readers who would want to read it. That was all they had in mind. They did not pretend to know what they were doing. They did not expect to make money, or reorder the priorities of American journalism, or change the world.

And yet, somehow, despite themselves, they did. When America was ready to come out of the deep sleep that was the 1950s, the paper that had done so much to keep cultural diversity alive during its slumber was ready to parade before it every new fad, every new movement, every new revolutionary breakthrough that made the 1960s what they were. In the process, it became an event itself. It became the headquarters of something called the New Journalism, something that attracted a generation of writers just coming of age to come to New York City and write, not about imaginary events and imaginary people in their heads, but about the real life out there in the streets that was outstripping everybody's capacity for imagination. The dream of someday writing the Great American Novel was over. The dream of someday writing for the Great American Newspaper had begun. It became a house of permanent and eternal dialogue. And the people who knew it loved it.

But, one day, all that began to change. The fever of the 1960s became the malaise of the 1970s. The members of the family that had grown up there together, free, now began to use that freedom to attack and quarrel with one another. And the newspaper that had never been intended to make money, that did everything supposedly "wrong," made, in a time when newspapers and magazines were falling all over the terrain like dinosaurs in a frost, almost too much money. Its two founders grew old. They grew tired. They decided at last to sell their paper, and when they did, they chose badly. They chose a man they thought they could trust with their paper, but who could not handle trust, or power, or honor, and they lived to regret what they had done. From that day forward, the *Village Voice* became not something there because of the need for it, to give a voice to voiceless people, but a prize of booty on the battlefield of venture capitalism, something to be looked at and fought over, put into the portfolio of a corporation, used by one individual on the make after another. The first man who had bought the paper gave it to another man to invade, and he did so with the ruthlessness of a dictator and the finesse of a gangster. He drove out the two men who had created it, and had made it all that it was. He uglified it. He defiled it. Until, at last, having ruined the paper and destroyed himself, that man was overthrown by another man, even more on the make than he was, by use of the very same methods. "I never understood the *Village Voice*," Clay Felker said about the newspaper, in the winter of 1977, after he was out of there. It was perhaps the only sensible statement about the paper he ever made.

First, it had been independent. Then it had become part of an empire. And, as of 1977, it had become part of a super-empire. And that seemed to be the way of things, in journalism, in America, in life. For the *Village Voice,* in 1977, the worst was over; but the best was behind it. The paper would never again, thanks to all that had happened, be the energy center or the magnet of talent or even the money-making enterprise it had once been. It would survive, somehow. But the magic and the glory that had been there would never return.

Thesis, antithesis, synthesis.

Epilogue

And then . . . at 6 P.M., Tuesday, January 11, 1977, Marianne Partridge met Rupert Murdoch at the *New York Post*. He informed her she was fired. She reminded him he was violating the agreement he had just made to keep her for two years. "I know," he said, "but . . ."

She refused to quit and went home. Michael Kramer, owner-editor of [*MORE*] Magazine and Murdoch's choice to replace her, phoned Jack Newfield with the news. Newfield threatened to kill Kramer. Kramer began having second thoughts. Karen Durbin began rousting the staff by phone. Newfield reached James Wechsler, *Post* editorial page editor, and Wechsler advised Murdoch to relent. Alex Cockburn reached Murdoch and told him that too. And, at 9, Newfield and Cockburn were waiting outside the door to Murdoch's apartment when he opened it and told them, "I'm going to take all the wind out of your sails. We're back to square one." He took them inside, explaining he had been badly advised and had already called Partridge—and Kramer, who was at her place—to tell her she could stay. "I feel duty-bound to attack Carter Burden every week in the paper now," Jack Newfield told him, "because he's such a scumbag." Smiled Murdoch: "Be my guest. The boy is a fool."

The next day, Rupert Murdoch, wearing a three-piece suit, parking a car whose length was more than the *Village Voice* building itself, and striding past a spray-painted "vv EXPLOITS LESBIANS" inscription on the outside wall, met the staff, took his lumps, was never—but for a few quiet business meetings—seen around there again, and kept his hands off. Until he was ready.

On Sunday, January 9, 1977, the staff of the *Village Voice* met and trooped over to the headquarters of District 65, Distributive Workers of America, to begin the process of unionization. Cards were signed. The union won an election that summer, 86 to 21, and, close to a strike deadline, negotiated its first contract with management in November.

In the January 17, 1977, *Village Voice*, Edward Sorel drew a mock monster movie ad in his strip: "Rupert Murdoch in 'IT CAME FROM DOWN UNDER.' It had devoured all of Australia and part of England but now it craved something a bit more ethnic," showing a skyscraper-eating Godzilla, and, in the lower corner, a ski bum on the slopes with a press badge on his suit—"with CARTER BURDEN." One week later, Jack Newfield attacked Carter Burden for his chronic absenteeism at the City Council. Burden responded. And letter-writer Philip Ryan of

West 16th Street asked, "How come Jack Newfield only now discovers what kind of councilman Carter Burden is?" Sporadic sniping, from Newfield, Geoff Stokes, and others, continued.

The *Village Voice* changed layout, back to an all-news front page, in July 1977, right after the Second Great New York Blackout, and, in March 1978, its typeface too. The paper's size was smaller. Its circulation steadied at 150,000. Its profits went back up to $1 million a year. There were comings: writers Michael Daly and Mark Jacobson and Ianthe Thomas and Denis Hamill, Pete's brother, and Leslie Harlib, to co-write Howard Smith's "Scenes," and Joe Conason, a Jack Newfield protégé imported from Boston's *Real Paper* to do "Runnin' Scared," and editor Jill Goldstein. Goings: Edward Sorel. Phil Tracy, to try screenwriting. Brian van der Horst, to flack for Werner Erhard's est. Joe Flaherty, after his articles stopped running; he told Marianne Partridge the paper had become "a campy rag," and she phoned his agent to tell him he was through. And, so he said, Paul Cowan, though his name stayed on the masthead and he still contributed. Returns: Clark Whelton and Margot Hentoff and Robin Reisig and, as managing editor, Alan Weitz. And switches: Karen Durbin, from editor to writer. Joel Oppenheimer and Jill Johnston, to punctuation and capitals.

The other new properties of Rupert Murdoch's did not fare so well. *New York* without Clay Felker was like the *Voice* without Dan Wolf. At *New West,* Murdoch, contract protection or no, sacked both top editors. And at the *New York Post,* he was everything that had been feared.

He performed one journalistic service. When Pete Hamill dropped Shirley MacLaine to squire Jacqueline Onassis, and attacked Murdoch one time too many in the *Daily News,* he dug up from the *Post* files and ran, in five installments, an unpublished column lambasting Jackie for her marriage to Onassis ("No courtesan . . . ever sold herself for more") under the head, "Who wrote this?" until he said who—Hamill, six years before. But otherwise, it was the pits.

He brought in new editors, except for Wechsler, and sacked them. He offered employees extra severance to get them to quit, complaining the paper was losing money, and set a lockout deadline against the union in the spring of 1978—bringing in workers from his San Antonio papers as standby scabs to back up his threat—unless it gave him a one-shot right to fire anyone "incompatible" with his "philosophy." He brought in Theodore Kheel, the ex-lawyer for *New York* he had sacked, to mediate. The matter went on to federal arbitration. And when a mass-murdering maniac calling himself "Son of Sam" was loose on the streets of New York, Rupert Murdoch pursued the story like a starving man who has just observed a sirloin steak through a plate-glass window. When a suspect was arrested, a *Post* photographer sneaked into his cell. SAM SLEEPS, blared the headline over a shot of a napping David Berkowitz.

"Many predicted that Sam's other natural functions would be given similar prominence on succeeding days," jousted Alex Cockburn in his column. For that and assorted other cracks throughout the year, Cockburn was, for once, unable to ingratiate himself with a new owner. As for his old owner, Clay Felker was ripped apart by Lucian Truscott in a piece, "Requiem for a Winner," in George Hirsch's *New Times.* In *High Times,* one "George R. Boz"—Ron Rosenbaum, so it was said— wrote a serial, "Murder at Elaine's," about a Felker-like figure shot to death at the East Side bistro. And WCBS-TV in New York stopped showing "Name of the Game" reruns, leaving Felker without much life left, real or reel. But in June, girlfriend Gail Sheehy came back with a piece in *Rolling Stone* that had to be the print medium equivalent of the Nixon-Frost interviews—all about how "Father" Clay Felker and his "Family," with the "Left Bank atmosphere" of *New York* and the "cake-and-eat-it-too Marxism" of the *Voice,* were betrayed by a "Conspiracy." Sample prose: "A week after having his life kicked apart Clay awoke on a Caribbean island with a shudder. 'I realize how fragile my life is,' he said. . . . Was there time to dream the great magazine of the Eighties? He began running the beach. We swam a mile in the morning. . . . A storm built up. . . . The sea turned wild. . . . The storm withdrew, leaving the brain stuporous." Stuporous indeed. In August, backed by English publishing magnate Vere Harmsworth, Felker bought, for $4.5 million, failing *Esquire,* launching it as a "fortnightly" for "the new success" the following February. "If it's a successful magazine there are protective clauses to prevent Mr. Felker from being pushed out," Harmsworth announced, familiarly.

Tom Morgan launched a magazine too—*Politicks,* with Carter Burden ($200,000) one of his investors. It folded after fourteen issues at a $900,000 loss.

On November 8, 1977, Edward Koch, Dan Wolf's old friend, was elected the 105th mayor of New York—with the *Village Voice,* the newspaper that had prospered with him, savaging him. The paper not only endorsed Jack Newfield's candidate, Secretary of State Mario Cuomo, it said that Koch "has revealed himself as a mere opportunist" for his support of the death penalty, and printed, on Primary Eve, a denigrating profile of Koch by Denis Hamill. Other, wilder attacks followed (Nat Hentoff: Koch's "moral collapse . . . is the single saddest thing I have ever seen in politics"). Koch loyalists—Andrew Sarris, Clark Whelton, and, in a letter, Joe Flaherty ("One didn't know whether to guffaw or gag when confronted with *The Voice*'s moral flatulence")—shot back in his support. But Rupert Murdoch swung the *Post* powerfully behind Koch—so powerfully sixty of his reporters protested his biased news coverage.

In the same election, Carter Burden gave up his seat to run for City Council president. He far outspent all opponents and failed even to make the runoff. Neither the *Voice,* nor Murdoch in the *Post,* supported him.

The election over, old *Voice*rs began taking jobs with Mayor Ed Koch. Clark Whelton, as a speechwriter. Annette Kuhn, as a City Hall aide. Mary Nichols, to run the city's radio and TV stations. And Dan Wolf, as a $1-a-year "special adviser" with a desk just outside the office of his friend the mayor, where he proceeded to exercise power as he had exercised it before—invisibly, masterfully. "Cronyism," charged Pete Hamill, incessantly. "Cronyism," charged Newfield, incessantly. Newfield even accused Koch of "trying to foment a religious war in New York between Christians and Jews" and his protégé Conason used "Runnin' Scared" to mug various Koch officials—all with the ultimate objective of tormenting Newfield's demon, Dan Wolf, who sat back at his desk at City Hall, smoked his pipe, and could not have cared less.

Carter Burden won the Democratic nomination to fill Ed Koch's seat in Congress at a disputed district convention. Bella Abzug sued and took it away from him—only to lose the election to the Republican. Carter Burden announced for the seat again in the fall election. There would always be new horizons to conquer, new buyers to be found.

And then, on Wednesday, May 10, 1978, Bill Ryan—a Felker holdover, made *Voice* publisher by Murdoch—called Marianne Partridge down to his office and fired her. Reprise of 1977, sort of. The staff rallied, walked her to work, and Jack Newfield, to Dan Wolf's amusement, went on television to call her "the best editor in the history of the *Voice*." Once again, she got to stay—till January 1979, when Murdoch's designee, David Schneiderman, would take over, and a new era might—or might not—begin.

Index

474

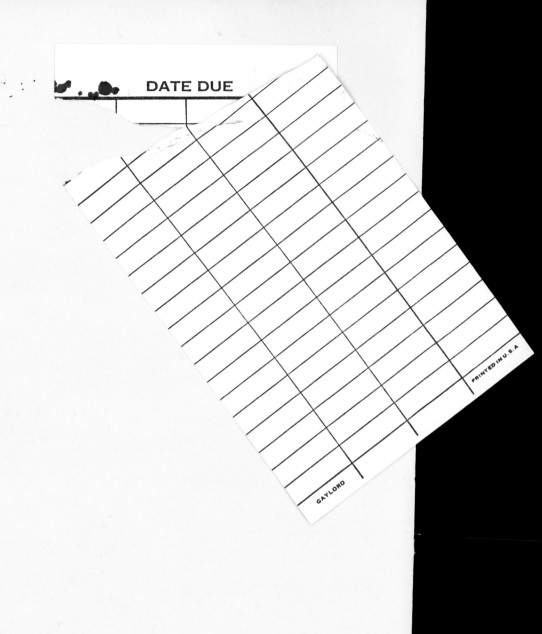

DATE DUE

PRINTED IN U.S.A

GAYLORD